"This volume is a meticulously researched text on pneumatology which does not confine itself to the traditional path but presents an innovative pneumatological paradigm which can be applied to today's problems. This volume would definitely inspire many readers to consider anew the doctrine of the Holy Spirit as it relates to all the facets of theological reflection and action."

Prof. Dr. Hans Schwarz,
Professor of Systematic Theology and Contemporary Issues and
Director of the Institute of Protestant Theology
University of Regensburg, Germany

"This is another classic on pneumatology, a remarkably well conducted research on its own kind by a young Pentecostal theologian, divulging the importance of pneumatology in systematic theology. This research contends that the discernment of the Spirit is not a dead issue of the past but rather it is very much alive giving responsible answers to humanity's pressing needs in today's context. This is worth reading".

Prof. Dr. Veli-Matti Karkkainen,
Professor of Systematic Theology
Fuller Theological Seminary, Pasadena, California

"Wilson Varkey has done those researching the doctrine of the Holy Spirit a tremendous service by providing a comprehensive analysis of the roots of the so-called renaissance of pneumatology today, peering into the intricate details of not one, nor two, but three of the most important Protestant systematic and dogmatic theologians of the twentieth century – Barth, Moltmann, and Pannenberg. Herewith he has accomplished the impossible: identifying from whence the winds of the Spirit have blown and charting trajectories to where they are going. The theological academy is in his debt."

Prof. Dr. Amos Yong,
J. Rodman Williams Professor of Theology and
Director of PhD Program in Renewal Studies
Regent University School of Divinity

Role of the Holy Spirit in Protestant Systematic Theology

A Comparative Study of Karl Barth,
Jürgen Moltmann, and Wolfhart Pannenberg

Wilson Varkey

MONOGRAPHS

© 2011 by Wilson Varkey

Published 2011 by Langham Monographs, an imprint of Langham Creative Projects
Zugl.: Regensburg, Univ., Dissertation, 2010.

Langham Partnership
PO Box 296, Carlisle, Cumbria, CA3 9WZ
www.langham.org

ISBN 978-1-907713-10-1

All rights reserved. No part of this publication may be reproduced, stored in a retrieval system, or transmitted, in any form or by any means, electronic, mechanical, photocopying, recording or otherwise, without the prior permission of the publisher or the Copyright Licensing Agency.

Scripture quotations marked (ESV) are from The Holy Bible, English Standard Version® (ESV®), copyright © 2001 by Crossway, a publishing ministry of Good News Publishers. Used by permission. All rights reserved.

British Library Cataloguing in Publication Data

Varkey, Wilson.
  Role of the Holy Spirit in Protestant systematic
  theology : A comparative study of Karl Barth, Jurgen
  Moltmann, and Wolfhart Pannenberg.
  1. Barth, Karl, 1886-1968. 2. Moltmann, Jurgen, 1926-
  3. Pannenberg, Wolfhart, 1928- 4. Holy Spirit--History of
  doctrines. 5. Protestant churches--Doctrines--History.
  I. Title
  231.3-dc22

ISBN-13: 9781907713101

Cover & Book Design: projectluz.com

Langham Partnership actively supports theological dialogue and a scholars right to publish but does not necessarily endorse the views and opinions set forth, and works referenced within this publication or guarantee its technical and grammatical correctness. Langham Partnership does not accept any responsibility or liability to persons or property as a consequence of the reading, use or interpretation of its published content.

Contents

Foreword ix

Acknowledgements xiii

Chapter One 1
Introduction
   1. What is Pneumatology? 1
   2. Why Pneumatology? 3
   3. Statement of the Problem 9
   4. Purpose of the Research 14
   5. Methodology of the Research 18
   6. Previous Researches 20
   7. Structure of the Research 23

Chapter Two 27
A Paradigm Shift: Brief Survey of Reformer's Pneumatology
   1. Introduction 27
   2. Reformation Defined 28
   3. A Milieu to the New Paradigm 32
   4. Pneumatology of the Right Wing Reformers 40
      4.1 Martin Luther (1483 – 1546) 40
      4.2 John Calvin (1509 – 1564) 45
   5. Pneumatology of the Left Wing Reformers 51
      5.1 Thomas Müntzer (1490 – 1525) 53
      5.2 Menno Simons (c. 1496 – 1561) 59
      5.3 Hans Denck (1500 – 1527) 65
      5.4 Caspar von Schwenckfeld (1489 – 1561) 69
      5.5 Sebastian Franck (1499 – 1542) 75
   6. Summary 80

Chapter Three 83
Pneumatology of Karl Barth (1886 – 1968)
   1. Introduction 83
   2. The Sitz-im-Leben of Karl Barth 84

2.1 The Socio-cultural Setting	84
2.2 The Political Setting	87
2.3 The Philosophical Setting	88
2.4 The Theological Setting	93
3. Pneumatology of Karl Barth	97
3.1 Role of the Holy Spirit in Revelation	98
3.2 The Divinity of the Holy Spirit	110
3.3 Holy Spirit and Christology	125
3.4 Holy Spirit and Anthropology	137
3.5 Role of the Holy Spirit in Redemption	142
3.6 Holy Spirit and Ecclesiology	152
3.7 Word of God and the Holy Spirit	167
3.8 Holy Spirit and Eschatology	176
4. Summary	183

Chapter Four 187
Pneumatology of Jürgen Moltmann (1926 -)

1. Introduction	187
2. The Sitz-im-Leben of Jürgen Moltmann	188
2.1 The Socio-cultural Setting	188
2.2 The Political Setting	191
2.3 The Philosophical Setting	192
2.4 The Theological Setting	195
3. Pneumatology of Jürgen Moltmann	197
3.1 The Divinity of the Holy Spirit	198
3.2 The Personhood of the Holy Spirit	208
3.3 The Shape of the Spirit's Personhood	215
3.4 The Trinitarian Personhood of the Holy Spirit	220
3.5 Holy Spirit and Christology	226
3.6 Holy Spirit and Anthropology	234
3.7 Holy Spirit and Redemption	240
3.8 Holy Spirit and Ecclesiology	249
3.9 Holy Spirit and Creation	265
3.10 Holy Spirit and Eschatology	272
4. Summary	277

Chapter Five — 281
Pneumatology of Wolfhart Pannenberg (1928 -)
   1. Introduction — 281
   2. The Sitz-Im-Leben of Wolfhart Pannenberg — 282
      2.1 The Socio-cultural Setting — 282
      2.2 The Political Setting — 283
      2.3 The Philosophical Setting — 284
      2.4 The Theological Setting — 285
   3. Pneumatology of Wolfhart Pannenberg — 287
      3.1 The Divinity of the Holy Spirit — 288
      3.2 Holy Spirit and the Doctrine of Trinity — 294
      3.3 The Holy Spirit and Christology — 308
      3.4 Holy Spirit and Anthropology — 318
      3.5 The Holy Spirit and Redemption — 330
      3.6 The Holy Spirit and Ecclesiology — 341
      3.7 Holy Spirit and Creation — 361
      3.8 Holy Spirit and Eschatology — 373
   4. Summary — 383

Chapter Six — 387
Come Creator Spirit: Towards A Theology of the Holy Spirit
   1. Introduction — 387
   2. Pneumatological Approaches — 389
   3. A Comparison of Pneumatological Approaches — 392
      3.1 Spirit: Cinderella in the Trinity — 392
      3.2 Pneumatology Subordinate to Christology? — 396
      3.3 Significance of the Spirit and Its Role Today — 397
      3.4 The Christian Spirituality — 405
      3.5 The Spirit and Imagination in Human Beings — 406
      3.6 The Spirit, Ecumenism, and a Theology of Religions — 408
      3.7 The Spirit and a Renewed Eco-theology — 410
      3.8 The Spirit and Feminist Pneumatology — 411
      3.9 Science and Religion: A Dialogue in the Spirit — 412
   4. Summary — 413

Bibliography — 415

Index — 441

Foreword

The Holy Spirit enjoys considerable attention among pentecostal and charismatic Christians. The same cannot be said about Christians coming from other traditions. This may have little to do with unfaithfulness to Christianity, but with the problematic personhood of the Spirit. Talking about the first person of the trinity one naturally thinks of God the father or, as some prefer to say, God the creator. Such talk immediately brings to mind a certain image to which the faithful can relate. The same is true about the second person of the trinity. Talking about Jesus Christ immediately brings to the fore an image of a person to whom one can easily relate. But when we mention the third person of the trinity, the Spirit, many people, Christians and others alike, wonder about such a spirit. Especially when one uses the somewhat antiquated term Holy Ghost, people could easily associate the Spirit with a ghost who supposedly haunts people or who dwells in ancient buildings and in forests. Even the term "spirit" is prone to misunderstandings when people think about an evil spirit or the spirit of the time. Therefore in the Christian tradition we find no talk about the person(ality) of the Spirit as is the case with God as person or with the person of Jesus Christ. We only speak of the personhood of the Spirit. When we mention the third person of the trinity we must immediately relate the Spirit to one of the other two members of the trinity to accord the Spirit personal quality. We see this very clearly in the Old Testament where the Spirit is intimately associated with God (the father) as God's Spirit.

At the same time the Spirit is by no means incidental. As we read for instance in the Nicene Creed, put in its final form at Constantinople at A.D. 381, the Spirit is the "life-giver" and Jesus Christ "was incarnate from the Holy Spirit". This means without the Spirit there is no life and without the Spirit there is no Jesus of Nazareth. Without Jesus of Nazareth there is also no redemption. The Spirit is essential for our life here and in the hereafter. Moreover, Christians are reminded to "walk not according to the flesh but according to the Spirit" (Rom 8:4, ESV). And they participate in the gifts of the Spirit. Yet wherever the Spirit becomes an independent agent, as occurred with some representatives of the so-called left wing of the Reformation then the Spirit loses its trinitarian anchorage. The results can be rather disastrous as we see with Thomas Müntzer or in an even more secular way with the ideology of Adolf Hitler's Third Reich. Therefore it is important to reflect responsibly on the role of the Holy Spirit.

One approach to doing this involves a comparison of three significant Protestant theologians, Karl Barth, Jürgen Moltmann, and Wolfhart Pannenberg, and how they describe the significance and working of the Holy Spirit. The author rightly claims that this "study is an innovative effort in the pneumatological discussion of Protestant Systematic Theology and is original in its kind." He does not start with these three theologians but first prepares the ground and asks how the Reformers saw the role of the Holy Spirit. This detour is important because Protestant theology whether it is cognizant of its roots or not is in some way or other indebted to the impulses provided by the Protestant Reformation. It becomes quickly evident that Karl Barth is from the Reformed tradition who in turn decidedly influenced Jürgen Moltmann. Wolfhart Pannenberg, however, as a Lutheran is much more indebted to the catholic tradition in its original sense, meaning the tradition of the whole church. Therefore he argues from a biblical base attempting to correlate the different ecclesial traditions and then establishes a pneumatology which is responsive to the issues of today. This effect he likens the Holy Spirit to a field showing that a field as in physics permeates all things, upholds them, and also allows the emerging of different movements and qualities. While Pannenberg may overextend the concept of a field at least he shows that a new conceptuality is needed to make the work of the Holy Spirit understood to a wider audience.

After tracing the explication of the doctrine of the Holy Spirit by these theologians the author now weds together their insights and presents his own approach to show the significance of the Holy Spirit for today. He emphasizes that the presence of the Spirit in creation disallows any dualism between God and nature, and between humans and nature. Furthermore, since the Spirit can be considered as feminine, this would counterbalance an exclusively masculine understanding of God. Finally, since the Spirit endows us with wisdom and imparts us with knowledge, an appreciation of the Spirit can also lead to a renewed dialogue between theology and the sciences, a dialogue in which both partners are in search for truth. These few examples show that a discernment of the Spirit is not a dead issue of a past age but is much needed in theology today to find responsible answers to humanity's pressing needs.

The author presents a text which is meticulously researched and which does not confine itself to tell us what others have said, though this is also done, but shows us his own insights which he has gathered from his readings and applies them to today's problems. One wishes this text many readers who may be inspired to consider anew the doctrine of the Holy Spirit as it relates to all the facets of theological reflection and action.

Prof. Dr. Hans Schwarz,
Professor of Systematic Theology and Contemporary Issues and Director
of the Institute of Protestant Theology
University of Regensburg, Germany.

Acknowledgements

While engaging in a project such as researching and writing a theological monograph, there are inevitably many people who contribute in various fashions along the way.

This book is the published version of a doctoral dissertation submitted to the University of Regensburg, Germany. I would like to sincerely thank my *Doktorvater*, Prof. Dr. Hans Schwarz, for his guidance, support, and immeasurable contribution to this work. He has read several previous drafts and has continued to be a theological encouragement to me even after my time in Regensburg came to a close. Prof. Dr. Mathias Heesch, and Prof. Dr. Martin Rothgangel were the dissertation examiners for the earlier version of this work, and their comments have been extremely insightful.

Frau Ferme, the secretary of Prof. Schwarz also contributed a lot during my stay and research in Regensburg. Whenever there was a need, she was always available to help and without her support this project would never have been easy.

I really thank Prof. Dr. Sathianathan Clark, who always has been a support and encouragement throughout my academic career and especially for insisting I continue my theological walk courageously. I would also like to thank Dr. Richard McLarry for reading through the proof of the earlier work and also for his friendship and support during this project. Mr. Ludwig Danneck was a great source of encouragement to me and has made valuable contribution to my academic and spiritual journey. I cannot skip the support of all the pastors and members of the *Freie evangelische Gemeinde*, Regensburg for their love, care, and support during the time I spent in Regensburg as a research student. If I name each one of them, the list will be lengthy.

I cannot forget the prayer and support of the various people who are associated with me in various capacities. The theological institutions where I did my basic theological studies and the association of my colleagues in India, Europe, and America were always a source of inspiration to me in accomplishing this project. I am indebted to my parents, siblings, and their families, parents-in-law, and other in-laws who have also contributed much for accomplishing this project successfully.

Finally, this work is dedicated to my beloved wife Jeena and our lovely children Agnes and Ashley, without whose support, care, constant encouragement, and prayers, this project would never have come to fruition. Naturally, whatever faults remain in the book are the responsibility of the author alone.

Wilson Varkey

CHAPTER ONE

Introduction

1. *What is Pneumatology?*

For almost two thousand years, Christendom has been engaged in the endeavor to unfold the meaning of the church's ancient confession, "We believe in the Holy Spirit, the Lord, the Giver of Life." Consequently, there were many teachings developed in the past in relation to the third person in the Trinity, and still the mystical entity of the Spirit[1] is an enigma, inviting attention continually to reflect upon its personality and role. Hence, throughout the history of Christian thought we find a swarm of conceptions regarding the Spirit. For example, in historical theology, the Spirit is conceived of as being an emotional and gift-giving force, as in Pentecostalism. In various forms of Catholicism, the Spirit is conceived to be the unseen authentication of the instruments of water, bread, and wine in the two sacraments. Or the Spirit is conceived to be the inspirer of the Word to the hearers, as in Reformation Protestantism. In Orthodoxy, the

---

1. The Hebrew term that denotes Holy Spirit is *ruah*. The Greek is *pneuma*. Both these terms are like the Latin *spiritus*, derived from roots which means "to breath" (Gen 1:7; 6:17; Ezek 37:5-6; or "wind" Gen 8:1; I Kgs 19:11; Jn 3:8). The Old Testament generally uses the term "Spirit" without any qualification, or speaks of "the Spirit of God" or "the Spirit of the Lord", and employs the term "Holy Spirit" only in Ps 51:11 and Isa 63:10-11. However, in the New Testament this has become a common designation of the third person in the Trinity. While the Old Testament repeatedly calls God "the Holy one of Israel" (Ps 71:22; 89:18; Isa 10:20; 41:14; 43:3; 48:17), the New Testament seldom applies the adjective "holy" to God in general, but uses it frequently to characterize the Spirit. This is probably due to the fact that it was especially in the Spirit and his sanctifying work that God revealed himself as the Holy one. See Louis Berkhof, *Systematic Theology* (London: Banner of Truth, 1971), 95.

Spirit is conceived to be the mediator of Christ's earthly presence through the icon.[2] Thus, in spite of such developed teachings[3] elucidating the work of the Spirit in creation, in the restoration of the human person, and as an inspiring reality, the person of the Spirit still remains a baffling reality with which theologians around the world struggle.

The starting point of the Christian experience and teaching about the Spirit is the New Testament account of Pentecost. Luke writes:

> This is what was spoken by the prophet Joel: "And in the last days it shall be, God declares, that I will pour out my spirit upon all flesh, and your sons and your daughters shall prophesy…, your young men…, and your old men; … yea … my menservants and my maidservants … shall prophesy. And I will show wonders in the heaven above and signs on the earth beneath …, before the day of the Lord comes…. And it shall be that whoever calls on the name of the Lord shall be saved." Men of Israel, hear these words: Jesus of Nazareth, a man attested to you by God with mighty works and wonders and signs…, you crucified and killed…. This Jesus God raised up…. Being therefore exalted at the right hand of God, and having received from the Father the promise of the Holy Spirit, he has poured out this which you see and hear. (Acts 2:16-33)

---

2. Paul F. M. Zahl, "The Spirit in the Blood," *Anglican Theological Review* vol. 83, no. 3 (Summer 2001), 496; Colin E. Gunton explains that there are at least three places where we find highly varying accounts of the person and work of the Holy Spirit. One is the mainstream dogmatic tradition, which tends to concentrate on the work of the Spirit as applying the benefits of Christ to the believer and the church. The second source for the modern identification of the Spirit is the charismatic movement. They tend to separate the Son and the Spirit from one another and identify the Spirit as the cause of particular religious phenomena. The third place is the modern identification of the Spirit, which is more broadly cultural than the other influences. They identify the Spirit with or in particular cultural and historical developments. See Colin E. Gunton, *Theology Through the Theologians: Selected Essays 1972-1995* (Edinburgh: T & T Clark, 1996), 105-108.

3. Origen is noted as the first Greek Father to have contributed to a systematic treatment of the Holy Spirit. Although Origen remains vague on nature and status, he describes the Holy Spirit in terms of a single reality. See Clint Tibbs, *Religious Experience of the Pneuma: Communication with the Spirit World in 1 Corinthians 12 and 14* (Tübingen: Mohr Siebeck, 2007), 63; for an excellent discussion on Origen, see P. Tzamalikos, *Origen: Cosmology and Ontology of Time* (Boston: Brill, 2006).

This account that Luke gives regarding the Spirit has raised a series of questions and various answers. Therefore, roughly speaking, the endeavor to give an explanation of the Spirit is the starting point of pneumatology. In other words, pneumatology is the study of the entity of the Spirit in response to its being, its position in the Trinity, and the role it plays in the divine blueprint in relation to the human beings and the rest of the world.[4] As a result, pneumatology is nothing other than the confession of the Christian faith and an elucidation of the experience of our encounter with the person and work of the Holy Spirit.

2. *Why Pneumatology?*

Theology is the cogent articulation of the knowledge of God. To put it in Anselm's well-known terminology, it is "faith seeking understanding." However, from this vantage point, the crucial concern is whether one can convincingly talk about God. This question has been answered throughout the centuries from a Christological point of view. Pannenberg, for example, writes:

> All theological statements win their Christian character only through their connection with Jesus. It is precisely Christology that discusses and establishes the justification and the appropriate form of theological reference to Jesus in a methodological way. Therefore, theology can clarify its Christian self-understanding only by a thematic and comprehensive involvement with Christological problems.[5]

---

4. The doctrine of the Holy Spirit intersects with at least three established sectors of Christian Theology. They are in relation to grace and sacramental life, church and ministry, and the distinctive Christian treatment of God as Father, Son, and the Holy Spirit. See David B. Burrell, "The Spirit and the Christian Life," in *Christian Theology: An Introduction to Its Traditions and Tasks*, eds., Peter C. Hodgson and Robert H. King (Philadelphia: Fortress, 1988), 304.
5. Wolfhart Pannenberg, *Jesus – God and Man*, trans. Lewis L. Wilkins and Duane A. Priebe (Philadelphia: Westminster, 1968), 11.

If Christology is the basis for theology, as Pannenberg argues, why can the Holy Spirit not be? What is the relationship between pneumatology and Christian theology?

Although it was ambiguous in the past, pneumatology is a definite form of theology today. There is a theological and systematic link between pneumatology and the doctrine of the Trinity. Hence, it is impossible to have a proper view of the Trinity without the Spirit, or *vice versa*. The core subject of pneumatology is the action and being of the Spirit of the triune God. The particularity of its action and being cannot be mentioned without considering its relationship with God the Father and the Son.[6] It is the Spirit that coordinates the inner life of God, providing the means whereby the Father is revealed in the Son, and the Son is revealed in the Spirit and the Spirit is revealed in the Father.[7] Gerard Longhlin writes that, "The Spirit 'narrates' the Son … one can say that the Spirit 'narrates' both Father and Son, and thus that the Father and Son 'proceed' as much as from the Spirit as that the Spirit 'proceeds' from one or both of them. There is a radical coinhering of the three stories or 'persons.'"[8] Pannenberg also recognizes the personhood of the Spirit and as the essence of the common deity. He writes:

> But the Spirit is not just the divine life that is common to both the Father and the Son. He also stands over against the Father and the Son as His own center of action. This makes sense if the Father and the Son have fellowship in the unity of the divine life only as they stand over against the person of the Spirit. Precisely because the common essence of the deity stands over against both – in different ways – in the form of the Spirit, they are related to one another by the unity of the Spirit.[9]

---

6. Sang-Hwan Lee, "The Relevance of St. Basil's Pneumatology to Modern Pentecostalism," *Cyber Journal for Pentecostal Research* (February 2000), http://www.pctii.org/cyberj/cyberj7/lee.html. 20.05.2008.
7. Travis Du Priest, "Spirit: Inner Witness and Guardian of the Soul," *Anglican Theological Review* vol. 83, no. 3 (Summer 2001), 391.
8. Gerard Longhlin, "Writing the Trinity," *Theology*, vol. 97, no. 776 (March–April, 1994), 82.
9. Wolfhart Pannenberg, *Systematic Theology* vol. 1, trans. Geoffrey W. Bromiley (Grand

In addition to that, pneumatology contains and promotes a theological-ontological congruence as well. That means that the incarnation belongs to the truth of Christ taught by the Spirit. Hughson writes that, "The Paraclete's witness to Christ transpires as a mystogogical induction into Christ's reality, above all through the Eucharist which educates disciples in practical affirmation of the incarnation."[10] The obligation to bear true witness is fulfilled by the *Paraclete,* whose substantiation (another *Paraclete*) of Christ's witness takes the form of the Spirit enlightening the disciples on the meaning of Christ. Indeed, the Spirit is Christ's true witness par excellence, as Christ had also borne witness to the Father.[11] Here one must remember the promise of Jesus that "when the Spirit of truth comes, He will guide you into all truth" (Jn 15:26, ESV), which takes us back to Jesus' claim that, "I am the way, and the truth, and the life" (Jn 14:6, ESV). Yet again, Jesus informed the disciples that the Spirit of truth "will teach you all things and bring to your remembrance all that I have said to you" (14:26, ESV). The statement in 15:26 has a forensic, somewhat defensive connotation that makes it an act of providing true testimony in adverse circumstances.[12] Therefore, it must be argued that the existence of Christology is based on the true witness of the Spirit and it leads us to realize the fact that there is a theological-ontological congruence between pneumatology and Christology. This train of thought takes us into another plane, to say that even the Christological affirmations in the Bible become authoritative only because the Spirit has spoken of it. The Bible contains the message that explains the revelation of God. In other words, the Bible is the human witness to the transcendent Word.[13] Therefore, as has been argued before, we have a Christology only because we have a pneumatology. As Stanley and John argue, "… it is the Holy Spirit announcing the good news about

---

Rapids: Eerdmans, 1991), 383-384.
10. Thomas Hughson, S. J., "Citizenship: Re-Minded by the Holy Spirit," *Anglican Theological Review* vol. 83, no. 3 (Summer 2001), 575.
11. Hughson, "Citizenship," 568.
12. Hughson, "Citizenship," 569.
13. Stanley J. Grenz and John R. Franke, *Beyond Foundationalism: Shaping Theology in a Postmodern Context* (Louisville: Westminster, 2001), 69.

Jesus Christ, which Word the church speaks in the Spirit's power and by the Spirit's authority, and which is thereby connected to Christ himself."[14]

Western Christianity has not given adequate attention to the togetherness of the Spirit and Christ in their theology. The Orthodox East has, however, consistently maintained the balance and complementarity between the work of the incarnate Son and the Spirit. In the writings of the Eastern Fathers, one can find an image that embodies this complementarity in the saying that the Son and the Spirit are the right and left hands of God.[15] Here the point is that the mission of the incarnate Lord in history is complemented by the free and unconditioned activity of the Spirit. To put it another way, the work of the Spirit serves as the needed counterpoint to the work of the Son by bringing new life and breath to individuals and institutions that would otherwise rigidify.[16]

From a hermeneutical point of view as well, pneumatology is vital to Christian theology. Traditionally, all Protestant theologians have agreed that the Bible is the norming norm of theology. The Evangelical theologian Bernard Ramm writes that, "The proper principle of authority within the Christian church must be ... the Holy Spirit speaking in the Scriptures, which are the product of the Spirit's revelatory and inspiring action."[17] This is very clear in the Westminster Confession of Faith:

> The Supreme Judge, by which all controversies of religion are to be determined, and all decrees of counsels, opinions of ancient writers, doctrines of men, and private spirits, are to be examined, and in whose sentence we are to rest, can be no other than the Holy Spirit speaking in the scripture.[18]

---

14. Grenz and Franke, *Beyond Foundationalism*, 71.
15. Louis Weil, "The Holy Spirit: Source of Unity in the Liturgy," *Anglican Theological Review* vol. 83, no. 3 (Summer 2001), 411; for a detailed study of Eastern approach on the Spirit, see Petro B. T. Bilaniuk, *Theology and Economy of the Holy Spirit: An Eastern Approach* (Bangalore: Dharmaram, 1980); Stanley M. Burgess, *Eastern Christian Traditions: The Holy Spirit* (Peabody: Hendrickson, 2000).
16. Weil, "The Holy Spirit," 412.
17. Bernard L. Ramm, *The Pattern of Religious Authority* (Grand Rapids: Eerdmans, 1959), 28.
18. John H. Leith, ed., *The Creeds of the Churches: A Reader in Christian Doctrine from the Bible to the Present*, 3rd ed. (Atlanta: John Knox, 1982), 196.

This link between the Scripture and the Spirit provides the foundation for understanding in what sense the Bible is the norming norm in theology, and it also advocates the essential prerequisite for reading the Bible as a text.[19] That means the Bible is authoritative only because it is the vehicle through which the Spirit speaks. Hence, "… the authority of the Bible is in the end the authority of the Spirit…"[20] Moreover, since the Spirit is speaking through the Word of God to the church even today, the Spirit becomes the ultimate authority in the faith community.[21] Achtemeier writes:

> If it is true, therefore, that the church, by its production of Scripture, created materials which stood over it in judgment and admonition, it is also true that Scripture would not have existed save for the community and its faith out of which Scripture grew. That means that church and Scripture are joint effects of the working out of the event of Christ.[22]

This "working out" is carried out under the guidance and illumination of the Spirit.[23] In short, the authority of Scripture and tradition is ultimately an authority derived from the work of the Spirit. Therefore, without an adequate recognition of the Spirit, one cannot construct a convincing theological locus based on Scripture.

The recognition of this vital relatedness between pneumatology and theology has been realized by theologians recently and there has been a renewal of interest in engaging the Spirit's presence and understanding the Spirit's activity. McGrath observes that the rise of the Charismatic movement within every mainstream church has ensured that the Spirit figures prominently on the theological agenda. A new experience of the reality and power of the Spirit has a major impact upon the theological discussion of the person and work of the Spirit.[24] Feminist, ecological, and

---

19. Grenz and Franke, *Beyond Foundationalism*, 65.
20. Grenz and Franke, *Beyond Foundationalism*, 65; Stanley J. Grenz, "The Spirit and the Word: The World Creating Function of the Text," *Theology Today* vol. 57, no. 3 (October, 2000), 357-374.
21. Grenz and Franke, *Beyond Foundationalism*, 75.
22. Paul J. Achtmeier, *The Inspiration of Scripture* (Philadelphia: Westminster, 1980), 116.
23. Grenz and Franke, *Beyond Foundationalism*, 117.
24. Alister E. McGrath, *Christian Theology: An Introduction* (Oxford: Blackwell, 1994), 240.

charismatic-Pentecostal movements have been harbingers of this rebirth. The theme of the 1991 Assembly of the World Council of Churches in Canberra, Australia, "Come, Holy Spirit – Renew the Whole Creation," represents a powerful symbol of this new consciousness.[25] Korean theologian Chung Hyun Kyung concluded her address to the assembly with these powerful words:

> Dear sisters and brothers, with the energy of the Holy Spirit let us tear apart all walls of division and the culture of death which separates us. And let us participate in the Holy Spirit's political economy of life, fighting for our life on this earth in solidarity with all living beings and building communities for justice, peace, and the integrity of creation. Wild wind of the Holy Spirit blow to us. Let us welcome her, letting ourselves go in her wild rhythm of life. Come Holy Spirit, renew the whole creation. Amen![26]

These observations confirm that pneumatology is essential for theology and this fact has been neglected in theological discussions in the past. This occurred simply because the church leaders and theologians were in the process of hammering out their understanding of other doctrines such as Christology and soteriology. While the average Christian had some understanding of the ministry of the Spirit and its importance in their lives, the doctrine was not systematized until more recently, nor was the emphasis on the Spirit given its proper place. Nonetheless, the Spirit is the Cinderella in the Trinity.[27] Perhaps realizing this, the twelfth century Calabrian abbot Joachim of Fiore (c. 1132-1202) envisioned a trinitarian history of humankind in three grand *statuses*, namely the age of the Father, the age of the Son, and finally, a third age yet to come, the age of the Holy Spirit.[28]

---

25. The theme is based upon the text of Psalm 104:30, which says "When you send forth your Spirit, they are created; and you renew the face of the ground."
26. Chung Hyun Kyung, *Christianity and Crisis*, 51 (15 July 1991), 223.
27. McGrath, *Christian Theology*, 240.
28. Delno C. West, ed., *Joachim of Fiore in Christian Thought: Essays on the Influence of the Calabrian Prophet* vol. 1 (New York: Burt Franklin, 1975), v; for an excellent discussion on this idea, see La G. Piana, "Joachim of Flora: A Critical Survey," in *Joachim of Fiore in Christian Thought: Essays on the Influence of the Calabrian Prophet* vol. 1, ed., Delno C. West (New York: Burt Franklin, 1975), 3-28.

As Christian theologians are engaged in reflecting upon the current secular and religious issues creatively, they must not forget Joachim's 'prophecy' which envisaged the third age of the Spirit. It challenges Christendom to reflect upon the doctrine of the Holy Spirit.

3. *Statement of the Problem*

It has already been noted that the doctrine of the Spirit is vital in constructing a theology in any context. Based on the above understanding, the researcher recognizes that there are vital issues to be solved with regard to the Spirit in Protestant systematic theology. Of course, in the New Testament, the Spirit[29] is the name for the actual presence of the divine reality in Christian experience and in Christian community. Therefore, as Pannenberg rightly pointed out, "one might expect nothing to be more familiar to every Christian than the reality of the Spirit."[30] In its strictest sense, the word Spirit itself implies the supernatural, and it is applied to God and to Christ in its divine nature. Prestige argues that "a being called 'the Spirit' *par excellence*, and sharply distinguished from other spirits, could hardly fail to be associated with the deity, even without the additions commonly made to His title, by which he became known as 'the divine Spirit', or 'God's Spirit' or 'the Spirit that is Holy.'"[31] However, most of the time, the person of Spirit was overlooked or disregarded in Protestant systematic theology throughout the centuries, especially in western Christianity.[32] Berkhof sup-

---

29. Spirit is regarded as the stuff or matter of which God consists. It is a synonym for "the divine nature." This term implies not only "the awful purity" which fills the minds of the Hebrew prophets, but also the mysteriously supernatural power of which they were not fully conscious. For a discussion on the Spirit, see Michael Green, *I Believe in the Holy Spirit* (Grand Rapids: Eerdmans, 1980), 18-31.
30. Wolfhart Pannenberg, Avery Dulles, and Carl E. Braaten, "The Working of the Spirit in the Creation and in the People of God," in *Spirit Faith and Church* (Philadelphia: Westminster, 1970), 13.
31. G. L. Prestige, *God in Patristic Thought* (London: SPCK, 1959), 81.
32. Priest writes that, "On most Sundays, and in most people's experience, the Spirit is the forgotten person of the Godhead." In the words of one theologian, Spirit seems nothing more than "an edifying appendage to the doctrine of God." John Macquarrie says the Spirit is "shadowy." Norman Pittenger calls the Spirit "anonymous." Thus Spirit became like an abandoned child and it has been forced to the outer realms of consciousness in the mainline churches and to the inner depths of forgetfulness for many Christians. See Priest, "Spirit: Inner Witness and Guardian of the Soul," 390.

ports this argument by saying that pneumatology is a neglected field in the systematic theology.[33] Pittenger says that, "The *Cosmic* significance of the Holy Spirit, in *all* history and in *all* nature, has been strangely neglected."[34] Johnson also writes that subordination of the Spirit, marginalization of women, and exploitation of nature have gone hand in hand in the history of the church.[35] Having all these arguments before us, now the crucial question can be: why was the person of the Spirit and its role in whole divine action with regard to human beings and the whole creation neglected so much in Christendom throughout the centuries?

Up to the fourth century, the deity of the Spirit, in contrast to that of the Son, did not receive either explicit assertion[36] or direct attack, because the Spirit did not raise a special problem in Christendom. In those days divine attributes were commonly ascribed to the Spirit, and its action was identified only with the process of biblical inspiration and the phenomena of Christian prophecy.[37] Whenever a question of the unity of God was embarked on, it was as simple as conceiving the significance of trinitarian controversies as being limited to the Father and the Son, without extending the range of dispute and the settlement of the problem to include the Spirit. Only the Father and the Son were found necessary to lead to a solution of the entire difficulty. Although the early church understood that the Spirit is a member of the Trinity, it was content to enjoy the benefits afforded through

---

33. Hendrikus Berkhof, *Theologie des Heiligen Geistes* (Neukirchen: Neukirchener, 1968), 10.
34. Norman Pittenger, *The Holy Spirit* (Philadelphia: United Church Press, 1974), 8.
35. Elizabeth A. Johnson, *She Who Is: The Mystery of God in Feminist Theological Discourse* (New York: Crossroad, 1992), 128-131.
36. It must be noted that up to about the middle of the second century, there has been a general decline both in the charismatic manifestations and in the vital sense of the living presence of the Spirit. A powerful reaction in the opposite direction came with Montanism. As Jaroslav Pelikan, the historian of early doctrines argues, by the time of Montanism, the extraordinary gifts of the Spirit seen in the New Testament church had died out both in frequency and in intensity. The apocalyptic and eschatological vision had become less vivid and the church's institutional structure more rigid. Therefore, the origin of Montanism seems to lie in disaffection with these developments, which its followers regarded as a settling and adjustment of the church to the world's terms. See D. F. Wright, "Montanism," in *Evangelical Dictionary of Theology*, 2nd edition, ed. Walter A. Elwell (Michigan: Baker Academic, 2001), 790; J. Robert Wright, "Holy Spirit in Holy Church: From Experience to Doctrine," *Anglican Theological Review* vol. 83, no. 3 (Summer 2001), 444.
37. Prestige, *God in Patristic Thought*, xxii.

it rather than attempting to develop a theology of the Spirit. The church leaders began to dig into the Scripture to develop a better understanding of the Spirit only when false teachings centered on the Spirit or Trinity arose.[38] A good fourth century illustration of this fact can be found in a passage from Apollinarius, who expressly gives his reasons for regarding the holy triad strictly as one God. However, actually his explanation extends only to the relations between the Father and the Son. That means the argument for the unity of two persons covers in principle the unity of the three.[39] Similar instance occurs in Tertullian's treatment of the problem and his argument is also in fact based on the unity and distinction of the Father and the Son alone.[40] Basil's pneumatology is one of the outstanding examples of this kind of development. It has been regarded as the most prominent and influential theology of the Spirit in the earliest stage of Christianity.[41] Therefore, pneumatology over against Christology was not at all a serious issue in the patristic writings.

Arguing from a Christological point of view, one can find Christological emphasis in western Christianity both in its theology and liturgical prayer.[42] This is seen, for example, in the debate between East and West on the inclusion of the *filioque* clause in the Nicene Creed: "Who (The Holy Spirit) proceeds from the Father and the Son," which the Eastern Church has never accepted as a legitimate addition. For the West, these words were

---

38. P. V. Joseph writes, "It seems true that pneumatology has been pushed to the periphery of Christian theologizing. However, 'this marginalization' of the Spirit was not intentional; rather it was because of the exigencies of the context where crucial doctrinal issues related to the second person of the Trinity were at stake." See P. V. Joseph, *Indian Interpretation of the Holy Spirit: An Appraisal of the Pneumatology of Appasamy, Chenchiah, and Chakkarai* (Delhi/Dehradun: New Theological College/ISPCK, 2007), 5.
39. Prestige, *God in Patristic Thought*, 80; John McIntyre notes that the formalization of the church's understanding of the Holy Spirit emerged from the third century onwards. See John McIntyre, *The Shape of Pneumatology* (Edinburgh: T & T Clark, 1997), 75.
40. Prestige, *God in Patristic Thought*, 80.
41. Basil Studer suggests that Basil's pneumatology is better than Athanasius', although the latter (359) is earlier than the former (374/5). Athanasius did not explicitly discuss the nature of the Spirit's origin that is the essential part of pneumatology, as Basil did. We could regard Basil as "the most prominent theology of the Holy Spirit in the Eastern Church. This honorary title is confirmed by the fact that the Second Ecumenical Council in its remaking of the Nicene Creed essentially restates St. Basil's teaching on the Holy Spirit." See Andrew Louth, ed., *Trinity and Incarnation* (Edinburgh: T & T Clark, 1993), 148-49.
42. Weil, "The Holy Spirit," 411.

an affirmation of the full divinity of the Son in its confrontation with the Arian heresy.[43] The inclusion of the *filioque*[44] in the West is indicative of the Christological prism through which the West interprets all divine action. That means, both the Western theological tradition and spirituality was shaped by this Christocentric orientation.[45] This leads to a real denial of the Spirit in Christian Theology. Therefore Johnson writes:

> What is most baffling about forgetfulness of the Spirit is that what is being neglected is nothing less than the mystery of God's personal engagement with the world and its history of love and disaster.... Forgetting the Spirit is ... ignoring the mystery of God closer to us than we are to ourselves, drawing near and passing by in quickening liberating compassion.[46]

Moreover, in the present theological climate, all the pressures are towards Christology[47] thinking that Christology is the vehicle for coping with the most tormenting questions of our age about the *humanum*. The death of Jesus in a sense is the only possible theological datum now and it is maintained that to avoid Christology is to avoid the human question of how to talk about God. From this perspective, pneumatology is viewed as evasive and triumphalist. Consequently, harsh remarks are sometimes made about the emergence of Pentecostalism and charismatic groups and

---

43. Weil, "The Holy Spirit," 411.
44. For an excellent discussion on *filioque*, see George A. Tavard, "A Clarification on the Filioque," *Anglican Theological Review* vol. 83, no. 3 (Summer 2001), 507-514; Charles P. Price, "Some Notes on *Filioque*," *Anglican Theological Review* vol. 83, no. 3 (Summer 2001), 515-535.
45. Weil, "The Holy Spirit," 411.
46. Johnson, *She Who Is*, 131.
47. I do not neglect the fact that nowadays there is a renewal in the focus of Christian theology in favor of pneumatology due to the emergence of Pentecostalism and charismatic movements. These powerful movements have brought the Holy Spirit into a position of prominence today.

their emphasis upon the Spirit[48] and its experiential theology,[49] because pneumatology can be seen as only raising the question of God and certain limited kinds of human experience.[50] But, on the other hand, Christology has priority simply because there the question of God and the human is most directly raised. Perhaps one can argue that it is a reductionism to say that Christology has priority over the other doctrines. Nevertheless, the major argument here is that due to the Christological focus of Christian theology, pneumatology has been disregarded.

Along with this aspect, another crucial issue with regard to the Spirit is the subjective method of approaching the personality of the Spirit.[51] Jesus Christ had appeared on earth, made history, and Jesus was tangible. And the Spirit is now dwelling in the hearts of human beings and continues to making history. It, however, is not recognized adequately because of its mystical personality. Only when people could look back upon historical results of its operation and correlate them with their own immediate experience, will they then be able to state explicitly that it was not only a gift or instrument of grace but its giver.[52] One should note that pneumatology is not as simple as Christology or any other doctrines, because the Spirit holds a mystical

---

48. Max Turner writes that, "Unlike the great churches of Reformation, Pentecostals have no profound deep-thinking founding fathers, to give them a stamp identity and theological direction; no prayer book to bring them uniformity; not even a common socio-cultural ethos. The diversity of Pentecostalism was no doubt increased by its lack of formal theological education, and its tendency to give priority to narrative (especially Acts), and to testimony, rather than to exposition of the epistles (with notable exception of 1 Cor 12-14)." Max Turner, "The Charismatic Movement and the Church – Conflict or Renewal?" *European Journal of Theology* vol. 10, no. 1 (2001), 49-61; George Mathew Nalunnakkal also maintains such a reductionist understanding. See George Mathew Nalunnakkal, "Come Holy Spirit, Heal and Reconcile: Called in Christ to be Reconciling and Healing Communities," *International Review of Mission* vol. 94, no. 372 (January 2005), 7-19. However, Clark Pinnock argues that, "One might expect the Pentecostals to develop a Spirit-oriented theology of mission and world religions, because of their openness to religious experience, their sensitivity to the oppressed of the Third World where they have experienced much of their growth, and their awareness of the ways of the Spirit as well as dogma." Clark Pinnock, *Flame of Love: A Theology of the Holy Spirit* (Downers Grove: Inter Varsity, 1996), 274.
49. Allan Anderson, "Pentecostal Approaches to Faith and Healing," *International Review of Mission* vol. 91, no. 363 (October 2002), 523-534.
50. Rowan Williams, *Challenges in Contemporary Theology: On Christian Theology* (Oxford: Blackwell, 2000), 108.
51. See a critique in Grenz and Franke, *Beyond Foundationalism*, 67-68.
52. Prestige, *God in Patristic Thought*, 81.

personhood and its activities are likewise mystical. This in turn leads to a curtailment in addressing pneumatology within Christian theology.

And of course, one should admit the fact that of all the themes of Christian theology, the Holy Spirit seems to be the most elusive and difficult facet. How can one speak at all adequately of the power that enables authentic discernment and speaking of God? How can one avoid reducing the Spirit of Jesus Christ crucified and risen to a mere item in a catalogue of the history of ideas?[53] One should not forget the fact that there has been a series of errors and it has always forced the church to purify and crystallize its theology in the past. Although there is much better understanding of the Spirit today, who it is and what it does, still there are widespread erroneous teachings concerning the Holy Spirit. This raises lot of apprehensions and most of the time it becomes safer to disregard pneumatology. However, the present study endeavors to look into the above noted major issues and to provide a new paradigm of pneumatology, establishing the significance and role of the Spirit in Protestant systematic theology.

4. Purpose of the Research

As noted earlier, in fact, the study of the Holy Spirit is not new in systematic theology. However, it seems that there has not been a favorable treatment of the Spirit in Christian theology. Hence Berkhof writes that, "The personality of the Spirit was denied in the early church by the Monarchians and the Pneumatomachians. In this denial they were followed by the Socinians in the days of the Reformation. Still later Schleiermacher, Ritschl, the Unitarians, present day modernists, and all modern Sabellians reject the personality of the Holy Spirit."[54] Moreover, one can find different positions that are taken by different churches with respect to the doctrine of the Spirit. Hendrikus Berkhof writes:

> Roman Catholicism preferably defines the Spirit from the view point of his place in the church, whose soul and animating

---

53. Alasdair I. C. Heron, *The Holy Spirit: The Holy Spirit in the Bible, the History of Christian Thought, and Recent Theology* (Philadelphia: Westminster, 1983), vii.
54. Berkhof, *Systematic Theology*, 95-96.

principle he is. In the tradition of orthodox Protestantism his essence is especially determined from his influence in the life of the individual in effecting faith and conversion, regeneration, and sanctification. Liberal Protestantism likes to start from the common content and structure of man's spiritual life, and to understand the Spirit as analogous to it.[55]

It proves the fact that each time one approaches pneumatology, different questions arise, inviting a fresh reflection. This factor challenges Christendom to make fresh and creative endeavors with respect to pneumatological problems from generation to generation.

Of course, there are innovative efforts in the field of pneumatology, because more than in the past, it is realized that pneumatology is a promising theological locus.[56] Hodgson writes that, "The resources for a theology of the Holy Spirit are rich and diverse, ranging from Eastern orthodoxy and classical western spirituality to New Age movements, folk and tribal religions, feminist, ecological, and liberation theologies, and new philosophies of Spirit."[57] However, as Moltmann says, a new paradigm of pneumatology has not yet emerged. Yet there are beginnings, and we are witnessing a transition from an anthropocentric to a holistic pneumatology, one that embraces the whole creation and recognizes in the Spirit the symbol of wholeness, relatedness, energy, and life.[58] This search for a new paradigm

---

55. Hendrikus Berkhof, *Christian Faith: An Introduction to the Study of the Faith*, trans. Sierd Woudstra (Grand Rapids: Eerdmans, 1979), 322.
56. For example, the Spirit-centric theme is very helpful in addressing the ecological issues of our times, and it would provide a cosmic vision of mission vis-à-vis healing and reconciliation. It is through the Spirit that God creates, reconciles, and saves the entire creation. Moreover, God is present in creation in the power of the Holy Spirit. The Holy Spirit is the breath and life of the world. The language of "Spirit" to refer to God helps us to transcend anthropocentrism, that itself is a major reason for the current ecological impasse. The fact that the Spirit is used as a feminine category in Semitic languages also provides us with an eco-feminist perspective for mission. God as Spirit is not understood as the controller of the universe, but rather as its source and breath. From this perspective, all worldly beings are seen as "entspirited" embodiments of God. See Nalunnakkal, "Come Holy Spirit," 7-19.
57. Peter C. Hodgson, *Winds of Spirit: A Constructive Christian Theology* (Louisville: Westminster, 1994), 277.
58. Jürgen Moltmann, *The Spirit of Life: A Universal Affirmation*, trans. Margaret Kohl (Minneapolis: Fortress, 1992), 1-2, 34-37.

makes pneumatology always significant, and that is what the whole concern of this research is.

In addition to that, the doctrine of the Spirit has aroused an interest within the life of the church recently, which is growing and extends incredibly. It fixates on the spiritual side of human nature. Swete writes, "It is possible that modern life, as it escapes from the control of a crude materialism, may be led to seek the solution of its perplexities in the Christian doctrine of a divine Spirit working in the world and in man."[59] Therefore, there are promising possibilities which pneumatology opens for the Christian church and the modern world in order to face the challenges before humanity and the universe as a whole. As a result, the present world has witnessed an unprecedented interest in the study of the Spirit, more so than at any time in the history of the church.[60] Kärkkäinen observes in one of his articles that today we are living in the midst of "a pneumatological renaissance" with writings and discussions on the Spirit abounding.[61] Thus those promising possibilities that the Spirit offers for today are the major concern of the present research.

Moreover, the Spirit is an eschatological reality that gives hope in the midst of a hopeless world. The pneumatological basis of the Bible faith communities is the linguistic and theological connection between "Spirit' and "breath," which the ancients linked phenomenologically to "life." The Biblical people came to see "Spirit" as the divine power creating (Gen 1:2; 2:27) and sustaining life (Ps 104:29; Isa 32:15; cf. Job 27:3; 34:14-15). Therefore, wherever the Spirit is present, life flourishes, and wherever the Spirit is absent, life ceases. Moreover, the biblical writings link the Spirit with the eschatological new life. As the one who raised Jesus from the dead, the Spirit will give life to our mortal bodies (Rom 8:11). As the author of life, the Spirit is the creator Spirit, the divine power at work fashioning the universe, and in this sense, the Spirit is the author of the world.[62] This realization will give a new sense of hope to the world that suffers from

---

59. Henry Barclay Swete, *The Holy Spirit in the Ancient Church: A Study of Christian Teaching in the Age of the Fathers* (London: Macmillan, 1912), 7.
60. Joseph, *Indian Interpretation of the Holy Spirit*, xvii.
61. Veli-Matti Kärkkäinen, *Pneumatology: The Holy Spirit in Ecumenical, International, and Contextual Perspective* (Grand Rapids: Baker Academic, 2002), 9.
62. Grenz and Franke, *Beyond Foundationalism*, 77.

fundamentalism, terrorism, and dehumanizing tendencies. One should note that the divine is the great creative Spirit within which wears the universe as its body. This great cosmic, creative Spirit underlies all that exists and moves the world toward its completion not by almighty power but by kenotic self-giving. Each of us in some way knows or intuits "this great cosmic, creative Spirit" which underlies the disparate compartmentalization of modern life.[63] As Bishop Holloway of the Episcopal Church in Scotland writes, "Some great self-giving love seems to haunt the universe."[64] When dealing with the pneumatology of Moltmann and Pannenberg, these aspects will be clearer and will be further reflected in the new pneumatological paradigm at the end of this study.

In addition to that, the notion that the Spirit is present in the world religions is heard more loudly today.[65] D'Costa writes that, "… the claim that the Spirit is at work in their religions should be taken neither as a phenomenological socio-historical description of a religion, not as a claim that will necessarily be well-received by a non-Christian. Rather it constitutes a theological evaluation that must spring from and lead to fresh practices within the church if the claim is to have any credence."[66] The recognition of the Spirit in other religions allows the church the possible discernment of Christ-like practice in the other, and in so much as Christ-like activity takes place, then this can also be through the enabling power of the Spirit.[67] That means, as Alan Jones writes, "The Spirit is calling us out of our tribal and national manifestations into a way of being in the world that truly expresses

---

63. Priest, "Spirit: Inner Witness," 387.
64. Richard Holloway, *Dancing on the Edge* (London: Harper Collins, 1997), 44.
65. The major works are, Amos Yong, *Discerning the Spirit(s): A Pentecostal-Charismatic Contribution to Christian Theology of Religions* (Sheffield: Sheffield Academic, 2000); Amos Yong, "Guests, Hosts, and the Holy Ghost: Pneumatological Theology and Christian Practices in a World of Many Faiths,'" in *Lord and Giver of Life: Perspectives on Constructive Pneumatology*, ed. David H. Jensen (Louisville: Westminster, 2008), 71-86; Amos Yong, *Beyond the Impasse: Toward a Pneumatological Theology of Religion* (Grand Rapids: Baker Academic, 2003); Veli-Matti Kärkkäinen, "Identity and Plurality: A Pentecostal Charismatic Perspective," *International Review of Mission* vol. 91, no. 363 (October 2002), 500-503.
66. Gavin D'Costa, *The Meeting of Religions and the Trinity* (Edinburgh: T & T Clark, 2000), 128.
67. D'Costa, *The Meeting of Religions*, 129.

the universal good news of love and reconciliation."[68] The Spirit and other religions is also an area where this research will be focusing.

In short, having understood the major reasons for the negligence of the Spirit, on the one hand, and the significance of the Spirit, on the other, in Protestant systematic theology, the present study discusses the pneumatology of Barth, Moltmann, and Pannenberg in order to answer the following pertinent questions. Firstly, what is the personhood of the Spirit and how is it related to the other persons in the Trinity? Secondly, what is the role of the Spirit in the whole divine action with regard to humanity and the whole creation? Thirdly, how should one approach the Spirit, i.e., whether subjectively, or is there any possibility of understanding the Spirit and its role as reasonably accommodating to the modern mind? Finally, how can we formulate a pneumatology, giving significance to the working of the Spirit in the Christian church, other religions, liberation movements, and contextual theologies? In short, this study looks for a new paradigm, maintaining the significance of pneumatology and arguing for a pneumatological perspective in Protestant systematic theology in order to present a new hope to the church and world alike.

5. *Methodology of the Research*

The success of any study is based on the methodology one uses. The methodology which pneumatology has to take into account on the one hand is "religious experience" because neither the "liberal" account nor the "cultural-linguistic" alternative will help the study of the Spirit. Their common drawback is that each posits a starting point or an *a priori*.[69] As Murphy argues, "Although propounded in an increasingly subtle and complex fashion, the experience-based approach to theology that is characteristic of liberalism continued to dominate mainline theology throughout

---

68. Alan Jones, "Falling in Love: The Work of the Holy Spirit," *Anglican Theological Review* vol. 83, no. 3 (Summer 2001), 379.
69. Charles Hefling, "*Gratia*: Grace and Gratitude: Fifty Unmodern Theses as Prolegomena to Pneumatology," *Anglican Theological Review* vol. 83, no. 3 (Summer 2001), 486.

the twentieth century."[70] Therefore, as Grenz and Franke argue, "Christian theology, in turn, is an intellectual enterprise by and for the Christian community. Through theological reflection, the community of those who the God of the Bible has encountered in Jesus Christ seeks to understand, clarify, and delineate its interpretive framework informed by the narrative of God's action on behalf of all creation as revealed in the Bible. In this sense, we might say that the specifically Christian experience facilitating interpretative framework, arising as it does out of the biblical narrative, is 'basic' for Christian theology."[71] On the one hand, this has been the methodology followed by Moltmann in his whole theological program and particularly in developing a pneumatology and hence, this study also is employing the experiential methodology of Moltmann.

Along with this experiential approach, the rationalistic approach is also very significant in undertaking the study of the Spirit. Many believe that the use of rationalism to expound and explain the facts of Christian theology is illegitimate.[72] They argue that the finite minds can never adequately theorize the infinite, and this argument, of course, is to a certain extend valid too. However, one should not forget the fact that the human reason is a valid instrument for unfolding the implications of human experiences. In other words, reason is a part of the equipment with which human nature has been endowed by God. As Pittenger maintains:

> It is a demand that our rational exercise, with the intellectualizing that follows from them, shall be seen in their context and with the most profound regard for the richness both of human experience and of the world-setting for that experience.... At best, the words are useful counters; we should use them

---

70. Nancey Murphy, *Beyond Liberalism and Foundationalism: How Modern and Post Modern Philosophy Set the Theological Agenda* (Valley Forge: Trinity Press International, 1996), 22-28.
71. Grenz and Franke, *Beyond Foundationalism*, 49.
72. For example, Harnack criticizes Christian rationalism by saying that it is a process of secularization or Hellenization of Christianity. For a discussion see E. P. Meijering, *Die Hellenisierung des Christentums im Urteil Adolf von Harnacks* (New York: North-Holland, 1985).

> carefully, criticize them, and employ whatever logic may be appropriate in respect to them ....[73]

Therefore, this study is following a rationalistic approach as well[74] in order to avoid the danger of mere superficial and experiential schema in approaching pneumatology. This has been the methodology followed by Pannenberg as well in his whole theological program in order to make a credible presentation of the Christian faith. Therefore, the present study also employs the rationalistic approach of Pannenberg as well. Moreover, a critical approach is very important when one undertakes an important research because there is greater space for misunderstanding when the data are uncriticised.[75] In short, this study will be following an experiential, rationalistic, comparative, and critical approach in order to develop a relevant pneumatological paradigm.

6. Previous Researches

There is no doubt that Barth is a theological giant among Protestant systematic theologians of the twentieth century. However, it seems that his pneumatology has not been truly explored due to the excessive attention given to his theology of revelation. However, the major work that explores the pneumatology of Barth is done by Rosato, under the title, *Karl Barth's Theology of the Holy Spirit*.[76] Although Barth is normally known as a Christocentric theologian, Rosato argues that, "Once Christ was firmly established in his theology, Barth became at heart a theologian who took man seriously as the object of the Father's love in the Spirit of His Son;

---

73. Pittenger, *The Holy Spirit*, 20-21.
74. The use of the term "reason" always has some ambiguity in modern discussions. Some view it as the only means of establishing unbiased truth. Some view it as simply one way to get from a premise to conclusion. However, my goal here is to explore the treatment of the Holy Spirit in Protestant systematic theology in order to present a fresh pneumatological paradigm. For an excellent discussion on reason, see Richard Lints, *The Fabric of Theology: A Prolegomenon to Evangelical Theology* (Michigan: Eerdmans, 1993), 117-135; Hodgson, *Winds of Spirit*, 121-132.
75. Prestige, *God in Patristic Thought*, xiii.
76. Philip Joseph Rosato, *Karl Barth's Theology of the Holy Spirit: God's Noetic Realization of the Ontological Relationship between Jesus and All Men*, Ph.D. Thesis (Tübingen: n.p., 1976).

in short, Barth became more and more a pneumatocentric theologian."[77] The whole focus of Rosato in this study is to prove the fact that Barth's pneumatology is the theology of God's Holy Spirit who noetically realizes in the Christian the ontological relationship between Jesus Christ and all humanity. In order to fulfill the task, Rosato makes a detailed thematic study of Barth's pneumatology. Rosato asserts that the possibility for an opening to other thought patterns in theology and outside of it can be found in Barth's Spirit theology more than in any other aspect of his thought. Moreover, Barth's theology of the Spirit consists of systematic thoroughness and depth. However, Rosato critiques Barth's pneumatology by arguing that, "Its failure is its tendency to submit the Spirit and man to the Word, so that the Spirit and man meet so uniquely in the one person, Jesus Christ, that that meeting alone has ontological significance; every other meeting of man and the Spirit is noetical and thus deprived of an independent ontological meaning of its own. Barth could never free the Spirit from the Word, or free man from the Spirit and the Word. Only by liberating man could Barth have liberated modern theology for a new understanding of God's Spirit. That Barth partly did and this is his great contribution to a future pneumatology."[78]

Although there are not many works published particularly on the pneumatology of Moltmann, one of the major works that needs attention is done by David Beck under the title *The Holy Spirit and the Renewal of all Things*.[79] This work explores the shape pneumatology takes when we develop the theology of the Holy Spirit within an eschatological framework that has a universal scope and an unlimited history. In such an attempt, one can find that pneumatology deriving from questions about what the Spirit does for us needs to give way to pneumatology that derives from questions about how the Spirit can draw us into the saving history of the triune God. Although Moltmann follows Barth to a certain extent, he critiques Barth for his Christocentricism. Beck writes that, "Although Barth's theology is exceedingly Christocentric, it nonetheless provides an example of the di-

---

77. Rosato, *Karl Barth's Theology of the Holy Spirit*, 107.
78. Rosato, *Karl Barth's Theology of the Holy Spirit*, 351.
79. T. David Beck, *The Holy Spirit and the Renewal of All Things: Pneumatology in Paul and Jürgen Moltmann* (Eugene: Pickwick, 2007).

rection of pneumatology can take place in the stream of Protestantism that I have called 'institutional.' In keeping with the trajectory of mainstream Western theology, Barth makes Christ the centerpiece of theology and subordinates the Holy Spirit to Christ in the process."[80] After providing a detailed discussion on different sorts of pneumatology and eschatology in Protestant thought, Beck focuses on the Spirit in the Pauline eschatological framework and maintains that Moltmann also shares these basic positions, although in a contemporary and modified form. One can thus note that his whole focus in this study is to examine Moltmann's theological views with particular interest in the ways his eschatological sensibilities inform his concept of the person and work of the Holy Spirit.[81] Beck concludes his work by suggesting contours of an eschatological pneumatology in the present context.[82] In short, the speciality of Beck's work is that he builds on a detailed study of the Apostle's eschatological framework in pneumatology and allows to absorb through interaction the numerous and rich flavors of Moltmann's own treatment of the very subject. Moreover, this work provides an excellent point of entry into the contemporary discussion of some of the most vital themes of the doctrine of the Holy Spirit. It clearly identifies the role that pneumatology has played in the Protestant tradition and the character of its development, as well as demonstrates why eschatology is now widely recognized as constituting the essential horizon of the doctrine.

To the best of my knowledge, no systematic studies have been done on the pneumatology of Pannenberg so far. Perhaps this is due to the fact that he has not produced a separate pneumatology in his systematics although it runs through Pannenberg's entire theological program. However, there is a work done by Graham J. Watts, which is worth mentioning.[83] Although Watts makes a brief analysis of the pneumatology of Pannenberg, his focus is to delineate the relationship between the doctrine of revelation and pneumatology in Pannenberg's theology. This is because, as Watts argues,

---

80. Beck, *The Holy Spirit*, 7.
81. Beck, *The Holy Spirit*, 85.
82. Beck, *The Holy Spirit*, 236-254.
83. Graham J. Watts, *Revelation and the Spirit: A Comparative Study of the Relationship between the Doctrine of Revelation and Pneumatology in the Theology of Eberhard Jüngel and Wolfhart Pannenberg* (Eugene: Wipf & Stock, 2005). See especially from 123-162.

Pannenberg seeks a *via media* between the concept of God gained through revelation and the nature of God conceived by human reason.[84]

In comparison with the previous researches, the present research distinguishes itself on the basis of its whole focus because, on the one hand, it looks into the pneumatology of the above mentioned theologians together, especially the role of the Spirit in the Protestant systematic theology. Secondly, this study makes a comparison between the pneumatology of these three theologians and involves a critical engagement with them in order to provide proposals for a fresh pneumatological paradigm in the present context. Therefore, the current study is an innovative effort in the pneumatological discussion of Protestant systematic theology and is original in its kind.

7. *Structure of the Research*

The following research seeks to unveil the role of the Spirit in Protestant systematic theology. It is apparent that one cannot deal with all the Protestant theologians in depth in a dissertation of this type. Hence, a selection among the notable Protestant systematicians has been made in this study. They are the prominent theologians of the twentieth century, namely Karl Barth, Jürgen Moltmann, and Wolfhart Pannenberg. In present day Protestant systematic theology, these names are familiar and they are contemporaries as well. According to the convenience of the study and to be more feasible, this research will have six different chapters.

The first chapter is an introduction to the research, sketching the issue and the relevance for undertaking a pneumatological study in today's context. As Jones writes:

> We are called in to a pilgrim community through the saving images of scripture, and we joyfully celebrate God's hospitality

---

84. Watts, *Revelation and the Spirit*, xvi; he asserts that through this *via media* the relationship between the doctrine of revelation and a trinitarian account of the person and work of the Spirit is expressed more openly and in some original ways. However, the main question is whether the resulting model of the Spirit is internally, logically coherent, and whether it accords with biblical testimony and theological orthodoxy? See Watts, *Revelation and the Spirit*, xvi; 148-162.

> in a community where the unqualified and rejected are the most welcome. The theater of the Spirit is history, which means that we are in an endless conversation with the mystery of what it is to be human in the context of thrilling images of love and mercy in a community centered around a table from which no one is excluded.[85]

Therefore, it is very important to critically engage in discussing the role of the Spirit in Protestant systematic theology in order to present a relevant pneumatology today.

The second chapter deals with the pneumatology of the Reformers, because the Christian doctrines did not emerge instantly; rather, they have been developed after a series of theological discussions in the past. As Barclay Swete writes:

> ... no Christian doctrine, as it is now expressed, can be rightly understood without some knowledge of the history of Christian thought. The Christianity of the present day has not been evolved directly out of the New Testament, but is the product of the gradual assimilation of the original deposit by a long succession of Christian generations.[86]

It reminds us that, when attempting to look into a systematic study of a subject like pneumatology in Protestant theology, it is necessary to look into the treatment of such doctrine in the Reformers' theology. Therefore, the writer discusses pneumatology in the writings of the right wing Reformers and the radicals. Since the focus of this study is to dig out the role of the Holy Spirit in Protestant systematic theology, especially in the writings of the above mentioned theologians, the writer will deliberately avoid discussions about the Spirit in the writings of the early church fathers.[87]

---

85. Jones, "Falling in Love," 380.
86. Swete, *The Holy Spirit in the Ancient Church*, 4.
87. There are studies that deal with the pneumatology of the early church fathers. See for example, Joseph, *Indian Interpretation of the Holy Spirit*; Stanley M. Burgess, *Ancient Christian Traditions: The Holy Spirit* (Peabody: Hendrickson, 2002); Burgess, *Eastern Christian Traditions*; Stanley M. Burgess, *The Holy Spirit: Medieval Roman Catholic and Reformation Traditions* (Peabody: Hendrickson, 1997).

The third chapter discusses the pneumatology of Karl Barth. Barth stands unchallenged as the leading theologian of the 1900s. Throughout the century, his towering frame casts its shadow across the theological landscape. Dorrien asserts regarding Barth's prominence that, "As the preeminent theologian of his century, Karl Barth was the single figure that all other twentieth-century theologians had to deal with, if not define themselves against."[88] Hence, it is essential to deal with such an eminent figure in this study.

The fourth chapter discusses the pneumatology of Jürgen Moltmann. Moltmann is the most decorated theologian since Barth. Meeks writes that, "It is difficult to imagine any theology in the near future which could function without being consciously or unconsciously influenced by Jürgen Moltmann's 'theology of hope' …. Perhaps it will be said in the future that he has initiated a new theological era."[89] Moltmann is one of the most read, most productive, and most relevant Christian theologians at work today.[90] Therefore, it is important to deal with the Pneumatology of Jürgen Moltmann as well.

The fifth chapter deals with the pneumatology of Wolfhart Pannenberg. No theologians in the last fifty years have displayed a greater intellectual breadth than Pannenberg. Stewart cites that, "the intellectual seriousness with which he treats the natural and social sciences" is a feature that distinguishes him "from other major theologians of the second half of the twentieth century."[91] Moreover, no contemporary theologians has made theology's claim to universality "more strongly, explored its methodological foundations more thoroughly, or pursued its implications more consistently" than Pannenberg.[92] Hence it is equally important to engage with the pneumatology of Pannenberg as well.

---

88. Gary Dorrien, *The Barthian Revolt in Modern Theology: Theology without Weapons* (Louisville: Westminster, 2000), 13.
89. M. Douglas Meeks, *Origins of the Theology of Hope* (Philadelphia: Fortress, 1974), xiii.
90. Cited in Stanley J. Grenz, *Rediscovering the Triune God: The Trinity in Contemporary Theology* (Minneapolis: Fortress, 2004), 73.
91. Jacqui A. Stewart, *Reconstructing Science and Theology in Postmodernity: Pannenberg, Ethics, and the Human Sciences* (Aldershot: Ashgate, 2000), 2.
92. Mark William Worthing, *Foundations and Functions of Theology as a Universal Science: Theological Method and Apologetic Praxis in Wolfhart Pannenberg and Karl Rahner* (Frankfurt am Main: Peter Lang, 1996), 3.

The final chapter is a critical and comparative study between the above mentioned Protestant theologians in order to develop a pneumatological paradigm in the present context. Moreover, this chapter consists of proposals and possibilities for a fresh pneumatological paradigm. In addition to that, this study is strictly a library research based on both primary and secondary materials available.

CHAPTER TWO

A Paradigm Shift: Brief Survey of Reformer's Pneumatology

1. Introduction

There are strong reasons to argue that the whole doctrine of the person and work of the Holy Spirit at large is a gift to the church from the Reformation. This has been taken into consideration by many theologians on the grounds that the upheaval of the Reformation precipitated a shift in pneumatological interest as dramatic as that ushered in by Augustine.[1] Although mainstream Protestant theology continued to preserve and maintain the established Western doctrine including the *filioque,* the Reformation particularly concentrated with a new intensity on what the Spirit enables and performs. Alasdair Heron writes that, "The presence and action of the Spirit in the life of the believer to represent Jesus Christ, to convey forgiveness, to illuminate and renew by divine spiritual energy – these themes take on a new centrality owing directly to the fundamental insights of the Reformation".[2] The

---

1. In the philosophy and theology of the Middle Ages, the thoughts of Augustine had a wide impact. The revival of Augustinianism at the time of Reformation exerted a great influence on the theology and life of the Protestant churches. Although during the fourteenth and fifteenth centuries the thoughts of Augustine were challenged, he was claimed anew with fresh ardor during the sixteenth century. See Irvin B. Horst, "Menno Simons and the Augustinian Tradition," *The Mennonite Quarterly Review* vol. 62, no. 4 (October 1988), 419-430; hereafter *MQR*; Augustine maintained a different outlook in his pneumatology than the Greek thought of trinitarianism. His treatment of the doctrine of the Spirit can be seen in the *De Trinitate*. For a discussion see Gunton, *Theology through the Theologians*, 105-128.
2. Heron, *The Holy Spirit*, 98.

emphasis that the Spirit received in the Reformation can be clearly seen in the words of Princeton theologian Benjamin Warfield, that "the developed doctrine of the work of the Holy Spirit is an exclusively Reformation doctrine."[3] Therefore, it is imperative to inquire into the fact of how pneumatology can be seen as a developed doctrine of the Reformation. Keeping this argument in mind, the following chapter makes a brief survey of the pneumatology of selected Reformers both from the right wing and the left wing.[4] At the very outset, this chapter will look into the whole question of Reformation as a theological issue. This discussion will follow the main current that influenced the Reformers and their pneumatology. Finally, the pneumatology of the Reformers themselves will be briefly discussed.[5]

2. *Reformation Defined*

Before entering into an inquiry of the pneumatology of the Reformers, it is imperative to discuss and understand the whole phenomenon of Reformation in the sixteenth century. The term "Reformation"[6] is used by

---

3. Benjamin B. Warfield, "Introductory Note," in *The Work of the Holy Spirit*, by Abraham Kuyper (Grand Rapids: Eerdmans 1979), xxxiii.
4. The essential line of division, which made the radicals "left" and the Protestants "right" could be drawn on the issue of church and state. From this angle one can see the left wing as "those who separated church and state and rejected the civil arm in matters of religion." The distinguishing characteristics of the radical sects came from their ethical, primitivist view of the church. They were often anti-intellectual, and some stressed community of possessions. See A. G. Dickens and John Powell, *The Reformation in Historical Thought* (Oxford: Blackwell, 1985), 224.
5. It has to be clarified that this chapter is not a detailed study of the pneumatology of the Reformers, but rather a brief historical survey. Therefore, the writer will not attempt to make an analysis or to critique the pneumatology of the Reformers in depth.
6. The word "Reformation" has a long history that on the one hand goes back to the classical times and on the other hand, in the contemporary undergraduate curricula, it is almost always associated with the "'Renaissance." The medieval use of *Reformation* may generally be understood in terms of the Eusebian rubric that older is better. Technically, the term was used in relation to the reestablishing of universities in their original condition, e. g., *reformatio in pristinum statum*. The fourteenth century conciliar movement used the phrase, "reformation of the church in head members," meaning by this an ethical appeal to self-reform of the church as an institution. In the sixteenth century "Reformation" developed further meanings of improvement and renewal in both ecclesiastical and profane usage. See Carter Lindberg, *The European Reformation* (Oxford: Blackwell, 1996), 9; Harbison notes that, if one considers the whole religious side of the picture, the century (refers to the sixteenth century) should be properly called "the Age of the Reformations." He defines Reformation as part of a wider "reorganization" of

historians and theologians to refer to the Western European movement, centering upon the individuals such as Martin Luther, Huldrych Zwingli, John Calvin, and others, concerned with the moral, theological, and institutional reform of the Christian church in that region.[7] The Scottish Presbyterian theologian William Cunningham, opened his massive study of Reformation theology with the bold claim that the Reformation of the sixteenth century "was the greatest event or series of events that has occurred since the close of the canon of scripture."[8] Although the Reformation history provides valuable insights to understand that period, as Timothy George writes, "we must recognize that the Reformation was essentially a religious event; its deepest concerns, theological."[9] Moreover, the idea of "religion" as a "spiritual" phenomenon outside the secular order of things first emerges in the Reformation.[10]

Today, however, it becomes increasingly difficult to define Reformation just as a movement. Although the popular assumption is that the Reformation began with Luther's famous nailing of the ninety-five thesis to the door

---

economic, political, and religious life which characterized the century. Harris Harbison, *The Age of Reformation* (New York: Cornell University Press, 1962), 1; see the collection of essays for an excellent historical analysis, Gerald Strauss, ed., *Enacting the Reformation: Essays on Institution and Reception* (Hampshire: Variorum, 1993).

7. McGrath, *Christian Theology*, 55.
8. William Cunningham, *The Reformers and the Theology of Reformation* (Edinburgh: T & T Clark, 1866), 1.
9. Timothy George, *Theology of the Reformers* (Nashville: Broadman, 1988), 18.
10. C. Scott Dixon, ed., *The German Reformation* (Oxford: Blackwell, 1999), 199.

of the Castle Church in Wittenberg in 1517,[11] it is simply inadequate[12] because Reformation was a "universal phenomenon," and the advent of modernity cannot be imagined without it. From a socio-cultural point of view, the Reformation brought an end to the existence and universality of the medieval church, and re-determined the relationship of religion to society and to the world of daily life, redefining the content and boundaries of the religious and spiritual, political and social, and moral and ethical order.[13] Hence Kramm writes:

---

11. It is common to assume the existence of forerunners of the Reformation, e. g., Wycliffe and the Lollards in England, John Hus and various Bohemian Reformation movements, the attempts by Gerson, Marsilius of Padua and others, attempting to raise the authority of general church councils above the authority of the Pope, to criticize abuses in the church, the immorality of her priests, and the stupidity of her monks, as exposed by the humanists. Some utterances of Luther himself may indicate that he believed Hus and the Bohemian brethren to be in the nature of spiritual predecessors of himself. Therefore, some historians assume that it only needed a spark to bring about the explosion of all the accumulated gunpowder. This conception is violently contrasted by others, who claim that the whole Reformation, or at least the start and direction of the Reformation, was exclusively born in Luther's mind and that no one could justifiably claim the name of a forerunner of the Reformation. See K. H. Kramm, *The Theology of Martin Luther* (London: James Clarke, 1947), 30; for an excellent history, see Marvin W. Anderson, *Evangelical Foundations: Religion in England, 1378-1683* (Frankfurt am Main: Peter Lang, 1987); it is also important to read the despair which Luther had in his life leading him to be the herald of Reformation. See John von Rohr, "Medieval Consolation and the Young Luther's Despair," in *Reformation Studies: Essays in Honor of Roland H. Bainton*, ed. Franklin H. Littell (Richmond: John Knox, 1962), 61-74; Scott H. Hendrix, *Recultivating the Vineyard: The Reformation Agendas of Christianization* (Louisville: Westminster, 2004).
12. The nailing of the ninety five theses to the door at the Castle Church is often popularly viewed as the event that pushed the Roman Catholic Church to the edge. However, it is important to remember that it was originally meant to provoke not revolt but discussion of the sale of indulgences. Harbison argues that there were four main conceptions of reform. The first conception looked to saintly individuals to spread the new life through the church by the congregation of their example. This conception was based on a conviction widely held in the Middle Ages that institutions were patterned by God and they could not be made better or worse. Therefore, the proper approach was to pray for the conversion of individuals rather than to attempt the futile task of reorganizing the church as an institution. The second conception of reform was strongly institutional. It was the conciliar theory that since the papacy the church as a whole should shoulder the burden of reform. It rested upon the belief that while parts of the church and even the papacy itself might be utterly corrupt, God's truth and grace were preserved in the church as a whole, in the whole company of the faithful. The third conception of reform was that it should be carried by the secular rulers. It was always assumed in medieval theory that the secular ruler had a wide responsibility for defending and protecting the church. The fourth conception of the reform was the program of a group of scholars who are now called Christian humanists. The essence of this conception was that the new learning would save the church. Harbison, *The Age of Reformation*, 41-46.
13. Richard van Dülmen, "The Reformation and the Modern Age," in *The German*

Luther's Reformation has – at least in Germany and Scandinavia – affected and changed all spheres of life. It affected doctrine, religious life, preaching, liturgy, music, and art; it affected church order, constitution, and finance; it affected the political sphere, especially the relation between church and state, but also between territorial princes and the German emperor; it affected schools and universities, training and moral life of ministers and laymen; and it affected many other spheres, including the creation of a commonly used "high German" language.[14]

Although there were many reasons for the outbreak of the Reformation in the sixteenth century, one cannot neglect the fact that Reformation was a protest against the theological stands of the church and its practices at this time. Therefore, the researcher also employs the word "Reformation" in this study in its conventional sense, particularly the rise of an evangelical Christianity called Protestantism[15] which could not accommodate itself in the old church theology and its ecclesiastical institutions. Since the Reformation of the late Middle Ages, as just noted, was primarily a theological issue[16], the major concern is of how the Reformers prized

---

Reformation: Essential Readings in History, ed. C. Scott Dixon (Oxford: Blackwell, 1999), 199.
14. Kramm, *The Theology of Martin Luther*, 18
15. The best description is still that of Ernst Troeltsch, who early in the twentieth century called Protestantism a "modification of Catholicism" in which the Catholic problems remain, but where different solutions are given. The four questions that Protestantism answered in a new way are: How a person is saved? Where does religious authority lie? What is the church? And what is the essence of Christian living? Protestant Reformers throughout sixteenth-century Europe came to hold similar convictions about these questions but fresh answers emerged first in Luther's personal conflict with Rome. Four major traditions marked in early Protestantism are Lutheran, Reformed, Anabaptist, and Anglican. See Bruce L. Shelly, *Church History in Plain Language* (Dallas: Word Publishing, 1982), 253, 256-257.
16. For an excellent discussion see David C. Steinmetz, "The Intellectual Appeal of the Reformation," *Theology Today* vol. 57, no. 4 (January 2001), 459-472; Luther provided relatively new answers to the four questions which go far back into the Christian history. Firstly, how a person is saved, and Luther answered, not by works but by faith. To the question where does religious authority lie, he answered, not in the visible institution known as the Roman Catholic Church, but in the word of God. To the question what is church, he answered, the whole community of Christian believers. And finally, what is the essence of Christian living, and he answers, serving God in one's calling, whether

the work of the Spirit in their theology. Hence, what follows is a brief discussion on the factors that influenced particularly the pneumatology of the Reformers.

3. A Milieu to the New Paradigm

While attempting to discuss the pneumatology of the Reformers, there are at least two important factors to be taken into consideration that rendered lasting influence in the theology of the Reformers one way or the other. They were, firstly, mysticism[17] and secondly, the teachings of the renowned mystic expositor of prophecy of the twelfth century, Joachim of Fiore. Hence, it is impossible to move forward without discussing these two factors and how they influenced the Reformers in their theology of the Spirit.

In fact, the two dominant forces in the theology of the later Middle Ages were mysticism and nominalism.[18] One way of using the word mysticism is to express the "type of religion which puts the emphasis on immediate awareness of relation with God, on direct and intimate consciousness of the divine presence."[19] In other words, mysticism is an intensely personal and individual thing, bringing the single soul face to face with God, without the intervention of the priests or sacraments. During the Middle Ages, three types or schools of mysticism developed: the Neo-Platonic; the Christ-mysticism of Bernard of Clairvaux; and the German Mysticism associated

---

secular or ecclesiastical, since all useful callings are equally sacred in the eyes of God. See Harbison, *The Age of Reformation*, 53.

17. The mystic is the one who claims to be able to see God and divine things with the inner vision of the soul. This has been the subjective principle of Protestantism. See Charles Beard, *The Reformation of the Sixteenth Century in its Relation to Modern Thought and Knowledge: Herbert Lectures* (London: Constable, 1927), 16-17.

18. Nominalism held that universals (general concepts representing the common elements belonging to individuals of the same genus or species) have a separate existence apart from the individual object, and reality is found only in the objects themselves. Roscellinus of Compiegne, a teacher and priest in Brittany in the eleventh century, has been called the father of nominalism. In the fourteenth century William Ockham devised a nominalistic system of theology which had lasting impact on the later theologies. See D. A. Rausch, "Nominalism," in *Evangelical Dictionary of Theology*, 2nd edition, ed. Walter A. Elwell (Grand Rapids: Baker Academic, 2001), 843.

19. Rufus M. Jones, *Studies in Mystical Religion* (London: Macmillan, 1923), xv.

with men like Tauler,[20] Suso,[21] and Eckhardt.[22] These mystics were more religious, and one of their ventures was to make the church spiritual.[23] They emphasized that the heart of religion is the union of the soul with God. It was exactly the same desire of the Reformers as well to get away from the mechanical and formal means of salvation offered by the church. Charles Beard writes:

> It could never be anything but a sporadic phenomenon because it was so intensely individual. While it satisfied the spiritual needs of many, it could never amalgamate with other forces of the time, either social or intellectual. As a philosophy or a creed it led not so much to solipsism as to a complete abnegation of the reason. Moreover, it was slightly morbid, liable to mistake giddiness of starved nerve and emotion for a moment of vision and of union with God.[24]

The same conviction can be seen in the words of Hillerbrand that, "The point of the Protestant proclamation was that religion was to be personal and creative. It called for personal involvement, not merely the affirmation of the dogma of the church or the external participation in its rites."[25] It is a fact that the Reformers were in a sense following this mystical tradition and it is explicit in their writings. For example, the Christian mysticism of Germany had a considerable share in the development of Luther's religious

---

20. Tauler interpreted the Bible allegorically. His sermons were filled with the constant admonitions that one must overcome the "darkness of the flesh" by searching for God who is already within human in the "divine spark" and by attaining complete "independence from creatureliness." See Dick Helander, *Johann Tauler als Prediger* (Lund: Almquist and Wicksells, 1923), 261.
21. Suso proclaimed humanity's inner conformity with God and Christ through the union between the divine "spark" in the human soul and the divine Word – expressed in the terminology of romantic love. See Henry Suso, "Das Büchklein der Wahrheit," in *Heinrich Seuse: Deutsche Schriften*, ed. Karl Bihlmeyer (Frankfurt: Minerva, 1961), 90-95.
22. Charles S. Anderson in his Introduction to Bengt Hägglund, *The Background of Luther's Doctrine of Justification in Late Medieval Theology* (Philadelphia: Fortress, 1971), vi; see this book for a detailed discussion on these different schools of thought.
23. Preserved Smith, *The Age of the Reformation* (New York: Henry Holt, 1920), 30.
24. Smith, *The Age of the Reformation*, 34.
25. Hans J. Hillerbrand, ed., *The Protestant Reformation* (New York: Torchbooks, 1968), xxiii.

opinions.[26] Charles Beard says that justification by faith, at least in its most spiritual form, is a mystical doctrine.[27] Moreover, one should realize the fact that the Christian mystics have taken their anchor on the teachings of Augustine. Since Luther was trained in Augustinian scheme, the mystical influence can be marked in his theology. In the same way, this same mystical influence can be seen in the writings of the other Reformers as well, particularly in the pneumatology of the radical Reformers.[28]

The second significant influence upon the Reformers and their pneumatology was the teachings of the twelfth century Calabrian expositor of prophecy, Joachim of Fiore. To be particular about Joachim, it was his explication of the Spirit that influenced the Reformers and their doctrine of the Spirit. Delno writes:

> The recurring influence of the twelfth century Calabrian expositor of prophecy, Joachim of Fiore, is one of the more interesting features of late medieval intellectual histories. The spread of Joachims's writings and men's belief in them must rank as a major milestone in the history of Western thought. His pronouncements have appeared again and again in the history of Western Civilization down to modern times, thus making Joachim of Fiore an important figure to Western ideas about time and human destiny.[29]

---

26. Martin Luther and Thomas Müntzer had an attraction towards the 13th century German Mystic, John Tauler. Luther, at least initially, held Tauler's theology in high esteem. His lectures on Romans would appear to confirm that he encountered Tauler sometime in 1516. Müntzer's intellectual development was also deeply influenced by Tauler. See Abraham Friesen, "Thomas Müntzer and Martin Luther," *Archive for Reformation History* vol. 79 (1988), 59-79.

27. Beard, *The Reformation of the Sixteenth Century*, 187; Luther was never primarily a mystic. However, he often quoted the medieval mystics. The emergence of his Evangelical theology and ethics cannot be understood without understanding his acceptance of the mystical theology. For a discussion see George Huntston Williams, "German Mysticism in the Polarization of Ethical Behavior in Luther and the Anabaptists," *MQR* vol. 48, no. 3 (July 1974), 275-304.

28. For a detailed discussion on the mystical influence upon Müntzer see, Reinhard Schwarz, "Thomas Müntzer und die Mystik," in *Der Theologie Thomas Müntzers: Untersuchungen zu einer Entwicklung und Lehre*, ed. Siegfried Bräur and Helmar Junghans (Göttingen: Vandenhoeck & Ruprecht, 1989), 283-301.

29. Delno C. West, "Introduction," in *Joachim of Fiore in Christian Thought: Essays on the Influence of the Calabrian Prophet* vol. 1, ed. Delno C. West (New York: Burt Franklin,

A Paradigm Shift: Brief Survey of Reformer's Pneumatology

As noted in the first chapter, Joachim divided history[30] into three ages associated respectively with the Father, Son, and the Holy Spirit. He asserted that the dawn of the third age would be heralded by the coming of a new order of spiritual men who would oppose the false hierarchy of the church and prepare the way for a new millennium of peace which would continue until the last judgment. Delno comments:

> An even more innovative aspect of Joachim's writings was his interpretation of the mission of the Holy Spirit. The church fathers had conceived the Holy Spirit as the force which developed and spread the teachings of Christ. Joachim, on the other hand, held that the Holy Spirit would complete the teachings of Christ and unlock God's last revelation before the end time.[31]

The Protestant Reformers carried the idea of the new age or the eschatological future[32] of Joachim further by mixing it with an identification of

---

1975), i.

30. Joachim considered the inquiry into history as another path to knowing God. He sensed that historical inquiry would provide the key which unlocks the hidden meaning in Scripture, not only to understand the past, but also to interpret the future. The Old and New Testaments are parallel halves of history which correspond in significant detail so that the astute observer and reader could extend these parallels and correspondences into the time from the resurrection to the twelfth century and into the future. See Delno C. West and Sandra Zimdars-Swartz, *Joachim of Fiore: A Study in Spiritual Perception and History* (Bloomington: Indiana University Press, 1983), xi-xii; two of Joachim's immediate predecessors, Rupert of Deutz, writing in the first quarter of the twelfth century, and Anselm of Haverlberg, in the second quarter, developed a concept of meaning within time itself by interpreting it as a progressive revelation of the Trinity. Each of them saw progressive stages of illumination, the work of the Spirit in history. See Marjorie Reeves, *Joachim of Fiore and the Prophetic Future* (SPCK: London, 1976), 2.

31. West and Zimdars-Swartz, *Joachim of Fiore*, 12, 78-98.

32. Roland Bainton, *The Reformation of the Sixteenth Century* (London: Hodder and Stoughton, 1965), 19; Reid argues that eschatology was a strong doctrine during the Middle Ages. This eschatological thought was rooted in the Scripture, especially in the apocalyptic passages in the Minor Prophets, Daniel, Mathew, and Revelation. Within these strains of biblical thought two themes predominated: the advent of the anti-Christ and a widespread hope based upon the return of the prophets Enoch and Elijah, who would come in the last days to preach against this anti-Christ. This eschatological vision was very strong in Luther and Müntzer. Both of their eschatological systems were shaped by their understanding of history. See Darrel R. Reid, "Luther, Müntzer, and the Last Day: Eschatological Hope, Apocalyptic Expectations," *MQR* vol. 69, no. 1 (January 1995), 53-74.

Rome as the apocalyptic Babylon and the Pope as an agent of the anti-Christ.[33] Moreover, the great Protestant compilers of historical anthologies saw Joachim and his disciples as the prophetic voices announcing the Roman Catholic Church as Babylon.[34] Consequently, the Protestant scholars ransacked the annals of the Roman Church for weapons to turn against her. The history of Joachim provided two splendid pieces from this armory.[35] One was Joachim's own pronouncement that the anti-Christ was already born in Rome. The other one was the scandal of the "eternal evangel'" which was used as evidence of the corruption of the Roman Church.[36] Burrell writes:

> By detaching the Spirit from the Son and by leaving the age of the Spirit to be determined, Joachim's typology gave to each charismatic leader who would emerge the opportunity of inaugurating this third age by giving a specific interpretation to the apocalyptic pronouncements in the New Testament.[37]

Matthias Flacius[38] picks out various supposed prophecies of Joachim which are damaging to the papacy and also emphasized his expectation of

---

33. West and Zimdars-Swartz, *Joachim of Fiore*, 107; by the end of the medieval period, the spirituality of the church was at low ebb. The secular interests of the clergy, the widespread absence of bishops from their diocese and the financial difficulties of the curia are further examples of factors which combined to compromise the moral and spiritual authority of the church at the time in a serious manner. It is obvious that there was considerable confusion within the late medieval church, undoubtedly exacerbated by a largely uneducated clergy, on matters of doctrine and the doctrine of justification in particular. See Alister E. McGrath, *Luther's Theology of the Cross* (Oxford: Blackwell, 1990), 8.
34. Reeves, *Joachim of Fiore*, 137.
35. Reeves, *Joachim of Fiore*, 136.
36. Reeves, *Joachim of Fiore*, 136-137.
37. David B. Burrell, "The Spirit and the Christian Life," in *Christian Theology: An Introduction to its Traditions and Tasks*, eds. Peter C. Hodgson and Robert H. King (Philadelphia: Fortress, 1988), 311; the next four hundred years in Europe heard the proclamation that the new age is upon them. Always appealing to the Spirit, these movements began with powerful preachers recalling the people to the purity of their faith in Jesus. The presumed vehicle of that faith that is the church and the clergy would be the evident target for the preacher's polemic, who would then be quite naturally drawn to proclaim the age of the Spirit in opposition to the now corrupted age of the Son. Burrell, "The Spirit and the Christian Life," 311.
38. Matthias Flacius (1520-1575) was a Lutheran theologian who developed a Lutheran teaching not only in distinction from Catholicism but also in opposition to the doctrine of the more moderate Lutherans.

the Reformation and saw the application of Joachim's third *status* to the Reformation.³⁹

The real Joachites among the Protestants were the visionaries who felt that they must interpret their religious experience in terms of a revolutionary new era of history. For example, in Basle, Curione shared his hopes with the humanist and biblical scholar, Sebastian Castellione, who maintained that the age of God announced in the Scripture must be awaited with expectation. In the Basle group we also find Bernardino Ochino who strongly emphasized the third age of the Spirit. Reeves writes:

> It is possible that his emphasis on the third stage of history now about to dawn, when the evangelical faith would be diffused throughout the whole world and all men would live in Christian liberty under the law of love, owed its inspiration to copies of works by Joachim and his disciples known to have been in the Sienese convent from which he started.⁴⁰

In their breakaway from an over-intellectualized dogma and their search for an imaginative vision of the work of the Spirit in history, some recognized Joachim, the antagonist Peter Lombard, as their forerunner. The most interesting example of these is Michael Servetus.⁴¹ He twice referred to Joachim in his polemic against metaphysical views of the Trinity. He came closer to the idea of what Cantimori has said, "the Joachimite vision of Christian history with the passion of the reformer in order to refute

---

39. Reeves, *Joachim of Fiore*, 138.
40. Reeves, *Joachim of Fiore*, 140.
41. Servetus was a Franciscan friar who rejected the belief of the Trinity as not based on the Bible but on the teachings of the Greek philosophers. He strongly advocated a return to a supposed simplicity of the gospels and the early church fathers. He hoped that the dismissal of the trinitarian dogma would also make Christianity more appealing to Judaism and Islam, which had preserved the unity of God in their teachings, whereas trinitarians, according to Servetus, had turned Christianity into a form of "tritheism," or belief in three gods. Servetus states his view clearly in the preamble to *Restoration of Christianity* (1553). He writes, "There is nothing greater, reader, than to recognize that God has been manifested as substance, and that His divine nature has been truly communicated. We shall clearly apprehend the manifestation of God through the Word and his communication through the Spirit, both of them substantially in Christ alone." See Michael Servetus, *Restitución del Cristianismo*, eds. Angel Alcalá and Luis Betés (Madrid: Fundación Universitaria Española, 1980), 119.

scholasticism."[42] He maintained that the reign of Christ began in the new liberty of evangelical truth, was indeed the third dispensation of history, the age of the Spirit, the humanist age of God.

One of the radical Reformers, who openly acknowledged his respect for Joachim, was Thomas Müntzer.[43] However, the question is how far Müntzer had really picked up the method of Joachim. It can be assumed beyond doubt that Müntzer had derived firstly, the method of interpreting the Scripture by concords in a pattern of threes; secondly, his belief that the third "state" of enlightenment would be brought in by the activities of men themselves.[44] In his Prague manifesto, Müntzer puts forth a program for the new church of the Spirit in which the elect would be directly instructed by a seven-fold outpouring of the Spirit, superseding all previous religious authority.[45] In Nuremberg Johann Herrgott, who was probably an adherent of Müntzer, wrote a pamphlet which opens with a clear statement of Joachim's three *statuses*:

> Three transformations have been seen in history: the first was instituted by God the Father in the Old Testament; the second transformation was instituted by God the Son in the word with the New Testament; the third transformation will be brought about by the Holy Spirit; with this future transformation the world will be changed from the evil in which it finds itself.[46]

Another significant figure in the radical Reformation, who followed the mystical tradition and asserted conversion and regeneration through the Spirit, is Menno Simons. Menno was the most outstanding leader of the

---

42. Reeves, *Joachim of Fiore*, 141.
43. Thomas Müntzer and the other radical Reformers perceived how explosive it was to claim the sanction of the Spirit to use the apocalyptic portions of the Scripture to fuel one's own cause. Spiritual illumination would replace learning as the Spirit overcomes a worldly church and a corruptible world. Thus the oppositions embedded in the early desert monastic challenge took on a new impetus, given the directing force of Joachim's ideology and the power of a mass movement. Burrell, "The Spirit and the Christian Life," 312; however there are people who argue that Joachimist influence on Müntzer has been overestimated. See Richard Bailey, "The Sixteenth Century's Apocalyptic Heritage and Thomas Müntzer," *MQR* vol. 57, no. 1 (January 1983), 27-44.
44. Reeves, *Joachim of Fiore*, 141.
45. Reeves, *Joachim of Fiore*, 142.
46. Cited in Reeves, *Joachim of Fiore*, 142.

Anabaptist branch of the radical Reformation.[47] Wenger notes that there are three important clusters of events and ideas in Menno's developing consciousness of the true church and his role in it. They were the issue of Lord's Supper, infant baptism, and finally the events surrounding the tragedy of Thomas Müntzer. Hans Denck, a moderate Anabaptist Reformer also followed the same mystical influence. Caspar von Schwenckfeld and Sebastian Frank, the notable spiritualists also were in line with the mystical tradition. All these Reformers asserted the Spirit not just as a person, but as a force as was envisaged by Joachim of Fiore.[48]

In short, along with many other factors, mysticism and the teachings of Joachim of Fiore had a lasting impact in shaping the pneumatology of the Reformers and their teachings. Hence, in the shadow of this background, one can move this discussion into the inquiry of the pneumatology of the Reformers to know what exactly was the pneumatology of the Reformers? To make this survey more feasible, the following discussion is divided into two parts. In the first part, the pneumatological discussion is centered on the right wing Reformers, namely Martin Luther and John Calvin. It follows a discussion on the pneumatology of the left wing Reformers, namely Thomas Müntzer, Menno Simons, Hans Denck, Caspar von Schwenckfeld, and Sebastian Franck.

---

47. Menno was neither the first nor the most original exponent of the Anabaptist tradition. One must note that the Swiss Anabaptism emerged out of the cradle of the Zwinglian Reformation. Its earliest leaders, namely Conrad Grebel and Felix Mantz, were radical disciples of Zwingli who felt that they were merely carrying the ideas they had learned from master Huldrych. Through their study of the Bible, they became convinced that the baptism they had received as infants was invalid and that, in defiance of Zwingli since he could not be persuaded, they had to restore true baptism of the believers only. See George, *Theology of the Reformers*, 255.

48. George H. Williams and Angel M. Mergal, eds., *Spiritual and Anabaptist Writers: Documents Illustrative of the Radical Reformers* (London: SCM, 1957), 35.

4. Pneumatology of the Right Wing Reformers

4.1 Martin Luther (1483 – 1546)

Luther did not make a separate study on pneumatology, although the Holy Spirit is a central thesis in the whole theology of Martin Luther[49] due to his realization that the arrival of the Spirit will equip the church for its final struggle with the adversary. Perry Hall writes that, "The Holy Spirit is a central doctrine in the theology of Martin Luther; his theology expresses his personal experience that he has been rescued in Christ by faith (*sola fide*); and the Holy Spirit comes through the physical means of the Word and sacrament (*sola scriptura*)."[50] Prenter also asserts that the concept of the Holy Spirit dominates Luther's theology although he has no systematic doctrine of the Spirit but rather a powerful living testimony of the Spirit.[51] There are three things that are important when dealing with the pneumatology of Luther, as follows; firstly, the Holy Spirit is a central doctrine in the theology of Luther; secondly, his theology expresses his personal experience of conviction of sin and forgiveness, the testimony of the Holy Spirit that he has been rescued in Christ by faith, and finally the Holy Spirit comes through the physical means of the Word and sacrament.[52]

---

49. The background of the doctrine of the Spirit in the writings of Luther is his study of Augustine's *de Trinitate,* which made a deep impression upon him, particularly in connection with the relationship between *dilectio* (or *caritas*) and the Spirit. For Luther, the concept of a created habit caused more problems than it solved, and he therefore attempted to resolve the dilemma on the basis of the lines indicated by Augustine himself. Setting aside hypothetical speculation Luther argues that it is impossible to separate the gifts of *caritas* and the Spirit. Both are given simultaneously and in conjunction with one another. Luther further argues that the relationship between *caritas* and the Spirit is to be regarded as analogous to that between *iustitia* and Christ. So he maintains that Spirit is *caritas*. Luther here reproduces an authentically Augustinian theme which had assumed increasing importance in later medieval theology. See McGrath, *Luther's Theology*, 81-85; also see Carl E. Braaten, *Principles of Lutheran Theology*, 2nd edition (Minneapolis: Fortress, 2007); Avery Dulles, S. J., *The Assurance of Things Hoped For: A Theology of Christian Faith* (Oxford: Oxford University Press, 1994), 44-46; also see a discussion by Scott Hendrix, "Martin Luther's Reformation of Spirituality," *Lutheran Quarterly* vol. 13, no. 1 (Spring 1999), 249-270.
50. Fred Perry Hall, *The Lutheran Doctrine of the Holy Spirit in the Sixteenth Century: Developments of the "Formula of Concord"* (California: Pasadena, 1993), 53.
51. See Regin Prenter, *Spiritus Creator*, trans. John M. Jensen (Philadelphia: Muhlenberg, 1953); ix; Larry Christenson, ed., *Welcome Holy Spirit* (Minneapolis: Augsburg, 1987), 173.
52. Hall, *The Lutheran Doctrine of the Holy Spirit*, 53.

First of all, Luther affirmed the divinity of the Spirit and its full personal participation in the divine essence and majesty, and maintained that the Spirit is a distinct person who proceeds from the Father and the Son.[53] Luther writes that, "The Father, generating, transfers his substance in the divinity to the Son. Thus the Father and the Son and the Holy Spirit are three distinct persons, and yet in truth one essence. These things can be believed but they will never be capable of being understood by human reason. However, I say that the Father, remaining the same God, transfers his divinity to the Son in such a way that the Son is the complete and perfect image and stamp of the Father."[54]

Having affirmed the divinity of the Spirit, Luther asserts that the Bible is "the Holy Spirit's book, namely the Holy Scripture in which one must seek Christ and find him."[55] Although it was written by human beings, it is neither of men nor from men, but from God. Luther makes his point clear by saying that there are many quotations which affirm that the Spirit speaks in the words of the Bible, as if he was the real author of the Bible or he moved the authors to write down the truth revealed by the Holy Ghost.[56] Moreover, the Spirit creates and gives faith through the preaching of the Word of God.[57] The Spirit brings awareness of Christ, faith, and confidence to those who believe, and bestows on them the merit of Christ. This is the testimony of the Spirit, witnessing to the authority of the Bible by using biblical preaching to create faith.[58] This faith from the Spirit through the Word is a gift of God which cannot be earned or achieved by human effort. Moreover, where Christ is not preached there is no Spirit to create, call, and gather the Christian church. But when Christ is preached as the prophets and apostles present him, then God speaks through the Word and the Spirit

---

53. Cf. Martin Luther, "Vom Abendmahl Christi. Bekenntnis" (1528), in *WA* 26: 505. 29ff.
54. Cf. Martin Luther, "Die Disputation über Job 1:14" (1539), in *WA* 39/2: 24, 9-14.
55. Martin Luther, "Spruche aus dem Alten Testament", in *WA* 48: 43. 3f.
56. Cf. Martin Luther, "Sprüche aus dem Alten Testament", in *WA* 48: 31. 24; Kramm, *The Theology of Martin Luther*, 117.
57. For an excellent discussion of Reformation Hermeneutics see, Peter Matheson, "Whose Scripture? A Foray into Reformation Hermeneutics," *MQR* vol. 70, no. 2 (April 1996), 191-202.
58. Kramm, *The Theology of Martin Luther*, 116.

produces faith, hope, love, and joyful new life.[59] Hence Luther advocated for the Word of God due to his conviction that the Spirit would lead people to Christ, works repentance and faith, and bestows the gifts of the Spirit through the spoken Word only.[60] Luther writes:

> No one can rightly understand God or His Word who has not received such understanding directly from the Holy Spirit. But no one can receive it from the Holy Spirit without experiencing, proving, and feeling it. In such experience, the Holy Spirit instructs us as in His own school.[61]

However, Luther warns that poor interpretation of Scripture will lead to the introduction of biblically unfounded doctrines and illegitimate devotional practices. But through a biblically legitimized Scripture interpretation, the required obedience to God's law can be fulfilled. It is possible only through the free gift of the Spirit.[62]

Luther makes a real effort to strengthen the authority of the ministry by relating the influence of the Spirit in the Christian ministry. Hence, Luther exhorted the Christian ministers to combine Word and Spirit in their ministry, especially prayers.[63] Such prayer includes the petition for the gift of the Spirit who uses the Word to accomplish a renewing and saving work in human hearts. Luther's approach to God in prayer in the Spirit is based on justification by faith where by the Spirit brings believers to God through the grace of forgiveness in Christ. Through grace the Spirit moves a person towards God in prayer and to rely upon the unmerited love of God in Christ.[64] Moreover, the Spirit will meet those who are discouraged

---

59. Fred W. Meuser, "Luther as Preacher of the Word of God," in *The Cambridge Companion to Martin Luther*, ed. Donald McKim (Cambridge: Cambridge University Press, 2003), 138.
60. Meuser, "Luther as Preacher of the Word of God," 141.
61. Cf. Martin Luther "Das Magnificat Verdeutschet und Ausgelegt" (1521), in *WA* 7: 546, 24-28.
62. Markus Wriedt, "Luther's Theology," trans. Katharina Gustavs, in *The Cambridge Companion to Martin Luther*, ed. Donald McKim (Cambridge: Cambridge University Press, 2003), 92.
63. Cf. Martin Luther, "Nam Quid oremus etc., nescimus," in *WA* 56: 376, 4-8; Cf. Martin Luther, "Auslegung deutsch des Vaterunsers für die einfältigen Laien" (1519), in *WA* 2: 115, 19-26.
64. Cf. Martin Luther, "Vom Missbrauch der Messe" (1521), in *WA* 8: 552, 536-553, 1.

with hope and comfort. Luther argues further that the Spirit establishes the corporate grouping of Christians for prayer in the church. And for Luther, the church's ministry is authoritative because in justification by faith the Spirit makes the redemptive merit of Christ operative in all members, and thus Christ's authority dwells in them.

According to Luther, salvation is the ultimate work of the Spirit. Luther writes:

> I believe that I cannot by my own reason or strength believe in Jesus Christ, my Lord, or come to Him; but the Holy Ghost has called me by the Gospel, enlightened me with his gifts, sanctified and kept me in true faith; even as He calls, gathers, enlightens and sanctifies the whole of Christian church on earth and keeps it with Jesus Christ in the one true faith: in which Christian church He daily and richly forgives all sins to me and all believers ....[65]

That means the task of the Spirit is to help Christians to find their way to Christ and to become one with Christ. In other words, Luther's position can be described such that in the Word God has given the Holy Spirit to offer and apply to humanity the treasure of salvation. Therefore to sanctify is nothing other than to bring humanity to Jesus Christ in order to receive the goodness of salvation made through Christ.[66] That means the Spirit brings the union of humanity with Christ into existence and produces love for God in them. Moreover, the Spirit preserves the human beings in this union of love until they are perfectly pure and holy people, full of goodness and righteousness, completely freed from sin, death, and all evil, living in new, immortal, and glorified bodies.[67] Thus the work of the Spirit continues throughout the whole life of a person until he/she is totally transformed into Christ and possesses the complete form of Christ.[68]

---

65. Martin Luther, "Der Kleine Katechismus" (1529), in *WA* 30/1: 296, 24-32 & 298, 1-4.
66. Simo Peura, "What God Gives Man Receives: Luther on Salvation," in *Union with Christ: The New Finnish Interpretation*, eds. Carl E. Braaten and Robert W. Jenson (Grand Rapids: Eerdmans, 1998), 90.
67. Peura, "What God Gives Man Receives," 91.
68. Peura, "What God Gives Man Receives," 91.

Luther asserted the continuous support of the Spirit in the life of a believer to lead a victorious Christian life. Therefore, he contends that the Spirit is given to battle sin in the conflict between the Spirit and the flesh which starts as soon as one begins to believe. But by the help of the Spirit, they can overcome. Moreover, the Spirit works in people to conform them to the character of Jesus Christ. Hall quotes Luther and writes that, "Christ has given us his Holy Spirit; He makes us spiritual and subdues the flesh, and assures us that we are still God's children, however hard sin may be raging within us, so long as we follow the Spirit and resist sin to slay it. Since, however, nothing else is so good for the mortifying of the flesh as the cross and suffering, He comforts us in suffering with the support of the spirit of love … the Spirit sighs within us … that we may be rid of the flesh and of sin."[69] Thus when a person is conformed to Christ, the Spirit gives him a new heart which reflects a love and pleasure for God's will and law with new desires to live a godly life. Hall argues that, "Luther broke from Augustine and the scholastics who saw the Holy Spirit as God prodding people's latent Godwardness to enable them to live God-pleasing lives. Luther's idea of the Holy Spirit began with the death of the old man and a new life in the Spirit, which collapsed the foundation of the Augustinian system."[70] This aspect of the real presence of God in the Spirit constitutes the core of Luther's theology.

According to Luther the Spirit is given only through the external means of the Word of God that is preaching, hearing, and believing the Word and the sacraments.[71] He writes:

> The Holy Spirit is now truly present among us and works in us through the Word and sacraments. He has covered himself with veils and clothing so that our weak, sick and leprous nature might grasp him and know him. If he came to us in his majesty, we would not be able to comprehend him and to bear so bright a light. So it is that He comes to us in his

---

69. See Hall, *The Lutheran Doctrine of the Holy Spirit*, 75.
70. Hall, *The Lutheran Doctrine of the Holy Spirit*, 77.
71. Cf. Luther, "Vom Missbrauch der Messe," 8: 541: 8f.

> prophets; and He is in truth bodily and substantially present in us through the Word and sacrament.[72]

Moreover, Luther insisted that where there is a holy, Christian church, all the sacraments and Christ himself will be there along with the Holy Spirit. It must be noted that Luther recognized only baptism and the Lord's Supper as sacraments because they only include the Scriptural promises attached to the physical signs.

In short, the Spirit is a central doctrine in the theology of Martin Luther. He identifies an incarnational dimension in the Spirit's visible coming to the world. Linking Christology with pneumatology, Luther maintained that pneumatology is foundational to Christian theology. Moreover, as an internal expression of his own experience of release and forgiveness, Luther emphasizes the internal testimony of the Spirit and the continual work of the Spirit in the life of a believer. And he recognizes the Word and sacraments as the means of the Spirit.

4.2 John Calvin (1509 – 1564)

As it was just noted in Luther, the Holy Spirit is a central doctrine in the theology of Calvin as well.[73] Zahman argues that, "He [Calvin] hoped to renew the knowledge of God in Jesus Christ through the Holy Spirit, not only in name, but in the experience of power, so that the faithful might know God as the author and fountain of every good thing, and be united to

---

72. Martin Luther, "Die Promotionsdispotation von Palladius und Tilemann" (1537), in *WA* 39/1: 244. 11-19.
73. Calvin is sometimes called the Thomas Aquinas of Protestantism to suggest that he played somewhat the same role of synthesizing and systematizing that St. Thomas performed three centuries earlier. Aquinas is one of the very few schoolmen whom Calvin quotes with respect in the *Institutes*. See E. Harris Harbison, *The Christian Scholar in the Age of the Reformation* (Philadelphia: Porcupine, 1956), 139; McGrath makes a detailed inquiry into the theological background of Calvin and maintains that he has been influenced by the *via moderna* and *schola augustiniana moderna*. See Alister E. McGrath, "John Calvin and the Late Medieval Thought: A Study in Late Medieval Influences upon Calvin's Theological Development," *Archive for Reformation History* vol. 77 (1986), 58-78; however, there are theologians who argue that Calvin was the greatest disciple of Luther. Historian Preserved Smith notes that first and foremost, Calvin depended on Luther. He also borrowed from Bucer, Erasmus, and Schwenckfeld. See Smith, *The Age of the Reformation*, 164.

God in eternal life."[74] Calvin's doctrine of the Spirit took a developed form in his renowned work entitled '*Institutes of Christian Religion.*'

Calvin treated the Spirit as the supreme God and not just as a third member in the Trinity. He affirms his point by referring to the history of creation. Calvin writes:

> And it is by no means an obscure testimony which Moses bears in the history of the creation, when he says that the Spirit of God was expanded over the abyss or shapeless matter; for it shows not only that the beauty which the world displays is maintained by the invigorating power of the Spirit, but that even before this beauty existed the Spirit was at work cherishing the confused mass.[75]

Thus he argues that in the same way Christ is the redemptive and creative Word of God, the Spirit is regenerative and creative.[76] All the particular attributes of the Godhead are ascribed to him in the same way as to the Son.[77] By means of the Spirit, according to Calvin, we become partakers of the divine nature and our justification is his work. It is from the Spirit that power, sanctification, truth, grace, and every good thought flow, only because all good gifts proceed from the Spirit alone. By taking anchor on 1 Cor 12:11, Calvin argues the divine power of the Spirit and demonstrates that he dwells hypostatically in God.[78] He is the true Jehovah, who dictated the prophecies.[79]

One of the specialties of Calvin's pneumatology is his representation of the person and work of Christ in constant reference to the Spirit, and the reality and work of the Spirit in constant reference to Christ. Therefore, Willis argues that, "Calvin's Christology is of course a 'Spirit-Christology'

---

74. Randall C. Zachman, "John Calvin (1509-1564)," in *The Reformation Theologians: An Introduction to Theology in the Early Modern Period*, ed. Carter Lindberg (Oxford: Blackwell, 2002), 184.
75. John Calvin, *Institutes of the Christian Religion,* trans. Henry Beveridge (Grand Rapids: Eerdmans, 1989), 1.12.14; 1.12.22; (Hereafter *Institute*).
76. David Willis, *Calvin's Catholic Christology: The Function of the So-called Extra Calvinism in Calvin's Theology* (Leiden: Brill, 1966), 121.
77. *Institutes* 1.12.14.
78. *Institutes* 1.12.14.
79. *Institutes* 1.12.15.

in the sense that it is so much a *Filioque-Christology* he never loses sight of the role of the Holy Spirit in the incarnation."[80] By referring to the *filioque* provision, Calvin underscores that the Son is never effectively active in creation or redemption without the Spirit.[81] Calvin argues that, it is through the Spirit that the humanity assumed by the eternal Son was sanctified for the office to be accomplished by the incarnate God.[82] It was not because Jesus was engendered without sexual intercourse that Jesus Christ was exempt from original sin, but because Jesus Christ was sanctified in his birth by the Spirit in such a way that he is true human, yet free from all fault and corruption.[83] Moreover, Calvin contends that in contrast to the prophets who went before him, Christ alone was given the Spirit without measure[84] and Christ alone received the Spirit in order to bestow it on all others.[85] Christ's uniqueness was that an unlimited abundance of Spirit had been poured out on him by the Father.[86] Christ received the Spirit not as the eternal Son but according to his manifestation in the flesh.[87]

---

80. Willis, *Calvin's Catholic Christology*, 82.
81. Willis, *Calvin's Catholic Christology*, 83.
82. Calvin maintained the view that during the life of Jesus Christ in Nazareth, the Word and Spirit were so joined that only those moved by the Spirit believed that Jesus, even after they saw his power demonstrated, was the messiah of God. Of course, only those so moved perceived, in the face of his humility when his power was not openly manifest, his true identity. The revelation was real enough, an unmistakable and concrete exhibition of divine power; but the revelation never became revelation for any one of Jesus' chronological companions except by the work of the Spirit. See Willis, *Calvin's Catholic Christology*, 116.
83. Charles A. M. Hall, *With the Spirit's Sword: The Drama of Spiritual Warfare in the Theology of John Calvin* (Zurich: EVZ Verlag, 1968), 86; *Institutes*, 2, 13-14; before his baptism, Jesus was indeed indwelt by the Spirit, but with the baptism he was clothed with a new power of the Spirit not so much for his own sake but rather to perform the office of redeemer for others. The appearance of the Spirit on that occasion was a reminder that nothing carnal was to be expected in Christ. He came from heaven as a divine being in whom the power of the Spirit reigned; so even as a servant and according to Jesus' human nature, here he was a heavenly power. See John Calvin, *Calvin's New Testament Commentaries*, eds. David W. Torrance and Thomas F. Torrance (Grand Rapids: Eerdmans, 1972), *Matthew* 3:16; (Hereafter *Commentary*).
84. *Commentary Luke* 1:15.
85. *Commentary Luke* 1:15.
86. *Commentary John* 3:34.
87. For Calvin, the power of Christ's Spirit, which came from the Father to renew human beings, was received according to Christ's humanity. The Spirit of the Father's love flowed into the human nature. This anointing with the Spirit equipped his humanity with gifts to accomplish the office of the redeemer.

Calvin, like Luther, maintained that the Bible is the inspired Word of God revealed in human language and confirmed to the believer by the inner witness of the Spirit. In other words, for Calvin, the Bible is the "school of the Holy Spirit." He writes that, "Although, as I have observed, there is this difference between the apostles and their successors, they were sure and authentic amanuenses of the Holy Spirit; and, therefore, their writings are to be regarded as the oracles of God…"[88] He continues that the Spirit at times uses both "eloquence" and "'a rude and unrefined style" in the Bible.[89] Calvin portrayed Mark as a genuine human author, who was uniquely inspired by the Spirit, not as a kind of programmed computer or automated typewriter.[90] Moreover, the human beings receive the saving knowledge of God only through the Word of God which is joined to the Spirit.[91] He adds that, humanity may contrive ways from Scripture for not coming to Christ.[92] However, the Spirit inwardly draws them, as it choses the prophets and apostles for the special witness of God's actions. The Scripture is the means of this particular vivifying revelation for us and the Spirit uses them to point to Christ.[93]

How could one know that the Bible is the Word of God? Calvin maintains that it is possible only when the same Spirit who inspired the prophets and apostles illuminates one's mind and confirms it. Against the demand for rational proof that Moses and the prophets were inspired and defending the inspiration of the biblical writers, Calvin writes:

> But I answer, that the testimony of the Spirit is superior to reason. For as God alone can properly bear witness to his own Words, so these Words will not obtain full credit in the hearts of men, until they are sealed by the inward testimony of the Spirit. The same Spirit, therefore, who spoke by the mouth of the prophets, must penetrate our hearts in order to convince

---

88. *Institutes*, 4.8.9.
89. *Institutes*, 1.8.2.
90. George, *Theology of the Reformers*, 195.
91. Willis, *Calvin's Catholic Christology*, 117.
92. *Commentary John* 7: 41.
93. Willis, *Calvin's Catholic Christology*, 119-120.

us that they faithfully delivered the message with which they were divinely instructed.[94]

Therefore, Calvin asserts that, the ability to recognize the Bible as the Word of God is not a skill acquired through the academic study or dogmatic presuppositions rather it is the free gift of God himself. That means the believers who are enlightened by the Spirit maintain a direct correlation between the moments of inspiration and illumination.[95] Thus, through the witness of the Spirit, the Scriptures authenticate themselves and disclose their proper interpretation to the diligent believer. Calvin contends that the Spirit will show his power only when the proper reverence and dignity are given to the Word. He writes, "… the Holy Spirit so cleaves to His own truth, as He has expressed it in scripture, that He then only exerts and puts forth His strength when the Word is received with due honor and respect."[96] Hence, Timothy George argues that, "All of Calvin's theology was carried out within these bounds: the objectivity of God's revelation in Holy Scripture and the confirming, illuminating witness of the Holy Spirit in the believer."[97] Moreover, Calvin asserted that, God operates in the life of his elected people through the Spirit. This is the form of God's operation by which he governs his faithful, living and reigning in them by God's Holy Spirit.

For Calvin, faith is the unique gift of the Spirit. It is "the principal work of the Holy Spirit," a supernatural gift that those who would otherwise remain in unbelief receive Christ by grace.[98] In other words, according to

---

94. *Institutes*, 1.7.4.
95. George, *Theology of the Reformers*, 197; Calvin maintained the unity of Word and Spirit and criticized the Catholic position. The Catholics downplayed the role of illumination by subordinating Scripture to the church. They took the words of Peter, "no prophecy of Scripture is of private interpretation," to prohibit any individual handling of the Bible and "to arrogate to their councils the final authority to interpret Scripture." Calvin argued that the word "private" in this context does not mean "individual" but humanly devised. He writes, "Let the whole world be unanimously agreed, and let all the minds of men be of one united opinion, what results would still be private and their own, because the subject is contrasted here with divine revelation, in that the faithful are enlightened by the Holy Spirit and acknowledge only what God wills in His Word." See Torrance and Torrance, eds. *Calvin's New Testament Commentaries*, 343.
96. *Institutes*, 1.9.3.
97. George, *Theology of the Reformers*, 197-198.
98. *Institutes* 3.1.4.

Calvin, faith is "a firm and sure knowledge of the divine favor towards us, founded on the truth of a free promise in Christ, and revealed to our minds, and sealed on our hearts by the Holy Spirit."[99] He adds, "… that until our minds are intent on the Spirit, Christ is in a manner unemployed, because we view him coldly without us, and so at a distance from us."[100] He maintained faith as "a lively awareness" by which we grasp the grace of our adoption as well as the newness of life and the other gifts of the Spirit. Thus for Calvin, there are two aspects of faith. Firstly, it is the work of the Spirit and secondly, it is the genuine human response by which those whom God has elected enter into their new life in Christ.[101]

Calvin, like Luther, perceived the work of the Spirit in the sacraments. While discussing the Lord's Supper, he agreed with Luther that the Lord's Supper is not an empty symbol, but a means of "true participation" in Christ in the Spirit.[102] How can Christ be at once at the Father's right hand and present at the "spiritual banquet" of communion? He argues that, "What our mind does not comprehend let faith conceive: that the Spirit truly unites things separated in space."[103] Moreover, Calvin maintained that ordination is a "solemn rite of institution" into the pastoral office. It is a sacrament and admitted that grace is conferred through this outward sign. It is a faithful token of the grace received from God's own hand, and it is a "legitimate act of consecration before God, something that could be done only by the power of the Holy Spirit."[104]

In short, as for Luther, the Spirit is also a central doctrine in the theology of Calvin. His treatment of the person and work of Jesus Christ in relation to the Spirit and *vice versa* can be prized as an innovative effort in systematic theology. Calvin's understanding of the illuminating witness of

---

99. *Institutes* 3.2.7.
100. *Institutes*, 3.1.3; while discussing about the revelation of God, Calvin asserts that, "When the divinity hidden by the flesh breaks out into open manifestation, there God is disclosing himself to those who are at the same time moved by the Holy Spirit to receive this manifestation of divine glory." Moreover he maintains that, our hearts are lifted up, by the way of the Holy Spirit's use of the flesh of Christ, to the acknowledgment of God's power and goodness. See Willis, *Calvin's Catholic Christology*, 113-114.
101. George, *Theology of the Reformers*, 225.
102. *Institutes* 4.17.10-11.
103. *Institutes* 4.17.10.
104. George, *Theology of the Reformers*, 242.

the Spirit in the lives of a believer resembles Luther's understanding of the internal testimony of the Spirit. However, it must be noted that the exercise of charismatic gifts do not hold much significance in the pneumatology of Calvin.

5. *Pneumatology of the Left Wing Reformers*[105]

The radical Reformation was a tremendous movement[106] of spiritual and ecclesial renewal which stood on the margins of the major territorial churches, Catholic, and Protestant during the great religious upheaval of the sixteenth century. However, this movement was neither marginal nor peripheral in its basic drives and spiritual vitalities. Embracing ecumenicity and sectarianism, violent revolution and pacific communalism, sublimating ascetical, mystical, and rationalist impulses from the late Middle Ages, the radical Reformation is considered as an entity that posed a thoroughgoing critique of the *Corpus Christianum* in both its mainline Protestant and Tridentine Catholic mutations.[107] Williams proposed the

---

105. Luther reversed the modern positioning, placing the Catholics on the left and the radicals on the right. Gordon Rupp argues that, "The Protestant left was the heir of the medieval underworld, to categories of thought and a vocabulary emerging from late medieval heresies, Waldensianism, the spiritual Franciscans, the German mystics, the modern devotion, the revival of Platonism, a varied vocabulary which pre-existed the Reformation and has its own power and momentum quite apart from Luther and from Wittenberg." See Gordon Rupp, "Word and Spirit in the First Years of the Reformation," *Archive for Reformation History* vol. 49 (1958), 13-25.
106. Roland H. Bainton likes to call radical Reformation a tendency. He writes, "It was so amorphous, varied, and vague that it can better be described as a tendency than as a movement." See Roland H. Bainton, *The Reformation of the Sixteenth Century* (London: Hodder and Stoughton, 1965), 123; however it is interesting to note the argument that, "Reformation was radical from the beginning and became moderate at a later stage." See for an excellent discussion, James M. Stayer, "The Passing of the Radical Moment in the Radical Reformation," *MQR* vol. 71, no. 1 (January 1997), 147-152.
107. George, *Theology of the Reformers*, 252; one reason for Catholic interest in the Anabaptists is explained like this: "The only subversive portion of their doctrine was that they held, with the Catholics, that the state is not responsible for religion." J.E.E.D. Acton, *The History of Freedom and Other Essays* (London: Mcmillan, 1907), 157; it is interesting to note that Luther was very critical of the radicals' position of the Holy Spirit. He complains, "with them all is Geist, Geist, Geist ... they are not obsessed with pneumatology, but more concerned with the contrast between the 'outer' and 'inner Word,' or between 'Spirit' and 'letter,' or the 'inward' and 'outer' man." See Rupp, "Word and Spirit," 13-25.

radical Reformation as a collective term for all those groups of religious innovators who remained in neither the Roman Catholic nor mainline Protestant churches.[108] Timothy George argues that radical Reformation "was instead a movement which gives birth to a new form of Christian faith and life."[109] Precisely this, together with the fact that for the most part the radicals were forced to develop their model of the Christian life outside the confines of the official churches, and gave their spirituality and church life a distinctive cast. In this sense, they were the "host of free spirits."[110] Richard Heath considers the sixteenth century religious radicals as primitive yet unconscious forerunners of modern socialism, people whose doctrines were nevertheless "retrograde" and "foredoomed to failure."[111]

In short, it was a new type of Christianity, or an existential Christianity, based on fellowship and love.[112] Among the dissidents in the radical Reformation, there are three main groupings: the Anabaptists, the Spiritualists,

---

108. Williams and Mergal, eds., *Spiritual and Anabaptist Writers*, 19-38.
109. George, *Theology of the Reformers*, 255; Bender argues that, "The Radicals provided the inspiration for a renewal of modern Christianity in believing that Jesus intended that the Kingdom of God should be set in the midst of earth here and now, and this they proposed to do forthwith." See H. S. Bender, "The Anabaptist Vision," *Church History* 13 (1944), 23-24.
110. A. G. Dickens and John Powell, *The Reformation in Historical Thought* (Oxford: Blackwell, 1985), 233; the radicals felt that the official Protestantism was not much better than medieval Catholicism. They agreed with Luther that what was needed was a restoration of the beliefs and practices of the early church, but they saw in the Lutheran churches simply a caricature of the ideal. So they used the word "reinstitution" by which they meant literally turning back to the first century and restoring the Spirit and institutions of the Apostolic Age. See Harbison, *The Age of Reformation*, 63.
111. The Marxist tendency to abstract Müntzer and other radicals from their spiritual context has been rightly criticized, yet the perilous association of religious radicalism with social and political radicalism has been equally emphasized by the Western historians. They argue that the religious radicals primarily represented the confused cause of the poor. Particularly many saw Anabaptists as the representatives of a true people's reformation and their hero was Thomas Müntzer, whom they regarded as the people's Luther. See Dickens and Powell, *The Reformation in Historical Thought*, 218, 230; the Soviet historian M. M. Smirin gave a Marxist interpretation of Müntzer, first published in Moscow, translated and published in East Germany as *Die Volksreformation des Thomas Müntzer und der grosse Bauernkrieg* (Berlin: Dietz, 1956). A similar work is by Alfred Meusel, *Thomas Müntzer und seine Zeit mit einer Auswahl der Dokumente des Grossen Deutschen Bauernkriegs* (Berlin: Aufbau-Verlag, 1952). However, Smirin's Russian colleague, O. G. Tschaikowskaja, denies the revolutionary character of the Peasant Movement. Another Russian, A. D. Epstejn, attempts to mediate between Smirin and Tschaikowskaja by calling the Peasants' War in Germany the "first bourgeois revolution."
112. Robert Friedmann, "Recent Interpretations of Anabaptism," *Church History* 24 (1955), 132-151.

and the Evangelical Rationalists. Although there are divergences in the theological positions of these groups, there is one thing which is common to all radical movements, namely the mystical character. Since the focus of this chapter is not to compare and contrast the theology of the Reformers, but rather to look into their pneumatology, what follows is a brief survey of the pneumatology of selected theologians in the radical Reformation.

5.1 Thomas Müntzer (1490 – 1525)

Thomas Müntzer was the prominent leader of revolutionary Anabaptism who stood in opposition to Luther and Wittenberg theology.[113] Although the doctrine of the Spirit is a leading theme in Müntzer's theology, over against the right wing Reformers Müntzer employed a very different scheme. Müntzer's pneumatology has to be seen as a reflection of his perception of the history as employed by Joachim of Fiore. To put it in the words of Hans-Jürgen Goertz, Müntzer believed that, "The 'transformation of the world' 'stood before the door.'"[114] His conviction that he was living in the final phase of history, forced him to anticipate the great transformation, a more radical and thoroughgoing reformation of Christianity - both its religious and secular aspects.[115] Moreover, he believed that Christ himself

---

113. Müntzer's confrontation with the theologians such as Augustine, German mystics, Martin Luther, and Augustinian-influenced theology of Luther's colleague, Andreas Bodenstein von Karlstadt provided him with some answers to the question of human nature and destiny. He was attracted by the mysticism of Suso and Tauler in his search for an answer to satisfy both his academic curiosity and his religious uncertainty. See Eric W. Gritsch, *Reformer without a Church: The Life and Thought of Thomas Müntzer* (Philadelphia: Fortress, 1967), 14-15; Gottfried Seebass, "Thomas Müntzer (c. 1490 – 1525)," in *The Reformation Theologians: An Introduction to Theology in the Early Modern Period*, ed. Carter Lindberg (Oxford: Blackwell, 2002), 339; he found in their tracts that a person must experience doubt and despair before he/she can be certain of the "birth of God" with themselves and their salvation. This mysticism, elaborated in systematic philosophical fashion by Eckhart, may have played a significant role in the theological development of Müntzer. Although Müntzer began as a follower of medieval theologians and mystics, it is in Zwickau, under the influence of Nicolas Storch and the Zwickau prophets, he turned to more radical doctrines. See Abraham Friesen, "Thomas Müntzer and Martin Luther," *Archive for Reformation History* vol. 79 (1988), 59-80; for Müntzer's experience with the Zwickau prophets, see Paul Wappler, *Thomas Müntzer in Zwickau und die Zwickauer Propheten* (Gütersloh: Gütersloher, 1966).
114. Hans Jürgen Goertz, "Thomas Müntzer: Revolutionary between the Middle Ages and Modernity," trans. James M. Stayer, *MQR* vol. 64, no. 1 (January 1990), 23-31.
115. Peter Matheson, ed. and trans. *The Collected Works of Thomas Müntzer* (Edinburgh: T & T Clark, 1988), 244.

would return in order to separate the pious elect from the godless establishing his kingdom and ruling on earth.[116] And this will be actualized only through the creative power of the Spirit. Hence, for Müntzer the Spirit was a significant aspect that actualizes transformation of the world. This realization makes the Spirit the central theme in his theology.

In contrast to other Reformers, Müntzer asserted the spiritual authority[117] of the Bible to point out the heresy of clericalism. This means that for Müntzer the authority of the Bible is spiritual rather than literal.[118] He argued for the direct subjective reception of the Spirit, mediated without any externals such as the priest's words, the sacraments of the church,[119]

---

116. Seebass, "Thomas Müntzer," 342; in a certain sense, the twentieth century more than any other was Thomas Müntzer's century. Up to then academic study of his person and work had been impeded by the long dominant misrepresentation of him by Luther and Melanchthon on the one side, and by the representatives of Anabaptism and mystical spiritualism on the other. Modern research began and prospered between the fronts of the so-called "bourgeois" and Marxist historiographies. Initially their perspectives were not essentially different in that both saw Müntzer as the revolutionary protagonist of the Peasants' War. The "bourgeois" perceptive branded him a prophet of murder and a revolutionary in light of his participation in the Peasants' War; the Marxist orientation extolled him for the same reason as a prophet of the aspirations of his time. In the West, the first partially positive views of Müntzer were stimulated by the theology of revolution, various liberation theologies, and the impact of the student revolutions in the 1960's. See Seebass, "Thomas Müntzer," 338.

117. With the question of authority in its religious, social and political dimensions, Müntzer first rejected the existing symbols of religious authority – the Catholic Pope and the Protestant Bible – claiming that to cling to such authorities is to flee from direct confrontation with the Spirit. In this sense, he put the testimony of an internal experiencing of the Spirit in the place of the old external authorities of Christendom. Assuming this experience to be universal, uniting all people in the same way since all are creatures of the same God, Müntzer created a broad theological basis for his revolutionary program. What also concerned him was the fact that Christendom was busying itself with externals such as the Bible, the sacraments, and rationalistic doctrine, instead of seeking a genuine encounter with God through the Spirit. See Gritsch, *Reformer Without a Church*, 115; although he constantly quoted the Bible to justify his reasoning, Müntzer asserted that the Bible is not a witness to the revelation of God given once-and-for-all in the historical Jesus, but only the ancient record of people who had experienced the power of the Spirit; only time separates their experience from that of contemporary human beings. See Gritsch, *Reformer Without a Church*, 187.

118. McLaughlin argues that Müntzer refuses to use visions in his theology and appeals instead to Scripture. He makes an excellent discussion rejecting the argument that Müntzer's theology was apocalyptic. See R. Emmet McLaughlin, "Apocalypticism and Thomas Müntzer," *Archive for Reformation History* vol. 95, (2004), 98-131; see also Hans-Jürgen Goertz, "Zu Thomas Müntzer's Geistverständnis," in *Die Theologie Thomas Müntzers: Untersuchungen zu seiner Entwicklung und Lehre*, eds. Siegfried Bräur and Helmar Junghans (Göttingen: Vandenhoeck & Ruprecht, 1989), 89.

119. For an excellent analysis of Müntzer's sacramental theology, see Ernst Koch,

or fruits of theological scholarship.[120] Müntzer followed the allegorical interpretation of Scripture, which is clear in his interpretation of "water" as the "Holy Spirit." However, one should note that this kind of interpretation was not unknown to medieval theology. In short, Müntzer's reflections concerning the relationship of Word and Spirit led him on the one hand to a new concept of religious authority that is the prophetic proclamation of the elect, and on the other to a new understanding of human nature and destiny. Thus, he saw the process of salvation as cooperation between human nature and divine Spirit. Using such colorful language of medieval German mysticism, Müntzer created the skeleton of an anthropology which undergirded his later revolutionary program.[121]

Concerning the origin of humanity's relationship to God in faith, Müntzer argues that this relationship begins not with an external act, such as the rite of baptism, but with the internal experiencing of the Spirit.[122] This baptism by the Spirit, marked by internal suffering and turmoil, is the only way in which God reaches humanity.[123] Müntzer writes that, "For

---

"Das Sakramentsverständnis Thomas Müntzers," in *Die Theologie Thomas Müntzers: Untersuchungen zu seiner Entwicklung und Lehre*, eds. Siegfried Bräur and Helmar Junghans (Göttingen: Vandenhoeck & Ruprecht, 1989), 129-155.
120. Gritsch, *Reformer Without a Church*, 60.
121. Gritsch, *Reformer Without a Church*, 189; for an excellent discussion on the mystical influence on Müntzer see, Abraham Friesen, "Thomas Müntzer and Martin Luther," *Archive for Reformation History* vol. 79 (1988), 59-80.
122. Müntzer writes, "Our scribes have not opened their eyes to the genuine truth, under the delusion that John 3 does not fit together with John 7, where the voice of truth says: 'If any man thirst, let him come to me and drink. He who believes in me,' as the Scripture has said, 'out of his body shall flow rivers of living water.' *This he said of the Holy Spirit, whom the believers will receive in the future.* You see, dear companion, the Evangelist interprets himself and speaks of the writers in the manner of the prophets, for the water is the stirring of our spirit in God's Spirit, as John himself explains, drawing on Isaiah in John 1.' Cited in Abraham Friesen, "Acts 10: The Baptism of Cornelius as Interpreted by Thomas Müntzer and Felix Manz," *MQR* vol. 64, no. 1 (January 1990), 5-22; this shows that Müntzer was concerned about the baptism of the Spirit, or the coming of the Spirit with transforming power into a person's soul and not the external signs.
123. Gritsch, *Reformer Without a Church*, 88; Maczka argues that "In Müntzer's writings, the work of the Holy Spirit in the individual is a three-stage process. The first stage he referred to variously as the beginning of the movement of the Spirit; the fear of God, or despair; or the individual beginning to search for God. Stage two is in response to contact with the Word of God; the searcher discovers that true faith is trust in God and a peaceful reliance upon Him. Stage three consists of striving, at the impulse of the Holy Spirit, to become more Christ-like, not in attaining moral perfection but in attaining conformity with the will with God." Romwald Maczka, "Retheologising Thomas Müntzer in the German Democratic Republic: 15 Years of Marxist and Non-Marxist Research," *MQR* vol.

without any experience of the arrival of the Holy Spirit, the overcomer of the fear of God, they fail to separate (in their disdain for divine wisdom) the good from the bad which is camouflaged under the appearance of good."[124] However, when individuals are certain that the Spirit is dwelling in their souls, they become instruments of God's will, leading others into the same experience.[125] That means that Müntzer wanted people to experience the descend of the Spirit into a person's soul.

Although Müntzer used this dialectic of "internal" and "external" against the Wittenberg theologians, when he later spoke of the relationship between human nature and God's revelation in Christ he transformed this argument into "spiritual" and "creaturely." He asserted that just as the "external" words of the Bible must be interpreted by those who experienced the Spirit in their soul, to have any religious value, the historical Jesus also must be interpreted spiritually as a force in the believer to become the real Christ and savior.[126] Therefore for Müntzer, the cross is no longer the experience of the historical Jesus of Nazareth, who actualized salvation through his historical death, but a spiritual experience, mediated through the Spirit. Müntzer thus "dehistorized" Jesus of Nazareth and his historical work into an inner religious experience through which the certainty of salvation is assured.[127]

One of Müntzer's peculiar contentions in his pneumatology is that the advent of the Spirit must always be preceded by suffering and despair.[128] Hence, he argued that the "justification by faith alone" is an invented doctrine, because Christ had come to fulfill the law. In this sense, the real "art" of preaching is to remind that the inner turmoil is just the beginning of salvation from sin, a salvation which is completed when the Spirit has converted sinful man into a willing instrument of God through the

---

63, no. 4 (October 1989), 345-366.
124. Thomas Müntzer, "Sermon Before the Princess," in *Spiritual and Anabaptist Writers: Documents Illustrative of the Radical Reformers*, eds. George H. Williams and Angel M. Mergal, (London: SCM, 1957), 56.
125. Gritsch, *Reformer Without a Church*, 116.
126. Gritsch, *Reformer Without a Church*, 189.
127. Gritsch, *Reformer Without a Church*, 61.
128. Goertz, "Zu Thomas Müntzer's Geistverständnis," 91; Gritsch, *Reformer Without a Church*, 70.

"justification by law."¹²⁹ This gospel of suffering which Müntzer preached became the battle cry of political revolution.¹³⁰ Interestingly enough, he declared in one of his sermons that only those who had experienced inner proof of their election would be saved. "… none may be saved unless the … Holy Spirit has previously assured one of salvation."¹³¹ In this sense, the Spirit becomes the chief instrument of a person's salvation. It gave life to the world when God created the universe, it effects the rebirth of fallen humanity, and it is the agent through which God erects his eternal kingdom.¹³² This Spirit is given only to those who hold a simple mind undistorted by the burden of complicated reasoning.

The Prague manifesto¹³³ contains the theological sketch of Müntzer's revolutionary program which he hoped would make him the leader of a reform movement more radical than Luther.¹³⁴ Gritsch writes that, "The praise of the Holy Spirit, clothed in the concepts of medieval German mysticism, was the theme of Müntzer's Manifesto, as well the basis for his attack on clericalism."¹³⁵ Müntzer realized that the church and the existing political power structures were unwilling to submit to the rule of the Spirit. Hence, he was impatient and called for a society of the elect thinking that these converted individuals representing the community of all those converted by the Spirit, would free themselves from the artifacts of the old world order.¹³⁶ When Müntzer headed for this revolutionary program, he founded a League¹³⁷ and regarded his League as the beginning of a world-

---

129. Gritsch, *Reformer Without a Church*, 90.
130. Gritsch, *Reformer Without a Church*, 91.
131. Müntzer, "Sermon Before the Princess," 51.
132. Gritsch, *Reformer Without a Church*, 189.
133. Müntzer prepared four different versions of his "Prague Manifesto," two in German, one in Czech and one in Latin. See an excellent discussion by Michael G. Baylor, "Thomas Müntzer's "Prague Manifesto,"" *MQR* vol. 63, no. 1 (January 1989), 30-57.
134. Gritsch, *Reformer Without a Church*, 56.
135. Gritsch, *Reformer Without a Church*, 56.
136. Gritsch, *Reformer Without a Church*, 117.
137. For Müntzer, the elect are those whom God has foreseen and ordained for salvation. However, it is very different from that of the major sixteenth century Protestant Reformers. He saw the elect in a universalistic way, including among the elect at least some members of non-Christian faiths and societies, individuals who have never heard the message of the gospel. Moreover, he included the common people also in the elect category. See for a discussion Michael G. Baylor, "Theology and Politics in the Thought of Thomas Müntzer: The Case of the Elect," *Archive for Reformation History* vol. 79 (1988), 81-102; moreover, he saw the League to be a transitional "church" between the end of the

wide movement that would eventually create a communistic society based upon biblical principles. For him the members of the League were the elect who hold an experience of the new birth in the spirit through the Holy Ghost.[138] He saw them as equal to Peter, Paul, John, or any other apostles or biblical authors because they also have experienced the Spirit in the same manner and power as they did. The League's military mission was to inflict punishment upon those who, in their godlessness, had refused to let God dwell in their hearts.[139] The paradox of his pneumatology can be seen here. That means, as Gritsch writes:

> What Müntzer had once described as the peaceful conversion of the individual through inner anxiety and despair, now became a political and military program for the creation of a society of the elect who would inflict physical suffering on those refusing to participate. The seeker for inner certainty had now become the crusader for, and executioner of, divine justice.[140]

In summary, like Luther and Calvin, Müntzer also dealt with the significance and role of the Spirit in his theology. However, he differs in many respects from the right wing Reformers in his treatment of the Spirit. His argument of the internal experiencing of the Spirit can be seen as an innovative doctrine. Moreover, the important characteristic of his pneumatology can be the understanding of the Spirit as the agent through which God erects his eternal kingdom, although he wrongly followed a military fashion to establish the kingdom of God.

---

old and the beginning of a new world governed by the Spirit. Just as individuals experience the purifying transfiguration of their hearts through the power of the Spirit, so must the entire world be changed from its weak state of "creatureliness" into a strong kingdom of God. He had the view that if persuasion, propaganda, and other peaceful means do not convince humanity to submit to the Spirit, then the will of God must be imposed upon the world by force through a military crusade executed by the League of the elect. See Gritsch, *Reformer Without a Church*, 190.
138. Bainton, *The Reformation of the Sixteenth Century*, 67.
139. Gritsch, *Reformer Without a Church*, 96.
140. Gritsch, *Reformer Without a Church*, 96.

5.2 Menno Simons (c. 1496 – 1561)

Menno Simons[141] is one of the prominent Anabaptist leaders in its early period, who was advocating a practical Christianity as Jesus Christ taught and lived over against the institutionalized form of Christianity during his time. It was this aspect that forced him to break with the Roman Catholic Church,[142] emphasizing the significance and role of the Spirit

---

141. There is a wrong conception that Menno Simons is the founder of the Mennonite Church. In reality, the Mennonite movement was initiated in Zurich, Switzerland in January 1525, by Conrad Grebel, Felix Manz, George Blaurock, and others, eleven years before Menno renounced Catholicism. Menno also did not found the church in Holland. Rather, it was Obbe Philips. However, Menno was duly ordained, probably by Obbe Philips, who with his brother Dirk had emerged as early leaders of the non-Müntzerite Dutch Anabaptists. As Williams notes, Menno, like many other former Roman Catholic priests, became not only an Anabaptist but also a reordinationalist. See George H. Williams, *The Radical Reformation* (Philadelphia: Westminster, 1962), 392-393; a few years after he had ordained Menno, Obbe Philips became disillusioned with the divisiveness of the Anabaptist movement and forsook the brotherhood altogether. George argues that "Had he remained steadfast in his leadership, the Dutch Anabaptist may well have been called "Obbenites" rather than Mennists or later Mennonites. However, Bender argues that, "There is good historical reason for Mennonite church to bear the name of Menno Simons, for in the time of greatest need, Menno Simon was the heaven-sent leader who rallied the scattered brethren and gave them the leadership in faith and Spirit and doctrine which they needed". See Harold Stauffer Bender, "A Brief Biography of Menno Simons," in *The Complete Writings of Menno Simons: c. 1496-1561*, trans. Leonard Wenger, ed. John Christian Wenger (Scottsdale: Herald, 1960), 28; Hereafter *The Complete Writings of Menno*.

142. In 1525, the very year that Grebel and Mantz were organizing the first Anabaptist congregations in Switzerland, Menno began to entertain doubts about the dogma of transubstantiation, that is, whether the bread and wine in the mass literally are the flesh and blood of the Lord. Such 'heretical' ideas were not so unusual because the real presence of Christ in the supper had been questioned among various circles in the Netherlands. For example, as early as 1521 Cornelius Hoen, a leader of the Dutch Sacramentalists, taught that the bread and wine in the Eucharist were merely symbols of Christ's suffering and death. It is not sure whether Menno had access to these teachings. But it is believable that he followed Luther in this issue. For example, in the *Babylonian Captivity of the Church*, Luther declared transubstantiation to be a figment of human opinion, since it was based neither on the Scripture nor sound reason. Menno later declared that Luther's writings had helped him to realize that "human injunctions cannot bind unto eternal death." See Cornelius Krahn, *Dutch Anabaptism: Origin, Spread, Life, and Thought (1450-1600)* (Nijhoff: The Hague, 1968), 171; the second issue for Menno was the infant baptism. As early as 1529 Menno read a book by a south German preacher, Theobald Billicanus, which cited Cyprian as an advocate of adult baptism. However, an event closer to home was really the catalyst for Menno's thinking on this subject. On March 20, 1531, in the city of Leeuwarden, capital of the Dutch province of Friesland, an itinerant tailor named Sicke Freerks was beheaded because he had been baptized a second time. He had been re-baptized by one of Hofmann's disciples at Emden. It prompted Menno to investigate the basis for infant baptism. He examined the arguments of Luther, Bucer, Zwingli and

to actualize such a Christian life. Therefore, the following survey will prove the fact that Menno makes a serious treatment of the Spirit in his writings and the central theme of his theology is the work of the Spirit in the life of a person.

Menno, like the other Reformers, asserts the divinity of the Spirit by stating that God is Spirit and he is closely associated to the humanity. He writes that, "He is a mystery to all mankind, incomprehensible, ineffable, and indescribable; divine with His divine attributes, proceeding from the Father through the Son, although he ever remains with God and in God, and is never separated from the being of the Father and the Son."[143] His conviction is that, although there are three distinct personalities, in reality they are one and one cannot exist without the other. The Father works everything through the Son in the power of the Spirit. The Son does not work without the Father and the Spirit. Moreover, the Spirit works with the Father and the Son. Therefore, one must remain on the other to avoid criticism of an imperfect God. He writes, "For if we deny the deity of Christ, or the true existence of the Holy Ghost, then we fashion a counterfeit God unto ourselves, a God who is without wisdom, power, life, light, truth, Word, and without the Holy Spirit."[144]

Menno notes that Christendom confesses the Spirit to be such a true real Spirit because we are brought to this by the Scripture. The role of the Spirit in the event of baptism is also prized by Menno because the Spirit descended upon Jesus Christ at the baptism, appeared to the apostles, and

---

Bullinger, but found them all lacking. Finally he searched the Scripture diligently and considered the question seriously but could find nothing about infant baptism. He came to the conclusion that "all were deceived about infant baptism." *The Complete Writings of Menno*, 8; the final issue was the events surrounding the tragedy of Müntzer. As early as 1532 some people in the area around Witmarsum had been re-baptized. Some of these had also been drawn into the vortex of the violent, revolutionary kingdom of the two Jans at Müntzer, including Menno's own brother, Peter Simons. On March 30, 1535, a group of some three hundred violent Anabaptists captured the Old cloister near Bolsward. For eight days they withstood the assaults of the authorities, but on April 7, the cloister was retaken and the radicals savagely slain. Among them was Menno's brother. This event precipitated a crisis in Menno's life. See George, *Theology of the Reformers*, 260; in the same month Jan of Leyden was tortured to death, and Menno made his decisive break with the Church of Rome.
143. *The Complete Writings of Menno*, 496.
144. *The Complete Writings of Menno*, 497; J. A. Oosterbaan, "The Theology of Menno Simons," *MQR* vol. 35, no. 3 (July 1961), 187-196.

also Christians are baptized in Jesus' name, as well as in the name of Father and Son. Moreover, Menno argues that the prophets ministered through the Spirit.[145] He writes, "… we believe the Holy Spirit to be the true, essential Holy Spirit of God, who adorns us with his heavenly and divine gifts, and through his influence, according to the good pleasure of the Father, frees us from sin, gives us boldness, and makes us cheerful, peaceful, pious and holy."[146] Hence, for Menno, Spirit is an entity that provides the gifts of God to human beings.

Menno asserts, like the other Reformers, a close link between the Spirit and the Word of God. He believes and accepts the Word of God as the truth because the Scriptures were written by the Spirit.[147] He finds God's Word as the sharp sword of the Spirit[148] and continuously refers to the Word as the "holy Word." Menno contends that the Spirit, doctrine, and life of Christ will not deceive us, for his Word is truth and his commandments are eternal life.[149] This Word of God must be taught, explained, and understood according to the true meaning of the Spirit.[150] Hence for Menno, the service of the New Testament is a service of the Spirit and not of the letter.[151] He finds the gospels as the blessed announcement of the favor and grace of God to humanity and forgiveness of sins through Christ Jesus and faith accepts this gospel through the Spirit.[152] Therefore, Menno argues that the preachers must have been called and urged by God into God's vineyard through the true love of God and their neighbor, and through the power

---

145. *The Complete Writings of Menno*, 496.
146. *The Complete Writings of Menno*, 496.
147. *The Complete Writings of Menno*, 81, 43; Cornelius J. Dyck, "Hans De Ries and the Legacy of Menno," *MQR* vol. 62, no. 3 (July 1988), 401-416; see also Christoph Bornhäuser, *Leben und Lehre Monno Simons: Ein Kampf um das Fundament des Glaubens (etwa 1496-1661)* (Neukirchen: Neukirchener, 1973), 60-62.
148. *The Complete Writings of Menno*, 200.
149. *The Complete Writings of Menno*, 201.
150. *The Complete Writings of Menno*, 259; on the one hand, Menno followed allegorical reading of the Scripture like Müntzer. He thought that such interpretation would allow problematic passages to be interpreted by other passages, but not by external authorities. On the other hand, he followed the literal understanding of Christ's commandments as well as other laws from the Old and New Testaments. See Beth Kreitzer, "Menno Simons and the Bride of Christ," *MQR* vol. 70, no. 3 (July 1996), 299-318.
151. *The Complete Writings of Menno*, 442.
152. *The Complete Writings of Menno*, 115.

of the Spirit.[153] Those who are not called by the Spirit "will never gather fruits in the vineyard of the Lord, no matter how eloquent they may be, how esteemed and equipped."[154] Moreover, Menno maintains that when the preachers obey the urge of the Spirit, there the Word will be taught unsullied and thereby the real children of the Spirit will be born.[155]

In addition to that, Menno argues that the regeneration and spiritual resurrection is possible only through the Spirit.[156] Without such a spiritual regeneration, no one can see the Lord. That means those who reject Christ and do not keep the Spirit can never be a Christian. Unless a person is born of water and the Spirit, he cannot enter into the kingdom of God.[157] Menno asserts that those who are regenerated and led by the Spirit become partakers of the divine nature and are made conformable to the image of his Son.[158] They have a spiritual king over them who rules them with his Spirit and Word. He clothes them with the garment of righteousness and refreshes them with the living water of the Spirit and feeds them with the bread of life. His name is Jesus Christ.[159] Moreover, for Menno, the need to become a new creation is to bring forth the fruits of the Spirit. He writes, those who "have put on Christ and are purified through the Holy Ghost

---

153. *The Complete Writings of Menno*, 160-161, 255; see a discussion concerning the ministry by Menno in Russel L. Mast, "Menno Simons Speaks Concerning the Ministry," *MQR* vol. 54, no. 2 (April 1980), 106-116.
154. *The Complete Writings of Menno*, 162.
155. *The Complete Writings of Menno*, 164.
156. *The Complete Writings of Menno*, 54; Menno was exhorting his followers to a holy life with repentance, new birth, discipleship, and even martyrdom. Therefore, he emphasized practical holiness and freedom from sin. See a discussion on sin in Menno's theology by Richard E. Weingart, "The Meaning of Sin in the Theology of Menno Simons," *MQR* vol. 41, no. 1 (January 1967), 25-39.
157. *The Complete Writings of Menno*, 90; regarding this regeneration by the Spirit, Cornelis Augustin argues that in this point there is a strong Erasmian impact. Erasmus had shown the way to a cleansed form of piety in which ceremonies have become unimportant or even dangerous, and the walk with God is consummated in the serenity of the soul. So the whole Erasmian call was to spiritualization of the religious life. See Cornelis Augustin, "Erasmus and Menno Simons," *MQR* vol. 60, no. 4 (October 1986), 497-508.
158. *The Complete Writings of Menno*, 58; throughout his writings Menno Simons clearly argues for a "new subjectivity." Central to his theology is the need for individual "rebirth," for "regeneration," for one to "put off the old man with his works." and put on the new man with his works. See Lawrence J. Altepeter, "The Asceticism of Menno Simons," *MQR* vol. 72, no. 1 (January 1998), 69-83.
159. *The Complete Writings of Menno*, 94; for a discussion on Menno's understanding of sanctification, see Egil Grislis, "Menno Simons on Sanctification," *MQR* vol. 69, no. 2 (April 1994), 226-246.

A Paradigm Shift: Brief Survey of Reformer's Pneumatology

in their consciousness from dead works to serve the Living God, bringing forth through the Spirit the fruits of the Spirit, whose end is eternal life."[160] Menno makes a bold statement that those who are forsaken by the Spirit are blind in divine things.[161] However, if a person is born of God in baptism and had received the Spirit as comforter, then certainly the new spiritual life and fruits will be manifested as it was with the saints from the beginning. But the Spirit refuses to dwell in a body enslaved to sin.[162] However, Menno did not argue for an outward baptism because it has no effect.[163] But on the other hand, he argues for spiritual baptism from above because that will render a good conscience to believers through the Spirit and the Word of God.[164] And this Spirit becomes the seal to the consciousness of the believer.

Menno argues that a person is led into the saving faith through the Word and the Spirit.[165] And also, one can understand the love of God which is manifested in Jesus Christ by the unction of the Spirit.[166] In this

---

160. *The Complete Writings of Menno*, 56.
161. Menno explains this by the story of David. David was a great prophet and a man after God's own heart. But when the Spirit departed him he lost all his divine natures and became a sinner. He was able to return to God only when the Spirit enlightened him through the prophets. This same thing happened also to Peter. When the Spirit forsook him for a while, he denied Christ. When the Spirit returned, he acknowledged his fall. See *The Complete Writings of Menno*, 82.
162. *The Complete Writings of Menno*, 97.
163. Critiquing infant baptism, Menno says that, "Since the believing or regenerate act rightly before God and diligently seek after and fulfill His holy will according to the grace they have received, therefore we must confess that we cannot be led to this godly gift of faith and of regeneration otherwise than by the Word of God through His Holy Spirit." See *The Complete Writings of Menno*, 271; those should be baptized who are roused by faith and impelled by the Spirit. Against infant baptism he argues that infants do not have the Spirit which justifies or regenerates. If it was there in them, it would surely manifest in their fruits. It is impossible that the Spirit of God, which of himself is living and fruitful, and by whom all true Christians are justified, taught led, and driven, should be idle, dormant, and futile in those in whom He dwells. See *The Complete Writings of Menno*, 125, 271-272; his argument is that "since infants are not so disposed and since the Spirit does not operate nor reveal himself to be in them, and since they cannot serve in the body of Christ as is required by the word of God, they should, therefore, not be baptized." *The Complete Writings of Menno*, 274.
164. *The Complete Writings of Menno*, 125.
165. *The Complete Writings of Menno*, 326; see for comparatively modest treatment of Menno's theology by Walter Klaassen, "Menno Simons: Molder of a Tradition," *MQR* vol. 62, no. 3 (July 1988), 368-386; Sjouke Voolstra, "True Penitence: The Core of Menno Simon's Theology," *MQR* vol. 62, no. 3 (July 1988), 387-400.
166. *The Complete Writings of Menno*, 328.

sense, Menno strongly emphasizes the experiential nature of faith[167] and asserts that incarnation was an act of God, "conceived and come forth of the Holy Ghost."[168] It was a miracle of the Spirit. Menno argues that, "God miraculously cleansed the seed of Mary of all sinful depravity at the conception of Jesus by his Holy Spirit."[169] The body of Mary was prepared by the Spirit so that it was fit to receive the intangible eternal Word according to the angel's announcement.[170] It is very interesting to note the clarification Menno makes about the birth of Jesus. He says that, "... I do not believe that Christ was *born* of the Holy Ghost, but that he was *conceived* by the Holy Ghost."[171] He continues, "But I simply teach that the blessed Christ Jesus is truly God and Man, a Son of God, and a son of man, conceived of the Holy Ghost, born of the virgin Mary, a poor, despised man, like unto us in all things, sin excepted."[172] This same Jesus is truly anointed by God and he is the first begotten son of God, whom the Father anointed with the holy oil, that is, with the Holy Ghost.[173] Therefore, Menno argues that Jesus taught in the power of the Spirit and was urged by the Spirit through an unquenchable love to the service of all mankind.[174]

Menno asserts that the Spirit is the true teacher of righteousness because it is the Spirit that quickens, pierces, and turns the hearts of the believers or hearers to the Word.[175] Therefore, only those whose hearts are quickened and turned by this Spirit through the Word of God must be baptized. Menno holds that we become the children of God firstly through the birth from above and then by water, by which the obedience of the children of God is signified. However, through the communion of the Spirit, we are assured in our hearts of the grace of God, remission of sins, and everlasting life through Jesus Christ.[176] Whosoever has put on Christ is dead to sin

---

167. Willis M. Stoesz, "The New Creature: Menno Simon's Understanding of the Christian Faith," *MQR* vol. 39, no. 1 (January 1965), 5-24.
168. *The Complete Writings of Menno*, 428; see a discussion by Irvin E. Burkhart, "Menno Simons on the Incarnation," *MQR* vol. 4, no. 3 (July 1930), 178-203.
169. *The Complete Writings of Menno*, 784.
170. *The Complete Writings of Menno*, 794.
171. *The Complete Writings of Menno*, 809.
172. *The Complete Writings of Menno*, 430.
173. *The Complete Writings of Menno*, 41.
174. *The Complete Writings of Menno*, 441.
175. *The Complete Writings of Menno*, 271.
176. *The Complete Writings of Menno*, 243.

and lives unto righteousness because they are led by the Spirit.[177] Menno contends that those who believe the gospel and are inwardly stirred by the Spirit comprise the church irrespective of nationality. In other words, they are the congregation of Christ who are truly converted by the operation of the Spirit.[178] According to Menno, all those who do not have the Spirit, love, and life of Christ, or do not sincerely desire them, have no share in the glorious Jerusalem of God that is in Christ's church.[179] Moreover, wherever human beings conform themselves to the Spirit of Christ, there the holy Christian church is founded.[180]

In short, Menno, like the other Reformers, realized the significance of the Spirit and its role as a divine entity. His novel contribution is that he envisaged the active role of the Spirit in the life of a person especially in the regeneration and sanctification. That means, he was advocating a practical Christianity or spiritual regeneration empowered by the Spirit over against the institutionalized form of Christianity.

5.3 Hans Denck (1500 – 1527)[181]

Hans Denck[182] belonged to the best age of Anabaptism, when it was deeply religious and a truly ethical movement. However, scholars of Denck argue

---

177. *The Complete Writings of Menno*, 269.
178. *The Complete Writings of Menno*, 300.
179. *The Complete Writings of Menno*, 448; Menno says, "If you want to be the true Church of Christ which boasts of the truth, grace, word, Spirit, and blood of the Lord, then first expel all your preachers who are driven by the unclean spirit and flesh, therefore are not of the church of Christ, namely, all those who are desirous of filthy lucre … Also, all drunkards, wranglers, flatterers, the proud, the envious, and the avaricious. For all these testify by their evident fruits that they have not the Spirit of Christ. And if they have not the Spirit of Christ, how can they, poor miserable men, teach and impress the Spirit, power, and will of God, the Word of grace, and the Word of eternal life, which they do not themselves possess and confess?" See *The Complete Writings of Menno*, 448-449.
180. *The Complete Writings of Menno*, 755.
181. In different books, different spellings are employed to write the name Hans Denck. Even Denck himself used different spellings to write his own name. See a discussion in Hans Denck, "Schriften," in *Quellen und Forschungen zur Reformationsgeschichte*, vol. 24 (Gütersloh: Bertelsmann, 1955), 16-18; hereafter *Schriften*.
182. Hans Denck was born in Heybach, in Bavaria. However, regarding his year of birth, there are inconsistencies. See *Schriften*, 8; when he died in 1527, he was described as still a young man. This drives us to the conclusion with some certainty that Denck was born in the last years of the fifteenth century. He lived in Nuremberg for a while, in Strasburg, Worms, and then in Augsburg. At Augsburg, he became the head of an Anabaptist community. At Strasburg he engaged in a public disputation with the Lutheran

that he was never a spiritualist, rather he followed the ordinary Anabaptist position. A thorough analysis of the theology of Denck reveals the fact that he focused on God's spiritual presence in the believer and on God's revelation of true love in Jesus.[183] Moreover, as the other Reformers, Denck also recognized God as the Spirit and argues that humanity should receive God as the Spirit through Jesus Christ, the son of God, because God is Spirit whom no fleshy eyes can see or hear.[184]

As noted above, in some respect Denck occupied the ordinary Anabaptist position and gave significance to the Spirit. The significance of his pneumatology is that he recognized the distinction between the outer and the inner Word, that is to say, the Word written in the Bible and that which is written in the heart, respectively. He writes:

> I esteem Holy Scripture above all human treasures, but not so highly as the Word of God which is living, powerful, eternal, free and independent of all elements of this world: for as it is God Himself, so is it Spirit and not letter, and written without pen and paper, so that it can never more be blotted out.[185]

---

preachers. See Beard, *The Reformation of the Sixteenth Century*, 204-205; Beard writes that, "everywhere, not only theological controversy and ecclesiastical unsettlement, but religious revival, followed Denck's steps." Beard, *The Reformation of the Sixteenth Century*, 206; people of his period were attracted by his sermons and were ready to follow his principles without any doubt. It is said that, "Men gathered eagerly about Denck, hung upon his lips, adopted his principles, and were afterwards not afraid to suffer for their faith." Beard, *The Reformation of the Sixteenth Century*, 206; Denck underwent the standard religious training of that day and to the new reform ideas. He was humanistically educated and had significant experience in Strasbourg. He was influenced deeply by the Bible, German medieval mysticism, and sixteenth century German humanism. The neo-Platonic influence which had been alive in medieval Italian philosophy found its way into German Mysticism and into the thought of Denck. See Claude R. Foster, Jr., "Hans Denck and Johannes Bünderlin: A Comparative Study," *MQR* vol. 39, no. 2 (April 1965), 115-124; for a discussion about the influence of humanism in Denck see, Thor Hall, "Possibilities of Erasmian Influence on Denck and Hubmaier in their Views on the Freedom of the Will," *MQR* vol. 35, no. 2 (April 1961), 149-170; moreover, he was influenced by Luther as well. For instance, in his doctrine of justification he was on Luther's side rather than the medieval side. Heinold Fast, "Hans Denck and Thomas Müntzer," *MQR* vol. 45, no. 1 (January 1971), 82-83.
183. *Schriften*, 35.
184. *Schriften*, 39.
185. Cited in Beard, *The Reformation of the Sixteenth Century*, 208.

The above statement does not mean that Denck rejected the Scripture totally. On the other hand, he asserted that Scripture and law in themselves are holy and good. However, without the help of the Spirit no human being is able to use them correctly. That means, according to Denck, the true believer becomes capable to listen to the whole testimony of the Scripture and to discern everything only by the anointing of the Spirit.[186] The discernment of the law through the letter of the Old and the New Testaments can never be achieved without God's Spirit. Moreover, Denck asserts that this Spirit points to Jesus as the perfect example of obedience to the law. When enmity toward God's law and unbelief are overcome through God's power in the Spirit, the law and the Gospel are heard and discerned with righteous ears.[187]

The above discussion proves the fact that Denck regarded Scripture as an external testimony to an internal truth. That means Scripture is not an instrument that God uses to create faith as Luther maintained. In other words, God's Spirit reveals God publicly and not only in private. This argument of Denck can be equated with the mystical tradition.[188] He writes:

> All commands, morals, laws, insofar as they are scripturally comprehended in the Old and New Testaments, are superseded for the true scholar of Christ, for he has a Word written in the heart by which he loves God alone and according to this he is able to judge what to do and what to leave alone even though he has nothing in writing .... It is expounded to him through the anointing of the Holy Ghost.[189]

Denck believed, in opposition to Luther and Calvin that the Spirit works in the inner being of a person without the precondition of external means. And this inner Word is present in the human beings from the very beginning. It is the new covenant which is written in the hearts of people

---

186. See Mathias Gockel, "A Reformer's Dissent from Lutheranism: Reconsidering the Theology of Hans Denck (ca.1500-1527)," *Archive for Reformation History* vol. 91 (2000), 127-148; *Schriften*, 36-38.
187. *Schriften*, 52-53.
188. Gockel, "A Reformer's Dissent from Lutheranism," 127-148.
189. Cited in Rupp, "Word and Spirit," 13-25.

by the Spirit.[190] However, in spite of the presence of the Spirit in the human beings, natural human beings are not sure of their own faith or do not realize the dwelling of this Word in them.[191] Denck developed this doctrine of the inner Word which links him with the *Theologia Germanica* and even more with Johannine theology.[192] For him the inner Word speaks clearly in every person, and in everything that is in them, that they may hear it and do God's Will, but they struggle against him.[193] So for him, Scripture is not univocally the Word of God, but a "witness" authenticated by the inner Word. On this account, Heinold Fast argues that one can find this problem in the pneumatology of Denck that he subordinates the Scripture to the Spirit.[194] However, Denck neglects the idea of incarnation of the divine Word in Jesus. Obviously, he is hesitant to bring God's spiritual being into immediate contact with any form of human bodily existence because God is a Spirit whom no fleshy eyes and ears can see or hear.[195]

One of the seminal arguments of Denck is that the Spirit is the rod by which God will chastise this world. He writes, "O Lord, my God! Let me be obedient unto thee and do to me whatever thou wouldst through thy most beloved Son, Jesus Christ, through whose Spirit the world will be chastised."[196] And also Denck believed that the kingdom of God is based only on the teaching and on the power of the Spirit.[197] Thus as noted earlier, the doctrine of the Spirit has been a key theme in the whole theology of Denck. His emphasis upon the inner Word over against the outer can be seen as a novel contribution. In other words, Denck's contention that the Spirit works in the inner being of a person without the precondition of external means is a clear detachment from the right wing Reformers'

---

190. *Schriften*, 59.
191. Fast, "Hans Denck and Thomas Müntzer," 82-83.
192. Rupp, "Word and Spirit," 13-25.
193. Rupp, "Word and Spirit," 13-25.
194. Fast, "Hans Denck and Thomas Müntzer," 82-83.
195. Cited in Gockel, "A Reformer's Dissent from Lutheranism," 127-148.
196. John Denck, "Whether God is the Cause of Evil," in *Spiritual and Anabaptist Writers: Documents Illustrative of the Radical Reformation*, eds. George H. Williams and Angel M. Mergal (London: SCM, 1957), 89.
197. Jan J. Kiwiet, "The Theology of Hans Denck," *MQR* vol. 32, no. 1 (January 1958), 3-27.

position. Thus he was arguing for God's spiritual presence in the believer and God's revelation of true love in Jesus actualized through the Spirit.

5.4 Caspar von Schwenckfeld (1489 – 1561)

Caspar von Schwenckfeld holds a much larger place than Hans Denck in church history. One of the reasons for this can be that he gave his name to a sect which long lingered in Germany and later survived in America.[198] He followed the mystic tradition[199] and stood in opposition to the later development of Lutheran theology.[200] His religious position, which in the eyes of partisans was neither Protestant nor Catholic, drew down upon him dislike and persecution from both sides.[201] He always remained faithful to Luther. However, Luther repulsed him with the bitterest reproaches. Melanchthon fulminated a decree of excommunication against both him and Sebastian Franck.[202] Although he was not an Anabaptist, he neverthe-

---

198. Beard, *The Reformation of the Sixteenth Century*, 212; Schwenckfeld had repeatedly denied any wish to establish a church. He had even instructed his sympathizers not to form a sect in his name. But by distinguishing themselves from their fellow citizens with their views and religious life, they became known as Schwenckfelders. They appear to have assembled for two kinds of low-key gatherings. There were firstly, frequent meetings for a kind of family worship to which friends and neighbors were invited, and secondly less frequent smaller meetings in various homes. Here they prayed, read the Scripture and Schwenckfeld's writings, and listened to expositions on various topics. See John Derksen, "The Schwenckfeldians in Strasbourg, 1533-1562: A Prosopographical Survey," *MQR* vol. 74, no. 2 (April 2000), 257-294.
199. Almost everything in Schwenckfeld belongs to the character of mysticism. The peculiarly Protestant character of his mysticism is shown in his doctrine of the deification of the flesh of Jesus, which was his way of explaining the difficulty of the real presence in the Eucharist. Jesus, sitting in the right hand of God, was in his heavenly humanity truly Lord and God, and the puzzle of the ubiquity of his body in the bread and wine upon the alter fell away of itself. This deified humanity of Jesus was a great point with Schwenckfeld. He thus puts forward a peculiar doctrine of the Eucharist. See Beard, *The Reformation of the Sixteenth Century*, 214.
200. Beard, *The Reformation of the Sixteenth Century*, 212; although Schwenckfeld was influenced by Luther initially, his whole perception concerning piety and religious reform appears to reflect the ideas of Erasmus's *Enchirion*, a book that was widely read in Silesia. It emphasized above all the necessity of the moral renewal of humankind and not that of the reform of the church. See Andre Seguenny, "Caspar von Schwenckfeld (1489-1561)," in *The Reformation Theologians: An Introduction to Theology in the Early Modern Period*, ed. Carter Lindberg (Oxford: Blackwell, 2002), 352; moreover, Adam Reissner left a lasting impact on the thoughts of Schwenckfeld. For a detailed study see, Peter C. Erb, "Adam Reissner: His Learning and Influence on Schwenckfeld," *MQR* vol. 54, no. 1 (January 1980), 32-41.
201. Beard, *The Reformation of the Sixteenth Century*, 213.
202. Beard, *The Reformation of the Sixteenth Century*, 213.

less associated much with them. On the one hand, they listened to him patiently, and on the other hand, he had a broad mind to believe that piety is not peculiar to a particular church. He was one of the prominent figures in the spiritualist circle.[203]

Schwenckfeld thought that the reason for the unchanging situation even after the Lutheran Reformation was due to the fact that people wrongly interpreted Lutheran principles such as justification by faith, the bondage of the will, the impossibility of achieving the commandments of God, the value of good works in the work of salvation, and finally, justification obtained by the grace associated with the sacrifice of Christ. The wrong interpretation of these principles further aggravated the crisis of piety and morality, and it was contrary to the intentions of the Reformer. Schwenckfeld, therefore, resumed analysis of these arguments, trying in an Erasmian spirit to draw out a positive meaning.[204] In other words, he was searching for a way that could lead people to authentic living faith by promoting true Christian piety in the hearts of the church.[205]

Taking a cue from the previous argument, one can insist that transformation of a person into a second Adam, into a spiritual person, was the principle subject of Schwenckfeld's reflections.[206] This principle has been always the same in his thought, that the definition of faith is an interior state that must lead the person to a transformation not only of the person's conscience but also body, soul, and flesh.[207] He argues that Jesus Christ was

---

203. It is certain that Theophrastus Paracelsus (1493-1541) exerted quite an influence on the genuine spiritualists. Paracelsus was a naturalist, philosopher, and physician of far reaching importance. He searched for basic divine elements in creation. Bünderlin, an Anabaptist leader and follower of Denck, came under the influence of this philosopher. Bünderlin maintained that God cannot be without the divine opposite, because God does not want to remain unknown. He continued that, human is essentially a spiritual being and therefore real religion must also be spiritual. Accordingly, there is no visible church, no external baptism and Lord's Supper. The Scriptures are given for the education to a pure inner religion. Sebastian Franck wrote enthusiastically about this new development of the Reformation. With Johannes Bünderlin and Sebastian Franck the spiritualist circles made a start. They spiritualized every concept; their basic principle was the inner Word or the inner light of all creation. Their world concept became some form of dualism. See Walther Köhler, "Die Spiritualisten," *Archive for Reformation History* vol. 41 (1948).
204. Seguenny, "Caspar von Schwenckfeld," 352.
205. Seguenny, "Caspar von Schwenckfeld," 351.
206. Paul Gerhard Eberlein, *Ketzer oder Heiliger? Caspar von Schwenckfeld: Der schlesische Reformator und seine Botschaft* (Metzingen: Ernst Franz, 1998), 165.
207. Seguenny, "Caspar von Schwenckfeld," 354-355.

not made in a fleshy act, but rather was engendered in an act by which the Word became a corporal reality. Hence, the body of Christ is the bearer of the Spirit of his Father. The body of Christ was from his birth a new flesh, immaculate, flesh of the Spirit, of grace and truth, although it was given by Mary.[208] Schwenckfeld contends that this ultimate incarnation of the Word in this manner was for the glorification of human beings in their soul and body. In other words, it is for the spiritual revival of a person. That means, the matter submits to the determination of the human will.[209] Thus he argues that when the spiritual renewal of a person is accomplished, then they are able to spiritualize matter and matter then becomes the body of the Spirit. Thus matter continues to exist in reality, but in so far as spiritual reality. Schwenckfeld argues that Christ, therefore, is perfectly human and perfectly God and he is a faithful image of his Father.[210]

Schwenckfeld contends that the spiritualization of the body of Christ permits him to be really present in the heart of the Trinity. There are two reasons why Schwenckfeld's findings are important. Firstly, that the natural human being, conscious in the faith of the identity of the nature of his flesh with that of Christ, can feel comforted since the spiritualization is also within human's reach. Secondly, that the creature transformed into the new person participates nonetheless, by the grace of Christ, in the mystery of the Trinity. This signifies not only the most complete identity between the creator and his work, but at the same time the acceptance, therefore, the justification of the person.[211]

Schwenckfeld argues that if the spiritualization is to be realized in the earthly human being, it is necessary that they loses their character of a creature made from dust. In other words, they must be reborn anew, accomplished by a spiritual act, in and by faith.[212] Their body must be changed into a spiritual body, that of Christ. Schwenckfeld argues that this is possible through the spiritual body of Christ, who like a ray of sun lights up and transforms all things, enlightens the whole body.[213] However,

---

208. Seguenny, "Caspar von Schwenckfeld," 356.
209. Eberlein, *Ketzer oder Heiliger?* 166.
210. Eberlein, *Ketzer oder Heiliger?* 168.
211. Seguenny, "Caspar von Schwenckfeld," 357.
212. Eberlein, *Ketzer oder Heiliger?* 166-167.
213. Andre Seguenny, *The Christology of Caspar Schwenckfeld: Spirit and Flesh in the Process*

Schwenckfeld asserts that the transformation cannot be defined as the act of creation, since the created being is already there. On the other hand, it concerns the creation itself, since it is the Creator who breathes the Spirit of God into the creation. Then the condition of the creature as an alienated object changes, and becomes the real expression of the Spirit in which God can be recognized as being himself. Thus the identity between the Creator and the spiritual human being is realized. In short, Schwenckfeld argues that the Word incarnate in Christ now incarnates itself in human being, to lead them to spiritualization.[214]

The strong spiritualistic outlook of Schwenckfeld undercuts the usefulness and necessity of the sacraments, the building blocks of the visible church.[215] Schwenckfeld's argument was driven by the dialectic of "inner" versus "outer," of "Spirit" versus "matter." For Schwenckfeld the inner and the spiritual always preceded the outer and material and gave them their meaning. Regarding baptism for example, this dialectic implies that the inner baptism, a spiritual rebirth, must precede the outer baptism if the physical rite has to get any meaning. In the same manner, in the Eucharist also the inner feeding in faith must precede the external consumption of bread and wine. Schwenckfeld maintained that the Spirit is the agent through which Christ invites the church into the Lord's Supper. He writes, "That the Lord Jesus Christ as the true heavenly high priest, through the Holy Spirit, himself invites to the supper and himself gives and distributes to all believers his body and blood unto eternal life …."[216] Thus Schwenckfeld argues that the sacraments are just symbols that merely reflect a precedent reality.[217]

---

of Life Transformation, trans. Peter C. Erb & Simone Nieuwolt (Lewiston: The Edwin Mellen, 1987), 88.
214. Seguenny, "Caspar von Schwenckfeld," 359.
215. Eberlein, *Ketzer oder Heiliger?* 172-173.
216. Caspar Schwenckfeld, "An Answer to Luther's Malediction," in *Spiritual and Anabaptist Writers: Documents Illustrative of the Radical Reformers,* eds. George H. Williams and Angel M. Mergal (London: SCM, 1957), 166.
217. R. Emmet McLaughlin, "The Politics of Dissent: Martin Bucer, Caspar Schwenckfeld, and the Schwenkfelders of Strasbourg," *MQR* vol. 68, no. 1 (January 1994), 59-78.

When one keenly observes, of course, there are conflicting statements in the theology of Schwenckfeld. For example, he says on the one hand that the Spirit is everything. He writes:

> First, justifying faith belongs to the order of spiritual, invisible, inner things; this no one doubts, for it is of God, of divine nature, yea, the work and gift of God. Hence its origin cannot be of physical things as of the external word, hearing, ministry, or letter, but it remains in its order as something higher and greater, issues from the inner Word which is Spirit and life, and must, according to its original state, precede all external ministrations .... Since all that is not of faith is sin, it follows that the external hearing of the gospel, if it be not preceded by faith, grace, love or good will, cannot be free from sin ....[218]

On the other hand, he implies that the careful reading of Scripture is central to the Christian experience. He writes:

> But holy Scripture is indeed a veritable storehouse and the true mine in Christ, in which, before all others, one should study, search and pore, reading and re-reading everything, chewing, pondering, turning it over in one's mind, studying all thoroughly. For within it are rich treasures prepared for the faithful, priceless pearls, gold and jewels; truly priceless noble things, which belong in heaven and in that eternal life, are offered through faith.[219]

Schwenckfeld asserts the active role of the Spirit in the incarnation of Jesus Christ. He argues that since Adam sinned and stopped the process of deification, Christ's incarnation was decreed by God in order to retrieve this situation.[220] With Christ the second Adam, the *Logos* assumed an even more important role. Schwenckfeld contends that through the agency of the Spirit, Jesus Christ's mother Mary conceived and gave birth to a non-created

---

218. Cited in R. Emmet McLaughlin, "Spiritualism and the Bible: The Case of Caspar Schwenckfeld (1489-1561)," *MQR* vol. 53, no. 4 (October 1979), 282-298.
219. Cited in McLaughlin, "Spiritualism and the Bible," 282-298.
220. Seguenny, *The Christology of Caspar Schwenckfeld*, 83.

human, the Son of God. Today other human beings achieve salvation by being engrafted into the body of Christ, by partaking of the heavenly flesh, and by becoming new persons in themselves.[221] This doctrine provides the basis for a thoroughgoing dualism which runs throughout Schwenckfeld's theology, a dualism which sharply distinguished old person and new person, Spirit and flesh, Spirit and letter.[222]

Therefore, when attempting to understand the pneumatology of Schwenckfeld, one must understand the complete dualism in his thoughts. He maintained that each believer is actually two persons, that means, the old creaturely person and the new deified person. For him they are the outer Word and the inner Word. Schwenckfeld argues that Christ is the inner Word and his ministry is exercised by the Spirit. And only this inner Word can save humankind.[223] Hence, Schwenckfeld attacked the other Reformers for preaching only the letter and not the Spirit of the gospel. The doctrine of the inner Word was a fruit of his preoccupation with the spiritual meaning of Scripture.[224]

In short, one can note that the doctrine of the Spirit is a key aspect in the whole theology of Schwenckfeld. In a sense, his explication of the inner and outer Word can be traced in line with that of Müntzer and Denck, who also emphasized the inner and outer Word in their theology as noted earlier. Thus by anchoring on the Spirit, Schwenckfeld was searching for an alternative way that could enable human beings to have an authentic living faith by promoting a true Christian piety in the hearts of the church. In that sense, Schwenckfeld's pneumatology can be highly prized.

---

221. He maintains that God works directly upon humans, dwelling within them. He needs no mediators, not even the Bible. Any reliance on such instruments would only limit the divine liberty. If Scripture could indeed have produced faith, an external material object would then have engendered something internal and spiritual. But in Schwenckfeld's dualism, only the Spirit could produce the spiritual. See McLaughlin, "Spiritualism and the Bible," 282-298.
222. McLaughlin, "Spiritualism and the Bible," 282-298.
223. McLaughlin, "Spiritualism and the Bible," 282-298; it is this principle which indicates Schwenckfeld's opposition to all forms of mediation between the human being and God. He writes, "In heaven at the side of the Father and nowhere else true faith needs to find Jesus Christ, our life and happiness, without exterior mediations." See Seguenny, *The Christology of Caspar Schwenckfeld*, 113.
224. McLaughlin, "Spiritualism and the Bible," 282-298.

5.5 Sebastian Franck (1499 – 1542)

Sebastian Frank was one of the Spiritualist Reformers,[225] who was more sympathetic with the Evangelical Anabaptists. A thorough analysis reveals the fact that his life resembles in many respects those of Hans Denck and Caspar von Schwenckfeld. Recognizing this similarity, Beard writes that, "There is the same untiring allegiance to theological opinions, the same wandering and harassed existence, the same result of contemporary fame and speedy forgetfulness."[226] At the time of Franck's arrival in Strasbourg[227] in 1529 or 1530, he was already a "programmatic Spiritualist."[228] Dipple writes:

> In his pre-Strasbourg writings, the relationships among biblical literarism, ceremonialism and sectarianism, and the ecclesiology of the Spiritualist church are presented in only rudimentary forms. These themes, which occupy central positions in his Strasbourg writings and in his thought generally,

---

225. One crucial issue in the interpretation of Franck's developing thought is whether or not Franck passed through an Anabaptist phase that rerouted to his particularly individualist variant of spiritualism. James Stayer, who has examined the Anabaptist/spiritualists debates from the broader perspective of the radical Reformation, has suggested that at this time spiritualists, who had earlier immersed themselves in the Anabaptist movements, now began to reappear as a distinct group. See James M. Stayer, "The Radical Reformation," in *Handbook of European History 1400-1600: Late Middle Ages, Renaissance and Reformation: Visions, Programs and Outcomes*, vol. 2, eds. Thomas A. Brady, Jr., Heiko A. Oberman, and James D. Tracy (New York: Brill, 1995), 263; scholars of Franck's writings have long debated the question of whether he passed through an Anabaptist phase in his intellectual and spiritual journey from Lutheranism to Spiritualism. Ernst Troeltsch suggests that at one stage Franck experimented with Baptist fellowship, and this interpretation has subsequently won significant, although not universal, support. See for a discussion, Geoffrey Dipple, "Sebastian Franck in Strasbourg," *MQR* vol. 73, no 4 (October 1999), 783-802.
226. Beard, *The Reformation of the Sixteenth Century*, 215.
227. Strasbourg in the years from 1528-1533 was the showplace of religious radicalism in Europe and the catch basin of dissidents in Germany. Possessed of relative political stability and economic well-being, the city was both able and willing to absorb waves of religious refugees who had been expelled by Catholic and Protestant regimes in Germany, Switzerland, France, and Italy. Major groups included the Swiss brethren who followed Michael Sattler, spiritualist Anabaptists of the Hans Denck stream, Augsburg refugees sympathetic to Hans Hutt, the circle around Pilgrim Marpeck, Melchorites led by Melchior Hoffman, intellectuals known as the Epicureans, and Schwenckfeldian spiritualists. For a discussion see, Dipple, "Sebastian Franck in Strasbourg," 783-802.
228. Dipple, "Sebastian Franck in Strasbourg," 783-802.

were hammered into their final forms in the imperial city and in the context of the Anabaptist/Spiritualist debates.²²⁹

Being a Spiritualist, the Holy Spirit has been a central aspect in the theology of Franck. One of the specialties of Franck's understanding of the Spirit is that, it is very much biblical. He writes, "Its power stands not in any external, pre-written, pre-spoken word or service, but rather in the invisible power of the living Word of God which is found in us and which brings the Holy Spirit with it, yes, is it itself."²³⁰ Therefore, he maintained that ceremonies and sacraments should be abandoned unless a new divine mandate for their restitution could be proven. As his spiritual journey led him from Lutheranism to spiritualism, he increasingly de-emphasized the significance of the reform of external elements of religious life, and maintained those sacraments and offices as hindrances to the spiritual reform.²³¹ Yet he remained committed to the possibility of a restitution of the apostolic church. He looked forward to a reformation in which the "Holy Spirit ... plans to erect a Christian church with the correct use of the sacraments, brotherly admonition, ban, and consequent betterment of Christian living."²³²

According to Franck, God is Spirit and the true world is that of the Spirit. Since God is Spirit and invisible, he works through the Spirit and stands in opposition to the world.²³³ For God, as Spirit, had first declared and then historically demonstrated his preference for working spiritually rather than sacramentally to achieve the mature fruits of the Spirit. These fruits, faith, penitence, and self-denial, can be realized by all people whether in or without organized Christianity.²³⁴ Franck maintains that there is neither outward church nor any sacrament existing in the world after the death of

---

229. Dipple, "Sebastian Franck in Strasbourg," 783-802.
230. Sebastian Franck, *Paradoxa*, trans. & intro. Siegfried Wollgast (Berlin: Academie Verlag, 1966), 289; hereafter *Paradoxa*.
231. R. Emmet McLaughlin, "Schwenckfeld and the Strasbourg Radicals," *MQR* vol. 59, no. 3 (July 1985), 268-278.
232. Cited in McLaughlin, "Schwenckfeld and the Strasbourg Radicals," 268-278.
233. *Paradoxa*, 40; Robert Wesley Brenning, *The Ethical Hermeneutic of Sebastian Franck, 1499-1542*, Ph. D. Thesis (London: Temple University Microfilms International, 1978), 75.
234. Sebastian Franck, "A Letter to John Campanus," in *Spiritual and Anabaptist Writers*, eds. G. H. Williams and A. M. Mergal (London: SCM, 1957), 146; *Paradoxa*, 148-155.

the apostles because the Spirit has been imparting all this to the believers. He writes that, "Therefore, I believe that the outward church of Christ, including all its gifts and sacraments, because of the breaking in and laying waste by the anti-Christ right after the death of the apostles, went up into heaven and lies concealed in the spirit and in truth .... But at the same time nothing has departed from the inner truth of baptism, the supper, the ban, and gathering for worship. Instead, the Spirit has imparted all this in truth to the faithful in whatever lands they may be ...."[235] Williams and Mergal note that Franck's attendance upon the living Spirit was like that of Thomas Müntzer but he was neither a revolutionary millennialist like him.[236]

One of the novel aspects of Franck's pneumatology is his treatment of the Spirit as the teacher of the new Covenant.[237] He writes:

> Therefore, even as the Spirit of God is alone the teacher of the New Covenant, so also he alone baptizes and alone avails himself for all things, namely, in the Spirit and in truth. And just as the church is today a purely spiritual thing, so also is all law, promise, reward, spirit, bread, wine, sword, Kingdom, life – all in the Spirit and no longer outward, etc. Therefore the unitary Spirit alone baptizes with fire and the Spirit all the faithful [all] who are obedient to the inner Word in whatever part of the world they are be.[238]

Franck continues that, "Since the outward arrangements and the sacraments were not wiped out by the laying waste of Antichrist after the time of the apostles, but rather were misused and sullied, God through the Spirit in truth provided by means of his spiritual church all things which the signs and outward gifts merely betokened."[239] He argues that God through the Spirit circumcises the hearts of his people, and "thus he establishes and perfects the whole New Testament and arranges all things in his fashion in the Spirit and in truth, so that nothing is fatuous or figurative, but rather

---

235. Franck, "A Letter to John Campanus," 149.
236. In their Introduction to Sebastian Franck's text. See Williams and Mergal, "A Letter to John Campanus by Sebastian Frank," in *Spiritual and Anabaptist Writers*, 146.
237. *Paradoxa*, 128-131.
238. Franck, "A Letter to John Campanus," 149; *Paradoxa*, 150.
239. Franck, "A Letter to John Campanus," 152.

all is truth."²⁴⁰ Against the enterprise of reinstalling the sacraments into the church, Franck warns that, "Cease therefore from thy enterprise and let the church of God remain in the Spirit among all peoples and pagans; let them be herein instructed, governed, and baptized by the doctor of the new Covenant, namely the Holy Spirit."²⁴¹

Franck contends that the Spirit that lives in human beings has the capacity to understand the Word that resides in them, thereby making the Word an internal experience. He writes that, "The Word of God issues directly from the mouth of God without intermediary and leads man directly to God. Christ is therefore not the intermediary between God and man, but is the very Spirit of God and also the spirit of man."²⁴² Franck argues that if the Spirit resides within a person, it cannot sleep but must act. This train of thought leads us to the conviction that for him the Spirit is the key to true religion. Eugene Peters writes that, "His emphasis on inner religion arose primarily from his rejection of the ritualistic, bibliocentric, and rationalistic approaches characterizing the religion of his age."²⁴³ Thus Franck turned to the inner authority, not as a result of purely theological theorizing, but to developing a nonsectarian religious orientation immune to the extremes of rigidity and enthusiasm that are characteristic of the various groups.²⁴⁴ For Franck, inner religion is the religion of the Spirit, the Spirit of God and humanity. He argues that the Spirit of God is the divine Word or the Word of God. And the spirit of humanity is their assimilation of the Word of God, which thereby becomes the inner Word. According to Franck, the Word of God is issued directly from the mouth of God without intermediary and leads humanity directly to God. Hence, Franck asserts that Christ is not the intermediary between God and human being but is the very Spirit of God and also the spirit of human being. Thus Christ is identical with the inner Word.²⁴⁵ The Spirit that comes to humanity through Christ from

---

240. Franck, "A Letter to John Campanus," 152.
241. Franck, "A Letter to John Campanus," 155-156.
242. Rudolph Kommoss, *Sebastian Franck and Erasmus von Rotterdam* (Berlin: Ebering, 1934), 57.
243. Eugene Peters, "Sebastian Franck's Theology of Religious Knowledge," *MQR* vol. 35, no. 4 (October 1961), 267-281.
244. Peters, "Sebastian Franck's Theology," 267-281.
245. Peters, "Sebastian Franck's Theology," 267-281.

God works against those who are living by the flesh rather than the Spirit. Thus he argues by quoting Paul's statement that one person is created with a living soul in the natural life and the other person is created with a living Spirit in the spiritual life.[246] Franck believed that the truth of life lay only in the being of the Spirit, the internal experienced Spirit. All other external existence is the work of the devil.[247]

Another notable point that Franck argues is that there exists a spiritual heart and a fleshy heart in every human being. As a result, there arises the necessity in human beings to turn either to the Spirit or to the flesh.[248] When a person wills to turn from evil to good, it is God who makes them do so because God grasps the heart of human beings so that they are naturally led to the spiritual heart. Franck insists that this turning should be understood as an inner force, not as an external compulsion. By turning to the spiritual heart, which is his genuine being, humanity leaves itself open to God because it is turning from the self-centeredness of the fleshy heart to God within. For Franck, once a person has decided for God, the Word of Christ, he/she becomes an invincible believer who is impervious to the world.[249]

The other characteristic of Franck's pneumatology is that he asserts the Spirit as the criterion of religious knowledge. It is because he maintains that the experience of God directly implies the intuitive knowledge of God. The motive power of Franck's intuitionism lies in his belief that the Spirit, the Word of God, is the ultimate criterion.[250] Reason or love may be employed sporadically as intermediate criteria, but ultimately the Spirit must prevail.[251] According to Franck, the Word of God, the Spirit, functions more as a formative power than as a theoretical norm. By the Word individuals can test everything within themselves but nothing in written or spoken discourse on specifically theological and doctrinal issues. In maintaining an intimate relation between Spirit and morality, Frank emphasized the importance of works of faith, although he refused to align himself with the

---

246. Brenning, *The Ethical Hermeneutic of Sebastian Franck*, 35.
247. Brenning, *The Ethical Hermeneutic of Sebastian Franck*, 71.
248. *Paradoxa*, 99-103, 118-120.
249. Peters, "Sebastian Franck's Theology," 267-281.
250. *Paradoxa*, 7.
251. Peters, "Sebastian Franck's Theology," 267-281.

position that human beings are justified by works. Thus for Franck, the Word is a norm of faith, a norm with the practical purpose of establishing a life of faith.[252] One can argue that for Franck, the Spirit or the epistemological criterion becomes the axiological criterion as well and neither is to be understood apart from the other.

In short, the active role of the Spirit in the life of an individual to turn them towards God is the key concept in the pneumatology of Franck. In many sense, Franck's pneumatology resembles the pneumatology of the other radical Reformers. However, the uniqueness of his pneumatology lies in the fact that he dealt with the living Spirit as an inner force that compels the transformation of human beings. Franck's argument of the Spirit as the key to true religion and the criterion of religious knowledge have to be duly recognized.

6. Summary

The main purpose of this chapter has been to make a brief survey to inquire and make out the pneumatology of the Reformers. The study shows the fact that pneumatology was quite significant in the theological discussions and articulations throughout the Reformation era, especially among the radical Reformers. Although Reformation started as a protest against the theological positions of the Roman Catholic Church in the late Medieval Age, the Reformers recognized in their theology the active role of the Spirit in the life of a person, in the church, in the sacraments, in the Christian ministry and so on, thereby making the Spirit a central doctrine of Reformation. Moreover, one of the greatest themes of sixteenth century theology and of the whole of the tradition stemming from the Reformation is the relationship between the Word and the Spirit. One cannot discuss either the spirituality of the Reformation or its doctrine of the Spirit as such a part from this theme. That means the intrinsic connection of the work of the Spirit in the church with the doctrine of the Word of God as written and preached constitutes the distinctive emphasis of the pneumatology of the Reformation. Both the right wing and left wing Reformers saw the

---

252. Peters, "Sebastian Franck's Theology," 267-281.

significance and relationship between the Word and Spirit working in the life of human beings in order to make them spiritual and new, although their understanding was different in many respects.[253] Nevertheless, numerous doctrines of the Spirit were developed in the Christian Church casting anchor upon these Reformers' pneumatology. One can also find this phenomenon in various present day churches like in Pentecostalism and charismatic movements. Thus the enormous possibility that the Spirit opens before the church and humanity has been recognized by the theologians irrespective of the church affiliation in the following centuries thereby making pneumatology an important locus in the systematic theology. They look into the person of the Spirit not just in relation to the Trinity as it was practiced in the past, but rather as a separate entity that actively functions in the spiritual and secular realm of the world. This realization of the role of the Spirit in the whole divine action with regard to the church and world is the focus of the following three chapters.

---

253. In comparison one can say that firstly, the challenge presented by the radical Reformation in their doctrine of the inner Word, apprehended by the Spirit, to the mainstream Reformation doctrine of the Word of God as publicly revealed in the Bible leads to the assertion of the link between the work of the Spirit and public discourse about the Bible. Secondly, thus public discourse can only affect the heart, or rise to the level of faith, by the inward work of the Spirit. Since faith is lodged in the divine promise, as revealed in the Word of God, and since faith is a gift of grace effected by the Spirit, faith has a certain primacy in all Reformation discussion of the Spirit. Thirdly, the doctrine of the inspiration of the Bible is thus highlighted, so that its importance extends beyond a simple concern for the authority of the Bible as the foundation of faith and practice. Finally, Reformation pneumatology is open in principle to the richer theme of mystical union with Christ. See Gary D. Badcock, *Light of Truth and Fire of Love: A Theology of the Holy Spirit* (Grand Rapids: Eerdmans, 1997), 92.

CHAPTER THREE

Pneumatology of Karl Barth (1886 – 1968)

1. *Introduction*

In the preceding chapter, we have briefly discussed the pneumatology of the left and right wing Reformers. Taking cue from these Reformers, especially from Calvin, the notable twentieth century patriarch Karl Barth developed a pneumatology which is the major concern of this chapter. It is beyond any doubt that the most interesting event in the post-war religious world has been the phenomenal suddenness with which the word of Barth has echoed in the ear of Europe and transformed the whole outlook of continental theology, in Germany, Switzerland, Holland, Denmark, and elsewhere.[1] Wherever the word of Barth has encountered doubt and criticism, it has always met with respect and with a certain longing and disappointment, a witness to the fact that there is a deep sense of need, a vacuum, in the Protestantism, calling out for a meaningful presentation of the Christian revelation. It has to be admitted that Barth has done his part brilliantly in presenting the Christian doctrines in a systematic manner. When taking the theology of Barth as a whole, the elucidation of

---

1. John McConnachie, *The Significance of Karl Barth* (London: Hodder & Stoughton, 1931), 13; Torrance equates Barth to Athanasius. He writes, "I believe that the far-reaching significance of Karl Barth for the universal church in the twentieth century may best be indicated by relating it to that of St. Athanasius in the fourth century." T. F. Torrance, "The Legacy of Karl Barth (1886-1986)," *Scottish Journal of Theology* vol. 39, no. 3 (August 1986), 289.

the doctrine of the Holy Spirit can be seen as one of the most beautifully articulated theological positions which ever has been made.² Therefore, the sole focus of this chapter is to dig into the pneumatology of Barth in depth. In order to make this endeavor possible, one needs to begin with the *Sitz-im-Leben* of Barth. Hence, this chapter begins with a survey of the socio-cultural, political, philosophical, and theological surroundings of Barth to discover the factors which influenced him to develop a pneumatology. This awareness is significant in this study particularly because Barth had to make use of what he learnt and experienced from his social, political, philosophical, and academic context in developing his pneumatology. Having briefly outlined his *Sitz-im-Leben*, the study will concentrate on the pneumatology of Barth thematically.

2. *The Sitz-im-Leben of Karl Barth*

2.1 The Socio-cultural Setting

Barth was born into a pious Christian family on May 10th 1886.³ Both of his grandparents were devoted and dedicated ministers.⁴ Barth's father, Fritz Barth, was a minister at the church in Reitnau located in the Canton of Aargau for seven years. Later he became a teacher at the *Predigerschule* in Basel on account of his book on the significance of Paul for Tertullian.⁵

---

2. Cochrane writes that, "Barth has always been reticent about describing himself as possessing the Spirit or even of being an instrument, channel, or means of grace." Arthur C. Cochrane, "Whether Karl Barth Changed My Mind," in *How Karl Barth Changed My Mind*, ed. Donald K. McKim (Grand Rapids: Eerdmans, 1986), 17; in response to a question whether he had been moved by the Spirit to leave Switzerland and to go to Scotland to deliver the Gifford Lectures, Barth replied that, *Ich will keine Apostelgeschichte über mein eigenes Leben schreiben* (I will not write an Acts of the Apostles about my own life). It means that he would not equate himself with an apostle. But he added that, "If the Word of God is spoken and heard in Scotland, then I was led by the Spirit to come here." See Cochrane, "Whether Karl Barth Changed My Mind," 17; see also Karl Barth, *Evangelical Theology: An Introduction*, trans. Grover Foley (London: Weidenfeld and Nicolson, 1968), 48-59.
3. Eberhard Busch, *Karl Barths Lebenslauf: Nach seinen Briefen und autobiographischen Texten* (Munich: Kaiser Verlag, 1975), 13, 17.
4. John Bowden, *Karl Barth* (London: SCM, 1971), 30.
5. David L. Müller, *Karl Barth: Makers of the Modern Theological Mind* (Waco: Word Books, 1972), 14.

When Barth was three years old, his father was appointed as professor in the University of Berne where he lectured in New Testament and Early Church History until his death in 1912.[6] Torrance writes that, "It was there that Karl grew up, went to school, and began his university training. There deep and lasting foundations were laid at home, in church, and at school, where his faith was nourished in positive evangelical theology, and there too sacred scholarship in the service of the Gospel entered, as it were, into his very blood."[7]

Karl Barth was greatly influenced by his father since he was an excellent *guru* to his children.[8] Moreover, his brother Heinrich exerted a great influence upon Karl with whom he had a good relationship. By profession, Heinrich was an outstanding philosopher[9] who worked in the philosophy department at the University of Basel.[10] Due to the close relationship between Heinrich and Karl, Heinrich helped Karl to understand philosophy better. Moreover, through the influence of his friend Thurneysen, Barth was introduced to the eschatological theology of Johann Christoph Blumhardt (1805-1880)[11] which influenced Barth immensely. When the elder Blumhardt died, his son Christoph took the leadership and through the personal contact with Christoph Blumhardt, Barth recognized the actual reality of the power

---

6. Thomas F. Torrance, *Karl Barth: An Introduction to His Early Theology, 1930 - 1931* (London: SCM, 1962), 15.
7. Torrance, *Karl Barth*, 15.
8. Barth also followed the same pattern in his family too. His Son Markus commends that, "He has always been my best friend, a close comrade who reflects and encourages true attachment and true freedom. The great knowledge he possesses, the books that he is producing, the direction he is giving to the thought and lives of many – all these ponderous gifts he has never used for exerting a formal authority over his children. He could teach us that 'mother is always right, precisely when it seems to you that she is wrong,' but he would make such a statement with a twinkle of the eye, and he would never make it about himself." Markus Barth, "My Father: Karl Barth," in *How Karl Barth Changed My Mind*, ed. Donald K. McKim (Grand Rapids: Eerdmans, 1986), 1.
9. Georg Merz, "Die Begegnung Karl Barths mit der Deutschen Theologie," *Kerygma und Dogma 2* (1956), 165.
10. Müller, *Karl Barth*, 14.
11. Johann Christoph Blumhardt was a pastor in Möttlingen in Swabia from 1838-1852. He was fully convinced of the present living power of God in Christ to set human beings free from the evils that imprison them. As he gained popularity, more believers who were hungry for spiritual food swarmed about him. This led him to establish a community at Bad Boll (1852-1880). James D. Smart, "Eduard Thurneysen: Pastor-Theologian," *Theology Today* 16, no. 1 (1959), 83; James Bentley, "Christoph Blumhardt: Preacher of Hope," *Theology* 78 (1975), 577.

and might of God which had concretely been witnessed in the healing performance and practice of the elder Blumhardt. The strong conviction of the Blumhardts in the redemptive and actualizing presence of God through Christ in the actual affairs of human life had strengthened Barth's faith and helped him to view Christ as the determinative point for talk of things human. For Barth, Christ appears like a vertical line intersecting the horizontal plane of history at a right angle.[12] Moreover, Barth's pastoral experience in Safenwil had a great impact upon him. Being a pastor, Barth had to give sermons every Sunday and it was a real challenge for him to meet the real needs and demands of the spiritual lives of the believers. When he came up against the practical problems of the pulpit, he discovered the inadequacy of his theology.[13] Thus Barth turned to the study of the Bible to escape from this predicament and sought for the voice of God to the church. Since he had to preach sermons in the church, he was busy with preparing messages which in turn made him a serious student of the Bible.[14] The new world of the Bible which Barth discovered was concerned with the whole human existence, their external as well as internal world. Thurneysen writes that, "Karl Barth's theological thinking was from the beginning directed to the life of man. The existence, the life of man, on the one side, and on the other the Word of God that meets this life, lays hold of it, and transforms it."[15] In short, Barth became convinced in the absolute authority of the Word and it enabled him to develop a pneumatology on the basis of the Word of God. Barth writes, "The knowledge of God occurs in the fulfillment of the revelation of His Word by the Holy Spirit, and therefore in the reality and with the necessity of faith and its obedience. Its content is the existence

---

12. Karl Barth, *Römerbrief* (Munich: Kaiser Verlag, 1924), 5.
13. McConnachie, *The Significance of Karl Barth*, 21.
14. Barth's exegesis covers the whole Bible and displays a great variety of hermeneutical skills and principles. See D. F. Ford, "Barth's Interpretation of the Bible," in *Karl Barth: Studies of His Theological Method*, ed. S. W. Sykes (Oxford: Clarendon, 1979), 56; see also Karl Barth, *The Epistle to the Romans*, trans. from 6th edition. Edwyn C. Hoskyns (London: Oxford University Press, 1968).
15. Eduard Thurneysen, "Introduction," in *Revolutionary Theology in the Making: Barth-Thurneysen Correspondence, 1914-1925*, trans. James D. Smart (London: The Epworth Press, 1964), 14; Godsey writes that, "What Barth was discovering in the Bible was something which liberal theology had tended to obscure, namely, the fundamental discontinuity between God and man." See John D. Godsey "Introduction," in Karl Barth, *How I Changed My Mind* (Richmond: John Knox, 1966), 23.

of Him whom we must fear above all things because we may love Him above all things; who remains a mystery to us because He Himself has made Himself so clear and certain to us."[16]

2.2 The Political Setting

One of the significant factors that exerted considerable influence upon the development of the theology of Barth is the political climate of the 19th and 20th centuries. This political context of Barth has to be seen firstly in the light of optimism over the human competence to shape their own history and to make use of nature for their own benefit, and secondly, the serious tragedies of the world wars that happened due to human failures. The wars and their after effects had left much impact upon the life and thought of Barth. Due to the worse political situation of that time, although with hesitation, Barth joined the Social Democratic Party in 1915 in order to contribute to the common people's rights.[17] Moreover, while National Socialism was surging in Germany, Barth was teaching at the University of Bonn. As a professor, he was employed by the state and supposed to take an oath of allegiance to Hitler. Because of his refusal, Barth was deposed from his post in 1934, six months after the Second Barmen Synod.[18] After being dismissed from his post, instead of hiding himself from the open realities of political fire, Barth continued to stay at the forefront of the opposition movement of the confessing Church against the National Socialist government. Moreover, he supported the battle with a fifteen thousand word pamphlet, written over a weekend, entitled *Theological Existence Today*. In the midst of the rising power of the Nationalist Socialist movement and their attack against the Christians, Barth was able to review the situation in the light of his understanding of divine command at the closest distance. It helped Barth to formulate an ideology about the church-state relationship in the light of his perception of the power of the freely given grace of God through Jesus Christ for the whole creation.[19] Barth asserted that the history

---

16. Karl Barth, *Church Dogmatics* 2/1, 3; in this study, the Edinburgh translation of *Church Dogmatics* (Edinburgh: T & T Clark) is followed; hereafter *CD*.
17. George Hunsinger, "Karl Barth and Radical Politics," *Studies in Religion* vol. 7, no. 2 (Spring 1978), 178; Bowden, *Karl Barth*, 68.
18. Bowden, *Karl Barth*, 73.
19. See for a description of Barth's understanding of church and society in E. Young,

of humankind and its cause is totally in the hands of God and whatever changes take place in it are directly or indirectly the political revolution of God in his handling of the cause of humankind.[20] Thus the political situation, particularly in Germany and Europe in general, had a lasting impact upon Barth, and it can be seen in the Barmen Confession[21] for it was Barth himself who was its architect.[22] Although the Barmen Confession was a theological response to the political realities of that time, it became just a brief theological definition of the question of church-state relationship. However, one should note that it points out the general atmosphere of the political context in which Barth found himself and his employment of the Word against the spiritual opponents of the time.[23]

2.3 The Philosophical Setting

Studies in the writings of Barth prove the fact that Barth had high esteem for philosophy and its principles. For Barth, everyone, even the simplest Bible reader, comes to the text of Scripture with some philosophical presuppositions.[24] Hence, for Barth, philosophy is not at all a danger to a theologian. However, when theologians do not realize that philosophy is just a contributing factor to the relativity of the hearing of the Word, then it is a danger.[25] For Barth, what both theologians and philosophers encounter

---

Church and State in the Theology of Karl Barth, Ph.D. Thesis (Michigan: University Microfilms, 1971).
20. Eduard Thurneysen, *Karl Barth: Theologie und Sozialismus* (Zurich: Theologischer Verlag, 1973), 23; Friedrich-Wilhelm Marquardt, *Theologie und Sozialismus: Das Beispiel Karl Barths* (Munich: Kaiser Verlag, 1972), 320.
21. It is an important declaration, in large part written by Karl Barth, agreed upon at the Synod of Barmen in 1934. It attempts to resist the subordination of the Christian gospel and church to any political or social movement as its writers believed the German Christians had done. See W. C. Regensburg, "Barmen, Declaration of (1934)," in *Evangelical Dictionary of Theology*, ed. Walter A. Elwell (Grand Rapids: Baker Academic, 2001), 141; Eberhard Busch, "Barmer Theologische Erklärung," in *Evangelisches Kirchenlexikon* vol. 1, eds. Erwin Fahlbusch, et. al. (Göttingen: Vandenhoeck & Ruprecht, 1986), 361; Busch, *Karl Barth's Lebenslauf*, 258.
22. William H. Gentz, *The Dictionary of Bible and Religion* (Nashville: Abingdon, 1986), 107.
23. See Busch, "Barmer Theologische Erklärung," 363; Thurneysen, *Karl Barth: Theologie und Sozialismus*, 19.
24. Karl Barth, *Die Christliche Dogmatik im Entwurf*, ed. Gerhard Sauter (Zurich: Theologischer Verlag, 1982), 403.
25. Barth, *Die Christliche Dogmatik*, 404-405.

in their existence is neither double-truth nor a half-truth, but rather a one truth.[26] That means the aim and task of theologians and philosophers is to find out the meaning of this one truth. Hence, they have a common starting point and goal in their speculative endeavor. However, there is a difference between theologians and philosophers on the basis of their approach to this one truth and how they perceive and interpret it. Macquarrie gives a testimony regarding Barth's understanding of the nature of the relationship between theology and philosophy. He writes:

> Philosophical and non-Christian ideas of God are therefore idolatrous. Yet Barth is anxious not to appear completely negative in his attitude to reason and philosophy. Like St. Anselm, Barth would acknowledge a *fides quaerens intellectum*, where faith leads the way and reason follows. He agrees that we are at liberty to use ideas taken from secular philosophy in the work of exegesis, and that such ideas can be legitimate and fruitful; always provided that they are kept subordinate to the text and follow after it.[27]

Thus Barth maintained that the ideas drawn from secular thought are different in principle from those of the text, about which only the Holy Spirit can enlighten a person. Moreover, philosophy cannot put the Word in question nor can it confirm the Word, but is itself always put in question by the Word. Theology is an autonomous science and has no obligation to harmonize findings with those of secular thought.[28] Barth writes that, "Theology is a free science because it is based on and determined by the kingly freedom of the Word of God."[29]

Having understood the position of Barth with regard to theology and philosophy, one has to analyze the philosophical influences on Barth. The

---

26. Karl Barth, "Philosophie und Theologie," in *Philosophie und Christliche Existenz*, ed. Gerhard Huber (Basel: Hebling & Lichtenhahn, 1960), 94.
27. John Macquarrie, *Twentieth-Century Religious Thought: The Frontiers of Philosophy and Theology, 1900-1980* (New York: Charles Scribner's, 1989), 322.
28. Colin Brown, *Philosophy and the Christian Faith* (Downers Grove: Inter Varsity, 1968), 322.
29. Karl Barth, *Dogmatics in Outline*, trans. G. T. Thomson (New York: Torchbooks, 1959), 5.

first philosophical system that impacted Barth was Karl Marx's (1818-1883) dialectical materialism. Marxism denied the reality of the spiritual world and considered that only the material thing has validity as a source for all realities of which people are conscious in their sensual experience. On this basis, Christianity and Judaism are the theoretical and practical forms of humanity's egoistic alienation. He asserted that Christianity served as a theoretical or "ideological" superstructure and justification for capitalism.[30] Moreover, Marx criticized religion so strongly arguing that, "Criticism has plucked the imaginary flowers from the chain, not so that man shall bear the chain without fantasy or consolation, but so that he shall cast off the chain and gathers the living flower. The critique of religion disillusions man so that he will think, act, and fashion his reality as a man who has lost his own true sun."[31] Along with Darwin's theoretical conception of evolution, the excessive anthropocentric type of thinking, which is generally termed as "scientific positivism," has influenced Barth a lot. The prime feature of this philosophical system is that it placed stress upon the reliability and accuracy of scientific method.[32]

When tracing the constructive influence of philosophy upon Barth's pneumatological thinking, one must go far back to Plato. Pauck states that, "If it can be said that Schelling has made a Platonian Gnostic out of Tillich, then it is not inappropriate to say that Plato has tempted Barth to develop a biblical-Christological theosophy or Gnostic."[33] The specialty of the idealist philosophy of Plato is that the world which we can see with our eyes and touch with our bodies is in reality only a world of shadows. It is a copy of the eternal world of spiritual forms.[34] Therefore Plato insisted that, if we want to know anything about the character and nature of real

---

30. Karl Marx, *Marx and Engels on Religion* (Moscow: Progress, 1957) 135; for Marx religion is false because its beliefs contradict the materialism, and it defends the interest of the ruling class. See Macquarrie, *Twentieth-Century Religious Thought*, 162; James C. Livingston, *Modern Christian Thought: The Enlightenment and the Nineteenth Century* vol. 1 (New Jersey: Prentice Hall, 1997), 230-233.
31. Michael Rosen, *On Voluntary Servitude: False Consciousness and the Theory of Ideology* (Cambridge: Polity, 1996), 177.
32. See for details, Macquarrie, *Twentieth-Century Religious Thought*, 95.
33. Wilhelm Pauck, *The Heritage of the Reformation* (Philadelphia: Harper & Row, 1961), 357.
34. Colin Brown, *Philosophy and the Christian Faith* (Downers Grove: Inter Varsity, 1968), 15.

and authentic reality, we must go beyond the boundary of our sensational perception and let ourselves plunge into the other side of the sensational world through speculative reasoning.[35] Only then will we arrive at a true knowledge of what the real truth is. In short, the visible world which we perceive through the means of our sensations is only a reflection of the spiritual world that lies at the other end of this world. In this way the true nature and meaning of the physical realm is shrouded in the garment of the spiritual realm. To understand the physical world, one must seek the answer not in it, but rather in the realm outside of it because Plato saw this physical world as an illusion.

In addition to Plato, Hegel's methodological influence on Barth deserves special attention. Barth himself writes that, "Hegel's philosophy is the philosophy of self-confidence."[36] Just as Hegel clothes his philosophy in the concept of the absolute idea and its self-differentiation, Barth also has embedded his theology in the matrix of a Christological concept. Moreover, Hegel's idea of history made a big impact on Barth's entire theology. For Hegel, history is the fall of the absolute Idea/Spirit into the plurality of the world,[37] or history is a paradigm in which the self-differentiation of the Spirit into the objective otherness in the circle of its evolution is materially pictured. He maintains that the kingdom of the Spirit is the goal of the entire process of history and is that moment which inaugurates the absolute or consummate religion. Christianity is the consummate religion, for in Christianity alone we see the actual dialectical process by which the Spirit (God) works itself out to full expression in history. Although Hegel insists that God is Spirit, in fact for him the Spirit is the process of life itself, or the life movement.[38] For him, the kingdom of the Spirit is the church or

---

35. Brown, *Philosophy and the Christian Faith*, 16.
36. Karl Barth, *Protestant Thought: From Rousseau to Ritschl*, trans. Brian Cozens (Freeport: Harper & Brothers, 1959), 275.
37. Jacob Taubes, "Theology and the Philosophic Critique of Religion," *Zeitschrift für Religions- und Geistesgeschichte* 8 (1959), 132.
38. Livingston, *Modern Christian Thought*, 125; according to Hegel, absolute Spirit develops and realizes itself according to a dialectical process that must be comprehended under a trifold determination. The idea goes forth into nature and actualizes itself as Spirit. It is for this reason that universal Spirit has found its adequate sensuous representation in the Christian religion under the name of the Holy Spirit. The divine Trinity is the sensuous representation of the dialectical process of the absolute Spirit, and in the kingdom of the Spirit (the synthesis of the Logic) the truths contained in the kingdoms of

the spiritual community. God, as fully actualized Spirit, is realizable only in a community of finite human minds because the Spirit achieves consciousness only through finite particularization or concretion. Since it is only through finite consciousness in its manifold forms that the absolute Spirit realizes itself, God as Father and as Son does not enjoy such perfection in consciousness. And if it is the case that God comes to explicit historical realization in and through the spiritual community of finite consciousness, then the naïve conception of God as a person must be left behind. The spirit actualized in a community of finite minds may have the unity of personality but certainly cannot be a person in our limited sense.[39] But on the other hand, Barth understands history as the material realization of the grace of God in Christ for the covenant relationship with humankind. Thus the Hegelian concept of the absolute Spirit has left a mark in Barth's thinking while writing his pneumatology.

In addition to the above mentioned philosophical influences, one of the other philosophers who greatly influenced Barth was Sören Kierkegaard.[40] McConnachie writes that, "Kierkegaard's somber message of the absolute contrast between God and man, a dualism defying all efforts of the reason to resolve his extreme individualism, his fierce criticism of the church and of civilization, found a loud echo in the heart of Barth."[41] Barth had an attraction towards Nietzsche as well, who was a radical prophet with his attacks on civilization, the church, and society.[42] Moreover, Dostojewski, the Russian novelist also had a great impact on the thoughts of Barth. One

---

the Father and the Son are reconciled and overcome. Moreover for Hegel, God only comes to *fulfill historical actualization* in the kingdom of the Spirit. The Spirit is the only member of the Trinity in which the reality of God is explicitly manifest. This is why Christianity is rightly called the "revealed" religion, for in the kingdom of the Spirit God is no longer an object "out there" or "back then" but is a God who is not only revealed but has come to conscious in and through the finite world. Thus, for Hegel, without the world God is not God. See Livingston, *Modern Christian Thought*, 125-126.

39. J. M. C. McTaggart, *Studies in Hegelian Cosmology* (Cambridge: University Press, 1918), 205ff.

40. For an explication of the relationship between Kierkegaard and Barth, see James Brown, *Kierkegaard, Heidegger, Buber and Barth: A Study of Subjectivity and Objectivity in Existentialist Thought* (New York: Collier Books, 1971); William Walter Wells, *The Influence of Kierkegaard on the Theology of Karl Barth*, Ph. D. Thesis (Michigan: University Microfilms, 1970).

41. McConnachie, *The Significance of Karl Barth*, 46.

42. McConnachie, *The Significance of Karl Barth*, 33.

cannot forget the name of Franz Overbeck, one of the radical masters of Barth who is spoken of as the 'skeptical church historian of Basle.' Overbeck raised disturbing questions in Barth's mind and led him to decisions regarding history and the basis of Christianity for which he has to contend down to the present day. Barth involved himself in serious study of Luther and Calvin and it had tremendous impact on the thoughts of Barth in his later theological thinking.[43]

2.4 The Theological Setting

Barth's desire to learn theology was not a sudden incident but rather, something which he really wanted to accomplish in his life.[44] While endeavoring to understand Barth's theological setting, one needs to begin with the student years Barth spent in Germany with the most famous liberal theologians of that time. After his studies in the University of Berne, Barth enrolled in the faculty of theology at the University of Berlin in the fall of 1906. In those days, its theological faculty was reputed to have the all-star faculty at the university,[45] due to the fact that the well-known theologians of that day occupied the chairs there.[46] However, what is important in this study is that it was Schleiermacher (1768-1834), who influenced Barth and his own teachers to a great extent. Hence it is essential to understand Schleiermacher's theological stance.

Initially, Barth stood in the deepest tension between two extremes of Neo-Protestantism and Roman Catholicism, which were equally alluring and equally inadequate for him. Rosato argues that, "Barth's task was to find a middle course between these two interpretations of Christianity which were for him ultimately one and the same, since they tended to make the proper object of faith not God in his revelation, but man himself believing

---

43. McConnachie, *The Significance of Karl Barth*, 33-42.
44. See for details, Torrance, *Karl Barth*, 15; Karl Barth, "Karl Barth and Oscar Cullmann on their Theological Vocation: On Systematic Theology," *Scottish Journal of Theology* vol. 14 (1961), 225.
45. H. Martin Rumscheidt, *Revelation and Theology: An Analysis of the Barth-Harnack Correspondence of 1923* (Cambridge: Cambridge University Press, 1972), 3.
46. The most famous among the faculty were Karl Holl, the notable church historian, Julius Kaftman, the well known dogmatician, Hermann Gunkel, the Old Testament scholar, Otto Pfleiderer, the New Testament scholar, and Adolf von Harnack, the historian of dogma. See Rumscheidt, *Revelation and Theology*, 4.

in the divine."⁴⁷ On the one side stood Neo-Protestantism, represented by Schleiermacher and his followers, which bestowed on "pious" human beings the honor of being both the object of faith and theology, instead of God himself. Roman Catholicism, represented by the whole tradition of Roman dogmatics depicted human being's real participation in God's being, as the distinctive Catholic principle of thought.⁴⁸ For Barth it was this principle which in the end joined Catholicism to Neo-Protestantism by bestowing the place of honor in faith and in theology not on God's Spirit, but rather on the "immaculate, infallible, and holy man."⁴⁹ Thus Barth's pneumatology arose from a reaction towards the philosophies which failed to distinguish the revelation of God's Holy Spirit from a philosophical or mystical principle, scholastic or idealistic, monastic or revivalist, and which thus claimed to possess in itself a pre-understanding of the uniqueness of that revelation.⁵⁰ Although there were theological shifts in Barth, one strain of thought that remained constant in his whole life was his association or disassociation with Schleiermacher.⁵¹ Hence, Barth's pneumatology has to be seen in the light of Schleiermacher's Spirit theology. Barth writes that, "It would be comfortless if all were to remain totally objective. There is also a subjective aspect, and one can understand the modern exaggeration of this subjective side, which had already begun in the middle of 17ᵗʰ century and which was brought to systematic order by Schleiermacher, as a tortured attempt to respect the truth of the third article."⁵² Moreover, Barth asserted that, "Pietism and Neo-Protestantism, which found its classic expression in Schleiermacher, could really both be understood as attempts to accentuate

---

47. Philip Joseph Rosato, *Karl Barth's Theology of the Holy Spirit: God's Noetic Realization of the Ontological Relationship between Jesus and All Men*, Ph. D. Thesis (Tubingen: 1976), 3.
48. Rosato, *Karl Barth's Theology of the Holy Spirit*, 3.
49. Hans Urs von Balthasar, *Karl Barth: Darstellung und Deutung seiner Theologie* (Köln: Verlag Jacob Hegner, 1951), 40.
50. Rosato, *Karl Barth's Theology of the Holy Spirit*, 4.
51. Friedrich Schleiermacher is generally considered as the most important Protestant theologian between John Calvin and Karl Barth. His theology is rightly acknowledged as the most impressive and systematic statement of the Romantic and liberal understanding of the Christian religion. See Livingston, *Modern Christian Thought*, 93; for an excellent collection of essays about the theology of Schleiermacher and Barth see, James O. Duke and Robert F. Streetman, eds., *Barth and Schleiermacher: Beyond the Impasse?* (Philadelphia: Fortress, 1988).
52. Karl Barth, *Dogmatik im Grundriß* (Zurich: Evangelischer Verlag, 1947), 162.

the truth of the third article that 'whoever understands the third article is able perhaps even to recognize Schleiermacher in it, and does not need think of him and of the theologians of the 19th century with wrathful indignation over their 'God in us' and all that was bound up with that assertion; he can recognize the true key to understanding Liberalism.'"[53]

At a key point in his essay on Schleiermacher, Barth stood before the question, "whether the divinity of the Spirit can be proved as the center of Schleiermacher's thought, that is, not only whether it was Schleiermacher's intention to do so, but whether it really is the divinity of the Holy Spirit which forms the proper center of his theology."[54] By the time of writing the third part of the *Church Dogmatics*, Barth was preoccupied with the question of whether Schleiermacher's theology could be adapted and developed in a very different direction as a theology of the subjective reality and possibility of revelation, which is not exclusive, but inclusive of its objective reality and possibility — a theology which, beginning with humanity, is intended as a theology of the Holy Spirit.[55] Thus Barth was trying to understand the very nature of Protestant theology and asserted that it must be precisely a theology of the Holy Spirit. Towards the end of Barth's life, it becomes clearer that he was taking a pneumatocentric stand. This is seen clearly in his later writings indicating that Barth was preoccupied up to the very end of his theological career with the question of a possible pneumatocentric reinterpretation of evangelical theology in general, Schleiermacher's theology in particular, and his own theology as well.[56] Barth stated that, evangelical theology as the modest, free, critical, and joyous science of the God who reveals Himself through the Word, through His witness and through His community "can only be understood as pneumatic theology; it can only exist in the courage which springs from the fact that the Spirit is the truth who both raises and answers the question

---

53. Karl Barth, *Die Christliche Lehre nach dem Heidelberger Katechismus* (Zurich: Evangelischer Verlag, 1948), 78.
54. Karl Barth, *Die Protestantische Theologie im 19. Jahrhundert: Ihre Vorgeschichte und ihre Geschichte* (Zurich: Evangelischer Verlag, 1947), 412.
55. Karl Barth, *Die Kirchliche Dogmatik*, 3/3 (Zürich: Evangelischer Verlag, 1961), 370-371.
56. Rosato, *Karl Barth's Theology of the Holy Spirit*, 10.

concerning the truth at the same time."[57] And finally Barth sums up his whole relationship to Schleiermacher precisely in terms of a theology of the Holy Spirit. He writes, "What I now and again have mentioned occasionally as an explanation of my relationship to Schleiermacher and what I here and there have indicated among friends, is that there might be the possibility of a theology of the third article – predominantly and decidedly, therefore, of the Holy Spirit."[58]

In the University of Berlin, Barth was particularly attracted to Adolf von Harnack (1851-1930) and never failed to attend his lectures. Although Barth had great attraction towards Harnack during his student years in Berlin, he stood always in contradiction to Harnack in his later theological thinking.[59] However, Harnack always had a lasting impact on Barth's theological outlook. Although there were differences in the understandings of Harnack and Barth, Harnack's analytical and critical skill was followed by Barth in his theological thinking. It helped Barth to look at things critically and analytically in order to formulate his theology with a clear form and shape. After his studies in Berlin, Barth moved to Marburg in the fall of 1908 to continue his theological studies under Wilhelm Herrmann (1846-1922). Herrmann happened to be the greatest teacher of his student life.[60] Even Barth remembers that it was Herrmann who led him to think independently in theology.[61] Barth also called Herrmann as the most pious liberal theologian of his day.[62] The impact of Herrmann's theological outlook upon Barth is distinctly reflected in the following remark of Barth that, "Herrmann is the one from whom I have learned something most basic, something which, once I followed it out to its consequences, caused me to say everything else in a wholly different way, even to interpret the most basic matter quite differently from him."[63]

---

57. Karl Barth, *Einführung in die Evangelische Theologie* (München: Siebenstern Taschenbuch Verlag, 1968), 48.
58. Karl Barth, *Schleiermacher-Auswahl mit einem Nachwort von Karl Barth* (München: Siebenstern Taschenbuch Verlag, 1968), 311.
59. See Adolf Harnack, *What is Christianity?* trans. T. B. Saunders (London: Hodder & Stoughton, 1901), 97.
60. Müller, *Karl Barth*, 16; McConnachie, *The Significance of Karl Barth*, 19-20.
61. McConnachie, *The Significance of Karl Barth*, 19.
62. Rumscheidt, *Revelation and Theology*, 4.
63. See Rumscheidt, *Revelation and Theology*, 4-5.

Moreover, it is Anselm who helped Barth to develop the theological method of the entire *Church Dogmatics*. Barth owed much to Anselm in realizing the fundamental nature and character of Christian theology.[64] Anselm took the statements of the Apostles' Creed seriously and gave them an extremely important place in his theology.[65] For Barth, like Anselm, the Creed is an articulation of faith-knowledge which the formulators acquired not on the basis of their human imagination and intellectual insight, but from God who encountered them.[66] Moreover, Kierkegaard's conception of the person of Jesus Christ as an absolute *Paradox*[67] exerted a powerful effect on Barth's theological thinking. Jesus Christ was for Kierkegaard an all-embracing truth not only for the talk of God but also for the solution of the riddle and perplexity human beings encounter in their own existence and nature. Perhaps due to this understanding of Kierkegaard's thought, Barth was greatly encouraged to take Jesus Christ as the norm and criteria for his entire theological method.

3. Pneumatology of Karl Barth

Having briefly surveyed the significant backgrounds of Barth's theological development, the major focus of this section is to make an in-depth treatment of Barth's pneumatology. In this endeavor we are following a systematic thematic study, focusing on the major aspects of Barth's theology of the Holy Spirit.[68]

---

64. Barth himself wrote a book about Anselm's theology. He gave the book the title *Fides Quaerens Intellectum*, which is the original title of Anselm's Proslogion. Later Barth said that his book about Anselm was the one which he wrote with greatest satisfaction. However, this book is among the least read of his books.
65. Karl Barth, *Fides Quaerens Intellectum* (Zurich: Theologischer Verlag, 1981), 25-28.
66. See Torrance, *Karl Barth: An Introduction*, 15.
67. For Kierkegaard's conception of *Paradox*, see Neil Thultrup and M. Mikulova Thultrup, *Bibliotheca Kierkegaardiana* 3 (Copenhagen: Reitzels Boghandel, 1980), 192-220.
68. For a systematic introduction of the themes of Karl Barth see, Geoffrey W. Bromiley, *Introduction to the Theology of Karl Barth* (Grand Rapids: Eerdmans, 1979); George Hunsinger, *How to Read Karl Barth: The Shape of His Theology* (New York: Oxford University Press, 1991); Herbert Hartwell, *The Theology of Karl Barth* (London: Gerald Duckworth, 1964).

3.1 Role of the Holy Spirit in Revelation

When one begins to analyze the pneumatology of Barth, the starting point should be the concept of revelation of God, the overarching subject in Barth's entire theology. Hence, the beginning theme of this study also is the concept of revelation and the role of the Holy Spirit in revelation.

3.1.1 The Concept of Revelation

Barth's concept of revelation is comprised of the concept of the Word of God. Hence, before beginning to discuss revelation seriously, Barth refers to the proclaimed Word and the written Word and discusses it in detail. Barth argues that the Bible is the concrete medium to know the past revelation and it promises the future revelation as well.[69] Thus, after making a ground to argue, Barth maintains that this future revelation is Jesus Christ himself, who was spoken and written of in the past. He writes, "… we are thus concerned with God's own Word spoken by God Himself. What we have in the Bible are in any case human attempts to repeat and reproduce this Word of God in human words and thoughts and in specific human situations…"[70] Thus revelation is originally and directly what the Bible and church have proclaimed, that is, the Word of God. Barth writes:

> Precisely in view of revelation, or on the basis of it, one may thus say of proclamation and the Bible that they are God's Word, that they continually become God's Word. But for this very reason one cannot say the same of revelation. One has to say the exact opposite, namely, that revelation becomes God's Word, i.e., in the Bible and proclamation, because it is this

---

69. *CD* 1/1, 111; one can look into the detailed discussion of the proclaimed Word of God and the written Word of God in *CD* 1/1, 88ff.

70. *CD* 1/1, 113; Barth maintained that in God's revelation, God's Word is identical with God. Among the three forms of the word of God this can be said unconditionally and with strictest propriety only of revelation. The word of God is mediated, first through the human persons of the prophets and apostles who receive it and pass it on, and then through the human persons of its expositors and preachers, so that the Scripture and proclamation must always become God's Word in order to be it. If the Word of God is God himself even in Scripture and Church proclamation, it is because this is so in the revelation to which they bear witness. In understanding God's Word as the Word preached and written, we certainly do not understand it as God's Word to a lesser degree. But we understand the same Word of God in its relation to revelation. See *CD* 1/1, 304.

Word in itself. It is this that "holds" the Bible and proclamation in that threefold sense. Revelation is itself the divine decision which is taken in the Bible and proclamation, which makes use of them, which thus confirms, ratifies and fulfils them. It is itself the Word of God which the Bible and proclamation are as they become it.[71]

For Barth, revelation is not a thing, a condition or an aspect of some nature. On the other hand, it is a relationship between the reality of God and our created world.[72] Thus revelation is the person of Jesus Christ and the reconciliation accomplished in him. In explicating his point clearly, Barth moves into a trinitarian schema by arguing that the doctrine of the Word of God is the basis for the concept of revelation. Barth insists that, "We can substitute for revelation, Scripture and proclamation the names of the divine persons Father, Son, and Holy Spirit and vice versa, that in the one case as in the other we shall encounter the same basic determinations and mutual relationships, and that the decisive difficulty and also the decisive clarity is the same in both …"[73] It proves the fact that the concept of "revelation" dominates the general and specific in Barth's account of the Trinity and the persons in the Trinity. This factor is very clear in his opening statement that we come to the doctrine of the Trinity by no other way than by the analysis of the concept of revelation.[74] Therefore for Barth, "The relationship is in fact reciprocal, for not only is the doctrine of the Trinity the interpretation of revelation, but revelation is the ground of the doctrine of the Trinity, while this reciprocity is rooted in the fact that the revelation attested to in the Scriptures, that is, to the self-revealing God, is understood

---

71. *CD* 1/1, 118; although Barth discusses the Word as proclaimed, written, and revealed, he maintains that it is one and the same whether we understand it as revelation, Bible, or proclamation. There is no distinction of degree or value between the three forms. See *CD* 1/1, 120.
72. For Barth revelation is historical in the sense that it happens within history, embracing and transforming particular features of created, fleshy existence. But it is not historical in the sense that its happening can be accounted for in terms of the normal cause and effect processes of nature and history. That it happens at all is pure miracle. See Trevor A. Hart, *Regarding Karl Barth: Essays towards a Reading of his Theology* (Cumbria: Paternoster, 1999), 26.
73. *CD* 1/1, 121.
74. *CD* 1/1, 304.

solely in Trinitarian terms."[75] Moreover, Barth argues that God reveals himself as the Lord, who is the root of the doctrine of the Trinity.[76] On this ground McIntyre argues that, "For Barth, biblical revelation in general and the revelation of God effected in the incarnation in particular, constitute the starting-point, the hermeneutic ambience and the normative control of all that he has to say about the doctrine of the Trinity."[77] This is clearly depicted in Barth's account of the doctrine of the Spirit. Barth writes that, "The one God reveals Himself to us according to Scriptures as Redeemer, i.e., as the Lord who sets us free. As such He is the Holy Spirit, by receiving whom we become the children of God, because, as the Spirit of the love of God the Father and God the Son, He is so previously in himself."[78] Thus the Spirit takes the central role in the whole revelation of God.

3.1.2 Hypostatic Model

We have already noted that Barth has understood God in a trinitarian scheme and he has declared his allegiance to the doctrine of the Triune God unequivocally. The trinitarian understanding of God can be found in the Scripture not as an impersonal power of the Spirit, but truly as a person. Barth writes that,

> "For it follows from the trinitarian understanding of the God revealed in Scripture that this one God is to be understood not just as impersonal lordship, i.e., as power, but as the Lord, not just as absolute Spirit but as person, i.e., as an I existing in and for itself with

---

75. John McIntyre, *The Shape of Pneumatology: Studies in the Doctrine of the Holy Spirit* (London: T & T Clark, 2004), 135; Barth clearly states that we mean by the doctrine of the Trinity the proposition that he whom the Christian church calls God and proclaims as God, the God who has revealed himself according to the witness of Scripture, is the same in unimpaired unity and yet also the same thrice in different ways in unimpaired distinction. Or, in the phraseology of the church's dogma of the Trinity, the Father, the Son, and the Holy Spirit in the biblical witness to revelation are the one God in the unity of their essence, and the one God in the biblical witness to revelation is the Father, the Son, and the Holy Spirit in the distinction of his persons. *CD* 1/1, 307-308.
76. *CD* 1/1, 314; for a beautiful analysis of the Trinity of Karl Barth, See Timothy Bradshaw, "Karl Barth on the Trinity: A Family Resemblance," *Scottish Journal of Theology* vol. 39, no. 2 (July 1986), 145-164.
77. McIntyre, *The Shape of Pneumatology*, 135
78. *CD* 1/1, 448.

its own thought and will. This is how He meets us in His revelation. This is how He is thrice God as Father, Son and Spirit."[79]

However, Barth is not interested in employing the concept of "person" as the hermeneutical principle for the foundation of the doctrine of the Trinity and affirms that he will not use the term "person" in his deployment of the nature and role of the members of the Trinity. Concerning this Hart argues that, "From what is at root an epistemological concern he is determined to avoid the danger of incipient Arianism which he sees as inherent in the very nature of all so-called social analogies for the Trinity. To suggest that there are in God three persons is to slide inevitably into Arianism, since a juxtaposition of human persons denotes a separateness of being which is completely excluded in God."[80] So the struggle Barth finds is that this terminology was never adequately clarified when it was introduced into the church's vocabulary for the first time. Moreover, even the interpretation that was given to this terminology, which was prevalent during the mediaeval and post-Reformation Scholasticism also, did not give the clarification.[81]

Thus, having made a lengthy discussion and protest against tritheism, Barth declares his preference for the notion "mode of being"[82] or modalism. However, by the use of modalism he means the same thing which should be expressed of a person.[83] He continues that what we have here are God's specific, different, and always very distinctive modes of being. It means that God's modes of being are not to be exchanged or confounded. In all three modes of being God is one both in himself and in relation to the world and human beings. In other words, he is successful at least to the extent that he affirms three simultaneous and not consecutive modes or ways of subsisting in God, and in as much as they utterly refute the suggestion that God has any other existence than that is perceived in these three simultaneous modes.[84] In short, the threeness is grounded in the one essence of the revealed God, because when we deny the threeness in the unity of God we

---

79. *CD* 1/1, 358-359.
80. Hart, *Regarding Karl Barth*, 102.
81. *CD* 1/1, 355.
82. *CD* 1/1, 355.
83. *CD* 1/1, 359.
84. Hart, *Regarding Karl Barth*, 104.

will be referring at once to another God than the God who is revealed in Scripture.⁸⁵ For this very reason this threeness must be regarded as irremovable and the distinctiveness of the three modes of being must be regarded as ineffaceable. Therefore, McIntyre argues that, "In fairness to Barth, it has to be said that as his presentation unfolds he does hold to that intention, and anyone charging him with Modalism would be relying on the evidence of a single phrase rather than on his total treatment of the Persons of the Trinity, as well as ignoring Barth's own statement that the doctrine of the Trinity is the denial of Modalism."⁸⁶ From this cue, one can spring into the theme of revelation more deeply from two aspects of objective revelation and subjective revelation. Christina Baxter writes that, "Revelation for Barth straddles objectivity and subjectivity, and is never completed or finished, for the relationship between God who is giving Himself to be known, and the human subject who is receiving the capacity to know God is a continuing relationship: it has to be "new every morning" or it is not knowledge of God at all."⁸⁷

3.1.3 Jesus Christ: The Objective Revelation

Having made the trinitarian base for his argument, Barth maintains that Jesus Christ is the objective revelation of God.⁸⁸ It is proved in the Word of God that God's revelation takes place in the fact that God's Word became a

---

85. *CD* 1/1, 360; the distinguishable fact of the three divine modes of being is to be understood in terms of their distinctive relations and indeed their distinctive genetic relations to one another. Father, Son, and Spirit are distinguished from one another by the fact that without inequality of essence or dignity, without increase or diminution of the deity, they stand in dissimilar relations of origin to one another. Moreover, formal distinctions in the three modes of being, and that which makes them modes of being, can indeed be derived from the concept of revelation. *CD* 1/1, 363.
86. McIntyre, *The Shape of Pneumatology*, 135
87. Christina A. Baxter, "The Nature and Place of Scripture in the Church Dogmatics," in John Thompson, ed., *Theology beyond Christendom: Essays on the Centenary of the Birth of Karl Barth, May 10, 1886* (Allison Park: Pickwick, 1986), 35.
88. When a question was asked to Barth of why does the Holy Spirit not appear more explicitly in the section on the revealed Word of God, Barth replied that, "You must remember the theological situation in 1932. At that time I wanted to place a strong emphasis on the objective side of revelation: Jesus Christ. If I had made much of the Holy Spirit, I am afraid it would have led back to subjectivism, which is what I wanted to overcome. Today, I speak more of the Holy Spirit …" John D. Godsey, ed., *Karl Barth's Table Talks,* trans. *John* Newton Thomas & Thomas Wieser (Richmond: John Knox, 1960), 27.

human and that this human has become God's Word. Thus, Jesus Christ, the incarnation of the eternal Word, is God's revelation.[89] After the fashion of Anselm and the Heidelberg Catechism, Barth maintains that human beings are indebted to God to pay for their sins. However, human beings are not able to pay it off since they are sinners.[90] Since no other creature is also able to pay it off for the human beings, there arises the need for a redeemer. That mediator and redeemer must be a true human, stronger than all creatures, i.e., true God. The redeemer must be a true person because human beings must do the paying, in order to be freed from sin. The redeemer must be a true God as well because in the power of his divinity he has to bear the wrath of God and must restore righteousness and life to the humanity.[91]

Although Barth does not neglect the significance of Anselm and the Heidelberg Catechism, he does not find it relevant to repeat what Anselm and the Heidelberg Catechism have taught. On the other hand, Barth prefers to follow Scripture in order to emphasize the revelation of God. He asserts that the reality of God's revelation can be seen in the constant reiteration of the name Jesus Christ in the Scriptures.[92] This revelation is a reality, temporally limited, and a quite unrepeatable event.[93] Moreover, this event is to be understood both in principle and in fact as future, as the end of all time. In other words, Jesus Christ who has come is also the one who is yet to come. The reality of revelation is not a determination of

---

89. *CD* 1/2, 1.
90. *CD* 1/2, 8.
91. *CD* 1/2, 9; Barth makes a detailed discussion regarding the divinity and humanity of Jesus Christ. Here Barth takes extra care to critique the docetic Christology and ebionite Christology. See *CD* 1/2, 15ff. Barth is careful to avoid the ebionite and docetic Christology. Ebionite Christology tends to identify the two natures and leads to historicism and the false attempt to assess Jesus only from his historical existence, and tends to adopt analogies of parity. Docetic Christology tends to separate the two natures, assumes that in Christ we have the personification of a familiar idea or general truth which can be grasped apart from faith and tends to adopt analogies of disparity. To avoid these errors Barth insisted on the priority of faith by stressing that there could be no exclusive interest in Christ's humanity on the one hand and by not allowing Christ's humanity to become the determinative element in Christology or in dogmatic on the other. Thus, faith recognizes that the Word is indeed the determinative element in the incarnation since it alone gives Jesus' humanity its true meaning. See Paul D. Molnar, "The Function of the Immanent Trinity in the Theology of Karl Barth: Implications for Today," *Scottish Journal of Theology* vol. 42, no. 3 (1989), 367-399.
92. *CD* 1/2, 10.
93. *CD* 1/2, 12.

all history or a part or section of the whole history, rather it is the history. Before Christ there was an age of prophecy about him, and after Christ an age of witness about him, but that before and after are governed by relation to the name of Jesus as the midpoint of time. Thus the real temporal pre-existence of Jesus Christ in prophecy and his real temporal post-existence in witness are identical with this once-for-all existence of him as the midpoint of time. The midpoint of time which, after all, belongs to time is the fulfillment of time.[94]

As noted earlier, Jesus Christ, the revelation of God, is very God and very human. In this unity he is the objective reality of divine revelation. His existence is God's freedom for humanity. In other words, God's freedom for humanity is the existence of Jesus Christ.[95] Thus Barth maintains that God is free for human beings in Jesus Christ, which is in the humanness of God and the God-ness of this human being.[96] Barth writes:

> Revelation and it alone really and finally separates God and man by bringing them together. For by bringing them together it informs man about God and about himself, it reveals God as the Lord of eternity, as the Creator, Reconciler and Redeemer, and characterizes man as a creature, as a sinner, as one devoted to death. It does that by telling him that God is free for us, that God has created and sustains him, that He forgives his sin, that He saves him from death. But it tells him that this God (no other) is free for this man (no other). If that is heard, then and not till then the boundary between God and man becomes really visible, of which the most radical skeptic and atheist cannot even dream, for all his doubts and negations. Since the boundary is visible, revelation, which crosses this boundary, is also visible as a mystery, a miracle, an exception.[97]

After exploring the revelation of God, Barth maintains that this revelation of God is the common work of the Father, Son, and Holy Spirit. He

---

94. *CD* 1/2, 12.
95. *CD* 1/2, 25.
96. *CD* 1/2, 28.
97. *CD* 1/2, 29.

writes that, "In view of the unity of God's nature, which is not disputed but confirmed by the threeness of His modes of existence as Father, Son, and Spirit, and in view of the mutual inner unity of these three modes of God's existence, it has to be said further that the Word or the Son does not become Man without the Father or without the Holy Spirit, but that the Word's becoming Man, like all the works of God, has to be regarded as the common work of the Father, the Son, and the Holy Spirit."[98] In this work of becoming a human person, common to the Father, the Son, and the Holy Spirit, the order in the Trinity is generally that the Father represents, as it were, the divine "who," the Son the divine "what," and the Holy Spirit the divine "how."[99] Thus Barth asserts that the revelation becomes an objective reality because the Spirit makes it possible since he is the divine "how."

3.1.4 Holy Spirit: The Subjective Revelation

After having explained the objective revelation of God, Barth moves to the subjective revelation of God by stating that to the objective particularity in revelation there corresponds a subjective.[100] Barth develops his point by stating that humanity achieves the state of revealedness of God through the Spirit. However Barth makes an imperative question that what is the meaning of revelation as the presence of God, not only as an event proceeding from God but also as an event that reaches the human beings? To what extent, in the occurrence of revelation, are human beings free for God, so that God can be revealed to them?[101] By taking anchor on the Scripture, the easy answer that Barth provides is the outpouring of the Holy Spirit.[102]

It is a fact that the content of the Scripture is the existence of a human being who renders faith and obedience to the Word of God and the response of the human beings to the divine act of revelation, Jesus Christ

---

98. *CD* 1/2, 33.
99. Hence for Barth a good theology can be based on any of the three articles of the creed. It could be based on the doctrine of the Holy Spirit. Barth maintains that a good doctrine of the Spirit would have been the best criticism of Schleiermacher and of all modernism. Schleiermacher must be understood as one who made a great attempt to center theology on the Holy Spirit, but in a wrong way. See Godsey, ed., *Karl Barth's Table Talks*, 27-28.
100. *CD* 1/2, 210.
101. *CD* 1/2, 204.
102. *CD* 1/2, 204.

as the incarnate Word of God.[103] However, Scripture does not attest to the existence and work, the deeds and words of God in Jesus Christ. Hence, he leaves the question of the result of it upon the human beings whom it is supposed to reach.[104] Barth writes:

> God and biblical man confront one another as the Lord confronts the servant, the Creator the creature, the Reconciler the pardoned sinner, the Redeemer the one who never ceases to expect His redemption, the Holy Spirit the Virgin Mary. It is this man who together with God (this God) constitutes the content of the Word of God attested in Scripture.... But in this sense and with this restriction Scripture does in fact have something quite definite to say not only about God but also about man, and with a like seriousness also about man. The Holy Spirit acting upon man is also God. Hence his work upon us is also revelation, and knowledge of him is knowledge of revelation, and therefore rests upon knowledge of the witness to revelation.[105]

Thus Barth maintains that the subjective revelation of God, which means the work of the Holy Spirit in the lives of human beings, is based on the Scripture. By God's election and calling, by his hearing of the Word, by the witness of the Spirit, this human being is distinguished not only invisibly and inwardly, but also and in spite of all that remains invisible and inward in the reality of the revelation which comes to him, very visibly and outwardly. Thus he stands at a definite place in history, which not by accident, but by a most definite necessity, is this particular place and not another.[106] The significant issue which Barth deals with in relation to the subjective revelation of God is how does the revelation come from Christ to human beings? His point is that, "The gift of the Holy Spirit is thus imparted to men who expect it with a quite definite awareness and by a quite definite method. They are already on Christ's side, since their existence is to be

---

103. *CD* 1/2, 206.
104. *CD* 1/2, 207.
105. *CD* 1/2, 207.
106. *CD* 1/2, 209.

given them from Christ's side."[107] By referring to Acts 1, Barth maintains that the Spirit was poured out upon those who were expecting the gifts of the Spirit with quite a definite awareness and by quite a definite method. They were already the believers, or on Christ's side. In short, Barth makes his point clear that God's revelation is real on God's side, that the Word has become flesh that Christ exists. Then in order to enable humankind to receive this revelation, a special presentation of revelation on human being's behalf is needed which is the subjective revelation, so that they receive and possesses the Spirit and with it the receptivity of Christ.[108]

3.1.5 *The Work of the Holy Spirit in Revelation*

In the previous paragraph we have noted that Barth presents the Spirit as the redeemer God. In this statement, two important aspects in relation to the work of the Spirit in revelation can be noticed. They are, firstly, the Spirit is "the Lord who sets us free" and "by receiving him we become children of God." One can argue that these two expressions are a clear summary of the witness of Scripture regarding the nature of the Spirit as an element of God's revelation in Jesus Christ.[109] Thus when Scripture speaks of the Spirit as an element in revelation, the word "freedom" implies specifically the ability which is given to humankind as the addressee of revelation and which in turn makes them the real recipient of revelation. Therefore, there arises no chance of asking the question of how human beings can believe? Barth maintains that the New Testament provides an unambiguous answer that, "It is the Holy Spirit who sets man free for this and for the ministry in which he is put therewith."[110]

On the other hand, the concept of divine sonship declares materially that when Scripture speaks of the Spirit as an element in revelation, the reference is to human beings, to whom this freedom or ability belongs. Barth writes that, "These men are what they can be. They can be what they are. It is thus that they are real recipients of revelation. It is thus that they can believe."[111] In short, human beings are not becoming children of God

---

107. *CD* 1/2, 222.
108. *CD* 1/2, 222-223.
109. *CD* 1/1, 456.
110. *CD* 1/1, 456.
111. *CD* 1/1, 457.

but rather, they are already children of God. Hence, they are free and as a result they can believe. Moreover, as they receive the Spirit, they become children of God. Hence, one can argue that human beings receive the Spirit because they are already God's children. Barth writes that, "At all events, in receiving the Holy Ghost he is what in himself and of himself he cannot be, one who belongs to God as a child to its father, one who knows God as a child knows its father, one for whom God is there as a father is there for his child. This is the second and material summary of the operations of the Holy Spirit in God's revelation."[112]

3.1.6 Significance of the Work of Holy Spirit in Revelation

After having discussed in detail the involvement of the Spirit in revelation, Barth tries to look into the significance of the Spirit in revelation. He maintains that the statements about the significance and work of the Spirit in the event of revelation in the New Testament can be arranged in three groups. This is because the work of the Spirit is very important for individuals with whom God is present in the Spirit and also for the church. Firstly, the Spirit guarantees humankind that it can personally participate in revelation. Barth argues that the act of the Spirit in revelation is the "Yes" to God's Word which is spoken by God for the human being. This "Yes" spoken by God is the basis of the confidence with which human beings can apply revelation to themselves. This "Yes" is the mystery of faith, the mystery of the knowledge of the Word of God, but also the mystery of the willing obedience that is well-pleasing to God. All these things, faith, knowledge, and obedience, exist for human beings in the Spirit.[113] Secondly, the Spirit guides and instructs human beings. Barth quite explicitly makes it clear that the Spirit is not identical with human beings. It is absolutely other and superior. We can only note what its "Yes" is to the Word of God. Moreover, as teacher and leader, the Spirit is in us, but not as a power of which we might become lords but rather the Spirit remains itself the Lord. Barth maintains that the Spirit is obviously not so much the reality in which God makes us sure of him as the reality in which he makes himself

---

112. *CD* 1/1, 457.
113. *CD* 1/1, 453.

sure of us, in which he establishes and executes his claim to lordship over humanity by his immediate presence.[114] Thirdly, human beings can witness Jesus Christ only with the Spirit of God. Through this witness of human beings God's revelation in Christ achieves a new actuality.[115] Barth writes that, "Exegetically most obscure but materially of crucial importance is the fact that the Spirit is the great and only possibility in virtue of which men can speak of Christ in such a way that what they say is witness and that God's revelation in Christ thus achieves new actuality through it."[116] The point that Barth makes here is that the revelation given to the human beings is not intended for their private delight or solely for their subjective salvation. On the contrary, it constitutes the qualification, equipment, and call to speak out to the world the great and wonderful deeds of God, in and through the life, death, and resurrection of his Son.[117] Thus Barth clarifies the fact that the Spirit is the medium through which the gospel is made available to every generation of human beings down through the ages.

In short, Barth believed that God is radically present and active in the world through the agency of the Spirit.[118] Consequently, the Spirit makes humankind free to be addressed by revelation and to embrace salvation. The Spirit makes them free because human beings are powerless and totally incapacitated to receive revelation. Thus by taking a cue from this significance of the Spirit in revelation, Barth provides the foundational principles for Liberation Theology.[119] Moreover, Barth makes it clear that the humans become children of God through the Spirit.[120] Thus Barth examines all that is involved in the *opus ad extra trinitatis* which has been appropriated to the Spirit, and which can be extrapolated when that *opus* is defined as fulfilling God's purposes in initiating the process of revelation in Jesus Christ. In Barth's judgment what he has been setting forth represents what the New Testament has to say about the operation by the Spirit. The operation of the Spirit was effective and successful so that the young church was able to

---

114. *CD* 1/1, 454.
115. *CD* 1/1, 454.
116. *CD* 1/1, 454.
117. *CD* 1/1, 456.
118. Hart, *Regarding Karl Barth*, 9.
119. McIntyre, *The Shape of Pneumatology*, 140.
120. McIntyre, *The Shape of Pneumatology*, 140.

make its classic confession "*Iesous Kurios*," "Jesus is Lord." Barth maintains that this declaration was made by faith through the work of the Spirit. Hence, this presence of the Spirit in the witness to Jesus by the church is an example of the Spirit's role in securing the manifestation of the revelation in Jesus.[121] Along with this aspect, Barth refers to the different occasions in the New Testament where the work of the Spirit is described to affirm the essential divinity of the Spirit, a mode of God's existence, in essential unity with the Father and the Son.[122]

3.2 The Divinity of the Holy Spirit

Barth makes all attempts to assert the divinity of the Holy Spirit without fail. Taking a cue from the Word of God, Barth argues that the Bible tells us who God is. It names and describes him as *Elohim, Yahweh, El Shaddai*, the Lord and protector of Israel, the creator of heaven and earth, the ruler of the world and its history, the holy and the merciful, and in the New Testament as the Lord of the coming kingdom, the Father in heaven, the Father of Jesus Christ, the redeemer, the Spirit, love, etc.[123] He continues that the God who has revealed himself according to the witness of Scripture, is the same in unimpaired unity and the same thrice in different ways in unimpaired distinction.[124] Or in the phraseology of the church's dogma of the Trinity, the Father, the Son, and the Holy Spirit in the biblical witness to revelation are the one God in the unity of their essence, and the one God in the biblical witness to revelation is the Father, the Son, and the Holy Spirit in the distinction of the persons.[125] Moreover, God who reveals himself according to Scripture is one in three distinctive modes of being subsisting in their mutual relations: Father, Son, and Holy Spirit. It is thus that He is the Lord, i.e., the "Thou" who meets human being's "I" and

---

121. One should note the fact that the major issue in the revealedness paradigm in pneumatology is that instead of beginning with the problem of the knowledge of revelation in the church, the relation between Jesus and the Spirit is regarded as the basic starting point. The noetic problem of faith is therefore secondary. The problem of Barth's pneumatology, therefore, is not that it is Christomonistic, but rather it is actually insufficiently Christological in character. See Badcock, *Light of Truth*, 184.
122. McIntyre, *The Shape of Pneumatology*, 141.
123. *CD* 1/1, 297.
124. *CD* 1/1, 307.
125. *CD* 1/1, 308.

unites himself to this "I" as the indissoluble subject and thereby and therein reveals himself to humans as their God.[126] While discussing the "Eternal Spirit," Barth makes a clear argument about the divinity of the Spirit by referring to the Nicene-Constantinopolitan Creed as the plane upon which to develop his case.

3.2.1 The Eternal Spirit

The doctrine of the deity and the autonomy of the Spirit's divine mode of being had been always a subject of interest to church historians. However, it is a fact that the doctrine of the Spirit achieved general understanding and acknowledgment in the church much later than the corresponding doctrine of the Son. It is true that during the first and second centuries, the church fathers endeavored to speak about the operation and gifts of the Spirit. But they maintained on the one hand the subordinationist view that it is a creature or creaturely force and on the other hand the modalist view that it is identical with the Son or Logos.[127] One can definitely argue that this circumstance was due to the absence of controversies within pneumatology. However, Barth offers another reason for the lateness of authenticated accounts of the person of the Holy Spirit. He locates the problem for pneumatology in human beings themselves. Human beings understand that the initiation of revelation has to come from the revealer himself who is outside humanity. Hence, the incarnate Lord cannot be confused with humanity.[128] However, when they accept revelation as an event which is so personal and inward to human beings, so much a part of their subjectivity, then resistance comes from human beings to any suggestion that for the acceptance of revelation, faith is required. It means that the acceptance of revelation, like the decision of God to reveal himself and of the Son to be

---

126. *CD* 1/1, 348.
127. *CD* 1/1, 467; at that time the position which later prevailed in both respects was understood with relative clarity and lack of ambiguity only by Tertullian, which is due to his relationship with Montanism. Even the Nicene Creed, though it uses ομοούσιος of the Son, it simply mentions the Holy Ghost as an object of faith without opposing Arianism at this point as well. It was again Athanasius who saw the connections and spoke the decisive word in this regard. Not without some hesitation the Neo-Nicenes and the Council of 381 followed him. But for the full development of the doctrine we shall have to look as late as the final reception of the *filioque* into the creed of the Western liturgy (1014) and the schism of the Eastern Church occasioned by the rejection of this addition.
128. *CD* 1/1, 467.

the bearer of that revelation, is not the work of human beings, but the work of God the Spirit. However, human beings in their self-pride are not able to accept it. Barth writes that, "The dogma of the Spirit means the knowledge, that in every respect man can only be present at God's revelation, as a servant is present at his master's action, i.e., following, obeying, imitating, serving; and that this relation is not wise and at no time reversed."[129] Thus the Spirit works this work of "manifestation" of the revelation in the Son subjectively in the hearts and lives of human beings because the Spirit is God antecedently to revelation and in himself.[130]

In order to explain the way how Barth deals with the "Eternal Spirit," one needs to consider the method which Barth follows. The subject of method is connected with his understanding of the relation of the immanent Trinity to the economic Trinity.

3.2.2 Immanent Trinity and the Economic Trinity

In order to understand Barth's treatment of the Holy Spirit, one has to understand the way he deals with the Trinity.[131] Barth rarely uses the expression immanent Trinity. It is familiar that the immanent Trinity infers the threefold self-manifestation of God as creator Father, redeemer Son, and sustainer Holy Spirit, relative to humanity.[132] Barth follows this functional line, replacing "economic Trinity," with his preferred term "modes of God's being." Barth understands these "modes of God's being" (creator, reconciler, or redeemer) as occurring within the context of God's revelation.[133] For Barth the immanent Trinity is the indispensable major premise of the economic Trinity.[134] Moreover, "One has to abide by the distinction and unity of the

---

129. *CD* 1/1, 468; here Barth takes his stance in opposition to all Pelagians, synergists, and what he comprehensively calls "modern Protestantism in its entirety."
130. McIntyre, *The Shape of Pneumatology*, 142.
131. Barth develops the doctrine of the Trinity as an explication of the Christian concept of revelation. His argument is that if God is the one whom we can and must come to know in the way of in which Christian faith claims to know God, then he is triune. See Robert Jenson, *God after God: The God of the Past and the God of the Future Seen in the Work of Karl Barth* (New York: The Bobbs-Merrill, 1969), 91.
132. Claude Welch, *In This Name: The Doctrine of the Trinity in Contemporary Theology* (New York: Scribner, 1952), 293.
133. Ben Leslie, "Does God have a Life?: Barth and Lacugna on the Immanent Trinity," *Perspectives in Religious Studies* 24, no. 4 (Winter 1997), 378.
134. The idea of the immanent Trinity refers to the relationship between the Father, Son, and Holy Spirit that is unaffected by the world and by humankind coming into existence.

modes of existence of God, as they meet us, according to the testimony of Scripture, in the reality of God in his revelation."¹³⁵ Barth's position is that "… Christian thinking about God must move from action to ontology, from the economic trinity to the ontological trinity, never *vice versa*. There is no possible retreat from the *Deus Revelatus* to a *Deus Absconditus*, no going behind God's own revelation of Himself in Jesus Christ."¹³⁶ McIntyre argues that there are two elements in Barth's argument here like explicit and implicit. The explicit argument holds that there is some hiatus between God as he is in revelation and God as he is antecedently in himself. It is based on the ultimate mysteriousness of God, and it is far beyond human understanding. Then there is the danger that somewhere behind the God of revelation there might stand "another reality of God," whose character was different from, or even contradictory to, that which has been revealed in the person and work of Jesus Christ through the Spirit.¹³⁷ On the contrary, Barth maintains that, "The reality of God in His revelation cannot be bracketed by an 'only,' as though somewhere behind His revelation there

---

The economic Trinity refers to the biblical testimony of God's participation with his creation, or the "economy of salvation" as Father, Son, and Spirit. This understanding is taken from Tertullian's distinction between the divine *substantia* (which is one) and divine *oikonomia* (multiple administrations, dispensations, or activities) of the Father, Son, and Holy Spirit. The Greek word *oikonomia*, meaning management of the household or economy, is used here in the sense of God's active involvement in the world, particularly the doings of salvation. This activity of the triune God within the history of salvation provides practical definition or understanding of the persons of the Trinity. See Robert W. Jenson, *Systematic Theology: The Triune God* vol. 1 (Oxford: Oxford University Press, 1997), 117–126; Leslie, "Does God have a Life?, 378; Cf., Welch, *In This Name*, 293.
135. *CD* 1/1, 479.
136. Godsey, ed., *Karl Barth's Table Talks*, 5; when he deals with Barth's logical movement from immanent Trinity to the economic Trinity, one can note the method adopted by Kant in his epistemological analysis of our perception of the external world, which he calls the, "transcendental deduction." For Kant, we perceive the external world with events occurring in time and in a variety of spatial relationships to one another. There are some conditions to be met and Kant describes these conditions of the possibility of such events. They are the institutions of space and time, the conceptual categories of the relationships of the relationships, and the ideas of reason. For Kant, the events that we perceive are as they are because they conform to these conditions. Barth's easy commitment to the relationship between the immanent and the economic Trinity, being a form of this "transcendental deduction," should prescribe what he will say about the Holy Spirit *ad intra* and define his attitude to several of the traditional questions surrounding the place of the Spirit in the Trinity. See, McIntyre, *The Shape of Pneumatology*, 144-145.
137. McIntyre, *The Shape of Pneumatology*, 143.

stood another reality of God; the reality of God which encounters us in his revelation is His reality in all the depths of eternity."[138]

The second aspect is the implicit element in Barth's argument for the relation of the "immanent Trinity" to the "economic Trinity." Barth maintained that the immanent Trinity is "the major premise" of the economic trinity. The point he makes is that the statements which are comprised within the account of the economic Trinity are true only when the statements comprising the immanent Trinity are true in the first place.[139] In other words, a right understanding of the elements of the doctrine of the economic Trinity, especially as it relates to the activity of God who is Father, Son, and Holy Spirit as recorded in the Scripture, commits us to the component elements of the doctrine of the immanent Trinity. One must be careful here that for Barth the immanent Trinity is a divine, identical image of the economic Trinity. In other words, the immanent Trinity is eternal in nature while the economic Trinity is deep-set in time, temporal occasions, and relations.[140] However, it would be wrong to maintain that the logical movement from the economic to the immanent Trinity conforms to any one of the acknowledged forms of logical reasoning, inductive, deductive or analogical, though there is a fair amount of all three at work, though none is dominant.[141] Here one has to be very careful about the mistake that normally happens to conceive the Spirit in terms of immanence. The essential distinction can be that God identifies himself with a part of his world in Jesus Christ. As Spirit, God is present to the world as transcendent. We speak of the Spirit as being present in our hearts – immanent in that sense – but not as them. The Spirit is not identified with no part of the world – though it mediates to us God's immanence as Word, because it is God bringing the world to its eschatological destiny.[142]

---

138. *CD* 1/1, 479.
139. McIntyre, *The Shape of Pneumatology*, 143-144.
140. For Barth, "Christology can only describe the mystery of God's action in Christ, any attempt to find this in human thought or experience circumvents faith and attempts to control the mystery of revelation as a general anthropological statement. Theology can only be faith seeking understanding because it is a miracle, i.e., an act begun, upheld, and completed by the Holy Spirit." See Molnar, "The Function of the Immanent," 372.
141. McIntyre, *The Shape of Pneumatology*, 144.
142. Colin E. Gunton, "The Triune God and the Freedom of the Creature," in *Karl Barth: Centenary Essays*, ed. S. W. Sykes (Cambridge: Cambridge University Press, 1989), 62.

3.2.3 Spirit in the Nicene-Constantinopolitan Creed

As we noted earlier, Barth affirms the divinity of the Holy Spirit based on the Nicene-Constantinopolitan Creed. Hence, it is important to refer to those arguments of Barth in order to make his point clear regarding the divinity of the Spirit. There are four aspects that Barth deals in relation to the creed to prove the divinity of the Spirit as follows.

3.2.3.1 Holy Spirit as the Lord

Barth asserts that the Holy Spirit, with the Father and the Son, is the bearer of the lordship of God which is not based on any higher lordship. With the Father and the Son it is the one sovereign divine subject, the subject who is not placed under the control or inspection of any other, and derives its being and existence from itself. It is neutral in the sense of being distinct from the Father and the Son, and their modes of being are reciprocal. But it is also neuter in the sense of relatedness to the Father and the Son, whose reciprocity is being to and from and with one another. This togetherness or communion of the Father and the Son is the Holy Spirit.[143] The specific element in the divine mode of being of the Spirit thus consists, paradoxically enough, in the fact that it is the common factor in the mode of being of God the Father and the Son. It is what is common to them, not in so far as they are the one God, but in so far as they are Father and Son.[144] Barth makes it clear that, "In a particularly clear way the Holy Spirit is what the Father and the Son also are. He is not a third spiritual Subject, a third I, a third Lord side by side with two others. He is a third mode of being of the one divine Subject or Lord."[145]

3.2.3.2 Holy Spirit as the Giver of Life

While explicating the deity of the Spirit, Barth refers to the fact that the Spirit is the subject of creation with the Father and the Son. He is not just the redeemer, although redemption stands in indissoluble correlation with the reconciliation. It is true that the reconciliation reaches its consummation only in redemption. This reciprocity between redemption

---

143. *CD* 1/1, 469.
144. *CD* 1/1, 469.
145. *CD* 1/1, 469.

and reconciliation reveals the fact that the Spirit is the reconciler with the Son. Just as in reconciliation, God the Father is revealed through the Son, i.e., God the creator, and the work of creation is shown to have happened through the same Word who became incarnate in Jesus Christ. Hence, now the Spirit is revealed as the one who in his own way co-operates in creation too. In order to support his argument, Barth refers to both the Old and New Testament references in which the Spirit is noted as the giver of life.[146] Barth maintains that, "The Holy Spirit is the Creator God with the Father and the Son in so far as God as Creator creates life as well as existence. From this standpoint we cannot avoid speaking of a presence and operation of the Holy Spirit which is presupposed in revelation, which is first and general, and which is related to the created existence of man and the world as such."[147] In short, the Spirit governs and gives life to what has been created by the Father through the Son.

3.2.3.3 Holy Spirit Proceeds from the Father and the Son

After affirming the lordship and creativity of the Spirit, Barth attempts to make two important clarifications. Firstly, he makes it clear that Spirit is not a creature. He asserts that although the third clause seems to say that the Spirit is a creature, he is not a creature because no creature can be said to have proceeded from God with divine essence. The universe or the human beings cannot be said to be an emanation from God because they are distinct from God having their own essence and not the divine essence. Since the essence of God cannot be divisible, what proceeds from God cannot go out from Him.[148] On this ground, the Spirit cannot be an emanation in the common sense of the term but only a mode of being of the one essence of God which intrinsically remains and is the same. Thus Barth argues that the third clause is a description of the Spirit with reference to its reality as a divine mode of being in its relation to the other divine modes of being.[149] Secondly, Barth maintains that the work of the Spirit in revelation has to be

---

146. *CD* 1/1, 471.
147. *CD* 1/1, 472.
148. *CD* 1/1, 473.
149. *CD* 1/1, 474.

differentiated from the Son or the Word of God. Though never separated from it, it should be distinguished by appropriation. Here Barth is trying to see the interrelation of the objective element of the Word in revelation and the subjective element of the Spirit in the essence of God, but not as modes of his being. In short, the Spirit, both in revelation and also antecedently in itself, is not just God, but in God independently, like the Father and the Son. In this unique revelation, the Son or Word represents the element of God's appropriation to human beings and the Spirit represents the element of God's appropriation by human beings. Thus there is a distinction between the reality of what the Son and the Spirit are antecedently in themselves, and this distinction should be maintained with the Father as well.[150]

3.2.3.4 Holy Spirit Is Worshipped

Barth maintains that although this final clause to a certain extent links up with the first clause, it emphatically shows that the Spirit is lord along with the Father and the Son. Hence, the Spirit also should be worshipped as lord together with the Father and the Son. Barth argues that there is no danger of tritheism when the Spirit also is worshipped as lord with the Father and the Son because here it does not say "alongside" rather "together with." Thus the Spirit is not a mere attribute of the Father and the Son, but rather they are to be worshipped and glorified together with the Holy Spirit.[151]

3.2.3.5 The Question of Procession of the Holy Spirit

When analyzing the Nicene Creed in order to emphasize the divinity of the Spirit, Barth notes the terminology "procession" used in the creed, which we have already noted. Since the procession of the Spirit has been a serious issue throughout the Christendom, it is important to discuss a little deeper with the position of Barth in relation to this aspect. Knowing the danger that such a word can arise, Barth asserts:

> It is neither chance nor carelessness that this term is one which in itself might well be applied to the origin of the Son from the Father, so that it does not specifically denote the distinctiveness of the origin of the Holy Spirit, but strictly and properly says

---

150. *CD* 1/1, 474.
151. *CD* 1/1, 487.

only that alongside the begetting of the Son or speaking of the Word the Holy Spirit has His own and "in some way" different "procession" in God.[152]

The peculiarity of this procession as compared with the begetting might be denoted by the term "breathing." However, the problem that Barth notes is that we are not able to make a distinction between the two terminologies.[153] Even the church has never defined the precise meaning of the term procession. Hence, we cannot establish how the divine processions are taken place and the divine modes of being. If we try to make such an attempt, then we are delimiting one from the other. But on the other hand, one can state that in revelation three who delimit themselves from one another are present, and these three who delimit themselves from one another are antecedently a reality in God.[154] However, when we use the phrase "breathing of the Spirit," it is used just for the sake of definition. This phrase also carries the same meaning as we call the "begetting of the Son." The necessity of these phrases is that they are just an attempt to express what they cannot essentially express.[155] However, Barth tries to further explain his point by taking anchor in the writings of Augustine.[156] Here two things are important to note. The first one is Augustine's concept of love specifically in the Spirit and the affirmation of the *filioque* in the Nicene Creed. Due to Barth's interest in Augustine and the immense influence of Augustine's trinitarian stance, it is very important to deal with these two important aspects while attempting to understand the divinity of the Spirit in the Barthian theology of the Holy Spirit.

3.2.3.5.1 Application of Attribution of Love to the Holy Spirit

Using his well-known doctrine of the *image of the Trinity* in the human soul, Augustine proposes the possibility that the genesis of the Spirit might be related to the Son in the same way as will or love is to knowledge in

---

152. *CD* 1/1, 474-475.
153. *CD* 1/1, 475.
154. *CD* 1/1, 476.
155. *CD* 1/1, 475.
156. *CD* 1/1, 475-476.

the soul.¹⁵⁷ The will proceeds from knowledge without being an image of knowledge. Similarly, the Spirit is generated from the Son.¹⁵⁸ Moreover, for Augustine the Spirit is the communion of the Godhead, the mutual affection and love of Father and Son.¹⁵⁹ The Scripture teaches that the Spirit belongs neither to the Father nor to the Son alone, but of both and his being suggests the mutual charity whereby the Father and the Son love one another.¹⁶⁰ After admitting that God is charity, Augustine endeavors to demonstrate the communion of the Godhead. By employing the psychological modes of memory, understanding of wisdom, and charity, and the human mental images, Augustine holds that, although they all apply to the whole Godhead, they can be better appropriated to one or the other persons. That means, one can attribute memory to the Father, wisdom to the Son (1 Cor 1:24) and charity to the Spirit.¹⁶¹ He maintains that the propriety of such application in the case of the Spirit can be clearly demonstrated from biblical sources, particularly 1 John 4:7 and Romans 5:5 where the Spirit is said to be the medium of the presence of the love of God and neighbor in the hearts of believers. Moreover, through that love kindled within them by the Spirit, they are enabled to dwell in God. This association of the Spirit with love in the economy of salvation is translated into its characterization within the Trinity. If charity is the mark of relationship between the Father and the Son, then it appropriates to the Spirit as well because it is the Spirit of both. Moreover, it is the source of the love that enables the indwelling of believers in God himself.¹⁶²

Barth, being greatly influenced by Augustine, is also arguing in the same line of thought. Thus, when Barth endeavors to describe the relationship of the Father to the Son in terms of love and the Spirit, he seems to be employing a purely intra-trinitarian argument with less emphasis laid upon the *opera ad extra trinitatis* as the basis for argument concerning the Spirit.¹⁶³

---

157. Aurelius Augustine, *The Trinity: The Works of Saint Augustine: A Translation for the 21ˢᵗ Century*, trans. Edmund Hill, ed. John E. Rotelle (New York: New City Press, 1991), XV: 32, 421; XV: 38, 425-426; hereafter *Augustine*.
158. Augustine, *The Trinity*, X: 17-19, 298-299; XV: 38, 425-426; XV: 41, 427.
159. Augustine, *The Trinity*, XV: 12, 403.
160. Augustine, *The Trinity*, XV: 32, 421.
161. Augustine, *The Trinity*, XV: 36-39, 424-426.
162. Augustine, *The Trinity*, XV: 32-33, 421-422.
163. It is interesting to note that the question of existence of God is never raised by Barth.

For example, he affirms without prior build-up that the specific feature of the mode of existence of the Spirit consists in its being "the common factor" between the mode of existence of the Father and the mode of existence of the Son. In other words, the Spirit is the communion, the community-ness, of the Father and the Son, the act in which the Father is the Father of the Son and the Son is the Son of the Father.[164] Moreover, Barth argues that the common being and operation of the Father and Son alongside the Father and the Son separately is the special mode of divine existence, which is the Spirit. Thus Barth maintains that Spirit is not a *third thing* which follows from the Father and the Son, but is present from the beginning within the Father-Son relationship.[165] Thus there exists a reciprocated love among the Godhead and the Spirit is the love that unites the Godhead as one. In support of his argument, Barth refers to 1 John 4:8 and argues that since God is love and that love is the love in which God "posits" himself as Father and Son, that love which goes forth from God is the Spirit.[166]

3.2.3.5.2 Application of the Filioque

When discussing the Nicene Creed in order to emphasize the divinity of the Spirit, Barth refers to the *filioque*, the procession of the Spirit from the Father and the Son. In order to understand Barth's position better, one has to understand Augustine's stance about the double procession because Barth has been following Augustine's line of thought. Augustine strongly defends the doctrine of the double procession which was introduced into the Nicene Creed. By referring to Scripture, Augustine argues that the Spirit who exists within the Trinity is the Spirit of both the Father and Son.[167] However, one can notice a logical gap between the statement that the Spirit is the Spirit of both Father and Son and the affirmation of the double procession. Hence, he strives to bridge the gap with two arguments. Firstly, he refers to John 15:26 to remind the promise of Jesus that he will send

---

Instead it is simply affirmed that the triune God exists as the one who freely loves, and his perfections are those of the divine loving, and divine freedom. See Godsey, ed., *Karl Barth's Table Talks*, 6.
164. *CD* 1/1, 360ff, 471.
165. *CD* 1/1, 366ff.
166. *CD* 1/1, 484ff.
167. Augustine, *The Trinity*, V: 12-13, 197-198; VI: 7, 209.

the Spirit to the disciples from the Father. Augustine asserts that it is a clear indication that the Spirit proceeds from the Father. Moreover, he refers to John 20:22 to argue that the Spirit proceeds from the Son because on the same evening of the resurrection, Jesus invited the disciples to receive the Holy Spirit.[168] Thus, when these two points are taken together, the double procession of the Spirit seems to be scripturally validated. However, there is a conceptual shift from *external works of the Trinity* to *internal works of the Trinity* without apparent awareness of the shift on Augustine's part.[169]

Along with the scriptural validation, Augustine provides a theological explanation about the double procession of the Spirit. He asserts that when the Father begets the only begotten Son, he imparted the common gift to the Son, which is the procession of the Spirit from the Son also. And he adds that the Son had never existed without this gift. Moreover, the begetting of the Son by the Father is an eternal generation, not temporal. Hence, the procession of the Spirit from the Father and the Son is equally eternal.[170] However, it seems that Augustine does not differ from the Eastern doctrine of the procession of the Spirit from the Father through the Son.[171] McIntyre argues that Augustine explicitly distanced himself from the single procession of the Spirit. Moreover, he refers to the Scriptures that he considers to be genuine in support of the double procession. Augustine argued that while begetting the Son, the Father did not impart his personal properties to the Son, rather he imparted the relational properties. Thus the Spirit proceeds from the Son as from the Father. However, Augustine seems to fail in distancing himself from the Eastern position about the double procession of the Spirit.[172]

Having surveyed the position of Augustine, it makes clear that Augustine supports the double procession of the Spirit. Similarly, Barth surveys the positions of the ancient fathers to dig out the significance of the *filioque* and supports it as Augustine did.[173] Barth writes:

---

168. Augustine, *The Trinity*, V: 12, 197; IV: 29, 174.
169. McIntyre, *The Shape of Pneumatology*, 149.
170. Augustine, *The Trinity*, IV: 29-30, 174-175.
171. McIntyre, *The Shape of Pneumatology*, 149.
172. McIntyre, *The Shape of Pneumatology*, 150.
173. *CD* 1/1, 476.

> The *Filioque* expresses recognition of the communion between the Father and the Son. The Holy Spirit is the love which is the essence of the relation between these two modes of being of God. And recognition of this communion is no other than recognition of the basis and confirmation of the communion between God and man as a divine, eternal truth, created in revelation by the Holy Spirit. The intra-divine two-sided fellowship of the Spirit, which proceeds from the Father and the Son, is the basis of the fact that there is in revelation a fellowship in which not only is God there for man but in very truth man is also there for God. Conversely, in this fellowship in revelation which is created between God and man by the Holy Spirit there may be discerned the fellowship in God Himself, the eternal love of God: discerned as the mystery, surpassing all understanding, of the possibility of this reality of revelation; discerned as the one God in the mode of being of the Holy Spirit.[174]

However, the case that Barth presents in support of the *filioque* has positive and negative components. Positively speaking, having already established that the Spirit is the love or the communion between the Father and the Son, he claims that the *filioque* clause is the expression of the knowledge of that relationship.[175] With regard to the *ad extra* trinitarian event of revelation, there is no possibility of it being accepted by human beings as if they were ready and able to do so. It is the work of the Spirit *ad extra* to empower human beings to receive the revelation from the Father of himself in the world through the Son, who reveals the Father.[176] Hence, as God is antecedently in himself what he is in revelation, the Spirit must be said to proceed from the Father and the Son in eternity also.[177] Barth also, like Augustine, makes the naïve argument that the Scripture points to the Spirit as being the Spirit of the Father as well as the Spirit of the Son. However,

---

174. *CD* 1/1, 480.
175. *CD* 1/1, 480.
176. *CD* 1/1, 480.
177. *CD* 1/1, 479.

Barth maintains that, "The Father is the Father and the Son the Son, that the former begets and the latter is begotten, is not common to them. In this respect they are different divine modes of being. But the fact is that between them and from them, as God's third mode of being, is the Spirit (which is love) and this they have in common. This third mode of being cannot result from the former alone, or the latter alone, or co-operation of the two, but only from their one being as God the Father and God the Son, who are not two 'persons' either in themselves or in co-operation, but two modes of being of the one being of God. Thus the one Godness of the Father and Son is, or the Father and the Son in their one Godness are, the origin of the Spirit."[178]

In short, in comparison with Augustine, Barth seems to declare the virtual identity of the immanent Trinity and the economic Trinity because what God is in revelation, he is antecedently in himself. Since the Spirit completes the work of revelation and reconciliation effected through the Son in obedience to the Father, therefore the Spirit, as far as the *opus ad extra trinitatis* is concerned, shares in the fullness of divine essence. What is true *ad extra* is equally true *ad intra*.[179] This argument is the core of his demonstration of the divinity of the Spirit and it conforms to the norm that the immanent Trinity is not different from the economic Trinity.[180]

At this moment, it is essential to throw an eye upon the negative arguments which Barth makes against the Eastern rejection of the doctrine. Barth charges that the Eastern theologians have unjustifiably isolated John 15:26 to affirm that the procession of the Spirit is from the Father alone. But in doing so, they have not given an equal weight to the other

---

178. *CD* 1/1, 486-487; one should also note that Barth takes an unusual step in refusing to characterize the procession of the Spirit from the Father *and* the Son, as a double procession from the Father and the Son in the form of two single processions. On the contrary, he says that the phrase *ex patre filioque* denotes a common origin from-the-Father-and-the-Son, and requires to be distinguished from the relations of the Father and the Son to one another, the one bringing forth and the other being brought forth – relations which are not common but reciprocal. What Father and Son have in common, what exists between them is the third mode of God's being of the Father and of the Holy Spirit. Thus the one God-being of the Father and of the Son is, or the Father and Son in their one God-being, are the origin of the Holy Spirit. See for details, *CD* 1/1, 485-486.
179. *CD* 1/1, 483.
180. McIntyre, *The Shape of Pneumatology*, 151.

texts which speak of the Spirit as the Spirit of the Son.[181] Hence, Barth argues that there should be mutual supplementation of biblical texts in the construction of a theology claimed to rest on the basis of Scripture. Barth continues his attack on the Eastern position on the ground of the external work of the Spirit. He argues that since the Spirit is the communion, the love, between the Father and the Son, this relationship is the "ground and confirmation" of the communion between God and human beings which is effected by the Spirit in the event of revelation. Through this same communion in revelation, the mystery of the eternal love in God becomes knowable.[182] However, if the *filioque* is denied, these positions are nullified. If the Spirit is the Spirit of the Son only in revelation, and not antecedently in the Godhead from all eternity, then this communion of God and human beings, of which Barth has been speaking, is gravely impaired to the point of lacking "objective ground and content,"[183] while revelation itself loses meaning. It is so because if the Spirit is not the Spirit of the Son within the Godhead, then that love which it is as the communion between Father and Son will be missing. Therefore the communion between God and human beings will have no ultimate ground in the being of God himself, and will yield no actual revelation of the content of God's being. Moreover, this communion between God and human beings will turn out to be a relation between creator and creature. With the omission of the Son — Spirit relationship and the mediatorial role which the Son would play in revelation and reconciliation would become as a form of immediate, unmediated "mystical union" of the creature with God the Father. Thus Barth asserts that the communion between God and human beings which is effected in the event of revelation is grounded in eternity in the love and communion between the Father and the Son which is the Holy Spirit.[184]

---

181. *CD* 1/1, 480.
182. *CD* 1/1, 480.
183. McIntyre, *The Shape of Pneumatology*, 154-155.
184. McIntyre, *The Shape of Pneumatology*, 155.

3.3 Holy Spirit and Christology

Barth is a well known Christocentric theologian.[185] However, he never attempts to discuss Christology without references to the Holy Spirit. Hence, in order to have an unmistakable understanding of the Christology of Barth, one has to be familiar with his pneumatology as well. Therefore, the focus of this section is to look into the selected themes of Christology and the role of the Holy Spirit in Barthian theology.

3.3.1 Role of the Holy Spirit in Incarnation

Barth begins his theology with the Word of God and God's concrete revelatory action in the event of Jesus Christ, who is the Word of God.[186] This objective revelation of God in Jesus Christ is the prime mystery for Barth because the revelation of God becomes the object of human knowledge and finds a way of becoming the content of their experience and thought by its own power[187] Barth maintains that, "The act of knowing it is distinctive as one which we actually can achieve, but which we cannot understand, in the sense that we simply do not understand how we can achieve it. We can understand the possibility of it solely from the side of its object, i.e., we can regard it not as ours, but as one coming to us, imparted to us, gifted to us."[188] Barth gives a definition to the revelation that the "incarnation of the Word" asserts the presence of God in the world and as a member of this world, as a human among the human beings. It is thus God's revelation to us, and our reconciliation with Him.[189] The very act of knowing this reality and of listening to the Christmas message, we have to describe the meeting of God and world, of God and human beings in the person of Jesus Christ and not only their meeting but their becoming one as inconceivable.[190] Barth maintains that there is remoteness between the world and God, between God's majesty and human kind's misery. Hence, even in the knowledge of the person of Jesus Christ we are speaking of something really

---

185. There are number of works that deal with Barth's Christology. See Charles T. Waldrop, *Karl Barth's Christology: Its Basic Alexandrian Character* (Berlin: Mouton, 1984).
186. Godsey, ed., *Karl Barth's Table Talks*, 4.
187. *CD* 1/2, 172.
188. *CD* 1/2, 172.
189. *CD* 1/2, 173.
190. *CD* 1/2, 173.

other. He argues that, "If the object of Christology, very God and very man, is objectively real for us, then all that we can arrive at by our experience and our thought is the realization that they are delimited, determined and dominated here by something wholly outside or above us."[191] Only through the expression of this knowledge, which is through confession, can we say that Jesus Christ is very God and very human. In acknowledgment and confession of the inconceivableness of this reality we describe it as the act of God. In the confession we must always acknowledge and confess together both the distance of the world from God and the distance of God from the world, both the majesty of God and the misery of humankind. It is the antithesis between these that turns their unity in Christ into a mystery. Thus we must ever acknowledge and confess the inconceivability of this unity. It is this mystery of Christmas which is indicated in Scripture and church dogma by reference to the miracle of Christmas. This miracle is the conception of Jesus Christ by the Spirit or his birth of the virgin Mary.[192]

3.3.1.1 Holy Spirit and the Virgin Birth

In order to explain the revelation of Jesus Christ, Barth refers to the doctrinal decisions and the Scripture. He refers to the passages with which the doctrinal decisions were promulgated such as Matthew 1:18-25 with its reference back to the sign of Emmanuel in Isaiah 7:14 and Luke 1:26-38, 34-35.[193] Although he refers to the dogma, he does it with apathy by stating that, "The respect paid in the Church to this dogma cannot be sufficient reason in itself for us to adopt it as our own. In dogma as such we hear merely the voice of the Church and not revelation itself."[194] Acknowledging the fact that there are lots of doubts about the dogma, in order to avoid

---

191. *CD* 1/2, 173.
192. *CD* 1/2, 173.
193. Barth refers to the formulation of the dogma by referring to the different stances. The Roman baptismal symbol of the 4th century according to Rufinus says, "who is born by the Holy Spirit of the virgin Mary." According to the Psalt. Aethelstani, "who is born by the Holy Spirit of the Virgin Mary." In the official form of the so-called Apostolicum, Apostle's Creed, "who was conceived by the Holy Spirit, and born of the Virgin Mary." In the Eastern form of the Apostle's Creed and in the Nicaea-Constantinople, "was made flesh by the Holy Spirit and the virgin Mary." In the Latin version of the Nicaea-Constantinople, "and was made flesh by the Holy Spirit of the virgin Mary." See *CD* 1/2, 174.
194. *CD* 1/2, 174.

confusions, Barth endeavors to clarify the exegetical position in the light of the doubts that have been cast upon the doctrine of the virgin birth.[195]

After dealing with the issues involved in the dogma, Barth argues that no one can dispute the existence of a biblical testimony to the virgin birth. However, the questions to be raised and answered are literary questions concerned with the tradition, the age, and the source-value of this testimony. It certainly was not their age and source-value that brought the narratives of the virgin birth into the text of the gospels and out of this text into the creed. But a certain inward, essential rightness, and importance in their connection with the person of Jesus Christ first admitted them to a share in the gospel witness. At first this was announced with great reserve but in the last resort quite definitely, and then admitted also to a share in church confession and dogma in contrast to some other elements in this testimony which outwardly (and apparently inwardly too) were much more distinctive.[196] The dogma of the virgin birth denotes not the Christological reality of revelation as the mystery of that reality, rather its character as a fact in which God has acted solely through God and in which God can likewise be known solely through God. The dogma of the virgin birth is not a repetition or description of the very God, very human, although in its own way it expresses and throws light upon it. As a formal dogma, which is required to explain the material, it states that when the event indicated by the name Emmanuel takes place, when God comes to us as one of ourselves to be our own, to be ourselves in our place, as very God and very human, this is a real event accomplished in space and time as history within history. In it God's revelation comes to us, and our reconciliation is taken place by God. The dogma of the virgin birth is thus the confession of the boundless hiddenness of the very-God, very-human and of the boundless amazement of awe and thankfulness called forth in us by this very God, very man.[197] In short, his earthly human origin is a mystery.[198] It can be understood only

---

195. *CD* 1/2, 175; for an exegetical note of virgin birth see, *CD* 1/2, 175-176.
196. *CD* 1/2, 176.
197. *CD* 1/2, 177.
198. Barth writes that, "If we wish to understand the meaning of 'conceived by the Holy Ghost' and 'born of the virgin Mary,' above all, we must try to see that these two remarkable pronouncements assert that God of free grace became man, a real man. The eternal Word became flesh. This is the miracle of Jesus Christ's existence, this descent of

as a unique and peculiar act of God. Moreover, the revelation of God as a whole is not an intellectual but a spiritual reality.[199]

Finally Barth turns to a theological explanation for the issue of virgin birth. For him, Jesus Christ is born of the virgin Mary. Since this statement does not ascribe to the sovereignty of God, Barth makes it clear that Jesus was born not because of male generation but solely because of female conception. It means, Mary was conceived by the Spirit, and it proves the sovereignty of God in the coming of God's Word into human existence.[200] However, Barth does not totally reject the significance of the usage of born of the virgin Mary because it states that the person Jesus Christ is the real son of a real mother, thus proving the perfect humanity of Jesus Christ.[201] Even Barth tries to bring in the involvement of Joseph in the birth of Jesus Christ by referring to Matthew 1:18-25 due to the understanding that the virgin birth is taken place by the Spirit. Barth argues that in the dream of Joseph's, conversation with the angel is directed towards helping Joseph over the stumbling-block which he must see to be involved in the pregnancy of Mary. Being born of the virgin, according to these texts, not only runs counter to nature in the biological sense, but deals positively with a genuine experience belonging to human as such. In that grace, Joseph is not a simple spectator of an unusual event, but to participate in an event which contradicts and withstands him.[202] Barth maintains that Joseph cannot accept this fact without pain, astonishment, and humiliation, which he can affirm and appreciate only in faith. Therefore, the emphasis in the creed that Jesus was conceived by the Spirit can be stressed in its interpretation.[203]

3.3.1.1.1 Conceived by the Holy Spirit

Barth argues that the phrase "conceived by the Holy Spirit" in the dogma states that the conception of Jesus Christ prior to his birth of the virgin Mary was the work of the Spirit. Hence, it was a miraculous birth and the

---

God from above downwards – the Holy Ghost and the virgin Mary. This is the mystery of Christmas, of the incarnation." Barth, *Dogmatics in Outline*, 96.
199. *CD* 1/2, 178.
200. *CD* 1/2, 185.
201. *CD* 1/2, 185.
202. *CD* 1/2, 187.
203. *CD* 1/2, 188.

sign of the incarnation of the eternal Word. The formula "conceived by the Holy Spirit" provides the answer indicated by the formula born of the virgin Mary. It indicates the ground and content, where the latter indicates the form and shape, of the miracle and sign.[204] Moreover, the mystery of the incarnation of the Word might also be expressed by saying that in the freedom and majesty appropriated to the merciful act of revelation and reconciliation, the human existence of Jesus Christ is totally the work of the Spirit.[205] Barth writes, "But even so, these two formula cannot be separated in such a way as to let the 'conceived by the Holy Spirit' refer to the thing signified, and the 'born of the virgin Mary' refer to the sign, because obviously it is the conceived by the Holy Spirit which is, so to speak, direct citation from the biblical account of the miracle in Matthew 1:18 or Luke 1:35, while the born of the virgin Mary (of course a reminiscence of Isa 7:14) gives, so to speak, dogmatic precision to it."[206] The reason why Barth makes such an emphasis upon the birth of Jesus Christ by the Spirit is due to two reasons. Firstly, in so doing we reject in anticipation the attempt to parallel the saying about the virgin birth of Christ by assertions from the realm of heathen mythology which sounds very similar.[207] Secondly, when we regard the Spirit by whom Jesus Christ is conceived, we are able to eliminate the possibilities of the saying about the virgin birth of Christ with any speculation from physics or scientific information of a biological sort. In other words, if we are clear that with the Spirit God is declared to be the author of the sign of the virgin birth, then we know that in acknowledging the reality of this sign we have at the outset renounced all understanding of it as a natural possibility, even when we are tempted to do so by a consideration so inviting as that of natural parthenogenesis.[208]

---

204. *CD* 1/2, 196.
205. *CD* 1/2, 196.
206. *CD* 1/2, 196-197.
207. *CD* 1/2, 197.
208. *CD* 1/2, 198; Barth makes a clear argument that the "conceived by the Holy Spirit" does not mean that Jesus Christ is the Son of the Holy Spirit according to his human existence. On the contrary, it states that Jesus Christ had no father according to his human existence. Because in this miracle, the Spirit takes the place of the male, this by no means implies that the Spirit is the human counterpart. In short, the idea is completely excluded that anything like a marriage took place between the Spirit and the virgin Mary. See *CD* 1/2, 200.

Moreover, by referring to Mark 1:9ff, Barth maintains that the sign of baptism in Jordan, like the virgin birth, points back to the mystery of Jesus' being which was real in itself, apart from this sign. The baptism in Jordan means that the Spirit is the mystery of this being. Secondly Barth refers to Romans 1:4 where his resurrection is mentioned as the sign of the installation of the human Jesus as the Son of God and this installation is also traced back to the Spirit.[209] The specific mention of the Spirit as a precise determination of the sign of the virgin birth is obviously significant in a twofold sense. Firstly, it refers back the mystery of the human existence of Jesus Christ to the mystery of God, as it is disclosed in revelation.[210] Secondly, it points back to the connection which exists between the reconciliation of the human beings and the existence of the reconciler, to the primary realization of the work of the Spirit.[211] It is on this ground that the preparation of human beings for God by God himself can happen in the form of pure grace, the grace manifested in Jesus Christ, which meets us and is bestowed upon us in him.

3.3.2 Holy Spirit and the Resurrection

Resurrection is one of the significant themes that Barth deals in relation to Christology. Barth writes, "That Jesus Christ is very God is shown in his way into the far country in which he the Lord became a servant. For in the majesty of the true God it happened that the eternal Son of the eternal Father became obedient by offering and humbling Himself to be the brother of man, to take His place with the transgressor, to judge him by judging Himself and dying in his place. But God the Father raised Him from the dead, and in so doing recognised and gave effect to His death and passion as a satisfaction made for us, as our conversion to God, and therefore as our redemption from death to life."[212] Barth maintains that Christ's death was once for all and Christians are commanded to attest this event in their own lives by their confession, suffering, repentance, prayer, humility, works, baptism, and the Lord's Supper. It is the one *mysterium*,

---

209. *CD* 1/2, 199.
210. *CD* 1/2, 199.
211. *CD* 1/2, 200.
212. *CD* 4/1, 157.

the one sacrament, and the one existential fact before and beside and after which there is no room for any other of the same rank.[213]

Thus after making the death of Jesus Christ as a mystery, Barth turns to the significance of Easter. Barth argues that the event of Easter was not a "timeless and non-historical truth" to the apostles and the first century church. But rather it was a real event in time and history, which gave rise to their faith and witness. Certainly it was a new coming of Christ. In other words, he came a second time in the incorruptibility and immortality which are proper to God alone. However, he came as the one who had come before, and therefore in space and time, in the "psycho-somatic totality of his temporal existence." His resurrection was the "concrete, visible, audible, and tangible new presence of Jesus the human being, who was crucified, died, and was buried."[214] Moreover, Barth maintains that Christ's resurrection and his Easter appearances were temporal events. The ascension was both their crowning conclusion and their end. It was their *crowning conclusion* in the sense that it pointed to the revelation which occurred in the resurrection.[215] It belongs to the resurrection as its "concluding form." It reveals Jesus Christ as the bearer of all power in heaven and on earth, and creates the church. Like the resurrection it only reveals it, for Jesus Christ from the moment of his incarnation as human being possesses this plenitude of power. Before it was hidden, now it is revealed. The ascension was the end of the Easter event in the sense that with it Christ's direct, "worldly" presence ceased. With it there ceased the time of revelation, the time of sight, and there began the time between the times, the time of the church, the time of the Holy Spirit. Christ continued to be present, but spiritually, through the mediation of recollection, tradition, and proclamation.[216]

---

213. *KD* 4/1, 326, 296; in this study, Barth's *Die Kirchliche Dogmatik* (Zurich: Evangelischer Verlag, 1957-1970) is followed. Hereafter *KD*.
214. *CD* 4/3, 311.
215. In the resurrection Barth sees the strange new world of grace breaking in from another dimension upon the world of flesh. The cross is the No of God on human sin. The resurrection is God's Yes, which can only be heard and understood by the soul which has accepted the No. However, in accepting the No we are sure of God's redeeming Yes. In being ready to die we are given the new life of the resurrection. In the word "resurrection" lies the whole of Christianity. The resurrection is the supreme revelation, the coming of God to us from the other side, the new world of which we can only say that it is *totaliter aliter*. See McConnachie, *The Significance of Karl Barth*, 110.
216. *CD* 4/1, 318.

Barth recognised the relationship between Jesus' death and resurrection and argued that in content these two events are one in reality. He argues that the resurrection was a new act of God. Its subject was God the Father. It was primarily God's free act of grace which happened to Jesus Christ, and only secondarily the active resurrection of Jesus Christ. It was the justifying judgment of the Father on his son, and on us in him. Barth argues that in raising him from the dead, he justified him, and in and with him God justified us.[217] This is the intimate relationship between Christ's death and resurrection. The "Yes" of God's reconciling will is effected and expressed in both. They are the two basic events of the one history of God with sinful humanity. The reconciliation of the world takes place in the son's obedience to the Father and in the son's reception of the Father's free and unmerited grace. It takes place in the sequence and correspondence of Christ's death and resurrection. It means that, in the death which aims at resurrection, and in the resurrection which has death as its negative presupposition, in the turning to and turning from, the putting off and putting on.[218]

Barth maintains that Jesus Christ was present in this world in the power of the Spirit even after his resurrection. That means the time which began after the ascension was not a time of Christ's absence. He was active as the contemporary of humankind through his Word and Spirit, awakening and calling them to life of discipleship.[219] Barth's point is that the true mediator is necessarily the light which effectively illumines the world. The basic form of his glory or power of revelation is his resurrection. But this power continues to shine in the time between his ascension and final coming. It does so, no longer in a visible, tangible form, but invisibly, spiritually, as the power of the Spirit. Jesus continues to be present spiritually in the

---

217. *CD* 4/1, 307.
218. *CD* 4/1, 307.
219. Barth argues that besides their togetherness in content, the death and resurrection of Jesus Christ are also together in time. His argument is based on the fact that the resurrection reveals that he who lived and died is the Lord of time. His being as the one who lived and died is his eternal being, and therefore his present being today. His death took place once for all. "His history did not become dead history. It was history in his time to become as such eternal history - the history of God with the men of all times, and therefore taking place here and now as it did there and then. He is the living saviour." See *CD* 4/1, 313-314.

accomplishment of his prophetic work which was, although perfectly accomplished in his resurrection, not yet concluded. Barth writes:

> In His prophetic work He moves from the one Easter Day to the day of all days, to the last day, to the day of His final and conclusive return.... The reconciliation of the world to God in Him was effected with this end in view. By way of anticipation, it is already reached in His resurrection, in Him as the Subject of the Easter event.... The new and future redeemed and perfected world is already present. In this commencement, however, the goal is not yet reached except in Him.... It is to this goal which is still to be reached outside Him, to the revelation of His own glory as the glory of the world reconciled in Him, of the man justified and sanctified in Him, that He moves in and from this beginning. In this conclusion of His return He Himself is still future. On the basis of the commencement in which it is already anticipated, He will certainly complete this revelation. But He has not yet completed it. He is on the way, moving and marching from the commencement to the completion. It is in this way, at this stage of His being and activity, that He encounters us in His resurrection.[220]

3.3.2.1 Promise of the Spirit

For Barth, the return of Jesus Christ in a middle form is his coming in the promise of the Spirit. This is his direct and immediate presence and action among, with, and in us.[221] The phrase "the promise of the Spirit" admits two meanings for Barth. Barth writes:

> In either case it is a matter of the Spirit, of the Holy Spirit, and of promise: of the Spirit to the extent that the Spirit is the particular mode of the coming again and therefore the presence and action of Jesus Christ in the place and time

---
220. *CD* 4/3, 327.
221. *CD* 4/3, 350.

between His resurrection and His final appearing; and of promise to the extent that the distinctive feature of His being in our sphere does materially consist in the fact that Jesus Christ as the hope of all is present to us as the One who promises and is promised.[222]

It means that for Christians Christ is present as the Spirit who promises. He is present and operative in them making the recipients and possessors of his final appearing and their redemption, and his presence and assistance in their temporal future.[223] To non-Christians he is present as the Spirit promised. He is not present and active as the Spirit who promises because they do not yet subjectively realise their objective reconciliation. But he is present and active for them too as the Spirit promised in the power of his resurrection. His power is already on the way to them and on the point of reaching them.[224] The form in which he is here and now manifest to the world in the time between these two times, the form in which he comes to us here and now, is the power of his coming in that first form, of the light which from it shines into this world. It is the form of his coming in which he is the hope of all people, namely, the promise of his Holy Spirit.[225]

For Barth, the form of Jesus Christ's presence which began with his ascension is the form of the Spirit. The Spirit is the third mode of being of the one indissoluble subject of revelation. Revelation is not revelation to humanity unless to the givenness of the revelation of the Father in the Son there is added a special act of manifestation of the Father or of the Son or of both. This special act is the Holy Spirit. It is God's power and freedom to be really present to human beings, to open him up for himself, to make him ready and capable to receive revelation, to effect the meeting between God and humanity. Without ceasing to be God he creates a relation to himself in the creature to himself outside the creature, and is thus the life of the creature.[226] He is no other than Jesus Christ himself acting and speaking in the power of his revelation as it begins in and with the power

---

222. *CD* 4/3, 351.
223. *CD* 4/3, 351.
224. *CD* 4/3, 355.
225. *CD* 4/3, 356.
226. *CD* 1/1, 514-516.

of his resurrection he continues his work among the human beings.[227] Jesus Christ is that Spirit, and he is the very sober and literal fulfilment of the promise that "I am with you always, even unto the end of the world" (Mt 28:20).[228]

This coming of Christ as the promise of the Spirit is his *parousia*, which is different from his first coming in the Easter event and the final coming as the judge. It is his direct and personal coming who is now in heaven at the right hand of the Father. It means that he is not present at a specific and limited point in creative space, nor is he extended over all points in creaturely space as maintained by the original *Ubiquitarianism* of the Lutherans.[229] But it also means that Christ is in full possession and exercise of the freedom of action, the authority of rule, and the disposal of the grace of God, and that he exercises them here and now in the form of the power of his resurrection and the promise of his Spirit.[230] The Spirit, or the sovereignly operative power of revelation proceeding from the resurrection of Christ, is the total exaltation of the whole person, both spiritually and materially. This power is the ontological and dynamic basis of a Christian and the knowledge and confessions of their being in Christ.[231]

3.3.2.2 Spirit as the Builder of *Oikos Pneumatikos*

The Holy Spirit is the power who is the exclusive and sovereign creator, founder, ruler, and fashioner of all individual and collective Christian being and essence.[232] It is the builder of the *oikos pneumatikos*. All the different *charismata* in the community rest on the variety of its distribution because they are the gifts of the same Spirit.[233] Hence, it guarantees their unity and cooperation. Moreover, Barth argues that it is Christ who sends the Spirit and he is the free active subject in this event. Before his resurrection, there

---

227. *CD* 4/2, 322ff.
228. *CD* 4/2, 129.
229. *Ubiquity* is the notion put forward by Martin Luther to explain his understanding of the Eucharist. Luther did not accept the Catholic idea of transubstantiation, nor was he happy with the idea that the bread and wine used were just memorials of the Last Supper. Instead he claimed that as Jesus Christ is present everywhere in his divine and human natures, so is he present in a real sense in the bread and wine of the Eucharist.
230. *CD* 4/3, 356-357.
231. *CD* 4/2, 310-320.
232. *CD* 4/2, 320.
233. *CD* 4/2, 325.

were no outpourings of the Holy Spirit, apostles, Christians, and church. In the New Testament the outpouring of the Spirit is depicted as a work supervening upon the completed *kerygma* of the life, death, and resurrection of Jesus. This brings out the non-identity between Christ and the Spirit apparent in 1 Corinthians 12:4f, 6:11; 2 Corinthians 13:14; 1 Peter 1:2. Even in 2 Corinthians 3:17 it is not a case of identifying Jesus Christ with the Spirit, but of asserting that to the Spirit belongs the divinity of the Lord. However, the above mentioned priority is not chronological. In John 2:11 the future must be thought of as already present. John 20:22 as well as Acts 2 must be regarded as testimonies to an event which chronologically was not limited, either backwards or forwards, to the precise day of Pentecost. Before his resurrection his followers did not know that God was in Christ.[234]

Barth further argues that the Spirit forms the undeniable basis of the New Testament's confidence in the coming of Jesus Christ to the human kind and their approach towards him. It means that the work of the Spirit is not an absolutely "subjective" illumination but points away from itself to Christ and therefore to the objective side of the Church. The work of the Spirit does not consist in a material addition by means of an immediate spiritual inspiration to the objective sign giving. Such a view is "concealed or open sectarianism."[235] The Holy Spirit is the Spirit of the Word, and comes to the humankind by the Word and its testimonies. We are tied to the sign giving. Thus for Barth, it is by the power of the Spirit that the children of God are enabled to live in the presence of Jesus Christ. He writes, "Thus the Spirit who makes Christians Christians is the power of this revelation of Jesus Christ Himself – His spirit. And for this reason, and in this fact, He is the Holy Spirit.... He legitimates and proves Himself as the Spirit of Jesus Christ."[236]

---

234. *CD* 4/2, 325-326.
235. *CD* 1/2, 236.
236. *CD* 4/2, 322ff.; Dawson argues that in making this claim, Barth seems to all but equate the Spirit with the resurrection. This coupled with his earlier interchangeable use of the "power of His resurrection in the Holy Spirit" and the "power of the Holy Spirit in the resurrection" (*CD* 4/1, 159, 163) seems to signal a severe reduction of the distinction between the two. Here Barth employs a more subtle form of description which does not force the identification of the two, but stresses their interrelationship. Barth's development of the doctrine of the Spirit in this manner does not negate an understanding of the Holy

3.4 Holy Spirit and Anthropology

After explicating the role of the Spirit in the incarnation, Barth deals with the significance of the Spirit for the act of divine revelation or reconciliation in relation to humankind.[237] For Barth, it is the Spirit who works in the lives of humankind to receive revelation by making them free.

3.4.1 Holy Spirit and the Freedom of Humankind

Barth asserts that human beings can receive revelation only through the Spirit. In other words, human beings allow God to work in their lives through the Spirit, to believe and to be the object of divine reconciliation.[238] In order to make the act of God effective in the lives of human beings, the Spirit provides freedom for the human beings. This freedom which the Spirit gives is its own freedom by which it makes humanity the children of God.[239] Barth writes that, "It is this freedom of the Holy Spirit and in the Holy Spirit that is already involved in the incarnation of the Word of God, in the assumption of human nature by the Son of God, the real ground of freedom of the children of God, the real ground of all conception of revelation, all lordship of grace over man, the real ground of the Church."[240] Thus through the Spirit human beings become free for God and they are assumed into unity with the Son of God.[241]

Moreover, it is through the Spirit the human nature is made the bearer of revelation, the recipient of it.[242] However, the main issue that Barth

---

Spirit in his own right, but demonstrates all the more clearly the unique character and role of the Holy Spirit in transition from Jesus Christ to others. See R. Dale Dawson, *The Resurrection in Karl Barth* (Hampshire: Ashgate, 2007), 149-150.

237. The major works that deal with the understanding of human in the theology of Barth are, David L. Müller, *Karl Barth's Critique of the Anthropological Starting Point in Theology*, Ph. D. Thesis (Duke University, 1958); Thomas Dunklin Parker, *The Concept of Human in Karl Barth's Theology*, Ph. D. Thesis (Princeton, 1965); Andrew Lidden Pate, Jr., *Man With God: A Study of the Doctrine of Man in the Theology of Karl Barth*, Ph. D. Thesis (Michigan: University Microfilms, 1968).

238. *CD* 1/2, 198.

239. *CD* 1/2, 198; Barth attempts to make validation to his argument by referring to John 1:12ff. and 3:3ff. One can note the authority bestowed upon the believers to become the children of God with a birth from above. And John 3:5ff. says very clearly that it is a birth of the Spirit. See *CD* 1/2, 198.

240. *CD* 1/2, 199.

241. *CD* 1/2, 199.

242. *CD* 1/2, 199.

deals with is how does the freedom in the human beings become possible? Barth maintains that there is an objective particularity in revelation and a subjective as well.[243] Human beings who receive the subjective revelation are special beings, who belong to the church in which Jesus Christ is present as the real acting subject. However, the membership in the church does not turn these people into recipients of revelation, rather God turns them into that.[244] Barth says that there is no question of something in the divine act in revelation which emanates from human's side, but only of something which is directed towards them. Thus the existence of humankind is an existence posited from God's side in the act of God's revelation. Since human beings cannot become the children of God by their own efforts, God takes the initiative which transcends their obscure creaturely being and makes them the children of God through the subjective reality of revelation. The basis is the divine movement towards them in revelation.[245] Barth has already maintained that the subjective reality of revelation consists in the fact that humanity has its being through Christ and in the church that humans are the recipients of the divine testimonies, and as a result they are the children of God. In other words, the being of the human being is the work of the Spirit. Therefore, the Spirit is the subjective reality of revelation.[246] He argues that the reality of the Spirit in its work on human beings has a strictly negative meaning. It is real in the Spirit that we are free for God. And this settles the fact that we are not free for God except in the Spirit. The work of the Spirit itself cuts away from us the thought of any other possibility of our freedom for God.[247]

Barth argues that the relationship between God and human beings can be seen in the objective and subjective relationship of the two. He writes:

> Objective revelation exists for us because God exists. And it exists in the way that God exists. But, of course, it also exists for us, and because we exist and in the way that we exist. For if God really exists for us, we also exist for Him. And this

---

243. *CD* 1/2, 209.
244. *CD* 1/2, 210.
245. *CD* 1/2, 235.
246. *CD* 1/2, 242.
247. *CD* 1/2, 243.

inconceivable event means no more and no less than that we are caught up together into the event of His revelation, not as co-workers but as recipients, not alongside God but by God and in God - and yet really caught up. Our own existence is revealed to us not as a divine but as a very human existence. Yet it is also revealed as an existence which God in His graciousness had adopted and assumed as such, as the existence of the children of God. This taking up of man into the event of revelation, on the basis of which he is revealed to himself as the child of God, is the work of the Holy Spirit or the subjective reality of revelation.[248]

Barth asserts that subjective revelation can consist only in the fact that objective revelation comes to human beings and is recognized by them, which is the work of the Spirit. Barth writes:

> It is God Himself who opens our eyes and ears for Himself. And in so doing He tells us that we could not do it of ourselves, that of ourselves we are blind and deaf. To receive the Holy Spirit means an exposure of our spiritual helplessness, a recognition that we do not possess the Holy Spirit. For that reason the subjective reality of revelation has the distinctive character of a miracle, i.e., it is a reality to be grounded only in itself. In the actual subjective reality of revelation it is finally decided that apart from it there is no other possibility of being free for God.[249]

In other words, the Spirit opens the blind eyes of the human beings to acknowledge the reality of revelation.[250] Thus the Spirit draws and takes the humanity into the reality of revelation by doing what they cannot do and assure them that they are in Christ by Christ.[251] Here there are four things that the Spirit does according to Barth. Firstly, the Spirit is the bond of peace by which Christ has bound the human beings to himself and united

---
248. *CD* 1/2, 237-238.
249. *CD* 1/2, 244.
250. *CD* 1/2, 239.
251. *CD* 1/2, 240.

them to himself just as the Father and the Son are united. Secondly, the work of the Spirit is nothing other than the work of Jesus Christ. It means, the Spirit is present in the world as the seed of heavenly life and through the Spirit God separates humanity from the world and gathers them to the hope of their eternal inheritance.[252] Thirdly, the Spirit provides confidence in human beings. And finally, the Spirit creates faith in the human beings that they are one with Christ.[253] Faith as the work of the Spirit is not a magical transformation. It is not a higher endowment with divine powers. It is simply that we acquire what we so much need, an inward teacher, a teacher of the truth within ourselves, by whose work in our minds the promise of salvation penetrates.[254]

3.4.2 The Holy Spirit Makes Human Beings the Abode of God

After arguing that the Spirit makes human beings free to receive divine revelation, Barth maintains that the Spirit makes the human being the abode of God as his own temple. In this reality, "God and man are separated with such power and finality, that their unity can no longer be understood except as the unity of the free grace of God with His unconditional adoration by man."[255] However, there is no contradiction between the offices of the Spirit as comforter and judge, between the unity and the distance which he creates. Barth writes, "For necessarily as the teacher of the Word who reconciles us to God, He informs us both about God and also about ourselves. God He sets before us as the almighty Lord, and His kindness as infinite, just because it is so unmerited, so absolutely unconditioned by our encounter with it."[256] Thus the Spirit puts God on the one side and humankind on the other. And then he calls this God the Father of human beings and the human beings the children of this Father.[257] Thus making the human beings the abode of God, Barth asks the major question how in

---

252. *CD* 1/2, 241; the grace of Jesus Christ does not exist except in the fellowship of the Holy Spirit (2 Cor 13:14), and the love of God is not poured out into our hearts except by the Holy Spirit (Rom 5:5). See *CD* 1/2, 241.
253. *CD* 1/2, 242.
254. *CD* 1/2, 242.
255. *CD* 1/2, 245.
256. *CD* 1/2, 245.
257. *CD* 1/2, 245.

the freedom of human beings it is possible for God's revelation to reach the humanity. Barth maintains that it is possible only in the outpouring of the Spirit. In order to support his argument, Barth makes a detailed discussion on the outpouring of the Holy Spirit.

Firstly, by the outpouring of the Spirit it is possible for God's revelation to reach human beings in their freedom, because in it the Word of God is brought to their hearing.[258] Barth maintains that the reason why human beings can receive revelation in the Spirit is that God's Word is brought to their hearing in the Spirit.[259] It means that there is an adequate basis for the faith of the human beings in Christ and their communion with him, because he is no other Spirit than the Spirit of Jesus Christ. It is, therefore, the subjective possibility of revelation because it is the process by which its objective reality is made subjective, namely, the life of the body of Christ, the operation of the prophetic and apostolic testimony, the hearing of preaching, the seeing of that to which the sacraments point.[260] In short, it is Christ, the Word of God, brought to the hearing of humanity by the outpouring of the Spirit, who is human being's possibility of being the recipient of divine revelation.

Secondly, by the outpouring of the Spirit it is possible in the freedom of humanity for God's revelation to meet them, because in it they are explicitly told by God's Word that they possess the possibility for such a meeting.[261] The Word of God which is revealed in revelation declares that human beings are not actually free for God. Hence, God comes forward to be the savior of human beings. Since humanity is in a dangerous and damaged state, they need a savior. Moreover, they do not possess the possibility of communion with God.[262] In this respect human beings are not free. When the Word of God is acknowledged, it is also acknowledged that humanity is not free for God. But when they acknowledge the Word of God, they become free for God.[263]

---

258. *CD* 1/2, 246.
259. *CD* 1/2, 246.
260. *CD* 1/2, 248.
261. *CD* 1/2, 257.
262. *CD* 1/2, 257.
263. *CD* 1/2, 258.

Thirdly, by the outpouring of the Spirit human beings become able in their freedom to be met by God's revelation, because in it the Word of God becomes their master.[264] It means that the freedom of the human beings for the Word of God depends on Jesus Christ. Therefore, Barth understands it as a miracle, and not in any sense as a natural freedom and capacity.[265] Moreover, Barth asserts that the subjective possibility of revelation is God's possibility, just as its objective and subjective reality is God's reality. We can never make the subjective revelation comprehensible as our own participation. However, human beings are given the possibility to comprehend it.[266] Barth maintains that the outpouring of the Spirit exalts the Word of God to be the master over humanity, and puts them under his mastery. The miracle of the divine revealedness, the power of Christ's resurrection in a person, consists in this event. In this event human beings are participators in the divine possibility.[267]

3.5 Role of the Holy Spirit in Redemption

The assertion of Barth that the Spirit is the redeemer God is his programmatic statement which helps us to know how Barth leads us into the work of the Spirit. Barth maintains that human beings are sinful, proud, and fallen. They are neither willing nor able to participate actively in the divine act of reconciliation. In order to make the reconciliation of human beings possible, Barth writes that, "It must be on the basis of a particular address and gift, in virtue of a particular awakening power of God, by which he is born again to this will and ability, to the freedom of this action, and under the lordship and impulse of which he is another man, in defiance of his being and status as a sinner. God in this particular address and gift, God in this awakening power, God as the creator of this other man, is the Holy Spirit."[268]

---

264. *CD* 1/2, 265.
265. *CD* 1/2, 265.
266. *CD* 1/2, 266.
267. *CD* 1/2, 270.
268. *CD* 4/1, 645.

3.5.1 Conversion of the Human Beings

Having discussed the concept of revelation and the work of the Spirit in revelation, Barth asks the question that how human beings can make the declaration that "Jesus is the Lord"? In other words, how they can believe in the Father through the Son and the Son through the Father? Barth argues that it is possible only through the manifestation of God. This manifestation and that something special is what Scripture speaks of as the Holy Spirit.[269] The conversion of human beings to God in Jesus Christ takes place firstly in the fulfilment and revelation of a verdict of God on human beings. The being of the new human person in the form of faith is such a person's recognition, acknowledgment, and acceptance of this verdict, the making of their own subjection to this verdict. In other words, human beings accept and bow to this verdict, which for Barth is the work of the Spirit making them Christian.[270] It is the faith which justifies a human in spite of their sin. It is their genuine conversion from themselves as a covenant-breaker and transgressor to the gracious and mighty God — a conversion in which they cease to be unrighteous and begin to be the righteous persons, pleasing to God and becoming God's dear child. Faith of this kind is the work of the Spirit which makes a person Christian.[271] But this is not the only form of the conversion of humankind to God accomplished in Jesus Christ. It is the first form. But there is also a second form, which is the placing of humankind under the divine direction or claim of God. The being of human beings in the form of Christian love consists in the fact that

---

269. *CD* 1/1, 449.
270. *CD* 4/1, 93.
271. *CD* 4/1, 99.

they accept the divine direction.²⁷² That also is another form of the work of the Spirit which makes a person Christian.²⁷³

3.5.2 Effectiveness of the Work of the Holy Spirit in Redemption

Barth makes a comprehensive analysis of how the manifestation is effected and the consequences which it entails. Barth writes that the Spirit

> ... is very generally God Himself to the degree that in an incomprehensibly real way, without on this account being any the less God, He can be present to the creature, and in virtue of this presence of His effect the relation of the creature to Himself, and in virtue of this relation to Himself grant the creature life. The creature needs the Creator to be able to live. It thus needs the relation to Him. But it cannot create this relation. God creates it by His own presence in the creature and therefore as a relation of Himself to Himself. The Spirit of God is God in His freedom to be present to the creature, and

---

272. According to Barth, the Spirit directs the humankind in three different yet complimentary ways. Firstly, it is a direction pointing the humankind to a very definite place of departure. Barth writes: "To receive and have the Holy Spirit has nothing whatever to do with an obscure and romanticised being. It is simply to receive and have direction. To be or to walk in Him is to be under direction, and to stand or walk as determined by it. And however it may be with the related spiritual experiences of enthusiasm or tranquillity, whatever similarity or dissimilarity the operation of the Holy Spirit may have to that of other spirits in the sphere of these experiences, the work of the Holy Spirit is always distinguished by the fact that it is and gives direction: the concrete direction which proceeds from the man Jesus, which is given us by the fact that this man lives; His direction as that of the eternal Son of God. The Christian community exists as the people which are built up under this direction." See *CD* 4/2, 362; secondly, by granting direction in terms of warning or correction. Barth writes: "It has to do with the possibilities selected and grasped by man, and therefore with the use or non-use of the freedom which he is granted at that point of departure. It is to be noted that there is no question of misuse - only of use or non-use. This freedom cannot be misused." See *CD* 4/2, 367; thirdly, instruction. This instruction is not limited merely to the information or considerations the Spirit advances. Barth writes that the Spirit "who actually reveals and makes known and imparts and writes on our heart and conscience the will of God as it applies to us concretely here and now, the command of God in the individual and specific form in which we have to respect it in our own situation." See *CD* 4/2, 372.
273. *CD* 4/1, 99; Barth writes that, "Through His Holy Spirit He has begotten me again, me who was in sin, unto a lively hope that I may recognize myself as His child – in my sin, my lost condition, my earthliness, may recognize myself as righteous before Him." See Karl Barth, *The Christian Life*, trans. J. Strathearn McNab (London: SCM, 1930), 14, 25.

> therefore to create this relation, and therefore to be the life of the creature. And God's Spirit, the Holy Spirit, especially in revelation, is God Himself to the extent that He can not only come to man but also be in man, and thus open up man and make him capable and ready for Himself, and thus achieve His revelation in him.[274]

One can definitely note some beautiful assertions that Barth tries to make here. First of all, in God's presence with his creature, the whole of God is present and not just some part of his being, or not just the "divine spark." It proves the fact that Barth is holding firmly to the deity of the Spirit. He writes that, "The Spirit is not, and does not become, identical with ourselves.... He remains Himself the Lord."[275] Secondly, Barth maintains that God who is present with his creatures is not simply God from above, but also God from within and from beneath. In other words, God from above is meeting God from below and the Spirit within the hearts and lives of human beings prepare and enable them to receive revelation. McIntyre observes that, "If the incarnation, death, and resurrection of Jesus Christ constitute the objective side of revelation, the Holy Spirit is the subjective side of the event of revelation, the presence of the revealed God happening within men and women."[276]

Here one has to be cautious because it seems that Barth is locating the Spirit already in the humankind before revelation takes place.[277] However a close analysis will prove that there is no complexity in the argument of Barth due to the following reasons. Firstly, one can accept the fact that the Spirit goes ahead of revelation and redemption preparing the way of the Lord. This role of the Spirit is part of its outgoing into the world, not just among the unbelievers who may become believers, but also among those who never will become believers.[278] Secondly, it seems that Barth is confining the role of the Spirit to more conventional terms. However, the purpose of Barth here is to make clear that the readiness of human beings

---

274. *CD* 1/1, 451.
275. *CD* 1/1, 454.
276. McIntyre, *The Shape of Pneumatology*, 137.
277. McIntyre, *The Shape of Pneumatology*, 137.
278. *CD* 1/1, 449.

to receive revelation depends not on their ability. On the other hand, their *imago dei* has to be renewed by God in Christ before the knowledge of God becomes a possibility. Thirdly, it draws attention to Barth's mention of biblical texts where the Spirit is spoken as making a "descent" (Acts 2:2; 10:44; 11:15) and as being a gift to the disciples from the Father, made at the request of the Son (Jn 14:16, 26) as well as being a gift sent to them by the Son himself (Jn 15:26).[279] This presence of God within and from below is described in other terms. For example, God's presence in this way is his guarantee that revelation will turn out to be revelation and that the salvation of the people for whom Christ lived, died, and was raised again will be accomplished.[280] Moreover, on the one hand, God makes us sure of him by ensuring that we participate in revelation, and on the other hand, he makes himself sure of us, by being so closely present to us that we do not run away from his grace.[281] Therefore Barth writes:

> The fact that God gives His *pneuma* to man or that man receives this *pneuma* implies that God comes to man, that He discloses Himself to man and man to Himself, that He gives Himself to be experienced by man, that He awakens man to faith, that He enlightens him and equips him to be a prophet or apostle, that He creates for Himself a community of faith and proclamation to which He imparts salvation with His promise, in which He binds men to Himself and claims them for Himself, in short, in which He becomes theirs and makes them His.[282]

From the above discussion, it is clear that Barth asserts that the Spirit is integrally involved in the process of revelation by making the work of Christ complete. Secondly, he maintains that the Spirit is the Spirit of the Father and the Son. When we try to understand Barth in this schema, it is very important to avoid misinterpretations. One should note the fact that the

---

279. *CD* 1/1, 450.
280. It is clear now why Barth finds it useful to speak of a person of the Trinity as a mode of God's existence.
281. *CD* 1/1, 450.
282. *CD* 1/1, 450.

Spirit should not be identified with the Son, with the Word of God, because the Spirit has a clearly distinguishable role to play in the event of revelation and its fulfillment. When Barth makes clear the distinction between the Spirit and the Son, it seems that he takes a narrow view of the work of the Spirit.[283] He asserts that, "Thus we find the Holy Spirit only after the death and resurrection of Jesus Christ or in the form of knowledge of the crucified and risen Lord, i.e., on the assumption that objective revelation has been concluded and completed. We have seen already that Christ is the revelation of the Father in His passage through death to life."[284] The reason for this assertion lies in Barth's insistence that the Spirit is God himself completing subjectively in the hearts of his people what he had initiated objectively before the foundation of the world, namely, his whole plan of salvation and revelation. However, Barth admits the existence of contrary New Testament texts, where references to Spirit-inspired events occur prior to the crucifixion, which in turn produces retrospective illumination upon the miracles of Jesus Christ and his whole life.[285] Even such a confession falls short on two counts. Firstly, it raises the finger against the references to the Spirit throughout the Old Testament, where we see the Spirit is involved in the salvific purpose of God. This may be comprehended with a "retrospective illumination" which Barth applied to the New Testament references.[286] Secondly, the references of the Spirit-related occasions mentioned in the Old Testament which Barth confines into the action of the Holy Spirit to post-resurrection occurrence, do not have a clearer connection with God's salvific action. Hence McIntyre argues that, "Barth, with all the weight of his authority and the persuasiveness of his scholarship, here reinforces what has been an element in Reformed theology from the sixteenth century, the defining of the role and work of the Holy Spirit exclusively in direct association with the person and work of Jesus Christ."[287]

---

283. McIntyre, *The Shape of Pneumatology*, 138.
284. *CD* 1/1, 451.
285. See *CD* 1/1, 466ff.
286. McIntyre, *The Shape of Pneumatology*, 139.
287. McIntyre, *The Shape of Pneumatology*, 140.

3.5.3 Election and the Holy Spirit

Election is one of the central themes of Barth which is reasonable to discuss along with the concept of redemption.[288] Barth writes that,

> The doctrine of election is the sum of the Gospel because of all words that can be said or heard it is the best: that God elects man; that God is for man too the One who loves in freedom. It is grounded in the knowledge of Jesus Christ because He is both the electing God and elected man in One. It is part of the doctrine of God because originally God's election of man is a predestination not merely of man but of Himself. Its function is to bear basic testimony to eternal, free and unchanging grace as the beginning of all the ways and works of God.[289]

Barth maintains that Jesus Christ is the electing God.[290] However, He does not elect alone, but in company with the electing of the Father and the Holy Spirit.[291] For Barth, the Spirit is not a private Spirit, but the power by which the Son of God has from the beginning of the world to the end assembled out of the whole human race, and preserves and maintains, an elect congregation. He assembles, preserves, and maintains them as a community of those of whom each one can individually recognise and confess by his power that he is a living member of the community. Thus salvation is ascribed to the individual in the existence of the community, and it is appropriated by the community in the existence of the individuals of which it is composed.[292] In short, Barth writes that, "It is in Him that the eternal election becomes immediately and directly the promise of our own election as it is enacted in time, our calling, our summoning to faith, our assent to

---

288. There are a number of works about election in the theology of Karl Barth. See for example, Mary Kathleen Cunningham, *What is Theological Exegesis? Interpretation and Use of Scripture in Barth's Doctrine of Election* (Pennsylvania: Trinity Press International, 1995).
289. *CD* 2/2, 3.
290. *CD* 2/2, 103; Barth bases his argument on John 1:1ff. and developed two statements concerning the election of Jesus Christ. The first is that Jesus Christ is the electing God. This statement answers the question of the subject of the eternal election of grace. And the second is that Jesus Christ is elected human. This statement answers the question of the object of the eternal election of grace. Strictly speaking, the whole dogma of predestination is contained in these two statements. See *CD* 2/2, 145.
291. *CD* 2/2, 105.
292. *CD* 4/1, 149.

the divine intervention on our behalf, the revelation of ourselves as the sons of God and of God as our Father, the communication of the Holy Spirit who is none other than the Spirit of this act of obedience, the Spirit of obedience itself, and for us the Spirit of adoption."[293]

3.5.4 Elected as Predestined

Barth maintains that the elected individuals are the predestined individuals also.[294] Hence, the affinity of the individual to God, which makes him the object of his election of grace, is based solely on the nature and activity of God alone. Thus the individuals are reached and encountered by the Word of God, summoned to faith and confession, baptised and gathered into the church. These "individuals" recognise the election of Jesus Christ as their own election. Moreover, the election of individuals reaches its consummation in the authority and operation of the Spirit in their hearts and in their free personal decisions.[295] Consequently, Barth's idea of the "individual" has a positive meaning that the Christian concept of election is more fundamentally "individualistic" than anything produced by secular individualism.[296] This election of individuals can be seen only in the light

---

293. *CD* 2/2, 106; although Barth tends to make both reconciliation and election universal for Christological reasons, Irving limits the universality to redemption for pneumatological reasons. According to him, election has to do with the mysterious activity of the Spirit, communicating the benefits of redemption to particular people at particular times. See Edward Irving, *The Collected Works of Edward Irving* vol. 5, ed. G. Carlyle (London: Alexander Strahan, 1864).
294. Traditional doctrines of predestination involved an inscrutable if not arbitrary divine will, and gave rise to agonizing questions. Why did God predestine only certain souls to salvation? Why, as in Calvin, God predestined some to damnation as well as some to salvation? Is grace partial? Is there a conflict between the saving God of grace revealed in Christ and some unrevealed, deep, hidden will of God? Barth addresses the problem from the conviction that God is fully revealed in Jesus Christ. There is no hidden remainder, no other will and nature of God which is undisclosed or in conflict with what is revealed in Jesus Christ. See Clifford Green, ed., *Karl Barth: Theologian of Freedom* (Minneapolis: Fortress, 1991), 31.
295. For Barth, predestination means God's eternal choice of all humankind to their salvation in heaven. In this election of all Barth follows Johannes Koch, a Protestant theologian of the 17th century and probably Kierkegaard. The reason why Barth does not accept the election of some and the reprobation of others, is his thesis of the election of Jesus Christ to whom the divine decree refers and who takes the place of all mankind. In other words, the object of election is Jesus Christ, and in him all others are also elected. See Sebastian A. Matczak, *Karl Barth on God* (New York: St. Paul Publications, 1962), 165.
296. *CD* 2/2, 314.

of the election of Jesus Christ and the humankind elected through him. However, individuals are not elected on the basis of their individuality or because of some merit, rather through the work of the Spirit each acknowledges through faith his election in Jesus Christ.[297]

For Barth predestined human is the one who is in and with God's choice justified by grace alone. They are not the object of divine election in virtue of a life which is acceptable and welcome to God, but on the other hand God encounters, covers, transforms, and renews their unworthy and rebellious life. In other words, the predestined human being is the one who is made usable to God by the Spirit.[298] However, one must note the fact that the election of the elect is realised in their faith in Jesus Christ.[299] It rests on Jesus Christ as the promise of divine compassion towards the ungodly, and it does so as a work and gift of the Spirit. Faith is the opening up of human beings for God as brought about by God himself. In faith human beings are the new subject which can no longer compete with God but can live only by him, and with him, and in conformity with him.[300]

Barth makes a distinction between the called human beings and others. According to Barth, human beings are potentially away from God and have earned the wrath of God. However when they respond to the call of Jesus, they become children of God.[301] It happens through the grace of Jesus Christ, which is the sole ground of their distinction as the children and friends of God. Since they are called by the Spirit, their election is

---

297. Müller, *Karl Barth*, 108.
298. *CD* 2/2, 315; to the distinction, peculiar to the elect, of God's relationship to them and their relationship to God, there corresponds objectively their difference from other human. This difference is their calling. But their calling - the work of the Holy Spirit - is that by means of the community the election of Jesus Christ may be proclaimed to them as their own election, and that they may be assured of their election by faith in Jesus Christ, in whom it was brought about. But we cannot put this the other way round and say what distinguishes other men from the elect. They lack this twofold possibility. They do not possess the Holy Spirit. They do not stand in the area of proclamation and faith. See *CD* 2/2, 346.
299. *CD* 2/2, 326.
300. *CD* 2/2, 326-327.
301. It is interesting to note what Barth writes, namely that, "The rejection of mankind is the rejection borne eternally and therefore for all time by Jesus Christ in the power of the divine self-giving." Therefore, to live as though one were rejected by God is to live a lie. However, the individual who lives in this way serves to remind the believer of the rejection which has been carried by Jesus Christ. See *CD* 2/2, 450, 449-506.

accomplished in their life.[302] Otherwise, they are unable to proclaim their election as it took place in Jesus Christ, or to determine themselves to believe in this proclamation. Proclamation and faith, and therefore everything that distinguishes them from others, are possible and actual by the Spirit. Without the Spirit, and therefore without their calling, they would necessarily be the same as others in all respects in which they are distinguished from them.[303]

3.5.5 Elected Human Beings as the New Creation

For Barth, the elected human beings are a new creation as well. While dealing with the subject of ethics, Barth talks about the life of the believers as a new creation. In comparison to the Ten Commandments, Barth says that the proclamation of the divine law in the Sermon on the Mount and in the other comparable parts of the New Testament is clearly one thing and the outpouring of the Spirit and the new life it inspires is quite another.[304] Barth writes:

> For all the difference between the Sermon on the Mount and the Ten Commandments, what we have in it is obviously the delimitation of the sphere in which the life of the divine community will be fulfilled under the control of the Holy Spirit. The fact that it is the people which is not only called, and under an obligation, to live in the sphere of the divine covenant of grace, but may and will actually live in it, receiving the Holy Spirit and being ruled by it, is something which is certainly affirmed and decided in the Sermon, for it manifests the kingdom, the person of Jesus and the new man as the conditions of life which are not only promised to it, but created and given by God.[305]

Barth maintains that the new human person should be obedient to the commandment of God. Moreover, they will be impelled by the Spirit,

---

302. *CD* 2/2, 348.
303. *CD* 2/2, 348.
304. *CD* 2/2, 699.
305. *CD* 2/2, 699.

although God's commanding and forbidding will pierce their lives. For this experience, they have to prepare themselves by a consideration of this collection of commands and prohibitions. They have neither to exceed nor to fall short of this revealed standard of the life of human being in the Messianic time between the death and resurrection of Jesus Christ and his return, because the commanding and prohibiting God who is the Lord of this time will always be the one who has here revealed himself as at once the law, the lawgiver, and the fulfiller of the law.[306] Moreover, "They will have to recognise the voice of the Spirit and to distinguish it from the voices of other spirits by the fact that, in repetition and confirmation, in elucidation and application of the Word of the Sermon on the Mount, He will lead them into all truth and from one truth to another. But this necessary repetition and confirmation, elucidation and application of the Word of the Sermon, and therefore their progress from one truth to another, will not be their own concern but that of the Holy Spirit."[307]

3.6 Holy Spirit and Ecclesiology

Ecclesiology is one of Barth's significant themes, and he affirms the fact that the Holy Spirit is the builder of the Christian church.[308] He dives into this argument by stating that God who is at work is not an anonymous God, rather he is concretely the man Jesus in the power of his Spirit. He is the one who builds the church. In other words, the church takes place as Christians being loved and integrated by God through the Spirit; in turn they mutually love one another and build themselves up for his service in the world.[309] The action in which this communion and up-building primarily and continually takes place is the community's common worship. Hence Barth writes:

> The work of construction in which the community is the true Church is at its centre, where it continually begins and is directly palpable and perceptible, the work in which, true to its name of *ecclesia,* the community comes together as the

---

306. *CD* 2/2, 699.
307. *CD* 2/2, 699.
308. *CD* 4/2, 632.
309. *CD* 4/2, 635-638.

congregation of the Lord and is at work and confesses and gives itself to be known as such before god and His angels and the world and not least itself and its individual members. This work is its common worship.... This is the point where in its totality it becomes a concrete event as a specific time and place."[310]

3.6.1 The Being of the Church

Barth maintains that the Spirit is the builder of the true church. He continues that, "The Holy Spirit, for whose work the community, and in and with the community the believing Christian, is thankful, is not the spirit of the world, nor is He the spirit of the community, nor is He the spirit of any individual Christian, but He is the Spirit of God, God Himself, as He eternally proceeds from the Father and the Son, as He unites the Father and the Son in eternal love, as He must be worshipped and glorified together with the Father and the Son, because He is of one substance with them."[311] This Spirit quickens the human beings when they hear the word of God to reconcile with God. Thus the Spirit intervenes and acts for humanity, addressing them in such a way that they would say "yes" to himself. In other words, the Spirit would make it possible that human beings would say "yes" to him.[312] Thus the church is a work which takes place among human beings in the form of a human activity by Jesus Christ through

---

310. *CD* 4/2, 638-639.
311. *CD* 4/1, 646; the word "holy" does not emphasise the fact that he is himself God. According to 1 Corinthians 8:5 there are many gods, and to attest to them there are many spirits. The real operation of these spirits is not a secret, but they can be understood as the many forms of the spirit of the world and human beings as they correspond to the nature of those gods. But the Holy Spirit is clearly marked off from these spirits of the world by the fact that it is the Spirit of God who acts in Jesus Christ, reconciling the world to himself and revealing himself in the world as the doer of this work. He attests to him the Son, who in obedience to the will of the Father took up and trod to the very end the way into the far country - his Judge who gave himself to be judged in his place. He attests the verdict of the Father on the world and himself as spoken in his death and revealed in his resurrection. He attests the grace of God as the righteousness of God and the righteousness of God as the grace of God. He is the Spirit of the Father and the Son who accomplishes and reveals the will of the Father. He is the Spirit of Jesus Christ, his power awakening humans to a knowledge of the God acting in him. In this way he is the Spirit of God. In this way he is holy, and he makes us holy. See *CD* 4/1, 647-648.
312. *CD* 4/1, 646.

the Spirit.[313] Barth writes that, "The Church is when these men subject themselves to the law of the Gospel, "the law of the Spirit of life" (Rom 8:2), when they become obedient to it, when they keep to the fact, as to an imperative which is true of all of them in common, that God was and is and will be faithful to man in His great wrath against man's unfaithfulness to Him, that He has given Himself up for him in His Son, that in this One He has re-established His own damaged right and the lost right of man, that in Him He has maintained and fulfilled His covenant and concluded eternal peace."[314] In short, the being of church is only in the particular relationship of these human beings, when it is possible and actual under the sovereignty of Jesus Christ in their common hearing and obeying, when they can make a common response with their existence to the work of Jesus Christ received by them as Word through the Spirit.[315]

3.6.2 Church as a "Historical Construct"

Although the Spirit is the builder of the church, Barth maintains that church is "a human, earthly historical construct" historically involving human actions.[316] However, Barth identifies it as "the Christian Church" for two reasons. Firstly, God is at work in it by his Spirit, who is the quickening power of Jesus Christ. Secondly, the human activity which takes place in the church is occasioned and fashioned by God.[317] Barth writes:

> Thus, to see the true Church, we cannot look abstractly at what a human work seems to be in itself. This would not be a genuine phenomenon but a false. The real result of the divine operation, the human action which takes place in the true Church as occasioned and fashioned by God, will never try to be anything in itself, but only the divine operation, the divine work of sanctification, the upbuilding of Christianity by the Holy Spirit of Jesus the Lord, by which it is inaugurated and controlled and supported. To the extent that it is anything in

---

313. *CD* 4/1, 650.
314. *CD* 4/1, 651.
315. *CD* 4/1, 651.
316. *CD* 4/2, 616.
317. *CD* 4/2, 616.

> itself, it is the phenomenon of the mere semblance of a Church, and it is only this semblance, and not the true Church, that we shall see when we consider this phenomenon.[318]

Thus Barth asserts the visibility of the true church through the victory of the Spirit over the sinfulness of human action and decision. It means that the work of the Spirit in the church is goal-oriented towards the building up of the community and the sanctification of humanity in Jesus Christ. Thus Barth defines the true church in terms of the creedal *communio sanctorum*, the men and women who are quickened by the power and action of the Spirit in conjunction with one another. But as members of the human race acting within the course of human history, they are still part of the *communio peccatorum*. Nevertheless, since they still live and act in the communion of the Spirit, they remain also the *communio sanctorum*, a provisional representation of the new humanity in the midst of the old.[319]

While Barth argues for the Spirit as the builder of the church, Barth never loses his Christocentrism which he maintains between the work of the Spirit and the work of Jesus Christ. Hence, he defines the being of the Spirit in the up-building of the church as the self-attestation of Jesus and that the Spirit causes the community to grow both in numbers and in depth of faith into the true church in the world.[320] Thus by his self-attestation through

---

318. *CD* 4/2, 616-617.
319. *CD* 4/2, 642; the up-building of the community can first be understood as the "communion of the saints." As many humans, through the power of the Holy Spirit, look backwards to their established unity and the unity of all humans, and move forward to this same unity, they are themselves united and act in common. This is the communion of the saints. We can distinguish a communion of the *sancti* and a communion in the *sancta*. The *sancti* are *peccatores* like all others, but are distinguished from all others by the fact that they are and act in this communion, providing a provisional representation of the new humanity in the midst of the old. The *sancta* are those things which distinguish the human being and activity of the *sancti*. The *communio sanctorum* is the event in which the *sancti* participate in *the sancta*. In this event the up-building of the community takes place. See *KD* 4/2, 641-643.
320. The communion of the saints or up-building of the community takes an analogous form to that of organic growth. It does not result from the action of God and humanity, but God and humanity build the community as a result, confirmation, concretion, glorification, and manifestation of this growth. From first to last the up-building of the community is a growth, a growth in its own sovereign power and manner. This is its secret, its distinctive character, indicated in the two parables of the seed and the sower. See *CD* 4/2, 644-645. The growth of this community is an intense, vertical and spiritual one. This extensive and intensive growth means simply that the community *lives* as the communion

the power of the Spirit, Jesus continues to work in the world and in the community of the church. Thus Barth speaks of the being of Jesus Christ as the one in heaven, and the earthly-historical being with sinners in the community as is his body.[321] However, these two forms of Jesus are one because the Spirit is subject to these dual descriptions as the sanctifying power from high, and the indwelling power who moves within history, exposed to all its ambiguities, whether ecclesiastical or theological.[322] Moreover, the nexus between the Spirit and Jesus is close. That has to be said because, as Barth expands upon the place of Jesus in church, imparting himself to them, being present with them, disclosing his unity with them, we are tempted to wonder whether the place of the Spirit has been ignored by implication. But it is not true. Barth writes:

> Thus the only content of the Holy Spirit is Jesus; His only work is His provisional revelation; .... But as the self-attestation of Jesus the Holy Spirit is more than a mere indication of Jesus or record concerning Him. Where the man Jesus attests Himself in the power of the Spirit of God, He makes Himself present; and those whom He approaches in His self-attestation are able also to approach Him and to be near Him. More than that, where He makes Himself present in this power, He imparts Himself; and those to whom He wills to belong in virtue of this self-presentation are able also to belong to Him. In the Holy

---

of saints. What is this indwelling or immanent power of life of the community expressed and fulfilled in its growth? It is Jesus Christ Himself, "Jesus is the power of life immanent within it; the power by which it grows and therefore lives." The human Jesus does not only exist in a heavenly form superior to human history. He also exists within human history in the community of Christians through the power of the Holy Spirit. In this second form he is the power of life and growth immanent to the community. See *KD* 4/2, 737.

321. *CD* 4/2, 653; according to Barth, the crucified and risen Jesus Christ has two forms of existence. Firstly, he exists in a heavenly form at the right hand of the Father, as the advocate and intercessor of human beings. Secondly, he lives in a special element of human history created and controlled by him. In other words, through his Holy Spirit he overcomes the unbridgeable abyss between heaven and earth and operates in time and history from that exalted status. He reveals Himself to certain human beings and enables them to know, love, and confess him. His self-attestation through the Spirit is not a mere indication or record of an absent Jesus. Through his Spirit he indwells and is immanent in history. His self-attestation is a self-presentation in which he enables those whom he approaches to approach him. See *CD* 4/3, 754.

322. *CD* 4/2, 653.

Ghost as His self-attestation He reveals and discloses Himself to certain men living on earth and in time as the Holy One who represents them before God and therefore in actuality, and also grants them the knowledge that He is theirs; the Holy One in whom they also are holy, and are His - holy in His holy person. He reveals and discloses and grants to them the knowledge of His unity with them and their unity with Him. In this knowledge they find that even on earth and in time they are with Him, and therefore at unity with one another. It is in this way, by this self-attestation, self-presentation and self-impartation, that He founds and quickens the community, which is the mighty work of the Holy Spirit.[323]

Thus, when Barth spins out his comprehensive accounts of the closeness of Jesus to the church, he is careful to affirm that it is all happening in the power of the Spirit. It proves the fact that Barth has a very thoroughgoing Christ-centered pneumatology.[324]

3.6.3 The Community Is an Event

For Barth, the community is an assembly which comes into being in response to a call in a definite place.[325] Moreover, the community shares the common interests which bind them together as a unity.[326] Thus the community is an event in which it fulfils its existence in its gathering, up-building, and mission. Barth writes that, "The essence of the Church (seen from within) is the event which is called in the New Testament 'the fellowship of the Holy Spirit.' The fellowship of the Holy Spirit is nothing other than the actual operative might and power of the work of the Lord Jesus Christ, which has become a Word, addressed to particular men and

---

323. *CD* 4/2, 654.
324. McIntyre, *The Shape of Pneumatology*, 157; Barth's position is that, "Jesus Christ is the same yesterday, today and forever. He Himself is the historical continuity of the Church. He is present in the Spirit. Suppose there is a history of the outpouring of the Spirit within the historical series of the events of the church. Then you have an unbroken continuity of the presence of the word of God. The visible church, the human efforts, is to be believed, but you must see more than this. You must see the work of the Holy Spirit." Godsey, ed., *Karl Barth's Table Talks*, 40.
325. *CD* 1/1, 18.
326. *CD* 4/1, 651.

has prompted their response. The fellowship of the Holy Spirit creates the living community."[327] This community has a history that they have been gathered by Jesus Christ through the Spirit.[328] It exists as community since it is continually quickened and built up and builds itself up in a common subjection to "the law of the Spirit of life" (Rom 8:12). Moreover, it exists as a missionary community since it is continually enlightened, called, and sent by Jesus Christ through the Spirit to preach the Gospel.

Moreover, Barth argues that the community is an event because the community is a confluence of divine and human action. It is a being and work of human beings, a historico-temporal human communal action, inaugurated, controlled, and supported by divine action. This divine action is the spiritual presence of the risen Jesus in power in the exercise of his prophetic office through his Spirit. This is always a history, an event, because Jesus himself lives eternally in the historical singularity of his way from Bethlehem to Golgotha. The community which is his earthly-historical form or reflection must be also a history, an event.[329] He is a living person who gathers, up-builds, and sends his community "at every moment."[330] At the same time, Barth asserts that the human action occasioned and fashioned by the Spirit is the action of human beings who are still prisoners to the flesh, sin, and death. That means we cannot abstract from the divine action and consider the human work for the existence of the community. Hence, Barth argues that church is an event due to the result of a divine operation which inaugurates, controls, and supports it.[331]

3.6.4 The Community Is Visible and Invisible

Barth maintains that the church is derived from the Word that became flesh.[332] In other words, "The existence of the church involves a repetition of the incarnation of the Word of God in the person of Jesus Christ in that area of the rest of humanity which is distinct from the person of Jesus

---

327. Karl Barth, *God here and Now*, trans. Paul M. van Buren (New York: Routledge, 2003), 80.
328. *CD* 4/1, 650.
329. *CD* 4/2, 695ff.
330. *CD* 4/2, 710.
331. *CD* 4/2, 617.
332. *CD* 1/2, 214.

Christ."³³³ Hence, the church, the subjective reality of revelation, is divine and human, eternal and temporal, and therefore invisible and visible. The community takes place in the form of a sequence and nexus of definite human, historical activities. It is the gathering and separation of certain human beings to a fellowship. This involves an ecclesiastical organisation, constitution, and order. Barth writes that, "The Christian community is a phenomenon which all men may perceive and assert like all others in the sphere of history and indeed of creation generally. It is an empirical and rationally comprehensible magnitude 'like the kingdom of France or the republic of Venice,' as they used to put it in the 16ᵗʰ century."³³⁴ In this sense, the church is never an invisible fellowship of the Spirit. Moreover, the visibility of the church is not something accidental. Barth maintains that as Jesus Christ was elected from and to all eternity as the *verbum incarnandum* in his concrete humanity and visibility, so in the same Jesus Christ, God has elected his community from and to all eternity in its very being and *ad extra*, in its visibility and worldliness.³³⁵ It can be a witness of Jesus Christ in the world since it is visible and worldly like him, and therefore like the world. The power of the Word made flesh creates it in his own image. Barth writes:

> The work of the Holy Spirit, to which it owes its existence, is something which is produced in a concrete earthly-historical form. It is the awakening power of the Word made flesh, of the Son of God, who Himself entered the lowliness of an historical existence in this world, who as very God became and is very man. Like begets like. The Christian faith awakened by Him is a definite activity and therefore a definite human phenomenon.³³⁶

The power of the Word made flesh, which is the invisible essence of the church, is dynamic and "conforming." It effects an earthly-historical form,

---

333. *CD* 1/2, 215.
334. *CD* 4/3, 722.
335. *CD* 4/3, 724.
336. *CD* 4/1, 652.

"pressing from within outwards, from invisibility to visibility."[337] Just as the individual Christian can exist only in time and space as a doer of the Word (James 1:22), and therefore in a concrete human form and basically visible to everyone, so also the Christian community can exist only in concrete and visible form through the common doing of the word which they have heard.[338] Thus, the presence and lordship of Jesus Christ in his congregation is visible, not hidden. The Spirit is the presence and lordship of Jesus Christ himself in the visible form of this witness.[339]

Just as the community called into being by the Spirit does not exist and must not be sought abstractly in the invisible, it neither exists nor must be sought abstractly in the visible.[340] Barth maintains that we can never see the real church directly as we see a state in its citizens and officials and organs and laws and constitutions. Although the mystery of the church and its spiritual character is manifested and there are analogies to its visible form, nevertheless there is no direct unequivocal identity between its real being and its historical manifestations.[341] The real essence and being of the community as the living community of the living Jesus Christ, the truth of its existence in time and space is not a matter of general but of a very special visibility. It is visible only in faith because it is in the hand of God.[342] Barth writes that, "The gathering and maintaining and completing of the community, as the mystery of what its visible form is on this level, is in the hand of God, and as His own work, as spiritual reality, its third dimen-

---

337. *CD* 4/3, 728.
338. *CD* 4/1, 653.
339. Barth, *God Here and Now*, 58.
340. The church is not only invisible in virtue of divine election, calling, illumination, justification, and sanctification, which turn the children of God into what they are. But in all these things it is also visible. The children of God are visible human beings. A visible event brings them together. A visible unity holds them to each other. The fact that they have received God's revelation is invisible, but they themselves are visible as those who have to remember that fact, and are glad to do so. That the event is the call of God is invisible; but the event of their being brought together is visible. That their unity is the Word heard is invisible; but that they belong together and keep together is visible. The problem of their existence as the church can be perceived with a perspicacity which is proportionate to our constant perception of the problem of the God-humanhood of Jesus Christ. See *CD* 1/2, 219.
341. *CD* 4/2, 619.
342. See a discussion on the authority and openness in the church by S. W. Sykes, "Authority and Openness in the Church," in *Karl Barth: Centenary Essays*, ed. S. W. Sykes (Cambridge: Cambridge University Press, 1989), 69-86.

sion, it is invisible, it cannot be perceived but only believed."[343] Moreover, Barth asserts that the true church is visible due to the free grace of God, the mighty act of the particular divine mercy that justifies, sanctifies, and reveals the basis and meaning of this sinful human action to faith, as much as we can see and read the dark letters of an electric sign when the current is passed through it.[344]

3.6.5 Community Is the Body of Christ

We have already noted that for Barth the being of the community is spiritual and invisible in nature. Moreover, its secret and mystery is described by saying that it is the earthly-historical form of existence of Jesus Christ, or in New Testament language as the body of Christ. Barth writes, "It is the work of the Holy Spirit that the Lord does do this in His mercy that he shines on men to give this knowledge of Jesus Christ and themselves. And in this knowledge, in and with Jesus Christ, His body is known as His community, His community as His body. It is known because this union has already been created in the eternal and temporal happening. It is known in such a way that its being precedes the knowledge of it, and the knowledge of it can only follow its being."[345] Thus Barth finds the relationship between Jesus Christ as the head of the community and the community as the body of Jesus Christ. He makes it very clear that the community is not Jesus Christ, but rather he is the community. He does not live because the community lives, but on the other hand, the community lives and continues to live because he lives. Thus in the work of the Holy Spirit there is a "real identity"[346] between the head and the body, between the kingdom of God and the communion of saints on earth. Moreover, Barth makes an interesting argument that Jesus Christ is a body. By nature Jesus Christ is not simply one, but one in many. He is this body as the one who in his death and resurrection has become the representative of all. In his bodily death all human beings are one dead body. In his risen body, made all alive through the Spirit, all human beings are one living

---

343. *CD* 4/1, 657.
344. *CD* 4/2, 619.
345. *CD* 4/1, 667.
346. See *KD* 4/2, 656.

body. Thus as his earthly-historical form of existence, the community is his body and Jesus Christ's body is the community.³⁴⁷ This equation is valid only with reference to the divine action in the creation and preservation of the community. In this action of Christ through his Spirit the community knows of its own justification and that of all humanity, in the death and resurrection of Jesus Christ.³⁴⁸

3.6.6 Subjective Revelation Takes Place in the Church

Barth asserts that the subjective revelation takes place in the church on the ground that the human beings who receive the revelation are special people. They are special not only invisibly and inwardly, but in their very existence, in their visible outward position.³⁴⁹ In the Old Testament they belong to the nation with which God has made his covenant, to the nation of Israel. In the New Testament they belong to the church in which Jesus Christ is present as the real acting subject, as the head of all the members gathered in the church with their definite tasks and functions. However, the membership of the nation or church does not turn these people into recipients of revelation. God turns them into that. However, God is not forced to turn them into that because of this membership. God and God alone turns human beings into a recipient of his revelation; he does so in a definite area, and this area, combining the Old and New Testaments, is the area of the church.³⁵⁰ This significance of the church for the subjective reality of revelation is not biblical and therefore of necessity a universally Christian doctrine. Barth's assertion is that Jesus by no means addresses human beings in any abstract individuality of their existence, but *a priori* as members of the community. To them the Spirit is promised (Acts 1:4f.) and upon them the Spirit poured out at Pentecost, with the result that they receive the gift of speech and that people of every nation can understand them.³⁵¹ Thus for Barth, the fundamental characteristic of the church is the outpouring of the Spirit. It means that, after God has become human in Christ for the human beings, he adopts them, makes them ready to listen

---

347. *CD* 2/2, 199; cf. *KD* 4/1, 666.
348. *CD* 4/1, 353; cf. *KD* 4/1, 744.
349. *CD* 1/2, 210.
350. *CD* 1/2, 210.
351. *CD* 1/2, 210.

to the Word, intercedes with them for himself, makes the speaking and hearing of his Word possible among them. Thus the existence of the church should be seen in the backdrops of the mystery of Pentecost.[352]

Therefore Barth maintains that the work of the Spirit in the church is nothing other than the work of Jesus Christ. The Spirit is present in his own as the seed of heavenly life, pointing them away from every here and now. By the Spirit he separates them from the world and gathers them to the hope of their eternal inheritance. In this way he creates his church. By the Spirit he calls prophets, pupils, and teachers of revelation towards him. By the Spirit all human beings go in the body of death to meet the resurrection. As the Spirit of Jesus Christ who, proceeding from him, unites human beings closely to him so that they might be one with them. He distinguishes himself from the Spirit of God who lives an animal life in creation, nature, and history, and to that extent in the godless as well. And just because he is Christ's Spirit, the work of Christ is never done without him. Nor is it done except by him. The grace of Jesus Christ does not exist except in the fellowship of the Spirit (2 Cor 13:14), and the love of God is not poured out into our hearts except by the Spirit (Rom 5:5).[353]

3.6.7 Subjective Revelation Happens through Objective Signs

Barth maintains that in the subjective reality, God's revelation consists of definite signs of its objective reality which are given by God. Among the signs[354] of the objective reality of revelation, there are certain definite events and relations and orders within the world in which revelation is an objective reality. The special determination of these events and relations and orders is that along with what they are and mean within this world, in themselves, and from the standpoint of immanence, they have another nature and meaning from the side of the objective reality of revelation, i.e., from the side of the incarnation or the Word.[355] Their nature and meaning from this transcendent standpoint is that by them the Word which entered

---

352. *CD* 1/2, 221.
353. *CD* 1/2, 241.
354. One of the signs that Barth deals with is the election of the people of Israel. See for details, *CD* 1/2, 225.
355. *CD* 1/2, 223.

the world objectively in revelation, which was spoken once for all into the world, now wills to speak further in the world. They are the instruments by which it aims at becoming a Word which is apprehended by humankind and therefore a Word which justifies and sanctifies them, by which it aims at executing upon humanity the grace of God which is its content.[356] This giving of signs is the objective side of the church as the sphere in which God's revelation is subjectively real.

Moreover, Barth finds that sacraments also are the objective side of the revelation in the church. The sacraments are emphatically described as holy acts. He finds the nature of baptism and the Lord's Supper as being the church's action as opposed to the church's word in preaching. Being instituted by Christ, sacraments are the signs of the divine grace in Christ. Their purpose is the sanctification and justification of human beings. Its function is to apply and seal the reconciliation that occurred and was expressed objectively, by the ministry of certain human beings.[357] Referring to the baptism and the Lord's Supper, Barth maintains that sacraments are an indispensable means of grace.[358] The sphere of subjective reality in revelation is the sphere of the sacrament. When the signs have been given, a person encounters and receives them as the signs of revelation, and therefore in and with them encounters and receives revelation itself.[359] Thus for Barth, on the one hand, God's revelation in its subjective reality is the person and work of the Spirit, and on the other hand the objective signs that happen through the Spirit.[360]

3.6.8 Holy Spirit and Christian Love

While dealing with the role of the Spirit in building up the church, we have already noted that Barth considers the Spirit as the quickening power in human beings. Thus Jesus Christ places humanity in his community by giving them freedom to submit themselves for God and to their fellows as God's witness, and enables them freely to obey God and to love others.[361] Thus the

---

356. *CD* 1/2, 223.
357. *CD* 1/2, 230.
358. *CD* 1/2, 232.
359. *CD* 1/2, 232.
360. *CD* 1/2, 233.
361. *CD* 4/2, 726.

beginning of Christian life in Barth's definition is that, "... God plunges us into this despair when He reveals Himself to us, when His Word is made flesh and the judgment of our flesh by the Holy Spirit, who opens our eyes and ears and therefore kindles our faith. When that occurs, the Christian life begins."[362] Thus human beings are reconciled to God through Jesus Christ, and they live in the knowledge that they belong to Christ and hold a part in that reconciliation effected in Christ. This reconciliation and all gifts given to the human beings are based on the faith effected in them by the Spirit. Being reconciled to God, members of the community have responsibilities to fulfill like Jesus Christ did, who came into the world as a servant. Here Barth's argument is that the Christians are supposed to obey and render service to God and the neighbor.[363] Barth makes it clear that, "Love to God is, therefore, necessarily love to the neighbor, because obviously I can only honor God by submitting to what He as Creator disposes regarding me and therefore by accepting my responsibility to the thou in the framework of His ordinances."[364] Barth maintains that to love the neighbor, is intended for the child of God in his not yet completed walk and activity as an earthly member of this heavenly head.[365] However, human beings cannot fulfill this task by themselves rather only through the quickening power of the Spirit, who not only confronts the new man and woman with the demand of the reality of conversion and discipleship, but "calls and transposes" them into it.[366]

---

362. *CD* 1/2, 372.
363. *CD* 4/2, 729; for Barth, in the biblical sense of the concept my neighbor is not this or that person as such. Nor is he/she a member of this or that larger or smaller group, or of the group which comprises the whole of humanity. On the contrary, my neighbor is an event which takes place in the existence of a definite person definitely marked off from all other human beings. My neighbor is my fellow-human being acting towards me as a benefactor. Not every person is my neighbor. My neighbor is the one who emerges from amongst all my fellow-human beings as this one thing in particular, my benefactor. I myself, of course, must be summoned by Jesus Christ, and I must be ready to obey the summons to go and do likewise, that is, to be myself a benefactor, if I am to experience as such the emergence of a fellow-man as my benefactor, and therefore to see and have him as my neighbor. Therefore I myself have a decisive part in the event by which a fellow-person is my neighbor. See *CD* 1/2, 420.
364. *CD* 1/2, 404.
365. *CD* 1/2, 409.
366. *CD* 4/2, 729.

Thus making a space to argue, Barth asserts that the quickening power of the Spirit is also present in the "second act," which is the act of "total giving, offering, and surrender, corresponding to this receiving."[367] Barth calls this love and argues that it stands in contrast to the faith of reception. For him, these two acts are indivisible though distinguishable elements in the Christian life. Justification and sanctification are two distinguishable though simultaneous components of one single divine action in the Christian life effected by Christ through the Spirit, just as humiliation and exaltation of Jesus Christ are two components of a single divine action. This self-giving love is the centre of Christian discipleship and obedience to God, and it is present in sinful humanity, through the quickening power of the Spirit and having its ultimate foundation in the being and nature of God.[368] Thus Barth makes the theology of love within the Trinity that "God is" and "God loves" are synonymous.[369] The Father loves the Son and the Son the Father, and the love and communion which exists between them and unites them is the Spirit. That love, which God is in himself from all eternity, is the basis of God's love for us.[370]

Moreover, by characterizing God's love as "electing" in which God gives himself freely to the sinful humanity to redeem them, Barth highlights his analysis of love as "creative." In other words, Barth asserts that God does not love humanity simply to be loved in return, but rather God sets them free to model our love upon him. That freedom also is effected through the Spirit.[371] However, Barth is very cautious that Christian love is not to be regarded as a kind of extension of God's love, which is poured into the

---

367. *CD* 4/2, 730.
368. Barth argues that, in responding to God's love and acting in love towards our fellows, we must not think that an attitude, a disposition, an emotion, or a thought will suffice. On the contrary, God showed his love in action, the suffering of crucifixion; therefore the response of Christian love must be action, action by the whole and not just simply internal. The essence of such love is self-impartation, for it is better to give than to receive, and it is grounded in the love of God and elicited in response to that love through the work of the Spirit. By arguing so, Barth reaffirms his central stance that as the Holy Spirit is the quickening power undergirding, energizing, directing, and realizing the whole scope of the Christian life as devoted to loving both God and its neighbor, so he commensurately equips the Christian with the freedom, the ability and the motivation to achieve its God-given goals. See *CD* 4/2, 826.
369. *CD* 4/2, 755.
370. McIntyre, *The Shape of Pneumatology*, 158.
371. *CD* 4/2, 755.

human action. In other words, the Spirit is not some overwhelming control which reduces the human element to servitude. Rather it is the work of the Spirit to liberate human beings for Christian love which are uniquely and peculiarly their own, and not those of some particle of God's love or of some puppet of his. Hence Barth writes:

> Christian love, as we have had to indicate already, is not a kind of prolongation of the divine love itself, its overflowing into human life which man with his activity has to serve as a kind of channel, being merely present and not at bottom an acting subject. It is not the work of the Holy Spirit to take from man his own proper activity, or to make it simply a function of His own overpowering control. Where He is present, there is no servitude but freedom. This false conception is contradicted by the great frailty of that which emerges as love in the life of even the best Christians. If it were merely identical with the flowing of the stream of divine love into human life, if our little love were a manifestation or particle of the love of God, it could not and would not be so weak and puny. But the work of the Holy Spirit consists in the liberation of man for his own act and therefore for the spontaneous human love whose littleness and frailty are his own responsibility and not that of the Holy Spirit.[372]

3.7 Word of God and the Holy Spirit

Work of the Spirit through the Word of God is one of the important themes of Barth. He is very keen to acknowledge the fact that the Word of God becomes the Word of God only because the Spirit works in it. There are different aspects in relation to the work of the Spirit in the Word which Barth attempts to deal with. Initially, we will see how Barth understands the important issue of inspiration.

---

372. *CD* 4/2, 785.

3.7.1 Inspiration and the Holy Spirit

Barth asserts that the Word of God is inspired by the Holy Spirit. For him, the Word is not given "by the will of man," "but in it men spoke as they were moved by the Holy Ghost."[373] By referring to 2 Timothy 3:14-17 and 2 Peter 1:19-21, Barth maintains that the decisive center to which these two passages point is in both instances indicated by a reference to the Spirit, and indeed in such a way that the Spirit is described as the real author of what is stated or written in Scripture.[374] Now Barth turns to discuss the church's statement about the inspiration of Scripture in relation to the sayings in 2 Timothy 3:16 and 2 Peter 1:20f. In the so-called doctrine of inspiration the issue is that on the basis of what relationship between the Spirit as God opening up human being's ears and mouth for his Word and the Bible, the latter can be read and understood and expounded as a human witness of his revelation as the Word and therefore in the strict sense as Scripture. He argues that, "The doctrine of inspiration will always have to describe the relation between the Holy Spirit and the Bible in such a way that the whole reality of the unity between the two is safeguarded no less than the fact that this unity is a free act of the grace of God, and therefore for us its content is always a promise."[375]

This refers to the "disposing act and decision of God himself," which gives to Scripture the role described by Paul (vv. 14-17) in the past and future lives of his hearers. In 2 Peter 1:19-21 also, our relationship to Scripture is described as one "between the times," and the reason given is that in it human beings speak as they are "moved by the Holy Spirit." The decisive center in both passages is that the Spirit is the real author of Scripture.[376] Barth argues:

> The statement that the Bible is the Word of God cannot therefore say that the Word of God is tied to the Bible. On the contrary, what it must say is that the Bible is tied to the Word

---

373. *CD* 1/2, 505.
374. *CD* 1/2, 505.
375. *CD* 1/2, 514; Barth makes a detailed discussion about the stance of the early church and the Reformers in order to show the significance of inspiration to the Word of God. See *CD* 1/2, 517ff.
376. *CD* 1/2, 513ff.

of God. But that means that in this statement we contemplate a free decision of God — not in uncertainty but in certainty, not without basis but on the basis of the promise which the Bible itself proclaims and which we receive in and with the Church. But its content is always a free decision of God, which we cannot anticipate by grasping at the Bible — even if we do it with the greatest faith of which we are capable, but the freedom of which we will have to recognize when we grasp at the Bible in the right way.[377]

Hence, the human church has no power or control over the Bible as the Word of God. If the church lives by the Bible because it is the Word of God, which means that it lives by the fact that Christ is revealed in the Bible by the work of the Spirit, that means it has no power or control over this work, rather it can grasp and honour the Bible.[378] The Bible is the Word of God to the church and this is owed solely to the work of the Spirit, to God's free grace, and the power of the heavenly Christ which "is the divine side of the life of the church."[379]

The doctrine of inspiration always has to describe the relation between Spirit and the Bible in such a way that both the reality of the unity between the two and the fact that this unity is a free act of the grace of God are safeguarded. The work of the Spirit in the inspiration of Scripture includes its hearing and understanding as well as its writing. The same Spirit, who disclosed the mystery to certain human beings and enabled them to speak of it, must bear witness also to its truth to those who hear and read it.[380] This self-disclosure in its totality is *theopneustia* (divinely inspired), the inspiration

---

377. *CD* 1/2, 513.
378. *CD* 1/2, 513.
379. *CD* 1/2, 514.
380. We must understand that the notion of inspiration need not be construed in such a way as to involve an inner text as such. And it cannot be limited to some past phenomenon resulting in a revelation which is subsequently to be had in codified and textually fossilized form. Rather we have to say that we must view inspiration as a single, timeless, or rather, contemporary act of God in both the biblical authors and ourselves. In this single event of the Spirit, then, the biblical witnesses themselves are in a sense made contemporary with us, and we are given to see and hear what they saw and heard for themselves. See Hart, *Regarding Karl Barth*, 45-46.

of the word of the prophets and apostles.[381] However Barth laments that very early in the church's history, due to the result of struggle and reaction against Montanism, interest was concentrated especially on the circle of inspiration, namely, the work of the Spirit in the emergence of the spoken or written Word. It excluded the work of the Spirit in the knowledge of the Scripture from the concept of inspiration. In accordance with the manifold witnesses of Scripture itself they emphasized the identity of the human and divine words. They reduced verbal inspiration to inspiredness. They made of it a phenomenon like all other natural and historical phenomena which can be ascertained and studied naturally. This is the doubtful element in the standard doctrine of inspiration. It gives the church authority and control over God's Word, violating God's majesty. Catholicism's relativization to tradition is in this sense quite understandable.[382]

Moreover, Barth is very particular about the canonicity of the Bible too. He recognizes that there are lots of writings that were not accepted into canon in the first century due to the fact that they were not apostolic. The first century criteria to accept a book into canon was the authenticity of the text in terms of Jesus Christ. Barth asks, "Do we hear the truth through these books or not? Thus the question is one of the Holy Spirit's speaking through them. If we found the manuscript of a new Gospel, the church would be faced with the question of its canonicity. If the Holy Spirit led the church to accept it, then it could be taken into the Canon."[383]

3.7.2 Holy Spirit as the Teacher of the Word of God

While dealing with subjective revelation, Barth maintains that the Spirit is the teacher of the Word. Although the Spirit is a unique person, it is not an independent divinity side by side with the unique Word. On the other hand, it is the teacher of the Word and the Word never exists without its teacher.[384] Since the Spirit is the teacher of the Word, the instruction of the Word also is the work of the Spirit. Without the work of the Spirit, there can be no instruction of the Word because the Word is never apart from

---

381. *CD* 1/2, 516.
382. *CD* 1/2, 517-519.
383. Godsey, ed., *Karl Barth's Table Talks*, 55.
384. *CD* 1/2, 244.

the Spirit.[385] Therefore Hart argues that, "Karl Barth's entire theological project might be legitimately described as a 'theology of proclamation.'"[386] Barth writes, "And it is by this very work of the Holy Spirit, and because in the Holy Spirit we recognize that God's Word is the truth, that we are convinced of the futility of the only remaining possibility, i.e., that in some sense we already have the Holy Spirit, in other words, that we have a prior knowledge of the Word of God, that we have been instructed in it from the very first, that we are even in a position to instruct ourselves in it."[387] Therefore, Barth's position is that, "When you go into the pulpit, go with the Bible and the Holy Spirit" and "it may be that our preaching is bad; nevertheless, it is possible that through our ineffectively preached words and bad language, the Holy Spirit may speak."[388] However, he does not say that the Spirit speaks only through the Bible. According to him, "the Holy Spirit has not retired. Calvin insisted on the omnipresence of the Holy Spirit. But if we must distinguish between the Holy Spirit and other spirits, then the Bible is the criterion."[389]

---

385. *CD* 1/2, 244.
386. Hart, *Regarding Karl Barth*, 28; the reason for this argument is based on the fact that Barth concerns himself as the only legitimate starting point for truly theological activity as the claim made by faith that God has proclaimed his word to humankind. This proclamation occurs in the humanisation of God's own Word as the human Jesus Christ, in the prophetic and apostolic testimony to this Scripture, and in the preaching of the church.
387. *CD* 1/2, 244.
388. Godsey, ed., *Karl Barth's Table Talks*, 38; Barth insists a special activity of the Spirit upon the prophets and apostles, commissioning them for their particular task of human witness; even in the midst of their "capacity of errors." Hart, *Regarding Karl Barth*, 45; it is very interesting to note that Barth was not much concerned with the hermeneutical methods. In a passage which is fraught with meaning for the task of hermeneutics, Barth explains that the modern historical-critical method of investigating the Bible has its rightful place, insofar as it is concerned with a preparation of the intelligence, but that the old doctrine of inspiration was concerned with an element which is even more crucial: the labor of understanding itself. He is glad that he does not have to choose between the two, but confess that his entire energy has been directed towards seeing through and beyond the historical into the spirit of the Bible, which is the eternal Spirit. See John D. Godsey, "Introduction," in *Karl Barth: How I Changed My Mind*, ed. Robert W. Funk (Richmond: John Knox, 1966), 24.
389. Godsey, ed., *Karl Barth's Table Talks*, 96.

3.7.3 Scripture as the Witness of Divine Revelation

Barth asserts that the Bible is the witness of divine revelation since the Bible has in fact answered our question about the revelation of God, bringing before us the lordship of the triune God.[390] The statement that the Bible is the witness of divine revelation is not limited by the fact that there is also a witness of the church which we have to hear, and in addition witness is also demanded from us. The possibility both of the witness of the church and of our own witness is founded upon the reality of which that statement speaks.[391] In this sense Barth seems to attack the authority of the Roman Catholic Church. Although the Word is the witness to revelation, Barth maintains that this Word is God's revelation in human words also. In other words, it is a human expression of God's revelation.[392] He writes that, "God's revelation in the human word of Holy Scripture is distinguished from everything else that is said to us by men by the fact that a majesty belongs to the one which obviously is radically lacking in the other, a majesty without which the latter would be meaningless if the former were only an exception and not the law and the promise and the sign of redemption which has been set up in the sphere of all other human words, and of all that is said by them."[393]

Barth's point is that Jesus Christ in his eternal presence as the Word is concealed from the human beings. He is revealed only in the sign of his humanity, and especially in the witness of his prophets and apostles. However, by nature these signs are not heavenly and human, but earthly and temporal-human. Therefore the act of their institution as signs requires repetition and confirmation. Their being as the Word requires promise and faith just because they are signs of the eternal presence of Christ. For if they are to act as signs, if the eternal presence of Christ is to be revealed to us in time, there is a constant need for the continuing work of the Spirit in the church and its members which is always taking place in new acts. If the church lives by the Bible because it is the Word, it means that church lives

---

390. *CD* 1/2, 462.
391. *CD* 1/2, 462.
392. *CD* 1/2, 473.
393. *CD* 1/2, 472.

by the fact that Christ is revealed in the Bible by the work of the Spirit.[394] The human side of the life of the church with the Bible rightly consists in all these things. But apart from these things, the human side of its life with the Bible can consist only in the fact that it prays that the Bible may be the Word here and now, that there may take place that work of the Spirit, and therefore a free applying of the free grace of God.[395]

Since Christ is revealed in the church, the church has to seek the divine revelation in the Word in the authority of the Spirit. Barth writes:

> If the Church can only serve the Word of God and if this service is only a human and, as such, a fallible service, we cannot escape this service, what it says to us in this service has authority, we have to accept it as at first normative for us, and therefore until we are better informed we have to approach the Holy Scripture laid before us by the Church — not otherwise, and in its full compass as presented to us, and therefore without addition or subtraction — the collection of those documents in which we too have to seek the witness of divine revelation. The Church with its existing and already attested faith promises us that we shall not seek this witness in it in vain. Except in its ministerial function, in a human way, by its preaching and instruction on the basis of this Canon, the Church cannot ensure that we shall find this witness in this Canon. We shall find this witness only in virtue of its self-witness, that is, in virtue of the authority of the Holy Ghost.[396]

Therefore, Barth maintains that the church's confession is a formulation and proclamation reached on the basis of common deliberation and decision.[397] However, there is no confession whose authority might not seem endangered by the history of its origination. But there is none whose authority might not have the testimony of the Spirit in spite of that history. Where there has been too little concern about church order is the making

---

394. *CD* 1/2, 513.
395. *CD* 1/2, 514.
396. *CD* 1/2, 598-599.
397. *CD* 1/2, 637.

of a confession, which has always been avenged in its history, in spite of the sin-forgiving witness of the Spirit.

3.7.4 Word of God and Faith

For Barth, the Word of God has a spiritual power to reach humankind so that it can hear the Word of God. The Word comes to human beings through the miraculous work of the Spirit.[398] Consequently, they become free to confess Jesus Christ to be believers and witnesses.[399] This is because the Spirit is the power of the Word which is inseparably linked to the Word and goes out to human beings to bring them to the Word. Barth writes that, "The Holy Spirit is the Lord not only of the Word itself, but also of its being heard. Thus I mean openness of mind. The Holy Spirit opens the mind of man to receive and hear the Word."[400] Moreover, the Spirit is inseparable from the Word and its power is not a power separate from the Word, but it lives in the Word and through the Word.[401] Thus according to Barth, the Spirit is the spiritual power of the Word that enables the Word to accomplish its end to encounter them and to bind them to himself. Barth writes that, "There is only one Word of God and that is the eternal Word of the Father which for our reconciliation became flesh like us and has now returned to the Father, to be present to His Church by the Holy Spirit."[402]

For Barth, God the Spirit incorporates the human beings to revelation through faith.[403] This faith comes from the Spirit because the Spirit speaks through the Word binding the Christian to its commands and directions.[404]

---

398. *CD* 1/2, 701.
399. *CD* 1/2, 702.
400. Godsey, ed., *Karl Barth's Table Talks*, 37.
401. *KD* 1/1, 155-156.
402. *CD* 1/2, 512-513.
403. It means that Barth sees faith not as a human activity in which something virtual is actualized, but rather as that action in which we joyfully embrace something which is already real and already has our name firmly stamped upon it. See Hart, *Regarding Karl Barth*, 67; for a beautiful interpretation see Robert Townsend Voelkel, *The Conception of Faith in the Theology of Karl Barth: A Critique of Barthian Theology*, Ph. D. Thesis (New York: Union Theological Seminary, 1962).
404. Christian life in the Spirit is the life of faith. Faith does not consist of an immanent changing of a person, even though it cannot exist without some transmutation which does indeed takes place through the work of the Spirit in the form of a new birth of human beings through God. Spirit carries the human beings to him through faith and holds them fixed at its goal. See Matczak, *Karl Barth on God*, 117.

Barth argues that it is the Spirit who is given not as the Spirit of the individual but as the Spirit of the whole community. It leads the Christian in the fellowship of this community and it orders its actions to obedience within the framework of this fellowship and its mission and service. At the same time, in its divine authority and within the limits of its own nature, the Spirit is the free Spirit of God moving where he himself wills and demanding of each individual his own individual obedience, demanding of each individual an obedience which is always new, and leading the community into new situations and laying upon it new tasks. Therefore there cannot really be any external statutes by which Christian obedience may ever be defined or determined absolutely.[405]

Moreover, the Word is not only revealed to human beings but also believed by them. That means the Word is uttered to humankind so that they can listen and make a response to the Word. Barth writes, "Without hesitation we must confess that, first of all and fundamentally, it is not we ourselves who decide. In every case, if we believe, we believe in the consummation of the sovereign act of the Word of God. In every case, it is the work of Holy Spirit."[406] The Bible and church dogma and the entire older theology, when they come to say of this event, speak of the Spirit. What that means for Barth is that the source of faith is not human himself, rather God is accomplishing the final phase of his revelation. In other words, it is the spiritual source, and it is so due to the fact that when the Word is believed by human beings, it becomes the ground of their belief and not their experience of believing. Thus Barth aims at the experience of faith as the source of the spiritual power of the Word. Faith is not the work of human beings, but rather the miracle brought about by the Spirit, who concretely and historically imparts the power of its own Word to the human beings.

Finally, Barth asserts that the Spirit is God who makes the Word heard in the human beings and identifies it as the third way of God's manifestation. Hence, he writes that, "The Lord of the language is also the Lord of our listening to it. The Lord who gives the Word is also the Lord who

---

405. *CD* 3/3, 255.
406. Barth, *God Here and Now*, 27.

gives faith. The Lord of our listening, the Word who gives faith, the Lord through whose act the openness and readiness of man for the Word is true and real — is not another God, but the one God in this way — and that is the Holy Spirit."[407] For Barth this is the third way of God's manifestation. The fact that there are actually human beings who subjectively or existentially hear the objective Word spoken to them reveals that there is a third way in which God acts. God acts as the imparter to himself, as the instigator of relationship, as an intermediary between an objective revelation and a subjective, existential, acceptance of the revelation.[408] Human beings know that despite the existential character of their faith, the ground of believing is not in themselves. Rather, they are touched by a spiritual mystery. Barth writes that, "But that this experience is the experience of faith, this attitude the attitude of faith and these thoughts the thoughts of faith which has heard the Word of God, is decided spiritually, i.e., is decided not by faith, but by the Word we believe in … because the Word of God is a mystery in that it really touches us spiritually, i.e., invariably only through the Holy Spirit, in full mediacy only immediately from God's side."[409]

3.8 Holy Spirit and Eschatology

We have already discussed the major aspects of Barth's pneumatology under different headings. Having considered all these points of view, our final

---

407. *KD* 1/1, 189-190; by calling the Spirit the Lord Barth means that the Spirit acts in revelation by relating human beings to the Word, so that they can utter a spiritual Word in human words. Human beings come to know their relationship to the Holy Spirit concomitantly as they come to faith. Human beings recognize the Spirit as the final form of God's self-revelation at the moment in which they find themselves related to God so that they believe. For they suddenly find themselves in reality a listener and a believer, a person related to God's Word, and attribute that listening and believing not to themselves, but to God, in so far as God brings them to faith and forms a relationship with him. The God who brings human beings to the point where they are open and ready to hear is God in this third form of existence, God the Holy Spirit. See *KD* 1/1, 494.
408. *KD* 1/1, 378.
409. *KD* 1/1, 190; human beings who believe in that the experiences, attitudes, and thoughts of faith become real meditative human acts, and also that faith, in so far as it is the spiritual hearing of a Word which is beyond the realm of human being's experience, is not their own work, but the immediate work of the Spirit in them as attested by the Scripture and by the church's proclamation. Hence, faith for Barth is not a thing, but rather an event, an act of encounter with the Holy Spirit of the Word, who causes real human actions to take on the character of mediators of a spiritual mystery, which is not immediate to human beings as such but which comes to them.

theme is eschatology and the Spirit in the theology of Barth. Dalferth argues that, "Barth's theological realism is a decidedly eschatological realism."[410] Hence, we are considering the eschatology of Barth from the point of view of Jesus Christ's final coming or *parousia*.[411]

Barth had learned from Franz Overbeck, the remarkable historian of the 19th century that "Christianity which is not entirely and completely eschatology ... is entirely and completely contrary to Christ."[412] He criticised modern Christianity and its attempt to harmonise Christian faith and modern culture as being totally incompatible with the original Christian faith.[413] However, Barth had learned from the two Blumhardts that it is possible to be true to the eschatological nature of the Christian faith without leaving or ignoring this world. "Jesus is victor" was the motto of Blumhardts which Barth also accepted to be the starting point and guiding principle of all Christian existence and theology. In short, for Barth the reality with which theology must deal is the reality of the risen and living Jesus himself, acting and speaking as a distinctive factor no less actual today than yesterday. For him it is the reality of the resurrection in which the eschatological kingdom of God became manifest and which, in the proclamation of the gospel, continuously represents itself by the power of the Spirit. Dalferth argues that, "Barth did not waver from this fundamental point: the reality to which theology refers is the eschatological reality of the risen Christ and the new life into which we are drawn by the Spirit."[414]

---

410. Ingolf U. Dalferth, "Karl Barth's Eschatological Realism," in *Karl Barth: Centenary Essays*, ed. S. W. Sykes (Cambridge: Cambridge University Press, 1989), 20.
411. We cannot treat Barth's conception of the future reality of the community in the *eschaton*. Unfortunately he has been unable to write the fifth volume of his *Church Dogmatics* which would have treated precisely this aspect. Here we are trying to look into the subjective reality of the community, seen between the times, and therefore in eschatological tension.
412. E. Jüngel, *Barth-Studien* (Zurich and Cologne: Benziger Güttersloher Verlagshaus, 1982), 71.
413. According to him, the first century Christians expected the present world order to be doomed to imminent annihilation and shapely contrasted the old reality and the new of the coming of the kingdom of God. They believed in such an eschatology on the basis of the resurrection of Christ as the beginning and promise of the general resurrection. Overbeck's problem was that he didn't see any way of overcoming this incompatibility in that either we remain Christian and thus must shut ourselves off from the modern world. Otherwise, we live in this world without being Christian. See Dalferth, "Karl Barth's Eschatological Realism," 20.
414. Dalferth, "Karl Barth's Eschatological Realism," 21.

3.8.1 The Three Forms of Jesus' Appearances

For Barth theology refers not to the past but to the present. Which means for him it is the personal presence of the risen Christ, the revelation of God's love towards the human beings through the Spirit by interrupting the continuities of our life and calling us into community with the living God. It is a presence in which God encounters the human beings immediately and creatively.[415] For Barth it is the presence of Christ communicating with human beings so that they would know God. This presence of Christ and his direct communication is continued by the power of the Spirit after Jesus' death and resurrection. Thus the true knowledge of God and Christ is rooted in the power of the resurrection and results from being drawn into the eschatological presence of God by the power of the Spirit.[416] Barth continues his argument by affirming that the New Testament talks about only one coming again of Jesus Christ in effective presence. However, this one coming again takes place in three different forms. Firstly, it took place in Christ's resurrection and Easter appearances. Secondly, it will take place its final and definitive form in Christ's return as the goal of the history of the church, the world and the individual, as the author of the general resurrection of the dead and the fulfiller of universal judgement. Both these types are one and the same event. In the words of Barth, they are, "The immediate visible presence and action of the living Jesus Christ Himself."[417] However, these two appearances are different forms because they are not visible to us as one and the same event. For Barth, the first occurred in a provisional, transitory, and particular form, whereas the last will occur in its perfect, final, and universal form. Thirdly, the *parousia* of Jesus Christ also takes place in a middle form as well between the first and final forms. It takes place in the time of the community in the form of the impartation of the Spirit. For Barth, it is a different form, due to the fact that in it Jesus Christ is really but invisibly and indirectly or directly present through the mediation of human words. Barth writes that, "There is the indispensability of an indirect and historical connection with Him in the

---

415. Karl Barth, *Der Römerbrief*, 1st ed. (1919) (Zurich: Theologischer Verlag, 1963), 97f.
416. Dalferth, "Karl Barth's Eschatological Realism," 22.
417. *CD* 4/1, 725.

service or as a garment of the true and direct connection which he Himself institutes and continues between Himself and us from the right hand of the father."[418]

Although Barth deals with these three forms of the presence of Jesus Christ, he asserts that these three forms are one identical event in substance, scope, and content. Therefore, he justifies his position by stating that Christ's coming in Spirit is genuinely his own direct and personal coming.[419] Barth writes that, "This, then, is His new coming in the glory and revelation of His mediatorial act, as the light and Word of life, in His prophetic office. In correspondence with the fact that it is the form of His coming between the commencement and the goal, and in correspondence with our historical place between, it is His coming as the hope of all men."[420] We say this when we say that it is his universally relevant coming in the Spirit and in the promise of the Spirit.[421] Thus it is made clear that each form of the appearance contains the other two by way of anticipation or recapitulation in analogy with the doctrine of the Trinity. In his resurrection Christ is already engaged in the outpouring of the Spirit, and in outpouring of the Spirit he is engaged in the resurrection of all the dead, and the execution of the last judgement.[422]

3.8.2 *The Outpouring of the Spirit in the End Time*

After having discussed the three forms of the appearance of Jesus Christ, Barth maintains that the beginning and goal of the return of Jesus Christ is also the beginning and goal of the time of the community. The time of the community is the "time between the times," that is, the time between the

---

418. *CD* 4/1, 325.
419. *CD* 4/3, 356ff.
420. Viewed as the condescension of God in his movement towards humanity in Jesus Christ, and in relation to human sin, the history of the incarnation is seen as God's vindication of his creation. Viewed as the movement of this humanity towards God, and in relation to the eschatological future of humankind, the history of the incarnation is seen as the exaltation, the sanctification of our humanity in the Spirit, a movement which extends beyond this particular history into the history of the church. See Hart, *Regarding Karl Barth*, 72.
421. *CD* 4/3, 356.
422. *CD* 4/3, 292ff.

time of Christ's ascension and final *parousia*.[423] In the first *parousia* of Jesus Christ, Barth writes:

> There began a time in which He was and continues to be and ever again will be directly present and revealed and active in the community by His Spirit, the power of His accomplished resurrection.... There began a time in which the community, Christians, are aware, and will and must always be aware, that they themselves, the hearers of the Word, those who are justified by it, the children of God, believers, the witnesses to the Crucified and Risen, are still in the world, and are still like it in the sphere of human perception, so that to themselves and one another they are not visible or audible or perceptible as those who are dead and resurrected to new life, they cannot be known outwardly or inwardly as such, they are still hidden, they can recognize in themselves as in others an altered world only in relation to Jesus Christ, only according to the verdict of the Holy Spirit, only by faith and not by sight.[424]

Hence, Barth maintains that the community must look upon Jesus Christ as the final future of the world and the human beings. The verdict of God wills this from them. Jesus Christ himself, empowered by the Father and operative by his Spirit, attests and proves himself to them not only as the first but also as the last (Rev 1:17; 2:8), and therefore as the one who comes (Rev 1:4-8). That alone is the necessity of expectation, and therefore of the differentiation of the times attested in the New Testament.[425]

After outlining the present time and the *parousia* of Jesus Christ, Barth moves to the new time which has commenced. It is the end time, or the *eschaton*. For Barth, the impartation of the Spirit is the coming of Jesus Christ in the last days. Moreover, it is the promise given to the church

---

423. *CD* 4/1, 319; Barth's eschatology takes shape as a development of his threefold depiction of the perfect time of Jesus Christ. He is really past, present, and future, but now in a way more specific to the perspectives of the church – He is past in his Easter time, present in the time of his Spirit, and future in the time of his consummate *parousia*. See Dawson, *The Resurrection in Karl Barth*, 81.
424. *CD* 4/1, 318-319.
425. *CD* 4/1, 324-325.

through the Spirit and therefore the community is supposed to do its mission while moving towards its end. Hence, the new coming of Jesus Christ has an eschatological character in this second form too. Barth argues that if the *parousia* is an eschatological event in its third and final stage as well, this means specifically that in it we have to do with the manifestation and effective presence of Jesus Christ in their definitive form, with his revelation at the goal of the last time.[426] Christ's first, middle, and last coming are all the one event of the *eschaton*. Barth maintains that the *eschaton* cannot refer merely to the final stage of the *parousia,* rather it denotes the last time as well. Hence Barth asks the question, "Is the time of the community not the other world in this world, the incorruptible within the corruptible, eternal life in temporal, the divine in the human? Is not the church itself the eschatological fact *par excellence.*"[427] Thus for Barth, the time between is the time of the community, the time spared and appointed for its gathering, up-building, and mission.[428] Barth's point is that God wills a human response corresponding to the reconciliation perfectly accomplished in Jesus Christ. Although God does not need this, in his friendliness God does not forego the praises of human beings. Hence, God does not hurry up for the final consummation until God has first received praise from the heart of his creation. This is the greatness of God's grace, the reach of his condescension. God wishes a subjective human realisation and correspondence. Thus, this time is the time for the work of the Spirit, time for the community. The community has not this time, and its existence in it, merely for its own sake. It has it for God and for the world.[429]

Moreover, Barth maintains that the final event had already taken place in the resurrection. For him, this is the meaning of the popular sayings of Jesus concerning his imminent coming and imminent consummation.[430]

---

426. *CD* 4/3, 296.
427. *CD* 4/3, 321.
428. The existence of an eschatological time means that even after his first *parousia* God did not cease to act in and with the world and humanity. It means that this time is still his time. In other words, he grants space to humanity in which it can still exist — surplus space, and a surplus existence, but still a possibility for being, and for real being. He grants it the possibility of development, of history — a history which is not only a "post-history," but real history.
429. *CD* 4/1, 735-739.
430. *CD* 4/1, 734.

Primarily it was the expectation of Jesus himself. He does not know the exact time of the revelation of the reality of the kingdom already present in him. All Christ knows is that it will come soon because it is the goal of the limited life in the time of Jesus of Nazareth. It will come suddenly because it is foreordained and foreknown by God alone, and will occur when human beings are not expecting it. In the form of his Spirit, Jesus Christ is really present in his community. Christ does not temporarily relinquish his Lordship in this time between, either to the church, Christianity or the Christian. He remains its direct Lord and head through his Spirit.[431]

Barth finally argues that the kingdom of God is the lordship of God established in the world in Jesus Christ, the rule of God as it takes place in him.[432] It is absolutely identical with Jesus Christ. In this sense, for Barth kingdom is the church.[433] However, he does not argue that the community is the kingdom. It will not be so before the final universal revelation. Jesus Christ alone is the kingdom, even in the relative sense in which the kingdom is the church. But in Christ's unique lordship, power, life, and work his kingdom is present in an earthly-historical form, namely the church. Therefore, Webster says that Barth presents "A depiction of the world of human action as it is enclosed and governed by the creative, redemptive and sanctifying work of God in Christ, present in the power of the Holy Spirit."[434] The being of the absolute kingdom is the being of the historical relative kingdom. In short, there is a real identity, not present in *abstracto*, but given by God and enacted in the mighty work of the Spirit, between the holy one, the kingdom of God as perfectly established in him, and the communion of saints on earth, which is also a communion of sinners.[435] The kingdom of God in heaven grows also on earth, and because and as it does so the Christian community grows after it.[436]

---

431. *CD* 3/2, 504-508.
432. *CD* 4/2, 655-656.
433. *CD* 4/2, 657.
434. J. B. Webster, *Barth's Ethics of Reconciliation* (Cambridge: Cambridge University Press, 1995), 2.
435. *CD* 4/2, 656.
436. *CD* 4/2, 655-659.

4. Summary

As we have made an in depth study of Barth's pneumatology, one thing is obvious. His theology of the Spirit was a corrective both to the Calvinist absolute decree and to the unhappy consciousness by a return to elements of biblical tradition which had been lost or overlaid. Although the Enlightenment was a movement that attempted to liberate the Spirit entirely from the trammels of ecclesiastic control, there were failures in that which Barth attempts to make out afresh. Moreover, the ecclesiastical control since Augustine had tended to make the Spirit immanent within the institution, which also was rejected by Barth. After the Enlightenment, immanence was transferred to human thought and action and it became secularized in human culture. Consequently, the Spirit is no longer the transcendent and eschatological Spirit which also was a concern for Barth.[437] Thus when attempts are made to see the pneumatology of Barth along this line of thought, one realizes the fact that his contribution is immense.

However, Barth's pneumatology has been criticized on various grounds. The major criticism levelled against Barth is that the work of the Spirit is not given adequate weight in Barth's Christology. Here Barth has failed to carry through his critique of the tradition, as his espousal of the *filioque* makes clear. For Orthodox theologians, the offence of that teaching lies mainly in the fact that it prevents us from seeing that Jesus is the *gift* of the Spirit as much as he is the giver. The Spirit is the source of Jesus' authentic humanity, and so the means by which the benefits of life are made available to us. It is this side of Christology which is underweighted in Barth, with the consequent loss on the side of the doctrine of Christ's humanity.[438] Moreover, Barth's pneumatology subsides into Christology, as if there's nothing the Spirit can do that Christ can't do better. As Jenson writes, "The personal agent of the [community's] work in fact turns out at every step of Barth's argument to be *not* the Spirit, as advertised, but Christ; the Spirit is denoted invariably by impersonal terms, chiefly the 'power

---

437. The Enlightenment and much nineteenth century theology with its tendency to locate God in the human spirit can in this light be seen as a return to a kind of pantheism, the identification of God with the world, and the route to slavery rather than liberation. See Gunton, "The Triune God," 66.
438. Gunton, "The Triune God," 63.

of Jesus Christ.'"[439] It also must be noted that Barth rendered the Spirit automatically identical with Jesus, or permissively reduces the Spirit to his power of promise. Moreover, although Barth announces the Spirit as an agent who sets us free, in reality Barth explains it in Christological terms.[440] There is nothing wrong in bringing other persons, whose act toward the world is indivisible. The issue is that Barth leaves the reader no reason to think you couldn't unpack the setting free in terms of Christ alone and the exposition abandons the Spirit to the rubrics.[441] Moreover, Barth pays full and detailed attention to the humanity of Christ, and to balance the teaching of the pre-temporal decision of God to redeem with an equally emphatic concentration on the centrality of the historical and particular. The Spirit of God is present to the world at particular times and places, giving to it the liberty to move into the future prepared for it.[442] However, his weakness is a weakness of balance. There is insufficient weight given to the distinctions between the three divine persons and, in particular, to the reality and distinctive functions of the Spirit, with the result that too much is thrown onto Christology, too much onto the immanent and eternal and so too little on the particularities of history.[443] It is often said that talk of the Spirit is also a way of conceiving the immanence of God. Gunton writes that, "In fact, it has been suggested that pneumatology is so attractive an alternative to Christology for this purpose, that we can dispense with traditional Trinitarian ways of speaking of God, confining ourselves to God as Spirit."[444] One cannot solve this problem by playing Word and Spirit Christologies against or alongside one another. Hence, it seems that it is a mistake to conceive the Spirit in terms of immanence. The essential distinction can be that in Jesus, God identifies himself as a part of the world through the Son. As Spirit, God is present to the world as other, as transcendent. In other words, "Spirit is present *in* our hearts and is not identified with no part of the world, although he mediates to us God's im-

---

439. Robert Jenson, "You Wonder where the Spirit Went," *Pro Ecclesia 2* (1993), 303.
440. Eugene F. Rogers Jr., *After the Spirit: A Constructive Pneumatology from Resources Outside the Modern West* (Grand Rapids: Eerdmans, 2005), 21.
441. Rogers Jr., *After the Spirit*, 15.
442. Gunton, "The Triune God," 64.
443. Gunton, "The Triune God," 64.
444. Gunton, "The Triune God," 62.

manence as Word, because he is God bringing the world to its eschatological destiny."⁴⁴⁵ Hence, Berkhof argues that, "If the Spirit is the bridge-builder between the Word and the world, the creator of an encounter between God and human existence, we have to prolong not only Christology in the direction of pneumatology but also pneumatology in the direction of anthropology (and perhaps even of sociology and cosmology)."⁴⁴⁶

---

445. Gunton, "The Triune God," 62.
446. Hendrikus Berkhof, "Beginning with Barth," in *How Karl Barth Changed My Mind*, ed. Donald K. McKim (Grand Rapids: Eerdmans, 1986), 23.

CHAPTER FOUR

Pneumatology of Jürgen Moltmann (1926 -)

1. Introduction

The major intent of the previous chapter has been to systematically delineate the pneumatology of Karl Barth. Having understood the major tenets of Barth's pneumatology, the present chapter looks into the pneumatology of Jürgen Moltmann, who is greatly influenced by Barth and his theology. Jürgen Moltmann had a meteoric rise in theology, establishing himself as one of the world's leading Protestant theologians with the publication of *Theology of Hope*. It would not be an exaggeration if one argues that at least for a decade no contemporary theological work was more widely read and discussed than Moltmann's. Recognising this significance of Moltmann, Harvey Cox points out that Moltmann began a new chapter in modern theology with his *Theology of Hope*.[1] In 1974, the editors of seven church periodicals in the United States and Canada cited Moltmann as one of the major shapers of current Christian thought and life, as "the most dominant theological presence of our time."[2] Various labels have been attached to the theology of Moltmann like theology of hope, theology of eschatology, dialectic theology, theology of the cross, political theology, liberation

---

1. Harvey Cox, "Gedanken über Jürgen Moltmanns Buch: Der gekreuzigte Gott," in *Diskussion über Jürgen Moltmanns Buch "Der gekreuzigte Gott,"* ed. Michael Welker (Munich: Kaiser, 1979), 126.
2. Dale Vree, *On Synthesizing Marxism and Christianity* (New York: Wiley, 1976), 90.

theology, the theology of the Trinity etc. Nonetheless, one theme that runs throughout all his writings is hope for the future based on the cross and resurrection of Jesus Christ and the role of the Spirit to establish the kingdom of God on the earth. Therefore, the central focus of this chapter is to dig into the pneumatology of Moltmann in depth. In order to materialize this endeavor, one needs to begin with Moltmann's *Sitz-im-Leben*. Hence, the current chapter begins with a brief survey of Moltmann's socio-cultural, political, philosophical, and theological surroundings in order to discover the factors which influenced him to develop a pneumatology. This awareness is significant in this study, particularly because Moltmann had to make use of what he learnt and experienced from his social, political, philosophical, and academic context in developing his pneumatology. Having briefly outlined his *Sitz-im-Leben*, the study will thematically concentrate on the pneumatology of Moltmann.

2. The *Sitz-im-Leben* of Jürgen Moltmann

2.1 The Socio-cultural Setting

Moltmann was born in Hamburg, Germany, on April 8, 1926. He was raised in a rather "enlightened secular" home. Therefore, he did not undergo very profound Christian socialization, but grew up with poets and philosophers of German Idealism like Lessing, Goethe, and Nietzsche.[3] Consequently, he was far from Christianity, the church, and the Bible. However, he always had an interest to discover and comprehend things for himself, especially things that others had already learned from an early age. Thus theology has always remained to him an incredible adventure. Moltmann writes:

> For me, Christian faith began with a despairing search for God and a personal struggle with the dark side of the "hidden face" of God. At the end of July 1943, as an air force auxiliary, I experienced the destruction of my home town Hamburg through RAF's "Operation Gomorrah," and barely survived

---

3. Randall E. Otto, *The God of Hope: The Trinitarian Vision of Jürgen Moltmann* (Maryland: University Press of America, 1991), 3.

the fire storm in which 40,000 people burnt to death. The friend standing beside me was blown to pieces by the bomb which left me unscathed. I come from a secular family, but that night I cried out to God for the first time "My God, where are you?"[4]

Moltmann had a religious conversion that began in a prisoner of war camp in Belgium. He started to read a Bible (a copy of the New Testament and Psalms), given to him by an American military chaplain. Though he began to read it largely out of boredom, he was surprised to find that the words of Scripture fed his imagination and emotional need. They opened his eyes to God who is with the broken-hearted and found God was present even in afflictions.[5] But whenever he tried to profess or grasp this experience of the presence of God, the experience evaded him. All that was left was an inward drive, a longing which provided the impetus to hope. His inexpressible experiences led Moltmann to become interested in theology. Fortunately he was allowed to study theology in a Protestant theologians' camp, Norton Camp, an educational camp run by the YMCA and supervised by the British army, near Nottingham in England. Since then, the experiences of the life of a prisoner have left a lasting mark on him, mainly the suffering and the hope which reinforce each other. Later Moltmann studied theology systematically and obtained his doctorate from Göttingen University and got married in 1952. Then he became pastor of the *Evangelical Church of Bremen-Wasserhorst*, where he served for five years. There he sought to bring restoration and renewal to a desolate people.[6] Moltmann writes that, "Renewal meant for us the acknowledgment of our guilt and a new hope born of forgiveness. We could withstand the crucifying experiences of life only through faith in the vicarious suffering and death of Christ our brother, and in the freedom conferred by his resurrection. That is what made us so christocentric."[7]

---

4. Jürgen Moltmann, *Experiences in Theology: Ways and Forms of Christian Theology*, trans. Margaret Kohl (London: SCM, 2000), 3-4.
5. Otto, *The God of Hope*, 3.
6. Otto, *The God of Hope*, 3.
7. Jürgen Moltmann, "Foreword" to *Origins of Theology of Hope* by M. Douglas Meeks (Philadelphia: Fortress, 1974), xii.

In 1957 Moltmann moved as a theology professor to the *Kirchliche Hochschule* at Wuppertal, an academy of the *Confessing Church*.[8] There he became a colleague of Wolfhart Pannenberg, who joined as professor of systematic theology in 1958 in the same *Hochschule*. This gave Moltmann new focus in his theological thinking. After working for a couple of years together, Pannenberg left Wuppertal in 1962 for university posts in systematic theology at Mainz and Munich. Moltmann also left the *Hochschule* to take up university posts at Bonn and Tübingen. One thing that runs through the thought of both theologians during their stay at the *Hochschule* was the concept of promise and both continued this thought in their later writings as well. On the one side, Pannenberg exchanged the promise/fulfilment motif in 1961 for the perspective of "the history of the transmission of tradition," citing "the judgment of historical science [that] the biblical 'fulfilments' do not correspond to the promises as perfectly as the dogmatic history of the biblical accounts would have it."[9] On the other side, Moltmann continued to focus on the promise motif as vital to his eschatological interpretation of God and the cross of Christ.[10] Although Moltmann distances with Pannenberg in many ways, he shares with Pannenberg that basic immanentistic, historical premise. In other words, Moltmann attempts "to think of God and history together."[11]

Since his marriage Moltmann has received help from his wife in doing theology. Continual discussion with her opened his eyes to many things which he should probably otherwise have overlooked. It also made him conscious of the psychological and social limitations of his male point of view and judgment.[12] Moltmann writes, "Since I came to know my wife during our study together in Göttingen, I have ceased to feel that I am an

---

8. Moltmann, *Experiences in Theology*, 5.
9. Wolfhart Pannenberg, *Basic Questions in Theology* vol. 1, trans. George H. Kehm (Philadelphia: Westminster, 1983), 79.
10. See Christopher L. Morse, *The Logic of Promise in Moltmann's Theology* (Philadelphia: Fortress, 1979).
11. Hans-Georg Geyer, "Ansichten zu Jürgen Moltmanns 'Theologie der Hoffnung,'" in *Diskussion über die "Theologie der Hoffnung" von Jürgen Moltmann*, ed. Wolf-Dieter Marsch (Munich: Kaiser, 1967), 78.
12. His wife, Elisabeth Moltmann-Wendel, the author of *The Women Around Jesus, A Land Flowing with Milk and Honey*, and *I am My Body*, etc., also has played an active part in feminist theology. See Moltmann, *Experiences in Theology*, 4-5.

'individual.' Our shared life began with a theological dialogue, and our marriage since then has been accompanied by a theological dialogue. This has brought a great depth of friendship to our marriage. ... I want to draw attention to the constant and fundamental conversation from which my theological work derives and without which it cannot be understood."[13]

2.2 The Political Setting

As a teenager, the major ambition of Moltmann was to study mathematics and physics. The heroes of his youth were Einstein, Planck, and Heisenberg.[14] However, Moltmann was drafted, at the end of 1944, into the German army at the age of eighteen to fight in World War II. At that time he took with him Goethe's poems and *Faust* as well as Nietzsche's *Zarathustra* for intellectual nourishment. In early 1945 Moltmann was captured by the British forces in Belgium. For the succeeding three years he was confined to prisoner-of-war camps in Belgium, Scotland, and England.[15] In the Belgium camp he saw how other prisoners collapsed inwardly giving up all *hope*, sickening and dying for the lack of it. About his experience in the war camps Moltmann writes that, "We lost our names and became numbers. We lost our home and our country; we lost our hope and our self consciousness; and we lost our community. What we experienced in those years was *ochlos*, an unorganized, uneducated, imprisoned, and suffering mass of people without a face, without freedom, without history."[16] However, Moltmann survived through the help of the Bible and the kindness of Scottish and English Christians. He writes, "I needed what the Heidelberg Catechism calls 'comfort in life and death,' and through the chance of reading the Bible and the undeserved kindness of Scottish and English Christians, I found that comfort in the Christ who in his passion from the dead awakened me too to a living hope."[17] These experiences made Moltmann a theologian of hope. He writes, "My experiences of death at the

---

13. Jürgen Moltmann, *History and the Triune God: Contributions to Trinitarian Theology*, trans. John Bowden (New York: Crossroad, 1991), 167.
14. Moltmann, *Experiences in Theology*, 4.
15. Otto, *The God of Hope*, 2.
16. Jürgen Moltmann, *The Passion of Life: A Messianic Lifestyle*, trans. M. Douglas Meeks (Philadelphia: Fortress, 1978), 97.
17. Moltmann, *Experiences in Theology*, 4.

end of the war, the depression into which the guilt of my people plunged me, and the inner perils of utter resignation behind barbed wire: these were the places where my theology was born. They were my first *locus theologicus*, and at the deepest depths of my soul they have remained so."[18]

2.3 The Philosophical Setting

Being one of Germany's most prominent leftist intellectuals[19] following from his emphasis on openness and his concern for synthesis, the liberal Reformed theology of Moltmann has taken root in differing types of intellectual soil. The influence on Moltmann's thought according to Otto "can be broken down into four: enlightenment theology, dialectical theology, secular theology, and Marxist revisionism."[20] In this section we focus briefly on the enlightenment theology since it is very important with regard to the theology of Moltmann.

The major figure to be mentioned in the enlightenment theology is first of all Immanuel Kant. His main argument was that mathematics can be *a priori* synthetical knowledge because it does not describe things as they are in themselves but only as they appear to humans. The form of these appearances is determined by the nature of human's sensibility. But the sensuous experiences or institutions of human beings are in space and time and hence everything that humans perceive is known *a priori* to fall under the forms of space and time and obey the laws thereof.[21] Moltmann draws a number of ideas from Kant. He fully acknowledges the destruction of metaphysics which Kant is said to have achieved. Moltmann does speak repeatedly of two distinct realities, that which exists and that which is coming, God dwelling in the latter.[22] Otto holds the view that, "The possibility has also been suggested that Moltmann utilizes the Kantian 'as if' in his

---

18. Moltmann, *Experiences in Theology*, 4.
19. Andrew Buchwalter, Translator's Introduction to *Observations on "the Spiritual Situation of the Age,"* ed. Jürgen Haberms (Cambridge: MIT Press, 1984), xiii.
20. Otto, *The God of Hope*, 13.
21. Otto, *The God of Hope*, 13.
22. Jürgen Moltmann, *Theology of Hope*, trans. James W. Leitch (New York: Harper & Row, 1993), 18.

own doctrine of God. Clearly, Moltmann does build on the foundation of Kantian revolution."[23]

The second major figure to be noted is Hegel. He followed the enlightenment dogma of the autonomy of human reason. He distinguished between the objective religion, ordered and doctrinal, and the subjective religion, which expresses itself only beyond in feelings and actions. For Hegel subjective religion was all that mattered. In his *Phenomenology of Spirit*, he followed strictly secular humanism.[24] Completely opposed to supernaturalism and wholly anti-metaphysical, Hegel reduced all questions of being to questions about the structures of human experience. For Hegel, there was nothing beyond the realm of conscious experience. For him "The phenomenology is a grand treatise in cosmic humanism; humanity is everything, in the guise of Geist, or 'Spirit,' and the purpose of Hegel's philosophy is to get us to appreciate ourselves as a unity, as all-embracing humanity, and bring about the 'self-realization of Spirit.'"[25] There can be no doubt that most prevalent criticism of Moltmann is his affinity with Hegel. Otto argues that, "Regardless of the philosophical dispute as to whether Hegel himself actually utilized the "thesis-antithesis-synthesis" dialectic which has become synonymous with his name, there can be no question that Moltmann understands the Hegelian dialectic in this way and utilizes it heavily in his work."[26]

When one tries to look into the enlightenment theology and the influence on Moltmann, there are other major figures like Ludwig Feuerbach, who is generally considered as the fountainhead of modern atheism and Karl Marx. Feuerbach maintained that, "The secret of theology is nothing else than anthropology."[27] According to Feuerbach, human being's ideas of God have two sources, intellectual and emotional. Intellectually, God is the objectification in an imaginary supernatural being of the higher characteristics within humanity. The objectification which creates God in the image of humanity is not only intellectual, but also emotional. Human

---

23. Otto, *The God of Hope*, 16.
24. Robert C. Solomon, *In the Spirit of Hegel* (Oxford: Oxford University Press, 1983), 5.
25. Solomon, *In the Spirit of Hegel*, 5.
26. Otto, *The God of Hope*, 19.
27. Ludwig Feuerbach, *The Essence of Christianity*, trans. George Eliot (New York: Harper & Row, 1957), 206.

being's earthly experience, filled with pain, frustration, and impending death, is given new hope in the illusion of a God who will conquer earthly evil and grant perfect bliss in the beyond. For Feuerbach, this God is but the externalization of human hopes. God is the nature of human feeling, unlimited, pure feeling, made objective. Moltmann is fully appreciative of the historical intent of Feuerbach's approach.[28] At the same time, Moltmann criticizes Feuerbach on various grounds, mainly for his divinization of human beings saying that Feuerbach's divinization of human beings makes them no longer human, but rather inhuman.[29]

If the beginning of the critique of religion lies with Feuerbach's referring all religions back to mysticism, the reversal of mysticism into revolution becomes the spear point of the Marxist criticism of religion.[30] For Moltmann, religion is put back on its feet when it acknowledges Marx's criticisms. He acknowledges the need in ecclesiology for a critique of ideology which reflects the true setting of churches, sees justification for a theological adoption of Marxist analyses and ideology critique in the ecumenical context.[31] Moltmann thus sees the aims and hope of Marxism and Christianity as one, which is for the real possibilities after which Marxists are striving are also possibilities for the Christians' struggle for freedom.[32] In short, it is a

---

28. Moltmann writes that, "This faith can have nothing to do with feeling the world, with resignation and with escapism.... In the words of Ludwig Feuerbach, it puts 'in place of the beyond that lies above our grave in heaven the beyond that lies above our grave on earth, the historic future, the future of mankind.'" See Moltmann, *Theology of Hope*, 21.
29. Otto, *The God of Hope*, 24.
30. Jürgen Moltmann, *Religion, Revolution, and the Future*, trans. M. Douglas Meeks (New York: Charles Scribner's, 1969), 94.
31. Otto, *The God of Hope*, 28.
32. Moltmann, *Religion, Revolution, and the Future*, 78; Moltmann maintains that Marxism, with its religious criticism of Christianity and with its transformation of the religious energy into its revolutionary counterpart, is entirely in line with the prophets and the Christian Puritans. Christianity understands the enslavement and dehumanization humanity in more than one dimension, seeing his economic, physical, spiritual, and psychological needs as a whole. Liberation thus embraces the various dimensions of suffering. It runs from the economic abolition of the exploitation which results from the rule of particular classes, or the political vanquishing of oppression and dictatorship and the cultural elimination of racialism, down to faith's experience of liberation from the compulsion of sin and the eschatological hope of liberation from the power of death. See Jürgen Moltmann, *The Church in the Power of the Spirit: A Contribution to Messianic Ecclesiology*, trans. Margaret Kohl (London: Harper & Row, 1975), 265, 17.

fact that when one looks into the theology of Moltmann, one can clearly see the impact of the enlightenment philosophies in his theology.

2.4 The Theological Setting

After his return to Germany in 1948, Moltmann began to study theology regularly at Göttingen University. He studied there under teachers who are strongly influenced by Barth and hence Moltmann also imbibed thoroughly the theology of Barth.[33] Therefore, he initially became a disciple of the great master of dialectical theology. Later, however, he saw some need to move beyond the narrow understanding of Barth and "Barmen orthodoxy" — *solus Christus* — when he wanted to give positive answers to the political possibilities and cultural challenges of the post-war period. Thus he became highly critical of Barth's neglect of the historical nature of reality, while remaining indebted to Barth.[34]

Bultmann was another major figure who influenced Moltmann to a great extent. Bultmann was associated with Barth from early on in the attack on the liberal theology of their day. In accord with Bultmann, Moltmann also sees demythologization as necessary for the activation of human hopes.[35] Following Feuerbach and Marx, Moltmann believes Christianity must combine demythologization with sensitivity to the nature of myth. Because Christian faith has not understood myth as an expression of the real misery of humans, demythologization has not arrived at the categorical imperative of transformation of the world in need. Otto writes that, "Moltmann therefore seeks to combine Bultmann's program of demythologization with

---

33. Otto, *The God of Hope*, 3.
34. For example, Moltmann resists Barth's emphasis on God as sovereign subject. He argues that, "In God there is no one-sided relationship of superiority and subordination, command and obedience, master and servant, as Karl Barth maintained in his theological doctrine of sovereignty, making this the starting point for his account of all analogously antithetical relationships: God and the world; heaven and earth; soul and body; and not least, man and woman too." See Jürgen Moltmann, *God in Creation: A New Theology of Creation and the Spirit of God*, trans. Margaret Kohl (London: SCM, 1985), 16-17; not withstanding his striking criticism of Barth, Moltmann stands in complete accord with the assertion of the early Barth that Christianity must be thoroughgoing eschatology. He is also of one accord with Barth in asserting that the triune God can only be known in the person and work of Jesus Christ. See Otto, *The God of Hope*, 35.
35. Jürgen Moltmann, "Hope without Faith: An Eschatological Humanism without God," in *Is God Dead?*, *Concilium* 16, ed. Johannes B. Metz (New York: Paulist, 1966), 31.

Marx's sensitivity for the nature of man's misery as expressed in religious symbols. In doing so Moltmann hopes to go beyond liberated subjectivity in a more practical and concrete application of demythologization."[36]

Through Bonhoeffer's work, Moltmann developed his concern for social ethics and the church's involvement in society. R. H. Fuller has said that Moltmann is one of "The chief representatives of the ecclesiological-christological school of Bonhoeffer interpretation."[37] It is true that when Walter Capps says that Moltmann's theology of Hope is "an elaboration, refinement, and extension of certain motifs either expressed or hinted at in Bonhoeffer's writings."[38]

As noted above, Moltmann began his theological studies in Göttingen and it can be said to be the most important fact in the genesis of the theology of hope because its real progenitors were the three Göttingen professors: Otto Weber (1902-1966), Hans Joachim Iwand (1899-1960), and Ernst Wolf (1902-1071).[39] In addition to that, he was also influenced by Luther and Hegel through Iwand. Luther and Iwand convinced him of the liberating truth of the Reformation doctrine of justification and the theology of the cross. Moreover, Hegel and Iwand helped him to develop his dialectical interpretation of the cross and resurrection. Through Weber, Moltmann's doctoral supervisor, he became immersed in Calvinism and the theology of Karl Barth. His professor Wolf helped Moltmann to understand the significance of social ethics.[40] In addition to that, he gained his solid grounding

---

36. Otto, *The God of Hope*, 39.
37. R. H. Fuller, Translators' Introduction to *Two Studies in the Theology of Bonhoeffer* by Jürgen Moltmann and Jürgen Weissbach (New York: Charles Scribner's, 1967), 15.
38. Walter H. Capps, *Time Invades the Cathedral* (Philadelphia: Fortress, 1972), 50.
39. All of them were leaders in the Confessing Church's struggles against compromises with the National Socialism of the Third Reich. Each insisted that the church convict itself co-guilty for the catastrophes of this century. All of them remained until their deaths critical of the restoration of the old forms and functions of the German churches after 1945. All were convinced that theology responsible to the church would have to become eschatological if it should have any identity over against the power of society. For them the task of theology was not apologetically to explain Christian truth claims to an increasingly secular and technological society, but rather polemically to say something new, both judging and promising, to this society out of the eschatological traditions of Bible and church. See Meeks, *Origins of the Theology of Hope*, 20; for Moltmann's testimony regarding the influence of teachers upon him, see Moltmann, *Experiences in Theology*, 87-92.
40. For more information on the influences on Moltmann, see Moltmann, *Experiences in Theology*, 88-92.

in biblical theology from Gerhard von Rad and Ernst Käsemann. Above all, Otto Weber, who supervised the doctorates of him and his future wife, Elisabeth Wendel, helped him gain the eschatological perspective of the church's universal mission toward the coming kingdom of God.[41]

3. Pneumatology of Jürgen Moltmann

Having briefly surveyed the significant backgrounds of the theological development of Moltmann, the major focus of this section is to make an in-depth treatment of the pneumatology of Moltmann. In this endeavor we are following a systematic thematic study focusing on the major aspects of Moltmann's theology of the Holy Spirit. Moltmann argues that it is important to dive into the study of pneumatology due to the fact that the Spirit's being is not forgotten in the modern times. He writes:

> Between the patristic pneumatology of the Orthodox church on the one hand, and the Pentecostal experience of the young churches on the other, there are also the still unsettled questions of modern European times – the age of "subjectivity" and "experience." Fired by Joachimite expectation, the classic German philosophers, Lessing, Kant, Fichte, and Hegel interpreted "Enlightenment" as the "third age" – that is to say, "the age of the Spirit." So there can be no question of the spirit's "being forgotten'" in the modern times. On the contrary: the rationalism and pietism of the enlightenment was every bit as Enthusiastic as Pentecostal Christianity today.[42]

Taking all these aspects into consideration, the major pneumatological work of Moltmann is *The Spirit of Life: A Universal Affirmation* which outlines the major thrust of his pneumatology. Although this English translation does not capture all the nuances of the original German, *Eine ganzheitliche Pneumatologie*, it suggests a pneumatology which is holistic, all encompassing, and comprehensive. The peculiarity of the pneumatology of Moltmann

---

41. For detailed information on the theological influences, especially by the Göttingen teachers on Moltmann, see Meeks, *Origins of the Theology of Hope*.
42. Moltmann, *The Spirit of Life*, 2.

is that firstly, he highlights the critical role of the Spirit of God in giving birth and sustaining life and secondly, he aims to create a pneumatology that does not exclude any area of life.[43] According to Kärkkäinen,

> What makes Moltmann's pneumatology so appealing and exciting is that in his discussion he takes note of a wide ecumenical array of materials, from the patristic pneumatology of the Orthodox Church to the Pentecostal experience of young churches. He places between these two opposite poles the questions of the contemporary (European) era, for example, questions related to subjectivity and experience. His approach is also ecumenical in that he notices the latest developments in the ecumenical movement, the work in which he has actively participated for many years, as has Pannenberg.[44]

Moltmann's basic argument is that wherever there is passion for life, there the Spirit of God is operating. Hence, his whole focus is to affirm life in the midst of injustice and marginalisation. Moltmann writes that, "So the essential thing is to affirm life – the life of other creatures – the life of other people – our own lives. If we do not, there will be no rebirth and no restoration of the life that is threatened. Anyone who really says "yes" to life says "no" to war. Anyone who really loves life says "no" to poverty. So the people who truly affirm and love life take up the struggle against violence and injustice. They refuse to get used to it. They do not conform. They resist."[45]

3.1 The Divinity of the Holy Spirit

When one begins to look into the pneumatology of Moltmann, one has to really see how Moltmann understands the Holy Spirit. He has no doubt that the Spirit is God himself. Hence he writes:

---

43. Kärkkäinen, *Pneumatology*, 126; Richard Clutterbuck has written a beautiful article saying that Moltmann is a doctrinal theologian. See Richard Clutterbuck, "Jürgen Moltmann as a Doctrinal Theologian: The Nature of Doctrine and the Possibilities for its Development," *Scottish Journal of Theology* vol. 48, no.1 (1995), 489-505.
44. Kärkkäinen, *Pneumatology*, 126.
45. Moltmann, *The Spirit of Life*, xii.

> The gift and the presence of the Holy Spirit is the greatest and most wonderful thing which we can experience – we ourselves, the human community, all living things and this earth. For with the Holy Spirit it is not just one random spirit that is present, among all the many good and evil spirits that there are. It is *God himself*, the creative and life-giving, redeeming and saving God. Where the Holy Spirit is present, God is present in a special way, and we experience God through our lives, which become wholly living from within.[46]

The Spirit of God is called the Holy Spirit because it makes our own life here something living, not because it is alien and estranged from life. The Spirit sets this life in the presence of the living God and in the great river of eternal life.[47]

3.1.1 Spirit – The Divine Energy of Life

Moltmann follows a semantic approach in order to establish that the Spirit of God is the *ruah* of Yahweh in the Old Testament. He maintains that the Greek word *pneuma,* the Latin s*piritus*, and the German *Geist* were always conceived as antithetical to matter and body. They mean something immaterial. When we consider Greek, Latin, German, or English terminologies, by the Spirit of God it means something disembodied, super sensory, and supernatural. Hence, it has been described from earliest times that the activity of the Spirit as a flowing, an outpouring, and a shining with the understanding that the Spirit is the source of life and the origin of the torrent of energy.[48] But the Hebrew word about Yahweh's *ruah* refers to God as a tempest, a cleavage between spirit and body, humanity, and nature.[49] Hence, when the word is applied to God, the tempest becomes a parable for the irresistible force of the creator's power, God's killing wrath, and life-giving mercy (Ezek 13:13; 36:26).[50] Because people saw the livingness of life in the inhaling and exhaling of air, *ruah* was also the breath of life

---

46. Jürgen Moltmann, *The Source of Life: The Holy Spirit and the Theology of Life*, trans. Margaret Kohl (London: SCM, 1997), 10.
47. Moltmann, *The Spirit of Life*, x.
48. Moltmann, *The Source of Life*, 69.
49. Moltmann, *The Spirit of Life*, 40.
50. Moltmann, *The Spirit of* Life, 41.

and the power to enjoy by human beings and animals. By taking cue from this argument, Moltmann insists that if *ruah* is associated with God and God with *ruah*, then Yahweh's *ruah* and Yahweh's *dabar* – his Word – are very close to one another.[51]

Moreover, *ruah* is thought of as the breath of God's voice. Consequently, if this unity of breath and voice is carried over to God's creative activity, then all things are called to life through God's Spirit and his Word.[52] It means that God creates everything through the Word, speaks in the creative energies of the *ruah*. Moltmann writes that, "Remembering the analogy of breath and voice, we might even say that the words of creation specify and define, but that they are spoken in the same breath, so that all creatures come to life through the one same *ruah*; and it is this that constitutes the community of creation. The masculine Word (*dabar*) and the feminine life force (*ruah*) necessarily complement one another."[53]

For Moltmann, *ruah* is not just the voice of God alone rather it is his "divine presence" as well. Hence, if we interpret *ruah* as the confronting event of God's presence, then we have to understand the happenings of God's presence as *ruah* as well. This proves the fact that every efficacious presence of God is determined by the *ruah* and has to be interpreted pneumatologically.[54] However, this theological person-formula for the *ruah* as God's presence is not a sufficient way of naming the power from which everything that has life lives. Hence Moltmann argues that, "The creative power of God is communicated to the beings he has created in such a way that in talking about *ruah* we are talking about the energy of their life too."[55] The *ruah* as Yahweh's *ruah* is of course transcendent in origin. But it is equally true to say that as the power of life in all the living it is immanently efficacious. In other words, the creative power of God is the transcendent side of the *ruah,* and the power to live enjoyed

---

51. Moltmann, *The Spirit of Life*, 41.
52. Moltmann, *The Spirit of Life*, 41.
53. Moltmann, *The Spirit of Life*, 42.
54. Moltmann, *The Spirit of Life*, 42.
55. The *ruah* is certainly present only when and where God wills it to be so. But with his will towards creation it is also present in everything and keeps all things in being and in life. When we think about *ruah* we have to say that God is in all things, and all things are in God – though this does not mean making God the same as everything else. See Moltmann, *The Spirit of Life*, 42.

by everything that is alive is its immanent side.⁵⁶ It is interesting to note that for Moltmann *ruah* is not just the confronting event of the personal presence of God and the life force immanent in all the living. It is related to *rewah* or breadth as well.⁵⁷ It means that *ruah* creates space. Hence, to experience the *ruah* is to experience what is divine not only as a person, and not merely as a force, but also as *space* of freedom in which the living being can unfold.⁵⁸ If God's Spirit is experienced as this broad, open space for living conferred on created beings, then it is easy to understand the spatial designations which declare that people live "*in*" God's spirit, and experiences God spatially as "breadth."⁵⁹

3.1.2 The Cosmic Spirit

Moltmann insists that there has been only a limited pneumatological approach in the past. He writes that, "In both Protestant and Catholic theology and devotion, there is a tendency to view the Holy Spirit solely as the Spirit of redemption. Its place is the church and it gives men and women the assurance of the eternal blessedness of their souls. This redemptive Spirit is cut off both from bodily life and from the life of nature."⁶⁰ Consequently, people turn away from "this world" and hope for a better world beyond. They then seek and experience in the Spirit a power that is different from the divine energy of life, which according to the Old Testament ideas interpenetrates all the living. Moltmann continues that, "The theological textbooks therefore talk about the Holy Spirit in connection with God, faith, the Christian life, the church and prayer, but seldom in connection with the body and nature."⁶¹ The result has been tragic. This limited view of the Spirit has impoverished and emptied the churches while the "Spirit emigrates to spontaneous groups and personal experiences."⁶²

Moltmann believes that the main reason for this neglect of the role of the Spirit in the world and creation has been the *filioque*. Theology has

---

56. Moltmann, *The Spirit of Life*, 42.
57. Moltmann, *The Spirit of Life*, 43.
58. Moltmann, *The Spirit of Life*, 43; Moltmann, *The Source of Life*, 71.
59. Moltmann, *The Spirit of Life*, 43.
60. Moltmann, *The Spirit of Life*, 8.
61. Moltmann, *The Spirit of Life*, 8.
62. Moltmann, *The Spirit of Life*, 2.

spoken of the Spirit of Christ and of redemption rather than of the Spirit of the Father, the creator. Consequently, Christ's Spirit and Yahweh's *ruah* have had nothing to do with each other. Thus, the continuity between the work of the Spirit in creation and in the new creation has been severed.[63] Hence, Moltmann welcomes new approaches to the study of the Spirit, such as ecological theology, cosmic Christology, the rediscovery of the body in theology, and so on. These approaches begin with the Hebrew understanding of the Spirit as the Spirit of creation.[64] It emphasizes that God's *ruah* is the life force immanent in all the living, in body, sexuality, ecology, and politics. Moltmann writes:

> The dynamic of the life process is always greater than the diversity of the forms of life and the living relationships which the process creates. Life is fathomless, and is more than any individual expression of life. It is these creative living energies which we call *the divine Spirit*, because it transcends all the beings it creates.[65] We call *the cosmic Spirit*, because it is the life in everything that lives. Because God is the Creator, his creative Spirit is the dynamic of the universe and the power that creates community in the widening, differentiating network of the living.[66]

Thus Moltmann radically expands the traditional notion of the "communion of the Holy Spirit" to encompass the whole "community of creation," from the most elementary particles to atoms to molecules to cells to living organisms to animals to human beings to communities of humanity. In this "fellowship as process," all human communities are embedded in the

---

63. Moltmann, *The Spirit of Life*, 8-9.
64. Moltmann writes that, "So experience of the life-giving Spirit in the faith of the heart and in the sociality of love leads to itself beyond the limits of the church to the rediscovery of the same Spirit in nature, in plants, in animals, and in the ecosystems of the earth." See Moltmann, *The Spirit of Life*, 9-10.
65. Moltmann, *The Spirit of Life*, 227.
66. Moltmann, *The Spirit of Life*, 227; Moltmann qualifies his statement by arguing that Chinese call this cosmic Spirit *chi*, Greek *eros*, Hebrew *ruah*. But for all that, we must not say that "though God is not the creator, he is no doubt the Spirit of the Universe." It would be rather true to say that because God is the creator, his creative Spirit is the dynamic of the universe and the power that creates community in the widening, differentiating network of the living. See Moltmann, *The Spirit of Life*, 227.

ecosystems of the natural communities and live based on the exchange of energy with them.[67] In short, Moltmann believes that God's Spirit is identical with the cosmic spirit. If the cosmic Spirit is the Spirit of God, then the universe cannot be viewed as a closed system. It has to be understood as a system that is open for God and for his future.[68] This realisation leads Moltmann to argue that the Spirit's suffering is identical with the world's suffering as well. He writes that, "The Spirit is ... God himself. If God commits himself to his limited creation, and if he himself dwells in it as 'the giver of life,' this presupposes a self-limitation, a self-humiliation and a self-surrender of the Spirit. The history of suffering creation, which is subject to transience, then brings with it a history of suffering by the Spirit who dwells in creation."[69]

3.1.3 Procession of the Spirit

When one tries to understand the divinity of the Spirit according to Moltmann, it is important to see how he deals with the procession of the Spirit as well. Moltmann insists that the Spirit proceeds both from the Father and the Son.[70] He tries to make his point clear by stating that the Son originated from the Father through the Spirit.[71] The Spirit's accompaniment of the eternal begetting of the Son by the Father is also called the "manifestation" of the Spirit through the Son.[72] That means the Spirit is present in the Son in all eternity. The hypostatic persons of the Spirit and the Son remain so united with one another that they exist indivisibly in one another in eternity and hence, the Son is inconceivable without the Spirit and the Spirit is inconceivable without the Son.[73]

Moreover, the Spirit who proceeds simultaneously from the Father with the birth of the Son, rests in the Son.[74] The Son is the recipient of the Spirit and his eternal resting place. The Son is born from the Father as the

---

67. Moltmann, *The Spirit of Life*, 225-226.
68. Jürgen Moltmann, *God in Creation: An Ecological Doctrine of Creation*, trans. Margaret Kohl (London: SCM, 2005), 103.
69. Moltmann, *God in Creation*, 102.
70. Moltmann, *The Church in the Power of the Spirit*, 53ff.
71. Moltmann, *The Source of Life*, 17.
72. Moltmann, *The Spirit of Life*, 307.
73. Moltmann, *The Spirit of Life*, 307.
74. Moltmann, *The Source of Life*, 17.

dwelling place for the Spirit, and the Spirit proceeds from the Father in order to dwell eternally in the Son.[75] The Spirit, who rests in the Son and indwells him, shines from the Son and through the Son. He sheds his eternal light from the Son to the mutual relations between the Father and the Son, bringing into God's eternal love God's eternal light. This eternal light brings eternal joy into God's being and his love. This is the transfiguration within the Trinity itself which proceeds from the Spirit. Moltmann argues that the Spirit also shines through the Son on whom he rests making the human beings "children of light" (Eph 5: 8ff).[76]

3.1.4 Objections to the Filioque

Moltmann rejects the traditional Western doctrine of *filioque,* which arose as a dispute over the statement that "I *will send* the Advocate or Spirit of Truth to you *from* the Father" (Jn 15:26). The West traditionally refuses to acknowledge that this verse supports the procession of the Spirit from the Father solely and favors a view of dual procession from the Father *and the Son.* As Barth emphasized, the belief does not confer the idea that the Spirit has two origins but, rather, the relationship of the Father and Son is the direct origin of the Holy Spirit.[77] Moltmann asserts that the defense of *filioque* "led to a one-sided trinitarian doctrine in the West, and hindered the development of a trinitarian pneumatology."[78] For Moltmann, this doctrine is at best superfluous and is at worst pernicious.[79]

---

75. Moltmann, *The Spirit of Life*, 307.
76. Moltmann, *The Spirit of Life*, 308; according to Moltmann, it is logical that the monarchical concept of the Trinity should lead to the introduction of the *filioque* into the Nicene Creed. For him, the Spirit proceeds "from the Father and the Son," since in salvation history, he is sent by the Father and the Son, and is experienced in this way by human beings. Moreover, his eternal procession in the "'immanent" Trinity as transcendent primordial ground must correspond to his *mission* in the economic Trinity as this is experienced. See Moltmann, *The Spirit of Life*, 293.
77. Barth, *CD* 1/1, 486.
78. Jürgen Moltmann, *The Trinity and the Kingdom,* trans. Margaret Kohl (London: SCM, 1981), 179.
79. Moltmann, *The Spirit of Life*, 306; here Moltmann breaks from Karl Barth who defended the doctrine vigorously – apparently to secure the sole revelatory role of Jesus Christ – because he objects to explaining the Spirit through a Christological filter, as can be a tendency of Barth. See Warren McWilliams, "Why All the Fuss about Filioque? Karl Barth and Jürgen Moltmann on the Procession of the Spirit," *Perspectives in Religious Studies* 22 (Summer 1995), 176. See a discussion in Moltmann, *The Trinity and the Kingdom,* 168-170.

Although Moltmann insists that the procession of the Spirit is both from the Father and the Son,[80] he never appreciates the addition of the *filioque* into the Nicene Creed. According to Moltmann, with the *filioque*, the Holy Spirit is once and for all put in third place in the Trinity, and subordinated to the Son.[81] As a result, the relationship of the Son and the Spirit can no longer be understood as a reciprocal relationship. The way always leads from the Son to the Spirit, no longer from the Spirit to the Son.[82] This makes it impossible to comprehend the salvation history adequately. It is true that this order applies to the sending of the Spirit through Christ on the foundation of the resurrection, but it does not apply to Christ's own history in the Spirit. If Christ was conceived by the Spirit, baptized with the Spirit, and ministered by virtue of the energies given him by the Spirit, then he presupposes the Spirit, and the Spirit precedes him. That is the truth of the synoptic Spirit Christology which in the course of history was driven out by the Christological pneumatology of Paul and John.[83]

Secondly, according to Moltmann, the addition to the Nicene Creed which maintains that the Holy Spirit proceeded from the Father and from the Son is *superfluous* and it contributes nothing new to the statement about the procession of the Spirit from the Father.[84] Moreover, the fatherhood of the Father cannot be thought without the sonship of the Son. If the Spirit proceeds from the fatherhood of the Father, then the Son is not uninvolved. His sonship participates indirectly in the direct procession of the Spirit from the Father.[85]

---

80. See a beautiful discussion in Moltmann, *The Trinity and the Kingdom*, 182-185.
81. Moltmann, *The Spirit of Life*, 293.
82. Moltmann, *The Spirit of Life*, 307.
83. Moltmann, *The Spirit of Life*, 293.
84. Moltmann insists that if the Spirit is said to proceed from the Father, this also says that it proceeds from the Father of the Son, for it is only in relation to the Son that the first Person of the Trinity has to be called "Father." That means if the Spirit proceeds from "the Father of the Son," then it has its origin in the Father's relation to the Son. It proceeds not only from the Father, but also from its fatherhood. See Moltmann, *The Spirit of Life*, 306.
85. Moltmann, *The Spirit of Life*, 306; the procession of the Spirit consequently presupposes the existence of the Father and the Son, as well as the reciprocal relationship of the Father and the Son: As soon as God is called Father, he is thought of as having a Son. Even though the primordial relations have to be distinguished from the *perichoretic* relations in the life of the Trinity, the Spirit's hypostatic existence is nevertheless given its imprint by the Father and by the Son: From the Father, as origin of the Godhead, the Spirit receives its hypostatic divinity, from the Son and from the Father and from

Thirdly, the Spirit accompanies the Son, rests in the Son, and shines from the Son. This corresponds better to the Spirit-history of Christ and the Christ-history of the Spirit about which the New Testament talks than the one-sided definition which pins the Spirit down to his procession from the Father and the Son because it corresponds only to the *kairos* after Christ's resurrection and since Pentecost. In fact it does not even correspond to this *kairos* properly, since there, too, the Son makes the Spirit accessible to us, and the Spirit procures our access to the Son. So the reciprocal relationship between the Son and Spirit is the only remaining conclusion. This is the most important theological objection to the *filioque*.[86]

Fourthly, clericalism is the non-theological factor which led to the insertion of the *filioque* and to the confining definition of the Spirit through the Son. If God is represented by Christ, Christ by the Pope, and the Pope by the bishops and priests, then by way of the *filioque* in the primordial relationships, the Spirit with all its charismata and energies in salvation history is tied down to the operative acts of the priesthood. The Spirit is then nothing other than the operation of "the spiritual pastors," their ministerial grace, their proclamation, pastoral cares, and administration of the sacraments. The congregation turns into the passive recipient of the gifts of the Spirit mediated through the church.[87]

Finally, Moltmann asserts that there is a tendency to view the Spirit solely as the Spirit of redemption which he never appreciates. This happens due to the far reaching decision in favour of the *filioque*. It means the Holy Spirit is understood solely as "the Spirit of Christ" and not at the same time as "the Spirit of the Father." As the Spirit of Christ, it is the redemptive Spirit. But the work of creation too is ascribed to the Father, so *the Spirit of the Father* is also *the Spirit of creation*. If redemption is placed in radical discontinuity to creation, then "the Spirit of Christ" has no longer anything to do with Yahweh's *ruah*. According to this notion, the soul is saved from this world and carried up into the heaven of the blessed spirits.[88] Moltmann

---

their reciprocal relationships it receives its inner-trinitarian configuration of gestalt. See Moltmann, *The Spirit of Life*, 306; Moltmann, *Experiences in Theology*, 307ff.
86. Moltmann, *The Spirit of Life*, 308.
87. Moltmann, *The Spirit of Life*, 294.
88. Moltmann, *The Spirit of Life*, 8.

maintains that this is not a Christian doctrine rather, it is Gnostic. It was in order to controvert them that the ancient church introduced *the resurrection of the body* into the third article of the Apostles' Creed.[89]

3.1.5 Objections to the Usage of "Hypostasis" and "Person"

Moltmann deliberately avoids the usage of terms like *hypostasis* and *person* to designate the Holy Spirit because he does not wish to blur the differences between the personhood of the Father, Son, and the Spirit by using a term for the person common to them all.[90] He insists that the Spirit has a wholly unique personhood, not only in the form in which it is experienced, but also in its relationship to the Father and the Son.[91] Moltmann writes:

> ... the Spirit is not an energy proceeding from the Father or from the Son; it is a subject from whose activity the Son and the Father receive their glory and their union, as well as their glorification through the whole creation, and their world as their eternal home. If the Holy Spirit means *the subject* who glorifies the Father and the Son, and unites the Father and the Son, then the "exegetical question" should be capable of solution as well; for in this respect Paul too in act understands the Holy Spirit as the centre of the act, which is to say as "person."[92]

Recognising the fact that the personhood of the Spirit was an unsolved problem from the very beginning, the problem is as difficult as it is fascinating. On account of the *experience* of the Spirit, it was symbolized mostly

---

89. Moltmann, *The Spirit of Life*, 9.
90. Moltmann, *The Spirit of Life*, 12.
91. Moltmann, *The Spirit of Life*, 12; Moltmann argues that after Barth, Karl Rahner too had departed from the concept of person in the doctrine of the Trinity, on the ground that in modern times this term has become open to misunderstanding. He talked instead about one God in these distinct modes of subsistence. But Barth and Rahner misunderstood the modern concept of person because they interpreted it individualistically. The modern philosophical personalism, defines person as primal distance and relationship. To be a person means "being-in-relationship." He talkedH These thinkers did not see even "subjectivity" in isolation, but view it in the social network of "inter-subjectivity." See Moltmann, *The Spirit of Life*, 13-14.
92. Moltmann, *The Trinity and the Kingdom*, 126.

with non-personal words and phrases like the Spirit is divine energy, wind and fire, light and wide space, inward assurance and mutual love.[93] In other words, because of what the Spirit effects, its nature was often described through analogies drawn from experiences. However, a direct address to the Spirit has to take place with such paraphrases because the addresses to the Spirit in prayer are rare compared to the addressing of God the Father and to Christ Jesus. Prayers to the Holy Spirit are always *epikleses* – pleas for the coming of the Spirit: *veni Creator Spiritus*. They seldom include thanksgiving or cries for help.[94]

Moltmann argues that theological assertions about the personhood of the Spirit were made in the patristic church in the dispute with the Pneumatochi.[95] However, Tertullian's famous Trinitarian formula, *una substantia – tres personae*, asserts the divine personhood of the Spirit, and puts it on the same level as the personhood of the Father and the Son. It secures for the Spirit the same worship and glorification as given to the Father and the Son. This is stated in the third article of the creed.[96] This divine personhood of the Spirit is only asserted and not demonstrated. But for all that, to assert the personhood of the Spirit in the theology of the Trinity leads in a different direction from statements based on the experiences of the Spirit. What the Spirit *effects* allows its subjectivity to be discerned (as the effector of a work), but not its personhood. Moltmann writes that, "Its personhood becomes comprehensible only from that which the Spirit *is*, in relation to the Father and the Son. For personhood is always being-in-relationship. But the relationships which constitute the personhood of the Spirit's must be looked for within the Trinity itself, not in the Spirit's outward efficacies."[97]

3.2 The Personhood of the Holy Spirit

As it is a fact, Moltmann also agrees that a precise discernment of the personhood of the Spirit is a difficult problem in pneumatology particular

---

93. Moltmann, *The Spirit of Life*, 10.
94. Moltmann, *The Spirit of Life*, 10.
95. These people interpreted the general Christian subordinationalism to mean that the Spirit is subordinated to the Son as the Son is subordinated to the Father.
96. Moltmann, *The Spirit of Life*, 11.
97. Moltmann, *The Spirit of Life*, 11.

and in the doctrine of the Trinity generally.[98] Since the personhood of the Spirit is asserted rather than proved and the concept of person derived from God the Father is simply transferred to the Spirit, Moltmann insists that, "Simply to transfer like this a concept of person acquired elsewhere, obscures rather than makes apprehensible the special personhood of the Spirit. Consequently, we have to reject any generalizing talk about the 'three Persons' of the Trinity."[99] Although Moltmann follows the lead of Barth, the major difference is that Moltmann starts with three different persons rather than with the substantialist unity of God.[100] He maintains that the Spirit is different from the Father and the Son and the Son and the Spirit exist from the Father. However, in its later development of trinitarian doctrine, Christian theology has replaced the interpretation of "person" in terms of substance by a relational and *perichoretic* understanding, and has, in the anthropological correspondence too, prepared the way for a self rich in relation and sociality.[101] However, even this development has not yet arrived at the unique personhood of the Spirit rather it has merely socialized the Spirit relationally as "the third in the bond." It means that the emphasis is given not to the divine persons in themselves but on their relationality and their unique community.[102] Then how one can understand the personhood of the Spirit without a previous concept of the person? Moltmann takes two angles here. Firstly he draws the metaphors with which experiences of the Spirit have been described and secondly, the relations of the Spirit in its origin and in the consummated Trinity. Here Moltmann is trying to start

---

98. Moltmann gives the reason for his position as follows. If we take the experience of faith as our starting point, then even in the New Testament it is already an open question whether God's Spirit was thought of as a person or a force. If we make the doctrine of the Trinity as the starting point, then the personhood of the Spirit is asserted rather than proved. It is because the concept of person is derived from God the Father which is simply transferred to the Spirit, or in other words, for doxological reasons, the Spirit – as in the Nicaeno-Constantinopolitan Creed declares – together with the Father and the Son is worshipped and glorified. See Moltmann, *The Spirit of Life*, 268.
99. Moltmann, *The Spirit of Life*, 268; see also Jürgen Moltmann, "The Fellowship of the Holy Spirit: Trinitarian Pneumatology," *Scottish Journal of Theology* vol. 37 (1984), 287-300; Jürgen Moltmann, "The Trinitarian History of God," *Theology* vol. 78 (1975), 632-646.
100. Ted Peters, *God as Trinity: Relationality and Temporality in Divine Life* (Louisville: Westminster, 1993), 103.
101. Moltmann, *The Spirit of Life*, 269.
102. Moltmann, *The Spirit of Life*, 269.

from what the Spirit *effects*, and try to combine this with that which the Holy Spirit *is*, in its constitutive relations to the Father and the Son.[103]

3.2.1 Holy Spirit Is Lord, Mother, and Judge

Moltmann uses three personal metaphors to introduce the person of the Holy Spirit. The first among them is the metaphor of *Lord*. According to the third article of the Creed, the Spirit is the Lord and giver of life. Behind the name "Lord" is the idea of freedom which we find in 2 Corinthians 3:17. "The Lord is the Spirit; but where the Spirit of the Lord is, there is freedom." Paul means the Spirit of the resurrection, which takes possession of believers here and now, freeing them from the compulsion of sin and power of death because it now already mediates to them eternal and imperishable life.[104] Moreover, he insists that if "Lord" is the name for the experience of liberation and for free life, this name should be complemented by the name of the one who gives and quickens life.[105] The second personal metaphor that Moltmann uses is mother. Moltmann argues after Paul that it is the raised Christ who has become the "life-giving" Spirit (1 Cor 15:45). For John, it is the *Paraclete*, who comforts as a mother comforts and from whom believes are "born anew" (Jn 3:3-6).[106] Human life is born, nurtured, and accompanied by the life of the mother. So it is useful to use feminine metaphors for corresponding experience of the Spirit. Freedom and life are the two key facts in experience of the divine Spirit. Freedom without new life is empty. Life without freedom is dead. The third personal metaphor that Moltmann uses is judge. He argues that living freedom and free life can endure only in justice and righteousness. In justice, human freedom ministers to life – the life shared by all living beings. In justice, human life struggles for the freedom of everything that lives, and resists oppression.[107] The experience of liberation and rebirth through the Spirit are joined by an inward necessity to the experience of the righteousness and justice of God

---

103. Moltmann, *The Spirit of Life*, 269.
104. Moltmann, *The Spirit of Life*, 270.
105. Moltmann, *The Spirit of Life*, 271.
106. Moltmann maintains that the femininity or motherliness of the Spirit has impact upon the community of men and women by making them a community of sisters and brothers, of free and equal people. See Moltmann, *The Source of Life*, 27.
107. Moltmann, *The Spirit of Life*, 271.

which itself creates justice, justifies, and rectifies. The Spirit of whom we are told convicts the world of its sins (Jn 16:8), does not come to condemn but to save (Jn 3:17). That is why to convict of sin becomes at the same time the conviction of sin's forgiveness.[108]

In short, these three experiences – the experiences of "being set free," of "coming alive," and of being made "just" – belong together and complement one another making up the fullness of life in the experience of God. Moreover these three names given to the source of these experiences also belong together and complement one another. Moreover, it is striking that these metaphors should trace back experience of the operation of the divine Spirit to determining subjects who are thought of in personal terms. It is true that "Lord," "mother," and "judge" are functions, not personal names, but in each of them a transcendent subject is named for the efficacies which are immanently experienced.[109]

3.2.2 Holy Spirit Is Energy, Space, and Gestalt

After delineating the personal metaphors of the Spirit, Moltmann focuses on the formative metaphors. For him there are three formative metaphors namely, energy, space, and *gestalt* and they describe forces which impose a profound impress. The first formative metaphor is Spirit as energy. As we noted earlier, the experience of the Spirit as energy goes back to the Hebrew *ruah* concept. This energy of the Spirit releases those who are touched by it from this earth and their own earthly bodies and works as protean to living things. The second formative metaphor is Spirit as space. Moltmann maintains that every life needs its corresponding *living space*. That is why the creation story already tells that spaces for living were prepared before the living things were created and put into them.[110] Moltmann tries to explain this "space" as liberty as well. Hence he writes that, "Between people it is essential to concede personal liberty.... In the warp and weft of social

---

108. Moltmann, *The Spirit of Life*, 272.
109. Moltmann, *The Spirit of Life*, 272-273.
110. Moltmann, *The Spirit of Life*, 276; for Moltmann, the Spirit of eternal life is first of all a further space for living in which life that has been cut short, or was impaired and destroyed will be able to develop freely. Even in this life before death, we experience the Spirit of life as the wide space in which there is no more cramping. See Jürgen Moltmann, *The Coming of God: Christian Eschatology*, trans. Margaret Kohl (London: SCM, 2005), 118.

relationships we find the freedom to move freely, and in these free spaces we discover our potentiality for development. The free spaces sustain our freedom, and invite us to our full unfolding."[111] The third metaphor that Moltmann uses is Spirit is *gestalt*. Out of the energies of life and in the free space of life, the multifarious *configurations of life* come into being. In the human sphere, the individual *Gestalt* is made possible and given its impress by inner genetic conditions and by the frame of reference imposed by ecology and cultural history. In the personal sphere, the important thing is always the way in which we mediate between our expectations of life and our experiences of life.[112] Moltmann insisted that the discipleship of Christ is a practical, personal way of living and we are "formed" by God's Spirit – that means, we are made like in form to Christ, the first born of God's children (Rom 8:29). In his Spirit we already participate here and now in his resurrection, "as dying, and behold we live" (2 Cor 6:9), and expect one day to be made "like in form to his glorious body" (2 Cor 6:9; Phil 3:21).[113]

In short, experience of the Spirit is experience of the divine life which makes our human life something truly living. That is why the Spirit as vital energy, as living space, and as the *gestalt* of every community for living belongs together. No one of them is enough by itself, but taken together they tell us something about the mystery of life – created life, life-giving life, and holy life.[114]

3.2.3 Holy Spirit Is Tempest, Fire, and Love

After discussing the formative metaphors of the Spirit, Moltmann discusses the movement metaphors of the Holy Spirit. He outlines three movement metaphors, namely tempest, fire, and love. Moltmann relates the movement metaphors of tempest and fire to the experience of life-affirming, life-giving love of God – that is, to the presence of the Holy Spirit.[115] Relating this metaphor with the *ruah* of Yahweh, Moltmann argues that, "The divine is the living compared with the dead, and what is moving compared with

---

111. Moltmann, *The Spirit of Life*, 276.
112. Moltmann, *The Spirit of Life*, 277.
113. Moltmann, *The Spirit of Life*, 278.
114. Moltmann, *The Spirit of Life*, 278.
115. Moltmann, *The Spirit of Life*, 279.

the things that are petrified and rigid. God's Spirit is the breath of God's life, which gives life to human beings and animals."[116] Referring to the Old Testament occurrences where the water and fire images are used, Moltmann maintains that the Spirit can be experienced as a tempest (Ps 104:4; Ezek 43:2; 1 Kgs 19:11ff.; Ex 3:2; Num 9:15).[117] According to the Pentecost experience, the "flaming fire" of the Spirit makes those it touches luminous in the presence of God. In Luke 12:49 it is written that Jesus came to cast fire upon the earth, which points to the fact that the dawn of the kingdom of God is at hand through the outpouring of the Spirit on all flesh. This is what John the Baptist is talking about that "He will baptize you with the Holy Spirit and with fire" (Mt 3:11; Lk 3:16, following Mal 3:2-3). It is the fire of purification in which everything is reforged, which is an image of the new creation of the world.[118] The third movement metaphor is that the Spirit is love. Moltmann insists that, "The images of the tempest and the raging fire are also images for the experience of the *eternal love* which creates life and energizes it from within, so that life can live."[119] If human love can become an experience of God, then the experience of God can be described as the experience of the divine love. The Pentecostal hymns beseech the Holy Spirit to "kindle a flame of sacred love" in us.[120] This shows how close the fire metaphor is to love and to the Holy Spirit.

3.2.4 Holy Spirit Is Light, Water, and Fertility

The final metaphors of the Spirit that Moltmann uses are the mystical metaphors namely "flowing light," "living water," and "fertility." He calls these descriptions as *mystical metaphors* because they are concepts charged by mystical experience, and they express so intimate union between the divine Spirit and human soul and between the human spirit and divine, a unity which cannot be distinguished between the two. For Moltmann, they complement one another in a meaningful way.[121] The first mystical metaphor is Spirit as light. It is this shining radiance of God's glory which

---

116. Moltmann, *The Spirit of Life*, 279.
117. Moltmann, *The Spirit of Life*, 279; Moltmann, *The Source of Life*, 12.
118. Moltmann, *The Spirit of Life*, 280.
119. Moltmann, *The Spirit of Life*, 280.
120. Moltmann, *The Spirit of Life*, 280.
121. Moltmann, *The Spirit of Life*, 281.

is said to have shone on the face of Christ (2 Cor 4:6; Jn 1:9; 8:12).[122] It is this same radiance that is attributed to the Spirit, who illuminates believers. Moreover, this divine light illuminates the whole of creation, so that the human beings perceive what things are and who they are.[123] Moreover, Moltmann insists that the divine light is also the stream of energy which we cannot see but sense, and which floods through us, transposing our life into vibrations and resonance. The divine light of the Spirit is not merely the cold light of rational knowledge. It is also the warm light of loving perception. The divine love draws the deity out of itself, so that the energies of the divine life brim over from the Godhead on to created beings, to transfigure them and make them eternally alive.[124] The second mystical metaphor is Spirit as water. The water metaphor is generally associated with the images of source, fountain, and well. What is meant is the water which comes out of the earth. Whereas the light metaphor describes the operation of the Spirit "from above," the metaphor of the source, spring, fountain, or well sees it as coming "from below."[125] The union of light and water is a necessity of life. Moltmann further finds the bond between the water and Spirit in baptism. People are born again "from water and Spirit" so that they may see the kingdom of God (Jn 3:5).[126] Recognising the link between light and water, Moltmann maintains that, "So it is just as appropriate to experience the operation of the divine Spirit as a 'flowing' or a 'flooding' light as it is to talk about the 'outpouring' of the Spirit on all flesh."[127] The third mystical metaphor is Spirit as fertility. The image of *fertility* emerges with inner logic from the link between the light and the water metaphors. Moltmann takes a link from the Old Testament to show that this image comes from the Old Testament. However, he refers to John 15 where Christ has been compared with the vine and believers with the grapes. Moltmann maintains that when the Spirit of flowing light and living water is experienced, the eschatological spring time of the new creation of all things begins, and the rebirth of the whole life. So the experience of the Spirit is the experience of a new vitality

---

122. Moltmann, *The Spirit of Life*, 281.
123. Moltmann, *The Spirit of Life*, 282.
124. Moltmann, *The Spirit of Life*, 282.
125. Moltmann, *The Spirit of Life*, 283.
126. Moltmann, *The Spirit of Life*, 283.
127. Moltmann, *The Spirit of Life*, 284.

which finds its truth in community with the living God. In the experience of the Spirit, men and women sense the creative breath of God and wake up, like nature in the spring.[128]

In short, in the mystical metaphors, the distance between a transcendent subject and its immanent work is ended. Moreover, the distinctions between causes and effects disappear. In the metaphors of light, water, and fertility, the divine and human are joined in an organic cohesion. Consequently, the divine becomes the all-embracing presence in which the human can fruitfully unfold. For Moltmann, this implies a closer relationship than suggested by the concept of emanation.

3.3 The Shape of the Spirit's Personhood

After expressing the operation and human experience of the Spirit through these metaphors, Moltmann tries to deduce the shape of the personhood of the Spirit. He admits the fact that this is only a deductive knowledge derived from the operation experienced and not a direct knowing face to face. Moreover, it is not a speculative intrusion into the depths of the Trinity in an attempt to understand the primordial relationships of the Spirit who proceeds from the Father and radiates from the Son.[129] Moltmann writes:

> In the primordial Trinitarian relationships, the Spirit must appear simply as he is. There, it is of course true that only the Father knows the Spirit whom he breathes out, and only the Son knows the Spirit whom we receive. But in the efficacies experienced and in the energies perceived, this primordial personhood of the Spirit is concealed from us, and we paraphrase the mystery of his life with many metaphors.[130]

However, the operation of the Spirit is different from the acts in creation which we ascribe to the Father, and different from the reconciling sufferings which we ascribe to the Son. From this difference in kind of its efficacy and energies, the unique character of its personhood is revealed. Hence Moltmann writes:

---

128. Moltmann, *The Spirit of Life*, 285.
129. Moltmann, *The Spirit of Life*, 285.
130. Moltmann, *The Spirit of Life*, 285.

If all God's activity in the world is pneumatic, and hence every human experience of God too (since according to the ancient "trinitarian order" the Father always acts through the Son/Logos in the Spirit, and the Son too acts in the name of the Father through the Spirit who rests on him), then in the operation of Spirit we experience the operation of God himself, and all the metaphors used for the Holy Spirit are metaphors for God in his coming to us, and in his presence with us. An understanding of the unique personhood of the Spirit is therefore decisive for the understanding of God in general.[131]

3.3.1 Spirit Is God's Presence and Counterpart

The prominent theme of the Spirit's personhood is that the Spirit can appear as either presence or counterpart. Moltmann writes that, "The Spirit is in us and round about us, and we are in him. In the Spirit, God is for us pure presence. In order to perceive him as "object," we have to distance ourselves from his presence …. Apparently the Spirit allows himself to be known as presence *and* counterpart, so that it is *only* in his presence that we can perceive him as counterpart at all."[132] That means some aspects of the Spirit's operations entail an experience of the Spirit appearing as close to us as we are to ourselves. Thus Moltmann tries to understand the personhood of the divine Spirit in the flow between his presence and his counterpart, his energies and his essential nature. Moreover, it is not uncommon for people to experience the Spirit as a counterpart who leads, challenges, encourages, and comforts them. Hence Moltmann argues that the personhood of the Spirit takes on further distinctive contours in the interplay between the Spirit's operations as presence and as counterpart.[133]

When Moltmann argues the Spirit as both presence and counterpart, one needs to understand that it is only in its presence one can perceive it as counterpart.[134] Which means, perceiving the Spirit as counterpart assumes as a necessary condition that the Spirit is already there as presence.

---

131. Moltmann, *The Spirit of Life*, 285-286.
132. Moltmann, *The Spirit of Life*, 287.
133. Moltmann, *The Spirit of Life*, 288.
134. Moltmann, *The Spirit of Life*, 287.

When Christians pray to the Spirit, they are already praying in the Spirit.[135] Moltmann concludes his discussion of the personhood of the Spirit as it is experienced by human beings in its efficacies. Firstly, it is not indivisible rather self-communicating. Secondly, it is not a "self-existence" (*substantia*), cut off from all relationships rather it is a social being, rich in relation and capable of relation. Finally, it does not manifest rational nature alone rather it is also the disclosure of the eternal divine life, as wellspring of the life of all created being. In short, for Moltmann, "The personhood of God the Holy Spirit is the loving, self-communicating, out-fanning and outpouring presence of the eternal divine life of the triune God."[136]

3.3.2 Experience of the Spirit

Since Moltmann tries to develop the personhood of the Spirit through the experience of the Spirit, it is significant to understand how Moltmann deals with this significant theological theme. There is no doubt that Moltmann has a number of reasons for constructing a pneumatology of experience.[137] Moltmann insists that, "If we proceed from the experiences of the Spirit, then we must not start with a hard and fast definition of experience, but must keep the concept open for the transcendent origin of experiences."[138] People call what they "experience" about God "the power of God" or "the Spirit of God." By making the power or the Spirit of God a substantive, more is evidently meant than merely a divine attribute. This is a reality in which God himself is present according to his will. So "Yahweh's *ruah*" is described as a "confronting event of the efficacious presence of God."[139] For Moltmann, it is a *mode of his presence* in his creation and in human history. However, Moltmann is not happy to term this "God in action," because by that way we are setting bounds to the perception of the Spirit.[140] Moreover, the mode of God's presence in human history comprehends not merely God in action but God in passion too. This touches both God's suffering

---

135. Beck, *The Holy Spirit*, 197.
136. Moltmann, *The Spirit of Life*, 289.
137. Beck deals extensively about why Moltmann wanted to develop a pneumatology of experience. See for a beautiful discussion, Beck, *The Holy Spirit*, 182-186.
138. Moltmann, *The Spirit of Life*, 11.
139. Moltmann, *The Spirit of Life*, 11.
140. Moltmann, *The Spirit of Life*, 11.

with his people, in whom he desires to be present, and also the "descent of the Spirit."[141] Thus for Moltmann, "When experiences of the Spirit leads us to talk about 'the power' of God, about wind, fire and light, or a wide space, we are talking about the *kenotic forms* of the Spirit, forms of his self-emptying. They are not objectifications of the Spirit, but as *kenotic forms* actually presuppose the personhood of the Spirit, as the determining subject of these forms."[142]

It is interesting to note that Moltmann chooses the "experience of the Spirit" as a way of understanding the intermediate state of every *historical experience* between remembered past and expected future.[143] The experience, life, and worship of God's Spirit come into being when Christ is made present and when the new creation of all things is anticipated. These things are resonances of Christ, and a prelude to the kingdom of God. The experience of the Spirit is never without the remembrance of Christ and never without the expectation of his future.[144] Moreover, in the harmony between this expectation and this remembrance, experience of the Spirit acquires a statute and a dignity which is so much its own, and so entirely without substitute, that is rightly called *experience of God*. In this sense pneumatology presupposes Christology, and prepares the way for eschatology.[145] Moltmann writes:

> This Spirit, the life-giver, is in community with Christ already experienced now, in this life, as "the power of resurrection." As this power, the Spirit of life is stronger than death and must therefore be called immortal. But the Spirit of life is the living Gestalt or configuration of life as a whole. In this Spirit, it is not just one part of life (whether it be the soul or the ego) that is already immortal here and now; it is the whole of this mortal life, because that life is interpenetrated by eternal life, as by the spring that is its source. The Christian experience of the Spirit means that we experience this life here as at once mortal

---

141. Moltmann, *The Spirit of Life*, 11.
142. Moltmann, *The Spirit of Life*, 12.
143. Moltmann, *The Spirit of Life*, 17.
144. Moltmann, *The Spirit of Life*, 17.
145. Moltmann, *The Spirit of Life*, 18.

and immortal, as at once transient *and* intransient, as at one temporal *and* eternal.[146]

This understanding of the experience of the Spirit takes us into another plane of thought that, "The operation of God's Spirit can be remembered [by human being] as a particular happening in the world through which God reveals himself in Jesus Christ. But in faith the act of the Spirit becomes 'the present of the world of the human being' for the present event of justification manifests the self-demonstration of the Creator in his Word, and gives the present world in general its particular quality."[147] Hence, experience of the presence of God's Spirit does not merely qualify the immediate self-consciousness; rather, it gives the world of human beings its special quality, too. Thus Moltmann discovers transcendence in every experience, not merely in experience of the self. For this, the term *immanent transcendence* offers itself.[148] He holds that every experience that happens to us or that we have possesses a transcendent, inward side. That means the *experience of God's Spirit* is not limited to the human subject's experience of the self. It is also a constitutive element in the experience of the "Thou," in the experience of sociality, and in the experience of nature.[149] Moltmann writes, "It is therefore possible to experience God *in, with, and beneath* each everyday experience of the world, if God is in all things, and if all things are in God, so that God himself experiences all things in his own way. If experience of God embraces experiences of life … then …, experience of life can also embrace experiences of God."[150]

The experience of God found in human experience of the self has its inalienable and indestructible character as well and the experience of God in the experience of sociality has its own particular character also.[151] This experience of God is the experience of the presence of God the creator in creation. Moltmann maintains that, "The possibility of perceiving God in all things, and all things in God, is grounded theologically on an

---

146. Moltmann, *The Coming of God*, 71.
147. Moltmann, *The Spirit of Life*, 32.
148. Moltmann, *The Spirit of Life*, 34.
149. Moltmann, *The Spirit of Life*, 34.
150. Moltmann, *The Spirit of Life*, 34.
151. Moltmann, *The Spirit of Life*, 34.

understanding of the Spirit of God as the power of creation and the wellspring of life."[152] Hence, every experience of a creation of the Spirit is also an experience of the Spirit itself. Every true experience of the self becomes also an experience of the divine Spirit of life in the human being.[153] In short, as David Beck says, "Moltmann's expansion of the definition of experience of the Holy Spirit's is a welcome move. It is innovative, and it greatly enriches the concept. Even though it runs the risk of making the concept of experience of the Spirit too broad so that it begins to lose its meaning, it is a desirable change, for it destroys the bifurcation of the Christian life into 'holy' and 'secular' spheres."[154]

3.4 The Trinitarian Personhood of the Holy Spirit

In the preceding discussion, we have already looked into the attempt of Moltmann to assert the personhood of the Holy Spirit through the operation of the Spirit. However, he insists that:

> It is one thing to work back from the operation of the Holy Spirit to his essential nature; it is quite another to perceive his essential nature from his constitutive relationships. The deduction from the deed to the doer of it begins with human experience of the Spirit, and draws conclusions about his transcendent origin. But this knowledge is always an indirect knowledge, and remains tied to the experiences which are its point of departure. Only the energies of the Holy Spirit can be perceived from the Spirit's operation, not his Being as it exists in itself and is in itself.[155]

It means that, if one attempts to assert the personhood of the Spirit through the experiences of the operation of the Spirit, it will never be possible to do

---

152. Moltmann, *The Spirit of Life*, 35.
153. Moltmann maintains that to experience God in all things presupposes that there is a transcendence which is immanent in things and which can be inductively discovered. It is the infinite in the finite, the eternal in the temporal, and the enduring in the transitory. Moreover, to experience all things in God also means passing from the all-embracing horizon of the world and perception to the individual things which appear against this background. See Moltmann, *The Spirit of Life*, 35-36.
154. Beck, *The Holy Spirit*, 186.
155. Moltmann, *The Spirit of Life*, 289.

more than paraphrasing the nature of the Spirit by way of metaphors. It was in this way that Moltmann has arrived at the singular personhood of the Spirit as *presence and counterpart*. However, the question about the nature of the Holy Spirit cannot be answered only by pointing to the operation of the Spirit. On the other hand, the nature of the Spirit can be perceived only in his relationships to the other persons of the Trinity.[156] Hence, Moltmann tries to approach the inner-trinitarian personhood of the Spirit by building-up his case on the previous doctrines of the Trinity held in the Western and Eastern churches, taking them as flexible conceptual frameworks. However, Moltmann deliberately abandons the conceptual framework like the pattern of essence and revelation, being and act, immanent and economic Trinity, and he proceeds from four different angles, namely the *monarchical Trinity*, the *historical Trinity*, the *Eucharistic Trinity*, and the *doxological Trinity*.[157] Here one should not forget the fact that Moltmann never believes in a distinction between the immanent Trinity and economic Trinity due to the fact that with respect to God, the choice of either liberty or necessity is a false dichotomy. For him, the immanent and economic Trinity cannot be distinguished in such a way that the first nullifies what the second says. The two rather form continuity and merge into one another.[158]

3.4.1 *The Monarchical Concept of the Trinity*
The monarchical concept of the Trinity was developed pre-eminently in the West. The starting point of the Monarchical Trinity is the event of the self-revelation of God which denotes the unity of God preceding the

---

156. Moltmann, *The Spirit of Life*, 289.
157. Moltmann adheres to Karl Rahner's thesis that, "The 'economic' Trinity is the 'immanent' Trinity and the 'immanent' Trinity is the 'economic' Trinity." See Karl Rahner, *The Trinity*, trans. Joseph Donceel (New York: Seabury, 1974), 22; there can be no differentiation between how we experience God and God's nature. Any experience of God necessarily presupposes participation with God in his divine being. We are partakers of the divine nature (2 Peter 1:4). However, Moltmann adds to these concepts, from the acceptance of Rahner's thesis, the doxological Trinity or what he calls the experience of trinitarian doxology. He writes, "Real theology, which means knowledge of God, finds expression in thanks, praise and adoration. And it is what finds expression in doxology that is the real theology … Here we know in order to participate. Then to know God means to participate in the fullness of the divine life." The economic Trinity then becomes the message of the kerygmatic proclamation of the church and the immanent Trinity the content of doxological theology. See Moltmann, *The Trinity and the Kingdom*, 152.
158. Moltmann, *Trinity and the Kingdom*, 152

triunity.¹⁵⁹ It is a single movement in which the one God reveals himself through himself and communicates God's own to humanity. This movement proceeds from the Father through the Son in the Spirit, and spreads out in creation through the manifold energies of the Spirit. Moltmann insists that the monarchical structure can be seen in all God's works that the Father always acts through the Son in the Spirit.¹⁶⁰ Moreover, the Father creates and redeems the world through the Son in the power of the Spirit. In short, all activity proceeds from the Father while the Son stands as its mediator and the Spirit the mediation.¹⁶¹ According to this monarchical pattern of Trinity, the "economic Trinity" is bound to correspond to the "immanent Trinity" – indeed must be identical with it because if God is truth, then God corresponds to himself in his revelation, thereby making his revelation dependable.¹⁶² However, Moltmann argues that the monarchical concept of the Trinity has tended to subordinate the Spirit, especially through the inclusion of the *filioque* clause in the creed. When we remove the *filioque* from the Western creed, it becomes possible to see the interdependence between the Spirit and the Son. David Beck notes that, "The origination of the Son presupposes the presence of the Spirit, and the origination of the Spirit presupposes the presence of the Son. … Not only is their origination an interrelated affair, their work is mutually dependant as well. In the monarchical concept of the Trinity, the Spirit's identity is highlighted by his interrelation with the Son."¹⁶³

---

159. Moltmann, *The Spirit of Life*, 290.
160. Moltmann, *The Spirit of Life*, 290.
161. Moltmann, *The Spirit of Life*, 291.
162. Moltmann, *The Spirit of Life*, 291; the objection that Moltmann raises against the immanent Trinity is that, what precedes revelation as its foundation is not "the immanent Trinity." If the doctrine of the Trinity describes only the transcendent primordial ground of salvation history, then it must infer the transcendent "primordial ground" from the historical operations, and can naturally find nothing in the "primordial ground" that fails to correspond to salvation history. This means that "the immanent Trinity" is related to "the economic Trinity" and identified with it. Moreover, there is no "immanent Trinity" that could exist independently in itself. There is only a Trinity open and prepared for revelation and salvation that Moltmann calls the "primordial Trinity." See Moltmann, *The Spirit of Life*, 291-292.
163. Beck, *The Holy Spirit*, 199.

3.4.2 The Historical Concept of the Trinity

The historical concept of the Trinity links to the monarchical concept, transposing it from the vertical eternity-time relation to the sequence of the times of the Father, the Son, and the Holy Spirit in salvation history.[164] It is only possible to talk about an "economic Trinity" if this is taken to mean the inner cohesion and dynamic thrust of all works of the Trinity in the economy of salvation.[165] This trinitarian concept links in sequence the times of the Father, the Son, and the Spirit in salvation history. Although from earliest times the work of creating the world has been ascribed to the Father, the work of reconciling the world to the Son, and the work of sanctifying the world of the Holy Spirit, these trinitarian works do not stand side by side without any relation to one another. They belong within the context of salvation history, because the work of sanctification presupposes the work of reconciliation, and both have the work of creation as a premise. In short, history begins with creation and ends with the transfiguration of the world. It begins in the Father and consummated in the Spirit.[166] Thus the identity of the Spirit revolves around bringing to completion the work of the Father and the Son.

3.4.3 The Eucharistic Concept of the Trinity

The Eucharistic concept of the Trinity is the logical consequence of the monarchical form of the Trinity because the experience of grace arouses gratitude. Here praise proceeds from the indwelling Spirit, which is mediated by the Son and directed to the Father. The Eucharistic direction of praise teaches that God not only works, but he receives as well. For Moltmann, "Here all activities proceed from the indwelling Spirit, all mediation takes place through the Son, and the Father is purely the recipient of the thanksgiving and songs of praise of his creatures. The Spirit glorifies the Son, and through the Son the Father. The Spirit unites us with the Son, and through

---

164. One has to remember that the historical interpretation of the doctrine of the Trinity in its bearings on the economy of salvation has been the major focus of Joachim of Fiore. It is a fact that his historical periodization of salvation history and his eschatological vision of its perfecting shaped the Western interpretation of history, particularly its modern form.
165. Moltmann, *The Spirit of Life*, 295.
166. Moltmann, *The Spirit of Life*, 298.

the Son with the Father."[167] The significance of the Eucharistic concept of the Trinity is that it is the reversal of the monarchical concept. It means that in the monarchical concept the divine movement is Father – Son – Spirit, whereas in the Eucharistic concept it is like Spirit – Son – Father. In each case, the three hypostases arrive at their unity through their unified movement. Moltmann insists that for the monarchical movement the expression of "the threefold God" fit better where as for the Eucharistic movement the most appropriate term can be "triunity." The energies of the Spirit flow back to the Son and to the Father. But this means that both patterns are economic concepts of the Trinity – indeed that they really sum up the two sides of salvation history, which comes "from God" and leads "to God."[168] What is essential here to note is that in the Eucharistic model, the Spirit is identified as the originator of praise directed to the Father.[169]

3.4.4 The Trinitarian Doxology

The trinitarian doxology leads beyond the other three conceptions of the Trinity. In this model, God is glorified for his own sake rather than thanked for what God has done. It is the ultimate destiny of humanity that it will eventually worship and glorify God in this way. The trinitarian doxology reveals a phenomenon that will take place in the *eschaton*. Moltmann argues that this phenomenon is accessible to us in our present state only in

---

167. Moltmann, *The Spirit of Life*, 298; it is interesting to note that here God's being is described not through what he does but through the way he receives. While the monarchical concept of the Trinity has its place in the sending for the proclamation of the gospel and the accomplishment of Christian obedience in the world, the Eucharistic concept of the Trinity has its place in the situation of the human beings which is the celebration of the Eucharist and the life which itself becomes the feast since it has been filled with grace and happiness. This concept was best developed by the Orthodox churches whose centre is the celebration of the Eucharist. See Moltmann, *The Spirit of Life*, 298.

168. Moltmann, *The Spirit of Life*, 300; Bauckham notes that for Moltmann, it is not in relation to human beings that the Spirit can be discerned to be a person, but in relation to the Father and the Son. In the monarchical form the mission of the church to the world continues the divine activity in the order Father-Son-Spirit. The Spirit is here the subject of the church's mission in that he inspires it. In the Eucharistic form of the Trinity, it is we who make the Son and the Father the objects of our praise, but our praise is inspired by the Spirit, who thereby glorifies the Father and the Son. Moreover, Spirit is a subject in a divine community of three persons because of his principle for knowing the Trinity. See Richard Bauckham, *The Theology of Jürgen Moltmann* (Edinburgh: T & T Clark, 1995), 160-161.

169. Beck, *The Holy Spirit*, 200.

the "eternal moment" – "an awareness of the present which is so intense that it interrupts the flux of time and does away with transience."[170] For Moltmann, this eternal moment is a fleeting state of ecstasy. In the eternal moment the Spirit is discerned in its *perichoretic* fellowship which it shares with the Father and the Son. This doxology is stated in the Nicene Creed in the clause about the Holy Spirit "who with the Father and the Son together is worshipped and glorified." Moltmann insists that anyone who is glorified "together with" others cannot be subordinated to these others.[171] Moreover, in trinitarian doxology the linear movements end and the circular movements begin.[172] This objectivity is expressed in the co-equality axiom of the Nicene Creed. According to Moltmann, if the Spirit "together with" the Father and Son is "at the same time worshipped and glorified," then the Spirit is seen in the *perichoretic* fellowship it shares with the Father and the Son, and this puts an end to his positions as "third Person" in the Trinity. At the same time it permits to "pre-" and no monarchical movement of God's self-communication of human beings to God, which is the self-circling and self-reposing movement of *perichoresis*.[173]

In short, it is apparent that the identity of the Spirit proceeding from trinitarian theology should form the context for ideas coming from religious experience. Although the personal nature of the Spirit is a persistent problem, we cannot solve the problem by simply trotting out a doctrine of the Trinity. However, it is true that the problem is ultimately unsolvable without trinitarian theology.[174] Moreover, for Moltmann, the Father, the Son, and the Spirit are by no means merely distinguished from one another by their character as persons, rather they are united with one another and in one another, since personal character and social character are

---

170. Moltmann, *The Spirit of Life*, 303.
171. Moltmann, *The Spirit of Life*, 301.
172. Moltmann, *The Spirit of Life*, 303.
173. Moltmann, *The Spirit of Life*, 304; for Moltmann, the Trinity in the glorification has to be described correspondingly; all activity proceeds from the Holy Spirit. The Holy Spirit is the one who glorifies; it glorifies both the Son and the Father. The Son can be glorified, but only through the Spirit; whereas the Son for his part can also glorify, but only the Father; the Father is glorified both through the Spirit and through the Son. See Jürgen Moltmann, *The Future of Creation: Collected Essays*, trans. Margaret Kohl (Minneapolis: Fortress, 2007), 88.
174. Beck, *The Holy Spirit*, 200-201.

only two aspects of the same thing. The concept of person must therefore in itself contain the concept of unitedness or at-oneness.[175] It means that the concept of God's unity cannot in the trinitarian sense be fitted into the homogeneity of the one divine substance or into the identity of the absolute subject either and least of all into one of the three persons of the Trinity. It must be perceived in the *perichoresis* of the divine persons. If the unity of God is not perceived in the at-oneness of the triune God, or as a *perichoretic* unity, then Arianism and Sabellianism remain inescapable threats to Christian theology.[176]

3.5 Holy Spirit and Christology

There is no doubt that Moltmann's theology has always been strongly Christocentric, though by no means Christomonistic.[177] However, when Moltmann discusses the earthly ministry of Jesus, he follows a Spirit Christology. Hence, Bauckham argues that, "Moltmann's use of Spirit-Christology enables him to see Jesus' personal identity not in isolation but as formed and discovered in relationships, and not as fixed from eternity but as coming to be in history (which is still open to the future)."[178] Moltmann maintains that the Synoptic gospels begin with *a Spirit Christology*. Paul and John also followed this premise and stressed *a Christological doctrine of the Spirit*.[179] However, recognition of the mutual relationship between the pneumatological Christology of the synoptics and the Christological pneumatology of Paul and John was largely ignored in the tradition of the Western church. Moreover, the Spirit was seen just as the Spirit of the Lord, and communicated only through the "spiritual pastors" of the church and the anointed apostolic majesties of the holy *imperium*.[180] However, Moltmann understands that these two perspectives are interrelated and

---

175. Moltmann, *The Trinity and the Kingdom*, 150.
176. Moltmann, *The Trinity and the Kingdom*, 150.
177. Richard J. Bauckham, "Moltmann's Messianic Christology," *Scottish Journal of Theology* vol. 44 (1991), 519.
178. Bauckham, "Moltmann's Messianic Christology," 526; see for more details, Jürgen Moltmann, *Jesus Christ for Today's World*, trans. Margaret Kohl (Minneapolis: Fortress, 1994).
179. Moltmann, *The Spirit of Life*, 58.
180. Moltmann, *The Spirit of Life*, 59.

mutually interpret each other. Hence, Moltmann develops his pneumatological Christology in a mutual relationship.

3.5.1 Relationship between Christ of the Spirit and the Spirit of Christ

The initial aspect that Moltmann deals with is the old question of the relationship between the Christ of Spirit and the Spirit of Christ. Moltmann argues that, "It already sees 'the historical Jesus' himself in theological terms, as God's messianic child, is led by the Spirit, acts, and ministers in the Spirit, and through the Spirit surrenders himself to death on the cross."[181] Hence for Moltmann, the historical Jesus is not the temporal precondition for the Christ of the proclamation, or a preliminary form of the risen Christ. On the other hand, he is Christ himself filled with the divine Spirit.[182] This emphasis Moltmann shows is that there is a mutual relationship between *the Christ of the Spirit and the Spirit of Christ*.[183] To understand Moltmann's position clearly, one needs to understand his argument of the Christ of the Spirit and the Spirit of Christ.

3.5.2 The Christ of the Spirit

Moltmann maintains that both chronologically and theologically, the operation of the divine Spirit is the precondition for the history of Jesus of Nazareth.[184] Moreover, the history of Christ and the history of the Spirit are dovetailed and indissolubly intertwined. Taking cue from the synoptic gospels, he argues that Jesus was conceived by the Spirit, performed miracles, and proclaimed the kingdom of God in the power of the Spirit. His suffering and death and resurrection were also through the Spirit.[185] That means, the dependence of Jesus on the power of the Spirit begins with the incarnation of the Word by the Spirit and continues through the

---

181. Moltmann, *The Spirit of Life*, 58; Moltmann, *The Church in the Power of the Spirit*, 53-54.
182. Moltmann, *The Spirit of Life*, 58-59; Moltmann, *The Source of Life*, 15.
183. One should note that since the Cappadocian Fathers, *the Tradition of the Eastern Church* has emphasised the reciprocity between pneumatological Christology and the Christological pneumatology. In Protestant theology, it was Hendrik Berkhof who worked out the double relationship between the Spirit and Christ.
184. Moltmann, *The Spirit of Life*, 60.
185. See Moltmann, *The Source of Life*, 15.

Spirit endowment of Jesus at his baptism, public ministry, sufferings, and resurrection. At the baptism of Jesus, he had special experience of the Spirit, and through this he perceived his own calling and mission.[186] There he realised the call to be the expected messiah of the end-time, on whom the Spirit of God rests according to Isaiah 61:1.[187] Moreover, the Spirit is the real determining subject of the special relationship of Jesus to God, and of God to Jesus.[188] Jesus' ministry and his power over sickness and demons demonstrated that the kingdom of God and the new creation of all things were beginning. Moltmann writes that, "The Spirit makes Jesus 'the kingdom of God in person,' for *in the power of the Spirit* he drives out demons and heals the sick; in the power of the Spirit he receives sinners, and brings the kingdom of God to the poor."[189] Moreover, for Moltmann, the death of Jesus on the cross is the point at which the Spirit of God becomes the Spirit of Christ. Moltmann writes, "Through the *shekinah*, the Spirit binds itself to Jesus' fate, though without becoming identical with him. In this way, *the Spirit of God* becomes definitively *the Spirit of Christ*, so that from that point onwards it can be called by and invoked in Christ's name."[190]

3.5.3 The Spirit of Christ

Moltmann asserts that according to the gospels, before Easter the activity of the Spirit was apparently confined exclusively to Jesus. That means, he preached and acted in the power of the Spirit, but the Spirit had not been transferred to the disciples.[191] As noted earlier, the Christ of the Spirit is the Spirit bearer. It means that he is the promised one who was filled with the Spirit and brought justice and salvation to Israel. But in the gospel of

---

186. Moltmann, *The Spirit of Life*, 60-61; the phraseology about the "descent" of the Spirit on Jesus, and its "resting" on him, suggests that the Spirit should be interpreted as God's *shekinah*. What is meant here is the self-restriction and self-humiliation of the eternal Spirit, and his feeling identification with Jesus' person and the history of his life and suffering, just as, according to the rabbinic idea, God's Spirit has committed itself to the history of Israel's life and suffering. See Moltmann, *The Spirit of Life*, 61.
187. Moltmann maintains that the liberty of Jesus' prayer to the Father reveals the sonship. Through the "Abba" prayer believers are taken into the fellowship of the Son with the Father. This happens through the Spirit. See Moltmann, *The Trinity and the Kingdom of God*, 73.
188. Moltmann, *The Trinity and the Kingdom*, 71; Moltmann, *The Spirit of Life*, 61.
189. Moltmann, *The Spirit of Life*, 61.
190. Moltmann, *The Spirit of Life*, 62.
191. Moltmann, *The Trinity and the Kingdom*, 122.

John, Jesus promised the disciples that although he was about to die, he would send the *Paraclete* in his place (Jn 16:4-15). The transition between "the Christ of the Spirit" and "the Spirit of Christ" took place as Christ transitioned from the "Spirit-bearer" to the "Spirit-sender." After the resurrection, Jesus became the subject of the sending of the Spirit to the church.[192] In sending the disciples out into the world with the mission of his Father, the risen Christ gave them the Holy Spirit (Jn 20:21f.).[193] Thus Jesus became the Spirit sender, and the Spirit became the Spirit of Christ. This transition took place in the cross. Moltmann notes that, "It is only with the resurrection and exaltation of Jesus that the relationship is reversed: the Son sends the Spirit and is himself present in the life-giving Spirit. In this respect pneumatology will be Christological pneumatology."[194] In short, the transition took place, signalling a complementary relationship between the Christ of the Spirit and the Spirit of Christ. The benefit of approaching Christology and pneumatology in this way is that one can avoid the pitfalls of Christomonism into which much of the Western traditions have fallen, and the enthusiastic tendency toward spiritualist pneumatology which has flourished on the fringes of the Western tradition as a reaction to the mainstream tradition.[195]

3.5.4 *The Spirit Accompanies Jesus in His Suffering*

After delineating the relationship between the Christ of the Spirit and the Spirit of Christ, Moltmann discusses the suffering of the Spirit in Jesus' living and dying. Here Moltmann is developing a *theologia crucis* (later developed also into a *pneumatologia crucis*) in which the cross reveals God's nature and being. Beginning with the temptation of Jesus in the

---

192. It is a fact that the early church maintained a close association between Christ and the Spirit. There could be no salvation through Christ outside the accompanying gift of the Holy Spirit, and there could be no enjoyment of the blessings of the Spirit without discipleship to Christ. Of course, none of this would have been possible without the sending of the Spirit to the believing community. It was by receiving the same Spirit that empowered Christ in his ministry that the church could take up its own ministry of power and righteousness. In other words, in order to become a body of true imitators of Christ, the church needed to be endowed with the necessary divine power in the person of the indwelling Spirit. See Beck, *The Holy Spirit*, 150-151.
193. Moltmann, *The Trinity and the Kingdom*, 122-123.
194. Moltmann, *History and the Triune God*, 84; Moltmann, *The Source of Life*, 17.
195. Moltmann, *History and the Triune God*, 84.

desert, Moltmann insists that it was the Spirit who drove Jesus into the desert. The temptations that Jesus faced in the desert were not levelled at his human weakness rather they are aimed at his relationship to God. It means that Jesus' messianic kingship is put on trial, and in that trial the kingship is precisely defined.[196] The Spirit is not only leading Jesus into temptation, the Spirit himself is Jesus' strength in suffering and even the indestructible life in whose power Jesus can give himself vicariously for many.[197] Moltmann argues that, "If the Spirit accompanies him, then it is drawn into his sufferings, and becomes his *companion* in suffering. The path the Son takes in his passion is then at the same time the path taken by the Spirit, whose strength will be proved in Jesus' weakness."[198] Thus the Spirit is the transcendent side of Jesus' immanent way of suffering. In other words, the surrender through the Father and the offering of the Son take place "through the Spirit." The Spirit is therefore the link in the separation. He is the link joining the bond between the Father and the Son, with their separation.[199] So the "*condescendence*" of the Spirit leads to the progressive *kenosis* of the Spirit, together with Jesus. Although the Spirit fills Jesus with the divine, living energies through which the sick are healed, it does not turn him into a superman. It participates in his human suffering to the point of his death on the cross. Through the *shekinah*, the Spirit binds itself to Jesus' fate, though without becoming identical with him. In this way *the Spirit of God* becomes definitely *the Spirit of Christ*, so that from that point onwards it can be called by and invoked in Christ's name.[200]

3.5.5 Weakness of the Spirit in the Death of Jesus

After delineating the *kenosis* of the Spirit that is seen in his *shekinah* in the suffering Jesus, Moltmann focuses on the weakness of the Spirit in relation

---

196. Moltmann, *The Spirit of Life*, 61; see a discussion on the suffering of Jesus in D. G. Attfield, "Can God be Crucified? A Discussion of J. Moltmann," *Scottish Journal of Theology* vol. 30 (1977), 47-57.
197. Moltmann, *The Spirit of Life*, 64.
198. Moltmann, *The Spirit of Life*, 62.
199. Moltmann, *The Trinity and the Kingdom*, 82; Moltmann never understands Jesus' death as the death of God but only as death in God. He speaks of the relationships of the Son and the Father and the Spirit at the point of the death of Jesus. See Jürgen Moltmann, *The Crucified God*, trans. R. A. Wilson and John Bowden (London: SCM, 2008), 213.
200. Moltmann, *The Spirit of Life*, 62.

to the death of Jesus Christ. His point is that, "Looking only at the power of the Spirit and not at this weakness too, then we are ascribing to the Spirit a merely external influence on the sacrifice which Christ brings the Father through his self-surrender."[201] In other words, it argues that the Spirit draws the Son out of the depths of this suffering, but he does not participate in the suffering itself. Evidently then the Spirit which descended upon Jesus must have forsaken him before the passion in order to bring "the incense of the offering" to God the Father. But Moltmann argues in line with Paul that it is not Jesus who brings the reconciling sacrifice to the Father rather "God was in Christ reconciling the world to himself" (2 Cor 5:19).[202] If God himself was in Christ, then according to Pauline language the Father suffered *with* and *in* the Son. He did so by virtue of his indwelling in the Son through the Holy Spirit.[203] In this sense, "If the Spirit is God's empathy, this means that the eternal Spirit is also involved, in profoundest and identifying suffering. It is precisely his suffering with the Son to the point of death on the cross which makes the rebirth of Christ from the Spirit inwardly possible. The Spirit participates in the dying of the Son in order to give him new "life from the dead." Because he accompanies Christ to his end, he can make this end the new beginning."[204]

3.5.6 *The Spirit of Christ and the Resurrection of Jesus*

Resurrection is one of the main themes of Moltmann.[205] He asserts that Jesus was raised by the power of the Spirit and the same Jesus continues to live in the presence of the Spirit. Moltmann writes that, the Spirit of God is not only the one who leads Jesus to his self-surrender to death on the cross. He is very much more the one who brings Jesus up out of death.[206]

---

201. Moltmann, *The Spirit of Life*, 67.
202. Moltmann, *The Spirit of Life*, 67; for Moltmann, in this happening God is revealed as the trinitarian God, and in the event between the surrendering Father and the forsaken Son, God becomes so "vast" in the Spirit of self-offering that there is room and life for the whole world. See Moltmann, *The Church in the Power of the Spirit*, 96.
203. Moltmann, *The Spirit of Life*, 68.
204. Moltmann, *The Spirit of Life*, 68.
205. For a beautiful delineation of the resurrection of Jesus Christ, see Jürgen Moltmann, *Theology and Joy*, trans. Reinhard Ulrich (London: SCM, 1973), 50-51.
206. Moltmann, *God in Creation*, 66-67; Moltmann, *The Spirit of Life*, 65; Moltmann maintains that true Easter faith is the work of the Spirit because believing in Christ's resurrection does not mean affirming a historical fact. It means being seized by the life

The resurrection of Jesus by the power of the Spirit assures the fact that the same Spirit will transform this transitory world into the new world of eternal life.[207] By taking cue from the early Christian traditions, Moltmann insists that the resurrection of Jesus must also be understood as an advance payment and beginning of the end-time new creation of the world.[208] Thus we find the marvellous work of the Spirit in bringing the eternal future into history. Moltmann writes:

> As the power of resurrection, the Spirit is the reviewing presence of the future of eternal life in the midst of the history of death; he is the presence of the future of the new creation in the midst of the dying life of this world and its evil state. In the Spirit and through the Spirit's powers the eschatological new thing – "Behold I make all things new" – becomes the new thing in history, reaching, at least in tendency, over the whole breadth of creation in its present wretchedness. That is why the energies of new life in the Spirit are as manifold and motley as creation itself.[209]

In another place, Moltmann argues the same theme. He writes that, "What men and women fragmentarily experience here and now, even before their deaths, in rebirths to true life in the energies and powers of love, happens in perfected form and right into mortal flesh in the resurrection of the dead. The person who is wholly and entirely seized and pervaded by the living power of the divine Spirit becomes immortal, because death loses its power over him."[210] Thus Moltmann insists that the Spirit who raised Christ from

---

giving Spirit and experiencing the powers of the world to come. Hence for him, there is no Easter theology without a theology of Pentecost, and no Pentecost theology without Easter theology. See Moltmann, *The Source of Life*, 16; Moltmann argues that when the disciples wanted to interpret the experiences of Christ's death on the cross and his appearances in glory, they talked about the raising of the crucified one which is to say an act of God upon him through the Spirit; or they spoke about the resurrection of Jesus who has died, that is a power of the Spirit in him; and they also used images about Christ being born again from the Spirit to eternal life. See Moltmann, *The Coming of God*, 77.
207. Moltmann, *The Spirit of Life*, 66.
208. Moltmann, *The Spirit of Life*, 66.
209. Moltmann, *Church in the Power of the Spirit*, 295-296.
210. Jürgen Moltmann, *The Way of Jesus Christ: Christology in Messianic Dimensions,* trans. Margaret Kohl (Minneapolis: Fortress, 1993), 257.

the dead gives new life to believers. Thus believers enjoy life on two levels simultaneously. One is the mortal life that all living creatures currently possess and the eternal life that only Christ possesses in full, which the believers possess in part because of the indwelling of the Spirit of resurrection.

Moltmann argues that the resurrection does not mean just the giving of eternal life alone but also transfiguration and glorification. He writes that, "Christ is raised from the dead into God's eternal life. That is what is meant by the word resurrection. But it also means at the same time the *transfiguration* of the humiliated and crucified Jesus into glory of God. Transfiguration means both a glorifying and a transformation."[211] The interesting thing is that this transfiguration is a total alteration of the person. Hence for Moltmann, resurrection must have this holistic character and argues that if the Spirit infuses the whole person in the present, then the Spirit raises the whole person to life in the future.[212] David Beck argues that, "Moltmann recognizes that the resurrection of Jesus is eschatological in that it brings new life to human beings, but he also recognises that an eschatological perspective is a cosmic perspective. In addition, he acknowledges the operation of the Holy Spirit in the resurrection, and in this way he opens up connections between eschatology and pneumatology in the event of the resurrection of Jesus, and by extension of all human beings."[213]

For Moltmann, since Christ is resurrected in the power of the Spirit, the life-giving Spirit continues the ministry of Jesus Christ.[214] Moreover, the Spirit frees the oppressed and exploited people from unjust structures and the brutality of human beings. Just as in the ministry of Jesus the Spirit gathers the impoverished and helpless people (*ochlos*), making them the people of the beatitudes, and thus Jesus continues to act in the Spirit and in the community of his people.[215] Finally, as the power of Christ's resurrection the Spirit gives life to our mortal bodies and will drive our godless death from creation because the Spirit of Christ is the power and energy of the resurrection.[216]

---

211. Moltmann, *The Trinity and the Kingdom*, 123.
212. Moltmann, *The Coming of God*, 71.
213. Beck, *The Holy Spirit*, 175.
214. Moltmann, *Experiences in Theology*, 147.
215. Moltmann, *Experiences in Theology*, 147.
216. Moltmann, *Experiences in Theology*, 148.

3.6 Holy Spirit and Anthropology

Moltmann has in fact developed a pneumatological anthropology which is in one sense comprehensive. Moltmann writes:

> The operation of God's Spirit "can be remembered by [human being] as a particular happening in the world through which God reveals himself in Jesus Christ." But in faith the act of the Spirit becomes "the present of the world of the human being", for the present event of justification manifests the self-demonstration of the Creator in his Word, and gives the present world in general its particular quality. So experience of the presence of God's Spirit does not merely qualify the immediate self-consciousness. It gives the world of human beings its special quality too.[217]

Recognizing the importance of the pneumatological anthropology, Moltmann critiques the dialectical theology of Barth, Brunner, Bultmann, and Gogarten on the ground that it is unfruitful.[218] Critiquing Barth, Moltmann argues that the real phenomenon is to be found neither in the Spirit's immanence nor in its transcendence, neither in the continuity nor in the discontinuity. It is to be found in God's *immanence* in human experience, and in the *transcendence* of human beings in God. For him Spirit is not simply the subjective side of God's revelation, and faith is not merely the echo of the word of God in the human heart. The Spirit is much more than that. It is the power that raises the dead, the power of the new creation of all things.[219] Thus two things become clear in Moltmann's anthropology the Spirit's immanence and transcendence in human beings.

---

217. Moltmann, *The Spirit of Life*, 32-33.
218. The dialectical theologians began by reproaching nineteenth-century liberal and pietistic theology for starting from human consciousness of God, not from the divine Word to humanity. This, they said, was theology "from below," not theology "from above." In the German tradition, Schleiermacher is regarded as the founder of the modern theology of consciousness and experience. See Moltmann, *The Spirit of Life*, 5.
219. Moltmann, *The Spirit of Life*, 7.

3.6.1 Immanent Transcendence in the Human Experience

Moltmann recognises that according to the modern constitution of reason one cannot make any objective experience of God.[220] However, one can still talk about the experience of God in the non-objective context of human experience of the self. This happens through the operation of the Spirit who binds together I and Thou and Us. Moltmann writes that, "The Spirit brings God into relationship to the whole person, body and soul, past and future and at the meeting point of that person's social and natural relationships. The Spirit brings the whole person into relationship with God, in the entire fabric of that person's life. In the Spirit we live 'before God,' just as 'the light of God's countenance' is turned towards us in the presence of his Spirit."[221] Hence, Moltmann abandons the modern concept of "self-consciousness" to discover transcendence in every experience and employs the term *immanent transcendence*. According to this understanding, "The experience of God found in human experience of the self has its inalienable and indestructible character; and the experience of God in the experience of sociality has its own particular character too."[222] Since Moltmann insists on the presence of the Spirit in all creation, the possibility of perceiving God in all things, and all things in God, is grounded theologically on an understanding of the Spirit of God as the power of creation and the wellspring of life.[223] Hence, every experience of a human being or creation is an experience of the Spirit itself. In short, to experience God in all things presupposes that there is a transcendence which is immanent in things and that can be inductively

---

220. Modern philosophy argues that God can be objectively neither known nor experienced. A God who "exists" in this objective sense does not exist at all, at least not as a God. The modern empirical sciences are in principle agnostic. According to Kant's *Critique of Pure Reason*, God is as hidden and unknowable as the *Ding an sich*. He is not only unknowable because he is not an object of possible experience. The limits of reason itself have actually made it impossible for him to reveal himself and to manifest himself in the world of experience. In the human world of experience he can never make himself known. See Moltmann, *The Spirit of Life*, 31.
221. Moltmann, *The Coming of God*, 75.
222. Moltmann, *The Spirit of Life*, 34.
223. Moltmann, *The Spirit of Life*, 35.

discovered. It is the infinite in the finite, the eternal in the temporal and the enduring in the transitory.[224]

3.6.2 God's Presence in the Spirit among His People

According to Moltmann, the Spirit of God is present among his people in two ways. Firstly, it is on a corporal ground. Referring to the book of Judges to talk about the historical activity of the Spirit in Israel's charismatic leaders, Moltmann insists that these leaders possessed the Spirit and were led by the Spirit. For Moltmann, this is the charismatic endowment of the Spirit.[225] However, when monarchy came into power, this spontaneous and temporally limited charisma came to an end. Thereafter, the Spirit became a permanent gift to God's anointed one. Thus the Spirit became a special divine presence to accompany the kings and prophets in Israel.[226]

The second mode of the Spirit's presence among the human beings is individual or the inward experience of the Spirit. Referring to Psalm 139, Moltmann argues that God's Spirit and God's face are seen together. Hence, when the psalmist talks about the Spirit, he refers to the commitment of God's own person. On the other hand, in the human beings the spirit is associated with the heart, so that what is meant is God's commitment to the human person. When God withdraws his Spirit, it is the same as if he turns away and hides his face.[227] The gift of the Spirit comes from the countenance of God. It is a gift that brings inward assurance in living, and new vital energies. Referring to Psalm 51, Moltmann argues that it is the "new heart" and the "new spirit."[228] Hence, Moltmann writes, "But for me theology also springs from God's love for life – the love for life that we experience in the presence of the life-giving Spirit and that enables us to move beyond our resignation and begin to love life here and now."[229] Experience of the Spirit on an individual level has a trinitarian dimension as well. Moltmann writes that, "Through the sending of the creative Spirit,

---

224. Moltmann, *The Spirit of Life*, 35; Moltmann, *The Source of Life*, 12.
225. Moltmann, *The Spirit of Life*, 43.
226. Moltmann, *The Spirit of Life*, 44.
227. Moltmann, *The Spirit of Life*, 45.
228. Moltmann, *The Spirit of Life*, 45.
229. Jürgen Moltmann, "Theology in the Project of Modern World," in *A Passion for God's Reign: Theology, Christian Learning, and the Christian Self*, ed. Miroslav Wolf (Michigan: Eerdmans, 1998), 2.

the trinitarian history of God becomes a history that is open to the world, open to men and women, and open to the future. Through the experience of the life-giving Spirit in faith, in baptism, and in the fellowship of believers, people are integrated into the history of the Trinity. Through the Spirit of Christ they not only become participators in the eschatological history of the new creation. Through the Spirit of the Son they also become at the same time participants in the Trinitarian history of God himself."[230]

3.6.3 From Anthropocentric Pneumatology to a Holistic Pneumatology

Although Moltmann emphasized the Spirit's immanence and transcendence in the human beings, he never argued for an anthropocentric pneumatology, rather argued for a holistic pneumatology. Moltmann argues that the anthropocentrism has induced human beings to seize power over nature and to destroy her. Hence, what we need today is a pneumatology which is not only anthropologically concentrated, rather an anthropology that is related to the consciousness and to the immediate consciousness.[231] An experience of God restricted to the immediate self-consciousness is not an experience of God at all. This brings us to the conclusion that it is literally essential for us to develop *a holistic doctrine of God the Holy Spirit*. It must be holistic in at least two ways. On the one hand, it must comprehend human beings in their total being, and sociality. On the other hand, it must also embrace the wholeness of the community of creation, which is shared by human beings. Moltmann asserts that if this holistic view is critically related to the existing cleavages in human beings themselves, to the divisions between human beings, and to the disjunction between human beings and nature, its effect can be therapeutic.[232]

3.6.4 Liberation of the Human Beings in the Spirit

According to Moltmann, the people whom the word of God calls forth and who are possessed by God's Spirit experience liberation in different sectors of their lives. This has been true in the case of the people of Israel who

---

230. Moltmann, *The Trinity and the Kingdom of God*, 90.
231. Moltmann, *The Spirit of Life*, 35.
232. Moltmann, *The Spirit of Life*, 37-38.

experienced liberation through the experience of God. In the same way, through faith in Jesus Christ, Christians also experience freedom in the Spirit. Moltmann insists that the experience of God and the experience of freedom are deeply fused that they belong indissolubly together.[233] In our experience of the Spirit we also experience liberating fellowship with Jesus. That means that through the Spirit believers have an experience of the history of Christ.[234] Moreover, if one wishes to comprehend the liberating experience of the Spirit, they must understand the Spirit as both "the Spirit of Christ" and "the Spirit of God" because faith comes into existence when God the Father and Jesus the Lord act together in the Spirit.[235] Thus for Moltmann, the experience of freedom in the Spirit is in fact the experience of God himself. There are three considerations that Moltmann provides here supporting his argument. Firstly, the Lord is the Spirit (2 Cor 3:17), the power in which people experience their inward and outward liberation.[236] Secondly, where the Spirit of the Lord is, there is freedom (2 Cor 3:17). Here it is not the Spirit itself who is the Lord rather the Spirit of Christ. That means, the experience of freedom encompasses a double experience of God: the Lord is the Spirit, and the Sprit is the Spirit of the Lord. Thus liberation reveals the fact that there is a reciprocal operation between God's Spirit and his Christ. Out of their cooperative activity comes the freedom.[237] Finally, freedom is present where Christ is experienced in the Spirit. This freedom has nothing to do with slavery.[238]

3.6.4.1 Freedom in the Spirit as Subjectivity

According to Moltmann, "Faith is not just a formal assent to the doctrine of the church, or participation in the church's faith or a 'blind obedience' to God's commandments. Rather, it is a *liberating faith* that takes us person-

---

233. Moltmann, *The Spirit of Life*, 99.
234. Moltmann, *The Future of Creation*, 84.
235. Moltmann, *The Spirit of Life*, 102.
236. Moltmann, *The Spirit of Life*, 120.
237. Moltmann, *The Spirit of Life*, 121; Moltmann holds the view that Pentecostal and charismatic experiences of the Spirit become spiritualistically insubstantial and illusory without the personal and political discipleship of Jesus. See Moltmann, *The Spirit of Life*, 120.
238. Moltmann, *The Spirit of Life*, 121.

ally captive."²³⁹ It means being possessed by the divine energy of life, and participation in that energy. Through trust in the God of the Exodus and the resurrection, the believer experiences and partakes this liberating power of God which raises to new life. God manifests his creative energies in the confronting historical events and the people touched by them are interpenetrated by these energies.²⁴⁰ Moreover, through faith, the unexplored creative powers of God are given to human beings. So faith means becoming creative with God and in his Spirit. Moreover, faith awakens trust in the unrealized possibilities in human beings – in oneself and in other people. So faith means crossing the frontiers of the reality which is existent now, and has been determined by the past, and seeking the potentialities for life which have not yet come into being.²⁴¹ However, this discovery of the subjectivity is not enough to take the soundings of freedom in God's Spirit adequately because subjective freedom involves social freedom too and subjective powers also require the objective scope of the possible. Otherwise there is no subjective development.²⁴²

3.6.4.2 Freedom in the Spirit as Sociality

Moltmann insists that the freedom is a qualification of the relationship in which and from which the people concerned live. This is the concept of communicative freedom. The truth of subjective freedom is mutual love. It is only in love that human freedom enters its free world.²⁴³ He writes, "I am free and feel free when I am respected and accepted by other people, and when I for my part respect and accept other people too. I become truly free if I open my life for other people and share with them, and if other people open their lives for me, and share them with me. Then the person is no longer the limitation of my freedom, but its extension."²⁴⁴ He holds

---

239. Moltmann, *The Spirit of Life*, 114.
240. Moltmann, *The Spirit of Life*, 115; for Moltmann, the coming kingdom of God is destined to be the kingdom of freedom for those who believe and through their perfected liberty non-human creation is destined to be free also. The liberty which believers lay hold through the Spirit is not an exclusive liberty from the created being and from the body. It is an inclusive liberty, for these things too. Moltmann, *God in Creation*, 68.
241. Moltmann, *The Spirit of Life*, 115.
242. Moltmann, *The Spirit of Life*, 117.
243. Moltmann, *The Spirit of Life*, 118.
244. Moltmann, *The Spirit of Life*, 118.

that life is communion in communication. When we give one another life, individuals become free beyond the borders of their individuality. This is the social side of freedom and it is love or solidarity.[245] The true human freedom is to be found in the love that longs for life. This leads to unhindered, open community in solidarity. This freedom as community or sociality is able to heal the wounds which freedom as dominion inflicts.

3.6.4.3 Freedom in the Spirit as Future

The faith of a Christian is essentially the hope of the resurrection. In the light of this hope, freedom is the creative passion for the possible. It is directed towards the future, the future of the coming God which is the limitless kingdom of creative possibilities.[246] Moltmann criticises that this future dimension of freedom has been overlooked because the freedom of the Christian faith was not understood as participation in God's creative acts and because Christianity was dominated by religious reverence rather than by messianic hope. But freedom in faith is the creativity in the forecourt of the possible which breaks down frontiers.[247]

3.7 Holy Spirit and Redemption

Moltmann's effort to view the Spirit holistically spills over into his pneumatological examination of Christian soteriology. Moltmann recognizes that the drawback of the traditional Protestantism is that Christ's redemptive work was seen one-sidedly in his death on the cross and rarely in his resurrection, his present lordship, and his *parousia*.[248] That means, Christ accomplished salvation on the cross, but did not confer it. "It was only in the appropriating work of the Holy Spirit that salvation was actually conferred, by way of word and sacrament. The objectification of Christology made this subjectification of pneumatology necessary. Christology and pneumatology together then added up to soteriology."[249] Here Moltmann's attempt is to get beyond the traditional Protestant pattern which simply adds together Christ and the Spirit or the objectivity of

---

245. Moltmann, *The Spirit of Life*, 118.
246. Moltmann, *The Spirit of Life*, 119.
247. Moltmann, *The Spirit of Life*, 119.
248. Moltmann, *The Spirit of Life*, 81.
249. Moltmann, *The Spirit of Life*, 81.

salvation and its subjective appropriation. However, before entering into such a discussion, it is important to discuss the position of Moltmann regarding sin and salvation.

3.7.1 Sin and Salvation: General or Specific

Moltmann insists that the Reformation doctrine of salvation is based on Paul's teaching that all have sinned and fall short of the glory of God (Rom 3:22). The Reformers were convinced that through original sin, the godless nature and unrighteousness of human beings have come upon the world. That means they insisted on the equal universality to all sinners.[250] The same way, the Pauline teaching about the justifying righteousness of God has the universality of sin as its premise, and the universality of salvation from sin as its objective. It points out that condemnation came upon all through one person's trespass, and therefore, acquittal and life for all came through one person's act of righteousness (Rom 5:18). In this sense, the atonement Christology sees both Christ's death and his resurrection as vicarious on behalf of all. Moltmann argues that this universal concept of sin and salvation is so widespread in the Protestantism although there is an alternative in the Synoptic gospels that they talk about sinners quite specifically and in a social context.[251]

Moltmann maintains that the doctrine of universality of sin is a metaphysical view of sin.[252] Consequently, this generality prevents many people from finding either the Catholic doctrine of grace or the Protestant doctrine of justification convincing. Hence, sin must be seen strictly within the therapeutical circle which embraces the knowledge of Christ, knowledge of our own misery, and the new life in faith. In this way, according to Moltmann, "The Protestant doctrine about the justification of sinners, and today's theology about the liberation of the oppressed do not have to be

---

250. Moltmann, *The Spirit of Life*, 124.
251. Moltmann, *The Spirit of Life*, 125.
252. Moltmann insists that the eating of the forbidden fruit in the Garden of Eden belongs to the world of myth, which offers a metaphysical interpretation of the physical history of the world. The myth about paradise and the fall never played as fundamental a role in Judaism as it did in Christianity. Judaism never deduced from it any doctrine of original sin. So it is important for Christians not merely to look at the mythical story, but to see the real history of injustice and violence as sin to find from God's Spirit the energy to act justly. See Moltmann, *The Spirit of Life*, 126.

antithetical. They can correct and enrich one another mutually. The full and complete Protestant doctrine of justification is a liberation theology: it is about the liberation of people deprived of justice, and about the liberation of the unjust, so that they may all be freed for a just society."[253] Thus for Moltmann, one must consider the structural sin as important instead of looking too exclusively at individuals.

3.7.2 Spirit and Justification

Justification occupies the opening subject in the course of his assessment of salvation. When delineating justification, Moltmann broadens the concept beyond the justification of sinners explicated by Paul in his epistles. Moltmann, writes that, "It is surprising that Protestant theology has not noticed the analogy between God's 'justifying' righteousness and his righteousness that 'creates justice'… for just as in Paul *the justification of the sinner* becomes the revelation of God's righteousness in the world, so in the Old Testament *the establishing of justice* for people deprived of it is the quintessence of the divine mercy, and hence of the divine righteousness."[254] Thus for Moltmann, the work of Messiah is not just salvific; rather, he *creates* justice as well (Isa 11:4; 32: 15ff.; 42:1, etc.). God, who is immanently with us in the Spirit, gives justice because he himself has been deprived of justice. God creates justice for the disenfranchised, marginalized, victimized, and oppressed "through his *solidarity* with them."[255] In short for Moltmann, justification is not just forgiveness of sins and hence he follows a more expanded account of justification.

Moltmann insists that justification is the work of the Holy Spirit. Then the immediate question is why Moltmann insists on justification as the work of the Spirit. This is due to the fact that the Spirit is judge for Moltmann. He makes his point clear with two arguments. Firstly, in negative terms, the Spirit is the Spirit of righteousness and justice.[256] Secondly, in positive terms, the Spirit of God is the presence of Christ among and in the victims of violence, who declares solidarity with them in the Spirit.[257] That

---

253. Moltmann, *The Spirit of Life*, 128.
254. Moltmann, *The Spirit of Life*, 129.
255. Moltmann, *The Spirit of Life*, 130.
256. Moltmann, *The Spirit of Life*, 142.
257. Moltmann, *The Spirit of Life*, 143.

means the Spirit is the atoning power of Christ's substitution among and in the perpetrators. This leads Moltmann to move away from the traditional doctrine of justification with new proposals.

Moltmann suggests three possible alterations in the doctrine of justification. Firstly, justification "must show the saving significance of Christ's death *and resurrection.*"[258] It means that being justified involves more than just forgiveness of sins and it leads to the regeneration of the individual and to the renewal of the cosmos. Secondly, justification "must from the outset be presented pneumatologically as *experience of the Spirit.*"[259] The reason is that the event of being justified must be a pneumatological event because it is through the work of the Spirit that the death and resurrection of Jesus is made universally efficacious. Finally, justification "must be *eschatologically oriented.*"[260] That means, justification never ends with the individual rather must be waiting for the new creation of everything in the *eschaton*. David Beck argues that, "Moltmann wants to expand the notion of justification to include other elements besides the cross and juridical pardon. He wants to include such dimensions as the new creation to life, the awakening of love and the rebirth to a living hope."[261] In short for Moltmann, experience of the Spirit must be Christologically oriented and eschatologically aligned. It must be trinitarian as well. Moltmann writes that the atonement reaches the human beings "out of the compassion of the Father, through the vicariously suffered God-forsakenness of the Son, and in the exonerating power of the Holy Spirit. It is a single movement of love, welling up out of the Father's pain, manifested in the Son's sufferings, and experienced in the Spirit of life. In this way God becomes the God of the godless."[262] Thus keeping a trinitarian order, Moltmann insists that justification is experience of the Spirit that is based on Christ's death and resurrection and is oriented towards the consummation of all things.

---

258. Moltmann, *The Spirit of Life*, 149.
259. Moltmann, *The Spirit of Life*, 149.
260. Moltmann, *The Spirit of Life*, 149.
261. Beck, *The Holy Spirit*, 189.
262. Moltmann, *The Spirit of Life*, 137.

3.7.3 Rebirth and Regeneration

We have already noted that justification is a pneumatological experience, which is accomplished in the work of Christ. But on the other hand, regeneration is a trinitarian event, which has taken place particularly in the divine Spirit. The typical passages to which Moltmann refers are Titus 3:5-7 and 1 Peter 1:3 which explain the trinitarian nature of rebirth. For Moltmann, it happens through the Spirit. He writes that, "... the eternal foundation of regeneration is the mercy of God, the Father of Jesus Christ. The historical foundation for regeneration is Christ, or to be more exact: the resurrection of Christ from the dead ... The medium of regeneration is the Holy Spirit ...."[263] The operation of the Spirit as we experience it is therefore a double one: it is the justification of the godless out of grace, and their rebirth to a living hope through their installation in their right to inherit God's future.[264] In short, referring to Titus 3:5-7 and 1 Peter 1:3 Moltmann concludes that, "In these texts the interpretation of regeneration or rebirth as new creation is christologically based, pneumatologically accomplished and eschatologically oriented. The experience of the Spirit makes Christ – the *risen* Christ – present, and with him makes the eschatological future present too. Precisely because of this, experience of the Spirit is the experience of the presence of eternity."[265]

According to Moltmann, the Christian tradition has viewed rebirth as a phenomenon affecting the individuals as an inward experience of the soul.[266] However, the Jewish apocalyptic tradition understood regeneration on an eschatological level due to the fact that it intended the rebirth of the entire creation for the kingdom of God. Moltmann writes that, "Neither the Reformation nor the Pietistic and revivalist theologians took this cosmic, apocalyptic character of 'rebirth' into account, however."[267] Hence, Moltmann insists that the Christian tradition can follow the Jewish apocalyptic tradition emphasising the eschatological nature of rebirth, even when talking about the rebirth of the individual. In this way, a

---

263. Moltmann, *The Spirit of Life*, 146; Moltmann, *The Source of Life*, 28.
264. Moltmann, *The Spirit of Life*, 146.
265. Moltmann, *The Spirit of Life*, 147.
266. Moltmann, *The Spirit of Life*, 145.
267. Moltmann, *The Spirit of Life*, 145.

Christian doctrine of regeneration can unite eschatology with Christology and pneumatology.[268]

3.7.3.1 Regeneration Makes Christ's Resurrection Present in the Spirit

Based on the Jewish apocalyptic tradition, Moltmann insists that Christians can also connect individual rebirth with cosmic eschatology through pneumatology. Moltmann writes that, "A coherent process issues from the rebirth of Christ from death through the Spirit, by way of the rebirth of mortal human beings through the Spirit, to the universal rebirth of the cosmos through the Spirit. In this process God the Father acts through the Spirit on Christ, and through Christ on the Spirit. The operations of his acts are the operations of the Spirit and are present in the Spirit."[269] Hence for Moltmann, regeneration makes the resurrection of Christ present and it is the opening of eternal life. Such a position gives pneumatology a justification of its own between Christology which is its premise and the eschatology towards which it is aligned. For Moltmann, resurrection is the beginning of the rebirth of the whole creation, and it is "the rebirth of Christ."[270] Believers are possessed by the Spirit of the resurrection and through it are born again to a hope for eternal life. Like resurrection, rebirth is inception of a new form of human life. It is the anticipation of the resurrected life that Christ already holds. Moreover, in the event in which believers are born again to become children of God and heirs of his kingdom, the efficacies of Christ and the efficacies of the Spirit interpenetrate. We can call it either justification, or regeneration, but still we are describing the operation of the Spirit.[271] Thus Moltmann concludes that experiences of the Spirit are unfathomable depth, because in them God himself is present in us, so that in the immanence of our hearts we discover a transcendent depth. If this Spirit of God is "the Spirit of the resurrection" then we are possessed by a hope which sees unlimited potentialities ahead, because it looks towards God's future.[272] In his words, "The transcendent depths of the divine Spirit

---

268. Beck, *The Holy Spirit*, 189.
269. Moltmann, *The Spirit of Life*, 153.
270. Moltmann, *The Spirit of Life*, 152; Moltmann, *The Source of Life*, 30.
271. Moltmann, *The Spirit of Life*, 153; Moltmann, *The Source of Life*, 28.
272. Moltmann, *The Spirit of Life*, 155.

and the eschatological breadth of the Spirit of the resurrection mean that we cannot talk about our 'rebirth' or 'regeneration' as if it were a one-and-for-all experience, something finished and done with that is now behind us. We are still involved in the experience of renewal, and the becoming-new travels with us."[273] In short, there is a growth in faith and a growth in the new life of the Spirit.

According to Moltmann, in rebirth, we are not experiencing the Spirit as a counterpart, but as a divine presence. He writes that, "If the new life is experienced and lived in the Spirit, then the Spirit is not itself the object of experience; it is the medium and space for experience."[274] The speciality of this kind of experience of the Spirit is that the Spirit can appear to be so mysterious not because it is far away rather because it is so close. Moreover, life in the Spirit is a life in the "broad place where there is no cramping" (Job 36:16). So in the new life we experience the Spirit as a "broad place" – as the free space for our freedom, as the living space for our lives, as the horizon inviting us to discover life. "The broad place" is the most hidden and most silent presence of God's Spirit in us and round about us.[275] Moltmann writes, "We explore the depth of this space through the trust of the heart. We search out the length of this space through extravagant hope. We discover the breadth of this space through the torrents of love which we receive and give. God's Spirit encompasses us from all sides and wherever we are (Ps 139). Christ's Spirit is our immanent power to live – God's Spirit is our transcendent space for living."[276]

3.7.3.2 Rebirth and Motherhood of the Spirit

Motherhood of the Spirit and the rebirth is a significant theme in the theology of Moltmann. It seems that the main reason for this affinity can be the influence of his wife who was active in the feminist movement. When dealing with the motherhood of the Spirit, Moltmann follows Makarios, a fourth century monk from Syrian tradition, and Zinzendorf, the founder of the first American community of brothers and sisters in Pennsylvania in

---

273. Moltmann, *The Spirit of Life*, 155.
274. Moltmann, *The Spirit of Life*, 157.
275. Moltmann, *The Spirit of Life*, 178.
276. Moltmann, *The Spirit of Life*, 178-179.

1741.²⁷⁷ Both of them have extensively dealt with the motherhood of the Spirit in their writings. Moltmann, basing on these two figures, interprets the experience of rebirth and divine comfort as revealing the feminity of the Spirit. Moltmann writes that, "If believers are 'born' again from the Holy Spirit, then the Spirit is 'the mother' of God's children and can in this sense also be termed a 'feminine' Spirit. If the Holy Spirit is 'the comforter' (*Paraclete*), it comforts 'as a mother comforts.' In this sense, it is the motherly comforter of believers."²⁷⁸

According to Moltmann, when this motherhood of the Spirit is emphasized, God is experienced as the "well of life."²⁷⁹ That means, God as the one who is giving birth, nourishing, protecting, and consoling. These are expressions to describe the relations of the Spirit to its children. Moreover, the motherhood of the Spirit proves the relationship of Jesus with the human beings as their brother since they are born anew of the Spirit. Moltmann argues that as Jesus was born through the medium of the Spirit, believers also experience their birth from the same Spirit. Hence, Mary becomes a type for the Spirit, because both of them carry out their motherly roles in the history of Christ and of the believers.²⁸⁰ In short, the motherly image of the Spirit helps Moltmann to achieve two important facts. Firstly, the personality of the Spirit can be grasped clearly with this image in comparison to others. Secondly, the motherhood of the Spirit will help to overcome patriarchalism in the image of God and male domination in the church. Moreover, it will open ways to enter into dialogue with feminist theologians.²⁸¹

3.7.4 The Sanctification and the Spirit

The life that has been born again and regenerated from God's Spirit must grow and arrive at its proper form.²⁸² For Moltmann, "If the primal experience of the Spirit is called rebirth, this metaphor – sanctification – itself

---

277. Moltmann, *The Source of Life*, 36.
278. Moltmann, *The Spirit of Life*, 157; Moltmann, *The Source of Life*, 27.
279. Moltmann, *The Spirit of Life*, 159.
280. Moltmann, *The Way of Jesus Christ*, 83-84.
281. Moltmann, *History and the Triune God*, 65.
282. Moltmann, *The Source of Life*, 33.

implies 'growth' in faith, in knowledge, and in wisdom."[283] Moltmann holds that sanctification implies "growth" in faith, in knowledge, and in wisdom. It is a progression in the life of believers to become adults in faith.[284] However, for Moltmann, there are two things that are important in this growth. Firstly, this growth of sanctification should not be interpreted individualistically. On the other hand, we experience life in the interplay between what is inward and what is outward.[285] That means, "Our biography is woven into our social history, and into the political history of our era; and it is only in relatively peaceful times that the naturalistic expression 'growth' is an appropriate way of describing history at all."[286] Secondly, this growth of sanctification should not be interpreted linearly.[287] It means that the perfection of a person is a complex thing which involves not just the alteration of conscious choices but the transformation of the whole person, including the unconscious realm. Moreover, Moltmann understands sanctification as harmony with God through the Spirit. Moltmann insists that sanctified lives are holy and happy and they seek harmony with other people and everything that God has created and in which his Spirit is present.[288] Sanctification for Moltmann is not just present world reality rather it is eschatological as well. Following Paul, Moltmann maintains that the Spirit experienced in the present is the advance payment on our complete sanctification. Hence, there is a greater fulfilment in the *eschaton*. Hence Moltmann insists that, "Sanctification is the beginning of glorification; glorification is the consummation of sanctification."[289]

There are some important aspects that Moltmann deals with when he discusses the significance of sanctification today. Firstly, sanctification today means rediscovering *the sanctity of life* and *the divine mystery of creation*, and defending them from life's manipulation, the secularization of nature, and the destruction of the world through human violence.[290] Secondly,

---

283. Moltmann, *The Spirit of Life*, 161.
284. Moltmann, *The Spirit of Life*, 162; Moltmann, *The Source of Life*, 33-34.
285. Moltmann, *The Spirit of Life*, 161.
286. Moltmann, *The Spirit of Life*, 162.
287. Moltmann, *The Spirit of Life*, 161.
288. Moltmann, *The Source of Life*, 48.
289. Moltmann, *The Spirit of Life*, 163.
290. Moltmann, *The Source of Life*, 49-52.

sanctification means integrating ourselves once more into the web of life from which modern society has isolated human beings.[291] Thirdly, there must be a reverence for life, which means respect for one's own life and the life of other creatures.[292] In short, Moltmann maintains that to sanctify life does not mean manipulating it religiously and morally. It means being freed and justified, loved and affirmed, and more and more alive. Life in God's Spirit is a life entrusted to the guidance and drive of the Spirit, a life that lets the Spirit come.[293] Separations from God and the mutual isolations of human beings are abolished where God's presence is experienced in the Spirit, and the divine energy interpenetrates body and soul once more, and makes them fruitful.[294]

3.8 Holy Spirit and Ecclesiology

The main theological work of Moltmann on the doctrine of church is *The Church in the Power of the Spirit*, which deals with the significance of the Spirit with regard to the church. For Moltmann, church is part of the history of the creative Spirit. It means that it is the concrete form in which human beings experience the history of Christ.[295] However, it has an eschatological orientation as well. That means the history of the Spirit, that is the church, will work as a way and a transition to the kingdom of God. Therefore, the present existence of the church is in the experience and practice of the Spirit from the eschatological anticipation of the kingdom. This experience of the Spirit mediates the presence of the history of Christ and the future of the new creation making the church its mediation.[296] Hence, for Moltmann, church, on the one hand, is the community of human beings for whom Christ is the Lord and on the other hand, it is the community of human beings who live and wish to live in expectation of his appearance.

For Moltmann, the church is also the community of the justified sinners.[297] It is the fellowship of the people in the Spirit who are liberated by

---

291. Moltmann, *The Spirit of Life*, 172.
292. Moltmann, *The Spirit of Life*, 173.
293. Moltmann, *The Spirit of Life*, 176.
294. Moltmann, *The Spirit of Life*, 176-177.
295. Moltmann, *The Church in the Power of the Spirit*, 35.
296. Moltmann, *The Church in the Power of the Spirit*, 35; Moltmann, *The Source of Life*, 94.
297. Moltmann, *The Church in the Power of the Spirit*, 33.

Christ and experience salvation in their life. Being such a fellowship, the church is on the way to fulfilling the meaning of the history of Christ. The church lives in the Spirit and it is the beginning and earnest of the future of the new creation.[298] As the historical community of Christ, therefore, the church is the eschatological creation of the Spirit. In this sense history passes into eschatology and eschatology into history. This transition is called the work of the Holy Spirit.[299]

According to Moltmann, in the concurrence of faith in Christ and hope for the *parousia*, this community grows in the sphere of the Spirit into a charismatic community, where potentialities and capabilities are brought to life.[300] The charismatically enlivened "body of Christ" sees itself as a "down payment" – as the advance pledge and beginning of the new creation of all things. In this manner, church is "the temple of the Holy Spirit."[301] Thus, for Moltmann, it is pneumatology that brings Christology and eschatology together. In his own words, "There is no mediation between Christ and the kingdom of God except the present experience of the Spirit, for the Spirit is the Spirit of Christ and the living energy of the new creation of all things. In the present of the Spirit are both origin and consummation."[302] Moltmann insists that since the sacramental happening cannot be "created" and calculated, the solution of the problem of faith and experience, hope and reality, the nature and form of the church, has to be looked in pneumatology. It will help us to perceive the history and promise of Christ through which we become aware of the coming rule of God in Word and sacrament and church, and through which we enter into the fellowship of the history of the triune God. This perception, awareness, and fellowship are taken place in the mediation of the Spirit.[303] There are two main headings under which Moltmann discusses the relationship between the Spirit and the church and they are firstly, church in the presence of the Spirit and secondly, church in the power of the Spirit.

---

298. Moltmann, *The Church in the Power of the Spirit*, 33.
299. Moltmann, *The Church in the Power of the Spirit*, 33.
300. Moltmann, *The Spirit of Life*, 69.
301. Moltmann, *The Spirit of Life*, 69.
302. Moltmann, *The Spirit of Life*, 69.
303. Moltmann, *The Church in the Power of the Spirit*, 28.

3.8.1 The Church in the Presence of the Spirit

The church lives in a history which finds its validation in the resurrection of Christ and whose future is the all-embracing kingdom of freedom. The living remembrance of Christ in the church directs the church's hope towards the kingdom, and the living hope in the kingdom leads back to the inexhaustible remembrance of Christ. According to Moltmann, the power of this remembrance is called "the power of the Holy Spirit" because the human beings cannot believe in Jesus as the Christ and hope for the future with their own strength, reason, and will. Faith in Christ and hope for the kingdom are due to the presence of God in the Spirit.[304] Moreover, the church understands the tension between faith and hope as the history of the Spirit that makes all things new. Its fellowship with Christ is founded on the experience of the Spirit which manifests Christ. Its fellowship in the kingdom of God is founded on the power of the Spirit, which leads it into truth and freedom. It is when the church, out of faith in Christ and in hope for the kingdom, sees itself as the messianic fellowship that it will logically understand its presence and its path in the presence and the process of the Holy Spirit.[305] When we discuss about the presence of the Spirit in the church, Moltmann discusses mainly three aspects here in relation to the Spirit.

3.8.1.1 Spirit and Sacraments

Since church is the history of the Spirit, Moltmann brings the ministries of the church and sacraments within the context of the history of the Spirit. For him sacraments are the definitive event that makes the church the church.[306] Moltmann never considers the ministries of the church as

---

304. Moltmann, *The Church in the Power of the Spirit*, 197.
305. Moltmann, *The Church in the Power of the Spirit*, 197; the presence and future of redemption, the church and the kingdom of God are framed and comprehended by belief in the Holy Spirit. History and eschatology are therefore parts of pneumatology. This means, conversely that pneumatology is developed historically and eschatologically, in the sense that the history of the church, the communion of saints, and the forgiveness of sins are to be interpreted as the history of the future. Also the eschatology of the resurrection of the body and life everlasting are to be seen as the future of history. That is why we understand this mediation of eschatology and history as the presence of the Holy Spirit. See Moltmann, *The Church in the Power of the Spirit*, 198.
306. Moltmann, *The Church in the Power of the Spirit*, 27.

somehow containing or mediating the presence of the Spirit. Rather for him, the sacraments and the ministries are the movement and the presence of the Spirit. Hence he writes that, "There is no 'Spirit of the sacraments' and 'no Spirit of the ministry,' there are sacraments and ministries of the Spirit."[307] Moltmann understands sacraments also in eschatological terms. He maintains that future and salvation become manifest to faith only as a mystery through the proclamation and the gift of the Spirit. It means, salvation and future are disclosed to faith through the Spirit and the Word. The Spirit and Word therefore point beyond themselves to the consummation.[308] On the basis of this eschatological Christology, which sees the coming of Christ as the dawn of the revelation of the divine secret or mystery in the last days, we are justified in finding the eschatological transition to the expectation of the future revelation of this mystery. The riches of God revealed in Christ are overflowing and spread beyond themselves. The use of the word "mystery" therefore spreads beyond Christology and flows into pneumatology, ecclesiology, and the eschatology of world history.[309]

Having established the point that the coming of Christ is the dawn of mystery, Moltmann develops the trinitarian concept of the sacrament. Moltmann maintains that, "The presence of the kingdom of God and the revelation of the divine mystery of the last days are to be found in the eschatological gift of the Holy Spirit. He reveals Christ and creates faith. Proclamation, fellowship, and the emblematic messianic acts take place in the power of the Holy Spirit. He is the power of the divine future and the one who completes the divine history."[310] This trinitarian concept of the sacrament includes on the one hand the eschatological history of God's dealings with the world in the "signs and wonders" of the Holy Spirit, and in the "signs of the end." In the eschatological gift of the Holy Spirit "word and sacrament,'" "ministries and *charismata*" become comprehensible as the revelations and powers of Christ and his future.[311] In the framework of the trinitarian concept of the sacraments we therefore understand the

---

307. Moltmann, *The Church in the Power of the Spirit*, 289.
308. Moltmann, *The Church in the Power of the Spirit*, 204.
309. Moltmann, *The Church in the Power of the Spirit*, 204.
310. Moltmann, *The Church in the Power of the Spirit*, 205.
311. Moltmann, *The Church in the Power of the Spirit*, 205.

proclamation, the sacraments, and the *charismata* as the "signs and wonders" of the history of the Spirit who creates salvation and brings about the new creation and who through Christ unites us with the Father and glorifies him.[312]

3.8.1.1.1 Spirit and Baptism

Since Moltmann deals with sacraments in trinitarian schema, he brings baptism also within the trinitarian history of God's dealing with the world. He writes that, "Through baptism in Christ's name believers are publicly set in Christ's fellowship; and through baptism in the name of the triune God they are thereby simultaneously set in the history of God."[313] For Moltmann, baptism is a public sign of the life of the Spirit, who unites believers with Christ and brings the new creation.[314] In contradiction to the Protestant tradition, in which baptism is presented in the framework of soteriology, Moltmann sets baptism in the context of eschatology emphasising its place in the overall history of God's dealing with the world. Moreover, Moltmann insists that baptism is pneumatological. In order to establish his case, Moltmann refers to the Synoptic gospels where it is reported that at the baptism of Jesus, the Spirit descended upon him and equipped him for the messianic mission. This operation of the Spirit can be seen all through his life until the death on the cross. Hence, Moltmann argues that, "The history of Christ and the history of the Holy Spirit are so interwoven that a pneumatic Christology leads with inner cogency to a christological pneumatology."[315]

3.8.1.1.2 Spirit and Lord's Supper

Moltmann looks at the Lord's Supper also in a trinitarian framework as he did with baptism. He understands the Lord's Supper as a repeatable sign of hope. He writes that, "Just as baptism is the eschatological *sign of starting out*, valid once and for all, so the regular and constant fellowship at the table of the Lord is the eschatological *sign of being on the way*. If baptism is

---

312. Moltmann, *The Church in the Power of the Spirit*, 206.
313. Moltmann, *The Church in the Power of the Spirit*, 226.
314. Moltmann, *The Church in the Power of the Spirit*, 226.
315. Moltmann, *The Church in the Power of the Spirit*, 236.

called the unique *sign of grace*, then the Lord's supper must be understood as the repeatable *sign of hope*."[316] Moreover, Moltmann insists that the Lord's Supper is an eschatological sign of history.[317] He explains that while the Eucharist is celebrated, the community thanks God the Father for the creation and redemption of the world and glorifies the triune God in its song of joy. It prays for the eschatological gift of the Spirit, so that the Spirit may fill it with the powers of the new creation and may descend on all flesh. It prays for the coming of his kingdom.[318] The important aspect of the Lord's Supper for Moltmann is that the Lord's Supper makes the risen Christ present in the community in the Spirit. He writes that, "Just as the remembrance of Christ's death makes the fellowship conscious of the 'openness' of his self-giving, so the prayer for the Spirit opens it for the perfecting power of his glory. In this way the Lord's Supper becomes the mark of the history of the Spirit."[319]

3.8.1.1.3 *Word of God and the Holy Spirit*

At the heart of Moltmann's contribution was his rediscovery that the Bible is oriented towards history, or more specifically, to eschatology.[320] Moltmann discusses the significance of Word under the sacraments because he finds proclamation also as a sacrament. According to Moltmann, there are no words of God without human experiences of God's Spirit.[321] Thus the words of proclamation spoken by the Bible and the church must also be related to the experience of people today, so that they are not merely hearers of the Word, but become spokespersons of the Word too.[322] But this is only possible if Word and Spirit are seen as existing in a *mutual relationship*, not as a one-way street. The Spirit is the subject determining the Word and not just the operation of the Word. Moreover, the efficacies of the Spirit

---

316. Moltmann, *The Church in the Power of the Spirit*, 243.
317. Moltmann, *The Church in the Power of the Spirit*, 243.
318. Moltmann, *The Church in the Power of the Spirit*, 247.
319. Moltmann, *The Church in the Power of the Spirit*, 257.
320. Grenz and Franke, *Beyond Foundationalism*, 245.
321. Moltmann criticises the concept of verbal inspiration. He writes, "To see the Spirit at work only in the verbal inspiration of scripture is a reduction of the mighty efficacy of God the Spirit which does not accord with the 'matter of scripture.'" See Moltmann, *Experiences in Theology*, 136.
322. Moltmann, *The Spirit of Life*, 3.

reach beyond the Word.[323] The indwelling of the Spirit in our hearts goes deeper than the conscious level in us. It rouses all our senses, permeates the unconscious too, and quickens the body, giving it new life (1 Cor 6:19f.).[324] A new energy for living proceeds from the Spirit. To blind the experience of the Spirit is solely one sided, and represses these dimensions. He maintains that the Word is bound to the Spirit, but that the Spirit is not bound to the Word, and that the Spirit and Word belong in a mutual relationship which must not be conceived exclusively, or in merely intellectual terms.[325]

For Moltmann, the church proceeds from the interaction between the Spirit and Word and also the Son and the Spirit. The purpose of the coming of Jesus Christ and his death is "the outpouring of the Holy Spirit on all flesh."[326] Moltmann asks the question, why it is from the Son and the Father that the Spirit comes upon all flesh? Here he finds that there is an interaction between the Spirit and the Word. In the interaction between the Spirit and the Word, the Spirit of Christ radiates from the Word of God that *has become flesh*. It is the earthly life of the bodily death, and the "glorified bodiliness" of the raised Christ (Phil 3:21) from which the Spirit shines, transfiguring the earthly world and "all flesh" through his radiance. The verbal presence of Christ in the proclaimed Word is important, because it names the name, however the figure of Christ and his taking this form upon himself among men and women goes beyond that.[327] Moreover, he understands the interactions between Christ and the Spirit as forces of historical movements. There is an objective for these interactions, and so there are also rhythms in the movements, rhythms which call forth Word and Spirit. The objective of Christ's history is in this respect the coming and outpouring of the Spirit upon all flesh. It means the quickening of all

---

323. Moltmann, *The Source of Life*, 93.
324. Moltmann maintains that, "In the New Testament 'the matter of scripture' is the unconditioned endorsement and universal enactment of God's promises through and in Christ, and the beginning of their fulfillment in the experiences of God's Spirit. The Christian scriptures are 'holy' inasmuch as they correspond to God's promise in Christ and in the Spirit; they are 'hallowed' or sanctified by their function for the proclamation of the gospel to the nations, and for the new life in the Spirit. They are writings on which the church is founded and life-renewing texts of the promise." See Moltmann, *Experiences in Theology*, 136.
325. Moltmann, *The Spirit of Life*, 3.
326. Moltmann, *The Spirit of Life*, 232.
327. Moltmann, *The Spirit of Life*, 233.

mortal beings through their fellowship with God's eternal life.[328] The goal of this history of the Spirit is the eschatological restoration of all things and their new creation for eternal glory.[329]

Moltmann insists that the Spirit of God is the real interpreter of the Word. It is the Spirit of truth, who reveals what is hidden. What the Spirit of truth communicates is knowledge of Christ and of the God who has raised him. But the facts that the Spirit communicates is something new and specific to the Spirit, over against what Christ and God the Father have done and do.[330] Moltmann even understands that Christ came to die and rise again to send the Spirit who sanctifies life and opens up the future of the eternal kingdom. Thus the faith which the Spirit awakens in the human beings is in content wholly related to Christ and God. It means faith then comes into existence when God the Father and Jesus the Lord act together in the Spirit.[331] Moltmann explains this in a beautiful manner. The experience of freedom always springs from a coincidence of the liberating Word and the proper time, the *kairos*. The divine Word becomes the word that binds or looses when it is spoken as the right word at the right time. Then the Word that comes from outside sets free the inner energies of faith, hope, and love. Moltmann calls this as the inward testimony of the Holy Spirit.[332] Through this faith the new day of God begins in their lives. Hence Moltmann holds that from time immemorial, the Spirit has been understood as the eternal light which enlightens and illuminates.[333] However, Moltmann does not want to see just the subjective working of the Spirit in the human beings because if the workings of the Spirit are seen only as the subjective operation of the objective Word of God in the hearts of believers, they are being too narrowly defined. Hence Moltmann insists that the *kairos* of a historical situation opens up external potentialities too. It means, the Spirit opens new chances and possibilities of the gospel through the circumstances of history. In the experienced reality of our lives, the two work together and show themselves to be one – the Spirit

---

328. Moltmann, *The Spirit of Life*, 233-234.
329. Moltmann, *The Spirit of Life*, 234.
330. Moltmann, *Experiences in Theology*, 145.
331. Moltmann, *The Spirit of Life*, 103; Moltmann, *The Source of Life*, 94.
332. Moltmann, *The Spirit of Life*, 103.
333. Moltmann, *Experiences in Theology*, 145.

of Christ and the Spirit of God, the Word and the *kairos*, inward powers and outward possibilities.³³⁴

3.8.2 *The Church in the Power of the Spirit*

After delineating the presence of Christ in the church, Moltmann focuses on the mission of the Church as an eschatological community. Moltmann maintains that the Spirit of the last days and the eschatological community of the saved belong together. The new people of God see themselves in their existence and form as being "the creation of the Spirit," and therefore as the initial fulfilment of the new creation of all things and the glorification of God. The Spirit calls them into life and makes effective its living powers and the ministries that spring from them.³³⁵ That means the new creation has a mission to fulfil in the Spirit. However, it is not the church that has a mission of salvation to fulfil rather it is the mission of the Son and the Spirit through the Father that includes the church. The Spirit "administers" the church with the events of Word and faith, sacraments and grace, offices and traditions.³³⁶ Moltmann writes:

> If the church understands itself, with all its tasks and powers, in the Spirit and against the horizon of the Spirit's history, then it also understands its particularity as one element in the power of the Spirit and has no need to maintain its special power and its special charges with absolute and self-destructive claims. It then has no need to look sideways in suspicion or jealousy as the saving efficacies of the Spirit outside the church; instead it can recognise them thankfully as signs that the Spirit is greater than the church and that God's purpose of salvation reaches beyond the church.³³⁷

In short, the mission of the church is to participate in Christ's messianic mission and in the creative mission of the Spirit for the liberation of creation. Wherever it takes place through the Spirit, there exists the church.³³⁸

---

334. Moltmann, *The Spirit of Life*, 103.
335. Moltmann, *The Church in the Power of the Spirit*, 294.
336. Moltmann, *The Church in the Power of the Spirit*, 64.
337. Moltmann, *The Church in the Power of the Spirit*, 64-65.
338. Moltmann, *The Church in the Power of the Spirit*, 65.

3.8.2.1 Christian Is Charismatic

Although Moltmann insisted that the mission belongs to the Son and Spirit, each member in the community has a mission to fulfil.[339] According to Moltmann, Paul states in 1 Corinthians 7 that there is one calling and many people are called. All are called to the peace of God, but everyone should remain in the particular calling to which he/she has been called. When a person is called, whatever he/she is and brings with him/her becomes a *charisma* through his/her calling, since it is accepted by the Spirit and put at the service of the kingdom of God.[340] Agreeing with the argument of Paul, Moltmann insists that whatever can be put at the service of Christ's liberating lordship is a *charisma*.[341] In other words, every Christian is charismatic in his/her own particular way because the Spirit is poured out upon all flesh to quicken it. Individual powers and energies become charismatic in the *relationships* which give form to the shared life-process.[342] The special *charismata* which are newly created by the Spirit are experienced for the first time in the discipleship of Jesus.[343] But today, the congregation is the place where the Spirit is revealed. Moltmann writes:

> If we sum up these charismata, we find the *kerygmatic charismata* of the female and male apostles, prophets, teachers, evangelists and exhorters, but also phenomena such as inspiration, ecstasy, speaking in tongues, and other ways of expressing faith. In addition there are the *diaconial*, or charitable, *charismata* of the deacons, the people who nurse the sick, the people who give alms, and the widows; but again there are special gifts too, such as the healing of sick bodies, exorcism, the healing of memories, and other kinds of help. Finally there are the *cybernetic charismata* of "the first" in faith,

---

339. For Moltmann, God's mission is the sending of the Holy Spirit from the Father through the Son into this world so that this world will live because Spirit is the source of life and brings life into this world. The sending of the Spirit is the revelation of God's indestructible affirmation of life and his marvellous joy in life. See Moltmann, *The Source of Life*, 19.
340. Moltmann, *The Spirit of Life*, 182; Moltmann, *The Source of Life*, 56.
341. Moltmann, *The Church in the Power of the Spirit*, 296.
342. Moltmann, *The Spirit of Life*, 182.
343. Moltmann, *The Spirit of Life*, 183.

the "presidents," shepherds and bishops; but there are also particular phenomena in the context of peace-making and building up community.[344]

For Moltmann, these tasks and functions emerge only when the church comes into being and they have to be seen as special gifts and tasks given by the Spirit.[345]

Moltmann says that it is historically indisputable phenomenon that the birth of the Christian congregations was accompanied by "speaking with tongues."[346] Accepting the fact that the speaking in tongues is still existing, Moltmann writes:

> I have no personal experience of this phenomenon, so I can neither explain nor dispute it. I can only describe it from the outside, from its effect on the people concerned. It would seem to me to be an inward possession by the Holy Spirit which is so strong that it can no longer find adequate expression in comprehensible language, so that it utters itself glossolalia – just an intense pain is expressed by unrestrained weeping, or extreme joy by jumping and dancing.[347]

However, Moltmann understands speaking in tongues as a powerful experience of the Spirit. He holds the view that speaking with tongues is the beginning through which a powerful experience of the Spirit loosens the tongues of people who have been dumb, so that they can express what moves them so much. First of all this is very important for the people affected, and then it is important for the whole congregation. These are personal expressions of a personal experience of the Spirit which exalts the people who are touched by it. And they are new ways of expressing experiences of the Spirit.[348]

---

344. Moltmann, *The Spirit of Life*, 183.
345. Moltmann, *The Source of Life*, 58.
346. Moltmann, *The Source of Life*, 60-61.
347. Moltmann, *The Spirit of Life*, 185.
348. Moltmann, *The Source of Life*, 61.

Nonetheless, Moltmann criticises the charismatic community for their escapist "spirituality," as David Beck puts it.[349] He wants the charismatic movement to be not just a non-political movement. Hence he asks the question, what about the neglect of *charismata*? Where are the *charismata* of the "charismatics" in the everyday world, in the peace movement, in the movements for liberation, in the ecology movement?[350] At the same time, he argues that all churches need to have this charismatic experience. Hence he writes, "The awakening of personally experienced and personally expressed faith is the 'charismatic experience' today. Before the mainline churches and the bishops and other leaders 'quench' the Spirit of the 'charismatic movement,' we should all make room for the Spirit, not only in church services, but in our bodies too, since those bodies are after all, supposed to be 'a temple of the Holy Spirit' (1 Cor 6:19)."[351]

3.8.2.2 The Church as the Sending Community

Moltmann argues that the people who experience the presence of the Spirit in their life must do two things, namely the gathering of Christians in the church, and secondly, sending out the church to Christians in the world.[352] That means Moltmann makes a distinction between the official church which is gathered and the Christians in the world who are not part of the official church. So church is the gathered congregation who come together for the sake of the Word and sacrament and the Christians in the world is church as it is dispersed in families, vocations, work, and friendships.[353] Hence, the meaning and scope of the church does not depend on the Sunday worship or church going rather it is much more than that. The gathered church has responsibility towards these Christians in the world and the laity are authorised for these Christians. So it is important to view life in the everyday world as just as important as the gathering of the congregation in the feast of worship.[354] Moltmann maintains that believers

---

349. Beck, *Holy Spirit*, 168.
350. Moltmann, *The Spirit of Life*, 186; Moltmann, *The Source of Life*, 62.
351. Moltmann, *The Spirit of Life*, 186.
352. Moltmann, *The Source of Life*, 95.
353. Moltmann, *The Spirit of Life*, 234; Moltmann, *The Source of Life*, 20.
354. Moltmann, *The Spirit of Life*, 234; Moltmann, *The Church in the Power of the Spirit*, 310.

must experience the presence of the Spirit in their homes too as they do in the church; otherwise, they will forget their individual and special callings and endowments.[355] Hence, for Moltmann, as gathering, sending into the world is also important. He writes that, "The gathering serves the sending, and the sending leads into the full life and the living fellowship of the Spirit. The sending acquires its concrete form from the need and distress of the world, which is threatened by injustice, violence, nuclear, and ecological annihilation. It acquires its hope from the horizon of future, the horizon of kingdom of God."[356]

3.8.2.3 The Spirit, Ecumenism, and Other Communities

Moltmann argues that, as far as experiences of the Spirit are concerned, we have to overcome the denominational divisions of the churches.[357] It means the difference between the Protestant definition of the church of Christ and the Orthodox idea of the church as *invocation and coming of the Holy Spirit*. These two perspectives must complement one another because where the Word is, there the Spirit is too – otherwise the Word is not the Word of God. And where the Spirit is, the Spirit shines from the Word and illuminates the understanding of faith – otherwise it is not God's Spirit.[358] The motivation towards ecumenical fellowship with the other churches and the prospect of a conciliar union of divided churches was often ascribed by the pioneers of the ecumenical movement to God's Spirit.[359] Hence today, there is a revolution of feeling that the other churches are not opponents or competitors rather they are partners on a shared path. Moltmann insists that this is possible only if we see the fellowship of the Spirit as something that transcends the denominational frontiers, and throws them open, so

---

355. Moltmann, *The Spirit of Life*, 235.
356. Moltmann, *The Spirit of Life*, 235; Moltmann writes that to grasp the missionary church theologically in a world-wide context means understanding it in the context of the *missio Dei*, mission comprehends the whole church. To proclaim the gospel of the dawning kingdom is the first and most important element in the mission of Jesus, the mission of the Spirit, and the mission of the church. It embraces all activities that serve to liberate creation from slavery. See Moltmann, *The Church in the Power of the Spirit*, 10.
357. Moltmann, *The Source of Life*, 93.
358. Moltmann, *The Source of Life*, 93.
359. Moltmann, *The Spirit of Life*, 4.

that we view Christians belonging to other churches as members of this great community of God.[360]

Along with the above discussed ecumenism, Moltmann argues for a co-operation between the church and other communities in the world, thereby opening itself for the wider operation of the Spirit in the world. Moltmann writes that, "The church above all, which listens to the word of Christ and confesses Christ, exists wholly in its receptivity for the Spirit's coming, for the influence of its energies and the radiance of its light. That makes Christianity alive to the operation of the Holy Spirit *extra muros ecclesiae* – outside the church as well – and prepared to accept the life-furthering communities which people outside the church expect and experience."[361] This means that the church exists in the fellowship of the Spirit, and this fellowship between people is the work of the Spirit which reaches beyond the church. He points out that the Spirit is to be "poured out upon all flesh." When Christ's church invokes the Spirit and pleads the presence of the Spirit, it is seeing itself as the beginning in history of this eschatological event, and it is placing itself in the cosmic context of this restoration of all things. When the church appeals exclusively to Christ, it experiences itself in the wider eschatological and cosmic dimensions of the coming of the Spirit. The Spirit is not tied to the church. The Spirit is concerned with the church, as he is with Israel, for the sake of the kingdom of God, the rebirth of life and the new creation of all things.[362]

3.8.2.4 The Fellowship of the Spirit

According to Moltmann, the inner being of the Spirit is capable of fellowship.[363] This significance of the fellowship of the Spirit leads us to look

---

360. Moltmann, *The Spirit of Life*, 4; Moltmann, *The Church in the Power of the Spirit*, 15ff.
361. Moltmann, *The Spirit of Life*, 230-231.
362. Moltmann, *The Spirit of Life*, 230; Moltmann, *The Source of Life*, 20.
363. Moltmann, *The Spirit of Life*, 217; Moltmann, *The Source of Life*, 89; Moltmann offers a definition to the term fellowship. He says that if we look at the word fellowship itself, we can say that fellowship does not take by force and possesses. It liberates, and draws others into the relationships that are essentially its own. Fellowship means opening ourselves for one another, giving one another a share in ourselves. It creates respect for one another. Fellowship lives in reciprocal participation and from mutual recognition. Fellowship comes into being when people who are different have something in common, and when what is in common is shared by different people. See, Moltmann, *The Source of*

into Moltmann's concept of fellowship of the Spirit. The fellowship of the Spirit begins with the Spirit's presence among his people which is expressed in the idea of *shekinah* in the Jewish theology. According to Moltmann, the basic idea of *shekinah* is "the descent and indwelling of God in space and time, at a particular place and a particular era of earthly beings and in their history. It is therefore useful at this point to compare the divine Spirit with the divine indwelling."[364] It means that the term *shekinah* refers to the full and personal presence of God with his people. Moltmann connects the divine indwelling of *shekinah* with the Spirit. However, this connection is not made in Jewish theology at all.[365] Following the kabbalistic thinkers, Moltmann offers three arguments for the connection between *shekinah* and the Spirit. Firstly, the doctrine of the Spirit makes the personal character of the Spirit clear. Secondly, the concept of the *shekinah* draws attention to the sensibility of God the Spirit. Finally, the idea of *shekinah* points towards the *kenosis* of the Spirit.[366] In short, for Moltmann *shekinah* is the presence of God, the Holy Spirit.

Moltmann insists that the special gift of the Spirit is its fellowship (*koinonia*), whereas grace is ascribed to Christ, and love to the Father. This is due to the fact that in his fellowship the Spirit evidently gives itself and enters into the fellowship with believers and draws them into its fellowship.[367] Moltmann argues that the New Testament phrase about "the fellowship of the Spirit" is all the more astonishing. It means both the fellowship with itself which the Spirit throws open, and the fellowship which human beings have with the Spirit. The subjective genitive – fellowship with the Spirit – will be the primal meaning. The objective genitive – fellowship with the Spirit – will be the secondary one.[368] Moreover, fellowship is always reciprocal too. The partners must have something in common, and must be able to share mutually in each other. In "the fellowship of the Holy Spirit," God the Spirit evidently enters into a relationship or reciprocity and mutuality with the people concerned and – in line with this – allows these people

---

Life, 33.
364. Moltmann, *The Spirit of Life*, 47.
365. Moltmann, *The Spirit of Life*, 48-49.
366. Moltmann, *The Spirit of Life*, 51.
367. Moltmann, *The Source of Life*, 90.
368. Moltmann, *The Spirit of Life*, 218.

to exert an influence on it, just as it exerts an influence on them.[369] This fellowship with the Spirit is trinitarian also. Moltmann writes that, "The Spirit does not merely bring about fellowship with himself. He himself issues from his fellowship with the Father and the Son, and the fellowship into which he enters with believers and corresponds to his fellowship with the Father and Son, and is therefore a *Trinitarian fellowship*. In the unity of the Father, the Son, and the Holy Spirit, the triune God himself is an open, inviting fellowship in which the whole creation finds room."[370]

For Moltmann, the fellowship of the Spirit is not just reciprocal and trinitarian, but rather it is something that transcends denominational frontiers. In fellowship with himself and through his creative energies, God the Spirit creates the network of social relationships in which life comes into being and becomes fruitful. In this sense the fellowship of the Spirit is the activity of the Spirit that confers fellowship or community.[371] This binds churches with other churches as members of the community of God paving the way for ecumenism. Besides the fellowship between churches, in the fellowship of the Spirit Moltmann also insists on community of generations.[372] Corresponding to the community of generations, Moltmann brings the community of the genders as well in the fellowship of the Spirit.[373] For Moltmann, this is a pneumatological aspect because "The eschatological hope for experience of the Spirit is shared by women and men equally."[374] David Beck writes, "Thus, fellowship between men and women finds two sources of unity. One is the commonality of being human beings by virtue of creation. The other is sharing in the same eschatological Spirit who indwells men and women equally."[375]

---

369. Moltmann, *The Spirit of Life*, 218.
370. Moltmann, *The Spirit of Life*, 218; Moltmann, *The Source of Life*, 91; the Spirit glorifies Christ in the world and the world in Christ to the glory of the Father. By effecting this it unites creation with the Son and the Father, as it unites the Son himself with the Father. As the force that glorifies, the Spirit is also the power of unification. See Moltmann, *The Church in the Power of the Spirit*, 60.
371. Moltmann, *The Spirit of Life*, 219; Moltmann, *The Church in the Power of the Spirit*, 306.
372. Moltmann, *The Spirit of Life*, 236ff.
373. Moltmann, *The Spirit of Life*, 239ff; Moltmann, *The Source of Life*, 23.
374. Moltmann, *The Spirit of Life*, 239.
375. Beck, *The Holy Spirit*, 161-162.

Finally, Moltmann argues that we must consider the communities found in nature also in the fellowship of the Spirit, because all human communities are embedded in the ecosystems of the natural communities, and live from the exchange of energy with them.[376] Community is not merely the particular character of the redeeming Spirit of Christ. It is already the essential nature of the creative Spirit of God and the Father too. All creatures are aligned towards community and are created in the form of communities. To form community is the life principle of created beings. Creation itself lives in the complexity of ever-richer communal relationships. That is why it is appropriate to talk about *the community of creation* and to recognise the operation of the life-giving Spirit of God in the trend of relationship in created things.[377] Thus for Moltmann, the community of creation is equally important as the creation of community. Moreover, pneumatology provides a way to develop important links between the human communities and the community of creation because both of them are related to each other through the Spirit. This emphasis of community will help to overcome the isolation of individuals and to direct the attention beyond the human social systems.[378]

3.9 Holy Spirit and Creation

The major work of Moltmann on creation is *God in Creation*, which deals with the divine presence in nature. Moltmann argues that:

> By the title "God in Creation" I mean God the Holy Spirit. God is "the lover of life" and his Spirit is in all created beings. In order to understand this, I have dropped the earlier divisions of theology, which followed the pattern of the three articles of the Apostles' Creed. Instead I have interwoven these three articles together in a Trinitarian sense so that I was able to develop a pneumatological doctrine of creation. This doctrine of creation, that is to say, takes as its starting point the indwelling divine Spirit of creation; and I hope that it may therefore also

---

376. Moltmann, *The Spirit of Life*, 225.
377. Moltmann, *The Spirit of Life*, 225.
378. Beck, *The Holy Spirit*, 162.

provide points of departure for a discussion with the old and new non-mechanistic, holistic philosophies of nature.[379]

Moltmann follows the biblical traditions to make his point clear that all divine activity is pneumatic in its efficacy.[380] Which means it is always the Spirit who first brings the activity of the Father and the Son to its goal. It follows that the triune God also unremittingly breathes the Spirit into his creation. Everything that is, exists and lives in the unceasing inflow of the energies and potentialities of the cosmic Spirit. This means that we have to understand every created reality in terms of energy, grasping it as the realized potentiality of the divine Spirit.[381] The reason why Moltmann emphasizes the significance of the Spirit in creation is that the Christian tradition has emphasized the first two persons of the Trinity in the act of creation but not the third. Hence he hopes to highlight the activity of the Spirit in creation neglecting any view of creation that does not consider the role of the Spirit. This is true not just in the act of creation alone rather also in the preservation of creation and the coming renewal of creation. In short, for Moltmann, "All things are therefore created 'by God,' formed 'through God' and 'exists in God.'"[382] In other words, creation is a trinitarian process that God the Father creates through the Son in the power of the Holy Spirit.[383]

According to Moltmann, the creation narrative in Genesis 1-2 begins by stating that the Spirit of God hovered over the waters. This is the biblical warranty to prove the fact that the Spirit of God is the creative power and the presence of God in his creation.[384] Moreover, Moltmann refers to Psalm 104:29-30 which states that, "When you hide your face, they are dismayed; when you take away their breath, they die and return to their

---

379. Moltmann, *God in Creation*, xii.
380. Moltmann, *The Source of Life*, 114.
381. Moltmann, *God in Creation*, 9.
382. Moltmann, *History and the Triune God*, 72; for a beautiful discussion on Moltmann's concept of history, see Abda Johnson Conyers, *Jürgen Moltmann's Concept of History* (London: University Microfilms International, 1981).
383. Moltmann, *The Source of Life*, 115; Moltmann maintains that the creation is God's play, a play of his groundless and inscrutable wisdom. It is the realm in which God displays his glory. See Moltmann, *Theology and Joy*, 41.
384. Moltmann, *God in Creation*, 99.

dust. When you send forth your Spirit, they are created; and you renew the face of the ground." This reference indicates that the Spirit is present in all living beings, and that all life depends on the Spirit. David Beck argues that, "Moltmann reads the Old Testament creation account with a Trinitarian theology in mind, and he concludes that God set forth the original creation through the Holy Spirit. This means that the Holy Spirit is God immanent in his creation, completing the creative process and giving life to creatures."[385]

For Moltmann, "God is not merely the Creator of the world. He is also the Spirit of the universe. Through the powers and potentialities of the Spirit, the Creator indwells the creatures He has made, animates them, holds them in life, and leads them into the future of His kingdom."[386] Through developing such an exposition of God and creation, Moltmann exhibits his theology to be panentheistic.[387] He writes that, "By taking up panentheistic ideas from the Jewish and Christian traditions, we shall try to think *ecologically* about God, man, and the world in their relationships and indwellings. In this way it is not merely the Christian *doctrine* of the Trinity that we are trying to work out anew; our aim is to develop and practice trinitarian thinking as well."[388] Here such a link between the creator and ecology is important for Moltmann because he sees humanity's exploitation of nature is creating a crisis. Hence Moltmann insists that this untraditional approach to create an ecologically-minded theology is important to inspire

---

385. Beck, *The Holy Spirit*, 209.
386. Moltmann, *God in Creation*, 14; Moltmann maintains that the world was created by God's free will. Unlike Barth, who sees freedom and love as complementary (the one who loves in freedom), implying that God could have decided not to create the world if he had so wished because he is self-sufficient in himself. Moltmann believes creation "out of freedom" means creation "out of love." See Moltmann, *God in Creation*, 75; Moltmann, *The Source of Life*, 24.
387. Paul D. Molnar, "The Function of the Trinity in Moltmann's Ecological Doctrine of Creation," *Theological Studies* 51 (1990), 674; Moltmann considers his acceptance of panentheism as the result of his social doctrine of the Trinity. According to Moltmann, if Christian faith looks back to creation in the beginning, it will already discover the presence of the Holy Spirit there, as the creative Spirit. Faith cannot develop any view of creation that excludes the Spirit. Creative energy only exists in the power of the Spirit, which has entered into it. It would perish if God withdrew his Spirit from it (Ps 104:29ff.). That is why the whole creation also sighs and longs for the revealing of the liberty of the children of God. It is the divine Spirit who cries out for redeeming freedom in enslaved creation (Rom 8:9ff). See Moltmann, *The Trinity and the Kingdom*, 111.
388. Moltmann, *The Trinity and the Kingdom*, 19-20.

renewed respect and reverence for the creation by reiterating God's presence in the creation.[389]

Although Moltmann constructs a trinitarian account of creation, he notices that there are some tensions in God himself during the process. It means that God creates the world *ex nihilo*, thereby being distinguished from it, but he also enters into it.[390] Moltmann finds the solution for this dilemma firstly in the doctrine of the Trinity. He writes that, "Through the Son, God creates, reconciles, and redeems his creation. In the power of the Spirit, God is himself present in his creation – present in his reconciliation and his redemption of that creation."[391] Moltmann maintains that God exists in a mutual relationship with creation. That means, he created it and influences it and at the same time he allows himself to be influenced by it. This mutuality mirrors the inner life of the Trinity. Such an idea helps Moltmann to present the *perichoresis* that exists between God and creation. Moltmann writes that, "Through the concept of *perichoresis*, the social doctrine of Trinity formulates the mutual indwelling of the Father, the Son, and the Holy Spirit, and the eternal community that is manifested through these indwellings."[392] The second solution to the dilemma is the doctrine of the *shekinah*. Moltmann uses the concept of *shekinah* for God's immanent presence within all of creation.[393] According to Moltmann, God is present in the *shekinah* in his people and the whole creation. In both cases it means that God constricts himself so as to be present in beings, objects, processes, and events which are circumscribed by linear time and finite space. For Moltmann, this self-constriction is the *kenosis* of the Spirit. The *kenosis* of the Spirit is foundational for the *shekinah* because without *kenosis*, there is no true divine immanence.[394] Just as God is immanent in all things, this *perichoretic* indwelling means that the presence of the infinite imbues

---

389. Moltmann, *The Source of Life*, 120; see also Jürgen Moltmann, "The Alienation and Liberation of Nature," in *On Nature*, ed. L. Rouner (Notre Dame: University of Notre Dame Press, 1984), 133-144; Jürgen Moltmann, "The Ecological Crisis: Peace with Nature," *The Scottish Journal of Religious Studies* vol. 9 (1988), 5-18.
390. Moltmann, *God in Creation*, 15.
391. Moltmann, *God in Creation*, 15.
392. Moltmann, *God in Creation*, 16.
393. Moltmann, *Experiences in Theology*, 315.
394. Beck, *The Holy Spirit*, 210.

everything and the community of all things with self-transcendence.[395] The *shekinah* is the principle of transcendence in all things. It is interesting to note that although Moltmann insists on the immanence of *shekinah*, it is still the presence of God himself, who remains transcendent beyond creation as its creator and sustainer.

3.9.1 The Spirit and Ongoing Creation

Moltmann asserts that there are two views that the Christian tradition has been following with regard to the creation. Firstly, God sustains what God has created and secondly, he repeats his original Yes to creation. These two ideas suggest the doctrine of preservation and the continuous creation respectively. However, these two ideas lack a complete understanding of creation, and they do not suggest the new creation of all things. Moltmann writes that, "The original creation and its preservation serve a goal. It is the consummation of creation in the realm of divine glory. All that is created longs to participate in the divine glory. What has been created is preserved for that. That is the goal of the continuation creation.... Every act which preserves creation from destruction is an act of hope for its future."[396] Moltmann's central argument is that God preserves his creation through the Spirit and continues to permeate creation. Moreover, the Spirit suffers along with the creation and raises its eyes to the future renewal of all things. In order to establish his point regarding the ongoing creation, Moltmann lists four manners in which we experience the operation of the Spirit in nature. Firstly, "The Spirit is the principle of creativity on all levels of matter and life. He creates new possibilities. ... In this sense, the Spirit is the principle of evolution."[397] The newness of birth experienced by his creatures (Jn 3:5; 2 Cor 5:17) is the same creative work that drives the course of biological evolution which has brought rise to the present condition of the earth. Secondly, God's Spirit is also "the holistic principle. At every evolutionary stage, he creates interactions ... and therefore a life of co-operation and community. The Spirit of God is the 'common Spirit'

---

395. Moltmann, *God in Creation*, 101.
396. Moltmann, *History and the Triune God*, 75; Jürgen Moltmann, "Schöpfung, Bund, und Herrlichkeit; zur Diskussion über Karl Barths Schöpfungslehre," *Evangelische Theologie* vol. 48 (1988): 108-127.
397. Moltmann, *God in Creation*, 100.

of creation."³⁹⁸ Thirdly, the Spirit is "the principle of individuation," in which each creature is unique without any differentiation.³⁹⁹ That means the creatures are not contradicting each other, rather complement each other. Finally, "all creations in the Spirit are in intention 'open.' They are directed towards their common future, because they are all, each in its own way, aligned towards their potentialities. The principle of intentionality is inherent in all open systems of matter and life."⁴⁰⁰ This is the eschatological yearning and waiting of all things for the Second Coming, which is the consummation of things.

3.9.2 The Spirit, Consummation, and the New Creation

Moltmann maintains that in the New Testament the Spirit is understood eschatologically. It is the power of the new creation. It is the power of the resurrection. It is the earnest and pledge of glory. Its present efficacy is the rebirth of humanity.⁴⁰¹ This proves the fact that creation and consummation are the history of God's interaction with his creation. It is a continuous story, because creation is continuous, and the eschatological era is just beginning. This means that when we examine the Spirit's relation to creation, it inevitably leads us beyond the original creation and ongoing creation to the Spirit's role in the consummation of all things. Moltmann writes that, "From the positive experiences of life ... we form conceptions of hope for the new creation of all things. So we speak of the 'kingdom of God' which will drive away the powers of chaos and death. We speak of the 'eternal life' which overcomes death. We hope for the 'divine righteousness' which will drive injustice and violence from the earth."⁴⁰² This is a positive expectation for the consummation and the new creation. In other words, it is a hope that in the Spirit death will eventually be overcome and peace, love, and justice will take hold in the world. This is not just an individual hope rather the hope of the whole creation.

---

398. Moltmann, *God in Creation*, 100.
399. Moltmann, *God in Creation*, 100.
400. Moltmann, *God in Creation*, 100.
401. Moltmann, *The Trinity and the Kingdom*, 89.
402. Moltmann, *History and the Triune God*, 78-79.

Moltmann argues that there is a sigh of created beings who want to live. Quoting Paul, Moltmann writes that the whole creation groans in travail together with us even now (Rom 8:22).[403] In this groaning of creation, the Spirit himself represents believers and creation in their sighs for liberty through his "sighs too deep for words" (Rom 8:26). Moltmann writes:

> The dumb sighs of nature and the uttered cry of human beings for liberty are gathered up by the Spirit into his own sighing. In the bondage of creation, in the pains of the body and in the yearning of believers, the Spirit is co-imprisoned and co-suffering and keeps the waiting and the hoping alive through his own wordless and inexpressible sighs. We can surely understand this as meaning that God the Creator, who has entered into his creation through his Spirit, himself holds created being in life. (Ps 104:30)[404]

This is an eschatological hope of the creation in the experience of the Spirit. This hope for the new creation has in fact begun before the outpouring of the Spirit on the church. This can be seen when Christ proclaimed the new creation of all things when he brought the kingdom of God to the poor, salvation to the sick, and divine justice to sinners. Moreover, the day of Christ's resurrection is the first day of the new creation.[405] This reveals

---

403. Moltmann, *The Source of Life*, 111; Moltmann believes that nature is the "sister" and travelling companion of hoping, searching human beings. It is not only human beings who live from hope and yearn for the redemption of the body from the dominion of death. All other earthly creatures and even the earth itself also groan under the power of transitoriness, and yearn for the glory that the "children of God" are already experiencing in their freedom. It is God's Spirit itself that groans within believers as well as in all transitory creatures for the new world of eternal life, and that reveals the suffering of this time to be the labor pains of that eternal home of all things. See Jürgen Moltmann, "Christianity and the Revaluation of the Values of Modernity," in *A Passion for God's Reign: Theology, Christian Learning and the Christian Self*, ed. Miroslav Wolf (Michigan: Eerdmans, 1998), 31-32.
404. Moltmann, *God in Creation*, 69; Jürgen Moltmann, "Creation and Redemption," in *Creation, Christ and Culture: Studies in Honor of T. F. Torrance*, ed. Richard W. A. McKinney (Edinburgh: T & T Clark, 1976), 119-134.
405. As the paradigm of new creation, the resurrection of the crucified Christ reveals his identity in death and resurrection. The same Jesus Christ who was died and raised, and correspondingly the resurrection of the dead and the new creation of all things is not the replacement of this creation by another but the renewal of this creation. See Moltmann, *Theology of Hope*, 29, 265.

the fact that the new creation takes place in the *eschaton* although it began with the resurrection of Christ and it is anticipated in the Christian experience of the Spirit of resurrection. In his Spirit everything comes alive and without his Spirit everything disintegrates. His eternal Spirit is the driving force and the vital spark in all things. Hence everything living cries out for God's Spirit, in which alone it can live.[406] And God the creator calls his creatures into life, and in his Spirit he preserves and quickens them.[407] When we wait together with earthly creation for the coming of the Spirit, we are awaiting liberation from injustice and violence and liberation from time and death.[408] Moreover, the presence of the Spirit in the church is the advance radiance and beginning of the presence of God's Word and Spirit in the new creation of all things. From its foundation and by its very nature, the church becomes cosmos-oriented.[409] It is significant to note that, in the sighs and groans of suffering creation God's Spirit itself sighs and groans and calls for redemption. The God who through his indwelling Spirit suffers with the creation is the firm hope of created beings. This hope is our assurance that the beings he has created have not been forsaken by their creator.[410] With the raising of Christ from the dead and the annihilation of death which took place in him, the eschatological process of the new creation of all transient and mortal being begins. Whoever out of the deadly perils of earthly creation cries out for the creator Spirit expects with the resurrection of Christ the resurrection of the body and the resurrection of nature also.[411]

3.10 Holy Spirit and Eschatology

Jürgen Moltmann's first major work was his *Theology of Hope*, first published in 1964, arguably one of the influential works of the last few decades. It changed the way Christian eschatology was understood over a wide spectrum of contemporary theology, quite apart from its mediated influence far

---

406. Moltmann, *The Source of Life*, 114.
407. Moltmann, *God in Creation*, 262.
408. Moltmann, *The Source of Life*, 114.
409. Moltmann, *The Source of Life*, 118.
410. Moltmann, *The Source of Life*, 120.
411. Moltmann, *The Source of Life*, 1123.

beyond the bounds of academic theology.[412] However, only in *The Coming of God* he finally wrote a systematic eschatology, which is his mature eschatological vision, innovative, and contextual. One can rightly argue along with Terry C. Dohm that, "Moltmann's eschatological approach is 'future-oriented,' but from a more cosmological perspective. What is important for him is not only that the world is 'on the way' to becoming a new creation, but also that Christians should be actively engaged in combating the causes of the suffering of humanity and the destruction of nature and the ecosystem until that day comes."[413] Schwarz argues that unlike Pannenberg, the main emphasis of Moltmann is on the implications of eschatology.[414]

The resurrection of Jesus Christ stands at the centre of the eschatological framework of Moltmann. The resurrection of the crucified Jesus precedes the general outpouring of the Spirit. On this date the eschatological era begins.[415] Hence, pneumatologically speaking, eschatology[416] is the work of the Spirit because through the Spirit the believer is determined by the divine future. The powers of the Spirit are the powers of life, which de-

---

412. Richard Bauckham, "Introduction," in *God will be All in All: The Eschatology of Jürgen Moltmann*, ed. Richard Bauckham (Minneapolis: Fortress, 2001), xiii; this work named *God will be All in All* is a beautiful discussion on the eschatology of Moltmann. It is unique in the sense that Moltmann responds to most of the articles written in this book. Hence, this book is a dialogue between Moltmann and the authors.
413. Terry C. Dohm, *The Rediscovery of Eschatology in the Message of Jesus and Its Impact on Theology in the Twentieth Century* (Regensburg: Roderer Verlag, 2003), 239; Dohm argues that, "The 'future-oriented' eschatological approaches of Jürgen Moltmann and Wolfhart Pannenberg developed in reaction to the transcendental approach of Barth and the existential approach of Bultmann, both of which were 'present-oriented'. Whereas Althaus and Brunner attempted to bring eschatology back into balance with the future, Pannenberg and Moltmann tipped the scales toward the future." Dohm, *The Rediscovery of Eschatology*, 239.
414. Hans Schwarz, *Eschatology* (Grand Rapids: Eerdmans, 2000), 146; Schwarz holds the view that Moltmann does not want to confine himself to a strictly theological treatise. On the other hand, he is much more interested in showing the practical consequences of a biblical eschatological perspective as they inform church life and the burning political issues, such as social justice, world peace, and personal freedom. He no longer wants to confine eschatology to discourse about the so-called last things which will happen in the end, but to consider the whole cause which drives toward this end. See Schwarz, *Eschatology*, 146; also see Hans Schwarz, *Theology in a Global Context: The Last Two Hundred Years* (Grand Rapids: William B. Eerdmans, 2005), 540-548.
415. Moltmann, *The Trinity and the Kingdom*, 122.
416. For a beautiful analysis of the eschatology of Moltmann, see Morse, *The Logic of Promise in Moltmann's Theology*; also see Tim Chester, *Mission and the Coming of God: Eschatology, the Trinity and Mission in the Theology of Jürgen Moltmann and Contemporary Evangelism* (Eugene: Wipf & Stock Publishers, 2006).

termine the present, extending their influence forward from the future of the new life. Consequently, the whole eschatology of the history of Christ can be described as the history of the Spirit, a result of the workings and indwelling of the Spirit through which the future enters into history.[417] Hence Moltmann insists that the sending of the Spirit is also the eschatology of the history of Christ. In short, when we say Pentecost is the *telos*, the highest goal of revelation in Christ, it is true as far as the gift of the Spirit is concerned. However, if we consider the fulfilment of the meaning of the history of Christ, we have to talk about the "history of the Spirit" because it is the beginning of the new time, the time of the direct and lasting presence of revelation in history.[418]

The fundamental passage that Moltmann refers to express his eschatological thesis is Revelation 1:4 that shows God *is*, God *was*, and God is *coming*. It means that God is not in the process of becoming, but rather God is "coming" towards the world. He writes that, "Through his promises and his Spirit (which precede his coming and announce it) God now already sets present and past in the light of his eschatological arrival, arrival which means the establishment of his eternal kingdom, and his indwelling in the creation renewed for that indwelling."[419] This coming of God in the Spirit offers eternal life and eternal time and it is eschatological as well. For Moltmann, the experience of God's Spirit awakens new and unexpected expectations about life like the eschatological longing for the completion of salvation, the redemption of the body and the new creation of all things. This experience of the Spirit makes Christians in every society restless and homeless, and in the search for the kingdom of God (Heb 13:14) in the present world.[420]

For Moltmann, there are two dimensions in the expectations of the Spirit. Firstly, the positive dimension. Moltmann writes that, "The more deeply the presence of the Spirit is experienced in the heart, and in fel-

---

417. Moltmann, *The Church in the Power of the Spirit*, 34; see a discussion of eschatology by Richard Bauckham, "Moltmann's Eschatology of The Cross," *Scottish Journal of Theology* vol. 30, (1977), 301-311.
418. Moltmann, *The Church in the Power of the Spirit*, 35; Moltmann, *The Trinity and the Kingdom of God*, 124.
419. Moltmann, *The Coming of God*, 23.
420. Moltmann, *The Spirit of Life*, 73.

lowship with one another, the more certain and assured the hope for the Spirit's universal coming will be."[421] That means the experience of the Spirit in the present is the beginning and advance pledge of the coming kingdom of glory (Rom 8:23; 2 Cor 1:22; 5:5; Eph 1:14).[422] Thus the new creation of all things is already experienced representatively and in anticipation. That is why experience of the Spirit is described as a rebirth of the whole cosmos. Moltmann writes that, "... he will *'spiritize'* all created beings, and the spheres in which they live in heaven and on earth. We cannot take this to mean the *spiritualization* of creation; it can only mean its *vitalization*."[423] This hope for the newly creating efficacy of the Spirit in everything that lives is not derived from any experience of deficiency in the present. It springs from the overflowing rapture of experience of the Spirit and extravagant joy over the coming of God.[424] Secondly, the negative dimension. Moltmann argues along with revelation that "God will wipe away every tear from their eyes, and death shall no more, neither shall there be mourning nor crying nor pain any more" (Rev 21:4). Moreover, God will make all things new (Rev 21:3, 5). Thus Moltmann insists that, "What is positive can at present be described only through a determined negation of the positive position that has been experienced. For nothing positive emerges of itself simply from the mere negation of the negative, since no positive conclusions can be deduced from negative premises."[425]

3.10.1 The Holy Spirit and the Kingdom of God

The eschatological fulfilment of the liberating lordship of God in history is termed the kingdom of God. The Greek word *basileia* can mean both the actual rule of God in the world and the universal goal of that divine rule.[426] When dealing with the kingdom of God, Moltmann follows Joachim's threefold division of the kingdom as three historical stages corresponding to Father, Son, and the Spirit. However, Moltmann never limits himself to these three stages; rather there is a fourth stage which is the glorification of

---

421. Moltmann, *The Spirit of Life*, 74.
422. Moltmann, *The Source of Life*, 11.
423. Moltmann, *The Spirit of Life*, 74.
424. Moltmann, *The Spirit of Life*, 74-75.
425. Moltmann, *The Spirit of Life*, 76.
426. Moltmann, *The Church in the Power of the Spirit*, 190.

God. Even here, he is following a trinitarian framework. Moltmann writes that, "We shall instead interpret the history of the kingdom in trinitarian terms: the kingdoms of the Father, the Son, and the Spirit means continually present strata and transitions in the kingdom's history."[427] The kingdom of the Spirit is experienced as a gift conferred on people liberated by the Son – the gift of the Spirit's energies. In the experience of the Spirit, people lay hold on the freedom for which the Son has made them free. Moreover, in the Spirit the new creation in the kingdom of glory is anticipated.[428] However, for Moltmann the kingdom of the Spirit is not the consummation of the kingdom; rather, "It presupposes the kingdom of the Father and the kingdom of the Son and, together with the kingdom of the Father and the kingdom of the Son, points in its own way towards the eschatological kingdom of glory."[429]

If the kingdom of the Spirit presupposes the eschatological kingdom, then what is the actual kingdom of God in the *eschaton*? It is the eschatological kingdom of glory. Moltmann writes that, "The kingdom of glory must be understood as the consummation of the Father's creation, the universal establishment of the Son's liberation, and as the fulfilment of the Spirit's indwelling."[430] That means, creation is the material promise of glory, the kingdom of the Son is the historical promise of glory and finally the kingdom of the Spirit is the actual dawn of the kingdom of glory. In short for Moltmann, "The trinitarian doctrine of the kingdom therefore sums up 'the works of the Trinity (creation, liberation, glorification) and points them towards the home of the triune God. The kingdom of glory is the goal – enduring and uninterrupted – for all God's works and ways in history."[431]

The major issue when one deals with the kingdom of God in the theology of Moltmann is, how does he understand the timing of the kingdom? This dilemma is due to the fact that Moltmann himself is not consistent in his position regarding timing. One can argue that he follows inaugurated

---

427. Moltmann, *The Trinity and the Kingdom*, 209; Moltmann, *The Source of Life*, 11.
428. Moltmann, *The Trinity and the Kingdom*, 211.
429. Moltmann, *The Trinity and the Kingdom*, 212.
430. Moltmann, *The Trinity and the Kingdom*, 212.
431. Moltmann, *The Trinity and the Kingdom*, 212.

eschatology because he writes that, "An anticipation is not yet fulfilment. But it is already the presence of the future in the conditions of history. It is a fragment of the coming whole. It is a payment made in advance of complete fulfilment and part-possession of what is still to come."[432] Some can argue that Moltmann follows consistent eschatology. It means that the kingdom of God is not yet here but it is so close impacting the present reality. That means the signs of the kingdom are already present, but the kingdom itself is not yet present although it influences the present reality.[433] Finally, Moltmann differentiates between the kingdom of God and the rule of God. The rule of God refers to the reign of God in the present. But the kingdom of God refers to the coming kingdom of God in the *eschaton*.[434] In short, "It is difficult to answer the question of Moltmann's timing of the kingdom. His position could end up being aligned with either consistent or inaugurated eschatology."[435]

4. Summary

As we have made an in depth study of the pneumatology of Moltmann, one thing is obvious that his pneumatology is an attempt to move away from the traditional understanding of the Spirit to develop an innovative theology of the Holy Spirit. In this attempt, Moltmann has been critical to Barth on the one side and the whole Western pneumatology. For example, regarding the relationship between the Spirit and Christ, Barth always insisted that the Spirit is the Spirit of Christ. In this sense, the Spirit has been subordinated to the Son. But on the other hand, Moltmann holds a mutual and bi-directional relationship between the Spirit and Christ.[436] At the same time, "Moltmann eschews the tendencies of German idealism to convey the Holy Spirit in terms of the human spirit or the 'spirit' of history.

---

432. Moltmann, *The Church in the Power of the Spirit*, 193.
433. See for example Moltmann, *The Way of Jesus Christ*, 97; Moltmann, *The Church in the Power of the Spirit*, 99-100.
434. Moltmann, *The Church in the Power of the Spirit*, 98.
435. Beck, *The Holy Spirit*, 138.
436. Beck, *The Holy Spirit*, 255.

Following Barth, Moltmann affirms a necessary division between the divine Spirit and creaturely humanity."[437]

The second significance of Moltmann's pneumatology is the trinitarian emphasis he maintains, thus clearly specifying the personhood of the Spirit.[438] Moltmann has clearly specified the Spirit's unique subjectivity in order to avoid possible misunderstandings that can arise from his own Spirit-Christology. Moreover, he never wanted to follow a hierarchical order in the Trinity rather as fulfilling each other. This forced him to interpret trinity as a union or *perichoresis*. In this sense, the Spirit is no more seen just as a third person in the Trinity but rather as equal with the other persons in the Trinity. It is a fact that the three theological premises that run throughout his theology is Christology, pneumatology, and eschatology. When discussing eschatology, Moltmann never considers Christ as the agent for the fulfillment of the future, but rather the Spirit. It is the Spirit who brings about the kingdom of God as a historical reality. However, when he argues for pneumatology, he never misses the trinitarian framework at all. Moreover, his concern for the creation and his concept of the motherhood of the Spirit has far reaching significance today. Although one can appreciate Moltmann in his attempt to develop a new paradigm of pneumatology, there are unavoidable issues involved in his pneumatology.

Although Moltmann tries to develop a personality of the Spirit, this has serious problems. He makes the attempt to deduce the shape of the Spirit's personhood. This is of course a deductive knowing derived from the operation experienced by the operator. Hence, the need is to move from experience to understanding. However, this is impossible with the Spirit of God because we cannot make whatever encompasses us an object without moving it. Here lies the problem because Moltmann does not consider its consequences through to the end. Geiko Müller-Fahrenholz notes that, "If any concept essentially has something to do with conceptualizing, and thus if any conceptualizing has as its presupposition something that is objectified, and if every attempt to understand God's Spirit has to do with the objectification of the Spirit and consequently has to be paid for

---

437. Timothy Harvie, *Jürgen Moltmann's Ethics of Hope: Eschatological Possibilities for Moral Action* (Surrey: Ashgate, 2009), 58.
438. Harvie, *Jürgen Moltmann's Ethics of Hope*, 59.

with a distancing from this Spirit, then paradoxically we are on the way towards becoming Spirit-less precisely in conceptualizing the Spirit."[439] Moreover, Moltmann gets into difficulties with his attempt at a conceptual definition of the *ruah* of God. Hence one should not seek anything else in respect of the Spirit of God because the Spirit of God transcends any conceptual frameworks that human beings make. The other main issue that one can find in the pneumatology of Moltmann is his Spirit Christology. It seems that he is unsuccessful in creating a Spirit Christology that frees the Spirit from the subordination to Christology despite his efforts. What is important today is the development of a pneumatology that sees the Spirit as an independent eschatological force, calling radically into question our ecclesiological and secular fellowships and institutions and opening them up to praxis in unexpected and truly miraculous ways.[440]

Finally, Moltmann's rejection of the "otherness" of God is one of the basic problems of his pneumatology. Barth maintained that a one-sided notion of God's otherness can create the kind of horrifying distance between God and life which Moltmann rejects. Yet God's otherness can also grant us an adequate appreciation for the ambivalence we often feel in the indepth encounter with God – both embraced and alienated, or both comforted and feared. This is because of God's awesome presence that lays claims to us in promise and hope can never be associated with created life, nor can it be demonstrated or manipulated. By way of contrast, the Spirit's presence described by Moltmann is indeed identified with life, despite his effort to include an element of divine transcendence that comforts us. Hence Macchia argues that, "With Moltmann's notion of life as 'emanating' from the Spirit, any 'confrontation' Moltmann might inject into the discussion will not grasp us very deeply and certainly will not provoke the *mysterium tremendum* that we Pentecostals have to value in our experience with God."[441]

---

439. Geiko Müller-Fahrenholz, *The Kingdom and Power: The Theology of Jürgen Moltmann* (London: SCM, 2000), 197.
440. Peter Althouse, *Pentecostal Eschatology in Conversation with Jürgen Moltmann* (New York: T & T Clark, 2003), 177-178.
441. Frank D. Macchia, "A North American Response," *Journal of Pentecostal Theology* vol. 2, no. 4 (1994), 26-27.

CHAPTER FIVE

Pneumatology of Wolfhart Pannenberg (1928 -)

1. Introduction

The central focus of the previous chapter has been to systematically delineate the pneumatology of Moltmann. Having understood the major tenets of Moltmann's pneumatology, the present chapter looks into the pneumatology of Wolfhart Pannenberg, who was, like Moltmann, greatly influenced by Barth and his theology. Since the publication of his first essays in the 1950s, Pannenberg's program has become the object of an intense debate spilling beyond the borders of Germany. Pannenberg is considered as the most creative of contemporary thinkers. Kärkkäinen argues that, "Since Karl Barth's publication of his massive *Church Dogmatics*, no other theologian except for Wolfhart Pannenberg has attempted to formulate a full-scale, comprehensive theological system."[1] Although Pannenberg is undeniably one of the most notable pneumatologists in the third millennium, interestingly enough, he has not produced a separate pneumatology. Rather, he incorporated his doctrine of the Spirit into his whole theological program, which is interwoven throughout his systematic, especially God, creation, anthropology, Christology, ecclesiology, and eschatology. His theology also contains a rich discussion of the Spirit with regard to salvation, but he avoids the dangers of privatization of the Spirit to only subjective

---

1. Kärkkäinen, *Pneumatology*, 117; see also Don H. Olive, *Wolfhart Pannenberg*, ed. Bob E. Patterson (Texas: Word Books, 1973).

areas.² Therefore, the central focus of this chapter is to dig out the pneumatology of Pannenberg in depth. In order to materialize this endeavor, one needs to begin with Pannenberg's *Sitz-im-Leben*. Hence, the current chapter begins with a brief survey of Pannenberg's socio-cultural, political, philosophical, and theological surroundings in order to discover the factors which influenced him to develop a theology of the Spirit. This awareness is significant in this study, particularly because Pannenberg had to make use of what he learnt and experienced from his own particular context in developing a pneumatology. Having briefly outlined his *Sitz-im-Leben*, the study will thematically make an in-depth treatment of the pneumatology of Pannenberg.

2. *The Sitz-Im-Leben of Wolfhart Pannenberg*

2.1 The Socio-cultural Setting

Pannenberg was born in 1928 as son of a German civil servant. He received the education usual for a gifted child of the solid middle class. However, it must be noted that Pannenberg was not reared in a devout Christian home.³ Hence James Robinson notes that, "Pannenberg's own road to Christianity had been more of rational reflection than of Christian nurture or a conversion experience."⁴ Nevertheless, in 1950, Pannenberg went to Basel and was strongly influenced by Karl Barth. Pannenberg continued his studies in Heidelberg in 1951 under the orthodox Lutheran theologians Peter Brunner and Edmund Schlink and also Hans von Campenhausen and Gerhard von Rad.⁵ During this period, Gerhard von Rad was constructing his argument that in the writings of the Hebrew Bible theology is at the same time an interpretation of history. Moreover, Pannenberg continued his philosophical studies with Karl Löwith, building on his previous work with Nicolai Hartmann and Karl Jaspers. Here it was that finally a circle of young theologians was formed that was called the "hope group." It served

---

2. Kärkkäinen, *Pneumatology*, 118.
3. Pannenberg, *Theology and the Kingdom of God*, 15.
4. Cited in Pannenberg, *Theology and the Kingdom of God*, 15.
5. Pannenberg, *Theology and the Kingdom of God*, 16.

to introduce the idea of the promise of God as a systematic principle.⁶ Against his wishes, this project in team theology became later identified with Pannenberg's name.⁷

Having finished his university studies, Pannenberg accepted a call to the church seminary at Wuppertal to be Professor of Systematic Theology. At this time, Moltmann also had been working as a professor in the same seminary. During the three years of his first lecture courses in Heidelberg, Pannenberg had focused on the history of theology in the nineteenth century.⁸ In his lectures in Wuppertal, Pannenberg developed the main body of his anthropology and Christology. Since 1961, when he went to Mainz and *Offenbarung als Geschichte* was published, his production has been prolific, ranging from philosophical exercises to popular radio addresses on the role of religion in society. Since 1967, Pannenberg has been professor of Systematic Theology at the University of Munich and became the head of the Institute of Ecumenical Theology.⁹ Pannenberg married Hilke Schütte in 1954. In spite of the services he rendered in Germany, he had visiting professorships at the University of Chicago, Harvard University, and the Claremont School of Theology.¹⁰

2.2 The Political Setting

Growing up during the Nazi era, like almost all the Germans of that time, he participated in the woeful effort to defend the *Vaterland* in the last desperate days of the *Third Reich*. Hence, his childhood memories of Nazism remain vivid and it had a great impact on his understanding of the instability of society in general and the German people's determination for democracy in particular.¹¹ Pannenberg writes:

---

6. Otto, *The God of Hope*, 4; E. Frank Tupper, *The Theology of Wolfhart Pannenberg* (Philadelphia: Westminster, 1971), 22.
7. Pannenberg, *Theology and the Kingdom of God* (Philadelphia: Westminster, 1970), 16; this group also included Martin Elze, Klaus Koch, Rolf Rendtorff, Dietrich Rössler, and Ulrich Wilkens. Their discussions eventuated in the book edited by Pannenberg, *Offenbarung als Geschichte* (Göttingen: Vandenhoeck & Ruprecht, 1961).
8. Pannenberg, *Theology and the Kingdom of God*, 16.
9. Pannenberg, *Theology and the Kingdom of God*, 17.
10. Tupper, *The Theology of Wolfhart Pannenberg*, 27.
11. Pannenberg, *Theology and the Kingdom of God*, 15.

> I went to be a soldier at the age of 16, was trained but saved by scabies from being kept for combat where the comrades of my unit were going to die a few days later, after the Russians had crossed the Oder river. Instead, I was sent with a hospital to Northern Germany, where I was taken prisoner by the British and spent the spring of 1945. Released in early summer, I returned to the East in the early fall, retrieved my family and went to school again for two more years, while we with all the people in that part of the Russian zone almost starved.[12]

It was an experience which prompted him to be cautious towards all ideological and political promises. His interest in religion developed after the war as the result of study and reflection during his university days.[13]

2.3 The Philosophical Setting

As noted earlier, Pannenberg had a great interest towards academics and he was intelligent too.[14] Hence he sought to understand his experience through reading the great philosophers and religious thinkers. Moreover, one of his teachers exerted considerable influence in Pannenberg's conversion to the Christian worldview. He encountered this teacher, who had been a member of the *Confessing Church* during the Third *Reich*, during his final years of high school. This instructor convinced Pannenberg to take a long hard look at Christianity, at a time that was a thoughtful period in Pannenberg's life.

---

12. Wolfhart Pannenberg, "An Autobiographical Sketch," in *The Theology of Wolfhart Pannenberg: Twelve American Critiques, with an Autobiographical Essay and Response*, ed. Carl E. Braaten and Philip Clayton (Minneapolis: Augsburg, 1988), 12.
13. One can look into his autobiography to know more about his political background which is quite interesting. Pannenberg, "An Autobiographical Sketch," 11-18.
14. Pannenberg is a relentlessly intellectual man. Yet his intellectual thrust toward the empirical makes necessary a lively exchange between experience and thought, an exchange that precludes dealing with ideas exclusively on their own terms, as it were. Pannenberg's theology argues for a continuity of events including the life of the mind. Ideas are shaped by experience, and experience is shaped by the ideas that are our equipment for reception and interpretation. In his writing and conversation, Pannenberg tends to understate the role of personal experience, holding himself primarily responsible to the ideas as such, both his own and those of others. This tendency must be attributed, not to a kind of arid intellectuality divorced from life context, but to his response to a theological situation in which psychological analyses and a preoccupation with the self-consciousness of the theologian have led to an obscuring of the theologian's contributions to the history of ideas. See Pannenberg, *Theology and the Kingdom of God*, 14.

It was then that he concluded that Christianity was the best philosophy. This "intellectual conversion" launched him into a vocation as a Christian theologian.[15] Moreover, while working as a *Privatdozent* at the University of Heidelberg in 1955, Pannenberg lectured on the history of theology in the nineteenth century, engaging in constructive "debate" with pivotal thinkers of the past, namely, Schleiermacher, Ritschl, Hegel, and Troeltsch.[16] Moving behind dialectical theology in the attempt to produce a new theological synthesis, Pannenberg entered still another notable phase of his Heidelberg experience – he became increasingly conscious of and impressed by the massive intellectual achievement of Hegel. Although he recognized the limitations of Hegel's philosophy, Pannenberg saw that Hegel's understanding of truth as history and its corollary of universal history offered the Christian theologian a unique opportunity for interpreting the biblical faith. Therefore, a critical dialogue with the giants of nineteenth century theology, especially Hegel, became one of Pannenberg's central concerns as he sought to forge a re-conception of Christian theology.[17] In short, the later writings of Pannenberg prove the fact that there is a close relationship between theology and philosophy in terms of truth. He regarded philosophy as very important for theology. As a matter of fact, he thought that there should be a dialogue between theology and philosophy, with special attention given to the perennial problem of faith and reason.[18]

2.4 The Theological Setting

Pannenberg insisted that it was rational reflection that led him to Christian faith. Due to his excitement towards Christianity, Pannenberg began his theological studies after the Second World War at the University of Berlin. He continued his theological investigations at the Universities of Göttingen and Basel as well. At the University of Heidelberg he completed his doctoral dissertation on the doctrine of predestination of the noted medieval

---

15. See for a beautiful delineation regarding the relationship between religion and philosophy, David Mckenzie, *Wolfhart Pannenberg and Religious Philosophy* (Washington: University Press of America, 1980). See also Wolfhart Pannenberg, *The Idea of God and Human Freedom* (Philadelphia: Westminster, 1973), 116-143.
16. Tupper, *The Theology of Wolfhart Pannenberg*, 25.
17. Tupper, *The Theology of Wolfhart Pannenberg*, 25.
18. Tupper, *The Theology of Wolfhart Pannenberg*, 50ff.

scholastic theologian John Duns Scotus under the supervision of the Lutheran Barthian Edmund Schlink. He completed his *Habilitationsschrift* in 1955 with an analysis of the role of analogy in Western thought up to Thomas Aquinas.[19]

While Pannenberg was at Basel, he studied under Karl Barth, the leading Protestant theologian of his day. Pannenberg appreciated Barth's Word of God theology which was a post-Kantian renewal of the Reformation theologies of John Calvin and Martin Luther. However, even as a student, Pannenberg sensed that Barth's stringent critique of natural theology was too radical. Moreover, his subsequent polemic against Barth's position, which is usually hidden but frequently explicit, is clearly the disagreement of a man who continues to respect Barth's magisterial command of the theological tradition.[20] Like Barth, Pannenberg intended to be a "church theologian" who holds himself responsible to the continuing tradition of Christian reflection. However, unlike Barth, Pannenberg believes that the church and her theology can only be understood as a part of the larger human community. It means that theology is clearly subject to the canons of rationality that are operative in this larger community.[21]

Like Barth, Hans von Campenhausen also exerted a creative impact upon Pannenberg and "the working circle," through his 1947 rectoral address, "Augustine and the Fall of Rome," in which he called for interdisciplinary theological interpretation of history that would present Jesus' life and destiny as the all-embracing centre of world history. Moreover, Campenhausen's affirmation of the importance of the historical event of Jesus' resurrection for Christian theology positively affected the position of the circle.[22] Pannenberg's study of medieval theology made him more sympathetic to God's general revelation in creation. He was able to work out this idea first in the field of history, through a neo-Hegelian philosophy of history, and later in his work in religion and science. Eventually he was able to draw these two threads together in his popular three volumes of systematic theology. Moreover, Gerhard von Rad provided the circle with

---

19. Tupper, *The Theology of Wolfhart Pannenberg*, 22ff.
20. Pannenberg, *Theology and the Kingdom of God*, 15.
21. Pannenberg, *Theology and the Kingdom of God*, 15.
22. Tupper, *The Theology of Wolfhart Pannenberg*, 24.

the methodological insight for overcoming the cleft between a *kerygmatic* and a historical-critical reconstruction of Israel's history, that is, the general theological distinction between "inner" and "outer" history. Consequently, von Rad's conception of history as the process of the transmission of traditions has proven integral to Pannenberg's understanding of the unity of historical event and its meaning.[23] In addition to that, the New Testament scholar Günther Bornkamm impressed "the working circle" with his early criticism of Bultmann and with this post-Bultmannian concern for relating the *kerygma* to the historical Jesus. However, moving beyond Bornkamm, Pannenberg interpreted "the history of Jesus" to include the resurrection and found in Jesus' history the ground and criterion for the church's *kerygma*.[24] Finally, Pannenberg is indebted to the confessional Lutheran theologian Edmund Schlink. Schlink provided Pannenberg the concept of the doxological structure of language about God and also an example of the ecumenical posture the Christian theologian should assume amid the divisions of the contemporary Christian church.[25]

3. Pneumatology of Wolfhart Pannenberg

As noted earlier, one of the particularities of Pannenberg's theological system is the significance given to the Holy Spirit. On this basis, Pannenberg is critical towards the secondary place given to pneumatology in theology since the Middle Ages and the restriction on the action of the Spirit with regard to soteriology in Reformation theology.[26] However, Pannenberg is careful to argue reasonably instead of following subjective explanations. He writes that, "The Spirit of which the New Testament speaks is no 'heaven of ignorance' (*asylum ignorantiae*) for pious experience, which exempts one

---

23. Tupper, *The Theology of Wolfhart Pannenberg*, 24.
24. Tupper, *The Theology of Wolfhart Pannenberg*, 24.
25. Tupper, *The Theology of Wolfhart Pannenberg*, 25.
26. Pannenberg maintains that contemporary theology lacks a doctrine of the Spirit that corresponds in breadth to the biblical concept of the Spirit. Such a doctrine would require a treatment of our present knowledge of the cause of life. The Christian statement about the Spirit can again receive full weight only through answering the question of life. Otherwise, they remain a dead piece of tradition or in any case – especially where the Spirit is restricted to the function of a supernatural principle of knowledge – do not correspond to the biblical idea of the Spirit. See Pannenberg, *Jesus – God and Man,* 171.

from all obligation to account for its contents. The Christian message will not regain its missionary power ... unless this falsification of the Holy Spirit is set aside which has developed in the history of piety."[27] Thus Pannenberg gave considerable significance to pneumatology and tried to avoid the easy talk with regard to the Holy Spirit. With this initial understanding, we endeavour to analyse his theology of the Spirit in detail and thematically.

3.1 The Divinity of the Holy Spirit

3.1.1 God as The Spirit

Pannenberg uses the term *Spirit* in two ways, God as Spirit and secondly the Spirit as the third person in the Trinity. When Pannenberg denotes God as Spirit, he defines God as infinite spiritual essence.[28] Traditionally, two approaches have been taken regarding the essence of God. On the one hand, the patristic interest in clarifying the otherness of God and rejecting the idea of God as physical because of the Stoic doctrines of physical *pneuma* led to the understanding of God as supreme reason.[29] This concern, however, is no longer an issue, since the *Spirit* is conceived as a nonphysical entity. On the other hand, in high scholasticism, the idea of God as reason was complemented with the idea of God as will.[30] Pannenberg is critical of these two concepts of God - God as reason and will - and sides with the biblical description of God as Spirit.[31] The biblical understanding of Pannenberg with regard to the Spirit leads him to affirm that the Spirit is the giver of life.

---

27. Wolfhart Pannenberg, "The Doctrine of the Spirit and the Task of a Theology of Nature," *Theology* 75, no. 1 (1972), 10; see also Pannenberg, *Theology and the Kingdom of God*, 86-87.
28. See for a detailed discussion in Pannenberg, *Systematic Theology* vol. 1, 370ff.
29. Pannenberg, *Systematic Theology* vol. 1, 372.
30. Pannenberg, *Systematic Theology* vol. 1, 380.
31. Pannenberg argues that the New Testament statements about the Spirit and its work should be understood in the light of the Jewish view. In the Jewish understanding, *ruah* is described as a mysteriously invisible natural force which declares itself especially in the movement of the wind. This is the background of the statement in John that the *pneuma* is like the wind that blows where it wills, and we hear its sound but do not know where it comes and where it goes. Pannenberg, *Systematic Theology* vol. 1, 370-378.

3.1.2 The Spirit Is the Giver of Life

According to Pannenberg, "In the New Testament, Spirit is the name for the actual presence of divine reality in Christian experience and in the Christian community. Therefore, one might expect nothing to be more familiar to every Christian than the reality of the Spirit."[32] Pannenberg contends that one can hardly point to the Holy Spirit as an obvious element in Christian individual experience or in the life of the Christian communities. The reality of the Spirit is not to be identified by looking for elements that separate Christian experience and Christian community from all other human experience and community. He argues:

> Perhaps we have to try it the other way round by looking for the divine Spirit in what Christian experience and Christian community have in common with all other human experience and communities. Then the particular working of the Spirit in the people of God could be explained as a particular modification of what can be said of all human communities and of all human experience. This would correspond to the fact that in the Bible the divine spirit is understood as origin of all life, and this universal power is said to be present in the Christian community in a special way.[33]

In defining the Spirit, Pannenberg recognises the universal meaning of the Spirit as origin of all life and the particular presence of the Spirit in the Christian community. After a detailed discussion of the Spirit in a general sense, Pannenberg comes to the conclusion that, "The Bible understood life as a function of the Spirit. In the Biblical conception the Spirit differs from the organic structure, although it is the Spirit who gives life to the organism. Thus the Spirit is not just the human spirit, but closely connected with

---

32. Wolfhart Pannenberg, Avery Dulles, S.J., Carl E. Braaten, "The Working of the Spirit in the Creation and in the People of God" in *Spirit, Faith, and Church* (The 1969 Walter and Mary Tuohy Chaira lectures), (Philadelphia: Westminster, n.d), 13; Pannenberg is clear that there is no other subject in modern theology so difficult to deal with as the doctrine of the Holy Spirit. The reason is that, it is hard to find out what kind of reality one is talking about in referring to the Spirit. See Pannenberg, "The Working of the Spirit," 13.
33. Pannenberg, "The Working of the Spirit," 14.

God."[34] Pannenberg insists that the human spirit is only a participation of the divine Spirit. Hence in Genesis the human body comes to life only when God "breathed into his nostrils the breath of life" (Gen 2:7). Thus Psalm 104 addresses God with reference to his creatures, "When you hide your face, they are terrified; when you take away their breath, they die and return to the dust. When you send your Spirit, they are created, and you renew the face of the earth." (104:29f.)[35] When exegeting the above noted verses, Pannenberg argues that here the same Hebrew word *ruah* is used to denote the breath of the creatures and the Spirit of God. As the last phrase of the quotation identifies the divine Spirit with those prolific winds that renew the surface of the ground in springtime, in the same way the prophet Ezekiel in a vision saw the dry and dead bones of his people came to life again when the divine wind breathed the Spirit of life into them (Ezek 37:5ff.). This Spirit is not identical with the idea of the soul as spiritual substance apart from the body. The Spirit is not the individual human. The human spirit is not an independent reality of its own, but a mere participation of the divine spirit, and a passing one.[36]

3.1.3 The Spirit as "the Field of Force"

We have already noted that Pannenberg holds the Spirit as the creative force, who gives life. However, the issue is that whether this idea allows reconciling the statement about the Spirit of God as the origin of life with the modern understanding? In the Bible, the Spirit is depicted as the life-giving principle to which all creatures owe life, movement, and activity. This is true of animals, plants, and humans. "When you send your Spirit, they are created, and you renew the face of the earth" (Ps 104:30). In keeping with this is the second creation account, which says that, God "formed the man from the dust of the ground and breathed into his nostrils the breath of life, and the man became a living being" (Gen 2:7). Conversely, all life perishes when God withdraws his Spirit (Job 34:13-15; Ps 104:29). The souls of all living things and the breath of all people are in the hands of the Spirit (Job

---

34. Pannenberg, "The Working of the Spirit," 16; Pannenberg, *Systematic Theology* vol. 1, 373.
35. Pannenberg, "The Working of the Spirit," 17.
36. Pannenberg, "The Working of the Spirit," 17.

12: 10).³⁷ Pannenberg asks how this biblical view of life can be reconciled with the modern biology in which life is a function of the living cell of the living creature as a self-sustaining and reproducing system.

In order to justify his argument that the Spirit is the creative force and to reconcile his statement with the modern understanding, Pannenberg depicts the Spirit in terms of a force field.³⁸ He writes that, "The antireligious ramifications of the reduction of the concept of force to the body and its inert mass enable us to see at once the theological relevance of the changed relation between force and body resulting from the growing significance of field theories in modern physics from the time of Michael Faraday."³⁹ Faraday believed that electric and magnetic fields are real physical "stuff." However, Faraday never spoke of fields of force but used the phrase "physical lines of force" to describe his concept of field theory. Although there has been some controversy as to what precisely Faraday's field concept was, its essential features would seem to be "that force is a substance, that it is the only substance and that all forces are interconvertible through various motions of the lines of force".⁴⁰ In fact, this idea of the field of force goes back by way of Stoicism to pre-Socratic philosophy to the teaching of Anaximenes that air is the *arche* and that all things originated as compression of air.⁴¹ The Stoic doctrine influenced not only the thought of Philo but also what early Christian theology had to say about the working of

---

37. Wolfhart Pannenberg, *Systematic Theology* vol. 2, trans. Geoffrey W. Bromiley (Grand Rapids: Eerdmans, 1994), 76-77.
38. With Pannenberg, several modern systematicians and pneumatologists have come to speak about the Spirit as "field of force/field of force," using a standard concept of modern physics. For example, Michael Welker, *God the Spirit*, trans. John F. Hoffmeyer (Minneapolis: Fortress, 1994); Brand Jochen Hilberath, *Pneumatologie* (Dusseldorf: Patmos, 1994); even Karl Rahner referred to the concept of "energy field" in his "Experience of Self," in *Theological Investigations* 13 (New York: Seabury, 1975), 122-132.
39. Pannenberg, *Systematic Theology* vol. 2, 80.
40. Nancy Nessian, "Faraday's Field Concept," in *Faraday Rediscovered: Essays on the Life and Work of Michael Faraday, 1971-1867*, ed. D. Gooding and F. James (London: Macmillan, 1985), 175ff., 183.
41. Pannenberg, *Systematic Theology* vol. 2, 81; Max Jammer thinks the Stoic doctrine of the divine *pneuma* was actually the direct precursor of the modern field concept. For the Stoics the *pneuma* was a very fine stuff that permeates all things, that holds all things in the cosmos together by its tension (*tonos*), and that gives rise to the different qualities and movements of things. This Stoic doctrine influenced not only the thought of Philo but also what early Christian theology had to say about the working of the divine Spirit as creator. See Pannenberg, *Systematic Theology* vol. 2, 81.

the Spirit in creation. In short, following Faraday, Pannenberg writes that, "But insofar as the field concept corresponds to the older doctrines it is not a mistake, but does justice to the history and concept of Spirit, if we relate the field theories of modern physics to the Christian doctrine of the dynamic work of the divine Spirit in creation."[42] Thus Pannenberg believes in combination with the biblical usage of *ruah/pneuma* that there are possibilities for agreement between the newer scientific theories and theological concepts.[43] He believes that, "Since the field concept as such corresponds to the old concept of *pneuma* … theologians should consider it obvious to relate the field concept of modern physics to the Christian doctrine of the dynamic presence of the divine Spirit in all of creation."[44]

However, Pannenberg cautions that he is proposing only a model and does not intend to equate the activity of the Spirit with the field theories of physics. He writes that, "To be sure, even a cosmic field conceived along the lines of Faraday's thought as a field of force would not be identified immediately with the dynamic activity of the divine Spirit in creation. In every case the different models of science remain approximations…. Therefore, theological assertions of field structure of the cosmic activity of the divine Spirit will remain different field theories in physics."[45] Mark Worthing critiques Pannenberg for his employment of the field concept. Worthing writes:

> Yet because he makes great effort to show the connections to the use of field theory in physics, it is not always easy to distinguish whether he means a field in the theological or physical sense. Pannenberg seeks to develop new conceptual models for the Trinity, the Holy Spirit, and angels in light of

---

42. Pannenberg, *Systematic Theology* vol. 2, 82.
43. Pannenberg notes that for theology there is in fact a closer relation between its doctrine of the divine *pneuma* and the field theories of modern physics than there was in the Middle Ages between this doctrine and the Aristotelian theory of motion. The renewing of the thought of the primacy in Leibniz (with Newton as a precursor) and the development of field theories in physics have made it possible again to relate the function of the divine Spirit in the creation of the world to the way in which physics describe nature. See Pannenberg, *Systematic Theology* vol. 2, 82.
44. Wolfhart Pannenberg, "The Doctrine of Creation and Modern Science," *Zygon* vol. 23, no. 1 (March 1988), 13.
45. Pannenberg, "The Doctrine of Creation," 14.

the concept of field theory. At some points, however, as in his doctrine of angels, he seems to identify these messengers of God with specific physical forces and fields and this confuses the theological and physical concepts of field. This difficulty can also be seen in his doctrine of God.[46]

3.1.4 The Spirit as the Third Person in the Trinity

Pannenberg asserts that the Spirit also denotes the third Person in the Trinity, the Holy Spirit. He makes this statement very clearly because he wants to affirm the personhood of the Spirit. For him, the persons of Father, Son, and Spirit are three forms of the existence of God in and over the world.[47] In the Father, Son, and Spirit the divine essence has the specific form of its existence – not merely the forms but the form, since the three persons constitute a single constellation. Materially, however, the specific form of the existence of God as Father, Son, and Spirit is identical with the unlimited field of God's non-thematic presence in his creation.[48] Pannenberg writes:

> The essence of the one God is revealed both Father and Son, and by their communion in a third, the Spirit who proceeds from Father and is received by the Son and given to his people. The Spirit is not just identical with the commonality of the divine essence which Father and Son share. He also mediates the fellowship of the Father and the Son as he proceeds from the Father and is received by the Son. In this function the

---

46. Mark William Worthing, *God, Creation, and Contemporary Physics* (Minneapolis: Fortress, 1996), 121; see for further reflections, Mark William Worthing, *Foundations and Functions of Theology as Universal Science: Theological Method and Apologetic Praxis in Wolfhart Pannenberg and Karl Rahner* (Frankfurt am Main: Peter Lang, 1996).
47. Pannenberg, *Systematic Theology* vol. 1, 359.
48. Pannenberg, *Systematic Theology* vol. 1, 359; in fact Pannenberg also introduces the concept of field theory into the understanding of the doctrine of God on the ground that God is spoken of in the Bible as "Spirit." This is significant because *pneuma*, the Greek word for Spirit, eventually became associated with the concept of fields of force in physics. In regard to the relation of the Spirit to the Father and the Son, Pannenberg develops his own "theological" field theory. See Worthing, *God, Creation, and Contemporary Physics*, 121; Pannenberg, *Systematic Theology* vol. 2, 104.

Spirit is a third form of the existence of the one divine essence alongside the Father and the Son.[49]

Moreover, for Pannenberg, "Although both the Father and the Son are differentiated from the essence of the Godhead that is Spirit, they are bound together through the Spirit, the third person of the Trinity. Likewise, in that the personal Spirit glorifies the others, that is, differentiates himself from them, he 'knows' himself as connected to the Father and the Son."[50] Pannenberg maintains that one must understand God as Spirit and as the third person in the Trinity. If the Spirit were solely the impersonal divine field, the divine essence (Spirit) would be impersonal. In the Bible, the Spirit is not only the common life of the Father and the Son but also appears as a personal centre of activity.[51] With this understanding of the Spirit as the third person in the Trinity, we are diving into an in-depth treatment of the Spirit in the Trinity.

3.2 Holy Spirit and the Doctrine of Trinity

One of the most distinctive features of Pannenberg's treatment of the doctrine of the triune God is that the Trinity precedes the unity of God.[52] Almost always the opposite is the case. This reversal is significant in view of the fact that the Trinity is not something added to the unity of God rather God in fact exists as the Trinity. Pannenberg makes use of Hegel, who derived the Trinity from the concept of God as Spirit. However, he differs from Hegel in one important respect that Pannenberg does not want to derive the Trinity from God's unity, be it as Spirit or otherwise, since it

---

49. Pannenberg, *Systematic Theology* vol. 1, 358.
50. Stanley J. Grenz, *Reason for Hope: The Systematic Theology of Wolfhart Pannenberg* (New York: Oxford University Press, 1990), 61.
51. Kärkkäinen, *Pneumatology*, 120.
52. Pannenberg, *Systematic Theology* vol. 1, 280-99; see a good discussion by Robert W. Jenson, "Jesus in the Trinity: Wolfhart Pannenberg's Christology and Doctrine of the Trinity," in *The Theology of Wolfhart Pannenberg: Twelve American Critiques, with an Autobiographical Essay and Response*, ed. Carl E. Braaten and Philip Clayton (Minneapolis: Augsburg, 1988), 188-206.

leads to modalism[53] or subordinationalism.[54] This understanding leads him to make a room for the cause of Trinity.

3.2.1 Basis for the Doctrine of the Trinity

Pannenberg makes a lengthy discussion to formulate a basis for the doctrine of the Trinity starting from Scholasticism to the modern Protestant theology. He writes:

> Any derivation of the plurality of trinitarian persons from the essence of the one God, whether it be viewed as spirit or love, leads into the problems of either modalism on the one hand or subordinationalism on the other. Neither, then, can be true to the intentions of the trinitarian dogma. The derivation from love is closer to the Christian concept of God and the doctrine of the Trinity than is derivation from the idea of a divine self-consciousness, since it leaves more room for a plurality of persons in the unity of the divine life. Yet this plurality cannot be deduced from an idea of divine love without relapse into a pretrinitarian monotheism, that of the subjectivity of the one God as the one who generates the other persons. In the concept of divine love it can find only their comprehensive unity.[55]

To find a basis for the doctrine of the Trinity, one must begin with the way in which the Father, Son, and the Spirit come on the scene and related to one another in the event of revelation.[56] Here lies the material justification

---

53. The view that the Trinitarian persons are not real persons but rather appearances or modes of acting.
54. The view that either the Son or the Spirit is subordinate to the Father.
55. Pannenberg, *Systematic Theology* vol. 1, 298.
56. Pannenberg notes that it was Barth who first saw the Trinity with full clarity and discussed it in relation to revelation. To base the doctrine of the Trinity on the content of the revelation of God in Jesus Christ, we must begin with the revelation of Jesus to the Father as it came to expression in his message of the divine rule. The New Testament statements about the deity of Jesus all presupposes his divine sonship and are ultimately grounded in his relation to the Father. The relation of his message and work to the Father forms the foundation of the confession of the divine sonship of Jesus by the Christian community in the light of the divine confirmation of his fullness of power by the Easter event. See Pannenberg, *Systematic Theology* vol. 1, 300, 304.

for the demand that the doctrine of the Trinity must be based on the biblical witness to revelation or on the economy of salvation. On this approach there is no material reason to append the doctrine of the Trinity to God's essence and attributes. The latter can be relevantly dealt with in the context of the trinitarian revelation of God as Father, Son, and the Spirit.[57] In other words, a systematic grounding and development of the doctrine of the Trinity must begin with the revelation of God in Jesus Christ, namely, on the way the Father, Son, and the Spirit come to appearance in the event of revelation. Therefore, the point of departure for trinitarian doctrine is Jesus' message of the fatherly care of God and the kingdom of God, his rulership over all creation.[58]

3.2.2 The Spirit and Self-differentiation in the Trinity

In keeping with the older concept of natural theology as what is in accordance with the nature of God, Pannenberg understands that God is revealed as three – Father, Son, and the Spirit – but as nevertheless a unity. Therefore, Pannenberg's understanding of God can be captured by two phrases: *the threeness of the one God* and *the unity of the triune God*.[59] At the heart of Pannenberg's doctrine is his concept of "self-differentiation" following Hegel that the essence of a person lies in the act of giving oneself to one's counterpart and thereby gaining one's identity from the other. Kärkkäinen notes that this is a correction of the traditional notion of trinitarian "self-differentiation," which refers to the bringing forth of the second and third trinitarian persons through the Father and so implies

---

57. Pannenberg, *Systematic Theology* vol. 1, 299.
58. Pannenberg, *Systematic Theology* vol. 1, 259-80.
59. Grenz, *Reason for Hope,* 43; Pannenberg notes that in many respects, the distinction between the Son and the Spirit was still unclear in the theology of the 2nd and 3rd centuries. On the one side the obscurities had to do with the relation to wisdom, whose pre-existence as an entity distinct from the creator is stressed in Proverbs 8:22ff. In addition to the lack of clarity regarding the relation of the Son and Spirit to wisdom there was also uncertainty as to which activities should be referred to the Son on one side and the Spirit on the other. Thus Old Testament prophecy and the birth of Jesus could be seen as the work of the Spirit but also as the work of the Logos. Both had a share in creation as the "two hands" of God. Thus it seems that the function of the Father, Son, and the Spirit, and especially Son and Spirit, are not clearly distinguishable. See Pannenberg, *Systematic Theology* vol. 1, 270; see also Wolfhart Pannenberg, "Father, Son, Spirit: Problems of a Trinitarian Doctrine of God," *Dialog* vol. 26, no. 4 (1987), 250-257.

the priority of the Father.⁶⁰ In short, the one who differentiates oneself from another is dependent on the other for one's identity. Subsequently, the Father's fatherhood is dependent upon the activity of the Son and the Spirit and vice versa. Following Athanasius, Pannenberg argues that, "The Father would not be the Father without the Son and vice versa."⁶¹ On this basis Kärkkäinen argues that even here it is clear that the Trinity is essential to God's ontological being.⁶²

However, Pannenberg argues that there is an assumption that the positing of different modes of working by the Father, Son, and Spirit is the only basis on which to contend for their differentiation. But this presupposition is neither self-evident nor keeping with the biblical facts.⁶³ The differentiation of Father and Son is grounded in one and the same event, which is the message of Jesus concerning God and his coming kingdom. What is said about the Spirit also relates to this event. Although the concept of Spirit is a familiar one from the Old Testament, only in connection with the relation of the Father and the Son is the Spirit seen to be an independent third principle of the divine reality. Decisive here is the differentiation of the Son from the Father.⁶⁴ This argument for a hypostatic distinction of Father, Son, and the Spirit does not begin with different spheres of operation but with the inner relations of the Son to the Father and the Spirit. The self-differentiation of the Son from the Father on the one side and the Spirit on the other forms a basis for thesis that there is a threefold distinction in the deity.⁶⁵ This understanding of the inner relation and distinction in the Trinity leads one to inquire the speciality of the unity of the Trinity.

3.2.3 *The Spirit and the Unity in the Trinity*
If there is distinction and relation in the Trinity, the pertinent issue is that how one can harmonize these with the monotheistic character of the biblical belief in God and the tradition of philosophical theology. Pannenberg holds that the early Christian theology had tried to prove the agreement of the

---

60. Kärkkäinen, *Pneumatology*, 121.
61. Pannenberg, *Systematic Theology* vol. 1, 273.
62. Kärkkäinen, *Pneumatology*, 121.
63. Pannenberg, *Systematic Theology* vol. 1, 272.
64. Pannenberg, *Systematic Theology* vol. 1, 272.
65. Pannenberg, *Systematic Theology* vol. 1, 272.

confession of the deity of the Son and Spirit with the Old Testament monotheism by expounding Old Testament passages as implicitly trinitarian. It stands in relation to the history of the exposition of such texts in Jewish thinking. It shows that the Christian view of the Son as a pre-existent hypostasis alongside the Father, and similar views concerning the Spirit which developed in the course of the formation of the doctrine of Trinity, were not opposed to Judaism and its belief in one God.[66] However, Pannenberg follows Hegelian understanding of the unity in the Trinity. Hegel understood the unity in the Trinity as the unity of reciprocal self-dedication. Thereby he conceived God's unity in an intensity and vitality never before achieved, not by striking off the threeness of persons, but precisely by means of the sharpest emphasis of the concept of the personality of Father, Son, and Spirit.[67] Pannenberg holds that Hegel's idea is suited to the relation of Jesus to the Father and Father to him, as well as to that of the Spirit, who glorifies both the Father and the Son as it is expressed in the New Testament. The relation of Jesus to the Father is entirely characterized by the dedication of the Son to the Father, which is the Father to Jesus by his acknowledgment of the Son in his raising Jesus from the dead.[68] Pannenberg writes that, "The Holy Spirit moves the believer to dedication to Jesus through believing trust and praise in the confession of him. Conversely, the dedication of the Son to humanity constitutes the content of this confession. Jesus is dedicated to men in obedience to the will of the Father who invites all men to trust in him, so that in Jesus' dedication to his mission the love of the Father to men as his children appeared."[69] Correspondingly, the Spirit mediates not only participation in Jesus through dedication to him, but also the community of the Son – and of the sons – with the Father. In the vital movement of such reciprocal dedication, the unity of the Father, Son, and the Spirit consummates itself in the historical process of the revelatory event. An intimation of this perception can be seen in the patristic

---

66. Pannenberg, *Systematic Theology* vol. 1, 275.
67. Pannenberg, *Jesus – God and Man*, 182.
68. Pannenberg, *Jesus – God and Man*, 183.
69. Pannenberg, *Jesus – God and Man*, 183.

doctrine of *perichoresis*, the reciprocal indwelling of the three persons in one another.[70]

Moreover, Pannenberg insists that the idea of the divine life as a dynamic field sees the divine Spirit who unites the three persons as proceeding from the Father, received by the Son, and common to both, so that precisely in this way the Spirit is the force field of their fellowship that is distinct from them both. As a field, the Spirit would be impersonal. The Spirit as person can be thought of only as a concrete form of the one deity like the Father and the Son. But the Spirit is not just the divine life that is common to both the Father and the Son.[71] It also stands over against the Father and the Son as its own centre of action. This makes sense if the Father and the Son have fellowship in the unity of the divine life only as they stand over against the person of the Spirit. Precisely because the common essence of the deity stands over against both – in different ways – in the form of the Spirit, they are related to one another by the unity of the Spirit. Pannenberg argues that, "If the union is to include the Spirit as person, it must be assumed that the personal Spirit, as he glorified the Son in his relation to the Father and the Father through the Son, knows that he is united thereby to both."[72] In short, the Spirit has a place in the eternal fellowship of the Father and the Son because Spirit is the condition and medium of their fellowship.[73] On this basis one can see the imparting of the Spirit to believers as their incorporation into the fellowship of the Son with the Father. Moreover, the personhood of the Spirit is a necessary premise of its work in the fellowship of the Son with the Father.[74] Pannenberg notes that the statement in Luke 10:21 that Jesus praised the Father in the Spirit for his sending and for the power that the Father had given him (10:22). It means that for Jesus

---

70. Pannenberg, *Jesus – God and Man*, 183.
71. Pannenberg, *Systematic Theology* vol. 1, 383.
72. Pannenberg, *Systematic Theology* vol. 1, 384.
73. That means there was a feeling that the Old Testament justifies a prior presentation of God as the supreme being (Exod 3:14) and also of his attributes. This thought was brought into relation to the New Testament concept of God as Spirit (Jn 4:24) and later replaced by it. In one way or another, the attributes of God were derived from the concept of God as the supreme being of the Spirit. The doctrine of the Trinity was then added to the existing idea of the one God as the specifically Christian revelation. See Pannenberg, *Systematic Theology* vol.1, 281ff. Pannenberg makes a detailed discussion about this aspect in his *Systematic Theology* vol. 1, 281ff.
74. Pannenberg, *Systematic Theology* vol. 1, 316.

himself, then, the work of the Spirit was to glorify the Father, and in this way glorifies the Son in his fellowship with the Father, and in this way glorifies the Father as well (16:14).[75]

3.2.4 Three Persons but only One God

The above discussion provides the answer for the previous question about the monotheistic character of the biblical belief. Pannenberg insists that, "If the trinitarian relations among Father, Son, and the Spirit have the form of mutual self-distinction, they must be understood not merely as different modes of being of the one divine subject but as living realizations of separate centres of action."[76] There is a divine consciousness subsisting in a threefold mode, and it does so in such a way that each of the three persons relates to the others as others and distinguishes itself from them.[77] Relations among the three persons that are defined as mutual self-distinction cannot be reduced to relations of origin in the traditional sense. The Father does not merely beget the Son. He also hands over his kingdom to him and receives it back from him. The Son is not merely begotten of the Father. He is also obedient to him and he thereby glorifies him as the one God. The Spirit is not just breathed. It also fills the Son and glorifies him in its obedience to the Father, thereby glorifying the Father. In so doing the Spirit leads into all truth (Jn 16:13) and searches out the deep things of Godhead (1 Cor 2:10-11).[78] When Scripture bears witness to the active relations of the Son and Spirit to the Father, it is not good enough to treat these as not constitutive for their identity and in this respect to look only at the reactions of begetting and proceeding (or breathing), viewing solely the relations of origin, which lead from the Father to the Son and the Spirit, as applicable to the constitution of the persons. None of the other relations is merely incidental to the Son and Spirit in their relation to the Father. All have a place in the distinctiveness and fellowship of the trinitarian persons.[79]

We may thus say of the richly structured nexus of relationship that binds together the Father, Son, and Spirit what a trinitarian theology has said

---

75. Pannenberg, *Systematic Theology* vol. 1, 316.
76. Pannenberg, *Systematic Theology* vol. 1, 319.
77. Pannenberg, *Systematic Theology* vol. 1, 319-320.
78. Pannenberg, *Systematic Theology* vol. 1, 320.
79. Pannenberg, *Systematic Theology* vol. 1, 320.

about the trinitarian relations, namely, that they constitute the different distinctions of the persons. The persons simply are what they are in their relations to one another, which both distinguish them from one another and bring them into communion with one another.[80] Yet the persons cannot be reduced to individual relations, as is done especially in the theology of West. Such reduction is ruled out by the fact that the nexus of relations between them is more complex than would appear from the older doctrine of relations of origin, i.e., the begetting of the Son by the Father and the procession or breathing of the Spirit from him. The persons cannot be identical simply with any one relation. Each is a catalyst of many relations.[81] In short, Pannenberg writes:

> Thus the Son says that only the Father as the one God is truly good (Mark 10:18) and therefore truly God. In keeping with this is the commitment of the Son to his mission in which he gives his own life in the service of the deity of the Father. The Spirit confirms and extols the Son as one with the Father in his obedience and as the Revealer of his love. The Father not only gives his Spirit to the Son, and by him sheds abroad his love in the hearts of believers (Rom 5:5), but also hands over his kingdom to the Son, so that the Son can be called the power and the wisdom of God (1 Cor 1:24).[82]

3.2.5 The Spirit Is the Power of Love in the Trinity

Although there is unity in the Trinity as noted earlier, how is this unity accomplished? Here Pannenberg follows the Augustinian understanding. Augustine described the Spirit as the eternal communion of the Father and the Son, as the love (*caritas*) that unites them. Following this statement, Pannenberg holds that there is a deeper truth in Augustine's view of the Spirit as the love that unites the Father and the Son.[83] Pannenberg writes, "According to 1 John 4:8, 16, love as the power manifests itself in

---

80. Pannenberg, *Systematic Theology* vol. 1, 320.
81. Pannenberg, *Systematic Theology* vol. 1, 320.
82. Pannenberg, *Systematic Theology* vol. 1, 321.
83. Pannenberg, *Systematic Theology* vol. 1, 316.

the mutual relations of the trinitarian persons is identical with the divine essence. It is the materially concrete form of 'Spirit' as the characteristic of God's essence. The two statements 'God is Spirit' and 'God is love' denotes the same unity of essence by which the Father, Son, and Spirit are united in the fellowship of the one God."[84] The statement that "God is Spirit" tells us what kind of Spirit it is whose sound (Jn 3:8) fills all creation and whose power gives life to all creatures. The Spirit is the power of love that lets the other be. This power can thus give existence to creaturely life because it is already at work in the reciprocity of the trinitarian life of God as in eternity each of the three persons lets the others by what they are.[85] Thus Spirit is the power and fire of love glowing through the divine persons, uniting them and radiating from them as the light of the glory of God.[86] Each person is ec-statically related to one or both of the others and has its personal distinctiveness or selfhood in this relation. In the person of the Father the sphere of the divine Spirit steps forth as the creative power of existence which takes its form only through the relation to the Son.[87] The coming forth of the Son from the Father is the basic fulfilment of divine love. It is so on the Father's part through the creative dynamic of the Spirit who is the essence of the Godhead. On the Son's part, the Spirit always participates in what happens, though not in every respect as the hypostatic Spirit. The essence of the Godhead is indeed the Spirit.[88] The Spirit comes forth as a separate hypostasis as it comes over against the Son and the Father as the divine essence, common to both, which actually unites them and also attests and maintains their unity in face of their distinction. If the Spirit is the love by which the Father and the Son are mutually related even if as a hypostasis he stands over against both as the Spirit of love who unites them in their distinction. As a hypostasis, the Spirit is distinct from both Father and Son. Hence Spirit can be at work in creation and can also be shed abroad in the hearts of believers as a gift.[89]

---

84. Pannenberg, *Systematic Theology* vol. 1, 427.
85. Pannenberg, *Systematic Theology* vol. 1, 427.
86. Pannenberg, *Systematic Theology* vol. 1, 428.
87. Pannenberg, *Systematic Theology* vol. 1, 428.
88. Pannenberg, *Systematic Theology* vol. 1, 429.
89. Pannenberg, *Systematic Theology* vol. 1, 429.

On the one side the Spirit and love constitute the common essence of deity and on the other they come forth as a separate hypostasis in the Spirit. Both Father and Spirit in their different ways represent the Godhead as a whole. This is true about the Son, because he partakes in the eternal deity only through his relation to the Father and as filled by the Spirit of the Father.[90] In the Spirit, too, the unity of the divine essence emerges as such, but the Spirit is seen to be an independent figure only in relation to the Father and the Son and in distinction from them. In the Son the inner dynamic of the divine life finds its concreteness as Spirit and love.[91] In this way, the divine persons are concretions of the divine reality as Spirit. They are individual aspects of the dynamic field of the eternal Godhead. This means that they do not exist for themselves but in ec-static relation to the overarching field of deity which manifests itself in each of them and in their interrelations.[92] In short, one can say that, "In the trinitarian persons, the Son is wholly himself in the relation to the Father and the Father in the relation to the Son, so that both are wholly what they are in the witness of the Spirit. The Spirit for his part, in his personal separateness, is simply the Spirit of the Father and the Son inasmuch as these are the object of his working, an object, however, that is always realized already in the eternal fellowship of the divine life."[93] Thus divine love constitutes the concrete unity of the divine life in the distinction of its personal manifestation and relations. Their personal distinction among Father, Son, and Spirit cannot be derived from an abstract concept of love. We may know them only in the historical revelation of God in Jesus Christ. But on this basis they and their unity in the divine essence make sense as the concrete reality of the divine

---

90. Pannenberg, *Systematic Theology* vol. 1, 429.
91. Pannenberg, *Systematic Theology* vol. 1, 430.
92. Pannenberg, *Systematic Theology* vol. 1, 430; in this sense, the Father and Son have their unity and their divine essence only through their relation to the Spirit. And the Spirit is a distinct hypostasis only by its relation to the distinction and fellowship of the Father and Son in their differentiation. For the Spirit has full potential independence, not as proceeding from the Father, as radiating from his divine essence, but only in its distinction from the Father and the Son in their differentiation. See Pannenberg, *Systematic Theology* vol. 1, 430.
93. Pannenberg, *Systematic Theology* vol. 1, 431.

love which pulses through all things and consummates the monarchy of the Father through the Son in the Spirit.[94]

3.2.6 Monarchy of the Father Is Established through the Spirit

When one argues that there is mutuality and mutual dependence between the persons of the Trinity, the pertinent question is whether the monarchy of the Father is at stake? Pannenberg argues that although there is mutuality and dependence in the Trinity with regard to their personal identity and deity, still the monarchy of the Father is not destroyed. Pannenberg writes:

> On the contrary, through the work of the Son the kingdom or monarchy of the Father is established in creation, and through the work of the Spirit, who glorifies the Son and the plenipotentiary of the Father, and in so doing glorifies the Father himself, the kingdom or monarchy of the Father in creation is consummated. By their work the Son and Spirit serve the monarchy of the Father. Yet the Father does not have his kingdom or monarchy without the Son and the Spirit, but only through them.[95]

It means that the monarchy of the Father is not established directly but through the mediation of the Son and the Spirit. Hence the unity of the divine lordship has its essence in the form of this mediation.[96] In short, the Son is not subordinate to the Father in the sense of ontological inferiority, but he subjects himself to the Father. In this regard he is himself in eternity the locus of the monarchy of the Father and one with the Father by the Spirit. The monarchy of the Father is not the presupposition but the result of the common operation of the three persons. It is thus the seal of their unity.[97] For Pannenberg, the unity of Father, Son, and Spirit certainly finds expression in the relations of salvation history which are determined by their mutual self-distinction, and especially in their joint working in

---

94. Pannenberg, *Systematic Theology* vol. 1, 432.
95. Pannenberg, *Systematic Theology* vol. 1, 324.
96. Pannenberg, *Systematic Theology* vol. 1, 327.
97. Pannenberg, *Systematic Theology* vol. 1, 325.

manifestation of the monarchy of the Father in creation. But this joint working of the persons and their mutual *perichoresis* must also be seen as an expression of the unity of the divine essence.[98]

3.2.7 *The Spirit and the Divine Action*

Since Pannenberg has already established the unity of the divine essence and the monarchy of the Father in relation to the Son and Spirit, he endeavors to see how the divine action is taken place in the universe? He maintains that the three persons of Father, Son, and the Spirit are primarily the subject of the divine action. By their cooperation, they are one God and this single divine subject acts in the world without restriction.[99] Pannenberg writes:

> The kingdom of God in the world is certainly the kingdom of the Father. The monarchy of the Father is God's absolute lordship. The Son serves it, and so does the glorifying of the Father and the Son by the Spirit. But the monarchy of the Father is mediated by the Son, who prepares the way for it by winning form for it in the life of creatures, and also by the Spirit, who enables creatures to honour God as their creator by letting them share in the relation of the Son to the Father. This is the action of the one God by the Father, Son and the Spirit as it may be seen in the light of the eschatological consummation of the kingdom of God in the world.[100]

Thus the action of Father, Son, and Spirit in the world is ascribed not merely to the three persons of the Trinity but also to the one divine essence.[101] The goal of God's action in the world by the working of Father, Son, and Spirit is twofold. Firstly, the creation of a creaturely reality that is distinct from God, and its consummation in encounter with the creator and secondly, the revelation of God's deity as creator of the world.[102] To this extent the action of God in the world is a repetition or reiteration of his eternal deity in

---

98. Pannenberg, *Systematic Theology* vol. 1, 334.
99. Pannenberg, *Systematic Theology* vol. 1, 388.
100. Pannenberg, *Systematic Theology* vol. 1, 388-389.
101. Pannenberg, *Systematic Theology* vol. 1, 389.
102. Pannenberg, *Systematic Theology* vol. 1, 389.

his relation to the world.[103] Pannenberg notes that, "By the common acting of the Father, Son, and Spirit the future of God breaks into the present of creatures, into the world of creation, and on the basis of this divine action the attributes are predicated not merely of the trinitarian persons but also of the divine essence that is common to them all."[104] These attributes may be seen equally in the divine works of creation, reconciliation, and redemption though they are articulated differently. From the identity of the attributes one can affirm that the God who acts in the creation, reconciliation, and consummation of the world is one and the same God.[105]

3.2.8 Question of the Procession of the Spirit

After delineating the issue of self-distinction and unity in the Trinity, Pannenberg focuses on the pertinent issue of begetting and breathing of the Son and the Spirit. He maintains that if the doctrine of the Trinity is an expression of the relation of Jesus to the Father and the Spirit, this has some incisive implications for the terminology which the classical doctrine of Trinity worked out to describe the trinitarian relations.[106] The processions according to the classical doctrine of the Trinity must be carefully distinguished from the sending of the Son (Rom 8:3; Gal 4:4; Jn 3:17; 8:16; etc.) and the Spirit (Jn 14:26; 15:26; 16:7), in which the issue is the relation of the eternal God to the world in the economy of salvation. The processions take place from all eternity in the divine essence, but the sending of the Son and the gift of the Spirit (Acts 2:38; 10:45) relates to those to whom the Son is sent or the Spirit given.[107] However, Pannenberg asserts that these sharp distinctions between begetting and breathing

---

103. Pannenberg, *Systematic Theology* vol. 1, 389.
104. Pannenberg, *Systematic Theology* vol. 1, 391.
105. Pannenberg, *Systematic Theology* vol. 1, 391-392.
106. Pannenberg, *Systematic Theology* vol. 1, 305; Pannenberg notes that in the East the doctrine followed Johannine terminology and distinguished between the "generation" of the Son (Jn 1:14; 3:16; cf. Lk 3:22) and the "procession" of the Spirit (Jn 15:26). On the other hand, Latin theology in the Middle Ages spoke of the procession of both Son and Spirit. There were thus two processions, the distinction is that the Son was begotten and the Spirit is breathed (Jn 20:22). These processions in the eternal divine substance resulted in the person of the Son and Spirit, who for their part are distinguished by relations (the Father actively begetting, the Son passively begotten and the Spirit passively breathed). See Pannenberg, *Systematic Theology* vol. 1, 305.
107. Pannenberg, *Systematic Theology* vol. 1, 305.

on the one side, sending and gift on the other, can perhaps be justified linguistically but can hardly be justified exegetically.[108] With regard to the breathing of the Spirit, the disciples were the recipients according to John 20:22. There is no reference to an eternal breathing. He argues that if there is an echo here of the imparting of the Spirit to Adam at creation (Gen 2:7), we obviously have an act in God's relation to created reality. It might be easier to find a distinction between the proceeding of the Spirit from the Father and the sending of the Son (cf. Jn 15:26). But modern exegesis sees the two expression as parallel in analogy to John 16:28, so that the subject is the same as in both cases, namely, the imparting of the Spirit to the disciples.[109] Hence, Pannenberg never argues based on John 15:26 that the Spirit proceeds from the Father. On the other hand, he maintains that the Spirit proceeds from the Father and is received by the Son. This does not rule out the fact that the Son gives the Spirit to his people, sharing with the Father in the sending of the Spirit in order to incorporate believers into his fellowship with the Father (Jn 16:7; cf. 14:6; 15:26).[110] By receiving the Spirit, believers share in the sonship of Jesus and this imparting of the Spirit takes place through the risen Lord (Jn 20:22), apostolic proclamation, and belief in the gospel of Jesus Christ (Gal 3:2). But this does not alter the fact that the Spirit originates and proceeds from the Father.[111] In short for Pannenberg, "Traditional Christian theology might well have worked this matter out correctly under the guidance of the Spirit of Christ even though it cannot be adequately proved from individual biblical verses. The relations between the person of Jesus, the Father, and the Spirit might well prove to be not just historical or economic but relations which characterize the eternal divine essence. That is

---

108. Pannenberg, *Systematic Theology* vol. 1, 305.
109. Pannenberg, *Systematic Theology* vol. 1, 306.
110. Pannenberg, *Systematic Theology* vol. 1, 317; how are we to think the unity of the divine essence if room is to be left for the Trinity of Father, Son, and Spirit? According to Pannenberg, "The essence of the one God is revealed by both Father and Son, and by their communion in a third, the Spirit, who proceeds from the Father and is received by the Son and given to his people. The Spirit is not just identical with the commonality of the divine essence which Father and Son share. He also mediates the fellowship of the Father and the Son as he proceeds from the Father and is received by the Son. In this function the Spirit is a third form of the existence of the one divine essence alongside the Father and the Son." See Pannenberg, *Systematic Theology* vol. 1, 358.
111. Pannenberg, *Systematic Theology* vol. 1, 318.

not to say, however, that we may reduce this description to the traditional concepts of procession, begetting, and breathing."[112]

3.2.9 Objections to the Filioque

Since Pannenberg has made a thorough discussion regarding the procession of the Spirit, he is critical towards the *filioque* clause. He holds that, "The theology of the Christian West has good cause not merely to regret the one-sided addition of the *filioque* clause to the third article of the Creed of 381, and to withdraw it as uncanonical, but also to recognise that the Augustinian doctrine of the procession of the Spirit from both Father and Son is inappropriate formulation of the fellowship of both Father and Son with the Spirit that Augustine rightly underscores."[113] It is inappropriate because it describes the fellowship in the vocabulary of a relation of origin. The mistaken formulation of Augustine points out in fact to a defect which plagues the trinitarian theological language of both East and West and sees the relations among Father, Son, and Spirit exclusively as relations of origin. With this view one cannot do justice to the reciprocity in the relations.[114] It is true that the concept of *perichoresis* or circumincession contains the idea of reciprocity and has been generally adopted as an expression of trinitarian unity. However, it had only a limited impact because of the one-sided view of the intratrinitarian relations as relations of origin.[115] In short, Pannenberg sees *filioque* as wrong because it presupposes that Father-Son is a primary relationship of origin to which the spiration of the Spirit is added. This makes the Spirit secondary and represents a subordination of the Spirit.[116]

3.3 The Holy Spirit and Christology

Having understood the whole question of the Spirit with regard to the Godhead, Pannenberg focuses on Christology and the important role it has played in the development of his whole theological program, especially pneumatology. The significance of his Christology in relation to pneumatology is that the Spirit plays a central role in his Christology. Although

---

112. Pannenberg, *Systematic Theology* vol. 1, 307.
113. Pannenberg, *Systematic Theology* vol. 1, 318.
114. Pannenberg, *Systematic Theology* vol. 1, 319.
115. Pannenberg, *Systematic Theology* vol. 1, 319.
116. Pannenberg, *Systematic Theology* vol. 1, 317-19.

Pannenberg discusses soteriology under Christology, in this study soteriology is addressed separately for the sake of convenience. The central focus of this section is to look into the role of the Spirit throughout the whole life of Jesus Christ.

3.3.1 Understanding of the Primitive Christianity Concerning Jesus and Spirit

Before entering into the discussion of the relationship between Jesus and the Spirit, we must be clear about the understanding of the primitive Christianity concerning Jesus and the Spirit. Pannenberg notes that primitive Christianity understood the Spirit primarily from the perspective of the Old Testament and Jewish tradition. Jewish tradition held the view that the Spirit of God is poured upon the charismatic leaders and prophets in ancient Israel and also upon those who received a special commission from Yahweh.[117] However, the predominant Jewish conception is that the Spirit has not been active after the end of the exile, rather has been absent in order to be poured out "on all flesh" in the *eschaton*.[118] Moreover, since the time of the prophets, the bringers of eschatological salvation in the future were expected as distinctive bearers of the Spirit of God, as the messiah of the last time (Isa 11:1ff.), the Son of man and the eschatological prophet. In short, the Jewish understanding has been that the special capacity and function of the bearer of salvation in the end time is the effect of God's Spirit, upon whom it will constantly partake.[119] Taking a cue from such expectations, primitive Christianity also understood Jesus as the bearer of the Spirit.[120]

---

117. Pannenberg, *Jesus – God and Man*, 116.
118. Pannenberg, *Jesus – God and Man*, 116.
119. Pannenberg, *Jesus – God and Man*, 116.
120. The tradition of Jesus' baptism and anointment with the Spirit is also originally rooted in the circle of Jewish tradition. The tradition of Jesus' anointment with the Spirit at baptism later became the connecting link to the concept of Jesus as the eschatological prophet. Moreover, the title *Christos* had been used only eschatologically for the function of the one who would return in power. But it was later associated with the earthly Jesus through the passion tradition and designated his whole activity. Because of his charismatic activity, Jesus was understood in Hellenistic Jewish Christianity as a "divine man", in which the Old Testament designation for the charismatic figures of ancient Israel fused with the Hellenistic evaluation of extraordinary men as "divine." In this sense the title "Son of God," which had been used for the resurrected Lord, was also applied to the pre-Easter Jesus. See Pannenberg, *Jesus – God and Man*, 117.

Along with this line, when dealing with the divinity of Jesus in relation to the divinity of the Father, Pannenberg argues Jesus' unity with God.[121] It is the presence of the Spirit in Jesus that makes him divine. Pannenberg contends:

> Probably the oldest attempt to express God's presence in Jesus was characterized by the concept of the Spirit. Through the Spirit, Jesus is not only connected with particular figures of Jewish expectation, with the prophet of the last times, the Son of Man, the Servant of God, or the Messiah, but directly with God himself. Naturally, no competition is asserted thereby between the concept of the Spirit and these titles; rather, the eschatological figures named were themselves understood as bearer of the Spirit in a special way.[122]

Thus Pannenberg argues that the fellowship of Jesus as the Son with God as the Father can obviously be stated only if there is reference to the Spirit, because the Spirit of God is the mode of God's presence in Jesus as he was formerly God's presence in the prophets or in creation.[123] Yet it is not present with eschatological ultimacy as an abiding gift which was the content of the eschatological hope of Israel, especially in the expectation of the Spirit-filled Messiah.[124]

3.3.2 Jesus Is the Son of God Due to the Operation of the Spirit

Since Jesus is the bearer of the Spirit of God according to primitive Christianity, the next main question can be on what ground Jesus is the Son of God? In order to answer this question, Pannenberg follows the New Testament understanding of the operation of the Spirit in Jesus Christ. He insists that, "The Gospels traced back the relationship of Jesus with the God whom he proclaimed to the presence and working of the Spirit within him."[125] Pannenberg refers to the gospels to establish his point clearly by

---

121. Pannenberg, *Jesus – God and Man*, 115.
122. Pannenberg, *Jesus – God and Man*, 116.
123. Pannenberg, *Systematic Theology* vol. 1, 267.
124. Pannenberg, *Systematic Theology* vol. 1, 267.
125. Pannenberg, *Systematic Theology* vol. 1, 266; one of the significant aspects that

arguing that in the story of the baptism of Jesus by John the Spirit was imparted to him on this occasion (Mk 1:10). The infancy story in Luke also traces back the sonship of Jesus to his birth and bases the description of Jesus as the Son of God by the operation of the Spirit, stating that he was conceived of the Spirit (1:35).[126] John also bears witness that Jesus, whose words were Spirit and life (6:63-64), was filled with the Spirit of God who enabled him to speak the words of God (3:33-34). The description of the words and works of Jesus in the gospels as expression of the presence of the Spirit within him has the function of denoting the close relation of Jesus with the Father. This is true even if Jesus himself does not appeal to the Spirit. But if the presentation of words and works of Jesus as the working of the Spirit describes the presence of God himself in him, then we cannot separate between God and the Spirit of God. In the working of the Spirit God himself is present.[127] In short, the Spirit of God is either presupposed or expressly named as the medium of the communion of Jesus with the Father and the mediator of the participation of believers in Christ.[128]

3.3.3 Incarnation as God's Self-actualization in the World

Pannenberg insists that incarnation of the Son is not irrelevant to the deity of the trinitarian God. It was significant for the eternal fellowship of the Father with the Son by the Spirit. It brings creation into the trinitarian

---

Pannenberg deals with in his eschatology is that Jesus is the eschatological figure. He insists that with regard to the theological presuppositions, the New Testament finds in the Spirit's presence with Jesus Christ and believers the decisive indication of the coming of the eschatological consummation. The powerful presence of the divine Spirit in the person of Jesus shows that he is the eschatological revealer of God through whom God's coming kingdom is already dawning. See Pannenberg, *Systematic Theology* vol. 2, 98.

126. For Pannenberg, the only New Testament support to the conception and birth of Jesus is in the Lucan account, where the message of the angel to Mary bases the divine sonship of Jesus on the act of conception in the power of the Spirit (Lk 1:35). Theology must evaluate this tradition in tension with the other New Testament accounts of the incarnation and sending instead of grounding its understanding of the incarnation solely on the birth story. We must recognize that according to the Lucan story Jesus was the Son of God from the very first and did not become so later, whether by his baptism or his resurrection. But this is not to say that we might equate the event of the incarnation with the isolated event of the birth. Instead, the significance of the birth is dependent on the story of his overall earthly course. See Pannenberg, *Systematic Theology* vol. 2, 302.

127. Pannenberg, *Systematic Theology* vol. 1, 267.

128. Pannenberg, *Systematic Theology* vol. 1, 266.

fellowship.[129] However, the creation of the world does not rest on any inner necessity of the divine nature that compelled God to make his creation; rather, it is a free act of God. But the creation of the world carries with it the incarnation of the Son, because it is the means of actualizing the royal rule of the Father in the world. Without Lordship over his creation, God would not be God.[130] The monarchy of the Father had been actualized already in the eternal fellowship of the Trinity. It did not need the existence of a world because in all eternity the Son gives the Father the honor of his kingly rule. However, the rule of the Father is eternal through the Son and Spirit. In other words, the rule of the Father is set up and brought to acknowledgement in creation through the Son and the Spirit.[131]

Pannenberg argues that through the incarnation of the Son, the Father is present to the world for its salvation. Moreover, the fatherly love is also revealed through the Son who has actualized the deity of God in the world and glorified in it God's name and kingly rule. Pannenberg writes that, "Certainly this glorifying of in the world presupposes constant glorifying in God's eternity. Yet in the world the kingly rule of the Father is first glorified by the Son and Spirit as the incarnate Son, by obedience to his mission, glorifies the name of the Father among us, and as the Spirit teaches us to see herein the mission of the obedient Son."[132] Pannenberg maintains that since the Father sends the Son and the Spirit for the fulfillment of the mission through the obedience of the Son and the work of the Spirit, the self-actualization of the trinitarian God has taken place in the world.[133] In this self-actualization of God, the threefold subjectivity of Father, Son, and Spirit works as both the origin and the result of the event. The one God acts through the trinitarian persons and precisely thereby creates the paradox. It is certainly true of all the persons specifically that they are there before the process of God's self-actualizing in the world of his creation by historical revelation.[134] It is also true that their deity is the result of this process. Yet the action of the trinitarian persons is not oriented directly to themselves

---

129. Pannenberg, *Systematic Theology* vol. 2, 389.
130. Pannenberg, *Systematic Theology* vol. 2, 389–390.
131. Pannenberg, *Systematic Theology* vol. 2, 390.
132. Pannenberg, *Systematic Theology* vol. 2, 392.
133. Pannenberg, *Systematic Theology* vol. 2, 393.
134. Pannenberg, *Systematic Theology* vol. 2, 393.

but to the other persons. In the economy of salvation the same is true in the sending of the Son by the Father, the Son's obedience to the Father, and in the glorifying of the Father and the Son by the Spirit. Hence the self-actualization of the one God is one of reciprocity in the relations of the persons and the result of their mutual self-giving to one another.[135]

3.3.4 The Spirit and the Resurrection of Jesus

Having understood the significance of the Spirit in the incarnation and life of Jesus Christ, Pannenberg makes a thorough treatment of the resurrection of Jesus Christ and the working of the Spirit in this unique event.[136] Hence, one can argue that one of the main aspects in the whole theology of Pannenberg is the significance of the resurrection of Jesus Christ and the role of the Spirit in this event. As noted earlier, Pannenberg understands that, "The Holy Spirit is the Almighty God himself and his breath blows through all creation. In the Old Testament, he is understood as the origin of all life. In this light, it is meaningful to speak of the Spirit of God as he who keeps all living creatures alive."[137] Moreover, the close connection that existed for Paul between the *pneuma* and the reality of the resurrection that appeared in Jesus and is hoped by Christians is demonstrated by the Old Testament understanding of the Spirit as the power of life. It was not accidental that Jesus was raised through the Spirit (Rom 1:4; 8:2, 11; cf. 1 Pet 3:18).[138] That means, the resurrection has taken place through the work of the Spirit. He continues:

> Once we understand this intimate connection between the whole range of the phenomena of life and the divine Spirit, we can understand the close kinship between New Testament statements about the Spirit and the proclamation of Jesus' resurrection. This kinship is notably accented in Paul who argues that, since a new life has appeared in Jesus' resurrection, the resurrection event pours forth the divine Spirit. The very

---

135. Pannenberg, *Systematic Theology* vol. 2, 394.
136. For Pannenberg, resurrection of Jesus is not a myth, rather it is a historical reality. See Wolfhart Pannenberg, *The Idea of God and Human Freedom* (Philadelphia: Westminster, 1973), 64ff.
137. Pannenberg, *Theology and the Kingdom of God*, 87.
138. Pannenberg, *Jesus – God and Man*, 171.

proclamation of this event is full of spiritual power, and faith in this proclamation receives the Spirit of life. The life received is the life that has overcome death.[139]

After making a safe ground to argue that the resurrection is the work of the Spirit, Pannenberg looks into the complexity of different statements in the New Testament regarding the resurrection. He asserts that the event of the crucifixion of Jesus does not merely bring the deity of the Father and the Son into question. It refers also to the work of the Spirit, who as the creator of all life raises Jesus from the dead.[140] In a pre-Pauline formula the resurrection is the work of the Spirit (Rom 1:4; 1 Tim 3:16b). This concept stands behind the statements in 1 Cor 15:44ff. concerning the pneumatic reality of the resurrection life.[141] Rom 8:11 also speaks of the work of the Spirit in the resurrection of the dead, although in such a way that it is the Father who will raise us up by the Spirit as he raised up Jesus. Similarly, in Acts 2:24, it is the Father who raised up Jesus, with no mention of the Spirit in this instance. In Luke and Paul there is little reference to the hypostatic distinction of the Spirit from the Father on the one hand or the Son on the other. This is clearly presented in John. For John, the Spirit is another advocate – *Paraclete* – whom the Father will send (Jn 14:16).[142] Thus looking into the complexity of the New Testament understanding about the resurrection of Jesus, Pannenberg asserts that the fathers found here a basis for their statements about the hypostatic distinction of the Spirit and could establish that the Spirit raised up Jesus from the dead. However, this does not rule out the Father's acting by the Spirit as he did in the sending of the Son, i.e., his acting by the mediation of the Spirit or Son.[143] Although Pannenberg insists that the resurrection is the work of the Spirit, he does not rule out the significance of trinitarian involvement in this event. Hence, he argues that, "The resurrection of Jesus may also be seen as an act of the Son of God himself, but again by the power of the Spirit. All

---

139. Pannenberg, *Theology and the Kingdom of God*, 87.
140. Pannenberg, *Systematic Theology* vol. 1, 315; Wolfhart Pannenberg, *Christianity in a Secularized World* (New York: Crossroad, 1989), 50.
141. Pannenberg, *Systematic Theology* vol. 1, 314.
142. Pannenberg, *Systematic Theology* vol. 1, 315.
143. Pannenberg, *Systematic Theology* vol. 1, 315.

three persons of the Trinity are at work in this event. Decisive significance attaches, however, to the work of the Spirit as the creative origin of all life. To that extent we may say that here the Father and the Son are referred to the working of the Spirit."[144]

3.3.5 The Significance of Jesus' Resurrection

Pannenberg does not limit his argument after establishing the role of the Spirit in the resurrection of Jesus Christ, but rather he looks into the universal significance of this event as well.[145] He insists that if Jesus has been raised from the dead, then the end of the world has begun. It means the universal resurrection of the dead and the judgment are imminent. In Pauline language, the resurrection of other humans, especially of believers, will immediately follow that of Jesus. Jesus is the first born among many brethren (Rom 8:29; 1 Cor 15:20).[146] Whoever believes the message of Jesus' resurrection has thereby already received the Spirit who guarantees to the believer the future resurrection from death because he has already raised Jesus (Rom 8:2-11). Thus the Spirit is the pledge of the Christian resurrection hope (2 Cor 1:22), the first fruits of the coming salvation (Rom 8:23).[147] To the nearness of the end which began with Jesus' resurrection belongs, as well, the early Christian conviction that the same Spirit of God by which Jesus has been raised now already dwells in the Christians. In early Christianity the Spirit had eschatological significance. The world designated nothing else than the presence of the resurrection life in the Christians.[148] Moreover, when Paul speaks of "spiritual" life, he has explicit reference to the Spirit. The spiritual life or spiritual body remains in unity with the Spirit and it will never die again. This is not true of the first and

---

144. Pannenberg, *Systematic Theology* vol. 1, 315; this fact emerges more clearly in the Johannine statements about the glorifying of the Son by the Spirit. As the Son glorifies the Father on earth, making manifest his deity (Jn 17:4), so the Spirit will glorify the Son (16:14). The prayer of Jesus to the Father that the Father will glorify him is thus answered by the sending and work of the Spirit. The Spirit manifests Jesus as the Son. It thus completes the revelation of the Father by the Son, since the Father is known only through the Son (14:6). Glorifying the Son, the Spirit also glorifies the Father and their indissoluble fellowship. See Pannenberg, *Systematic Theology* vol. 1, 315.
145. For a detailed discussion on this aspect, see Pannenberg, *Jesus – God and Man*, 66-73.
146. Pannenberg, *Jesus – God and Man*, 172.
147. Pannenberg, *Jesus – God and Man*, 172.
148. Pannenberg, *Jesus – God and Man*, 67.

ordinary life. The first life yearns for eternity, it is true, but it is also doomed to death, because it has separated itself from the origin of all life, from the divine Spirit. And yet eternity is the mystery in all life, present in it for the time it lasts. The present mystery of eternity can only be brought to fulfillment by the eternal Spirit. In this bringing to fulfillment, the Spirit perfects our present existence by giving to it its wholeness and integrity. This same Spirit is indeed present and creative in all life.[149] But it has entered into a lasting unity with the resurrected Lord and therefore, is poured into the hearts of those who have communion with Jesus the Lord by faith.[150]

3.3.5 Spirit Glorifies Jesus in the Believers

We have already noted that the rule of God is actualized in the world through the Son. However, to extend God's rule among the humanity, the Son needs the Spirit who glorifies him (Jn 16:14). The Spirit of truth who proceeds from the Father bears witness to Jesus (15:26).[151] It teaches the disciples all things and reminds them of all that Jesus said (14:26). It leads them into all truth (16:13), namely the truth of God that is manifest in the Son. It thus glorifies the Son in Jesus as the Son has glorified the Father on earth (17:4). When the Johannine Christ prays that the Father will glorify the Son (17:1, 5), he means the glorifying by the Spirit referred to in 16:4 because the Spirit proceeds from the Father (15:26). When it is said that the Spirit will take what is the Son's and proclaim it, the reference is not just to the history and words of Jesus. All creation is to be summoned to glorify the Son, for all that the Father has is his (16:15). Hence, the glorifying of the Son by the Spirit serves the glory of the Father. With the prayer for glorifying by the Father who sends the Spirit, the Johannine Christ acts to complete his own sending – "that the Son may glorify You" (17:1). In short, everything in the conduct of the Son and the work of the Spirit ultimately serves to glorify the Father and enhance the irruption of his kingdom into the world.[152]

---

149. Pannenberg, *Theology and the Kingdom of God*, 87.
150. Pannenberg, *Theology and the Kingdom of God*, 88.
151. Pannenberg, *Systematic Theology* vol. 2, 394.
152. Pannenberg, *Systematic Theology* vol. 2, 395.

There is no doubt that the Spirit glorifies the Son through the Easter event. However, Pannenberg asserts that the Spirit does not merely give the knowledge that Jesus is the Messiah of Israel and the Son of the eternal Father. On the other hand, the knowledge imparted rests on the fact that it creates life.[153] We find this in John 6:63 and Rom 8:2. The life-giving work of the Spirit relates primarily in this context to Jesus himself, for by the Spirit he was raised from the dead (Rom 8:11; cf. 1:4 and 1 Pet 3:18). The same Spirit, then, can guarantee the hope of new life to believers (Rom 8:11). As the creator of new life from the resurrection, the Spirit leads to knowledge of the sonship of Jesus in the light of the confirmation and vindication of his pre-Easter work (1 Tim 3:16). In Johannine terms, we have here the divine glorifying of Jesus in believers.[154] Pannenberg continues that, "The glorifying of Jesus by the Spirit is mediated by the apostolic message, which in virtue of its content goes out in the power of the Spirit (1 Thess 1:5; cf. 1 Pet 1:12), and by which those who believe in it receive the gift of the Spirit (Gal 3:2) that establishes in them hope in death - defeating new life in fellowship with the Crucified, whom God raised again."[155] Hence the Spirit gives believers not merely knowledge of the divine dignity of the Son but also, with this knowledge, the beginning of a new filial life in the Spirit, in a fellowship that has a part in the filial relation of Jesus Christ to the Father.[156] The glorifying of the Father and the Son in believers is the work of the Spirit which aims at the reconciliation of the world with God. It is linked to the overcoming of morality and consummation by participation in the eternal life that by the Spirit unites the Son to the Father and that has already comes as the future of creation in his resurrection from the dead.[157]

3.3.6 Returning of Christ and the Spirit

How does the eschatological work of the Spirit relate to the return of Christ? Referring to Paul and Peter, Pannenberg holds that as we see the glory of God, we are changed into this image from one glory to another

---

153. Pannenberg, *Systematic Theology* vol. 2, 395.
154. Pannenberg, *Systematic Theology* vol. 2, 395.
155. Pannenberg, *Systematic Theology* vol. 2, 395.
156. Pannenberg, *Systematic Theology* vol. 2, 395.
157. Pannenberg, *Systematic Theology* vol. 2, 396.

(2 Cor 3:18). It is the Spirit who does this changing. Hence, the work of the Spirit will be constitutive for the event of the return of Christ as it was also for the resurrection of Jesus and his institution of divine sonship (Rom 1:4). However, there will be a difference that at his coming again Jesus will no longer be a mere object of the Spirit's creative dynamic, since the life of the risen Lord is already wholly permeated by the Spirit and radiates the Spirit.[158] He maintains that, "The exalted Christ is present in the Spirit's work, and conversely the Spirit's work finds fulfillment in the return of Christ for the renewing of his fellowship with believers." [159] Moreover, the renewal and consummation of the world by world-changing judgment, and all under the sign of the divine glory will be manifested as the glory of Jesus Christ (1 Pet 4:13) by completing his reconciling of believers for participation in his life. Thus Jesus will be manifested as the Lord to the glory of Father (Phil 2:11; cf. 1:11). The Father's own glory, his deity, will thus be made manifest by consummating the lordship of Christ that is identical with his own *doxa* (1 Thess 2:12). In this way it will be shown again that all things are gathered together in him, but especially by the glorification of believers. This in turn will bring it about that by the power of the Spirit believers will glorify Jesus Christ and the Father and will themselves be changed from glory to glory by the knowledge of the glory of God in the face of Christ (2 Cor 3:18).[160]

3.4 Holy Spirit and Anthropology

Anthropology is a major theological treatise within Pannenberg's entire theology. While incorporating many aspects in his anthropology, Pannenberg focuses on the significance of the role of the Spirit in humanity as well. Those references would help us to develop a pneumatology of Pannenberg in relation to his anthropology, especially in terms of the working of the Spirit in human beings.[161]

---

158. Wolfhart Pannenberg, *Systematic Theology* vol. 3, trans. Geoffrey W. Bromiley (Grand Rapids: Eerdmans, 1998), 627.
159. Pannenberg, *Systematic Theology* vol. 3, 627.
160. Pannenberg, *Systematic Theology* vol. 3, 627.
161. See F. Leron Shults, *The Postfoundationalist Task of Theology: Wolfhart Pannenberg and the New Theological Rationality* (Grand Rapids: Eerdmans, 1999), 203-235.

3.4.1 Human Beings as Unity of Soul and Body

Following modern thought, Pannenberg maintains that, "Prevailing trends in modern anthropology see the soul and body as constitutive elements of the unity of human life that belong together and cannot be reduced to one another. The soul and consciousness are deeply rooted in our corporality. Conversely, the body is not a corpse. It is an ensouled body in all its expressions in life."[162] However patristic anthropology did not attain fully the biblical idea of psychosomatic unity for it was limited by its model of a linking of two substances.[163] He understands that High Scholasticism's Christian Aristotelianism, as presented through Aquinas, advanced the thesis that the soul is the essential form of the body.[164] On this view, the soul is not just a partial principle but that which makes us human in our bodily reality. Conversely, the body is the concrete form in which our humanity, the soul, finds appropriate expression. However, Pannenberg does not follow Aquinas fully since Aquinas does not explore the biblical reality of the bodily reality in terms of the soul. According to Pannenberg, the second creation story could use "living soul" (*nephesh hayya*) for this reality (Gen 2:7) and the real difference lies in the understanding of the soul, and especially its spiritual or intellectual character. The biblical account certainly relates the soul to Spirit, but in a very different sense.[165] Pannenberg writes:

> In Genesis 2:7 the soul is not merely the vital principle of the body but the ensouled body itself, the living being as a whole. Hence it does not have the autonomy expressed by the Aristotelian-Thomistic concept of substance. The description

---

162. Pannenberg, *Systematic Theology* vol. 2, 182.
163. Pannenberg maintains that wherever the New Testament writers speak independently and in an explicitly theological way, they always conceive of the Spirit as the divine counterpart to the human soul. In keeping with this, the Christian fathers too look upon human beings as not having by nature any share in the divine Spirit, not even in virtue of their being rational creatures. Only rebirth through faith and baptism gives them a participation in the Spirit and therewith the pledge of a new and immortal life that will be revealed in Christians at the resurrection of the dead, as it has already been revealed in Jesus Christ (2 Cor 1:22; Rom 8:23). See Wolfhart Pannenberg, *Anthropology in Theological Perspective*, trans. Mathew J. O'Connell (Philadelphia: Westminster, 1985), 523; see also Wolfhart Pannenberg, *What is Man? Contemporary Anthropology in Theological Perspective*, trans. Duane A. Priebe (Philadelphia: Fortress, 1970), 47ff.
164. Pannenberg, *Systematic Theology* vol. 2, 184.
165. Pannenberg, *Systematic Theology* vol. 2, 185.

> of Adam as *nephesh hayya* represents him as needy and therefore desirous; his life has the form of need and desire. The basic meaning of *nephesh* as throat, gullet, or larynx has in view the dry throat or hungry gullet .... A human being as *nephesh* is a being of desires oriented to things that might meet the desires, and one that is searching for them. Hence an ensouled body does not live of itself but by the Spirit of God who breathes life into it.[166]

Hence for Pannenberg, in the biblical sense "Spirit" does not mean intellect but vital creative force. Its nature is that of the wind. This is the obvious point of Genesis 2:7.[167] God blows into Adam the breath of life and this gives life to what he has formed (Job 33:4). Only the creator's breathing makes him a living being, a living person, a living individual. The wind of the Spirit or the breath of God is something that the creature always needs. It does not control the blowing of this wind.[168] If the wind stops, death follows. If God "should take back his Spirit to himself, and gather himself his breath, all flesh would perish together, and humanity would return to dust" (Job 34:14ff.). This happens when we die. "The dust returns to the earth as it was, and the *Spirit* (*ruah*) returns to God who gave it."[169] Hence the texts quoted show that the breath of life (*nishmat hayyim*) to which Genesis 2:7 refers cannot be separated from the Spirit (*ruah*). These two terms describe the same reality (cf. Gen 6:17). The mortality of human life results from the fact that the Spirit of God is not always at work in it (Gen 6:3). As "flesh" we are perishable like all other living creatures. Conversely,

---

166. Pannenberg, *Systematic Theology* vol. 2, 185.
167. Pannenberg, *Systematic Theology* vol. 2, 185.
168. Pannenberg, *Systematic Theology* vol. 2, 185.
169. Pannenberg, *Systematic Theology* vol. 2, 186; the Spirit was regarded in ancient Israel as first and last the creative Spirit of God (Gen 1:2). When Isaiah contrasts "Spirit" as life-giving power with the transient flesh (Isa 31:3), he is evidently speaking of the divine reality. The Spirit of God gives life to creatures, both plants and animals (Ps 104:30), and their life lasts as long as God permits his Spirit to work in them. Human beings too have life because God breathes his own breath into their nostrils (Gen 2:7). But because of their arrogance he willed that his Spirit should not abide in them forever (Gen 6:3), and therefore their lives, like those of other creatures, last for only a limited period. In death they give "their" Spirit back to God, who gave it to them, while their bodies return to the earth, from which they were taken (Eccl 12:7). See Pannenberg, *Anthropology*, 522.

as long as human life lasts, it is due to the continued activity of the breath of life that comes from the Spirit of God.[170] In short, "The working of the Spirit in living creatures does not mean that he is a constituent part of the creature. Rather, it means that creaturely life has an eccentric character, that it is referred to the divine power of the Spirit that works upon it. Living creatures have the breath of life in them, but it is not at their disposal. God is always the Lord of creaturely life."[171]

3.4.2 Spirit and Reason in Human Beings

Pannenberg argues that Paul did not say that the living soul was breathed into the first Adam by the Spirit of God. On the other hand, Paul's mention is that, the life-giving Spirit (*pneuma zoopoioun*) is not at the creation of the first human, but it is a distinctive feature of the eschatological man. But how is it that the natural human being, who is after the manner of the first Adam, can be or have *pneuma* (1 Cor 2:11) if he was created only as a living soul without the Spirit, and when the Spirit is reserved for the eschatological human?[172] Pannenberg notes that on the basis of Genesis 2:7 Hellenistic Judaism developed the inbreathing of the breath of life into Adam as imparting of the divine Spirit. Typical of this line of interpretation is the linking of the imparting of the Spirit to the knowledge of God.[173] One can find this in the Qumran texts. It understood wisdom as a charisma that the Spirit of God imparts to us.[174] The number of years does not

---

170. Pannenberg, *Systematic Theology* vol. 2, 186.
171. Pannenberg, *Systematic Theology* vol. 2, 186; based on the Old Testament sayings, Pannenberg holds that what is depicted is a special measure of the divine Spirit in some people as a *charisma* conferred upon them, which has some degree of independence vis-à-vis the transcendence of the Spirit of God. This independence is particularly noticeable in the case of what we might call a negative charisma, e.g., the evil *ruah* sent by God to king Saul (1 Sam 16:14; cf. 1 Kgs 22:20ff.; Isa 19:14); in a broader generalization the Spirit that works for a limited time in us might also be called "our" spirit. However, nowhere does the Old Testament make any basic distinction between the divine *ruah* and the independent creaturely *ruah* as an essential constituent of living things. It was Hellenism that first brought into Jewish thinking the idea of the vital process as functions of essential constituents of human beings and their souls. The *pneuma* that works in us could then be regarded either as an essential creaturely element or as an essential divine part of the creaturely soul. See Pannenberg, *Systematic Theology* vol. 2. 186-187.
172. Pannenberg, *Systematic Theology* vol. 2, 187.
173. Pannenberg, *Systematic Theology* vol. 2, 187.
174. In Christian anthropology the statement that "human has spirit" must be understood as meaning that the spirit is something that comes to humans, something not essentially

impart wisdom. Pannenberg notes that, "The Spirit enlightens men, the breath of the Almighty makes them understand (Job 32:8; cf. Deut 34:9). The Wisdom of Solomon even equates wisdom with the Pneuma. Hence humans, having received the breath of life, ought to know God instead of worshiping idols (Wis 15:11). Linking Spirit and wisdom according to a Hellenizing interpretation suggests that reason should be viewed as the divine Pneuma that is breathed into us at creation."[175] The imparting of Genesis 2:7 as an imparting of reason by the Creator was the basis of equating the human spirit and reason, which led Christian theology to see in the spirit-soul a higher part of our human constitution. But this theology rejected the idea that the spirit-soul is divine. Christian Gnosticism might have played an important role in this regard.[176] In short, Pannenberg argues that there is reason in human beings when compared to other creatures of God. Like all other expressions of human life, the work of reason is referred to as the life-giving working of the divine Spirit.[177] However, the life-giving working of the divine Spirit in us is not the same as our reason. Like all other living functions, our reason, too, needs to be actualized by the creator Spirit of God. This fact does not rule out, however, a natural disposition of reason for such actualization nor a leading role for it, as the dominant function of the human soul, in the relation of the whole person to the Spirit.[178]

3.4.3 Imagination and Spirit in Human Beings

While elucidating the significance of reason in human beings, Pannenberg insists the crucial role of the life of imagination, which unites receptivity and freedom. Moreover, in the activity of reason and understanding,

---

their own but to be received and actually received by them. Human beings are body and soul, but they are not spirit in the same way. The Spirit is the source of their life and is at work in them. "But while He is in man, He is not identical with him. For to say that the human beings is such only through the Spirit is the same as to say, "that he is man, and therefore soul of his body, not without God but by God, i.e., by the ever new act of God." See Pannenberg, *Anthropology*, 523.

175. Pannenberg, *Systematic Theology* vol. 2, 188.
176. Pannenberg, *Systematic Theology* vol. 2, 188.
177. Pannenberg, *Systematic Theology* vol. 2, 190; see also Wolfhart Pannenberg, "Spirit and Mind," in *Toward a Theology of Nature: Essays on Science and Faith*, ed. Ted Peters (Kentucky: Westminster, 1993), 148-161.
178. Pannenberg, *Systematic Theology* vol. 2, 190.

imagination helps to elucidate the dependence of reason on the working of the Spirit as the basis of our subjective freedom.[179] In order to make his argument clear, Pannenberg deals with the relation of the Spirit to the general functions of consciousness. He argues that, "The feeling of life as an expression of the presence of the Spirit with that of the indefinite totality of life that precedes and overarches the subject-object distinction underlines, then, the formation of the field of consciousness within which a survey of different contents is possible. In the experience of encounter with others, this world of consciousness is ascribed to one's own ego and is thus relativized as the world of this ego as distinct from others."[180] He continues that, "The presence of the infinite ground of being, the Spirit, which declares itself in the feeling for life, transcends, however, the difference of subjects; nor is this true only of one's own I, since awareness of this I is itself a product of the differentiating of the unity of the feeling for life in the process of experience."[181] For Pannenberg, this "I" is not just the physical individuality of the speaker; rather, "if we are to view the living body as ensouled inasmuch as it is living, then the term 'soul' must cover more than the inner world of the consciousness."[182] It must include the unconscious, which is related to one's own corporeality and its history. It is possible here to relate the idea of the soul that is oriented to experience of an inner world of consciousness with the concept of the soul as the vital principle of the body.[183]

Taking cue from the above argument, Pannenberg argues that, "Since the exact determining of what is distinct itself depends on an awareness of the unity, the perceptions of the imagination must relate both to the different members in their particularity and to the unity that binds them together for all their distinctiveness."[184] Grasping the unity in distinction is a function of the ability to keep one's distance in an awareness of otherness.

---

179. Pannenberg, *Systematic Theology* vol. 2, 192; see Pannenberg, *What is Man?*, 23ff; see also Anita Marie Hyslop, *The Theology of Image and Imagination in the Theology of Wolfhart Pannenberg* (Michigan: University Microfilms International, 1977).
180. Pannenberg, *Systematic Theology* vol. 2, 193.
181. Pannenberg, *Systematic Theology* vol. 2, 193-194.
182. Pannenberg, *Systematic Theology* vol. 2, 194.
183. Pannenberg, *Systematic Theology* vol. 2, 194
184. Pannenberg, *Systematic Theology* vol. 2, 195.

The unity of what is distinct is thus a different thing from the consciousness. Moreover, we can distinguish the infinite from the finite only on the condition that it is not just something other than the finite, in which case it would itself be finite, but that also comprehends everything finite. This thought of the infinite one gives expression to that which is always present to the consciousness as the indefinite infinite. It thus forms the mental space in which there can be distance from the other and definition of its otherness and relationship, of the space that is opened thereby for the consciousness.[185] Pannenberg argues that the multiplicity of the world and the living reality of the individual in distinction therefrom are opened up to the consciousness by the infinity of the feeling for life that underlines the difference of subject and object in the consciousness and thus transcends them in every situation in life. In this respect we should perhaps redefine the relation between spirit and consciousness if the feeling for life expresses the living presence of the creator Spirit in living creatures. Not the I but the divine Spirit is the ultimate basis for the interrelatedness of that which is distinct in the consciousness. It is also the basis for the interrelatedness of the I and the things of the world, especially similar living creatures.[186]

Thus for Pannenberg, in grasping the finite there is always a nonthematic sense of the infinite as that which is other than the finite. We are aware of the infinite in the religious awareness of a divine power at work in every finite phenomenon.[187] Here Pannenberg finds the working of the Spirit in human beings. In spite of the perversion due to sin, human beings are related to the self-distinction of the Son from the Father. In turn, Pannenberg writes:

> As the Son, in his self-distinction from the Father, is united with him by the Spirit in the unity of the divine life, and as, in his creative activity, he unites what is distinct by the power of the Spirit, so the differentiating activity of human reason needs the Spirit who enables it, by mediating the imagination, to name each thing in its particularity, and in all the distinction

---

185. Pannenberg, *Systematic Theology* vol. 2, 195.
186. Pannenberg, *Systematic Theology* vol. 2, 196.
187. Pannenberg, *Systematic Theology* vol. 2, 196.

to be aware of the unity that holds together what is different. In the process human reason is not of itself filled with the Spirit. In its creatureliness it needs, like every other vital function, to be quickened by the living power of the Spirit if it is to be active, and it also needs the inspiration that lifts it above its own finitude and that in all its limitation makes it aware of the presence of truth and totality in the individual.[188]

The biblical view of the Spirit of God as the creative principle of everything living insofar as it has soul and has life in itself may also be explained in terms of the varied nature of the consciousness and the activity of reason. The "ecstasy" of consciousness – that it "stands outside" – means enhanced and more inward life and therefore more intense participation in the Spirit, the creative origin of all life.[189] It expands the soul by experience of the world, which the Spirit creatively permeates, and especially by the experience of human fellowship in face of the infinite ground of the world.[190]

3.4.4 *Spirit and Personality of Human Beings*

For Pannenberg, personality is to be understood as a special instance of the working of the Spirit, a special instance of the anticipatory presence of the final truth of things.[191] He maintains that personality has to do with the manifestation of the truth and totality of individual life in the moment of its existence. The personality is grounded in the destiny that transcends our empirical reality. It is primarily experienced in the other, the Thou, as the secret of an inwardness that goes beyond all that we perceive outwardly of the other, so that this other meets us as a being that is active not merely of itself but in terms of a ground of existence that we cannot finally see externally.[192] Pannenberg notes:

> We all are persons in our psychosomatic totality as this finds manifestation at each moment of our existence. Totality and personhood are linked, for as we understand it today, "person"

---

188. Pannenberg, *Systematic Theology* vol. 2, 197.
189. Pannenberg, *Systematic Theology* vol. 2, 197.
190. Pannenberg, *Systematic Theology* vol. 2, 198.
191. Pannenberg, *Anthropology*, 528.
192. Pannenberg, *Systematic Theology* vol. 2, 198.

means not an exchangeable role but the human self. Selfhood, however, means identity in all individual life. This is true even over a stretch of time, hence selfhood never achieves definitive manifestation in life. It does not yet appear who we truly are, but now we exist as persons. This is possible only in anticipation of the truth of existence, which is mediated to us now through the Spirit by means of our feeling for life.[193]

According to Pannenberg, true personal identity of a person emerges only through a series of ecstatic events of spiritual experience, integrating all the different aspects of an individual life.[194] But even in this case a provisional form of spiritual unity is often mistaken as definite, or the true meaning of a situation is missed. Moreover, faith and hope are fixed on narrow and shaky objectives. All these ambiguities of self-identity in self-transcendence can be traced back to the fact that in the present form of human life there is no pre-established harmony between the Spirit and the personal self. Hence, the personal self separates itself from the Spirit and consequently, human beings have to transcend themselves in order to find themselves. The separation between the empirical self and the Spirit again and again separates human beings from the future of life and exposes their personal life to death.[195] On this ground, Pannenberg argues that, "While the Spirit is working in all life as the vitalizing principle, the lure to self-transcendence and as the inspirative power of ecstasy – the Christian community lives on the basis of the message of a new life, which is no longer separated from the spiritual origin of all life."[196] Thus when human beings receive faith, love, and hope, it elevates them beyond themselves and liberates them from narrow-mindedness. Thus for Pannenberg, the formation of a sound personality is the work of the Holy Spirit.[197]

---

193. Pannenberg, *Systematic Theology* vol. 2, 200.
194. Pannenberg, "The Working of the Spirit," 22.
195. Pannenberg, "The Working of the Spirit," 23.
196. Pannenberg, "The Working of the Spirit," 23.
197. Pannenberg, "The Working of the Spirit," 23-24.

3.4.5 Spirit and the Human Community

For Pannenberg, insofar as the soul is the life of its body it is an effect of the life-giving Spirit. The divine creative Spirit causes human beings to have life within them, and to that extent the Spirit is internally present to them, although it does not on that account become a "part" of them.[198] Conversely, the movement of life or the "soul" that is in every living things consists in a movement beyond the limited corporal life of the individual into the environment in which that life is lived. In this process the life of the soul is characterized by "neediness."[199] Moreover, in this neediness, and not simply in the satisfaction of need, the life-giving action of the Spirit manifests itself, since the living being is thereby enabled to act on its own and seek its food and other satisfactions from its environment or, as the case may be, "from God" (Ps 104:21).[200] Pannenberg argues that all life in this sense is ecstatic and to that extent spiritual. But the ecstatic character found in all life reaches a new level of intensity, a new high point, in human beings. To the extent that human beings exist exocentrically in a presence to what is other than themselves, precisely as other, and experience themselves from that vantage point, the life-giving power of the Spirit, which raises them above their own finitude, manifests itself in an intensified form. This specific kind of action by the Spirit finds expression especially in human consciousness, which is tied in with the behavioral structure. For by reason of their consciousness human beings exist outside themselves to a greater degree than do other living things. Human consciousness is therefore in an especially close relation to the action of the Spirit only because, and to the extent that, human beings realize their exocentric mode of being primarily in their conscious life.[201] However Pannenberg makes a distinction between the lifeless things and the living things. He insists that while lifeless things are grounded only in themselves and in a truth that transcends what is now manifested in them, living beings related actively to their perdurance, identity, and truth, which transcend what is manifested in them. To that extent, the Spirit is more intensely present in the ecstatic movement of

---

198. Pannenberg, *Anthropology*, 523.
199. Pannenberg, *Anthropology*, 524.
200. Pannenberg, *Anthropology*, 524.
201. Pannenberg, *Anthropology*, 524.

love and is, in addition, present in a special way in human consciousness as the medium of the presence of the person's own identity, as distinct from, though united with, the truth of things. Thus, in the medium of the human soul and in the place that is the ensouled body, the presence of the Spirit constitutes the identity of the person as a presence of the self in the instant of the ego.[202]

Thus when dealing with the personhood of human beings, Pannenberg focuses on one particular element in the authentic operation of the Spirit, which is the formation of a community. This can be seen in the fact that the ecstatic movement of life reaches beyond the particular being. The movement is accompanied by a tendency to share in that to which it is directed. This ecstatic movement of life in union with others is always concerned at the same time with the unity of that life itself, and this not only in the sense of preserving the unity of the particular life and its peaceful relations with its environment but also in the sense of preserving the species.[203] It is therefore part of the nature and operation of the Spirit to bring about a community that will transcend and overcome the isolation of individuals. In short, certain imperfection of the spirit manifests itself in every formation of a community. People are correct therefore when they talk of the Spirit of a family of a school or a team, but also of the Spirit of a period, an age, or a culture. In each case this "Spirit" is an always unique manifestation of the Spirit of God that is at work in all living things but that can also, as in human individuals, be cut off from its relation to God and become demonic. In fact it is especially easy for the Spirit – wherever a corporate spirit or the spirit of the age – that prevails in social life to take on demonic traits so that human beings become blind to the demands of reason and deaf to the voice of love.[204] Despite this danger of demonic perversion, harmony, and community remain marks of the true Spirit. At the same time, however, the harmony and the community must be concrete forms of that comprehensive unity and community which are consonant with faith

---

202. Pannenberg, *Anthropology*, 528.
203. Pannenberg, *Anthropology*, 529.
204. Pannenberg, *Anthropology*, 530.

in the one God and which for their criterion the universality of reason and the limitlessness of love.[205]

3.4.6 *The Spirit as Immanent in Human Beings*

One of the significant arguments of Pannenberg in his anthropology is that the Spirit is transcendent and immanent in human beings. The reason Pannenberg argues that the Spirit is immanent is due to the fact that only the Spirit grants personal identity and fulfillment to human life.[206] When we speak of the spirit of a person or an action or an institution, we point to the principle vitalizing them and they are regarded as a whole in itself. On the other hand, this unity in Spirit is immanent in a person or a social group only insofar as they transcend themselves. Hence, to speak of the Spirit of a person or a group or an action is to characterize them by an ecstatic unity that integrates the life of the individual or the group. Here Pannenberg finds the way to contrast Spirit with mood. For Pannenberg, a mood is never ecstatic.[207] When a person is in a certain mood, this certainly characterizes the person in his/her totality. That means, the mood refers to "the frame of mind" of a person. However, although the mood belongs to the given situation of a person, it has no liberating power as Spirit, which also concerns the totality of a person, but in relation to his self-transcendent activity. There is, however, a point of contact between mood and Spirit.[208] In a cheerful mood, a person is in a disposition for being grasped by the action of the Spirit. On the other hand, in a depressed mood a person cannot make contact with the Spirit.[209]

3.4.7 *The Spirit as Transcendent in Human Beings*

After the discussion that the Spirit is immanent in the human beings, Pannenberg focuses on the transcendence of the Spirit. He argues that, "The

---

205. Pannenberg, *Anthropology*, 530.
206. Pannenberg, "The Working of the Spirit," 20.
207. Pannenberg, "The Working of the Spirit," 20.
208. Pannenberg, "The Working of the Spirit," 20.
209. Pannenberg, "The Working of the Spirit," 21; Pannenberg argues on the other hand that when one speaks of a person as being in bad spirits, it means that the human participation in spirit is dominated by non-spiritual factors, but in such a way that an analogy develops to genuine spiritual ecstasy, except in the liberating effect of the latter. Such is the phenomenon referred to as obsession. See Pannenberg, "The Working of the Spirit," 21.

element of transcendence in spirit suggests that after all it might be neither necessary nor wise to admit a fundamental distinction between a human spirit and a divine Spirit."[210] The ecstatic, self-transcendent character of all spiritual experience brings sufficiently to bear the transcendence of God over against all created beings. The Spirit never belongs in a strict sense to the creature in its immanent nature, but the creature participates in the divine Spirit by transcending itself, by being elevated beyond itself in the ecstatic experience that illustrates the working of the Spirit.[211] Hence, for Pannenberg, "The spirit is not the mind, but the human mind comes to life only when he is touched by the spirit. And the same seems to be true of all living beings."[212] In short, Pannenberg argues that the idea of immanence and transcendence allows doing justice to the transcendence of God and at the same time explains its immanence in its creation. However, Pannenberg is not happy in making a distinction between the human spirit and divine Spirit due to the fact that theology would lose the chance to describe the immanence and transcendence of God in creation.[213]

3.5 The Holy Spirit and Redemption

In fact, Pannenberg deals with the doctrine of soteriology along with the doctrine of anthropology and Christology. Since we have already looked into Pannenberg's anthropology and Christology, this section focuses only on the doctrine of soteriology and the role of the Spirit. When endeavoring to understand the doctrine of redemption, at the very outset, one needs to be clear about the understanding of sin according to Pannenberg, which

---

210. Pannenberg, "The Working of the Spirit," 21.
211. Pannenberg, "The Working of the Spirit," 21.
212. Pannenberg, "The Working of the Spirit," 21.
213. Pannenberg, "The Working of the Spirit," 21; Pannenberg notes that the main reason to adopt the distinction between human spirit and divine Spirit was to secure the divine transcendence. But this argument can arise only when the ecstatic character of human spiritual experience is mistaken for something that belongs to the natural equipment of human beings. Human experience, even in its ecstatic self-transcendence, does not perceive the divine Spirit, but only participates in some way on his action. Therefore, the action of the Spirit can be received in perverted ways, the most extreme of which is known as possession or obsession. Without the working of the divine Spirit, the self-transcendent activity of life and this life itself must pale, but the "breath" of the spirit does not necessarily exclude the ambiguities of life precisely in the process of its self-transcendence. See Pannenberg, "The Working of the Spirit," 22.

he discusses clearly.[214] One can define the concept of sin according to Pannenberg simply as the alienation of the humanity from the Logos.[215] In other words, the relation of the created destiny of humanity to the incarnation of the Logos in Jesus is not a direct disposition and actualization because the way from disposition to actualization is broken by sin. Hence, Pannenberg insists that since the Logos is the epitome of the world's order and our relation to God, it is only through Jesus that humanity can get back to God.[216] In order to make this possible and to be received by God, they must be born anew by the Spirit of God. Moreover, Pannenberg asserts that dark forces have been at work in life and therefore by means of anxiety and desire there is death and resurrection. We cannot achieve liberation from these sinister forces merely by breaking the fetters that oppressors put on us from outside because that might bring only temporary alleviation. On the other hand, we achieve liberation from sin and death only where the image of the Son takes shape in human life through the operation of the Spirit of God.[217] This understanding of Pannenberg helps us to look into the redemptive work of Jesus Christ and the role of the Spirit in this activity. In this study, two understandings of Jesus are important as follows.

3.5.1 Jesus as the New Human Being

The first thing that Pannenberg deals with when he approaches the doctrine of redemption is that Jesus is the new human being in contrast to the old one. He notes that John perceived Jesus as the incarnate Logos, but on the other hand, Paul saw him as the eschatological figure, who has appeared in Jesus Christ. Pannenberg maintains that, "If the God of redemption who is revealed in Jesus Christ is the same as the Creator of the world and the human race, then we must view his saving work as an expression of his faithfulness to his creative work. In that case the sending of the new eschatological man must be seen in relation to the creation of Adam at the

---

214. See for a detailed discussion, Pannenberg, *Systematic Theology* vol. 2. 231ff.
215. Pannenberg, *Systematic Theology* vol. 2. 295; following Augustine, Pannenberg also notes that sin is turning away from God and unbelief is the root of sin. See Pannenberg, *Anthropology*, 93.
216. Pannenberg, *Systematic Theology* vol. 2, 295.
217. Pannenberg, *Systematic Theology* vol. 2, 275.

first. In harmony with this is the idea of a salvation history that aims at human fulfillment in Jesus Christ ..."[218]

3.5.2 Jesus as the Author of a New Humanity

The second thing that is significant according to Pannenberg is that Paul's view of Jesus Christ as the new eschatological or last Adam has a social reference oriented to the human community. It tells that "we" all shall "bear" the image of the new and heavenly humanity (1 Cor 15:49). As the last Adam, Jesus Christ is thus the original bearer of a new humanity that is made anew in his image by participation in his obedience, death, and resurrection.[219] The important thing in this argument is that Pannenberg notes along with the early Christology that Jesus was sinless. Although Jesus was tempted as all human beings, he was without sin.[220] Moreover, after Easter the overcoming of death by the new life of resurrection became the essence of the future of salvation, because participation in the divine lordship was the message of Jesus. Materially there is no difference here because the new life by resurrection from the dead is life in fellowship with God by the Spirit.[221] In particular, the character of the eschatological future is the same in both definitions of salvation, which is a future reality and also it is already present in the case of believers. This eschatological reference characterizes the New Testament term for salvation and underlies the other soteriological concepts of the New Testament, e.g., what Paul says about justification, redemption, reconciliation, and liberation by Christ, in which believers now share.[222]

3.5.3 The Suffering of Jesus Christ

The above understanding that Jesus is the new human being and the author of a new humanity leads Pannenberg to establish the significance of the suffering and death of Jesus Christ for the salvation of humanity. Pannenberg notes that although Jesus appeared as the incarnation of God in order to convert the covenant people to God, he and his message met with rejection

---

218. Pannenberg, *Systematic Theology* vol. 2, 297.
219. Pannenberg, *Systematic Theology* vol. 2, 304.
220. Pannenberg, *Systematic Theology* vol. 2, 306.
221. Pannenberg, *Systematic Theology* vol. 2, 398.
222. Pannenberg, *Systematic Theology* vol. 2, 399.

from his own people. However, interestingly enough for Pannenberg, it was not Jesus but his mission that was rejected by his people.[223] That is the reason why Jesus went to the cross and suffered and became the savior of the nations. Only as the crucified and risen Lord can Jesus become the new and eschatologically definitive figure. Pannenberg writes, "Precisely by the event of the passion he became a figure that transcends the national and religious differences between Jews and non-Jews (Eph 2:14). Because of his rejection by his own people, salvation has come to the Gentiles (Rom 11:11)."[224] Pannenberg notes that by depicting Jesus as the new eschatological Adam, and therefore as the definitive form of a new humanity, Paul has given expression to the universal significance of the person and history of Jesus in the light of the Easter event – a significance that reaches far beyond the people of Israel. He writes, "As the Messiah who does not exercise dominion through political power but through his vicarious suffering for human sins, Jesus not only changed the Jewish hope in the consciousness of his disciples but also opened it up with a view to the reconciliation of the Gentile world with Israel and its God."[225]

3.5.4 Reconciliation as the Work of Son and Spirit

Although Pannenberg attempts to expose that reconciliation as a trinitarian act, he believes that reconciliation is the work of the Son and the Spirit without excluding the Father. Pannenberg writes that, "To be sure, 2 Corinthians 5:18 causes us in the first instance to think specifically of an action of the Father in the death of Christ. But it may quickly be seen that the Son and Spirit also participated."[226] As Jesus is united to the Father as

---

223. Pannenberg, *Systematic Theology* vol. 2, 311.
224. Pannenberg, *Systematic Theology* vol. 2, 312; Pannenberg notes that Jesus experienced the death of sinners on the cross. As the Son he suffered dereliction much more profoundly than anyone else. Yet in the light of the Easter event the judgment of God in the crucifixion of Jesus proved to be a sign of the judgment of God on the world that rejected the Father himself in the Son. At the same time, this judgment in the cross of the Son became for the world its access to salvation. See Pannenberg, *Systematic Theology* vol. 2, 392.
225. Pannenberg, *Systematic Theology* vol. 2, 315.
226. Pannenberg, *Systematic Theology* vol. 2, 437; God as creator does not will the death of sinners (Ezek 18:23). He wills the existence and life of his creatures. In this sense his deity is tied to the sending of the Son, who with the Spirit is already present to all creatures from creation, but who himself also took the creaturely form in order that by his message the future of God might be present to the world, to its salvation and not its judgment. In

the Son precisely in his self-distinction from him, he vicariously reconciles in his own person the independence of humans and all creatures to God. According to Pannenberg, we cannot identify the salvation of the world as an aim that Jesus set himself in the historical humanity of his work, rather we must describe the atoning function of his death with a view to the world's salvation as the object and goal of the Son of God, who was at work in the history of Jesus. These kinds of statements have a prophetic structure as well. The relevance for all humanity that they ascribe to the special person and history of Jesus anticipates the outcome of human history. In other words, the truth of the content of such statements depends on the work of the Spirit, who will glorify Jesus in human hearts as the Son of God.[227] The Christological statements themselves arose in this way as an expression of the initial work of the Spirit in the believing community of primitive Christianity. This is true already in the titles such as "Messiah," "Kyrios," or "Son of God." Each of these titles relates to the specific figure of Jesus to all humanity, and above all to its future. Each is implicitly soteriological.[228] Moreover, according to Pannenberg, if the human and historical level of the history of Jesus is transparent to the presence of the incarnate Son of God concealed in it, as became clear in the light of the exaltation of the crucified, then the messianic dignity of Jesus in virtue of his kingly office is present in hidden form in his earthly appearance.[229] Hence, the execution of Jesus also must be seen as an act of the self-offering by the incarnate Son of God who is at work in this history. This is the content of the activity of the exalted Lord who rules the world by the word of the

---

this way, the Son glorifies the Father in the world and completes the work of creation. See Pannenberg, *Systematic Theology* vol. 2, 392.

227. Pannenberg, *Systematic Theology* vol. 2, 442.

228. Pannenberg, *Systematic Theology* vol. 2, 443; Pannenberg argues that the activity of the exalted Christ as Priest, King, and Prophet could not, of course, be seen as coincident with the content of the earthly history of Jesus as it is presented in the witness of the Spirit. It was simply described from the standpoint of a phase of Christ's mediatorial office that objectively follows his earthly history. Hence the older Protestant doctrine did not think the mutual relation between the work of the ascended Christ and the Spirit. We see here the one-sidedly Christological objectivism of the older doctrine of Christ's office as reconciler, which prevented it from doing justice to the interrelation of three different levels of meaning in the statements of primitive Christianity regarding Christ's saving work. See Pannenberg, *Systematic Theology* vol. 2, 448.

229. Pannenberg, *Systematic Theology* vol. 2, 448.

gospel and the power of the Spirit. Thus he creates faith in the gospel and assembles the believers, preparing the way for the kingdom of the Father in the world, as he had already in his earthly work made the coming rule of God present to believers.[230]

3.5.5 The Completion of Reconciliation in the Spirit

We have already noted that reconciliation is the joint work of the Son and the Spirit and not excluding the Father. But how can human beings share in the reconciliation that was achieved in exemplary fashion by the incarnation and death of Jesus Christ? Pannenberg asserts that they can do so only as they are taken up into fellowship with the Father of the Son who became human in Jesus Christ. This taking up is not merely in the sense of something that happens to them from outside but as a liberation to their own identity through the Spirit. That means, through the Spirit reconciliation of the humanity with God is not coming to them solely from outside rather they are entering into it.[231] Pannenberg writes that, "As the one self-offering of the Son for the reconciliation of the world and his being offered up by the Father are one and the same event and form a single process, so we are to see the work of the exalted Christ and that of the Spirit in us as different aspects of one and the same divine action for the reconciliation of the world."[232] On this ground, according to Pannenberg, there are some important aspects to be noted here in relation to the working of the Spirit in the human beings.

3.5.5.1 The Spirit Lifts Human Beings above Their Finitude

The first thing that the Spirit does with the reconciliation of human beings is that it lifts them above their finitude so that in faith they can share in

---

230. Pannenberg, *Systematic Theology* vol. 2, 448.
231. Pannenberg, *Systematic Theology* vol. 2, 450.
232. Pannenberg, *Systematic Theology* vol. 2, 450; we see this in Paul and in John's gospel. The work of the Spirit and the exalted Kyrios are to a large extent parallel; in fact they seem to be interchangeable in content. Paul could thus summon us to walk in the Spirit or put on Christ, and materially these two things are one and the same. The dwelling of the Spirit in believers (Rom 8:9) is having the Spirit of Christ, and directly afterward we read of Christ in us (v. 10). Paul thus sees his whole proclamation as a work of the Spirit, which is tantamount to saying that Christ himself is speaking through the apostles (2 Cor 5:20; cf. 2:17 and 12:19; 13:3). Pannenberg, *Systematic Theology* vol. 2, 451f.

Jesus Christ and his death as he is outside of them. As they are in Christ, believers are "ecstatic," i.e., outside themselves (Rom 6:6, 11). Thus Christ is also in them (8:10).[233] Pannenberg holds that, "There is nothing unnatural about this 'ecstasy,' because our spiritual life may well be inherently 'ecstatic' and may thus actualize in a special way the distinctiveness of living things."[234] Human consciousness in its ability to be itself among others has a thoroughly "ecstatic" structure, and precisely in this way it is given life by the Spirit.[235] Moreover, in "ecstatic" being with Christ, believers are not in bondage to another, because Jesus as the Son of the Father is fully God and human who gives himself up for others. Pannenberg writes:

> As believers are with Jesus through the Spirit, they participate in the filial relation of Jesus to the Father, in his acceptance of the world in virtue of the goodness of God as creator, in his love for the world. Those who believe in Jesus are thus not estranged from themselves, for with Jesus they are with God, who is the origin of the finite existence of all creatures and their specific destiny. For this reason being outside the self through the Spirit and in faith in Jesus Christ means liberation, not merely in the sense of elevation above our own finitude, but also in the sense of attaining afresh by this elevation to our own existence as the creator has affirmed it and reconciled it to himself. It means liberation from the bondage of the world, sin, and the devil for a life in the world in the power of the Spirit.[236]

---

233. Pannenberg, *Systematic Theology* vol. 2, 451.
234. Pannenberg, *Systematic Theology* vol. 2, 451.
235. Pannenberg argues that as self-consciousness, it knows its own being among others, and by nature it is thus itself when among others, for being with others determines its nature. Not all being outside the self, of course, enables us in a higher sense to come to ourselves by lifting us above our particularity. In this way we may also be estranged from ourselves in phenomena of bondage and addiction that lead structurally to the basic form of concupiscence. At the same time self-forgetfulness may be also be the supreme form of self-fulfillment when those that forget themselves are wholly dedicated to that which is their destiny as human beings as persons. This is how it is with faith in Jesus Christ. See Pannenberg, *Systematic Theology* vol. 2, 452.
236. Pannenberg, *Systematic Theology* vol. 2, 452.

3.5.5.2 The Spirit Allows Self-distinction from Jesus

The second aspect is that although believers are "ecstatically" lifted above themselves by the Spirit in order to be in Christ through faith, it does not mean that through mystical union, they merge into Christ or through him into Christ and form God and they are no longer aware of their own distinction from Christ and God. Instead, believers know very well that their own existence is different from Jesus Christ in whom they believe, even though they are united to him by faith.[237] He writes that, "An irrevocable part of their union with Christ in faith is awareness of the difference between their own existence and him their head, just as believers who in Christ share in the filial relation of Jesus to the Father differentiate themselves therein from the Father as Jesus did."[238] This self-distinction from God is the condition of the fellowship of Jesus himself with the Father and the basis of his own divine sonship. Here lies the difference between Jesus and the first Adam, who wanted to be as God and who thus lost both the God who is infinitely above all creatures and also his own creaturely life. Believers share in the filial relation of Jesus to the Father and therefore in his self-distinction from this Father, which found definitive actualization in the incarnation of the Son.[239]

The other important part of the sharing in the sonship of Jesus is the realization of believers that they differ from Jesus not only as he is another human but also as the one who alone in person is the Son of the Father. Precisely in the awareness of this distinction, and through acceptance of their own creatureliness, believers in Christ share in his sonship in relation to the Father. In other words, participation in the filial relation of Jesus to the Father frees believers for immediacy in relation to God as their Father. This immediacy to God is to be lived out in the particularity of their own life-fulfillment.[240] By the Spirit, believers are capable of this self-distinction from Jesus because the Spirit differentiates itself from the Son by not openly glorifying himself but glorifying Jesus as the Son of the Father and the Father in the Son. The Spirit, who is God, brings with it fellowship with

---

237. Pannenberg, *Systematic Theology* vol. 2, 452.
238. Pannenberg, *Systematic Theology* vol. 2, 452-453.
239. Pannenberg, *Systematic Theology* vol. 2, 453.
240. Pannenberg, *Systematic Theology* vol. 2, 453.

God, but only as it distinguishes itself from the Father and the Son, and with himself all those whose hearts it fills and lifts up to God. Even the "ecstatic" working of the Spirit does not mean that self-distinction from God is no longer a condition of fellowship with him. It makes it possible for humanity to rejoice in this distinction through peace with God.[241]

Moreover, although Jesus himself was filled with the Spirit of God, it was only after he left the disciples that they received the Spirit as an abiding gift. His absence put them in a position in which they could independently recognize the glory of Jesus in his humility and lowliness and thus be reconciled to God in their own lives by accepting his life as paradigmatic for them. Hence the Johannine Christ could say that it was good for them that he should leave them (Jn 16:7), for they could attain the independence of their own relation to the Father by perceiving the glory of the Son in his death and passion. The pain of finitude could then no longer separate them from God, who let his own Son die on the cross to make expiation for the sin of the world and also acknowledging his Son in death. Thus the Spirit completes the reconciliation of humanity with God by enabling them through faith in Jesus Christ to accept their own finite existence before God.[242]

3.5.5.3 Human Beings Are Given New Life by the Spirit

The final significant thing that the Spirit does in the reconciliation of human beings is that they are given new life. Traditionally, this understanding was associated with the future consummation of salvation. However Pannenberg argues along with the life and message of Jesus that the future salvation is mediated in the present by Jesus.[243] That means, the primary reference now is not to the deliverance of believers at the coming judgment

---

241. Pannenberg, *Systematic Theology* vol. 2, 453; the distinction and self-distinction of the Spirit from the Son are first clearly presented in John's gospel, though Christ and the Spirit are not absolutely identical in Paul. In John, Jesus announces the coming of the Spirit as the *parakletos* (14:26). It will come only when Jesus has parted from his own (7:39; 16:4). Whereas Jesus was with them only for a short time and will come again only at the consummation (13:33; 16:14; 17:24), the Spirit will stay with them always (14:16). The main point of distinction is that the Spirit will show the disciples the true significance of Jesus (14:26; 16:13) by reminding them of what he said (14:26) and glorifying him (16:14). See Pannenberg, *Systematic Theology* vol. 2, 453-454.
242. Pannenberg, *Systematic Theology* vol. 2, 454.
243. Pannenberg, *Systematic Theology* vol. 2, 402.

but on the historical event of resurrection from the life of sin for a new life by the Spirit (Titus 3:4ff.).[244] Paul had associated with deliverance at the coming judgment a definition of *soteria* in terms of participation in the glory of the new life manifested already in Christ (Phil 3:20; cf. Rom 5:10; 8:30). However, sharing of the new life in Christ is no longer determined primarily by deliverance at the last judgment. Hence, present salvation is now the initial reality of the new life itself which had come into this world through Jesus Christ.[245] Thus believers are freed from the tyranny of sin and death and enjoy freedom. At the same time, it has a future aspect as well. That means believers are free from sin and death in hope of the new life from God that was manifested in the resurrection of Jesus.

In short, fellowship with God and his eternal life gives individuals independence of the world and its powers in all the relation of dependence in which they live their finite lives.[246] It also sets them at a distance from themselves, which enables them to fulfill their individual callings in service to God and to the world, to which his love is addressed. This is the freedom of a new immediacy to God that believers have as his children (Gal 4:4-6). It is mediated by the sending of the Son and his vicarious death. However, it is actualized by the Spirit of sonship in believers themselves.[247] The Spirit thus brings the mission of the Son to completion. John writes that there is true freedom only through the Son (8:36) but that it is good for Christ's own that he should go away and that the Spirit should come (16:7ff.). For the Spirit will lead them into the truth (16:13), which makes them free (8:32). In this regard John agrees with Paul when the latter says that "where the Spirit of the Lord is, there is freedom" (2 Cor 3:17). Where there is this freedom of the Spirit, the reconciliation of humanity to God has reached its goal.[248]

---

244. Pannenberg, *Systematic Theology* vol. 2, 402.
245. Pannenberg, *Systematic Theology* vol. 2, 402; two things are important for Pannenberg namely, salvation is linked to the future of God, which is already present in this world in Jesus Christ, though its consummation is still ahead. Secondly, participation in salvation is mediated through the history of Jesus and especially his crucifixion. See Pannenberg, *Systematic Theology* vol. 2, 402-403.
246. Pannenberg, *Systematic Theology* vol. 2, 436.
247. Pannenberg, *Systematic Theology* vol. 2, 436.
248. Pannenberg, *Systematic Theology* vol. 2, 437.

3.5.6 The Sotereological Work of the Spirit in Creation

For Pannenberg, in all its forms the activity of the trinitarian God in creation is an activity of the Father by the Son and Spirit, an activity of the Son in obedience to the Father, and the glorifying of both in the consummation of their work by the Spirit. God's Spirit is not only active in human redemption rather the Spirit is at work already in creation as God's mighty breath. Only against this background of the activity of the Spirit as the creator of all life can we rightly understand on the one hand its work in the ecstatics of human conscious life, and on the other hand its role in the bringing forth of the new life of resurrection of the dead.[249] Conversely, the same Spirit of God who is given to believers in a wholly specific way, namely, so as to dwell in them (Rom 5:9; 1 Cor 3:16), is none other than the creator of all life in the whole range of natural occurrence and also in the new creation of the resurrection of the dead. Only when we see its imparting to believers in this comprehensive context can we judge what the event of the outpouring of the Spirit means in truth.[250] The work of the Spirit in the church and believers serves the consummating of its work in the world of creation. Pannenberg writes:

> For the special mode of the presence of the divine Spirit in the gospel and by its proclamation, which shines out from the liturgical life of the church and fills believers, so that Paul can say of them that the Spirit "dwells" in them, is a pledge of the promise that the life which everywhere from the creative work of the Spirit will finally triumph over death, which is the price paid for the autonomy of creatures in their exorbitant clinging to their existence, in spite of its finitude, and over against its divine origin.[251]

---

249. Pannenberg, *Systematic Theology* vol. 3, 1.
250. Pannenberg, *Systematic Theology* vol. 3, 2.
251. Pannenberg, *Systematic Theology* vol. 3, 2; Pannenberg notes that theology has often neglected the relation between the soteriological operations of the Spirit in believers and its activity both as creator of all life and also in its eschatological new creation and consummation. This is particularly true of the theology of the Christian West whose views of the work of the Spirit have concentrated mainly on its function as the source of grace or faith. See Pannenberg, *Systematic Theology* vol. 3, 2.

In short, by the Spirit creatures will be made capable of independence in their relation to God and at the same time integrated into the unity of God's kingdom. The imparting of the Spirit as gift thus characterizes the distinctiveness of the soteriological phase of its work in the event of reconciliation. The form of the gift does not mean that the Spirit comes under the control of creatures but that it comes into them and thus makes possible our independent and spontaneous entry into God's action of reconciling the world and our participation in the movement of its reconciling love toward the world. As the Spirit who "indwells" believers (Rom 8:9ff; 1 Cor 3:16), it lifts them above their own particularity and it is always more than a gift, namely, the quintessence of the ecstatic movement of the divine life.[252]

3.6 The Holy Spirit and Ecclesiology

In the whole theological program of Pannenberg, ecclesiology plays a significant role. As Kärkkäinen notes, it is interesting that Pannenberg begins the third volume of his *Systematic Theology* with the theme of ecclesiology and pneumatology and the chapter is entitled as "The Outpouring of the Spirit, the Kingdom of God, and the Church." He notes that Pannenberg's ecclesiological vision sees an integral, dialogical relationship between the Spirit and the Son.[253] This is true in the statement of Pannenberg that, "The Christological constitution and the pneumatological constitution do not exclude one another but belong together because the Spirit and the Son mutually indwell one another as Trinitarian persons."[254] With this preliminary understanding, we dive into the pneumatological ecclesiology of Pannenberg indepth.

3.6.1 The Church as the Creation of the Son and the Spirit

In the doctrine of redemption, we have already noted the significance of the special nature of the soteriological work of the Spirit in relation to creation.

---

252. Pannenberg, *Systematic Theology* vol. 3, 12; Pannenberg, *Systematic Theology* vol. 2, 274-275.
253. Kärkkäinen, *Pneumatology*, 123.
254. Pannenberg, *Systematic Theology* vol. 3, 16-17.

Taking a cue from this argument, one can endorse that for Pannenberg the formation of the church is the joint work of the Son and the Spirit. Pannenberg writes:

> Everywhere the work of the Spirit is closely related to the Son, from creation to salvation to the consummation of creation in the eschaton. The Logos and Spirit work in creation in such a way that the Word of creation is the fashioning principle, while the Spirit is the source of the movement and life of all creatures. In the eschatological consummation the Spirit is active as the enabling and transfiguring power that gives creatures a share in the glory of God, while the Son, as the agent of the last judgment, is the criterion for belonging to God and his kingdom or for incompatibility with them.[255]

Pannenberg maintains that both Father and Son work together in sending the Spirit. Whoever sends the Spirit, whether Father or the Son, in both cases the purpose of the sending of the Spirit is to continue Jesus' work of revealing. That means the sending of the Spirit by the Son relates to the special nature of his work in connection with the revelation of salvation.[256] Moreover, the Spirit glorifies Jesus as the Father's Son by teaching us to recognize the revelation of the Father in Jesus' words and work. This does not mean that the Spirit is the power in which Jesus Christ bears witness to himself. Instead, Jesus is referred to as the witness of the Spirit, who teaches us to know the Father's Son in him.[257] However, Pannenberg maintains that there is a distinction that arises between the Spirit and the Son due to the fact that in the New Testament testimonies and in Paul, Jesus Christ himself is seen as a *recipient* of the Spirit and his work, already in his baptism, and especially because the Spirit raised him from the dead (Rom 1:4; 8:11).[258]

---

255. Pannenberg, *Systematic Theology* vol. 1, 4; in accomplishing the work of reconciliation and the historical mediation of its saving effects, the incarnation of the Son, his earthly work, death, and resurrection, precede the imparting of the Spirit to believers. Only in this connection can we speak of the Son "sending" the Spirit who in eternity proceeds from the Father (Jn 15:26-27; 16:7). See Pannenberg, *Systematic Theology* vol. 1, 4.
256. Pannenberg, *Systematic Theology* vol. 3, 5.
257. Pannenberg, *Systematic Theology* vol. 3, 5.
258. Pannenberg, *Systematic Theology* vol. 3, 5; it is because the risen Lord is wholly permeated by the Spirit of life and this Spirit proceeds from him and the Christian Easter

Conversely, the Spirit can reveal the eschatological meaning of the history of Jesus because Spirit itself is eschatological reality.[259] The Spirit is not just the origin of all living things but also the source of the new life that has broken in the resurrection of Jesus Christ and that distinguishes itself from earthly life by the fact that it is linked to the divine source of life and may thus be called a *soma pneumatikon* and immortal (1 Cor 15:44-45).[260]

3.6.2 The Spirit as a Gift to the Church

One of the chief features of the primitive Christian understanding of the Spirit is that the gift of the *pneuma* is an eschatological gift and its working in the community is an eschatological event. The Spirit's work on believers is not just an external, invisible, and incomprehensible field of force. The Spirit is given to them as a gift. Here lies the special nature of its function relative to the salvation event. The gift of the Spirit has a soteriological function as an anticipation of the eschatological outpouring of the Spirit and is defined as a gift by the fact that Jesus Christ has given it to believers, the eschatological future of salvation having dawned already in his own person and history, so that he or she is aware that the Spirit he or she has received is the Spirit of Jesus Christ (Phil 1:19; cf. Rom 8:9).[261] The basic form of the Spirit's work is creative activity in the bringing forth of life and movement. It is thus in keeping with the Spirit's nature as "wind," and this is also the first thing to notice when it is said to proceed from the Father (Jn 15:26; cf. 14:16).[262] However, Pannenberg notes that the Spirit is not

---

message, so that the risen Lord can impart the Spirit to others also as long as they have fellowship with him.
259. According to Pannenberg, as the risen Lord Jesus is inseparably linked to the Spirit and its life, and that in the light of the Easter event and his pre-Easter life too, he is seen to be filled by God's Spirit (Jn 1:33; Lk 4:1). In both cases we have an expression of the breaking in of God's eschatological future in the person and history of Jesus, for in this connection Jewish hope expected the outpouring of God's Spirit on his people (Ezek 39:29; Zech 12:9-10; Joel 2:28). See Pannenberg, *Systematic Theology* vol. 3, 6.
260. Pannenberg, *Systematic Theology* vol. 3, 6.
261. Pannenberg, *Systematic Theology* vol. 3, 7.
262. Pannenberg, *Systematic Theology* vol. 3, 7; in an extended sense the breath of life that is already given to humanity at creation (Gen 2:7) may be seen as endowment of God's Spirit. Beyond that, special manifestations in the course of life display specific and more intensive forms of endowment by God's Spirit, like special capacities for insight, artistic gifts, prophetic inspiration, and leadership *charisma*. We do not think only of the momentary ecstatic experience here but the forms of lasting endowment of the Spirit of God. See Pannenberg, *Systematic Theology* vol. 3, 9.

always imparted and received as a gift. We must find the trinitarian basis for this in the fact that in the trinitarian life of God the Son is in eternity the recipient of the Spirit who proceeds from the Father. But only to the degree that the Son is manifested in creaturely life does the work of the Spirit in creation take on the form of a gift. This is definitively so only in relation to the incarnation of the Son. Hence, it is said of Jesus Christ that the Spirit is given him "without measure," i.e., without restriction (Jn 3:4). For believers, then, the Spirit as a gift is related to their becoming sons and daughters in baptism by fellowship with Jesus Christ (Rom 5:15; 6:3ff.).[263]

3.6.3 The Church as the Fellowship of Believers in the Spirit

In fact, for Pannenberg, the church is a community formulated by the Son and Spirit, who is given the Spirit as a gift. The aim of such a community of the Spirit is the fellowship of believers. Hence Pannenberg writes, "The gift of the Spirit is not just for individual believers but aims at the building up of the fellowship of believers, at the founding and the constant giving of new life to the church."[264] He continues that by linking to the one Lord by which all believers receive a share in his sonship, and hence also in the Spirit of Christ, they are at the same time integrated into the fellowship of believers. In the Spirit "the resurrected Lord" manifests himself with his resurrection power, which is more than mere power of ecstasy and of miracle, and reaches into the world leading to the new creation. Thus the Spirit incorporates humanity into the worldwide body of Christ. Moreover, Jesus himself is the unity of the body composed of the bearers of the gift of the Spirit (1 Cor 12) and who finally brings about the resurrection of the dead.[265] This relationship of humanity to the one Lord and to all believers takes place through faith in Jesus Christ. Pannenberg continues that the story of Pentecost in Acts 2:1ff. gives expression to the fact that the Spirit does not simply assure each individual believer of the fellowship with Jesus Christ, and therefore a share in future salvation; rather, it affirms the fellowship of believers. This reference demonstrates that the Spirit was

---

263. Pannenberg, *Systematic Theology* vol. 3, 9.
264. Pannenberg, *Systematic Theology* vol. 3, 12.
265. Pannenberg, *Jesus – God and Man*, 172.

given to all the disciples in common and that was where the church had its beginning.²⁶⁶

Having said that the church is the fellowship of believers, Pannenberg focuses on the paradox in the New Testament writings regarding the foundation of the church. According to Paul, Jesus Christ is the foundation of the church (1 Cor 3:11), and especially from the perspective of the relation between building and foundation. This thought led him to consider that believers are members of the one body of Christ, by which they are integrated into the fellowship of the church.²⁶⁷ In Luke, however, the church seems to be founded by the "power" of the Spirit, which is different from Jesus Christ even though promised and sent down from heaven by him (Lk 24:49), it being assumed that there is a continuity of the band of disciples that will be empowered for missionary proclamation by reception of the Spirit. Recognizing this paradox, Pannenberg insists that Christian theology should not see alternatives in these various ideas nor suppress awareness of the differences by harmonizing. Each theological concept of the church must integrate into itself the material aspects articulated in these different conceptions to form an intrinsically unified view of the constituting of the church by Jesus Christ and the work of the Spirit, and consequently, an interpretation of the relation between church and Spirit that cannot be treated as identical with any one New Testament concept because of a compulsion to erase the differences.²⁶⁸ Thus Pannenberg supports the Johannine statements about the Spirit due to the fact that they share with Luke an interest in the Spirit as an independent entity and also deal with

---

266. Pannenberg, *Systematic Theology* vol. 3, 13.
267. Pannenberg, *Systematic Theology* vol. 3, 15.
268. Pannenberg, *Systematic Theology* vol. 3, 15; although Pannenberg notes the paradox in the explanation about the beginning of the church in the different gospels and in the writings of Paul, he maintains that the Johannine statements about the Spirit are helpful because they share with Luke an interest in the Spirit as an independent entity and yet at the same time deal with the theme of the link between his work and Jesus Christ. This link is forged by the fact that the Spirit's work is to lead to knowledge of Jesus as the truth of God. The Spirit will not speak of itself but will glorify Jesus (Jn 16:13-14). But as that takes place, Jesus himself, by the Spirit's work, is with his own, being "in" them as they are in him (14:20). As the Spirit bears witness in believers to Jesus as the truth of God, they themselves are ecstatically ruptured and are outside themselves in Jesus, while conversely Jesus is in them to bind them in fellowship with one another, and along with Jesus the Father also takes up his dwelling in believers (14:23). See Pannenberg, *Systematic Theology* vol. 3, 15-16.

the link between the Spirit's work and Jesus Christ. In short, these sayings are remarkably close to Rom 8:14-16. The Spirit of adoption which Paul speaks here corresponds to the Johannine concept of the Son's dwelling in believers. And if in John the Father, too, takes up his dwelling in believers along with the Son, this corresponds to Paul's statement that the Spirit of adoption enables believers to call on God as Father as children may do.[269] It is clear from Paul that the Father's "indwelling" can take place only in such a way that like the Son believers differentiate themselves from the Father and subject themselves to him in prayer and praise. Conversely, the Johannine statements show that participation in adoption is already the work of the Spirit who glorifies Jesus in humanity. On the other hand, Paul in Rom 8:15 calls the Spirit itself as the "Spirit of sonship," and in Gal 4:6 he calls the gift of the Spirit as the result of adoption that believers have received. In 1 Corinthians 12:13 he also describes the work of the Spirit as incorporating the believers into the one body of Christ by baptism, by which they also receive sonship.[270]

The above discussion proves the fact that Jesus Christ dwells in believers by the Spirit. Hence, he is precisely the one Lord who in the unity of his body binds together his own into the church's fellowship because he is the foundation of the church due to the work of the Spirit. Moreover, the work of the Spirit is to glorify the Son by teaching us to know the Father in the Son through whom we have access to him.[271] Here one should note the fact that the Christological and pneumatological constitution of the church do not exclude one another but belong together because the Spirit and the Son mutually indwell one another as trinitarian persons. However, one must not overlook the special function and significance of the Spirit in the life of the church. As the Father raised Jesus from the dead by the Spirit, so it is only the Spirit who in the light of the eschatological future of God teaches us to see him as the Messiah of the eschatological people of God. Because the Spirit, as creator of the new life with no death, is himself an eschatological reality, it can also manifest the eschatological significance

---

269. Pannenberg, *Systematic Theology* vol. 3, 16; cf. Pannenberg, *Jesus – God and Man*, 173.
270. Pannenberg, *Systematic Theology* vol. 3, 16.
271. Pannenberg, *Systematic Theology* vol. 3, 16; cf. Pannenberg, *Jesus – God and Man*, 177.

of the coming and history of Jesus.[272] This work of the Spirit takes place in full and continuous connection with its work in the world of nature as the origin of all life, and especially in humans as the source of the spontaneity of their "spiritual" activities that lift them ecstatically above their own particularity and thus enable them to grasp that which is beyond themselves and distinct for their own existence.[273] Thus Pannenberg maintains that in the knowledge of Jesus Christ as the Son and Messiah, the Spirit binds together all believers into the fellowship of the church in unity with him and with one another. Moreover, with the content of this faith (Gal 3:2), the Spirit is conferred as a lasting gift upon believers in the fellowship of the church of Christ, a pledge of the hope beyond death whose fulfillment has already broken in with the resurrection of Jesus.[274]

While dealing with the church as a fellowship of believers, Pannenberg makes an important observation regarding the significance of the role of the Spirit in the church. He notes that, "We rightly define the Spirit's significance for the church's life and proclamation only if we pay constant heed to the relation to creation on the one side and the eschatology on the other. Only thus can we avoid a defective constricting of pneumatology from a christological angle that finds the Spirit's work in the fellowship of believers and hence often unrealistically exaggerates this work."[275] In the same way, relating the Spirit's testimony to Jesus Christ acts as a brake on the unregulated enthusiasm that with an appeal to the dynamic of the Spirit breaks free from the church's tradition and institutional order as though it alone counted as a sign of spiritual vitality. In light of the eschatological consummation of creation, the Spirit enables us to see the universal truth of the sending of Jesus and glorifies Jesus as the Messiah and the new human. The Spirit's specific work in the church always relates to Jesus and to the eschatological future of God's kingdom that has dawned already in him.[276]

---

272. Pannenberg, *Systematic Theology* vol. 3, 17.
273. Pannenberg, *Systematic Theology* vol. 3, 17.
274. Pannenberg, *Systematic Theology* vol. 3, 17.
275. Pannenberg, *Systematic Theology* vol. 3, 19-20.
276. Pannenberg, *Systematic Theology* vol. 3, 20.

3.6.4 Church as the Sign of Future Kingdom in the Spirit

One of the specialties of Pannenberg's ecclesiology is that he recognizes the church as the sign of the future kingdom of God. He maintains that if we derive the church's existence from the outpouring of the Spirit at Pentecost according to the Lucan account, we still have to show what this means. Acts depicts Pentecost as the basis of the church's existence, yet it is not merely as an act of collective enthusiasm but as the starting point of the proclamation of the resurrection of the crucified one and his installation to a position of eschatological power as Son of God and Kyrios.[277] Corresponding to the eschatological character of this event on the side of believers is the assurance that in them the outpouring of the Spirit that is promised for the eschatological consummation has occurred already and given them power to proclaim the gospel of the resurrection of the crucified one as God's act of deliverance for his people and for all humanity.[278] Pannenberg holds that, "The eschatological reality of the resurrection from the dead that had come already with Jesus and the awaited end-time event of the outpouring of the Spirit formed partial aspects of the all-embracing event of the consummation of the kingdom of God that was already dawning."[279] However, as Jesus in his earthly proclamation humbly distinguished himself from the Father and the future of his kingdom, so the church must distinguish its own existence from the future of the kingdom of God. Only in the spiritual poverty and humility of this self-distinction is it the place at which, by the power of the Spirit, the eschatological future of God's lordship is already present and at work for human salvation. Only as it renounces exclusive claims for its own specific form can it plainly be a sign of the universality of the kingdom of God and an instrument of the reconciliation of human beings with one another and with God, transcending all the differences that separate people from one another and from the God of Israel.[280]

In short, for Pannenberg, the church is not identical with the kingdom of God. Rather, it is a sign of the kingdom's future of salvation because

---

277. Pannenberg, *Systematic Theology* vol. 3, 27.
278. Pannenberg, *Systematic Theology* vol. 3, 27-28.
279. Pannenberg, *Systematic Theology* vol. 3, 28.
280. Pannenberg, *Systematic Theology* vol. 3, 32.

this future of God is already present in it and it is accessible to people through the church, through its proclamation and its liturgical life. To this extent Christians are already translated into the kingdom of God's Son by the Spirit of the Father (Col 1:13), so that by him they are already redeemed from sin (v. 14). In this sense the kingdom of God was present already in the work of Jesus (Lk 11:20) and by him it is also at work in his church.[281] Pannenberg argues that the community in its "institutional" form does not control the presence of God's saving future. This presence becomes an "event" in it by the Spirit, an "event" mediated through the Word of the Christian proclamation of the gospel.[282] This relation of Word and "event" undoubtedly has its most intensive form in the celebration of the Lord's Supper, in which the community is assured by Jesus' own words of his presence in it.[283] Moreover, the church as the community that awaits the *parousia* of its risen Lord is called to give missionary witness to the world. Hence it cannot be an end in itself. One must anchor this fact in the concept of the church's nature that "the church is a sign or sacrament of the kingdom, a definition that the church does not fit in and for itself but only as the body of Christ in the power of the Holy Spirit."[284] The messianic people of the coming kingdom is the church due to its function as an anticipatory sign of the destiny of humanity in the future of the kingdom of God that God alone will bring in. This future is already present in the church after the manner of a sign in a proleptic way.[285]

3.6.5 Church as an Eschatological Community in the Spirit

When dealing with the kingdom of God, one must not forget the fact that the church is an eschatological community as well. The early understanding of the church was that of an eschatological community, a community of high expectation and hope. In other words, the church was regarded as an anticipation of the new humanity, a humanity under the rule of God and

---

281. Pannenberg, *Systematic Theology* vol. 3, 37; see also Pannenberg, *Christianity in a Secularized World*, 23.
282. Pannenberg, *Systematic Theology* vol. 3, 37.
283. Pannenberg, *Systematic Theology* vol. 3, 38.
284. Pannenberg, *Systematic Theology* vol. 3, 46.
285. Pannenberg, *Systematic Theology* vol. 3, 46.

his Spirit.[286] This renewing Spirit of God was expected to be poured out in the last days upon everyone, but it was also believed that the Spirit is now present in the church. Therefore, in both an anticipatory and present sense, the church thought of itself as the new people of God and the new Israel. Only if we take these eschatological titles seriously can we understand the nature and vocation of the church in relation to the kingdom of God, which is the future of the entire world. In this sense the existence of the church is of utmost significance for all humanity, not simply for those who are members of the institution.[287] Moreover, the presence of the eschatological future in the life of the church is in a special way the work of the Spirit. The life of the faithful and the life of the Eucharistic community, that is the church, are characterized by an anticipatory participation in the final destiny of human beings through a sharing in the Spirit. The Spirit is the first fruit and pledge of the new and immortal life that has already manifested itself in the risen Christ (Rom 8:23; 2 Cor 1:22). The new life is no longer separated from its source in the divine Spirit. Rather, it is permeated by this Spirit (1 Cor 15:44ff.) and is precisely for that reason immortal. The presence of the truth of human life and the world, and also the presence of eternity in the consciousness of our own identity and the being of things within the totality of all that is, this presence will be made perfect in the final and definitive union of Spirit and body in the *eschaton*.[288]

---

286. Pannenberg, *Theology and the Kingdom of God*, 74; through Jesus, the Spirit opens the way to communion with God. Therefore, the Spirit of Christ demonstrates itself as the Spirit of communion with God. That means the Spirit makes Christians the children of God, just as Jesus has been designated to be the Son of God through the Spirit (Rom 1:4; 8:23; Gal 4:6). The difference is only that Christians becomes children of God not immediately but through participation in the sonship of Jesus – not by nature, but by adoption. In that the Spirit is essentially the Spirit of Sonship, even as it is imparted to Christians, in that the Spirit is the Spirit who joins the Son with the Father, so the Spirit of God is here recognizable as the Spirit of the community of Father and Son. This is the most inclusive concept of the Spirit in the revelation of God and thus in his eternal essence as well. See Pannenberg, *Jesus – God and Man*, 176.
287. Pannenberg, *Theology and the Kingdom of God*, 74.
288. Pannenberg, *Anthropology*, 532.

3.6.6 Church as the Mystery of Salvation in Christ and the Spirit

Pannenberg maintains that we might also understand the interrelation of Christ and the church in the concept of the mystery of salvation as an expression of the fellowship of the Son and Spirit in the work of reconciliation. To that extent one might call the mystery of salvation as the sacrament of the Spirit so long as the point is not to differentiate the church from Christ in the concept of the sacrament.[289] Pannenberg's argument is that the church is not a sacrament of the Spirit as distinct from the Son. Rather, Jesus Christ by the witness and work of the Spirit in his body, the church, is the one divine mystery of salvation that we might call the sacrament of the kingdom, because the saving work of both the Son and the Spirit are comprised in this term. Their common work advances the actualizing of the kingdom of God in his creation.[290] While dealing with the church as the mystery of salvation in Christ, he deals with the significance of the new law given by Jesus Christ.[291] Although there are lots of contradictions to the exposition of Paul with regard to the law, the gentile church soon came to see in Jesus the giver of a new law in keeping with a series of typological contrasts between the old covenant and the new. In this way Paul's teaching about the end of the Torah came to be related to the idea of a new law that is promulgated for Christians, that Paul called the law of the Spirit

---

289. Pannenberg, *Systematic Theology* vol. 3, 42.
290. Pannenberg, *Systematic Theology* vol. 3, 42.
291. He insists that Paul contrasted the law with faith (Rom 3:21ff., 4:13ff., 10:5) or grace (6:14-15) or the Spirit (7:6; cf. 8:2) but never with the gospel, although the message of faith which, as the source of the Spirit, Gal 3:2 sets in opposition to the "works of the law," is materially identical with the gospel. Paul here places the accent not on the form of the message but on the new reality of faith, grace, and the Spirit that does away with the law and its works. On the basis of Rom 10:4 Paul expected that those who are dead to self-seeking in Christ, by the Spirit will keep the righteous demands of the law (Rom 8:4), so that at least implicitly there is agreement with its moral requirements. Love is the fulfilling of the law (Rom 13:10; cf. Gal 5:14). Paul did not usually appeal to the authority of the law's requirements but sought to derive the content of his practical directions from the believer's relationship to Christ (Phil 2:5). The freedom acquired through Christ must not become a pretext for self-seeking (5:13; cf. Rom 8:12), to which Christians are dead in virtue of their fellowship with Christ. The Spirit of Christ finds expression in modes of conduct that the law does not oppose (Gal 5:22-23; Rom 8:1ff.). For Christians these rest not on the letter of the law but on fellowship with Christ by the Spirit. See Pannenberg, *Systematic Theology* vol. 3. 61, 68-69.

(Rom 8:2) or the law of Christ (Gal 6:2).[292] This new law of the gospel is no longer for either of them a demand that confronts us but the power of the Spirit itself at work in the heart.[293] This new law is characterized by the work of the Spirit and grace.[294]

3.6.7 In the Church Believers Enjoy Freedom in the Spirit

In fact, Pannenberg discusses the freedom in the Spirit in his major work on anthropology while discussing the sin and its impact upon the human beings.[295] However, in his systematic theology, Pannenberg discusses freedom along with the church.[296] Nevertheless, what is important for Pannenberg is that freedom is the work of the Spirit. But it is not in the sense that human beings have the freedom to sin because they are responsible to their sins.[297] Pannenberg notes that, "freedom" in the New Testament is not something that human beings have from the beginning and "by their nature" but as an effect of the redemptive presence of Christ and his Spirit (Jn 8:36; 2 Cor 3:17).[298] It means Christian freedom is the work of the Spirit in believers. But one should note the fact that the Spirit is not just working among the human beings or in the sphere of living things. On the other hand, the freedom of believers express the fact that the Spirit of God is permanently given to them, and this rests on their participation in the filial relation of Jesus to the Father, because only to the Son is the Spirit given without reservation or restriction (Jn 3:34). As the origin of all life the Spirit of God pledges to believers, to whom is given as a lasting gift, participation in the eternal life of God and the resurrection from the dead (8:11).[299] Moreover, Pannenberg insists that the liberation by the Spirit, who is given as a lasting gift with the acceptance of believers into filial relationship with the Father, is the basis of a freedom that no longer consists of being able to do this or that. On the other hand, we attain the authentic freedom only when those

---

292. Pannenberg, *Systematic Theology* vol. 3, 70.
293. Pannenberg, *Systematic Theology* vol. 3, 72.
294. Pannenberg, *Systematic Theology* vol. 3, 75.
295. Pannenberg, *Anthropology*, 104ff.
296. Pannenberg, *Systematic Theology* vol. 3, 129ff.
297. Pannenberg, *Anthropology*, 110.
298. Pannenberg, *Anthropology*, 111.
299. Pannenberg, *Systematic Theology* vol. 3, 129.

alienated from God are reconciled to God, so that alienation of the human identity is also overcome.[300] Humanity achieves this freedom by participation in the filial relation of Jesus to the Father in faith. In fellowship with the eternal God believers are freed from anxiety about their finite existence, from fear of others, and from the powers of this world. Thus the Spirit grants freedom not only by liberating us from fixation on our own ego and lifting us above our own finitude, but by becoming lastingly ours as it gives us a share in the sonship of Jesus Christ (Rom 8:13-14).[301]

Moreover, as noted earlier, for Pannenberg the Spirit is also the basis of the fellowship of believers in the unity of the body of Christ. Hence, where the Spirit of Christ rules, we cannot play off the freedom of faith against the fellowship of believers and the duty of maintaining it. In addition to that under the lordship of the Spirit of Christ, the communication of the gospel cannot take the form of clerical domination that does not let believers attain the true freedom of immediacy to God but keeps them dependent.[302] In short, Pannenberg argues that, "The work of the Spirit releases and reconciles the tension between the fellowship and the individual in the concept of the church, and with it the underlying anthropological tension between society and individual freedom that in sign at least is meant to be experienced as overcome in the church in anticipation of the future of God's kingdom."[303] Thus for Pannenberg, the Spirit's work is ecstatic not merely in individual Christians but also in the life of the church, leading to its center in worship and then radiating out from there into everyday life. In this process the relation to the Spirit does not mean that in every respect the church is different from other forms of the society, because God's Spirit is at work in all living things, especially human souls, and also in social structures.[304] In short, for Pannenberg the Spirit is the medium of the im-

---

300. Pannenberg, *Systematic Theology* vol. 3, 129.
301. Pannenberg, *Systematic Theology* vol. 3, 130.
302. Pannenberg, *Systematic Theology* vol. 3, 130.
303. Pannenberg, *Systematic Theology* vol. 3, 130.
304. Pannenberg, *Systematic Theology* vol. 3, 133-134; the ecstatic nature of his work finds expression in every society whose individual members are united by dedication to a common cause. In this kind of common spirit, the creative Spirit of God is at work only in a more or less broken form. The common cause that unites individuals may be most unholy. Even where that it is not so, as in such natural forms of social life as marriage and family, state and people, the ecstatic feature of the Spirit's work finds only limited

mediacy of individual Christians to God as it lifts them up to participation in the sonship of Jesus Christ and grants them the Christian freedom (Rom 8:15). Secondly, the Spirit binds believers together in the fellowship of the body of Christ and thus constitutes the church as the Spirit is presented to it as a lasting gift (1 Cor 12:13).[305] Thirdly, the fellowship of the believers in the church is a fellowship by the Spirit. (Rom 8:23; 2 Cor 1:22; 5: 5).[306] Thus the fellowship of the church can be a significant prefiguration of the eschatological fellowship of a humanity that is renewed in the kingdom of God.

3.6.8 The Basic Saving Works of the Spirit in Individual Christians

According to Pannenberg, every creature lives by existing outside itself, namely, in and by the world around it. This is true with the human beings as well because the Spirit gives life by lifting individuals above their particularity and finitude.[307] There are three important factors with regard to the basic saving work of the Spirit in individual Christians. The first aspect is faith. According to Pannenberg, faith is a form of the way human beings relate to truth.[308] In other words, faith lifts them above their entanglement in the vicious circle of sin and death by uniting them to Jesus and giving them a share in his Spirit.[309] The second aspect is hope. For Pannenberg, faith and hope is related to each other and Christian hope rests on faith. Those believers in Christ, to whom they are united in the ecstatic "outside-the-self" of faith, acquire a hope beyond death. He writes, "The imparting of hope by faith in Jesus Christ frees us from this imprisonment in self and lifts us above the self. Faith thus gives rise to a

---

fulfillment, because in the autarchy of these structures the cause that unites the members takes its own form. The situation differs in the Spirit fellowship of the church as a symbolically and sacramentally defined fellowship, for the "cause" that finds depiction in it, that of the coming divine rule, lies outside it. The kingdom is present only in the event of the proclamation of what God has done for us and all *extra nos*, in Jesus Christ, and in the significatory form of the sacraments. Precisely thus the Spirit of God is granted to the church as an end-time gift. See Pannenberg, *Systematic Theology* vol. 3, 134.
305. Pannenberg, *Systematic Theology* vol. 3, 134.
306. Pannenberg, *Systematic Theology* vol. 3, 134.
307. Pannenberg, *Systematic Theology* vol. 3, 135.
308. Pannenberg, *Systematic Theology* vol. 3, 136.
309. Pannenberg, *Systematic Theology* vol. 3, 177.

hope that is concerned not merely about one's own well-being but is bound with the cause of God in the world that has the salvation of all humanity as its goal and embraces the believer's I only in this broad context."[310] The third aspect is love. Pannenberg notes that hope and love belong together. Hence, "Our elevation to God by the Spirit of faith and hope, which is the basis of a new being of believers outside the self in Christ and by him in God, is already implicitly love of God, a response to the message of the love God showed for us in the sending of Jesus Christ, and it leads beyond this to participation in the dynamic of God's love for the world."[311] The ecstatic feature in faith and hope that relates us to the God revealed in Jesus Christ finds fulfillment in love. This is the love with which God has loved us and which is imparted to us by the Spirit who is given us as he bears witness to God's love for us (Rom 8:16).[312]

3.6.9 Sacraments and the Spirit

As noted earlier, Pannenberg maintains that it is the church which mediates the fellowship of individual believers with Jesus Christ. This occurs through the working of the Spirit in the life of the individuals and thus they share in the body of Christ as members of the community. Moreover, by the church's mediation individual Christians achieve the relation of immediacy to Jesus Christ. The immediacy of fellowship with Jesus Christ by the Spirit in which the aim of the event of reconciliation with God is reached comes into effect basically as faith, hope, and love. On this ground we need to see the life of the church and the sacraments.

3.6.9.1 The Spirit and Baptism

While discussing the ministry of the church, Pannenberg deals with the doctrine of baptism in detail and considers its significance. Pannenberg notes the significance of baptism due to the fact that through the content of the regeneration or reconstitution of the person by baptism, the baptized are related to Jesus Christ and thus to the triune God. This takes place by baptizing the candidates in the "name" of Jesus Christ or in the "name" of

---

310. Pannenberg, *Systematic Theology* vol. 3, 179.
311. Pannenberg, *Systematic Theology* vol. 3, 182.
312. Pannenberg, *Systematic Theology* vol. 3, 183.

God the Father, the Son, and Holy Spirit (Mt 28:19). Moreover, baptism in the name of Jesus, or by ancient church custom, in the name of the triune God, is an act of transfer. It means, the baptized are no longer their own but God's (Rom 6:10) or Christ's (7:4). This is the original point of viewing baptism as a seal (2 Cor 1:22) which as a distinguishing mark will also assure the baptized of eschatological deliverance at the coming world judgment, a sign of their election and hope.[313] By the link to Jesus Christ baptized Christians share in the fruit of his death and in the new and eternal life that his resurrection manifested and that vanquished death. Pannenberg notes that the primitive Christianity even related baptism to the forgiveness of sins, the atoning effect of the death of Jesus, and also to the eschatological gift of the Spirit, by whom the new life of the resurrection of Jesus is already present to the baptized and its future consummation is guaranteed.[314] Moreover, in the Spirit the baptized are received as the children of God and that enables them to follow their own specific calling, and to accept the consequence as Jesus did. As the sending of Jesus served to proclaim God's reign and its representation in the fellowship of his disciples, each Christian is summoned by the baptism of Jesus to make a special contribution to witness to God's reign in the fellowship of the church.[315]

Having affirmed the significance of baptism, Pannenberg focuses on the relationship between baptism and the reception of the Spirit on the basis of Jesus' baptism. He argues that Paul has already depicted a connection between reception of the Spirit and the filial relation of Christians to God as this finds expression in their addressing God as Abba, Father (Gal 4:6; Rom 8:15). In some way this filial relation might well go back to Jesus' own addressing God as Father, as Jesus also taught his disciples to do in the Lord's Prayer. Thus the link between baptism, reception of the Spirit, and addressing God as Father, with at least the implied thought of a filial

---

313. Pannenberg, *Systematic Theology* vol. 3, 239.
314. Pannenberg, *Systematic Theology* vol. 3, 240; the tradition of the baptism of Jesus and the form in which the story is told were obviously quite soon and increasingly influenced and shaped by Christological interest on the one side, which traced back Jesus' title as Son to baptism, and by the church's baptismal practice on the other. The primitive Christian tradition thus viewed Jesus' baptism already as the model of Christian baptism, especially with regard to the link between baptism and reception of the Spirit. See Pannenberg, *Systematic Theology* vol. 3, 279.
315. Pannenberg, *Systematic Theology* vol. 3, 282.

relation of God, refers the baptismal practice of primitive Christianity back to Jesus' own baptism.[316] Moreover, according to Pannenberg, in the enacted sign of baptism believers are buried in Christ's death (Rom 6:4) and their future death is anticipated here after the manner of a sign and linked to the death of Christ. In this way a relation is set up between baptism and all the earthly life that is still ahead for the baptized as the whole is seen in the light of its future end. The story of the life of Jesus between his own baptism and death is something that what is anticipated in the sign of baptism is to imitate. In terms of baptism the Christian life is a process of dying with Christ, and at the same time, by the Spirit, the new humanity, the resurrection life, is already at work in Christians (Rom 6:9ff.).[317]

3.6.9.2 The Spirit and the Lord's Supper

Pannenberg notes that, since the beginning of primitive Christianity, the celebration of the Lord's Supper stood at the heart of the Christian worship and gave it its distinctive character. At the breaking of the bread the primitive Christian community was aware of continuing table fellowship with its crucified and risen Lord. Jesus' disciples knew that for this they had the authority of Jesus himself, who before his death had promised them continued fellowship with himself at the common meal. Both Luke (24:30-31, 41; Acts 10:41) and John (21:13) tell us that the risen Lord appeared to his disciples to share a common meal with them.[318] However, the Lord's Supper is not just a commemorative meal because as Pannenberg writes, "After Easter the gift of the Spirit definitively actualized that which was implicit at the Last Supper. Yet it is also true of the celebration of the Lord's Supper itself that the presence of the risen Lord by the Spirit means that the church's Eucharistic worship is more than just a commemorative meal."[319] In fact, then, the church's existence is made possible only by God's own action in the resurrection of the crucified one and the eschatological gift of the Spirit. Nevertheless, it has its foundation in the concept of the new covenant that is related to the Last Supper.[320] In short, what is con-

---

316. Pannenberg, *Systematic Theology* vol. 3, 280.
317. Pannenberg, *Systematic Theology* vol. 3, 243.
318. Pannenberg, *Systematic Theology* vol. 3, 283.
319. Pannenberg, *Systematic Theology* vol. 3, 291.
320. Pannenberg, *Systematic Theology* vol. 3, 291.

stitutive for the being of the church is not its organizational form but the significatory action of Jesus' Supper, which the church celebrates with the assurance based on the gift of the Spirit.[321] In the Lord's Supper, the risen Jesus is present by his Spirit and it makes the Lord's Supper a fellowship with Jesus Christ.[322]

3.6.9.2.1 Eucharistic Anamnesis and Epiclesis

After delineating the significance of the Lord's Supper, Pannenberg discusses the manner of the celebration of the Lord's Supper in the church. Pannenberg argues that in the context of the church's Eucharistic celebration, Christ's presence is mediated by the recollection of its institution by Jesus himself on the night of his betrayal and death. This recollection takes place in the light of Easter faith and it is related to the prayer for the presence for Jesus Christ by his Spirit in fulfillment of what was promised in the words of institution. Thus *anamnesis* and *epiclesis* characterize the liturgical form of the Lord's Supper.[323] According to Pannenberg, Eucharistic *anamnesis* is not just an act of human remembering of which we are still subjects, but the self-representing of Jesus Christ by the Spirit. In Eucharistic *anamnesis* too, the Spirit's work expresses itself in the form of ecstatic elevation. It takes place in the act of believing recollection. Thus *anamnesis* begins with the summons "Lift up your hearts."[324] Liturgical participants, in faith, are outside themselves with Christ as they recall their Lord's passion. Only as they are outside themselves with Christ in the act of recollection is Jesus Christ, the one whom they remember, present to them. Hence recollection takes place after the manner of thanksgiving in which thanks for the gifts of creation mingles with thanks for the sending of the Son and his reconciling death. Thanksgiving leads to recollection of the institution of the Lord's Supper, at which bread and wine become the medium of Christ's presence.[325]

---

321. Pannenberg, *Systematic Theology* vol. 3, 292.
322. Pannenberg, *Systematic Theology* vol. 3, 304.
323. Pannenberg, *Systematic Theology* vol. 3, 305.
324. Pannenberg, *Systematic Theology* vol. 3, 307.
325. Pannenberg, *Systematic Theology* vol. 3, 308.

As noted earlier, in the power of the divine lordship and its future, the risen Lord is present in the meal of his community. Consequently the difference in time is overcome that separates the community from the days of the earthly ministry of Jesus. But this does not occur by human recollection alone. Hence Pannenberg insists that *anamnesis* has to pass over into prayer for the Lord's coming, as it happened in the primitive Christian worship. The cry "Come, Lord Jesus" (1 Cor 16:22; cf. Rev 22:20) is to be viewed not merely as a request for the eschatological coming of the ascended Lord to consummate his kingdom but also as a request for his coming for table fellowship in anticipation of God's coming kingdom. The cry can be constructed as a petition but also as a proclamation of the Lord's presence in the Supper.[326] Moreover, Pannenberg notes that the theological statements of the Greek fathers about the importance of the invocation of the Spirit in Eucharistic celebrations adduce especially parallels to the incarnation. As the Spirit mediated the union of the Logos with the human nature of Jesus, so it also effects the presence of Jesus Christ in bread and wine.[327] Pannenberg insists that we grasp the significance of the invocation of the Spirit in the context of Eucharistic celebrations only when we relate it primarily to the raising again of Jesus by the Spirit and hence to recollection of the Lord who went to his death. Linking *epiclesis* to *anamnesis* gives representation to the resurrection of the crucified one in eucharistic worship and with it anticipates his future return and the future consummation of God's kingdom. In short, it is always by the Spirit alone that the spiritual reality of the risen Lord is present to believers, and it is only in this way that it can be a living reality in the church's worship. Hence the liturgy of the Greek church rightly calls on the Spirit to make Jesus Christ present to us in the form of bread and wine according to his promise in the words of institution.[328]

---

326. Pannenberg, *Systematic Theology* vol. 3, 320; however, one should not forget that at eucharistic celebrations the Spirit is not springing into action at the *epiclesis*. It is already at work in the whole process of liturgical thanksgiving and *anamnesis*, and by the Spirit Jesus Christ himself is present to his community according to his promise (Matt 18:20). See Pannenberg, *Systematic Theology* vol. 3, 323.
327. Pannenberg, *Systematic Theology* vol. 3, 320.
328. Pannenberg, *Systematic Theology* vol. 3, 321; Pannenberg insists that rediscovery of the *epiclesis* and its importance for eucharistic celebration can enrich Western eucharistic theology in many ways. He says, *epiclesis* means prayer although it does not effect Christ's

Pannenberg notes that there are two important results in celebrating the Lord's Supper since Jesus is present in it through the Spirit. Firstly, the Spirit enables the Christians to lift up their hearts and give thanks to God because the Spirit is the power behind all Christian prayer (Rom 8:15).[329] Moreover, the believers are enabled to dedicate their own bodily lives as living and holy sacrifices that are pleasing to God in the service of God and his future kingdom (Rom 8:12, 1:1ff.). They are "transformed" in this way as the crucified Christ was transformed by the Spirit into a new life toward which Christians are moving as they await the "changing" of this mortal life into a life with no death that is permeated by God's Spirit of life (1 Cor 15:51ff.).[330] Secondly, the transforming work of the Spirit relates not merely to the eucharistic elements. This work embraces the participants as well in significatory anticipation in the eschatological world change. Only God's Spirit can effect the transforming of human life through bread and wine and they are drawn into the movement of the life of Jesus. This happens in the form of a sign in the celebration of the Lord's Supper. The consummation of the world and life of humanity by the Spirit is still ahead. It has already begun in the mission and resurrection of Jesus, and its presence in the form of the significatory action of the Eucharist. It involves also the ramifications for everyday life of the making of the eucharistic prayer at the celebrations of the liturgy.[331]

3.6.10 The Ministry of the Church and the Spirit

Having made a detailed discussion of the church and the role of the Spirit in the church and individual believers, Pannenberg finally comes to the mission of the church. He notes that in worship, individual Christians are united with others in the church's fellowship by the "ecstatic" fellowship

---

presence in bread and wine. Only the Spirit to whom prayer is made can do that. This is precisely what is expressed by prayer for the Spirit. Moreover, *epiclesis* does not compete with the words of institution because the Spirit should effect Christ's presence in bread and wine and it is related to the words of institution as their fulfillment. Hence the prayer can be made only with confidence that it will be heard. Secondly, reflection on the function of *epiclesis* at eucharistic celebration is important for the understanding of Christ's presence at the Supper because he has already promised that he would be present to his disciples in the bread and the wine of the Supper. See Pannenberg, *Systematic Theology* vol. 3, 322-323.
329. Pannenberg, *Systematic Theology* vol. 3, 324.
330. Pannenberg, *Systematic Theology* vol. 3, 324.
331. Pannenberg, *Systematic Theology* vol. 3, 324.

with Jesus Christ that lifts them above themselves. The fellowship of believers comes to realization at worship as a sign of our future fellowship in God's kingdom for the praising and glorifying of God to all eternity. But individual Christians as believers are not only lifted above themselves in Christ. They have to live in this world as those in whom Christ is present and at work by his Spirit.[332] Pannenberg notes that in church life there are many offices and ministries corresponding to the many tasks, the individual gifts, and abilities that are at work as gifts of the Spirit (*charisms*) in serving Christ's church and its mission.[333] However, there is no fixed number of *charisms* because new ones emerge in situations with new needs. Hence, according to Pannenberg, Paul's list in 1 Corinthians 12 does not claim to be complete, and not all the gifts he mentions there may be necessary at every period in the church's life. The main point of Paul's list lies in the unity of the body of Christ that is to be preserved notwithstanding the spontaneous variety of *charisms*, because the many believers are all members of this one body. Different *charisms* may appear more or less spontaneously, but they are meant to serve the unity of the body.[334] In short for Pannenberg, the various offices or ministries of the church have as their presupposition and basis the one common office or ministry of the church. This common calling of Christians is to continue the mission of Jesus in witness to the lordship of God.[335]

3.7 Holy Spirit and Creation

Creation is a significant doctrine in the whole theology of Pannenberg. When he deals with the doctrine of creation, his whole focus is on the significance of the Spirit in the creative action of God. Evaluating the position of Pannenberg, Grenz notes that Pannenberg calls for a "new understanding of the Spirit in relation to the biblical statement of his role in creation."[336] One should not forget the fact that the field theory as noted earlier lays the background for Pannenberg's idea of creation.

---

332. Pannenberg, *Systematic Theology* vol. 3, 370.
333. Pannenberg, *Systematic Theology* vol. 3, 372.
334. Pannenberg, *Systematic Theology* vol. 3, 372.
335. Pannenberg, *Systematic Theology* vol. 3, 372.
336. Grenz, *Reason for Hope*, 82; see Niels Henrik Gregersen, ed., *The Historicity of Nature: Essays on Science and Theology* (Pennsylvania: Templeton Foundation, 2008).

3.7.1 Creation as a Trinitarian Act

At the very outset, Pannenberg insists that creation is a free divine action.[337] The reason why Pannenberg makes such a bold statement is due to the fact that he finds creation in trinitarian scheme on the ground that the trinitarian relations between Father, Son, and Spirit are themselves actions. However, Pannenberg asserts that creation of the world is a different kind of divine action, which can be explained as outward actions.[338] It is the result and expression of a free act of divine willing and doing. Pannenberg continues that although God is active in himself in the mutual relations of the Father, Son, and Spirit through the creation of the world, God is active in new way. That means, with the creation of the world, all the persons, acting together, move out of what they have together, namely, the divine essence. Thus the creation of the world, with the related economy of the divine action, differs from the activity of the living God in the mutual relations of Father, Son, and Spirit.[339] According to Pannenberg, the temporal order in which the creaturely things and events stand as such enables us to describe their relation to the divine action in terms of a plan (Isa 5:19 etc.) – a plan that God himself follows in the process of history. If the destiny of all creaturely occurrence and existence is oriented to fellowship with God himself, then this idea takes the conceptual form of a plan of salvation. At this point the relation of the outward divine action to a goal acquires the form of trinitarian mediation inasmuch as the fellowship of creatures with their creator is to be thought of as participation in the fellowship of the Son with the Father through the Spirit.[340]

Delineating the traditional Protestant doctrine, Pannenberg argues that creation does not necessarily proceed from the fatherly love of God that is oriented from all eternity to the Son. The basis of its possibility is the

---

337. Pannenberg, *Systematic Theology* vol. 2, 1.
338. Pannenberg, *Systematic Theology* vol. 2, 1; the acts of the trinitarian persons in their mutual relations must be sharply differentiated from their common outward actions. This differentiation finds support in the rule that posits an antithesis between the inseparable unity of the trinitarian persons in their outward action relative to the world and the distinctiveness of their inner activities relative to one another, which is the basis of the personal distinctions of Father, Son, and Spirit. See Pannenberg, *Systematic Theology* vol. 2, 1.
339. Pannenberg, *Systematic Theology* vol. 2, 5.
340. Pannenberg, *Systematic Theology* vol. 2, 7.

free self-distinction of the Son from the Father although the Son moves out of the unity of deity, he is still united with the Father by the Spirit (2 Cor 3:17).[341] Pannenberg argues that although the Father sends the Son, he does not lay on him any compulsion to follow a command of fatherly love as though by outer constraint. But on the other hand, in a free act of fulfilling his sonship, the Son himself moves out of the divine unity by letting the Father alone be the one God.[342] Even in this act of freedom, the Son is one with the will of the Father and it can be understood only in the light of the fellowship of the Spirit that unites the two. Pannenberg writes that, "Thus creation is a free act of God as an expression of the freedom of the Son in his self-distinction from the Father, and of the freedom of the fatherly goodness that in the Son accepts the possibility and the existence of a creation distinct from himself, and of the freedom of the Spirit who links the two in free agreement."[343]

We have already noted that the Spirit is the uniting link between the Father and the Son and this understanding leads Pannenberg to argue that the creatures also can be related with the Father. Pannenberg writes, "As in the intratrinitarian life of God the self-distinction of the Son from the Father is the condition of his unity with the Father through the Spirit, so creatures are related to their Creator by their distinction from God and to one another by their distinctions from one another."[344] The distinctions do not have to take the form of separation or conflict, which is what happens when they fall out of the fellowship with God in which they were created by the Son and the Spirit of God. In his linkage with the Spirit the Son acts in creation as the principle not merely of the distinction of the creatures but also of their interrelation in the order of creation. He gathers the creatures into the order that is posited through himself (Eph 1:10) for participation in his fellowship with the Father. But this takes place only through the Spirit, for the creative work of the Son is linked at every point to that

---

341. Pannenberg, *Systematic Theology* vol. 2, 30.
342. Pannenberg, *Systematic Theology* vol. 2, 30.
343. Pannenberg, *Systematic Theology* vol. 2, 30; see Wolfhart Pannenberg, "The Doctrine of the Spirit and the Task of a Theology of Nature," in *Toward a Theology of Nature: Essays on Science and Faith*, ed. Ted Peters (Kentucky: Westminster, 1993), 123-137.
344. Pannenberg, *Systematic Theology* vol. 2, 31.

of the Spirit.[345] In addition to that, Pannenberg insists that the creatures need participation in God not merely because their existence differs from God but also in their life's movement insofar as life finds fulfilment in transcendence of its own finitude. This life of creatures as participation in God that transcends their own finitude is the special work of the Spirit in creation – a work that is very closely related to that of the Son.[346] The movement of such self-transcendence, especially its internalising, may be described as the participation of creatures in the God who gives them life. Thus Pannenberg writes that:

> The evolution of life as a process of producing increasingly complex and therefore increasingly internalised forms, and the sequence of forms may be seen as an expression of the increasing intensity of the participation of the creatures in the divine Spirit of life. At no stage does this growing participation in the Spirit eliminate distinction from God, for the creatures share in their life of the Spirit only by moving out of their own finitude. Hence they participate in the divine life only to the extent that self-distinction from God (and therefore the Son) takes shape in them. The work of the Spirit in creation thus converges on the incarnation of the Son, which in the scriptural testimony is in a special way the work of the Spirit, in which creation finds fulfilment by the full manifestation of the divine likeness in humanity.[347]

For Pannenberg, preservation also goes with the creation because it is a living occurrence, continued creation, and a constantly new creative fashioning that goes beyond the given original existence.[348] In short, according to Pannenberg:

> Creation, preservation, and overruling thus form a unity whose structural relation has yet to be defined more closely. By the doctrine of the Trinity all three are set in relation to

---

345. Pannenberg, *Systematic Theology* vol. 2, 32.
346. Pannenberg, *Systematic Theology* vol. 2, 33.
347. Pannenberg, *Systematic Theology* vol. 2, 34.
348. Pannenberg, *Systematic Theology* vol. 2, 34.

the saving economy of the divine action in the world. God's action, then, is seen to be a single act that embraces the whole cosmic process, that includes at the same time many individual acts and phases, and that thus leaves room for a plurality of creatures. Conversely, the creatures in their plurality, which is an expression of their finitude, can participate, each in its own place, in the movement of the divine action that permeates all creation, in the taking shape of the Word and the moving of the Spirit.[349]

3.7.2 *The Spirit and the Dynamic of Natural Occurrence*

In delineating the work of the Spirit in natural occurrences, Pannenberg begins his discussion with the biblical understanding of life. According to Pannenberg, the Spirit of God is the life-giving principle, to which all creatures owe life, movement, and activity. This is particularly true of animals, plants, and humans, of which Psalm 104:3 states: "When you send your Spirit, they are created, and you renew the face of the earth."[350] In keeping with this is the second creation account, which says that God "formed man of dust from the ground, and breathed into his nostrils the breath of life and man became a living being" (Gen 2: 7; cf. Job 33:4). Conversely, all life perishes when God withdraws his Spirit (Ps 104:29; Job 34:14ff.). The souls of all living things and the breath of all people are in the hands of the Spirit (Job 12:10).[351] However, Pannenberg argues that at a first glance this biblical view of life is hard to reconcile with modern ideas because the direct symbolism of God breathing breath into creatures seems to be more poetic than explanatory to the modern mind. Hence the issue is whether the metaphor carries a deeper meaning that might be illuminating even for the modern understanding of natural processes.[352] If it provides

---

349. Pannenberg, *Systematic Theology* vol. 2, 34-35.
350. Pannenberg, *Systematic Theology* vol. 2, 76.
351. Pannenberg, *Systematic Theology* vol. 2, 77.
352. Pannenberg notes that for modern theology, life is a function of the living cell or of the living creatures as a self-sustaining and reproducing system and not the effect of a transcendent force that gives life. Therefore, it might be suggested that the relevant biblical notions must be regarded merely as the expression of an archaic and outdated

a deeper meaning even for today, it is vital to explore this understanding because Paul's statement about the new life of the resurrection as a work of the divine Spirit (Rom 8:11; cf. 1:4; 1 Cor 15:44ff.) presuppose the Old Testament and Jewish concepts of the relation between the divine Spirit and life (cf. also Ezek 37:5ff.).[353] This argument has complexity because the first creation story extends the creative work of the Spirit beyond the giving of life to plants and animals and refers to the whole work of creation (Gen 1:2). The statement about original chaos leads on to the saying that "the Spirit of God was moving over the face of the waters."[354] Recognising the exegetical issues related to the usage of Spirit and wind in the Bible, Pannenberg asks that "in distinction from other OT passages, the divine breath is not itself life-giving or active?"[355] For him, the Spirit-wind does at least have the function of moving over the waters of chaos. The Spirit of God is the creative principle of movement as well as life. The Old Testament developed no general conception of cosmic movement to denote the various movements and activities of creatures. But there is an approach to this in the idea of the creative dynamic of the Spirit of God.[356]

---

understanding of the world, like many other biblical views on the natural phenomena. See Pannenberg, *Systematic Theology* vol. 2, 77.

353. Pannenberg, *Systematic Theology* vol. 2, 77.

354. Pannenberg, *Systematic Theology*, vol. 2, 77; Pannenberg notes that the exact meaning of *ruah elohim*, translated the "Spirit of God" has been the subject of much debate among exegetes, but only in regard to this one instance. In other occurrences, it is always rendered as "Spirit of God" and not here. Since we have a carefully considered text that in other places uses *elohim* as a divine name, we may rightly describe the idea that the reference is to an extremely powerful storm or a hurricane. It seems more likely that an existing theological view of the divine Spirit is at work in Genesis 1:2, one that we can hardly reconcile with the mere physical mobility of the wind. But why do we have to regard "Spirit" and "wind" as alternatives? The link to *elohim* suggests that God's Spirit is depicted here in terms of wind, as in Ezekiel 37:9ff. This view is close to the common idea of the life-giving breath of God, for with both wind and breath we have a movement of air that is otherwise still. As regards Genesis 1:2, we should not distinguish wind and breath rather we must plainly associate the reference to the Spirit of God with the creative speaking of God that immediately follows. See Pannenberg, *Systematic Theology* vol. 2, 78.

355. Pannenberg, *Systematic Theology* vol. 2, 78; See for discussion, Wolfhart Pannenberg, "Spirit and Energy," in *Toward a Theology of Nature: Essays on Science and Faith*, ed. Ted Peters (Louisville: Westminster, 1993), 138-147.

356. Pannenberg, *Systematic Theology* vol. 2, 79.

3.7.2.1 The Spirit and the Force Field

But still the question remains whether the above understanding helps us to reconcile the statements about the Spirit as the origin of life with the modern understanding? Here Pannenberg brings the significance of the concepts of force and field from modern physics. However, he notes that, "The principal differences between the ways of describing reality in physics and in theology prohibit us from offering a direct theological interpretation of the field theories of physics."[357] His position is that theology has to have its own material reasons for applying a basic scientific presentation. Only then is it justified in developing such concepts in a way appropriate to its own themes and independently of scientific usage. The reason why Pannenberg introduces field concept into theology is to present the Spirit of God as a dynamic field that is structured in trinitarian fashion, so that the person of the Spirit is one of the personal concretions of the essence of God as Spirit in the distinction from the Father and the Son.[358] According to Pannenberg, "The person of the Holy Spirit is not himself to be understood as the field but as a unique manifestation (singularity) of the field of the divine essentiality. But because the personal being of the Holy Spirit is manifest only in distinction from the Son (and therefore also from the Father), his working in creation has more of the character of dynamic field operations."[359] Pannenberg notes that in distinction from the Son's mediatorship in creation and its significance for the distinction and otherness of every creature, it relates to the link and movement that connects the creatures to one another and to God. To this extent the Spirit's work in creation is by nature more than a field of divine essentiality. It relates plainly to the specificity of the person of the Spirit in distinction from the Son, so that we may rightly refer to the third person of the Trinity.[360]

---

357. Pannenberg, *Systematic Theology* vol. 2, 83; Pannenberg notes that in accordance with the nature of scientific perception, these theories can be seen only as approximations to the reality that is also the subject of theological statements about creation. Pannenberg, *Systematic Theology* vol. 2, 83.
358. Pannenberg, *Systematic Theology* vol. 2, 83.
359. Pannenberg, *Systematic Theology* vol. 2, 83-84.
360. Pannenberg, *Systematic Theology* vol. 2, 84.

3.7.2.2 The Spirit, Space, and Time

Pannenberg asserts that when the first creation story speaks of the "moving" of the Spirit of God over the face of the waters (Gen 1:2), the idea of a surging force is hardly possible without time and space. The storm wind can develop its dynamic only in space, and to sweep forward it needs time. The same is true with the sending forth of the divine breath that renews life on earth (Ps 104:30).[361] In creating, God gives creatures space alongside himself and over against himself. That means, the eternal contemporaneity of the three persons in their mutual relations might suggest the idea of spatial distinctions and relations in God. The trinitarian distinctions, however, are not fixed divisions. In the act of self-distinction each of the persons is one with the other from whom it is distinguishing itself.[362] Hence, we cannot regard the bringing forth of creatures as though creatures were an object of divine self-distinction. Only indirectly do they proceed from the self-distinction of the Son from the Father. In the same way they are willed and affirmed by the Father in his self-distinction from the Son, by which he also accepts the Son in his distinction. The Father wills and accepts them as an expression of the overflowing of the divine love with which the Father loves the Son.[363] Pannenberg argues that, "Differences in the creaturely world take the form of division, of divided existence, though not to the exclusion of relations between things divided. The space of creatures is constituted by the fact that they are related precisely by their finitude and in their limitation. From this standpoint space is the epitome of relations between divided spaces, between points of space."[364]

Moreover, for Pannenberg, the differentiation of space from time is also a work of reflection that distinguishes the togetherness of things in space

---

361. Pannenberg, *Systematic Theology* vol. 2, 84-85; Pannenberg notes that spatial ideas occur elsewhere in biblical statements about God's relation to creation. The Bible says that God dwells in heaven. From there his power, or God himself, is manifested on earth. The idea of God's transcendence also demands space if it is not to be reduced to the logical distinction of the infinite from everything finite. The same way, incretion also has to be seen as God's entry into the sphere of creaturely being, which implies a spatial difference that can be overcome only in a temporal process. It is inappropriate to localize God in a space, but we cannot avoid this by limiting the idea of space to God's relations with his creatures. See Pannenberg, *Systematic Theology* vol. 2, 85.
362. Pannenberg, *Systematic Theology* vol. 2, 87.
363. Pannenberg, *Systematic Theology* vol. 2, 87.
364. Pannenberg, *Systematic Theology* vol. 2, 87.

from their following one another in time. The concept of time process is basic in this regard because it is constitutive for the space. The simultaneity of what is different constitutes space and this space is time.[365] The implied reduction of space to time is a presupposition for a theological interpretation of the presence of God in space as the dynamic operation of the divine Spirit.[366] Pannenberg notes that the constitutive significance of simultaneity for the concept of space renders philosophical plausibility in order to link space and time in an idea of space-time as a multidimensional continuum.[367] Here Pannenberg brings the relativity theory and argues that from the standpoint of the observer the spatial measurements are also relativized. Relative simultaneity means what is not simultaneous in itself. Here what is important for Pannenberg is that spatial measurements are made possible by the phenomenon of the present that bridges time.[368] Taking cue from this argument Pannenberg asserts that the present of creaturely events for God as also bridging time. Pannenberg writes:

> On the level of its own creaturely reality, that which is present to God belongs to different times. But before God it is present. In this regard God's eternity needs no recollection or expectation, for it is itself simultaneous with all events in the strict sense. God does not need light to know things. Being omnipresent, he is with every creature as its own place.[369]

When dealing with the Spirit and time, Pannenberg further links the theme of time with the eschatological consummation. He maintains that with the completion of God's plan for history in his kingdom, time itself will end (Rev 10:6ff.) in the sense that God will overcome the separation of the past from the present and the future and therefore the separation of the present from the past and the future that is a feature of cosmic time

---

365. Pannenberg, *Systematic Theology* vol. 2, 90.
366. Pannenberg, *Systematic Theology* vol. 2, 90.
367. Pannenberg here notes that the concept of absolute simultaneity has difficulties from the standpoint of relativity theory because many observers insist that there can be no strict simultaneity in many reference systems because determining time depends on light. See Pannenberg, *Systematic Theology* vol. 2, 91.
368. Pannenberg, *Systematic Theology* vol. 2, 91.
369. Pannenberg, *Systematic Theology* vol. 2, 91.

in distinction from eternity.[370] The powerful presence of the Spirit in the person of Jesus shows that he is the eschatological revealer of God through whom God's coming kingdom is already dawning. In short, the Spirit's function as the origin of all life is not viewed as preparation for the completion of his work by bringing the new eschatological life (1 Cor 15:45ff.). Pannenberg argues that, "The power of the future that manifests itself in the dynamic of the divine Spirit is not merely to be understood as the origin of the contingency of individual events. It must be seen also as the origin of lasting forms and of the unvarying regularity and reliability in the process of natural occurrences, without which there can be no lasting forms. The future at issue is in the dynamic of the divine Spirit is the entry into time of the eternity of God."[371] In short, the dynamic of the Spirit is a working field linked to time and space – to time by the power of the future that gives creatures their own present and duration, and to space by the simultaneity of creatures in their duration. From the creature's perspective, origin from the future of the Spirit has the appearance of the past. But the working of the Spirit constantly encounters the creature as its future, which embraces its origin and its possible fulfillment.[372]

3.7.3 Cooperation of Son and Spirit in the Work of Creation

Having said that the concrete order of the cosmic process is related to the incarnation of the Logos and the Spirit's field operations are temporally structured, so that each new event proceeds from the future of God from which all creaturely forms take their origin and seek their fulfillment,

---

370. Pannenberg, *Systematic Theology* vol. 2, 95.
371. Pannenberg, *Systematic Theology* vol. 2, 101-102; Pannenberg notes that the unity of life that we see only partially in the sequence of moments in time and that can find actualization as a whole only in eternal simultaneity, can be attained in the process of time only from the future, which brings its reality. It can be attained only as the integration of moments and events that are always contingent and therefore apart and separate in time. The emergence of contingent individual events from the possibility field of the future constitutes, then, only the elementary aspect in the creative dynamic of the Spirit, the beginning of its development. It culminates in the integration of events and moments into a unity of form. In short, the goal of the Spirit's dynamic is to give creaturely forms duration by a share in eternity and to protect them against the tendency to disintegrate that follows from their independence. See Pannenberg, *Systematic Theology* vol. 2, 102.
372. Pannenberg, *Systematic Theology* vol. 2, 102.

Pannenberg focuses on the cooperation of the Son and Spirit in the work of creation. He notes that Psalm 33:6 describes both Word and Spirit are organs of God's creative activity. Moreover, Genesis 1:2ff. claims that God's creative speaking is in the power of his Spirit or by his powerful breath. In agreement is the fact that the Son is the recipient and bearer of the Spirit. Genesis 1:2ff. justifies the assumption that the same applies to the work of creation. The Son's meditorial role in creation takes place in such a way that it is in the power of the Spirit that he is the origin of the different creatures in their specific distinctiveness.[373] As a field of force, the creative working of the Spirit of God is linked to time and space in its sphere of operations. It proves that there is interrelation of divine and creaturely reality, because creaturely existence proceeds from God's creative futurity with its own duration, which like all else subsists in the relations of space. On this ground, the idea of a vital creative dynamic is not sufficient to make intelligible to us the uniqueness of creaturely existence in its distinction from all else and its relation to it. For this we need a principle of distinction such as we find in the self-distinction of the Son from the Father, i.e., of the divine Logos. Whereas the creative dynamic in the events of creation relates to the Spirit, the Logos is the origin of the distinguishing form of the creature in the totality of its existence and in the ensemble of distinctions and relations of creatures in the order of nature.[374]

However, Pannenberg argues that we cannot separate the creative dynamic and the specific form of its expression. The two go together in the act of creation. In the first creation story this fact comes to expression in

---

373. Pannenberg, *Systematic Theology* vol. 2, 110.
374. Pannenberg, *Systematic Theology* vol. 2, 110; according to the biblical witness the Spirit was at work in creation (Gen 1:2), especially as the origin of life in the creatures (Gen 2:7; Ps 104:29ff.). On the one side the Spirit is the principle of the creative presence of the transcendent God with his creatures. On the other side it is the medium of the participation of the creatures in the divine life, and therefore in life as such. Its working, then, is closely related to that of the Son, though also characteristically different. For the independence and distinction of the creatures relative to God goes back to the self-distinction of the Son, but the Spirit is the element of the fellowship of the creatures with God and their participation in his life, notwithstanding their distinction from him. To be sure, in the Son, too, self-distinction from God and union with him belong closely together, for self-distinction from the Father is the condition of fellowship with him. Nevertheless, we see here the indissoluble interrelation of the Son and the Spirit. The Son is not the Son without the Spirit. See Pannenberg, *Systematic Theology* vol. 2, 32.

the idea of the creative speaking of God by which the dynamic of his Spirit becomes the origin of the specific creaturely reality. In the field concepts of science the same fact finds expression in the working of the field dynamic by natural laws.[375] In this respect the general rules in scientific description can be only approximations to an explanation of the concrete event in its uniqueness. Moreover, Pannenberg asserts that the creative dynamic of the Spirit has an element of indeterminacy. In it the distinctive form that comes forth from it is concealed before it takes concrete shape in the creature. Nevertheless, it is from the Spirit's dynamic, according to the relations of the Logos, that the distinct, independent, and self-centered form of creaturely operation arises.[376] Thus through the Logos, everything acquires its appropriate form and place in the order of creation. In this regard the Spirit mediates the working of the Logos in creation as also in the incarnation.[377]

3.7.4 Creation and Eschatology

Pannenberg contends that the goal of all creation, not just humanity, is to share in the life of God. However, the creation is sighing under the burden of corruption (Rom 8:21ff.).[378] Exactly like in the case of the human fall, one must view this sighing as an expression of the presence of the life-giving Spirit of God in creatures. The creative Spirit is vitally at work throughout creation, but also suffers with his creatures on account of their corruptibility prior to taking creative shape in humanity, in one human being.[379] Pannenberg notes that creation's destiny to be in fellowship with God, in the sense of sharing in the fellowship of the eternal Son with the Father through the Spirit, has not yet found direct fulfillment in the existence of each individual creature. Hence, all creation is waiting for the manifestation of sonship (Rom 8:5) in us, by which the creatures themselves will also be "sons" (Rom 8:19; cf. Gal 4:5ff.). This will take place through the last eschatological figure who appeared in the person of Jesus Christ for he will

---

375. Pannenberg, *Systematic Theology* vol. 2, 110.
376. Pannenberg, *Systematic Theology* vol. 2, 110.
377. Pannenberg, *Systematic Theology* vol. 2, 114.
378. Pannenberg, *Systematic Theology* vol. 2, 136.
379. Pannenberg, *Systematic Theology* vol. 2, 136.

be accepted by the Spirit into the fellowship of the Son with the Father (cf. 1 Cor 15:45ff.).[380]

Along with this understanding, one must see the consummation of creation as well. The same applies to Paul's theology that the Spirit who is imparted to believers guarantees them a share in the future consummation (Rom 8:23; 2 Cor 1:22; 5:5; Eph 1:13ff.).[381] The basis of this thesis is that the Spirit is the creative origin of the new life of resurrection (Rom 8:11). In this way the Jewish view of the Spirit as the origin of all life is seen from the new perspective of the eschatological future. The Spirit's function as the origin of all life is not viewed as preparation for the completion of his work by bringing forth the new eschatological life (1 Cor 15:45ff.).[382] Pannenberg argues that, "We have to regard the dynamic of the Spirit in creation from the very outset in terms of the coming consummation, i.e., as an expression of the power of his future. This is true even where the connection with the final eschatological future is not apparent. In the life of creatures this connection is concealed from both general observation and scientific description."[383]

3.8 Holy Spirit and Eschatology

In fact, one can definitely argue that the whole theology of Pannenberg leads to the doctrine of eschatology and it is the central focus of his theology.[384] One can note that Jesus' resurrection is the basis on which Pannenberg develops his eschatology because in the resurrection of Jesus, the eschatological reality itself became an event that occurred in him in proleptic anticipation.[385] Pannenberg writes that, "The eschatological

---

380. Pannenberg, *Systematic Theology* vol. 2, 138.
381. Pannenberg, *Systematic Theology* vol. 2, 98; Pannenberg, *Systematic Theology* vol. 3, 454.
382. Pannenberg, *Systematic Theology* vol. 2, 98; according to Pannenberg, "The theologically based idea of a dynamic of the divine Spirit working creatively in all events as the power of the future is by no means alien to a philosophy of nature. It stands in a demonstrable relation to the basic data of science. Indeed, it can set scientific descriptions in a new light by putting them on a different plane of argumentation." See Pannenberg, *Systematic Theology* vol. 2, 101.
383. Pannenberg, *Systematic Theology* vol. 2, 98.
384. See Christiaan Mostert, *God and the Future: Wolfhart Pannenberg's Eschatological Doctrine of God* (London: T & T Clark, 2002).
385. Wolfhart Pannenberg, *Basic Questions in Theology: Collected Essays*, vol. 1, trans.

salvation at which Christian hope is directed fulfills the deepest longing of humans and all creation even if there is not always a full awareness of the object of this longing. Yet like the reality of God it transcends all our concepts."[386] For Pannenberg the Spirit is the agent who leads creation into this *eschaton*. Before focusing on the role of the Spirit and eschatology, one needs to explore the understanding of the primitive church with regard to eschatology and Spirit.

3.8.1 Eschatology and the Primitive Church

Pannenberg asserts that the Spirit was an eschatological reality for primitive Christianity. Israelite prophecy had promised that the Spirit would be poured out at the end of history, and they experienced this eschatological reality as already present in the gift of the Spirit. Through the *pneuma* the *doxa* promised for the eschatological consummation is already poured out now on Christians.[387] Pannenberg insists that in order to understand the unique character of the Spirit's reality in primitive Christianity, one must go back to the significance of the Spirit in the Old Testament. In the Old Testament, the Spirit was not primarily a source of supernatural knowledge, rather the ground of life in the most inclusive sense.[388] The conceptual association of Spirit, wind, air, and breath must be noted in this connection (Ps 104:29-30; cf. Gen 1:2; 2:7; Ezek 37:5ff.). Moreover, the extra-ordinary works of the Spirit which provided the basis for the Israelite charismatic phenomena also must be understood from this perspective because the Israelites believed that a special endowment of the creative Spirit is necessary for outstanding activities, as in the case of the heroes, prophets, singers, and artists. This always involves a special working of the Spirit in which all life has its origin.[389] Moreover, for Israel, the distinction between

---

George H. Kehm (Philadelphia: Westminster, 1983), 179; see also Pannenberg, *Systematic Theology* vol. 2, 316.
386. Pannenberg, *Systematic Theology* vol. 3, 527; see Pannenberg, *The Idea of God*, 192-210.
387. Pannenberg, *Jesus – God and Man*, 169.
388. Pannenberg, *Jesus – God and Man*, 170.
389. Pannenberg, *Jesus – God and Man*, 170; at the end of history, according to Israelite expectation, the Spirit of God will become effective in a special way. According to Isaiah 11:2, the Messiah not only will be filled and driven by the Spirit but the Spirit will be continually joined with him, will rest upon him. Third Isaiah (Isa 61:1) also understood the Messiah as the bearer of the Spirit: the Spirit rests upon him. According to Second Isaiah (Isa 42:1), not only the Messiah but all Israel will share in God's Spirit in a new way

the eschatological and the present working of the Spirit consisted in the fact that in the *eschaton* the Spirit will be poured out and will rest upon humanity. In other words, he will be completely given to them. Therefore, we can expect that life in the *eschaton* will be a higher life in comparison to the earthly condition in which humanity do not really have the Spirit of God but can only be driven by him.[390]

3.8.2 Eschatology Is Actualized through the Spirit

According to Pannenberg, salvation has not yet been definitively actualized for humanity merely by the mission of the Son. Salvation will be actualized only when the work of the Spirit completes it because the work of the Spirit is to bear witness and glorify the Son and his work in the hearts of believers.[391] Pannenberg notes that Jesus Christ is not identical with the eschatological people of God that is formed with the coming of God's kingdom.[392] Certainly this people belongs so closely to Jesus as the Messiah that in the representation of the eschatological Supper it can be called his body. Yet it is the Spirit who by its work builds up this body and testifies to Jesus Christ in the hearts of believers.[393] In this sense, it is from the Spirit of God that the Christian world expects the eschatological fulfillment of believers, the changing of our mortal life into the new life of the resurrection of the dead (Rom 8:11).[394] Moreover, creation's waiting for the manifestation of the children of God (v. 19) suggests that its own corruptibility will be vanquished by the power of the life-creating Spirit as the world is transformed

---

at the end of history (cf. Ezek 36:27; Isa 44:3). In his last vision in night Zechariah saw the Spirit of Yahweh come upon all peoples; the wagons of the winds bear *ruah Yahweh* into the four corners of the world (Zech 6:1-8). Finally, Joel also promises the pouring out of God's Spirit on "all flesh" for the end time (2:28). Luke understood this prophecy as fulfilled in primitive Christianity (Acts 2:17ff.). The Spirit of God was understood in all this as power of life, not primarily as the source for knowledge which could not otherwise be attained. This remained true in postexilic Judaism. Wisdom and insight, called effects of the divine Spirit in Isaiah 11:2 were also understood in Judaism as one effect of the divine Spirit of life among others. See Pannenberg, *Jesus – God and Man*, 170.
390. Pannenberg, *Jesus – God and Man*, 171.
391. Pannenberg, *Systematic Theology* vol. 3, 551.
392. It seems that here Pannenberg is emphasizing the role of the Spirit in the eschatological salvation of human beings. However, one should note that Pannenberg never neglects the significance of the Son in the act of eschatological salvation at all. See for example Pannenberg, *Systematic Theology* vol. 3, 531f.
393. Pannenberg, *Systematic Theology* vol. 3, 551.
394. Pannenberg, *Systematic Theology* vol. 3, 551.

into the new creation of a new heaven and a new earth, just as the first creation already was created by the power of the Spirit. Of course, this work of the Spirit is closely related to Jesus Christ.[395]

Pannenberg notes that the distinctive nature of the eschatological gift of the Spirit consists of the fact that by the conferring of the Spirit as a lasting possession of believers, participation in the eternal life of God is made possible and also their resurrection to a new life in fellowship with God is guaranteed. The basis for this is that the Spirit is mediated by the Son incarnate in Jesus Christ, and in such a way that with faith in Jesus comes also a granting and receiving of participation in his sonship.[396] Thus the mediating of the gift of the Spirit by the Son and its eschatological content as participation in the death-defeating life of God go hand in hand. The gift of the Spirit to humanity at creation and the *charisms* of the old covenant as well are simply anticipatory signs of this eschatological gift. By this gift alone the Spirit binds itself to the lives of the recipients in such a way that even death can no longer separate these lives from its creative power.[397]

Moreover, Pannenberg notes that the subject of eschatology has a special relation to the work of the Spirit and it is clear when we consider that the Spirit is at work in both individuals and society. This is true already of its work in creation, because in virtue of its ecstatic nature of the life of individuals it is linked in many ways to others and their fellowship. Similarly, the redemptive work of the Spirit relates to both individuals and society.[398] If by baptism individuals receive the Spirit as an abiding gift, the gift is not for each in isolation, rather it binds all of them into the fellowship of the

---

395. Pannenberg, *Systematic Theology* vol. 3, 551; Schwarz argues that Pannenberg was one of the first systematic theologians in the twentieth century to show that the eschatology of Jesus had significance beyond our existential now. He directed our attention again to the relationship of eschatology and time and to the necessity of integrating nature and existence. See Schwarz, *Eschatology*, 145-146.
396. Pannenberg maintains that the Christ event is an eschatological event and it is spiritual. It is the reality of the new *aeon*. For this reason, Christians have a share in the Spirit to the extent that they share in the Christ event – in their confession to Jesus as the *Kyrios* (1 Cor 12:3), in the active verification of their belonging to him, in trust in him, and in the hope in one's own future participation in the life that has appeared in Jesus; resurrection from the dead. Because Jesus Christ, as the revelation of God, is one with the essence of God, the Spirit of Christ dwelling in Christians and going out from Jesus is the Spirit of God. See Pannenberg, *Jesus – God and Man*, 174.
397. Pannenberg, *Systematic Theology* vol. 3, 10.
398. Pannenberg, *Systematic Theology* vol. 3, 552.

church (1 Cor 12:13). This twofold function of the Spirit for the lives of individuals and the establishing of fellowship among them relates his work to the twofold form of eschatological hope, which on the one side aims at the totality of individual life and on the other side at the consummation of fellowship through peace in righteousness. The consummating work of the Spirit integrates these two aspects and in this way overcomes the antagonism between individuals and society that holds sway in this present world.[399] The linking of the future to the present through the reconciling of individuals and society on the basis of reconciliation with God by confession of Jesus Christ is the work of the Spirit. By the Spirit the eschatological future is present already in the hearts of believers. His dynamic is the basis of anticipations of eschatological salvation which is already in the incomplete history of the world. This was so in the incarnation of the Son in time, which took place by the Spirit's power, in his baptism and finally in the confirmatory event of the resurrection of the crucified one. In the same way the gift of the Spirit, as the pledge of future glory (2 Cor 1:22; 5:5; Eph 1:14; cf. Rom 8:23), constitutes the eschatological assurance of salvation for those who are linked to Jesus by faith and baptism.[400]

In short for Pannenberg, pneumatology and eschatology belong together because the eschatological consummation itself is ascribed to the Spirit, who as an end-time gift already governs the historical present of believers.[401] Conversely then, eschatology does not merely have to do with the future of consummation that is still ahead. It is also at work in our present by the Spirit. Hence, the presence of the Spirit also means already the overcoming of sin and death. If sin and death are to be finally overcome only in the eschatological consummation, victory over them is already in process in the present work of the Spirit, and above all in its presence as a gift in believers. Thus we experience the presence of the eschatological consummation itself as proleptic manifestation of the Spirit who in the eschatological future will transform believers, and with them all creation, for participation in the glory of God.[402]

---

399. Pannenberg, *Systematic Theology* vol. 3, 552.
400. Pannenberg, *Systematic Theology* vol. 3, 552.
401. Pannenberg, *Systematic Theology* vol. 3, 553.
402. Pannenberg, *Systematic Theology* vol. 3, 553.

3.8.3 Eschatology as the Final Phase of Salvation in the Spirit

Pannenberg notes that in the early church the confession of faith ascribed the work of creation to the Father, reconciliation to the Son, and the appropriating of salvation and consummation to the Spirit. However, "These so-called appropriations were seen to be right only on the basis of the principle of the unity of the Trinity in all its outward works, but they give expression to the fact that each of the three phases in the divine economy of salvation stand in this particularity close relation to one of the three divine persons, so that in this economy of the divine action, as it takes its course, we find expressed the inner differentiation of the Trinitarian life of God."[403] According to Pannenberg, the third and final phase of the economy of salvation is accomplished by the Spirit because it is the Spirit of fellowship between the Father and the Son and also fulfills the unity of the Trinity. Moreover, the Spirit enables the eschatological participation of creation in the life of the Trinity by its glorification. Hence, the glorification of God by creatures and the creatures by God are the two sides of one and the same event.[404] Pannenberg notes that the Spirit is the origin of life and the prophetic inspiration who stands in relation to the work of the creation. The third period in the economy of salvation was then ascribed to the Father because only in the eschatological consummation will there be full knowledge of the Father (1 Cor 13:12). If the tripartite division and relating of the third and concluding phase of the economy of salvation to the Spirit prevailed in the early symbols, it was because the Spirit is not only the creator of earthly life and the Spirit of prophecy but also the creator of the new life and as such is now given to believers as the pledge of their future glorification. Without losing their distinction from God, creatures receive through him a share in the life of God.[405] This takes place in two ways: by the gift of the Spirit in believers and his outpouring on the fellowship of the church on the one side, and by transfiguring the world and life in the eschatological consummation on the other. The question of the meaning

---

403. Pannenberg, *Systematic Theology* vol. 3, 554.
404. Pannenberg, *Systematic Theology* vol. 3, 554.
405. Pannenberg, *Systematic Theology* vol. 3, 554.

of this twofold nature constitutes the core of the problem when we ask concerning the relation between pneumatology and ecclesiology.[406]

Moreover, Pannenberg advocates that participation in the eternity of God is vital because it can overcome the disintegration of human life into moments that are sundered by the march of time and integrate such moments into unity and totality. Unbroken participation in eternity presupposes acknowledgement of the deity of God by creatures as they thank him as their creator and invoke and extol his deity.[407] To do this they must overcome the separation from God that the ego wants to be as God has caused in order that in the creatures' relation to God there may be manifested that of the Son to the Father. Overcoming this separation takes place by the working of the Spirit. The Spirit lifts the ego above itself and in confession of Jesus Christ as the Son of the eternal Father gives it a share in his filial relation to the Father. It thus becomes possible for humanity to take their life as a whole from the hand of the creator in self-distinction from God and hence in acceptance of other creatures too. Nevertheless, Christians also expect a future in which all their temporal life will be permeated by praise of God and will be glorified as incorruptible fellowship with this eternal God.[408] Pannenberg notes that the resurrection of the dead and renewal of creation may be seen as the act by which God through his Spirit restores to the creatures' existence that is preserved in his eternity the form of being-for-themselves. Here the identity of creatures needs no continuity of their being on the time line but is ensured by the fact that their existence is not lost in God's eternal present.[409] All individuals go into eternity at the moment of death, the eternity that means judgment as well as salvation and transfiguration. However, it is only at the end of the ages that all those who sleep in Christ receive in common by the Spirit of God the being-for-self of the totality of their existence that is preserved in God, and thus live with all others before God.[410] As the kingdom of God is already present by faith, so the future of God is also present already as regards to purging by the fire

---

406. Pannenberg, *Systematic Theology* vol. 3, 555.
407. Pannenberg, *Systematic Theology* vol. 3, 601.
408. Pannenberg, *Systematic Theology* vol. 3, 602.
409. Pannenberg, *Systematic Theology* vol. 3, 606.
410. Pannenberg, *Systematic Theology* vol. 3, 606-607.

of the divine judgment. Purging from sin takes place already by penitence and baptism for the forgiveness of sins. Thus purging is anticipated by judgment.[411] It takes place through baptism insofar as baptism anticipates the sign of death that the baptized will die as the consequence of sin. Since they are here linked to the death of Christ, this act is also the basis of the hope of new life that has been manifested in Jesus and that is now operative by the Spirit, so that another life is opposed to the life of sin that has fallen victim to death, a life that will grow as that which is subject to sin withers away.[412]

3.8.4 Role of the Spirit in Judgment and Transfiguration

Pannenberg contends that in primitive Christian testimonies the importance of the Spirit in the event of final consummation is not so plain as the function of the gift of the Spirit as an anticipation of eschatological salvation. Yet it would be a mistake to conclude that the Spirit will have no decisive function any longer at the eschatological consummation itself. Instead, the gift of the Spirit can have for the believer's present the significance of an anticipation and pledge of future salvation only because the Spirit is also the power of God effecting future salvation.[413] We find a clear starting point for this truth in what is said about the hope of the resurrection from the dead. Such statements are also basic for an understanding of the gift of the Spirit in the believer's present. Romans 8:11 tells that the indwelling of the Spirit who raised up Jesus Christ guarantees believers that God will raise up their mortal bodies, doing so indeed through the Spirit of Christ who is already imparted to them.[414] That means the Spirit is the creative source of the resurrection of life both in relation to the resurrection of Jesus and in relation to others. In this regard we must recall that the biblical stories view the Spirit as the source of all life already at creation. It is not surprising,

---

411. Pannenberg notes that according to the New Testament message, future judgment is already at work in the present (Rom 1:18; 12:31). But only in the case of penitence and baptism does it take place in the sense of salutary cleansing from sin. See Pannenberg, *Systematic Theology* vol. 3, 612.
412. Pannenberg, *Systematic Theology* vol. 3, 612.
413. Pannenberg, *Systematic Theology* vol. 3, 622.
414. Pannenberg, *Systematic Theology* vol. 3, 622.

then, that the same Spirit should be thought of as also the divine origin but will be wholly penetrated by the Spirit and remains related to him. This is why Paul calls the new eschatological life a spiritual life, a life wholly permeated by the divine creator Spirit (1 Cor 15:42-46), a life that will also be immortal by virtue of this indissoluble reaction to the divine Spirit as the source of life (vv. 50ff.).[415]

Following the above argument, Pannenberg notes that the work of the Spirit is at all events fundamental for the eschatological salvation event of the resurrection of the dead. Now for Paul resurrection also means change into a new life (vv. 51-52), and there thus results a relation between the Spirit's work and the theme of judgment as well. This mortal cannot without change acquire a share in immortality (cf. v. 50). But if we are right that the idea of a changing of this earthly life carries with it a link to judgment, then the work of the Spirit stands related also to the executing of judgment. For this reason John the Baptist proclaimed that the coming Son of man would baptize with the Spirit and fire (Lk 3:16; Mt 3:11) in contrast to the water baptism that John himself administered as a sign of this future event. Thus the Spirit does in any event have a function at the judgment (Isa 11:4; 2 Thess 2:8). Moreover, according to Paul, the Spirit enables us to judge ourselves and others (1 Cor 2:13ff. cf. 11:31), and present self-judgment of this kind preempts a sentence of condemnation at the last judgment (11:31; cf. 5:5). Perhaps associated with this Spirit-given ability to judge is the idea sometimes found in Paul that in company with Christ believers will judge the world and even angels (6:2-3) at the coming judgment.[416]

Thus it becomes obvious that the Spirit is the source of salvation, of the new and eternal life, and also the organ of judgment. The whole compass of its eschatological work comes into view if we think of it as distinctively a work of glorification.[417] The thought of glorification links the new life of resurrection to the moment of judgment that carries with it the transfiguration of this earthly life by means of relation to God the Father and to the praise of God. The glorifying of God in this comprehensive sense is the proper and final work of the Spirit, who is also the creator of life, the

---

415. Pannenberg, *Systematic Theology* vol. 3, 622.
416. Pannenberg, *Systematic Theology* vol. 3, 623.
417. Pannenberg, *Systematic Theology* vol. 3, 623.

source of all knowledge, as also of faith and hope and love, and therewith, too, of freedom and peace, and hence of the common life of creatures in mutual recognition that is perfected in the kingdom of God and that finds expression already in sign in the fellowship of the church. In all these areas the work of the Spirit always aims at the glorifying of God in his creation, and in his eschatological work this aspect will come to the fore in an overwhelming way, gathering together and transforming all else.[418]

3.8.5 Eschatological Glorification and the Spirit

Pannenberg notes that the divine light of glory brings believer's liberation from the scum of sin and death even as the wicked have to fear it as a consuming fire. The power at work here is the Spirit of God, who will lead creatures to the eschatological praise of God by which they glorify God, just as they for their part participate in the glory of God through Christ (Rom 8:18; Phil 3:21; cf. 1 Pet 5:1).[419] In the eschatological consummation the glorification will be mutual. On both sides, this mutual glorification is the work of the Spirit. But we are led to the ultimate profundities of this event by the recollection that in the depiction offered in John's gospel this mutual glorification marks the relation between the Father and the Son. The Son has glorified the Father (17:4) by proclaiming his lordship. He now asks the Father to glorify him by reaccepting him into his original fellowship with the Father (v. 5). In this way, and by the participation of believers in the common glory of the Son and the Father (v. 22), the glorifying of the Father by the Son will come to fulfillment. This event, however, is mediated by the work of the Spirit, who will glorify the Son in believers (16:14) by bringing their remembrance of Jesus and his message, and therewith the Father.[420] The Spirit has a part already in the mutual glorification of the Father and the Son, for the Son glorifies the Father in the power of the Spirit who rests on him (1:32), and the Father answers the request for the glorifying of Jesus as his Son not merely by raising him from the dead but also by sending the Spirit, who glorifies the Son in believers. The glorifying of believers, however, their transforming by the light of the divine glory,

---

418. Pannenberg, *Systematic Theology* vol. 3, 624.
419. Pannenberg, *Systematic Theology* vol. 3, 625.
420. Pannenberg, *Systematic Theology* vol. 3, 625.

draws them into the eternal fellowship of the Father and the Son by the Spirit. It is the same Spirit who is already conferred on believers by their baptism and who enables them, as they participate in the filial relationship of Jesus Christ to the Father, to call on God as their Father, and in so doing to have a foretaste of their own eschatological consummation as participation in the eternal life of the trinitarian God in the fellowship of the Son and the Father by the Spirit.[421]

4. *Summary*

We have already dealt with the pneumatology of Pannenberg profoundly. While dealing with his theology of the Spirit, one thing is clear that on both sides of the Atlantic the theology of Pannenberg has opened a new front in a theological sense. A good many issues that theologians had widely assumed to be more or less settled have suddenly been brought vigorously to the fore. While much contemporary work continues to build upon the foundations established by the dialectical theology of the twenties, Pannenberg takes a critical look at those foundations and proposes a quite different direction for theological development.[422] This statement is somewhat true with regard to the pneumatology of Pannenberg as well because Pannenberg has clearly shown the integral connection of pneumatology to the rest of systematic topics. Thus the critical role of the Spirit of God in all God's dealings with us is shown, from creation to sustenance, to life, to salvation, to Christian community, and to the consummation of creation at the *eschaton*. Kärkäinen makes a beautiful evaluation of the pneumatology of Pannenberg by stating that he has been quite successful in approaching several key systematic topics from a distinctively pneumatological perspective, the doctrine of God being the prime example, and anthropology, Christology, ecclesiology, and eschatology being other obvious instances.[423] Moreover, one should appreciate Pannenberg for framing an integral connection between God's

---

421. Pannenberg, *Systematic Theology* vol. 3, 626.
422. See Tupper, *The Theology of Wolfhart Pannenberg*, 253.
423. Veli-Matti Kärkäinen, "The Working of the Spirit of God in Creation and in the People of God: The Pneumatology of Wolfhart Pannenberg," *The Journal of the Society for Pentecostal Studies* vol. 26, no.1 (Spring 2004), 31.

original purposes (creation), present work (providence and salvation), and future consummation (eschatology) with the Spirit.[424] Another significant point is that Pannenberg has saved the doctrine of the Spirit from being limited to the narrow portals of individual salvation. He has revived the biblical idea of the Spirit as life force underlying and sustaining all life, rather than considering the Spirit as divorced from the corporeal or creaturely.[425] Pannenberg's use of the concept of "ecstatic" has advanced the perennial problem of the "one and many" because both in his doctrine of the Trinity as well as in his ecclesiology and eschatology, his specific formulation of the doctrine of the Spirit would help to grasp the dynamic relationship between the individual and community.[426]

Although one can recognize the positive contributions of Pannenberg and appreciate that his suggestions are creative and evocative, there are certain theological issues in his pneumatology as well. Firstly, Pannenberg's discussion of personhood within the field theory description seems less agreeable. This is due to Pannenberg's use of the natural sciences extending beyond theological descriptions of creation and applying them to the divine Godhead. This transposition of categories from observable phenomena in the physical world to explication of the divine being leads in this case to theologically unsatisfactory results. In other words, Pannenberg's field theory seems to become more than simply a model or a paradigm for theological reflection, inasmuch as he seems to make an actual identification between various physical fields of force and angels. Is there ultimately a qualitative distinction between Pannenberg's proposal to understand angels as physical force fields and identifying God with the sum total of physical laws of forces in the universe? Is not it a danger in Pannenberg's program

---

424. Kärkäinen, "The Working of the Spirit," 31.
425. A corollary advantage here is that Christian theology once again is able to talk to the issues of contemporary science, which, with its post-Newtonian mindset (and significant advances especially in the new physics' understanding of matter approaching the spirit/spiritual), is again turning to philosophy and perhaps to some kind of religious discourse to explore the mystery of life. Pannenberg's vision of theology as a public discipline, while out of vogue among the postmodernists with their own private discourses, is a powerful call to Christian theology to engage the public arena. Pannenberg's bold attempt to utilize the field concept of modern physics and his dialogue with science to penetrate the origins of the cosmos are most welcome advancements. See Kärkäinen, "The Working of the Spirit," 31.
426. Kärkäinen, "The Working of the Spirit," 32.

that angels, the Spirit, and ultimately God could be reduced to metaphors for physical realities?[427] It does not mean that theologians should not use natural sciences seriously, but rather their relevance should perhaps be more limited to describing created, rather than uncreated realities. Secondly, although Pannenberg's whole endeavor is to move away from the subjective description of the Spirit, it seems that he also falls into the same trap. For example, Pannenberg also maintains that human beings must be brought to reason into order to perceive the Jesus as the revelation of God. However, this reason itself must be illuminated by the Spirit to recognize the truth of the *kerygma* and shows itself as the power of the word. Thus Pannenberg also identifies the Spirit with pious subjectivity, "an unaccountable *asylum ignorantiae*, a tendency that thwarts the life and power of the church."[428] Finally, from a Pentecostal point of view, Pannenberg has totally neglected the existence of Pentecostal/charismatic movements although he dealt with the pneumatology in all crucial topics in his *Systematic Theology*. Moreover, even though he speaks of the ministry of the Spirit in the church or individual life, he makes only a marginal discussion with regard to *charism* which is very important when we construct a pneumatology. Even when he argues for an appropriate balance between pneumatology and Christology as a proper foundation for the church, Pannenberg does not give ample weight to the charismatic structure of the church, which is received by ecumenical theologians also apart from the Pentecostal/charismatic communities.[429]

---

427. Worthing, *God, Creation, and Contemporary Physics*, 123.
428. Tupper, *The Theology of Wolfhart Pannenberg*, 267.
429. Kärkäinen, "The Working of the Spirit," 33-34.

CHAPTER SIX

Come Creator Spirit: Towards A Theology of the Holy Spirit

1. *Introduction*

We are living in the midst of a pneumatological renaissance and hence one of the most exciting developments in theology recently has been an unprecedented interest in the person and work of the Holy Spirit.[1] The Roman Catholic theologian Elizabeth Dreyer describes this renewed enthusiasm clearly. She writes:

> Renewed interest in the Holy Spirit is visible in at least three contexts: individual Christians who hunger for a deeper connection with God that is inclusive of all of life as the needs of the world; the church that seeks to renew itself through life-giving disciplines and a return to sources; and the formal inquiry of academic philosophy and theology. In effect, one can hear the petition, "Come Creator Spirit" on many lips these days.[2]

This particular interest led to this study, starting with the question of the person and role of the Spirit in the Protestant systematic theology with

---

1. Kärkäinen, *Pneumatology*, 11.
2. Elizabeth A. Dreyer, "Resources for a Renewed Life in the Spirit and Pneumatology: Medieval Mystics and Saints," in *Advent of the Spirit: Orientations in Pneumatology*, Conference Papers from a Symposium at Marquette University, 17-19 April, 1998 (Unpublished), 1.

the assumption that the Spirit has not been given adequate consideration in its theological endeavor. Moreover, the Spirit and its role has been a neglected field in Western Christianity and its theological articulations due to its concentration on Christology. Having discussed Western systematic theology and its development throughout the centuries, especially in the twentieth century, the study proves that the person of the Spirit and its role cannot be subordinated to Christology or neglected without consideration due to the significance of its role in the divine action with regard to humanity and the universe.

One cannot overlook that there was neglect of the person[3] and role of the Spirit in the initial centuries of the church. However, as noted in the second chapter, there was a big shift in Reformation theology which contributed a new paradigm to pneumatology. A significant theme of the Reformation theology was the relation between Word and Spirit. One cannot discuss either the spirituality of the Reformation or its doctrine of the Spirit apart from this theme. Badcock argues that, "If the doctrine of the *deity* of the Spirit is the central concern of the fathers of the fourth century, and if the *filioque* preoccupies medieval pneumatologists, then the intrinsic connection of the work of the Spirit in the church with the doctrine of the Word of God as written and preached constitutes the distinctive emphasis of the pneumatology of the Reformation."[4] One can note here that the emphasis shifted away from the doctrine of the deity of the Spirit, though it is obviously acknowledged, to the real point of interest, the doctrine of the work of the Spirit in the subjective appropriation of the content of the gospel of grace by the believer. There is no pure reduction of the Spirit to Word, whether outer or inner, but instead a fairly expansive view of the Spirit as mediating the incorporation of the believer into Christ, so that a theology of the head of the church and its

---

3. It is a fact that the concept of "person" developed much later with regard to the three "persons" in the Trinity. However, the concept of "person" is referred to here in order to show how seriously the Spirit has been neglected in the initial centuries of the church. I do not neglect that the fourth-century theologian Gregory of Nyssa has developed a very sophisticated concept of the person in the context of his attempts to clarify the paradox of the Trinity – a single God comprising three distinct persons. See, Lucian Turcescu, *Gregory of Nyssa and the Concept of Divine Persons* (New York: Oxford University Press, 2005).
4. Badcock, *Light of Truth*, 86.

members emerges, in keeping with the strongly Christocentric character of the theology of the Reformation.[5]

The new pneumatological paradigm presented by the Reformation theology was questioned with the emergence of liberal theology in the West. The liberal theological trend, which emerged during the Enlightenment era associated with Schleiermacher, claimed that the trinitarian doctrine of the Spirit is both misleading and unnecessary.[6] On the one hand, it does not match up with the religious facts, and on the other, it is not essential to explicate the significance of the person and work of the Spirit. In response to this liberal trend, much of both nineteenth and twentieth century theology has been a running argument against the virtues and vices of such a theology. The leading figure in this movement was Karl Barth and the others who were influenced by his theology, namely theologians like Moltmann and Pannenberg. Since their pneumatology already has been extensively discussed in the preceding chapters, the intent here is to briefly compare their pneumatological approaches and positions in order to outline what the Protestant pneumatology can learn from them today.

2. *Pneumatological Approaches*

In response to liberal theology, the basic theological position which Barth employed is neo-orthodoxy. This neo-orthodox stance of Barth is clearly reflected in his pneumatology as well. In a sense, one can argue that Barth's entire theology is an elucidation of the third article of the Nicene Creed, beginning with the Christian existence in the Spirit and necessarily including a theology of the Son and the Father as well. In other words, Barth holds a theology of the subjective aspect of revelation which is parallel to Christology and falls expressively under the heading of the Spirit. As noted earlier, the impulse of Barth's pneumatology was a reaction to 19th

---

5. See Badcock, *Light of Truth*, 92.
6. One should note that the doctrine of the Holy Spirit traditionally has been concerned with the doctrine of the person of the Spirit and its divinity. The doctrine of the Trinity has served as the framework within which this question has been addressed in Christian thought. The attack of liberal Protestantism was against this traditional framework. See Badcock, *Light of Truth*, 109.

and 20th century idealistic, scholastic, and existential theologies, which were intellectually obliged to employ a philosophical anthropology as the necessary propaedeutic to a theology of the Christian faith.[7] Moreover, it springs from a pneumatic reinterpretation of neo-Protestantism, Roman Catholicism, and Christian existentialism. Thus one can conclude that the pneumatological approach of Barth can be said to be an appreciation for and a corrective of the rightly formulated bipolar (history and faith) structure of these theologies which must be mediated some way.[8] Thus Barth proposes an elliptical model for Christian theology in which the two are interrelated, but absolutely different. It focuses on God's revelation in history and human's subjective apprehension of that revelation in faith. The mediating principle of this bipolar structure is the work of the Spirit and not human's consciousness, ecclesiastical life, or their self-understanding.[9] In addition to that, Barth's pneumatology attempts to answer Hegelian, Thomistic, and Bultmannian exaggerations in the direction of an unbiblical, overly anthropological notion of the Spirit as well.

Over against Barth, Moltmann's pneumatology is holistic in nature, which is apparent in his critique of the manifold forms of captivity to which the doctrine of the Spirit has been subjected throughout history, especially to the anthropocentric, the ecclesiocentric, and the Christocentric forms. The *anthropocentric* captivity sees the Spirit operating only in the interiority of the human subject and excludes the whole realms of the body, social relations, and nature as pneumatologically irrelevant. The *ecclesiocentric* captivity confines the role of the Spirit to the church, the Word and sacraments, its authority, its institutions, and ministries, and dismisses history and nature as possible loci of the activity of the Spirit. The *Christocentric* captivity restrains the Spirit only as the Spirit of Christ and thus subordinates its role to the subjective side of God's self-revelation in Christ like in Barth's pneumatology. Hence, Moltmann's theological imperative is to liberate the Spirit from these confinements and to restore it as *the liberating power of the humanity and the universe.* In sum, Moltmann presupposes a holistic and liberating pneumatology, comprising a holistic anthropology

---

7. Rosato, *Karl Barth's Theology of the Holy Spirit*, 352.
8. Rosato, *Karl Barth's Theology of the Holy Spirit*, 353.
9. Rosato, *Karl Barth's Theology of the Holy Spirit*, 353.

and theology of creation which comprehends human beings in their totality and embraces the wholeness of the community of creation of both humanity and nature.[10] Moltmann's pneumatological approach focuses on the immanence of God in creation and stresses the coinherence of God and the world by the presence of the Spirit in sufferings and the anticipation of the eschatological rebirth of all things through the Spirit.[11]

In comparison to Barth and Moltmann, Pannenberg's pneumatological approach is quite different. His entire focus is to show that the Christian understanding of God is crucial to the pursuit of knowledge. Hence he attempts to construct a bridge between theology and science via the idea of contingency and the concept of field. His whole focus is to develop a new synthesis of theology and human scientific learning rivaling the great intellectual construction of the Middle Ages.[12] In this process he lays theological claims to scientific understandings. By pointing out the intellectual impossibility of conceiving the universe as a completely autonomous system and by asserting the importance of contingency in physical processes, Pannenberg steadfastly refuses to allow science to declare its independence from theology.[13] This is apparent in his "field pneumatology" which lies in the biologically based idea that life is essentially ecstatic.[14] Each organism lives in an environment that nurtures it and it is oriented by its own drives beyond the immediate environment on which it is dependent for its future. These dimensions are aspects of the presence of the Spirit. Thus for Pannenberg, life in the Spirit is the destiny of all creation – most specifically the human person – and that the fullness of this life is an eschatological reality.[15] In sum, Pannenberg's pneumatology is an attempt to provide ways

---

10. Anselm Kyongsuk Min, *The Solidarity of Others in a Divided World: A Postmodern Theology After Postmodernism* (New York: T & T Clark, 2004), 204.
11. Bauckham, *The Theology of Jürgen Moltmann*, 22.
12. Carol Rausch Albright and Joel Haugen, eds., *Beginning with the End: God, Science, and Wolfhart Pannenberg* (Peru, Illinois: Open Court, 1997), 31.
13. Stanley J. Grenz, "Scientific" Theology/"Theological" Science: Pannenberg and the Dialogue between Theology and Science," *Zygon* vol. 34, no. 1 (March 1999), 160.
14. See a discussion in Bernd Oberdorfer, "The Holy Spirit – A Person? Reflection on the Spirit's Trinitarian Identity," in *The Work of the Spirit: Pneumatology and Pentecostalism*, ed. Michael Welker (Grand Rapids: Eerdmans, 2006), 36ff.
15. Grenz, "Scientific" Theology, 164.

3. A Comparison of Pneumatological Approaches

Having discussed the pneumatological approaches of Barth, Moltmann, and Pannenberg, this section endeavors to make a brief conversation between the pneumatological approaches of these theologians with the intention of outlining the major results of current research. This would lead to a presentation of some of the major aspects carved out from the pneumatology of these theologians which is beneficial for the Protestant pneumatology today and also for further researches and reflections.

3.1 Spirit: Cinderella in the Trinity

While dealing with pneumatology, one of the main questions to arise is about the divinity of the Spirit and its position in the Trinity. This has been an issue even from the fourth century of Christianity onwards particularly with regard to Arianism. Consequently, one can argue that the greatest achievement of the patristic era in pneumatology was the definition of the divinity of the Spirit at the council of Constantinople in 381, from which we have what is traditionally called the Nicene Creed. Thus two things are important when dealing with the Trinity, namely, the divinity of the Spirit and the *filioque* clause in the Nicene Creed. In Barth's pneumatology, in agreement with the Nicene Creed, one can find the virtual identity of the immanent Trinity and the economic Trinity because what God is in revelation, he is antecedently in himself. Since the Spirit completes the work of revelation and reconciliation effected through the Son, in obedience to the Father, therefore the Spirit, as far as the *opus ad extra trinitatis* is concerned, shares in the fullness of the divine essence. What is true *ad extra* is equally true *ad intra*. This argument is the core of his demonstration of the divinity of the Spirit and it conforms to the norm that the immanent Trinity is not different from the economic Trinity. However Barth does not accept the Eastern position of the procession of the Spirit from the Father alone. But on the other hand, Moltmann affirms the divinity of the Spirit and strongly rejects the addition of the *filioque* clause into the

Nicene Creed and the Western defense for this clause. However, he admits along with Barth that the Spirit proceeds from both the Father and the Son. Moltmann understands Spirit as the divine energy of life and the cosmic energy by which it expands the traditional notion of the communion of the Spirit to encompass the whole community of creation. Pannenberg also follows the same line of thought as does Moltmann and affirms the divinity of the Spirit and never supports the *filioque* clause due to the fact that it presupposes that Father-Son constitutes a relation of origin in the Godhead to which the spiration of the Spirit is secondary, and thus it entails a type of subordinationism in the Trinity. His rejection of *filioque* leads to a fuller pneumatology than that often found in Western theology, as is evident throughout the dogmatic literature.[16] Although the *filioque* clause has been an issue in Christendom for a long time, what is significant for today is to realize how decisively the collective voice of Christendom (on both sides of the schism between the East and the West) expressed the conviction that the Spirit was distinct from the Son and the deity must be described in trinitarian terms.[17] This is what is important for today as well.

Having discussed the divinity of the Spirit and the *filioque* clause – the two significant aspects in Trinity – the major focus now is to discuss the doctrine of Trinity itself. Barth's doctrine of the Trinity shows that God who reveals himself according to Scripture is one in three distinctive modes of being and subsisting in their mutual relations: Father, Son, and the Holy Spirit. His epistemological concern is to avoid the danger of incipient Arianism which he sees as inherent in the very nature of all so-called social analogies of the Trinity. Although this formulation seems to achieve the described balance between oneness and threeness in God, the rendering of *persona* as "mode of being" is problematic. That means this notion to suggest that there are three persons in God in the sense of three human persons slides inevitably into Arianism, because a juxtaposition of human persons denotes a separateness of being which is completely excluded in God.[18] Barth's position is that we do not have to do with three distinct selves in God, or three separate self-conscious agents. Rather we have to do

---

16. Grenz, *Reason for Hope*, 51.
17. C. F. D. Moule, *The Holy Spirit* (London: Continuum, 2000), 49.
18. Hart, *Regarding Karl Barth*, 102.

with one divine subject who exists in three distinct ways or "modes" both in relation to the created other, and in relation to himself. And Spirit is "the common factor" between the mode of existence of the Father and the mode of existence of the Son. Thus God is one personal entity subsisting in three internal self-relations. The trinitarian "persons" do not have their own distinct subjects of inherence rather they are modes of existence of one common divine subject. Although this statement would sound like Sabellian modalism, it affirms three simultaneous and not consecutive modes or ways of subsisting in God, namely, one divine subject exists now and eternally as Father, Son, and Holy Spirit in creation. However, Barth does not provide an adequate model for trinitarin thinking, and the charges of Sabellianism can be leveled against his doctrine of Trinity.[19]

Moltmann has worked out his own trinitarian position in polemical response to Barth. The logic of Barth's trinitarian ontology when pushed to its natural and logical conclusion transfers the subjectivity of action to a deity concealed behind the three persons.[20] Over against this Moltmann resists any reduction of the concept of "person" to the concept of "relation" and stresses the absolute hypostatic diversity of Father, Son, and the Spirit. Thus Moltmann insists that there are three unique and irreducible subjects in God and not one and emphasizes the diversity of hypostatic prerogatives. For him Father, Son, and the Spirit are ultimately distinct in their activities, both in their relationship to the created other, and in relation to one another in the eternal life of God. This relationship is possible only through the Spirit. He advocates the unity of the Trinity as a unity of *koinonia*, a unitedness, or at-one-ment of the three distinct persons, a *perichoretic* unity in which the persons "indwell" one another.[21] This can be noted in his social doctrine of the Trinity which makes it clear that the divine persons are all subjects in relation to each other and there is no fixed order in the Trinity. The traditional descending order Father-Son-Spirit is only one of the changing patterns of trinitarian relationships in God's history within the world.[22] In short, for Moltmann the unity of God is unity of persons

---

19. Hart, *Regarding Karl Barth*, 104.
20. Moltmann, *The Trinity and the Kingdom of God*, 135.
21. Hart, *Regarding Karl Barth*, 111.
22. Bauckham, *The Theology of Jürgen Moltmann*, 16.

in relationships. They are both three and one in their mutual indwelling (*perichoresis*), and as a *perichoresis* it is a unity which can open itself to and include the world within itself. Thus a social trinitarianism grounds a relationship of freedom and equality.[23]

In many respects, Pannenberg's doctrine of the Trinity is strikingly similar to Moltmann's. For Pannenberg, God is revealed as three – Father, Son, and the Spirit – but nevertheless as a unity who are bound together through the Spirit. Pannenberg's description of the Trinity can be captured by two phrases: the threeness of the one God and the unity of the triune God.[24] He advocates that the doctrine of Trinity must be grounded on revelation, that is, on the economy of salvation – on the way that the Father, Son, and the Spirit come to appearance in the event of revelation and relate to each other. This doctrine cannot be developed from a consideration of the being and attributes of God. Instead, the latter can only be considered in connection with the trinitarian revelation of God as Father, Son, and the Spirit.[25] Pannenberg looks to Jesus' relationship to the Father, especially as it was expressed in his message concerning the rulership of God, for an understanding both of Jesus as the Son and of the Spirit as a third form different from, yet bound to, Father and Son. In this way the doctrine of the Trinity ultimately becomes the interpretation of the relationship of Jesus to the Father and to the Spirit.[26]

In conclusion one can argue that the Spirit is the *Cinderella* in the Trinity who cannot be subjugated or pushed into third place. Moreover, the trinitarian sharing teaches that the Christian life is fundamentally a sharing in the Son's relationship with the Father in the power of the Spirit through the economic earthing of that same relationship in the particular flesh of Jesus of Nazareth. We do not share in the persons of the Son, but precisely in the relationship which he has with the Father and the Spirit in the triune life of *koinonia*. This is the trinitarian shape of the *kerygma* and the Christian experience of God. Yet if the incommunicability of the threeness in God is denied, and persons are defined as modes of subsistence

---

23. Bauckham, *The Theology of Jürgen Moltmann*, 17.
24. Grenz, *Reason for Hope*, 45.
25. Grenz, *Reason for Hope*, 48.
26. Grenz, *Reason for Hope*, 49.

of just one ontological divine subject, all this takes on a decidedly different and problematic hue.[27] The study proves that Pannenberg's concept of the Trinity seems to be more consistent in holding together the being of God and his acts without losing the former in the latter, which is a theological task of great difficulty.[28]

3.2 Pneumatology Subordinate to Christology?

In the Christian theology, the person and work of the Spirit has generally been understood to be somehow hidden beneath Christ. Consequently, the Spirit has not received the degree of sustained treatment in the history of theology that Christ has been given. This aspect has already been discussed in detail in the first chapter. Nevertheless the present study proves that the Spirit cannot be subordinate to Christology because the Spirit plays a special role in Christology. The analysis of Barth's pneumatology proves this argument because his pneumatology is closely knit together with Christology. He insists the active involvement of the Spirit in the whole life and ministry of Jesus Christ which culminates in his death and resurrection through the Spirit. Moreover, he emphasizes the presence of Christ in the Spirit even after his ascension. That means Christ is active in the world through the Word and Spirit, awakening and calling human beings to life of discipleship. Barth does not limit the work of the Spirit in the church alone rather advocates that the Spirit is present as the Spirit promised to non-Christians as well.

In this respect, it is not Barth alone, but Moltmann also develops a Spirit Christology[29] which stresses the life and ministry of Jesus as the messianic prophet, which takes place in the power of the Spirit. This emphasis belongs

---

27. Hart, *Regarding Karl Barth*, 108.
28. See a discussion in Roger Olson, "Trinity and Eschatology: The Historical Being of God in Jürgen Moltmann and Wolfhart Pannenberg," *Scottish Journal of Theology* vol. 36, no. 2 (1983), 213-227.
29. I realize that "Spirit Christology" might not be the right term to use. Spirit is used by liberals to refer to the divine in Jesus, not to the third person of the Trinity dwelling in him. "Spirit Christology" as used by them refers to an inspirational, not an incarnational, Christology. When I refer to Spirit Christology, I do so in an orthodox way that preserves the trinitarian distinctions. Spirit Christology enriches but does not replace *Logos* Christology. See Paul W. Newman, *A Spirit Christology: Recovering the Biblical Paradigm of Christian Faith* (Lanham: University Press of America, 1987).

within Moltmann's mature view of the trinitarian history of God with the world, in which the trinitarian persons interrelate in changing and reciprocal ways. He understands the history of Jesus not in a narrowly Christological framework, but rather in a fully trinitarian way, in which Jesus lives in relation to his Father and the Spirit. The uniqueness of Jesus' trinitarian relationship to the Father and the Spirit prevents this Spirit Christology from being a degree Christology as other forms of Spirit Christology have often been.[30] Moreover, Moltmann's Christology deals with the old question of the relationship between the Christ of the Spirit and the Spirit of Christ. Thus one can see the significance of the Spirit in the Christology of Moltmann as well. Pannenberg also is not different from Moltmann in his Christology, because for Pannenberg as well the whole life and mission of Jesus Christ is linked to the Spirit. He understands that it is the presence of the Spirit in Jesus that makes him divine and hence one cannot separate God and the Spirit of God. Moreover, since the Father sends the Son and the Spirit for the fulfillment of the mission through the obedience of the Son and the work of the Spirit, the self-actualization of the trinitarian God is taking place in the world. The main aspect in the whole theology of Pannenberg is the significance of the resurrection of Jesus Christ and the role of the Spirit in this event. For Pannenberg the Spirit is the almighty God and its breath blows through all creation. Pannenberg insists on the universal significance of resurrection and establishes the universal resurrection of the dead and the judgments in the *eschaton*. In short, the study proves that one cannot keep the Spirit hidden behind Christ like before, but rather the role of the Spirit in the whole person and life and work of Jesus Christ must be adequately established. Moreover, one should not forget that we have a Christology today because we have a pneumatology. Thus without considering the role of the Spirit in the whole person and life and work of Jesus Christ, we cannot develop a Christology at all.

3.3 Significance of the Spirit and Its Role Today

We have already discussed the whole dilemma of Trinity and Christology with regard to the Spirit because a clear understanding of the person and

---

30. Bauckham, *The Theology of Jürgen Moltmann*, 20.

role of the Spirit in the Trinity and Christology is very important since the whole activity of the Spirit in the world is always trinitarian. Having understood the relationship and role of the Spirit in the Trinity and Christology, the following discussion will attempt to focus particularly on the work of the Spirit on different planes.

Anthropology is a social science developed into a discipline during the modern era and assumed many of the presuppositions of Enlightenment thinking. However, the anthropology of liberal Protestantism was diverse and invited criticism particularly from a theological conservative angle. For example, Barth's whole theology can be seen as a response to this new development marking his early dialectical theology.[31] Since the focus of this study is the person and role of the Spirit, Barth, Moltmann, and Pannenberg have recognized the role of the Spirit in human beings in a unique manner. Beginning with the dialogical relationship between God and human beings, Barth insists that human beings are sinful and astray from God. Since God is transcendent, no one can see him without God's willingness to reveal himself. Having dealt with the role of the Spirit in the revelation of God, Barth insists that the Spirit makes human beings free to receive divine revelation and makes them the abode of God as God's own temple. While Barth insisted on the transcendence of God, Moltmann's anthropology insisted on God's *immanence* in the human experience, and the *transcendence* of human beings in God. Although Moltmann emphasizes the Spirit's immanence and transcendence in human beings, he never argued for an anthropocentric pneumatology, rather argued for a holistic pneumatology. However, his emphasis upon the religious experience of human beings is significant when dealing with anthropology and the Spirit. In comparison to Barth and Moltmann, Pannenberg frames an innovative anthropology and working of the Spirit in human beings which is very significant for today due to the following reasons: firstly, soul and body are

---

31. In their doctrine of the Spirit, the liberals confused the Spirit of God with the human spirit, since their intention was to speak of God only from the standpoint of human religious sensibility. This assessment of liberal pneumatology is a view that has heavily influenced Barth's followers, who regularly describe the liberal tradition as erring by identifying the Spirit with the religious and ethical aspects of the human mind, thus treating the Spirit as merely a cipher for the realm of moral and spiritual values. See Badcock, *Light of Truth*, 11-112; see also Heron, *The Holy Spirit*, 113.

constitutive elements of human life that belong together and cannot be reduced to one another. Secondly, creaturely life has an eccentric character, which is referred to the divine power of the Spirit that works upon it. Thirdly, Pannenberg equates the work of reason to the life-giving working of the divine Spirit although he makes a distinction between the two. Fourthly, Pannenberg insists on the crucial role of the life of imagination, which unites receptivity and freedom (This aspect would be dealt in detail in another section). Finally, Pannenberg understands personality as a special instance of the working of the Spirit which is the anticipatory presence of the final truth of things. Like Moltmann, Pannenberg also insists that the Spirit is transcendent and immanent in human beings because it allows doing justice to the transcendence of God and at the same time to explain God's immanence in his creation.

Taking a lead from anthropology, it is reasonable to look into the doctrine of redemption in the theology of Barth, Moltmann, and Pannenberg. Barth argues that human beings are sinful and hence they need a redeemer. This redeemer is the revelation of God in Jesus Christ. Although Jesus is the redeemer, the actualisation of redemption is fulfilled through the joint working of the Son and the Spirit because there must be a particular awakening power of God in human beings, which is the Holy Spirit. Thus the Spirit within the hearts and lives of human beings prepares and enables them to receive revelation and to have fellowship with God. On the other hand, Moltmann's attempt is to get beyond the traditional Protestant pattern which simply adds together Christ and the Spirit or the objectivity of salvation and its subjective appropriation. Moltmann insisted that it was only in the appropriating work of the Spirit that salvation was actually conferred, by way of Word and sacrament. Thus for him the Spirit is the atoning power of Christ's substitution among and in the perpetrators. This leads Moltmann to move away from the traditional doctrine of justification with new proposals. That means, for him justification is not just forgiveness of sins but rather it should lead to the regeneration of the individual and to the renewal of the cosmos. It must be an *experience of the Spirit*, and also *eschatologically oriented*. The significance of Moltmann's doctrine of redemption is the Spirit's active role in theodicy. Moltmann understands the suffering of God on the cross as God's loving solidarity with the world in suffering. Thus Moltmann extends the traditional soteriological interest in the cross to embrace both the question of human guilt and liberation from it, and also the question of human suffering and liberation from it.[32] Thus Moltmann lets the divine love reach humanity through Jesus Christ's identification on the cross with humans in their condition. His resurrection represents salvation for them only because he died for them, identified with them in their suffering of God's absence.[33] By recognizing God's presence, as the incarnate son of God, in the abandonment of the cross, Moltmann brings the dialectic of cross and resurrection within God's own experience. In all these, it is the Spirit who makes the whole life and mission of the Son fruitful and effective in the world. The study shows that to a certain extent Pannenberg comes closer to Moltmann in his delineation of redemption and reconciliation, because he believes that reconciliation is the work of the Son and Spirit without excluding the Father. Moreover, Pannenberg also extends redemption towards the cosmos as well and hence he insists that God's Spirit is not only active in human redemption rather the Spirit is at work already in creation as God's mighty breath.

The doctrine of anthropology and redemption finally leads to the whole pneumatological question of the church. Does the church's authority underlie theology, or is the Bible the immediate instrument of the Holy Spirit? Is the Holy Spirit as the gift of grace mediated through the church, or is the Spirit in a more fundamental sense the Lord of the church? Does the Spirit work in the church in such a way as to make a continuing revelation possible? Barth has dealt with these issues in detail and finds the church as a work which takes place among human beings in the form of a human activity by Jesus Christ through the Spirit. When Barth spins out his comprehensive account of the closeness of Jesus to the church, he is careful to affirm that it is all happening in the power of the Spirit. Barth recognized the fundamental characteristic of the church as the outpouring of the Spirit and insists that the existence of the church should be seen in the backdrop of the mystery of Pentecost. On the other hand, Moltmann finds the church as part of the history of the creative Spirit. It means that it is

---

32. Bauckham, *The Theology of Jürgen Moltmann*, 11.
33. Bauckham, *The Theology of Jürgen Moltmann*, 11.

the concrete form in which human beings experience the history of Christ. Moltmann describes his ecclesiology alternatively as "messianic ecclesiology" or "relational ecclesiology." Both terms serve to situate the church within God's trinitarian history with the world, more specifically, within the mission of the Son and the Spirit on their way to the eschatological kingdom. Moltmann insists that the Spirit mediates the eschatological future to the world between the history of Jesus and the coming of kingdom. Hence church is an anticipation of the messianic kingdom, because it is created by and participates in the mission of the Spirit. Its defining characteristics are therefore not its own, but those of the presence and activity of Christ and the Spirit.[34] The relational ecclesiology of Moltmann indicates that because of its place within the trinitarian history, the church does not exist for itself, but only in relationships and can only be understood in its relationships.[35] It participates in the messianic history of Jesus and lives in the presence and powers of the Spirit, existing as a provisional reality for the sake of the universal kingdom of the future. Since the mission of the Spirit on the way to the kingdom includes but is not confined to the church, the church cannot absolutize itself, but must fulfill its own messianic role in open and critical relationships with other realities, its partners in history, the other world religions, and the secular state.[36]

In comparison to Barth and Moltmann, Pannenberg's ecclesiology is basically pneumatological due to his understanding that the Spirit who works in salvation is the Spirit of creation. Thus he finds a continuity between the order of life in creation and the order of higher life in the church. This lends a rational flavor to the Christian conception of salvation, because the soteriological activity of the Spirit marks the completion of the Spirit's creative work. At the same time, like Moltmann, Pannenberg also insists that the Spirit of salvation is the eschatological Spirit who makes present the future reality of the kingdom of God. This eschatological orientation lends a hopeful character to ecclesiology.[37] Pannenberg holds that the church is not identical with the kingdom of God but rather, it is a sign of the kingdom's

---

34. Bauckham, *The Theology of Jürgen Moltmann*, 13.
35. Bauckham, *The Theology of Jürgen Moltmann*, 13.
36. Bauckham, *The Theology of Jürgen Moltmann*, 14.
37. Grenz, *Reason for Hope*, 151.

future of salvation because this future of God is already present in it and it is accessible to people through the church, through its proclamation and its liturgical life. Thus he realized the church as a proleptic sign of the kingdom, and the people of God live from the proleptic presence of the future among them mediated by the Spirit.[38] Like Moltmann, Pannenberg also found the church as a community constituted by the Son and the Spirit, to which the Spirit is given as a gift. The aim of such community of the Spirit is the fellowship of the believers. While dealing with the church as a fellowship of believers, Pannenberg insists on the significance of the relationship between the creation on the one side and eschatology on the other. He makes such a connection to avoid a defective constricting of pneumatology from a Christological angle that finds the Spirit's work in the fellowship of believers only and hence often unrealistically exaggerates this work. It seems that the present day churches are away from the influence of the Spirit and this is a big issue. Hence the concern today is very important when we deal with the position of the Spirit in the present day churches. McIntyre writes:

> This ubiquitous presence of the Holy Spirit in the life and faith of the early Church and its members imparted a definable character to the whole Church which I find to be missing from the Church of today. Further, it was so integral to the very nature of the Church and of Christianity as the New Testament understood it, that to lose that centrality of the Spirit and to abandon it as if it were a product of first and second century cultural conditioning would be, if proved, to commit a treason which could become endemic to modern Christianity.[39]

The study proves that the role of the Spirit in creation should be given more consideration due to the fact that the creation is in fact an activity of the Spirit. This is obvious in the mature pneumatology of Moltmann that deals with the creator Spirit and the role of the Spirit in the whole creative activity of God. In his doctrine of creation, Moltmann advocates a sense

---

38. Grenz, *Reason for Hope*, 151.
39. McIntyre, *The Shape of Pneumatology*, 72.

of human community with nature, respecting nature's independence and participating in mutual relationship with it. Human beings, as the image of God, have a distinctive place within nature, but they are not the owners or rulers of nature. They belong with nature in a community of creation which is not anthropocentric but theocentric.[40] In order to theologically ground this emphasis on mutual relationships in nature, Moltmann appeals to his doctrine of God, whose own trinitarian community provides the model for life of God's creation as an intricate community of reciprocal relationships.[41] Moltmann's position is that not only is the trinitarian God a *perichoretic* community as well as God's creation is a *perichoretic* community, but also God's relationship to his creation is one of mutual indwelling. With this dominant notion of the Spirit in creation, Moltmann is able to take the non-human creation into his general concept of the trinitarin history of God. The Spirit in creation co-suffers with creation in its bondage to decay, keeping it open to God and to its future with God. Humanity's eschatological goal does not lift us out of the material creation but confirms our solidarity and relatedness with it. In all this Moltmann achieves a strong continuity between creation and redemption, and between the creative and salvific activities of the Spirit.[42] One of the significant aspects in Moltmann's pneumatology is that he understands the Spirit as the divine source of life. This emphasis serves a number of important purposes for today. Firstly, it breaks the narrow association of the Spirit with revelation, which was the characteristic of Barth's theology, and so enables Moltmann, in one of his more emphatic rejections of Barthian positions, to give experience – the experience of God in the whole of life and of all things in God – a place in theology, not as alternative to but in correlation with the revelatory word of God. The Spirit of life is God experienced in the profoundity and vitality of life lived in God. As the Spirit is the wellspring of all life, so all experience can be a discovery of this living source in God.[43] Secondly, "a holistic pneumatology" corresponds to Moltmann's holistic Christology and soteriology. As the Spirit of life, the Spirit is not related to the "spiritual" as opposed to

---

40. Bauckham, *The Theology of Jürgen Moltmann*, 17.
41. Bauckham, *The Theology of Jürgen Moltmann*, 18.
42. Bauckham, *The Theology of Jürgen Moltmann*, 18.
43. Bauckham, *The Theology of Jürgen Moltmann*, 22.

the bodily and material, or to the individual as opposed to the social, or to the human as opposed to the rest of creation.[44] The Spirit is the source of the whole of life in bodiliness and community. Life in the Spirit is not a life of withdrawal from the world into God, but the vitality of a creative life out of God, which is characterized by love of life and affirmation of all life.[45]

Over against Moltmann, Pannenberg calls for a new understanding of the Spirit in relation to the biblical statement of its role in creation. One should not forget that the field theory of the Spirit lays the background for Pannenberg's idea of creation. Pannenberg asserts that the creation of the world is a different kind of divine action, which can be explained as outward action. In opposition to Barth, Pannenberg argues that creation does not necessarily proceed from the fatherly love of God that is oriented from all eternity to the Son. For Pannenberg, preservation also goes with creation because it is a living occurrence, continued creation, and a constantly new creative fashioning that goes beyond the given original existence. Pannenberg tries to reconcile the statements about the Spirit as the origin of life with a modern understanding. Here Pannenberg brings in the significance of the concepts of force and field from modern physics. Moreover, his introduction of space and time in the working of the Spirit is an innovative effort to be expounded further today. When dealing with Spirit and time, Pannenberg further links the theme of time with the eschatological consummation. Pannenberg's linking of theology and science is apparent especially in the doctrine of creation which opens possibilities for dialogue between theology and science.

The pneumatology of Barth, Moltmann, and Pannenberg finally leads to the eschatological reality which is very important to all of them. Barth's theological realism is a decidedly eschatological realism. For him it is the reality of the resurrection in which the eschatological kingdom of God became manifest and which, in the proclamation of the gospel, continuously represents itself by the power of the Spirit. Barth did not waver from this fundamental point that the reality to which theology refers is the eschatological reality of the risen Christ and the new life into which

---

44. Bauckham, *The Theology of Jürgen Moltmann*, 22-23.
45. Bauckham, *The Theology of Jürgen Moltmann*, 23.

we are drawn by the Spirit. Barth understands *parousia* as the goal of the history of the church, the world and the individual, as the author of the general resurrection of the dead and the fulfiller of universal judgement. In comparison to Barth, Moltmann's eschatological approach develops from a cosmological perspective. What is important for him is not only that the world is "on the way" to becoming a new creation, but also that Christians should be actively engaged in combating the causes of the suffering of humanity and the destruction of nature and the ecosystem until that day comes. Like Barth, the resurrection of Jesus Christ stands at the centre of the eschatological framework of Moltmann. Moltmann's eschatology is predominantly a theology of hope whereas Pannenberg focuses much on a theology of the future. They are in strong agreement about the central importance of eschatology in Christian faith and theology.[46] Like Barth and Moltmann, Jesus' resurrection is the basis on which Pannenberg develops his eschatology because in the resurrection of Jesus, the eschatological reality itself became an event that occurred in him in advance. It is from the Spirit of God that the Christian world expects the eschatological fulfillment of believers, the changing of our mortal life into the new life of the resurrection of the dead. The linking of the future to the present through the reconciling of individuals and society on the basis of reconciliation with God by confession of Jesus Christ is the work of the Spirit. By the Spirit the eschatological future is present already in the hearts of believers. Thus the presence of the eschatological consummation itself is a proleptic manifestation of the Spirit who in the eschatological future will transform believers and all creation for participation in the glory of God.

3.4 The Christian Spirituality

In the study of pneumatology, one cannot overlook the significance of spirituality of a person since a person's spirituality is in fact life in the Spirit. In other words, "Christian spirituality is the study and experience of what happens when the Holy Spirit meets the human spirit."[47] Christian spirituality involves a choice we make to "know and grow" in our daily relationship with

---

46. See an analysis in Mostert, *God and the Future*, 4ff.
47. Edith M. Humphrey, *Ecstasy and Intimacy: When the Holy Spirit Meets the Human Spirit* (Grand Rapids: Eerdmans, 2006), 31.

Jesus Christ by submitting to the ministry of the Spirit in our lives. Spirit and spirituality go hand in hand. Barth has given considerable significance to the aspect of spirituality and the role of the Spirit in the life of human beings. Of course, one should remember that spirituality is not only a Christian phenomenon, for it appears in Buddhist, Hindu, Muslim, Jewish, and neo-Platonist forms. Moreover, it is a form without theistic connotations of any kind as well, since the subject and the practice have acquired other meanings too. Nevertheless, the bonding of the Spirit to spirituality and its appropriations are to be understood on the analogy between the spirit that is in humans and distinguishes them from the rest of creation, and the Holy Spirit as the third person of the Trinity.[48] One should remember that spirituality is a characteristic of all human beings and it happens where the human spirit fully realises that spirituality.[49] Spirituality is the domain of the Spirit and the accomplishment of spirituality. It is the purpose of all human beings because spirituality is the *catharsis*, the renewal, the reintegration of the human spirit and even its salvation. A theology that is really a theology of the Holy Spirit must be, in addition to all else, capable of opening up new dimensions of the spiritual life and a theology of the experience of God. This will be, from this point of view, concerned more with life than with truth, the life lived "in God."[50]

3.5 The Spirit and Imagination in Human Beings

We have already noted that imagination is one of the main themes of Pannenberg with which he deals extensively in relation to anthropology. This aspect has to be considered seriously when dealing with the pneumatology for today because the Spirit fulfills an imaginative role in human beings. In other words imagination is the medium which the Spirit employs in achieving certain purposes in the lives of human beings. The Spirit uses the medium of imagination in fulfilling certain important things in the lives of human beings as follows: The Spirit stimulates, controls, and confirms the imagination in human beings by alerting them to situations in which human imagination might act. Perhaps human reason can be devious and

---

48. McIntyre, *The Shape of Pneumatology*, 279.
49. McIntyre, *The Shape of Pneumatology*, 279.
50. Badcock, *Light of Truth*, 143-144.

wayward as human imagination, but the presence of the Spirit in both cases powerfully controls them and brings them within the influence of redemption from sin and error.[51] Moreover, imagination is the medium which the Spirit employs in enabling human beings to understand, interpret, and appropriate Scripture because Scripture is not a single, homogeneous entity but composed of different forms of literature – history, myth, poetry, prayer, and praise – and the imagination works in different ways in relation to each.[52] This imaginative role of the Spirit is the clue to one way of expressing the mystery of the presence of Jesus Christ in the sacraments. The significance of prayer which is the *epiklesis* in the Eucharistic office is that the Spirit may once again be active in the fusion of imagination which Christ enacted once, so that a person by receiving the bread and wine may by faith be made a partaker of his body and blood.[53] Moreover, the Spirit has employed imagination to enable us to transcend our rootedness in time. For the present, our interest is in the belief in the communion of saints and what it means. The communion of saints, as we may understand it in the light of the concept of presence-in-absence, is constituted by the Spirit, who stimulates the imagination to hold as present in those "whom we have loved and lost awhile." The consequence is that this fellowship is not at the mercy of our reminiscences, which may come and go, but bonded by the love of the Spirit itself.[54] Yet another area in which the Spirit uses the imagination is to create space, that is, to create a space for ourselves, for each one of us. Each one needs space in the midst of pressure and demands of modern life and it is not only legitimate but also necessary. What is important in the demand for space is the opportunity for people to come to terms with themselves, to execute an honest self-assessment, to think about the way ahead, to analyse relations to friends and colleagues, to undo the pressures and to seek a measure of self-peace, or alternatively to prepare for a course of action.[55]

---

51. McIntyre, *The Shape of Pneumatology*, 270.
52. McIntyre, *The Shape of Pneumatology*, 271.
53. McIntyre, *The Shape of Pneumatology*, 273-274.
54. McIntyre, *The Shape of Pneumatology*, 274-275.
55. McIntyre, *The Shape of Pneumatology*, 275-276.

3.6 The Spirit, Ecumenism, and a Theology of Religions

One of the major areas in which the Spirit can work is in the unity of the divided churches if the churches are ready to accept the move of the Spirit. It is wrong to adopt a sectarian approach and despise insights of others which have been the experience for long centuries now. Recognising this aspect, Barth, Moltmann, and Pannenberg have advocated the unity of churches by recognising the move of the Spirit in the churches. In their understanding, we need to be catholic in space and time loving the church of every century and every continent because the Spirit desires unity in Christ's body. They recognise that there is variety in theology to celebrate, and each tradition has its logic and grammar. Of course there are strengths and weakness in them, but theology is enriched when matters are considered ecumenically. Moreover there are gifts of God scattered over a wide variety of places in the church. They need to be gathered together which will be possible only when the churches are ready to recognise the move of the Spirit.[56] Everyone should understand that the unity of the church stems from unity in Christ because the members of the church are united with one another in Christ. However, this is possible only in the move of the Spirit because the Spirit has a special way of bringing people together.[57] The Spirit brings people together in freedom, without coercion, pressure, or persuasion. This does not mean that the unity that is advocated is uniformity, since this can be brought about only by imposition. On the other hand, the Spirit unites the greatest diversity, while respecting it.[58] The Spirit promotes unity by infusing Christians with a powerful inclination towards others, a movement of friendship which forms the true basis of unity. The church contains a wellspring of friendship which is stronger than all the factors making for dispersion or hostility in it.[59] Thus unity is possible when the churches are ready to respect each other by recognising the move of the Spirit in the churches.

---

56. Pinnock, *Flame of Love*, 238.
57. Jose Comblin, *The Holy Spirit and Liberation*, trans. Paul Burns (New York: Orbis Books, 1989), 96.
58. Comblin, *The Holy Spirit and Liberation*, 96.
59. Comblin, *The Holy Spirit and Liberation*, 97.

While advocating for the unity of the churches, Barth, Moltmann, and Pannenberg also note the question of a theology of religions. The major query of the theology of religion can be, is there salvation, or are there at least salvific elements, outside the church/Christ? In a sense Barth, Moltmann, and Pannenberg strongly talk about non-Christians and other religions or human communities which leads to this pertinent question of other religions and the Spirit. The study proves that Christians should learn to appreciate an unlimited ministry of the Spirit in the cosmos.[60] That means the Spirit's work in salvation should not be read as a denial of the creative work on which it is based. Clark Pinnock outlines some helpful tips in support here. Firstly, appreciating the creator Spirit one must see that God is involved in creation down to the last detail.[61] Secondly, the creator Spirit keeps links between creation and redemption open and alive. The Spirit is the power of redemption only because it is first the power of creation. Pinnock writes that, "By acknowledging the work of the Spirit in creation, we are actually allowed a more universal perspective where Spirit can be seen as seeking what the Logos intends and where one can believe and hope that no one is beyond the reach of grace. A foundation is laid for universality if indeed the Spirit pervades the world and if no religion is closed to his influence."[62] Thirdly, if the whole world is the field of the Spirit's activity, recognition of the creator Spirit gives us the opportunity to relate theology to the origins of the world and its environment in fresh ways.[63] Amos Yong also advocates a theology of religions from a pneumatological point of view.[64] He maintains that Christians must be open to learn from other religious traditions similarly to the ways in which Christians have learned from the findings of the sciences over the centuries. Christian theologies have adjusted to scientific advances, sometimes easily, other times with considerable difficulty and struggle. Why not with religions, which themselves are not static entities but are dynamically reconstituting themselves even as Christian traditions are? So Christians should be open

---

60. Pinnock, *Flame of Love*, 49
61. Pinnock, *Flame of Love*, 62.
62. Pinnock, *Flame of Love*, 63.
63. Pinnock, *Flame of Love*, 63-64.
64. See Amos Yong, *Beyond the Impasse: Toward a Pneumatological Theology of Religions* (Grand Rapids: Baker Academic, 2003).

to learn from other religious traditions because of the unfinished character of Christian identity.⁶⁵ He sets three "axioms" for the development of a pneumatological theology of religions in a trinitarian framework. Firstly, God is universally present and active in the Spirit. Secondly, God's Spirit is the life-breath of the *imago Dei* in every human being and the presupposition of all human relationships and communities, and finally the religions of the world, like all else that exists, are providentially sustained by the Spirit of God for divine purpose.⁶⁶ I am not arguing that other religions are salvific as such, but rather, other religions are important for the Christian church because they can help the church to penetrate more deeply into the divine mystery. The acknowledgment of the gifts of God in other religions by virtue of the presence of the Spirit – as well as the critical discernment of these gifts by the power of the same Spirit – means a real trinitarian basis to Christianity's openness toward other religions. It also enables the church to enter into dialogue with other religions.

3.7 The Spirit and a Renewed Eco-theology

It seems that there is a big shift from the anthropocentric theology to an ecocentric theology today. This is obvious in the theology of Moltmann and Pannenberg as well. The present-day ecological crisis points Christianity and Judeo-Christian traditions to Genesis 1:26 and such related texts. That means, nature has served humans and Christianity has sanctioned an exploitative ethic allowing science and technology to serve as instruments of exploitation. Recognising this issue, Moltmann strongly argues against this tradition and insists that human beings and animals should be able to live on the earth equally. Moltmann's "immanent transcendence" helps us to focus on the integral relationship between the Spirit and nature. The Father is the creating origin of creation, the cosmic Christ is the ground for the existence of creation and the Spirit of life is the life-giving origin. Thus the immanence of the Spirit undercuts the dualism of God and nature that has

---

65. Amos Yong, *The Spirit Poured Out on All Flesh: Pentecostalism and the Possibility of Global Theology* (Grand Rapids: Baker Academic, 2005), 240.
66. See Veli Matti Kärkäinen, ""How to Speak of the Spirit Among Religions": Trinitarian Prolegomena for a Pneumatological Theology of Religions," in *The Work of the Spirit: Pneumatology and Pentecostalism*, ed. Michael Welker (Grand Rapids: Eerdmans, 2006), 54.

characterised Western tradition. There is also an eschatological emphasis: it is not enough to affirm the goodness of creation in the past. We must also affirm the anxious waiting of creation under futility as the Spirit "groans" for the liberation of creation and its children.[67] Sallie McFague also appreciates the role of the pneumatology in earth healing because it reveals the immanent presence of God in creation through the Spirit.[68] Mark Wallace also advocates for an ecological pneumatology on the basis of the biblical literary images like water, light, dove, mother, fire, breath, and wind.[69] He writes that, "My conviction is that the role of theology in the current situation should be to reconstitute a biblical rhetoric that will serve the desires of all species to survive and flourish .... The Spirit comes with healing in her wings to a world that cries out for transformation and renewal. The Spirit comes to a world in need of refreshment as the breath of God and the water of life. The Spirit comes to a world fragmented by violence and suffering with the promise of health and wholeness for all creation."[70]

3.8 The Spirit and Feminist Pneumatology

When considering an alternative pneumatology, one cannot overlook the significance of the sexist language as an issue in Christian theology. Since we are living in an age of "hermeneutics of suspicion" what was comfortable before is questioned today. Hence, the argument is that the language of God as Father can lead to the social oppression of women. Hence there are theologians who try to address the Spirit as feminine.[71] Although the current study does not directly talk about a feminist pneumatology, there are discussions made by Moltmann and Pannenberg on the rights of women. Elizabeth Johnson does not follow the addressing of the Spirit as feminine for this practice subordinates women to men by reducing their identity and limiting them to roles that involve mothering or service. Hence Johnson insists that we need to model our relationships on Sophia,

---

67. See Moltmann, *Spirit of Life*, 31-38.
68. See Sallie McFague, *Models of God: Theology for an Ecological, Nuclear Age* (Philadelphia: Fortress, 1987), 72.
69. See Mark Wallace, *Fragments of the Spirit: Nature, Violence, and the Renewal of Creation* (Harrisburg: Trinity Press International, 2002), 4.
70. Wallace, *Fragments of the Spirit*, 225-226.
71. See a discussion in Comblin, *The Holy Spirit and Liberation*, 49ff.

in whose "inner relatedness" there is no subordination. Sophia herself is "unknowable mother of all."[72] That means there is a mutual relationship between women and Sophia in the sense that a woman is the image of Sophia and Sophia herself is the image of women. Johnson insists that naming God as feminine Sophia "points to the mystery of triune Holy wisdom as *imago feminae*."[73] As noted earlier Moltmann and Pannenberg have discussed the significance of Spirit of God in wider perspective which includes the feminine aspect as well. Pushing this argument further, one must not limit in framing an alternative pneumatology with the woman alone rather must focus further on the ecofeministic pneumatology. In the words of Johnson, "The exploitation of the earth, which has reached crisis proportion in our day, is intimately linked to the marginalisation of women, and that both of these predicaments are intrinsically related to forgetting the Creator Spirit who pervades the world in the dance of life."[74] Thus linking the challenges of women and creation from a pneumatological perspective is quite necessary today.

3.9 Science and Religion: A Dialogue in the Spirit

Theology and science should be partners in the search of truth. Science helps theology to understand the physical world, and theology helps science to detect the meaning and mystery of what is. Theology is fruitful for science because it raises issues that go beyond science. Science is important for theology because it helps us to connect the biblical text with created reality.[75] Integrating scientific learning with theological insight is an important challenge for serious theology. This has been one of the major concerns of Moltmann and Pannenberg, which is largely absent in Western dogmatics.[76] However, belief in the creator Spirit gives a perspective that is consonant with the biblical witness and new understandings of the universe. The doctrine of the Spirit may provide a conceptual way for understanding

---

72. Johnson, *She Who Is*, 51-53; 143-144.
73. Johnson, *She Who Is*, 215.
74. Elizabeth A. Johnson, *Women, Earth and Creator Spirit* (New York: Paulist Press, 1993), 2.
75. Pinnock, *Flame of Love*, 65.
76. See Pannenberg, *Systematic Theology* vol. 2, 76-115 and also the major pneumatological works of Moltmann.

continuing creation. Thus theology and science can be better integrated with the help of the Spirit. Pinnock notes that, "The dynamic order that we are glimpsing in science calls out for understanding in terms of the wisdom and creativity of God. On the horizon is a reinvigorated natural theology based on the life-giving work of the Spirit."[77] Moltmann also summarizes that, "The Spirit is the principle of creativity on all levels of matter and life. She creates new possibilities and in these anticipates new designs and blueprints for material and living organism. In this sense the Spirit is the principle of evolution."[78] Thus the Spirit opens possibilities for theology to enter into conversation with science which would in turn make a contribution to the clarification of the Christian faith today.

4. Summary

We are living in a world of pneumatological renaissance today, inviting us to seriously consider the person and work of the Spirit in our theological endeavours. The current study proves this aspect clearly, and hence we cannot hide behind and spend time always pulling hairs with theological jargon such as the Trinity or Christology. We need to engage in a serious consideration of the person and role of the Spirit with fresh interpretations for a world that is suffering from extremism, fundamentalism, eco-crisis, and such issues. Hence it is time for us to pray together in one accord; come Holy Spirit and blow where you will, transforming the lives of human beings and renewing the whole creation for accomplishing a new world that is free from sufferings of any kind, but filled with joy and peace.

---

77. Pinnock, *Flame of Love*, 67.
78. Moltmann, *God in Creation*, 100.

Bibliography

Primary Sources

Barth, Karl. *Protestant Thought: From Rousseau to Ritschl*. Trans. by Brian Cozens. Freeport: Harper & Brothers, 1959.

———. "Karl Barth and Oscar Cullmann on their Theological Vocation: On Systematic Theology." *Scottish Journal of Theology.* Vol. 14 (1961): 225-233.

———. *Der Römerbrief.* 1st ed. (1919). Zurich: Theologischer Verlag, 1963.

———. *Die Christliche Lehre nach dem Heidelberger Katechismus*. Zurich: Evangelischer Verlag, 1948.

———. *Die Christliche Dogmatik im Entwurf.* Edited by Gerhard Sauter. Zurich: Theologischer Verlag, 1982.

———. *Die Protestantische Theologie im 19. Jahrhundert: Ihre Vorgeschichte und Ihre Geschichte*. Zurich: Evangelischer Verlag, 1947.

———. *Dogmatics in Outline*. Trans. by G. T. Thomson. New York: Torchbooks, 1959.

———. *Dogmatik im Grundriß*. Zurich: Evangelischer Verlag, 1947.

———. *Einführung in die Evangelische Theologie*. München: Siebenstern Taschenbuch Verlag, 1968.

———. *Evangelical Theology: An Introduction*. Trans. by Grover Foley. London: Weidenfeld and Nicolson, 1968.

———. *Fides Quaerens Intellectum*. Zurich: Theologischer Verlag, 1981.

———. *God Here and Now*. Trans. by Paul M. van Buren. New York: Routledge, 2003.

_____. *Schleiermacher-Auswahl mit einem Nachwort von Karl Barth*. München: Siebenstern Taschenbuch Verlag, 1968.

_____. *The Christian Life*. Trans. by J. Strathearn McNab. London: SCM, 1930.

_____. *The Church Dogmatics*. Vol. 1/1. Edited by Geoffrey William Bromiley & Thomas Forsyth Torrance. Translated by Geoffrey William Bromiley. Edinburgh: T & T Clark, 1975.

_____. *The Church Dogmatics*. Vol. 1/2. Edited by Geoffrey William Bromiley & Thomas Forsyth Torrance. Translated by George Thomas Thomson and Harold Knight. Edinburgh: T & T Clark, 1956.

_____. *The Church Dogmatics*. Vol. 2/1. Edited by Geoffrey William Bromiley & Thomas Forsyth Torrance. Translated by T. H. L. Parker, W. B. Johnston, Harold Knight, J. L. M. Haire. Edinburgh: T & T Clark, 1957.

_____. *The Church Dogmatics*. Vol. 2/2. Edited by Geoffrey William Bromiley & Thomas Forsyth Torrance. Translated by Geoffrey William Bromiley, J. C. Campbell, Iain Wilson, J. Strathearn McNab, Harold Knight, R. A. Stewart. Edinburgh: T & T Clark, 1957.

_____. *The Church Dogmatics*. Vol. 3/2. Edited by Geoffrey William Bromiley & Thomas Forsyth Torrance. Translated by Harold Knight, Geoffrey William Bromiley, J. K. S. Reid, R. H. Fuller. Edinburgh: T & T Clark, 1960.

_____. *The Church Dogmatics*. Vol. 3/3. Edited by Geoffrey William Bromiley & Thomas Forsyth Torrance. Translated by Geoffrey William Bromiley and R. J. Ehrlich. Edinburgh: T & T Clark, 1960.

_____. *The Church Dogmatics*. Vol. 4/1. Edited by Geoffrey William Bromiley & Thomas Forsyth Torrance. Translated by Geoffrey William Bromiley. Edinburgh: T & T Clark, 1956.

_____. *The Church Dogmatics*. Vol. 4/2. Edited by Geoffrey William Bromiley & Thomas Forsyth Torrance. Translated by Geoffrey William Bromiley. Edinburgh: T & T Clark, 1958.

_____. *The Church Dogmatics*. Vol. 4/3. Edited by Geoffrey William Bromiley & Thomas Forsyth Torrance. Translated by Geoffrey William Bromiley. Edinburgh: T & T Clark, 1961.

_____. *The Epistle to the Romans*. Trans. from 6th edition by Edwyn C. Hoskyns. London: Oxford University Press, 1968.

———."Philosophie und Theologie." In *Philosophie und Christliche Existenz*. 93-106. Edited by Gerhard Huber. Basel: Hebling & Lichtenhahn, 1960.

———. *Die Kirchliche Dogmatik*. Vol. 1/1. Zurich: Theologischer Verlag, 1980.

———. *Die Kirchliche Dogmatik*. Vol. 3/3. Zurich: Theologischer Verlag, 1980.

———. *Die Kirchliche Dogmatik*. Vol. 4/1. Zurich: Theologischer Verlag, 1980.

———. *Die Kirchliche Dogmatik*. Vol. 4/2. Zurich: Theologischer Verlag, 1980.

Moltmann, Jürgen. "Christianity and the Revaluation of the Values of Modernity." In *A Passion for God's Reign: Theology, Christian Learning and the Christian Self*. 23-44. Edited by Miroslav Wolf. Michigan: Eerdmans, 1998.

———. "Creation and Redemption." In *Creation, Christ, and Culture: Studies in Honor of T. F. Torrance*. 119-134. Edited by Richard W. A. McKinney. Edinburgh: T & T Clark, 1976.

———. "Foreword." In M. Douglas Meeks. *Origins of Theology of Hope*. xi-xii. Philadelphia: Fortress, 1974.

———. "Hope without Faith: An Eschatological Humanism without God." In *Is God Dead? Concilium* 16. Edited by Johannes B. Metz. New York: Paulist, 1966: 25-40.

———. "Schöpfung, Bund, und Herrlichkeit; zur Diskussion über Karl Barths Schöpfungslehre." *Evangelische Theologie*. Vol. 48 (1988): 108-127.

———. "The Alienation and Liberation of Nature." In *On Nature*. 133-144. Edited by L. Rouner. Notre Dame: University of Notre Dame Press, 1984.

———. "The Ecological Crisis: Peace with Nature." *The Scottish Journal Religious Studies*. Vol. 9 (1986): 5-18.

———. "The Fellowship of the Holy Spirit: Trinitarian Pneumatology." *Scottish Journal of Theology*. Vol. 37 (1984): 287-300.

———. "The Trinitarian History of God." *Theology*. Vol. 78 (1975): 632-646.

———. "Theology in the Project of Modern World." In *A Passion for God's Reign: Theology, Christian Learning and the Christian Self*. 1-22. Edited by Miroslav Wolf. Michigan: Eerdmans, 1998.

_____. *Experiences in Theology: Ways and Forms of Christian Theology*. Trans. by Margaret Kohl. Minneapolis: Fortress, 2000.

_____. *God in Creation: A New Theology of Creation and the Spirit of God*. Trans. by Margaret Kohl. London: SCM, 1985.

_____. *God in Creation: An Ecological Doctrine of Creation*. Trans. by Margaret Kohl. London: SCM, 2005.

_____. *History and the Triune God: Contributions to Trinitarian Theology*. Trans. by John Bowden. New York: Crossroad, 1991.

_____. *Jesus Christ for Today's World*. Trans. by Margaret Kohl. Minneapolis: Fortress Press, 1994.

_____. *Religion, Revolution, and the Future*. Trans. by M. Douglas Meeks. New York: Charles Scribner's, 1969.

_____. *The Church in the Power of the Spirit: A Contribution to Messianic Ecclesiology*. Trans. by Margaret Kohl. London: Harper & Row, 1975.

_____. *The Coming of God: Christian Eschatology*. Trans. by Margaret Kohl. London: SCM, 2005.

_____. *The Crucified God*. Trans. by R. A. Wilson and John Bowden. London: SCM, 2008.

_____. *The Future of Creation: Collected Essays*. Trans. by Margaret Kohl. Minneapolis: Fortress, 2007.

_____. *The Passion of Life: A Messianic Lifestyle*. Trans. by M. Douglas Meeks. Philadelphia: Fortress, 1978.

_____. *The Source of Life: The Holy Spirit and the Theology of Life*. Trans. by Margaret Kohl. London: SCM, 1997.

_____. *The Spirit of Life: A Universal Affirmation*. Trans. by Margaret Kohl. Minneapolis: Fortress, 1992.

_____. *The Trinity and the Kingdom*. Trans. by Margaret Kohl. London: SCM, 1981.

_____. *The Way of Jesus Christ: Christology in Messianic Dimensions*. Trans. by Margaret Kohl. Minneapolis: Fortress, 1993.

_____. *Theology and Joy*. Trans. by Reinhard Ulrich. London: SCM, 1973.

_____. *Theology of Hope*. Trans. by James W. Leitch. New York: Harper & Row, 1993.

Pannenberg, Wolfhart. "The Doctrine of the Spirit and the Task of a Theology of Nature." In *Toward a Theology of Nature: Essays on Science and Faith*. 123-137. Edited by Ted Peters. Louisville: Westminster, 1993.

_____. "An Autobiographical Sketch." In *The Theology of Wolfhart Pannenberg: Twelve American Critiques, with an Autobiographical Essay and Response*. 11-19. Edited by Carl E. Braaten and Philip Clayton. Minneapolis: Augsburg, 1988.

_____. "Father, Son, Spirit: Problems of a Trinitarian Doctrine of God." *Dialog*. Vol. 26, no. 4 (1987): 250-257.

_____. "Spirit and Energy." In *Toward a Theology of Nature: Essays on Science and Faith*. 138-147. Edited by Ted Peters. Louisville: Westminster, 1993.

_____. "Spirit and Mind." In *Toward a Theology of Nature: Essays on Science and Faith*. 148-161. Edited by Ted Peters. Louisville: Westminster, 1993.

_____. "The Doctrine of Creation and Modern Science." *Zygon*. Vol. 23, no. 1 (March 1988): 3-21.

_____. "The Doctrine of the Spirit and the Task of a Theology of Nature." *Theology*. Vol. 75, no. 1 (1972): 8-21.

_____. Avery Dulles and Carl E. Braaten. "The Working of the Spirit in the Creation and in the People of God" in *Spirit, Faith, and Church*. (*The 1969 Walter and Mary Tuohy Chaira lectures*). 13-31. Philadelphia: Westminster, n.d.

_____. *Anthropology in Theological Perspective*. Trans. by Mathew J. O'Connell. Philadelphia: Westminster, 1985.

_____. *Basic Questions in Theology: Collected Essays*. Vol. 1. Trans. by George H. Kehm. Philadelphia: Westminster, 1983.

_____. *Christianity in a Secularized World*. New York: Crossroad, 1989.

_____. *Jesus – God and Man*. Trans. by Lewis L. Wilkins and Duane A. Priebe. Philadelphia: Westminster, 1968.

_____. ed., *Offenbarung als Geschichte*. Göttingen: Vandenhoeck & Ruprecht, 1961.

_____. *Systematic Theology*. Vol. 1. Trans. by Geoffrey W. Bromiley. Grand Rapids: Eerdmans, 1991.

_____. *Systematic Theology*. Vol. 2. Trans. by Geoffrey W. Bromiley. Grand Rapids: Eerdmans, 1994.

_____. *Systematic Theology.* Vol. 3. Trans by Geoffrey W. Bromiley. Grand Rapids: Eerdmans, 1998.

_____. *The Idea of God and Human Freedom.* Philadelphia: Westminster, 1973.

_____. *Theology and the Kingdom of God.* Philadelphia: Westminster, 1970.

_____. *What is Man? Contemporary Anthropology in Theological Perspective.* Trans. by Duane A. Priebe. Philadelphia: Fortress, 1970.

Secondary Sources

Augustine, Aurelius. *The Trinity: The Works of Saint Augustine: A Translation for the 21st Century.* Trans. Edmund Hill. Edited by John E. Rotelle. New York: New City Press, 1991.

Achtmeier, Paul J. *The Inspiration of Scripture.* Philadelphia: Westminster, 1980.

Acton, J. E. E. D. *The History of Freedom and Other Essays.* London: Macmillan, 1907.

Albright, Carol Rausch. and Joel Haugen. eds. *Beginning with the End: God, Science, and Wolfhart Pannenberg.* Peru, Illinois: Open Court, 1997.

Altepeter, Lawrence J. "The Asceticism of Menno Simons." *The Mennonite Quarterly Review.* Vol. 72, no. 1 (January 1998): 69-83.

Althouse, Peter. *Pentecostal Eschatology in Conversation with Jürgen Moltmann.* New York: T & T Clark, 2003.

Anderson, Allan. "Pentecostal Approaches to Faith and Healing." *International Review of Mission.* Vol. 91, no. 363 (October 2002): 523-534.

Anderson, Charles S. "Introduction." In Bengt Hägglund. *The Background of Luther's Doctrine of Justification in Late Medieval Theology.* Philadelphia: Fortress, 1971.

Anderson, Marvin W. *Evangelical Foundations: Religion in England, 1378-1683.* Frankfurt am Main: Peter Lang, 1987.

Attfield, D. G. "Can God be Crucified? A Discussion of J. Moltmann." *Scottish Journal of Theology.* Vol. 30 (1977): 47-57.

Augustin, Cornelis. "Erasmus and Menno Simons." *The Mennonite Quarterly Review.* Vol. 60, no. 4 (October 1986): 497-508.

Badcock, Gary D. *Light of Truth and Fire of Love: A Theology of the Holy Spirit.* Grand Rapids: Eerdmans, 1997.

Bailey, Richard. "The Sixteenth Century's Apocalyptic Heritage and Thomas Müntzer." *The Mennonite Quarterly Review*. Vol. 57, no. 1 (January 1983): 27-44.

Bainton, Roland H. *The Reformation of the Sixteenth Century*. London: Hodder and Stoughton, 1965.

Barth, Markus. "My Father: Karl Barth." In *How Karl Barth Changed My Mind*. 1-5. Edited by Donald K. McKim. Grand Rapids: Eerdmans, 1986.

Bauckham, Richard J. "Moltmann's Messianic Christology." *Scottish Journal of Theology*. Vol. 44 (1991): 519-531.

_____. "Introduction." In *God will be All in All: The Eschatology of Jürgen Moltmann*. xiii-xv. Edited by Richard Bauckham. Minneapolis: Fortress, 2001.

_____. "Moltmann's Eschatology of The Cross." *Scottish Journal of Theology*. Vol. 30 (1977): 301-311.

_____. *The Theology of Jürgen Moltmann*. Edinburgh: T &. T Clark, 1995.

Baylor, Michael G. "Thomas Müntzer's 'Prague Manifesto.'" *The Mennonite Quarterly Review*. Vol. 58, no. 1 (January 1989): 30-57.

_____. "Theology and Politics in the Thought of Thomas Müntzer: The Case of the Elect." *Archive for Reformation History*. Vol. 79 (1988): 81-102.

Beard, Charles. *The Reformation of the Sixteenth Century in its Relation to Modern Thought and Knowledge: Herbert Lectures*. London: Constable, 1927.

Beck, T. David. *The Holy Spirit and the Renewal of All Things: Pneumatology in Paul and Jürgen Moltmann*. Eugene: Pickwick, 2007.

Bender, H. S. "The Anabaptist Vision." *Church History*. Vol. 13 (1944): 23-24.

_____. "A Brief Biography of Menno Simons." In *The Complete Writings of Menno Simons: c. 1496-1561*. 3-29. Trans. by Leonard Wenger. Edited by John Christian Wenger. Scottsdale: Herald, 1960.

Bentley, James. "Christoph Blumhardt: Preacher of Hope." *Theology 78* (1975): 577-583.

Berkhof, Hendrikus. *Christian Faith: An Introduction to the Study of the Faith*. Trans. by Sierd Woudstra. Grand Rapids: Eerdmans, 1979.

_____. "Beginning with Barth." In *How Karl Barth Changed My Mind*. 19-26. Edited by Donald K. McKim. Grand Rapids: William B. Eerdmans, 1986.

_____. *Theologie des Heiligen Geistes*. Neukirchen: Neukirchener Verlag, 1968.

Berkhof, Louis. *Systematic Theology.* London: The Banner of Truth, 1971.

Bilaniuk, Petro B. T. *Theology and Economy of the Holy Spirit: An Eastern Approach.* Bangalore: Dharmaram, 1980.

Bornhäuser, Christoph. *Leben und Lehre Monno Simons: Ein Kampf um das Fundament des Glaubens (etwa 1496-1661).* Neukirchen: Neukirchener, 1973.

Bowden, John. *Karl Barth.* London: SCM, 1971.

Braaten, Carl E. *Principles of Lutheran Theology.* 2nd edition. Minneapolis: Fortress, 2007.

Brenning, Robert Wesley. *The Ethical Hermeneutic of Sebastian Franck, 1499-1542*, Ph. D. Thesis. London: Temple University Microfilms International, 1978.

Brown, Colin. *Philosophy and the Christian Faith.* Downers Grove: Inter Varsity, 1968.

_____. *Kierkegaard, Heidegger, Buber, and Barth: A Study of Subjectivity and Objectivity in Existentialist Thought.* New York: Collier Books, 1971.

Buchwalter, Andrew. Translator's Introduction to *Observations on "The Spiritual Situation of the Age."* i-xxxv. Edited by Jürgen Haberms. Cambridge: MIT Press, 1984.

Burgess, Stanley M. *Ancient Christian Traditions: The Holy Spirit.* Peabody: Hendrickson, 2002.

_____. *Eastern Christian Traditions: The Holy Spirit.* Peabody: Hendrickson, 2000.

_____. *The Holy Spirit: Medieval Roman Catholic and Reformation Traditions.* Peabody: Hendrickson, 1997.

Burkhart, Irvin E. "Menno Simons on the Incarnation." *The Mennonite Quarterly Review.* Vol. 4, no. 3 (July 1930): 178-203.

Burrell, David B. "The Spirit and the Christian Life." In *Christian Theology: An Introduction to Its Traditions and Tasks.* 302-327. Edited by Peter C. Hodgson and Robert H. King. Philadelphia: Fortress, 1988.

Busch, Eberhard. "Barmer Theologische Erklärung," in *Evangelisches Kirchenlexikon* Vol. 1, 362-363. Edited by Erwin Fahlbusch, et. al. Göttingen: Vandenhoeck & Ruprecht, 1986.

_____. *Karl Barths Lebenslauf: Nach seinen Briefen und autobiographischen Texten.* Munich: Kaiser Verlag, 1975.

Calvin, John. *Calvin's New Testament Commentaries*. Edited by David W. Torrance and Thomas F. Torrance. Grand Rapids: Eerdmans, 1972.

_____. *Institutes of the Christian Religion*. Trans. by Henry Beveridge. Grand Rapids: Eerdmans, 1989.

Capps, Walter H. *Time Invades the Cathedral*. Philadelphia: Fortress, 1972.

Chester, Tim. *Mission and the Coming of God: Eschatology, the Trinity and Mission in the Theology of Jürgen Moltmann and Contemporary Evangelism*. Eugene: Wipf & Stock, 2006.

Christenson, Larry. ed., *Welcome Holy Spirit*. Minneapolis: Augsburg, 1987.

Clutterbuck, Richard. "Jürgen Moltmann as a Doctrinal Theologian: The Nature of Doctrine and the Possibilities for its Development." *Scottish Journal of Theology*. Vol. 48, no.1 (1995): 489-505.

Cochrane, Arthur C. "Whether Karl Barth Changed My Mind." In *How Karl Barth Changed My Mind*. 15-18. Edited by Donald K. McKim. Grand Rapids: Eerdmans, 1986.

Comblin, Jose. *The Holy Spirit and Liberation*. Trans. by Paul Burns. New York: Orbis, 1989.

Conyers, Abda Johnson. *Jürgen Moltmann's Concept of History*. London: University Microfilms International, 1981.

Cox, Harvey. "Gedanken über Jürgen Moltmanns Buch: Der Gekreuzigte Gott." In *Diskussion über Jürgen Moltmanns Buch "Der gekreuzigte Gott."* 126-139. Edited by Michael Welker. Munich: Kaiser, 1979.

Cunningham, Mary Kathleen. *What is Theological Exegesis? Interpretation and Use of Scripture in Barth's Doctrine of Election*. Pennsylvania: Trinity Press International, 1995.

Cunningham, William. *The Reformers and the Theology of Reformation*. Edinburgh: T & T Clark, 1866.

Dalferth, Ingolf U. "Karl Barth's Eschatological Realism." In *Karl Barth: Centenary Essays*. 14-45. Edited by S. W. Sykes. Cambridge: Cambridge University Press, 1989.

Dawson, R. Dale. *The Resurrection in Karl Barth*. Hampshire: Ashgate, 2007.

D'Costa, Gavin. *The Meeting of Religions and the Trinity*. Edinburgh: T & T Clark, 2000.

Denck, Hans. "Schriften." In *Quellen und Forschungen zur Reformationsgeschichte*. Vol. XXIV. 14-21. Gütersloh: Bertelsmann Verlag, 1955.

Denck, John. "Whether God is the Cause of Evil." In *Spiritual and Anabaptist Writers: Documents Illustrative of the Radical Reformation*. 86-111. Edited by George H. Williams and Angel M. Mergal. London: SCM, 1957.

Derksen, John. "The Schwenckfeldians in Strasbourg, 1533-1562: A Prosopographical Survey." *The Mennonite Quarterly Review*. Vol. 74, no. 2 (April 2000): 257-294.

Dickens, A. G. and John Powell, *The Reformation in Historical Thought*. Oxford: Blackwell, 1985.

Dipple, Geoffrey. "Sebastian Franck in Strasbourg." *The Mennonite Quarterly Review*. Vol. 73, no 4 (October 1999): 783-802.

Dixon, C. Scott. ed., *The German Reformation*. Oxford: Blackwell, 1999.

Dohm, Terry C. *The Rediscovery of Eschatology in the Message of Jesus and Its Impact on Theology in the Twentieth Century*. Regensburg: Roderer Verlag, 2003.

Dorrien, Gary. *The Barthian Revolt in Modern Theology: Theology without Weapons*. Louisville: Westminster, 2000.

Dreyer, Elizabeth A. "Resources for a Renewed Life in the Spirit and Pneumatology: Medieval Mystics and Saints." In *Advent of the Spirit: Orientations in Pneumatology*, Conference Papers from a Symposium at Marquette University, 17-19 April, 1998 (Unpublished).

Dülmen, Richard van. "The Reformation and the Modern Age." *The German Reformation: Essential Readings in History*. 193-220. Edited by C. Scott Dixon. Oxford: Blackwell, 1999.

Duke James O. and Robert F. Streetman, eds. *Barth and Schleiermacher: Beyond the Impasse?* Philadelphia: Fortress, 1988.

Dulles, Avery. S. J. *The Assurance of Things Hoped For: A Theology of Christian Faith*. Oxford: Oxford University Press, 1994.

Dunklin Parker, Thomas. *The Concept of Human in Karl Barth's Theology*. Ph. D. Thesis. Princeton, 1965.

Dyck, Cornelius J. "Hans De Ries and the Legacy of Menno." *The Mennonite Quarterly Review*. Vol. 62, no. 3 (July 1988): 401-416.

Eberlein, Paul Gerhard. *Ketzer oder Heiliger? Caspar von Schwenckfled: Der schlesische Reformator und seine Botschaft*. Metzingen: Ernst Franz Verlag, 1998.

Erb, Peter C. " Adam Reissner: His Learning and Influence on Schwenckfeld." *The Mennonite Quarterly Review*. Vol. 54, no. 1 (January 1980): 32-41.

Fast, Heinold. "Hans Denck and Thomas Müntzer." *The Mennonite Quarterly Review*. Vol. 45, no. 1 (January 1971): 82-83.

Feuerbach, Ludwig. *The Essence of Christianity*. Trans. by George Eliot. New York: Harper & Row, 1957.

Ford, D. F. "Barth's Interpretation of the Bible." In *Karl Barth: Studies of His Theological Method*. 55-87. Edited by S. W. Sykes. Oxford: Clarendon, 1979.

Foster, Claude R. Jr. "Hans Denck and Johannes Bünderlin: A Comparative Study." *The Mennonite Quarterly Review*. Vol. 39, no. 2 (April 1965): 115-124.

Franck, Sebastian. "A Letter to John Campanus." In *Spiritual and Anabaptist Writers*. 145-147. Edited by George H. Williams and Angel M. Mergal. Philadelphia: Westminster, 1957.

_____. *Paradoxa*. Trans. & intro. by Siegfried Wollgast. Berlin: Academie Verlag, 1966.

Friedmann, Robert. "Recent Interpretations of Anabaptism." *Church History*. Vol. 24 (1955): 132-151.

Friesen, Abraham. "Acts 10: The Baptism of the Cornelius as Interpreted by Thomas Müntzer and Felix Manz." *The Mennonite Quarterly Review*. Vol. 64, no. 1 (January 1990): 5-22.

_____. "Thomas Müntzer and Martin Luther." *Archive for Reformation History*. Vol. 79 (1988): 59-79.

Fuller, R. H. "Introduction." In Jürgen Moltmann and Jürgen Weissbach. *Two Studies in the Theology of Bonhoeffer*. New York: Charles Scribner's, 1967.

Gentz, William H. *The Dictionary of Bible and Religion*. Nashville: Abingdon, 1986.

George, Timothy. *Theology of the Reformers*. Nashville: Broadman Press, 1988.

Geyer, Hans-Georg. "Ansichten zu Jürgen Moltmanns 'Theologie der Hoffnung.'" In *Diskussion über die "Theologie der Hoffnung" von Jürgen Moltmann*. 40-80. Edited by Wolf-Dieter Marsch. Munich: Kaiser, 1967.

Gockel, Mathias. "A Reformer's Dissent from Lutheranism: Reconsidering the Theology of Hans Denck (ca.1500-1527)." *Archive for Reformation History*. Vol. 91 (2000): 127-148.

Godsey, John D. "Introduction." In Karl Barth, *How I Changed My Mind*. 17-33. Edited by Robert W. Funk. Richmond: John Knox, 1966.

_____. ed., *Karl Barth's Table Talks*. Trans. *John* Newton Thomas & Thomas Wieser. Richmond: John Knox, 1960.

Goertz, Hans Jürgen. "Thomas Müntzer: Revolutionary between the Middle Ages and Modernity." Trans. by James M. Stayer. *The Mennonite Quarterly Review*. Vol. 64, no. 1 (January 1990): 23-31.

_____. "Zu Thomas Müntzer's Geistverständnis." In *Die Theologie Thomas Müntzers: Untersuchungen zu einer Entwicklung und Lehre*. 84-99. Edited by Siegfried Bräuer and Helmar Junghans. Göttingen: Vandenhoeck & Ruprecht, 1989.

Green, Clifford. ed., *Karl Barth: Theologian of Freedom*. Minneapolis: Fortress, 1991.

Green, Michael. *I believe in the Holy Spirit*. Grand Rapids: Eerdmans, 1980.

Gregersen, Niels Henrik. ed., *The Historicity of Nature: Essays on Science and Theology*. Pennsylvania: Templeton Foundation, 2008.

Grenz, Stanley J. and John R. Franke, *Beyond Foundationalism: Shaping Theology in a Postmodern Context*. Louisville: Westminster, 2001.

_____. "Scientific" Theology/"Theological" Science: Pannenberg and the Dialogue between Theology and Science." *Zygon*. Vol. 34, no. 1 (March 1999): 159-166.

_____. "The Spirit and the Word: The World Creating Function of the Text." *Theology Today*. Vol. 57, no. 3 (October, 2000): 357-374.

_____. *Reason for Hope: The Systematic Theology of Wolfhart Pannenberg*. New York: Oxford University Press, 1990.

_____. *Rediscovering the Triune God: The Trinity in Contemporary Theology*. Minneapolis: Fortress, 2004.

Grislis, Egil. "Menno Simons on Sanctification." *The Mennonite Quarterly Review*. Vol. 69, no. 2 (April 1994): 226-246.

Gritsch, Eric W. *Reformer without a Church: The Life and Thought of Thomas Müntzer*. Philadelphia, Fortress, 1967.

Gunton, Colin E. *Theology Through the Theologians: Selected Essays 1972-1995*. Edinburgh: T & T Clark, 1996.

_____. "The Triune God and the Freedom of the Creature." In *Karl Barth: Centenary Essays*. 46-68. Edited by S. W. Sykes. Cambridge: Cambridge University Press, 1989.

Hall, Charles A. M. *With the Spirit's Sword: The Drama of Spiritual Warfare in the Theology of John Calvin*. Zurich: EVZ Verlag, 1968.

Hall, Fred Perry. *The Lutheran Doctrine of the Holy Spirit in the Sixteenth Century: Developments of the "Formula of Concord."* California: Pasadena, 1993.

Hall, Thor. "Possibilities of Erasmian Influence on Denck and Hubmaier in their Views on the Freedom of the Will." *The Mennonite Quarterly Review.* Vol. 35, no. 2 (April 1961): 149-170.

Harbison, E. Harris. *The Christian Scholar in the Age of the Reformation.* Philadelphia: Porcupine, 1956.

_____. *The Age of Reformation.* New York: Cornell University Press, 1962.

Harnack, Adolf. *What is Christianity?* Trans. by T. B. Saunders. London: Hodder & Stoughton, 1901.

Hartwell, Herbert. *The Theology of Karl Barth.* London: Gerald Duckworth, 1964.

Hart, Trevor A. *Regarding Karl Barth: Essays Toward a Reading of His Theology.* Cumbria: Paternoster, 1999.

Harvie, Timothy. *Jürgen Moltmann's Ethics of Hope: Eschatological Possibilities for Moral Action.* Surrey: Ashgate, 2009.

Hefling, Charles. "*Gratia*: Grace and Gratitude: Fifty Unmodern Thesis as Prolegomena to Pneumatology." *Anglican Theological Review.* Vol. 83, no. 3 (Summer 2001): 473-491.

Helander, Dick. *Johann Tauler als Prediger.* Lund: Almquist and Wicksells, 1923.

Hendrix, Scott H. *Recultivating the Vineyard: The Reformation Agendas of Christianization.* Louisville: Westminster, 2004.

_____. "Martin Luther's Reformation of Spirituality." *Lutheran Quarterly.* Vol. 13, no. 1 (Spring 1999): 249-270.

Heron, Alasdair I. C. *The Holy Spirit: The Holy Spirit in the Bible, the History of Christian Thought, and Recent Theology.* Philadelphia: Westminster, 1983.

Hilberath, Brand Jochen. *Pneumatologie.* Dusseldorf: Patmos, 1994.

_____. ed., *The Protestant Reformation.* New York: Torchbooks, 1968.

Hodgson, Peter C. *Winds of Spirit: A Constructive Christian Theology.* Louisville: Westminster, 1994.

Holloway, Richard. *Dancing on the Edge.* London: Harper Collins, 1997.

Horst, Irvin B. "Menno Simons and the Augustinian Tradition." *The Mennonite Quarterly Review.* Vol. 62, no. 4 (October 1988): 419-430.

Hughson, Thomas. S. J. "Citizenship: Re-Minded by the Holy Spirit." *Anglican Theological Review.* Vol. 83, no. 3 (Summer 2001): 557-578.

Humphrey, Edith M. *Ecstasy and Intimacy: When the Holy Spirit Meets the Human Spirit*. Grand Rapids: Eerdmans, 2006.

Hunsinger, George. "Karl Barth and Radical Politics." *Studies in Religion*. Vol. 7, no. 2 (Spring 1978): 167-191.

_____. *How to Read Karl Barth: The Shape of His Theology*. New York: Oxford University Press, 1991.

Hyslop, Anita Marie. *The Theology of Image and Imagination in the Theology of Wolfhart Pannenberg*. Michigan: University Microfilms International, 1977.

Irving, Edward. *The Collected Works of Edward Irving*. Vol. 5. Edited by G. Carlyle. London: Alexander Strahan, 1864.

Jenson, Robert W. "Jesus in the Trinity: Wolfhart Pannenberg's Christology and Doctrine of the Trinity." In *The Theology of Wolfhart Pannenberg: Twelve American Critiques, with an Autobiographical Essay and Response*. 188-206. Edited by Carl E. Braaten and Philip Clayton. Minneapolis: Augsburg, 1988.

_____. *God after God: The God of the Past and the God of the Future Seen in the Work of Karl Barth*. New York: The Bobbs-Merrill, 1969.

_____. "You Wonder where the Spirit Went." *Pro Ecclesia 2* (1993): 296-304.

_____. *Systematic Theology: The Triune God*. Vol. 1. Oxford: Oxford University Press, 1997.

Johnson, Elizabeth A. *She Who Is: The Mystery of God in Feminist Theological Discourse*. New York: Crossroad, 1992.

Jones, Alan. "Falling in Love: The Work of the Holy Spirit." *Anglican Theological Review*. Vol. 83, no. 3 (Summer 2001): 375-386.

Jones, Rufus M. *Studies in Mystical Religion*. London: Macmillan, 1923.

Joseph, P. V. *Indian Interpretation of the Holy Spirit: An Appraisal of the Pneumatology of Appasamy, Chenchiah, and Chakkarai*. Delhi/Dehradun: New Theological College/ISPCK, 2007.

Jüngel, E. *Barth-Studien*. Zurich: Benziger Güttersloher, 1982.

Kärkkäinen, Veli-Matti. "How to Speak of the Spirit Among Religions: Trinitarian Prolegomena for a Pneumatological Theology of Religions." In *The Work of the Spirit: Pneumatology and Pentecostalism*. 47-70. Edited by Michael Welker. Grand Rapids: Eerdmans, 2006.

_____. "The Working of the Spirit of God in Creation and in the People of God: The Pneumatology of Wolfhart Pannenberg." *The Journal of the Society for Pentecostal Studies*. Vol. 26, no.1 (Spring 2004): 17-35.

_____. "Identity and Plurality: A Pentecostal Charismatic Perspective." *International Review of Mission*. Vol. 91, no. 363 (October 2002): 500-503.

_____. *Pneumatology: The Holy Spirit in Ecumenical, International, and Contextual Perspective*. Grand Rapids: Baker Academic, 2002.

Kiwiet, Jan J. "The Theology of Hans Denck." *The Mennonite Quarterly Review*. Vol. 32, no. 1 (January 1958): 3-27.

Klaassen, Walter. "Menno Simons: Molder of a Tradition." *The Mennonite Quarterly Review*. Vol. 62, no. 3 (July 1988): 368-386.

Koch, Ernst. "Das Sakramentsverständnis Thomas Müntzers." In *Die Theologie Thomas Müntzers: Untersuchungen zu einer Entwicklung und Lehre*. 129-155. Edited by Siegfried Bräur and Helmar Junghans. Göttingen: Vandenhoeck & Ruprecht, 1989.

Köhler, Walther. "Die Spiritualisten." *Archive for Reformation History*. Vol. 41 (1948): 164-186.

Kommoss, Rudolph. *Sebastian Franck and Erasmus von Rotterdam*. Berlin: Ebering, 1934.

Krahn, Cornelius. *Dutch Anabaptism: Origin, Spread, Life, and Thought (1450-1600)*. Nijhoff: The Hague, 1968.

Kramm, K. H. *The Theology of Martin Luther*. London: James Clarke, 1947.

Kreitzer, Beth. "Menno Simons and the Bride of Christ." *The Mennonite Quarterly Review*. Vol. 70, no. 3 (July 1996): 299-318.

Kyongsuk Min, Anselm. *The Solidarity of Others in a Divided World: A Postmodern Theology after Postmodernism*. New York: T & T Clark, 2004.

Kyung, Chung Hyun. *Christianity and Crisis*. Vol. 51 (15 July 1991): 220-223.

Lee, Sang-Hwan. "The Relevance of St. Basil's Pneumatology to Modern Pentecostalism." In *Cyber Journal for Pentecostal Research* (February 2000). http://www.pctii.org/cyberj/cyberj7/lee.html. 20.05.2008.

Leith, John H. ed., *The Creeds of the Churches: A Reader in Christian Doctrine from the Bible to the Present*. 3rd ed. Atlanta: John Knox, 1982.

Lidden Pate, Andrew. Jr., *Man With God: A Study of the Doctrine of Man in the Theology of Karl Barth*. Ph. D. Thesis. Michigan: University Microfilms, 1968.

Lindberg, Carter. *The European Reformation*. Oxford: Blackwell, 1996.

Lints, Richard. *The Fabric of Theology: A Prolegomenon to Evangelical Theology*. Michigan: Eerdmans, 1993.

Livingston, James C. *Modern Christian Thought: The Enlightenment and the Nineteenth Century*. Vol. 1. New Jersey: Prentice Hall, 1997.

Longhlin, Gerard. "Writing the Trinity." *Theology*. Vol. 97, no. 776 (March–April, 1994): 82-89.

Louth, Andrew. ed., *Trinity and Incarnation*. Edinburgh: T & T Clark, 1993.

Luther, Martin. "Das Magnificat Verdeutschet und Ausgelegt" (1521). In *WA* 7. 546-604.

_____. "Auslegung deutsch des Vaterunsers für die einfältigen Laien" (1519). In *WA* 2. 81-130.

_____. "Vom Abendmahl Christi. Bekenntnis" (1528). In *WA* 26. 242-509.

_____. "Der Kleine Katechismus" (1529). In *WA* 30/1. 241-424.

_____. "Die Promotionsdispotation von Palladius und Tilemann" (1537). In *WA* 39/1. 198-257.

_____. "Sprüche aus dem Alten Testament." In *WA* 48. 1-224.

_____. "Vom Missbrauch der Messe" (1521). In *WA* 8. 475-563.

_____. "Die Disputation über Job 1:14" (1539). In *WA* 39/2. 1-33.

_____. «Nam Quid oremus etc., nescimus.» In *WA* 56. 1-375.

Macchia, Frank D. "A North American Response." *Journal of Pentecostal Theology*. Vol. 2, no. 4 (1994): 25-33.

Macquarrie, John. *Twentieth-Century Religious Thought: The Frontiers of Philosophy and Theology, 1900-1980*. New York: Charles Scribner's, 1989.

Maczka, Romwald. "Retheologising Thomas Müntzer in the German Democratic Republic: 15 Years of Marxist and Non-Marxist Research." *The Mennonite Quarterly Review*. Vol. 63, no. 4 (October 1989): 345-366.

Marquardt, Friedrich-Wilhelm. *Theologie und Sozialismus: Das Beispiel Karl Barths*. Munich: Kaiser, 1972.

Marx, Karl. *Marx and Engels on Religion*. Moscow: Progress, 1957.

Mast, Russel L. "Menno Simons Speaks Concerning the Ministry." *The Mennonite Quarterly Review*. Vol. 54, no. 2 (April 1980): 106-116.

Matczak, Sebastian A. *Karl Barth on God*. New York: St. Paul, 1962.

Matheson, Peter. "Whose Scripture? A Foray into Reformation Hermeneutics." *The Mennonite Quarterly Review*. Vol. 70, no. 2 (April 1996): 191-202.

_____. ed., & trans. *The Collected Works of Thomas Müntzer*. Edinburgh: T & T Clark, 1988.

McConnachie, John. *The Significance of Karl Barth*. London: Hodder & Stoughton, 1931.

McFague, Sallie. *Models of God: Theology for an Ecological, Nuclear Age*. Philadelphia: Fortress, 1987.

McGrath, Alister E. "John Calvin and the Late Medieval Thought: A Study in Late Medieval Influences upon Calvin's Theological Development." *Archive for Reformation History*. Vol. 77 (1986): 58-78.

_____. *Christian Theology: An Introduction*. Oxford: Blackwell, 1994.

_____. *Luther's Theology of the Cross*. Oxford: Blackwell, 1990.

McIntyre, John. *The Shape of Pneumatology*. Edinburgh: T & T Clark, 1997.

Mckenzie, David. *Wolfhart Pannenberg and Religious Philosophy*. Washington: University Press of America, 1980.

McLaughlin, R. Emmet. "Apocalypticism and Thomas Müntzer." *Archive for Reformation History*. Vol. 95 (2004): 98-131.

_____. "Schwenckfeld and the Strasbourg Radicals." *The Mennonite Quarterly Review*. Vol. 59, no. 3 (July 1985): 268-278.

_____. "Spiritualism and the Bible: The Case of Caspar Schwenckfeld (1489-1561)." *The Mennonite Quarterly Review*. Vol. 53, no. 4 (October 1979): 282-298.

_____. "The Politics of Dissent: Martin Bucer, Caspar Schwenckfeld, and the Schwenkfelders of Strasbourg." *The Mennonite Quarterly Review*. Vol. 68, no. 1 (January 1994): 59-78.

McTaggart, J. M. C. *Studies in Hegelian Cosmology*. Cambridge: Cambridge University Press, 1918.

McWilliams, Warren. "Why all the Fuss about *Filioque*? Karl Barth and Jürgen Moltmann on the Procession of the Spirit." *Perspectives in Religious Studies*. Vol. 22 (Summer 1995): 167-182.

Meeks, M. Douglas. *Origins of the Theology of Hope*. Philadelphia: Fortress, 1974.

Meijering, E. P. *Die Hellenisierung des Christentums im Urteil Adolf von Harnacks*. New York: North-Holland, 1985.

Merz, Georg. "Die Begegnung Karl Barths mit der Deutschen Theologie." *Kerygma und Dogma 2* (1956): 157-175.

Meusel, Alfred. *Thomas Müntzer und seine Zeit mit einer Auswahl der Dokumente des Grossen Deutschen Bauernkriegs*. Berlin: Aufbau, 1952.

Meuser, Fred W. "Luther as Preacher of the Word of God." In *The Cambridge Companion to Martin Luther*. 136-148. Edited by Donald McKim. Cambridge: Cambridge University Press, 2003.

Molnar, Paul D. "The Function of the Trinity in Moltmann's Ecological Doctrine of Creation." *Theological Studies* 51 (1990): 673-697.

Morse, Christopher L. *The Logic of Promise in Moltmann's Theology*. Philadelphia: Fortress, 1979.

Mostert, Christiaan. *God and the Future: Wolfhart Pannenberg's Eschatological Doctrine of God*. London: T & T Clark, 2002.

Moule, C. F. D. *The Holy Spirit*. London: Continuum, 2000.

Müller, David L. *Karl Barth: Makers of the Modern Theological Mind*. Waco: Word Books, 1972.

_____. *Karl Barth's Critique of the Anthropological Starting Point in Theology*. Ph. D. Thesis. Duke University, 1958.

Müller-Fahrenholz, Geiko. *The Kingdom and Power: The Theology of Jürgen Moltmann*. London: SCM, 2000.

Müntzer, Thomas. "Sermon before the Princess." In *Spiritual and Anabaptist Writers: Documents Illustrative of the Radical Reformers*. 47-72. Edited by George H. Williams and Angel M. Mergal. London: SCM, 1957.

Murphy, Nancey. *Beyond Liberalism and Foundationalism: How Modern and Post Modern Philosophy Set the Theological Agenda*. Valley Forge: Trinity Press International, 1996.

Nalunnakkal, George Mathew. "Come Holy Spirit, Heal and Reconcile: Called in Christ to be Reconciling and Healing Communities." *International Review of Mission*. Vol. 94, no. 372 (January 2005): 7-19.

Nessian, Nancy. "Faraday's Field Concept." In *Faraday Rediscovered: Essays on the Life and Work of Michael Faraday, 1971-1867*. 175-188. Edited by D. Gooding and F. James. London: Macmillan, 1985.

Newman, Paul W. *A Spirit Christology: Recovering the Biblical Paradigm of Christian Faith*. Lanham: University Press of America, 1987.

Oberdorfer, Bernd. "The Holy Spirit – A Person? Reflection on the Spirit's Trinitarian Identity." In *The Work of the Spirit: Pneumatology and Pentecostalism*. 27-46. Edited by Michael Welker. Grand Rapids: Eerdmans, 2006.

Olive, Don H. *Wolfhart Pannenberg*. Edited by Bob E. Patterson. Texas: Word Books, 1973.

Olson, Roger. "Trinity and Eschatology: The Historical Being of God in Jürgen Moltmann and Wolfhart Pannenberg." *Scottish Journal of Theology*. Vol. 36, no. 2 (1983): 213-227.

Oosterbaan, J. A. "The Theology of Menno Simons." *The Mennonite Quarterly Review*. Vol. 35, no. 3 (July 1961): 187-196.

Otto, Randall E. *The God of Hope: The Trinitarian Vision of Jürgen Moltmann*. Maryland: University Press of America, 1991.

Pauck, Wilhelm. *The Heritage of the Reformation*. Philadelphia: Harper & Row, 1961.

Peters, Eugene. "Sebastian Franck's Theology of Religious Knowledge." *The Mennonite Quarterly Review*. Vol. 35, no. 4 (October 1961): 267-281.

Peters, Ted. *God as Trinity: Relationality and Temporality in Divine Life*. Louisville: Westminster John Knox, 1993.

Peura, Simo. "What God Gives Man Receives: Luther on Salvation." In *Union with Christ: The New Finnish Interpretation*. 76-95. Edited by Carl E. Braaten and Robert W. Jenson. Grand Rapids: Eerdmans, 1998.

Piana, La G. "Joachim of Flora: A Critical Survey." In *Joachim of Fiore in Christian Thought: Essays on the Influence of the Calabrian Prophet* Vol. 1. 3-28. Edited by Delno C. West. New York: Burt Franklin, 1975.

Pinnock, Clark. *Flame of Love: A Theology of the Holy Spirit*. Downers Grove: Inter Varsity, 1996.

Pittenger, Norman. *The Holy Spirit*. Philadelphia: United Church Press, 1974.

Prenter, Regin. *Spiritus Creator*. Trans. by John M. Jensen. Philadelphia: Muhlenberg, 1953.

Prestige, G. L. *God in Patristic Thought*. London: SPCK, 1959.

Price, Charles P. "Some Notes on *Filioque*." *Anglican Theological Review*. Vol. 83, no. 3 (Summer 2001): 515-535.

Priest, Travis Du. "Spirit: Inner Witness and Guardian of the Soul." *Anglican Theological Review*. Vol. 83, no. 3 (Summer 2001): 387-401.

Rahner, Karl. "Experience of Self." *Theological Investigations*. Vol. 13. New York: Seabury, 1975: 122-132.

Rahner, Karl. *The Trinity*. Trans. by Joseph Donceel. New York: Seabury, 1974.

Ramm, Bernard L. *The Pattern of Religious Authority*. Grand Rapids: Eerdmans, 1959.

Rausch, D. A. "Nominalism." In *Evangelical Dictionary of Theology*. 2nd edition. 843. Edited by Walter A. Elwell. Grand Rapids: Baker Academic, 2001.

Reeves, Marjorie. *Joachim of Fiore and the Prophetic Future*. London: SPCK, 1976.

Reid, Darrel R. "Luther, Müntzer and the Last Day: Eschatological Hope, Apocalyptic Expectations." *The Mennonite Quarterly Review*. Vol. 69, no. 1 (January 1995): 53-74.

Rogers, Eugene F. Jr., *After the Spirit: A Constructive Pneumatology from Resources Outside the Modern West*. Grand Rapids: Eerdmans, 2005.

Rohr, John von. "Medieval Consolation and the Young Luther's Despair." In *Reformation Studies: Essays in Honor or Roland H. Bainton*. 61-74. Edited by Franklin H. Littell. Richmond: John Knox, 1962.

Rosato, Philip Joseph. *Karl Barth's Theology of the Holy Spirit: God's Noetic Realization of the Ontological Relationship between Jesus and All Men*. Ph. D. Thesis. Tübingen: n.p, 1976.

Rosen, Michael. *On Voluntary Servitude: False Consciousness and the Theory of Ideology*. Cambridge: Polity, 1996.

Rumscheidt, H. Martin. *Revelation and Theology: An Analysis of the Barth-Harnack Correspondence of 1923*. Cambridge: Cambridge University Press, 1972.

Rupp, Gordon. "Word and Spirit in the First Years of the Reformation." *Archive for Reformation History*. Vol. 49 (1958): 13-25.

Schwarz, Hans. *Eschatology*. Grand Rapids: Eerdmans, 2000.

_____. *Theology in a Global Context: The Last Two Hundred Years*. Grand Rapids: Eerdmans, 2005.

Schwarz, Reinhard. "Thomas Müntzer und die Mystik." In *Die Theologie Thomas Müntzers: Untersuchungen zu einer Entwicklung und Lehre*. 283-301. Edited by Siegfried Bräur and Helmar Junghans. Göttingen: Vandenhoeck & Ruprecht, 1989.

Schwenckfeld, Caspar. "An Answer to Luther's Malediction." In *Spiritual and Anabaptist Writers: Documents Illustrative of the Radical Reformers*. 161-181. Edited by George H. Williams and Angel M. Mergal. London: SCM, 1957.

Seebass, Gottfried. "Thomas Müntzer (c. 1490 – 1525)." In *The Reformation Theologians: An Introduction to Theology in the Early Modern Period*. 338-350. Edited by Carter Lindberg. Oxford: Blackwell, 2002.

Seguenny, Andre. "Caspar von Schwenckfeld (1489-1561)." In *The Reformation Theologians: An Introduction to Theology in the Early Modern Period*. 351-362. Edited by Carter Lindberg. Oxford: Blackwell, 2002.

_____. *The Christology of Caspar Schwenckfeld: Spirit and Flesh in the Process of Life Transformation*. Trans. by Peter C. Erb & Simone Nieuwolt. Lewiston: The Edwin Mellen, 1987.

Servetus, Michael. *Restitución del Cristianismo*. Spanish edition by Angel Alcalá and Luis Betés. Madrid: Fundación Universitaria Española, 1980.

Shelly, Bruce L. *Church History in Plain Language*. Dallas: Word Publishing, 1982.

Shults, F. Leron. *The Postfoundationalist Task of Theology: Wolfhart Pannenberg and the New Theological Rationality*. Grand Rapids: Eerdmans, 1999.

Smart, James D. "Eduard Thurneysen: Pastor-Theologian." *Theology Today* 16, no. 1 (1959): 74-89.

Smirin, M. M. *Die Volksreformation des Thomas Müntzer und Der grosse Bauernkrieg*. Berlin: Dietz Verlag, 1956.

Smith, Preserved. *The Age of the Reformation*. New York: Henry Holt, 1920.

Solomon, Robert C. *In the Spirit of Hegel*. Oxford: Oxford University Press, 1983.

Stayer, James M. "The Passing of the Radical Moment in the Radical Reformation." *The Mennonite Quarterly Review*. Vol. 71, no. 1 (January 1997): 147-152.

_____. "The Radical Reformation." In *Handbook of European History 1400-1600: Late Middle Ages, Renaissance and Reformation: Visions, Programs, and Outcomes*. Vol. 2. 249-282. Edited by Thomas A. Brady, Jr., Heiko A. Oberman, and James D. Tracy. Leiden: Brill, 1995.

Steinmetz, David C. "The Intellectual Appeal of the Reformation." *Theology Today*. Vol. 57, no. 4 (January 2001): 459-472.

Stewart, Jacqui A. *Reconstructing Science and Theology in Postmodernity: Pannenberg, Ethics, and the Human Sciences*. Aldershot: Ashgate, 2000.

Stoesz, Willis M. "The New Creature: Menno Simon's Understanding of the Christian Faith." *The Mennonite Quarterly Review*. Vol. 39, no. 1 (January 1965): 5-24.

Strauss, Gerald. ed., *Enacting the Reformation: Essays on Institution and Reception*. Hampshire: Variorum, 1993.

Suso, Henry. "Das Büchklein der Wahrheit." In *Heinrich Seuse: Deutsche Schriften*. 90-95. Edited by Karl Bihlmeyer. Frankfurt: Minerva, 1961.

Swete, Henry Barclay. *The Holy Spirit in the Ancient Church: A Study of Christian Teaching in the Age of the Fathers*. London: Macmillan, 1912.

Sykes, S. W. "Authority and Openness in the Church." In *Karl Barth: Centenary Essays*. 69-86. Edited by S. W. Sykes. Cambridge: Cambridge University Press, 1989.

Taubes, Jacob. "Theology and the Philosophic Critique of Religion." *Zeitschrift für Religions und Geistesgeschichte*. Vol. 8 (1959): 129-138.

Tavard, George A. "A Clarification on the *Filioque*." *Anglican Theological Review*. Vol. 83, no. 3 (Summer 2001): 507-514.

Thultrup, Neil. and M. Mikulova Thultrup. *Bibliotheca Kierkegaardiana* 3. Copenhagen: Reitzels Boghandel, 1980.

Thurneysen, Eduard. "Introduction." In *Revolutionary Theology in the Making: Barth-Thurneysen Correspondence, 1914-1925*. Trans. by James D. Smart. London: The Epworth Press, 1964.

_____. *Karl Barth: Theologie und Sozialismus*. Zurich: Theologischer Verlag, 1973.

Tibbs, Clint. *Religious Experience of the Pneuma: Communication with the Spirit World in 1 Corinthians 12 and 14*. Tübingen: Mohr Siebeck, 2007.

Torrance, T. F. "The Legacy of Karl Barth (1886-1986)." *Scottish Journal of Theology*. Vol. 39, no.3 (August 1986): 289-308.

_____. *Karl Barth: An Introduction to His Early Theology, 1930 – 1931*. London: SCM, 1962.

Tupper, E. Frank. *The Theology of Wolfhart Pannenberg*. Philadelphia: Westminster, 1971.

Turcescu, Lucian. *Gregory of Nyssa and the Concept of Divine Persons*. New York: Oxford University Press, 2005.

Turner, Max. "The Charismatic Movement and the Church – Conflict or Renewal?" *European Journal of Theology*. Vol. 10, no, 1 (2001): 49-61.

Tzamalikos, P. Origen: *Cosmology and Ontology of Time*. Boston: Brill, 2006.

Urs von Balthasar, Hans. *Karl Barth: Darstellung und Deutung seiner Theologie*. Köln: Verlag Jacob Hegner, 1951.

Voolstra, Sjouke. "True Penitence: The Core of Menno Simon's Theology." *The Mennonite Quarterly Review*. Vol. 62, no. 3 (July 1988): 387-400.

Vree, Dale. *On Synthesizing Marxism and Christianity*. New York: Wiley, 1976.

Wallace, Mark. *Fragments of the Spirit: Nature, Violence, and the Renewal of Creation*. Harrisburg: Trinity Press International, 2002.

Regensburg, W. C. "Barmen, Declaration of (1934)." In *Evangelical Dictionary of Theology*. 141. Edited by Walter A. Elwell. Grand Rapids: Baker Academic, 2001.

Voelkel, Robert Townsend. *The Conception of Faith in the Theology of Karl Barth: A Critique of Barthian Theology*. Ph. D. Thesis. New York: Union Theological Seminary, 1962Waldrop, Charles T. *Karl Barth's Christology: Its Basic Alexandrian Character*. Berlin: Mouton, 1984.

Walter Wells, William. *The Influence of Kierkegaard on the Theology of Karl Barth*. Ph. D. Thesis. Michigan: University Microfilms, 1970.

Wappler, Paul. *Thomas Müntzer in Zwickau und die Zwickauer Propheten*. Gütersloh: Gütersloher Verlagshaus, 1966.

Warfield, Benjamin B. "Introductory Note." In *The Work of the Holy Spirit*, by Abraham Kuyper. xxv-xxxix. Grand Rapids: Eerdmans, 1979.

Watts, Graham J. *Revelation and the Spirit: A Comparative Study of the Relationship between the Doctrine of Revelation and Pneumatology of the Theology of Eberhard Jungel and Wolfhart Pannenberg*. Eugene: Wipf & Stock, 2005.

Webster, J. B. *Barth's Ethics of Reconciliation*. Cambridge: Cambridge University Press, 1995.

Weil, Louis. "The Holy Spirit: Source of Unity in the Liturgy." *Anglican Theological Review*. Vol. 83, no. 3 (Summer 2001): 409-415.

Weingart, Richard E. "The Meaning of Sin in the Theology of Menno Simons." *The Mennonite Quarterly Review*. Vol. 41, no. 1 (January 1967): 25-39.

Welch, Claude. *In This Name: The Doctrine of the Trinity in Contemporary Theology*. New York: Scribner, 1952.

Welker, Michael. *God the Spirit*. Trans. by John F. Hoffmeyer. Minneapolis: Fortress, 1994.

West, Delno C. "Introduction." In *Joachim of Fiore in Christian Thought: Essays on the Influence of the Calabrian Prophet.* Vol. 1. i-xv. Edited by Delno C. West. New York: Burt Franklin, 1975.

_____. and Sandra Zimdars-Swartz. *Joachim of Fiore: A Study in Spiritual Perception and History.* Bloomington: Indiana University Press, 1983.

_____. ed., *Joachim of Fiore in Christian Thought: Essays on the Influence of the Calabrian Prophet.* Vol. 1. New York: Burt Franklin, 1975.

Williams, George H. and Angel M. Mergal. eds., *Spiritual and Anabaptist Writers: Documents Illustrative of the Radical Reformers.* London: SCM, 1957.

_____. *The Radical Reformation.* Philadelphia: Westminster, 1962.

_____. "German Mysticism in the Polarization of Ethical Behavior in Luther and the Anabaptists." *The Mennonite Quarterly Review.* Vol. 48, no. 3 (July 1974): 275-304.

_____. "A Letter to John Campanus by Sebastian Frank." In *Spiritual and Anabaptist Writers.* 145-146. Edited by George H. Williams and Angel M. Mergal. London: SCM, 1957.

Williams, Rowan. *Challenges in Contemporary Theology: On Christian Theology.* Oxford: Blackwell, 2000.

Willis, David. *Calvin's Catholic Christology: The Function of the So-called Extra Calvinism in Calvin's Theology.* Leiden: Brill, 1966.

Worthing, Mark William. *Foundations and Functions of Theology as a Universal Science: Theological Method and Apologetic Praxis in Wolfhart Pannenberg and Karl Rahner.* Frankfurt am Main: Peter Lang, 1996.

_____. *God, Creation, and Contemporary Physics.* Minneapolis: Fortress, 1996.

Wriedt, Markus. "Luther's Theology." Trans. by Katharina Gustavs. In *The Cambridge Companion to Martin Luther.* 86-119. Edited by Donald McKim. Cambridge: Cambridge University Press, 2003.

Wright, D. F. "Montanism." In *Evangelical Dictionary of Theology.* 2nd Edition. 190. Edited by Walter A. Elwell. Michigan: Baker Academic, 2001.

Wright, J. Robert. "Holy Spirit in Holy Church: From Experience to Doctrine." *Anglican Theological Review.* Vol. 83, no. 3 (Summer 2001): 443-454.

Yong, Amos. "Guests, Hosts, and the Holy Ghost: Pneumatological Theology and Christian Practices in a World of Many Faiths." In *Lord and Giver of*

Life: Perspectives on Constructive Pneumatology. Edited by David H. Jensen. Louisville: Westminster, 2008.

———. *Beyond the Impasse: Toward a Pneumatological Theology of Religions.* Grand Rapids: Baker Academic, 2003.

———. *Discerning the Spirit(s): A Pentecostal-Charismatic Contribution to Christian Theology of Religions.* Sheffield: Sheffield Academic, 2000.

———. *The Spirit Poured Out on All Flesh: Pentecostalism and the Possibility of Global Theology.* Grand Rapids: Baker Academic, 2005.

Young, E. *Church and State in the Theology of Karl Barth.* Ph. D. Thesis. Michigan: University Microfilms, 1971.

Zachman, Randall C. "John Calvin (1509-1564)." In *The Reformation Theologians: An Introduction to Theology in the Early Modern period.* 184-197. Edited by Carter Lindberg. Oxford: Blackwell, 2002.

Zahl, Paul F. M. "The Spirit in the Blood." *Anglican Theological Review.* Vol. 83, no. 3 (Summer 2001): 493-498.

Index

A

absolute Paradox 97
Adam 69, 70, 73, 307, 320, 321, 331, 332, 333, 337, 424
ad extra 109, 119, 122, 123, 159, 392
ad intra 113, 123, 392
adoption 50, 149, 194, 346, 350
allegorical interpretation 55
Anabaptism 39, 52, 53, 54, 59, 65, 425, 429
analogical 114
Anamnesis 358
anointing 47, 67
Anselm 3, 35, 89, 97, 103, 391, 429
anthropocentric 15, 90, 237, 390, 398, 403, 410
Anthropocentric 237
anthropocentrism 15, 237
anthropology 55, 185, 193, 234, 237, 281, 283, 318, 319, 321, 329, 330, 352, 383, 390, 398, 399, 400, 406
Anthropology 137, 234, 318, 319, 320, 322, 325, 327, 328, 329, 331, 350, 352, 398, 419, 420
apocalyptic 10, 35, 36, 38, 54, 244, 245
Apocalyptic 35, 38, 421, 434
Aquinas, Thomas 45, 286
Arianism 101, 111, 226, 392, 393
Aristotelianism 319

Athanasius 11, 83, 111, 297
atonement 241, 243
Augustine 27, 34, 40, 44, 53, 118, 119, 120, 121, 122, 123, 183, 286, 301, 308, 331, 420

B

baptism 39, 45, 47, 55, 59, 60, 63, 70, 72, 77, 130, 164, 214, 228, 237, 253, 254, 309, 311, 319, 342, 344, 346, 355, 356, 357, 376, 377, 380, 381, 383
Baptism 55, 253, 355, 425
Barmen Confession 88
Barmen orthodoxy 195
Barth, Fritz 84
Barth, Karl x, 20, 21, 23, 25, 83, 84, 85, 86, 87, 88, 89, 91, 92, 93, 94, 95, 96, 97, 99, 100, 101, 102, 103, 105, 109, 112, 113, 114, 120, 125, 131, 137, 144, 148, 149, 150, 157, 158, 160, 169, 170, 171, 174, 177, 178, 179, 180, 185, 187, 195, 196, 204, 281, 282, 286, 389, 390, 393, 394, 396, 415, 416, 421, 422, 423, 424, 425, 426, 427, 428, 430, 431, 432, 434, 436, 437, 439
beatitudes 233

begetting 118, 121, 203, 300, 301, 306, 308
begotten 64, 121, 123, 144, 300, 306
Berkhof, Hendrik 227
Blumhardt, Johann Christoph 85
body of Christ 63, 71, 74, 141, 161, 250, 344, 345, 346, 349, 353, 354, 355, 361
Body of Christ 161
Bonhoeffer, Dietrich 196, 425
Bornkamm, Günther 287
bread 1, 59, 62, 69, 72, 77, 135, 357, 358, 359, 360, 407
breath 1, 6, 15, 16, 199, 200, 213, 215, 266, 290, 313, 320, 321, 322, 330, 340, 343, 365, 366, 368, 371, 374, 397, 400, 410, 411
breathing 118, 300, 301, 306, 307, 308, 320, 365
broad place 246
Brunner, Peter 282
Bultmann, Rudolf 195, 234, 273, 287

C

Calvin, John 29, 39, 45, 46, 47, 94, 286, 426, 431, 439
Hans von Campenhausen 282, 286
canon 29, 170
Canon 170, 173
canonicity 170
capitalism 90
Caspar, von Schwenckfeld 39, 69, 70, 71, 72, 75, 435
Catholicism 1, 14, 31, 36, 52, 59, 93, 94, 170, 390
charismata 135, 206, 252, 253, 258, 260
charismatic movement 2, 260
Charismatic movement 7
charity 119
Christ-history 206

Christian existentialism 390
Christology 3, 4, 5, 8, 11, 12, 13, 45, 46, 47, 48, 50, 71, 73, 74, 103, 114, 125, 126, 130, 183, 184, 185, 202, 205, 218, 226, 227, 229, 232, 240, 241, 245, 250, 252, 253, 278, 279, 281, 283, 294, 308, 309, 330, 332, 383, 385, 388, 389, 396, 397, 398, 403, 413, 418, 421, 428, 432, 435, 437, 438
Christomonistic 110, 226
church x, 1, 2, 3, 6, 7, 8, 10, 11, 14, 16, 17, 18, 24, 27, 28, 29, 30, 31, 33, 35, 36, 37, 38, 39, 40, 41, 43, 45, 49, 52, 55, 57, 59, 65, 69, 70, 72, 74, 75, 76, 77, 78, 80, 81, 83, 84, 85, 86, 87, 88, 92, 93, 98, 100, 101, 108, 110, 111, 118, 126, 127, 131, 136, 138, 149, 152, 153, 154, 155, 156, 157, 158, 159, 160, 161, 162, 163, 164, 168, 169, 170, 171, 172, 173, 174, 175, 176, 178, 179, 180, 181, 182, 187, 188, 196, 197, 201, 202, 206, 207, 208, 221, 224, 226, 229, 238, 247, 249, 250, 251, 252, 254, 255, 257, 258, 259, 260, 261, 262, 271, 272, 273, 283, 286, 287, 340, 342, 344, 345, 346, 347, 348, 349, 350, 351, 352, 353, 354, 355, 356, 357, 358, 359, 360, 361, 374, 377, 378, 382, 385, 387, 388, 389, 390, 396, 400, 401, 402, 405, 408, 409, 410
Church 9, 10, 11, 13, 16, 17, 24, 30, 31, 36, 52, 53, 54, 55, 56, 57, 58, 59, 60, 65, 80, 81, 85, 87, 88, 95, 97, 98, 102, 111, 126, 136, 137, 152, 153, 154, 155, 157, 160, 162, 169, 172, 173, 174,

177, 189, 190, 194, 196, 198,
  203, 227, 231, 232, 249, 250,
  251, 252, 253, 254, 257, 258,
  260, 261, 262, 264, 274, 275,
  277, 281, 284, 289, 341, 343,
  344, 348, 349, 351, 352, 360,
  374, 402, 416, 418, 419, 421,
  425, 426, 433, 435, 436, 437,
  438, 439
Church Dogmatics 87, 95, 97, 102,
  177, 281, 416
communio peccatorum 155
communio sanctorum 155
Community 157, 158, 161, 260, 265,
  327, 349
conception 30, 59, 64, 90, 92, 97,
  126, 128, 137, 167, 177, 285,
  287, 289, 309, 311, 366, 401
concept of emanation 215
concept of revelation 98, 99, 102,
  112, 143
Confessing Church 190, 196, 284
congregation 30, 65, 148, 153, 160,
  206, 258, 259, 260
Constantinople ix, 126, 392
consummation 115, 149, 175, 181,
  243, 248, 250, 252, 269, 270,
  276, 305, 306, 311, 317, 318,
  338, 339, 340, 342, 347, 348,
  356, 359, 360, 369, 373, 374,
  377, 378, 380, 382, 383, 384,
  404, 405
Consummation 270
continental theology 83
correlation 49, 115, 403
cosmic Christology 202
cosmic Spirit 202, 203, 266
Cosmic Spirit 201
Counterpart 216
Covenant 77, 78
Cox, Harvey 187
Creation 8, 9, 151, 195, 203, 225,
  231, 238, 239, 265, 266, 267,
268, 269, 270, 271, 272, 289,
  292, 293, 340, 341, 361, 362,
  364, 370, 372, 383, 385, 411,
  413, 417, 418, 419, 429, 432,
  437, 438
cross 44, 56, 131, 187, 188, 190,
  196, 227, 228, 229, 230, 231,
  232, 240, 243, 253, 333, 338,
  399, 400
crucifixion; 166

D

day of Pentecost 136
deductive 114, 215, 278
deification 69, 73
demythologization 195, 196
Denck, Han 39, 65, 66, 67, 68, 69,
  75, 425, 429
dialectical materialism 90
dialectical process 91
divine action 10, 12, 18, 81, 158,
  162, 166, 305, 306, 335, 362,
  365, 378, 388, 404
divine energy 201, 208, 239, 249,
  393
divine essence 41, 116, 123, 293,
  294, 302, 303, 305, 306, 307,
  362, 392
divine persons 99, 184, 209, 226,
  302, 303, 378, 394
divine substantia 113
divinity of the Spirit 41, 60, 95, 110,
  111, 115, 117, 118, 120, 123,
  203, 392, 393
divinization 194
docetic Christology 103
Doctrine of the Trinity 112, 294, 295,
  428, 437
Dostojewski 92
double procession 120, 121, 123
doxological Trinity 221
dualism x, 70, 74, 92, 410
dual procession 204

E

Easter 131, 133, 135, 178, 180, 228, 231, 232, 295, 309, 317, 332, 333, 342, 343, 357, 358
Easter theology 232
ebionite Christology 103
Ecclesiology 152, 194, 249, 341, 418
ecological 7, 15, 202, 261, 410, 411
ecology 202, 212, 260, 267
economic Trinity 112, 113, 114, 123, 204, 221, 222, 223, 392
Ecstasy 405, 428
Ecumenism 261, 408
Election 148, 423
elliptical model 390
Elohim 110
Elze, Martin 283
Emmanuel 126, 127
Energy 199, 211, 366, 419
enlightenment theology 192, 193
Epiclesis 358
epistemological criterion 80
eschatological 10, 16, 21, 22, 35, 85, 114, 177, 178, 179, 181, 183, 185, 190, 194, 196, 197, 214, 223, 232, 233, 237, 244, 246, 248, 249, 250, 252, 253, 254, 256, 257, 262, 264, 270, 271, 272, 273, 274, 275, 276, 279, 305, 309, 310, 311, 315, 317, 321, 331, 332, 333, 340, 342, 343, 346, 347, 348, 349, 350, 354, 356, 357, 359, 360, 369, 370, 372, 373, 374, 375, 376, 377, 378, 380, 381, 382, 383, 391, 401, 403, 404, 405, 411
eschatological prophet 309
eschatology 22, 35, 177, 180, 187, 195, 218, 233, 245, 250, 251, 252, 253, 254, 272, 273, 274, 277, 278, 281, 311, 347, 373, 374, 376, 377, 383, 384, 402, 405

eschaton 177, 180, 181, 224, 243, 248, 272, 276, 277, 309, 342, 350, 374, 375, 383, 397
eternal Son 47, 130, 144, 372
Eternal Spirit 111, 112
eternity 104, 114, 122, 124, 159, 166, 203, 223, 226, 244, 302, 304, 306, 312, 316, 342, 344, 350, 361, 362, 369, 370, 379, 404
Ethical 34, 76, 79, 422, 438
Eucharist 5, 59, 69, 72, 135, 224, 254, 360
Eucharistic Trinity 221
Evangelical 6, 10, 20, 30, 32, 34, 53, 75, 84, 88, 189, 415, 420, 430, 434, 437, 438
Evangelical Rationalists 53
evangelical theology 85, 95
event of revelation 108, 122, 124, 139, 145, 147, 295, 296, 395
exaltation 135, 166, 179, 229, 334
existential Christianity 52
experience 2, 3, 7, 9, 13, 18, 19, 37, 40, 42, 45, 53, 54, 56, 58, 66, 73, 78, 79, 86, 90, 114, 125, 126, 128, 152, 165, 175, 176, 189, 191, 193, 194, 197, 198, 199, 201, 202, 207, 209, 210, 211, 212, 213, 214, 215, 216, 217, 218, 219, 220, 221, 223, 225, 228, 232, 234, 235, 236, 237, 238, 243, 244, 246, 247, 248, 249, 250, 251, 254, 255, 256, 259, 260, 261, 262, 264, 269, 271, 272, 274, 275, 276, 278, 281, 282, 284, 285, 287, 289, 323, 325, 326, 327, 330, 343, 377, 395, 398, 399, 400, 401, 403, 405, 406, 408

F

Faith 6, 9, 13, 15, 40, 64, 89, 90, 91, 140, 143, 150, 174, 175, 195, 238, 251, 267, 289, 322, 354, 363, 366, 396, 417, 419, 420, 421, 422, 424, 432, 436, 437

Faraday, Michael 291, 432

Father 2, 3, 4, 5, 8, 10, 11, 20, 35, 38, 41, 47, 50, 60, 61, 64, 71, 74, 85, 92, 99, 100, 101, 102, 104, 105, 110, 112, 113, 114, 115, 116, 117, 119, 120, 121, 122, 123, 124, 130, 132, 134, 135, 140, 143, 146, 147, 148, 149, 153, 156, 166, 174, 180, 202, 203, 204, 205, 206, 207, 208, 209, 210, 215, 216, 222, 223, 224, 225, 228, 229, 230, 231, 238, 243, 244, 245, 253, 254, 255, 256, 257, 258, 263, 264, 265, 266, 268, 275, 276, 293, 294, 295, 296, 297, 298, 299, 300, 301, 302, 303, 304, 305, 306, 307, 308, 310, 311, 312, 313, 314, 315, 316, 317, 318, 324, 333, 334, 335, 336, 337, 338, 340, 342, 344, 345, 346, 348, 349, 350, 352, 353, 356, 357, 362, 363, 367, 368, 371, 372, 373, 378, 379, 381, 382, 383, 389, 392, 393, 394, 395, 397, 400, 410, 411, 419, 421

fellowship 4, 52, 75, 122, 140, 157, 158, 159, 163, 175, 202, 225, 228, 237, 238, 249, 250, 251, 252, 253, 254, 256, 261, 262, 263, 264, 265, 274, 293, 299, 300, 302, 303, 307, 308, 310, 311, 312, 315, 317, 318, 325, 332, 335, 337, 338, 339, 343, 344, 345, 346, 347, 351, 353, 354, 355, 356, 357, 358, 359, 360, 361, 362, 363, 371, 372, 373, 376, 377, 378, 379, 382, 383, 399, 402, 407

Feminist 7, 10, 411, 428

fertility 213, 214, 215

Fertility 213

Feuerbach, Ludwig 193, 194

Field of Force 290

Filioque 12, 47, 120, 122, 204, 308, 431, 433, 436

Fiore, Joachim of 8, 32, 34, 35, 36, 37, 38, 39, 53, 223, 433, 434, 438

Fire 81, 212, 420

forgiveness 27, 40, 42, 45, 61, 189, 211, 242, 243, 251, 356, 380, 399

Frank, Sebastian 39, 75, 77, 438

Freedom 51, 66, 114, 137, 149, 210, 238, 239, 240, 285, 313, 352, 420, 426, 427

fruits of the Spirit 62, 63, 76

G

general and specific 99

generation 15, 109, 121, 128, 306

Gentiles 333

Gerhard, von Rad 197, 282, 286

Gestalt 211, 212, 218

Giver of Life 1, 17, 115, 289, 438

Glorification 382

Godhead 9, 46, 119, 120, 124, 205, 214, 294, 300, 302, 303, 308, 384, 393

Goethe 188, 191

gospel 57, 61, 65, 73, 74, 88, 109, 127, 177, 224, 228, 255, 256, 261, 307, 335, 338, 340, 348, 349, 351, 352, 353, 382, 388, 404

Göttingen University 189, 195

Grace 18, 427

H

Harnack, Adolf von 93, 96
Hartmann, Nicolai 282
Hegel 91, 92, 193, 196, 197, 285, 294, 296, 298, 435
Heidelberg 103, 191, 282, 283, 285
Heidelberg Catechism 103, 191
heresy 12, 54
hermeneutical principle 101
hermeneutics 171, 411
Herrmann, Wilhelm 96
Historical Construct 154
historical Trinity 221
History 14, 31, 34, 35, 45, 51, 52, 53, 54, 55, 57, 67, 70, 75, 85, 191, 209, 229, 247, 251, 266, 269, 270, 417, 418, 420, 421, 423, 424, 425, 427, 429, 431, 434, 435, 438
Hitler x, 87
Holy Ghost ix, 17, 41, 43, 58, 60, 62, 64, 67, 108, 111, 127, 128, 156, 168, 173, 438
Holy Spirit ix, x, xi, 1, 2, 3, 4, 5, 6, 8, 9, 10, 11, 12, 13, 14, 15, 16, 18, 20, 21, 22, 24, 27, 28, 35, 38, 40, 41, 42, 43, 44, 45, 47, 48, 49, 50, 51, 55, 56, 57, 60, 61, 63, 64, 72, 76, 78, 81, 84, 86, 89, 91, 94, 95, 96, 98, 99, 100, 102, 105, 106, 107, 108, 110, 111, 112, 113, 114, 115, 116, 117, 118, 121, 122, 123, 125, 126, 128, 129, 130, 131, 133, 134, 135, 136, 137, 139, 140, 141, 142, 143, 144, 145, 147, 148, 149, 150, 151, 152, 153, 154, 155, 156, 157, 158, 159, 161, 164, 165, 166, 167, 168, 170, 171, 172, 174, 175, 176, 180, 182, 197, 198, 199, 201, 202, 204, 205, 206, 207, 208, 209, 210, 211, 212, 213, 216, 217, 220, 221, 222, 223, 224, 225, 226, 229, 231, 233, 234, 237, 240, 242, 243, 244, 245, 247, 249, 250, 251, 252, 253, 254, 255, 256, 258, 259, 260, 261, 262, 263, 264, 265, 266, 267, 268, 272, 275, 277, 278, 287, 288, 289, 293, 294, 298, 308, 313, 318, 327, 330, 341, 349, 356, 361, 367, 373, 387, 389, 390, 391, 393, 394, 398, 399, 400, 402, 405, 406, 408, 411, 413, 417, 418, 421, 422, 423, 426, 427, 428, 429, 432, 433, 434, 436, 437, 438
humiliation 128, 166, 203, 228
hypostasis 207, 298, 302, 303
hypostatic 203, 205, 297, 302, 314, 394
Hypostatic 100

I

illumination 7, 35, 38, 49, 136, 147, 160
imagination 97, 189, 322, 323, 324, 399, 406, 407
Imagination 322, 323, 406, 428
imago dei 146
immanent 112, 113, 114, 123, 156, 174, 183, 184, 201, 202, 204, 215, 219, 220, 221, 222, 230, 235, 246, 267, 268, 329, 330, 392, 399, 410, 411
immanent Trinity 112, 113, 114, 123, 221, 222, 392
incarnate God 47
incarnation 5, 47, 64, 68, 71, 73, 100, 103, 125, 128, 129, 131, 137, 145, 158, 163, 179, 227, 311, 312, 313, 331, 332, 335, 337, 342, 344, 359, 364, 370, 372, 377

Incarnation 11, 64, 125, 311, 422, 430
inductive 114
inner Word 51, 66, 67, 68, 70, 73, 74, 77, 78, 81
inspiration xiv, 10, 37, 48, 49, 52, 81, 136, 167, 168, 169, 170, 171, 254, 258, 325, 343, 378
Inspiration 7, 168, 420
intra-trinitarian 119
invisible 73, 76, 106, 159, 160, 161, 288, 343
Invisible 158
Iwand, Hans Joachim 196

J

Jaspers, Karl 282
Jesus ix, 2, 3, 5, 6, 12, 13, 14, 16, 19, 20, 21, 27, 36, 43, 44, 45, 47, 50, 52, 54, 56, 59, 60, 61, 62, 63, 64, 66, 67, 68, 69, 70, 72, 73, 74, 87, 94, 97, 98, 99, 102, 103, 104, 106, 107, 109, 110, 113, 114, 116, 120, 121, 125, 126, 127, 128, 129, 130, 131, 132, 133, 134, 135, 136, 137, 138, 140, 141, 142, 143, 144, 145, 147, 148, 149, 150, 151, 152, 153, 154, 155, 156, 157, 158, 159, 160, 161, 162, 163, 164, 165, 166, 170, 171, 172, 174, 177, 178, 179, 180, 181, 182, 183, 184, 188, 190, 195, 204, 208, 213, 219, 226, 227, 228, 229, 230, 231, 232, 233, 234, 238, 243, 244, 247, 251, 253, 255, 256, 258, 261, 271, 273, 277, 286, 287, 294, 295, 296, 297, 298, 299, 300, 303, 306, 307, 309, 310, 311, 313, 314, 315, 316, 317, 318, 319, 331, 332, 333, 334, 335, 336, 337, 338, 339, 342, 343, 344, 345, 346, 347, 348, 349, 350, 351, 352, 353, 354, 355, 356, 357, 358, 359, 360, 361, 370, 373, 374, 375, 376, 377, 379, 380, 382, 383, 385, 395, 396, 397, 399, 400, 401, 405, 406, 407, 418, 419, 424, 428, 434
Judaism 37, 90, 241, 298, 321, 375
Judge 6, 153, 210
judgment 7, 35, 109, 132, 165, 190, 315, 318, 333, 338, 339, 342, 356, 379, 380, 381
Judgment 380
justice 8, 58, 210, 211, 228, 242, 270, 271, 273, 292, 308, 330, 334, 399
justification 3, 34, 36, 42, 43, 46, 56, 66, 70, 71, 90, 160, 162, 164, 194, 196, 219, 234, 241, 242, 243, 244, 245, 295, 332, 399
Justification 33, 166, 242, 420

K

Kantian revolution 193
Kant, Immanuel 192
Kärkkäinen, Veli-Matti 16, 17
Käsemann, Ernst 197
kenosis 230, 263, 268
kenotic forms 218
kerygma 136, 287, 385, 395
Kierkegaard, Sören 92
kingdom 54, 57, 58, 60, 62, 68, 91, 92, 110, 151, 159, 161, 177, 182, 188, 197, 213, 214, 218, 227, 228, 239, 240, 244, 245, 249, 250, 251, 252, 254, 256, 258, 261, 262, 267, 270, 271, 274, 275, 276, 277, 278, 296, 297, 300, 301, 304, 305, 311, 316, 335, 341, 342, 347, 348, 349, 350, 351, 353, 354, 359, 360, 361, 369, 370, 375, 379, 382, 401, 402, 404

Kingdom 52, 77, 204, 205, 207, 221, 226, 228, 229, 230, 233, 237, 267, 270, 273, 274, 275, 276, 279, 282, 283, 284, 286, 288, 313, 314, 316, 341, 348, 350, 394, 418, 420, 432
Kingdom of God 52, 228, 237, 274, 275, 282, 283, 284, 286, 288, 313, 314, 316, 341, 350, 394, 420
Kirchliche, Hochschule 190
Koch, Johannes 149
Koch, Klaus 283
koinonia 263, 394, 395

L

Lessing 188, 197
liberalism 18
Liberalism 19, 95, 432
Liberation Theology 109
life force 200, 201, 202, 384
Light 81, 110, 213, 388, 389, 398, 406, 420
living soul 79, 319, 321
living Spirit 77, 79, 80
Logos 73, 111, 216, 296, 331, 342, 359, 370, 371, 372, 396, 409
Lombard, Peter 37
Lord 1, 2, 6, 17, 39, 43, 45, 50, 59, 62, 65, 68, 69, 70, 72, 100, 104, 106, 107, 108, 110, 111, 115, 130, 132, 136, 140, 143, 145, 147, 152, 153, 154, 157, 161, 164, 174, 175, 176, 182, 210, 211, 226, 238, 249, 253, 254, 256, 307, 309, 316, 318, 321, 333, 334, 339, 342, 343, 344, 346, 349, 356, 357, 358, 359, 360, 400, 438
Lordship 182, 312
Lord's Supper 39, 45, 50, 70, 72, 130, 164, 253, 254, 349, 357, 358, 360
love xiii, 12, 17, 18, 20, 24, 33, 37, 42, 43, 44, 47, 52, 61, 63, 64, 65, 66, 69, 73, 79, 87, 100, 110, 118, 119, 120, 122, 123, 124, 140, 143, 152, 153, 156, 163, 164, 165, 166, 167, 178, 198, 202, 204, 208, 212, 213, 214, 232, 236, 239, 240, 243, 246, 256, 263, 267, 270, 295, 298, 301, 302, 303, 304, 312, 326, 328, 329, 336, 339, 341, 355, 362, 363, 368, 382, 400, 404, 407
Love 13, 18, 24, 81, 118, 164, 165, 212, 301, 351, 408, 409, 412, 413, 420, 428, 433
Löwith, Karl 282
Lutherans 36, 135
Luther, Martin 29, 30, 31, 34, 39, 40, 41, 42, 43, 45, 53, 55, 135, 286, 425, 427, 429, 432, 438

M

manifestation 37, 47, 50, 110, 112, 134, 143, 144, 155, 167, 175, 176, 181, 203, 303, 305, 325, 326, 328, 364, 367, 372, 375, 377, 405
Marxism 90, 187, 194, 437
Marxist revisionism 192
Marx, Karl 90, 193
McGrath, Alister 431
Melanchthon 54, 69
Mennonite Church 59
messiah 47, 228, 309
Messiah 242, 310, 317, 333, 334, 346, 347, 374, 375
Middle Ages 27, 30, 31, 32, 35, 51, 53, 75, 287, 292, 306, 391, 426, 435
Ministry 62, 360, 430
miracle 64, 99, 104, 114, 126, 127, 129, 139, 142, 175, 344

Mission 13, 17, 273, 420, 423, 429, 432
modalism 101, 295, 394
Modalism 102
modalist view 111
mode of being 101, 111, 115, 116, 122, 123, 134, 327, 393
modernism 105
monarchical Trinity 221
monarchy 236, 304, 305, 312
Montanism 10, 111, 170, 438
morality 70, 79, 317
mother 73, 85, 128, 210, 211, 247, 411, 412
Mother 210
motherhood 246, 247, 278
Motherhood 246
Thomas Müntzer x, 34, 38, 39, 52, 53, 54, 55, 56, 57, 66, 68, 77, 421, 425, 426, 430, 431, 432, 434, 435, 437
mutual relations 110, 204, 302, 362, 368, 393
mutual relationships 99, 403
mystery 12, 24, 60, 71, 87, 104, 108, 114, 122, 124, 125, 126, 127, 128, 129, 130, 131, 160, 161, 163, 169, 176, 212, 215, 248, 252, 316, 351, 384, 400, 407, 410, 412
mystical spiritualism 54
mystical union 81, 124, 337
mysticism 32, 33, 39, 53, 55, 57, 66, 69, 194
Mysticism 32, 34, 66, 438
mythology 129

N

National Socialism 87, 196
neighbor 61, 119, 165, 166
Neo-Nicenes 111
Neo-Protestantism 93, 94
new covenant 67, 357

New Creation 151, 270
new humanity 155, 332, 333, 349, 357
Nicene-Constantinopolitan Creed 111, 115
Nicene Creed ix, 11, 111, 117, 118, 120, 204, 205, 225, 389, 392, 393
Nietzsche 92, 188, 191
noetic problem 110
nominalism 32
Nominalism 32, 434
Gregory of Nyssa 388, 436

O

objective revelation 102, 105, 125, 139, 147, 176
Objective revelation 138
obsession 329, 330
Ockham, William 32
oikonomia 113
oikos pneumatikos 135
ontological being 297
Operation Gomorrah 188
Origen 2, 437
original sin 47, 241
Orthodox church 197
orthodoxy 15, 23, 195, 389
Orthodoxy 1
outer Word 74
outpouring 38, 105, 136, 141, 142, 151, 157, 162, 179, 199, 213, 214, 217, 255, 271, 273, 340, 343, 348, 378, 400
Outpouring 179, 341
Overbeck, Franz 93, 177

P

panentheistic 267
Pannenberg x, 3, 4, 9, 17, 18, 20, 22, 23, 25, 190, 198, 273, 281, 282, 283, 284, 285, 286, 287, 288, 289, 290, 291, 292, 293, 294,

295, 296, 297, 298, 299, 300,
301, 302, 303, 304, 305, 306,
307, 308, 309, 310, 311, 312,
313, 314, 315, 316, 317, 318,
319, 320, 321, 322, 323, 324,
325, 326, 327, 328, 329, 330,
331, 332, 333, 334, 335, 336,
337, 338, 339, 340, 341, 342,
343, 344, 345, 346, 347, 348,
349, 350, 351, 352, 353, 354,
355, 356, 357, 358, 359, 360,
361, 362, 363, 364, 365, 366,
367, 368, 369, 370, 371, 372,
373, 374, 375, 376, 377, 378,
379, 380, 381, 382, 383, 384,
385, 387, 389, 391, 392, 393,
395, 396, 397, 398, 399, 400,
401, 402, 404, 405, 406, 408,
409, 410, 412, 413, 419, 420,
426, 428, 429, 431, 432, 433,
435, 436, 437, 438
Pannenberg, Wolfhart x, 3, 4, 9, 22,
23, 25, 190, 273, 281, 282, 283,
284, 285, 286, 287, 288, 289,
291, 292, 293, 294, 296, 313,
314, 318, 319, 322, 323, 363,
366, 373, 383, 385, 391, 396,
419, 420, 426, 428, 429, 431,
432, 433, 435, 436, 437, 438
pantheism 183
Paraclete 5, 210, 229, 247, 314
passion 191, 236, 271, 417, 418
Passion 191, 236, 271, 417, 418
patristic pneumatology 197, 198
Peasants' War 52, 54
Pentecostalism 1, 4, 12, 13, 81, 391,
410, 428, 429, 433, 439
perichoretic 205, 209, 225, 226, 268,
394, 403
perichoretic fellowship 225
person ix, 1, 2, 3, 4, 7, 9, 10, 11, 21,
22, 23, 27, 31, 39, 41, 42, 43, 44,
46, 50, 53, 54, 55, 56, 57, 60, 62,

63, 65, 67, 68, 70, 71, 74, 78, 79,
80, 81, 89, 92, 97, 99, 100, 101,
103, 105, 111, 113, 125, 127,
128, 135, 142, 143, 144, 146,
147, 151, 157, 158, 164, 165,
170, 174, 176, 195, 200, 201,
207, 209, 210, 224, 226, 228,
229, 232, 233, 235, 236, 239,
241, 248, 258, 278, 288, 294,
296, 299, 302, 306, 307, 311,
320, 322, 326, 328, 329, 333,
334, 337, 343, 355, 367, 368,
370, 372, 387, 388, 389, 391,
394, 396, 397, 398, 405, 406,
407, 413
Person 205, 207, 225, 293, 391, 433
personality 1, 13, 14, 92, 247, 278,
298, 325, 326, 399
Personality 325
personhood ix, 4, 14, 18, 207, 208,
209, 215, 216, 217, 218, 220,
221, 278, 293, 299, 325, 328,
384
Personhood 208, 215, 220
Philips, Obbe 59
pietism 197
Pietism 94
pietistic theology 234
Platonism 51
pneumatocentric 21, 95
Pneumatochi 208
pneumatologia crucis 229
Pneumatology 1, 3, 4, 11, 16, 17, 18,
21, 22, 25, 27, 40, 51, 83, 97,
100, 102, 109, 110, 112, 113,
114, 121, 123, 124, 145, 147,
157, 166, 184, 187, 197, 198,
209, 237, 281, 282, 287, 294,
297, 341, 383, 387, 391, 396,
402, 406, 407, 410, 411, 417,
421, 424, 427, 428, 429, 431,
433, 434, 437, 439
post-existence 104

Prague Manifesto 57, 421
prayer xiv, 11, 13, 42, 43, 130, 201, 208, 228, 254, 315, 316, 346, 358, 359, 360, 407
Prayer 356
predestination 148, 149, 285
Predigerschule 84
pre-existence 104, 296
presence x, 2, 7, 9, 10, 27, 32, 44, 59, 66, 68, 69, 86, 105, 109, 110, 116, 119, 125, 131, 133, 134, 136, 144, 145, 146, 157, 158, 160, 172, 178, 179, 181, 187, 189, 199, 200, 201, 212, 213, 215, 216, 217, 219, 221, 222, 231, 232, 234, 235, 236, 242, 244, 246, 249, 250, 251, 252, 255, 257, 260, 261, 262, 263, 265, 266, 267, 268, 269, 272, 274, 277, 279, 289, 292, 293, 310, 311, 315, 323, 324, 325, 327, 328, 334, 340, 349, 350, 352, 357, 358, 359, 360, 369, 370, 371, 372, 377, 391, 396, 397, 399, 400, 401, 402, 405, 407, 410, 411
Presence 216, 236, 251
preservation 162, 266, 269, 364, 404
proceed 4, 46, 122, 205, 217, 223, 343, 362, 368, 404
procession 117, 118, 120, 121, 123, 203, 204, 205, 206, 301, 306, 308, 392
proclaimed Word 98, 255
proclamation 33, 36, 55, 98, 99, 131, 146, 150, 151, 171, 173, 176, 177, 206, 221, 224, 227, 252, 253, 254, 255, 307, 313, 314, 335, 340, 345, 347, 348, 349, 354, 359, 402, 404
Proclamation 151, 252

Protestantism 1, 15, 22, 31, 32, 45, 52, 83, 93, 94, 112, 240, 241, 389, 390, 398
Protestant theology x, 24, 27, 95, 227, 242, 295

Q

quickening power 154, 164, 165, 166
Qumran 321

R

radical Reformation 38, 39, 51, 52, 53, 75, 81
Radicals 52, 76, 431
rapture 275
Reason 79, 235, 294, 296, 321, 361, 393, 395, 401, 402, 426
rebirth 8, 57, 62, 72, 198, 210, 214, 231, 243, 244, 245, 246, 247, 262, 270, 275, 319, 391
Rebirth 244, 246
reciprocal relationship 205, 206
reconciliation 15, 18, 99, 115, 116, 123, 124, 125, 127, 129, 130, 132, 133, 134, 137, 142, 149, 164, 165, 174, 181, 223, 268, 306, 317, 332, 333, 335, 338, 339, 341, 342, 348, 351, 355, 377, 378, 392, 400, 405
Reformation x, 1, 13, 14, 24, 27, 28, 29, 30, 31, 32, 33, 34, 35, 37, 38, 39, 40, 41, 45, 46, 51, 52, 53, 54, 55, 57, 58, 59, 66, 67, 68, 69, 70, 75, 80, 81, 90, 101, 196, 241, 244, 286, 287, 388, 389, 421, 422, 423, 424, 425, 427, 429, 430, 431, 433, 434, 435, 436, 438, 439
Reformers x, 24, 28, 29, 31, 32, 33, 34, 35, 38, 39, 40, 48, 49, 50, 51, 52, 53, 54, 56, 57, 58, 60, 61, 65, 66, 69, 72, 74, 75, 80,

81, 83, 168, 241, 423, 425, 432, 435, 438
regeneration 15, 38, 62, 63, 65, 243, 244, 245, 246, 355, 399
Regeneration 244, 245
Regensburg xi, xiii, xiv, 88, 273, 424, 437
relational 121, 209, 401
relativity theory 369
Renaissance 28, 75, 435
Rendtorff, Rolf 283
resurrection 35, 62, 109, 121, 130, 131, 132, 133, 134, 135, 136, 142, 145, 147, 152, 153, 161, 162, 163, 177, 178, 179, 180, 181, 188, 189, 196, 205, 206, 207, 210, 212, 218, 227, 228, 229, 231, 232, 233, 234, 239, 240, 241, 243, 244, 245, 246, 251, 270, 271, 272, 273, 286, 287, 311, 313, 314, 315, 317, 318, 319, 331, 332, 339, 340, 342, 343, 344, 347, 348, 352, 356, 357, 359, 360, 366, 373, 375, 376, 377, 379, 380, 381, 396, 397, 400, 404, 405
Resurrection 130, 137, 180, 231, 245, 313, 315, 423
Revelation 22, 23, 35, 93, 96, 98, 99, 102, 104, 105, 107, 108, 134, 162, 163, 172, 274, 434, 437
rewah 201
Ritschl 14, 91, 285, 415
Roman Catholicism 14, 93, 94, 390
Romantic 94
Roscellinus of Compiegne 32
Rössler, Dietrich 283

S

Sabellianism 226, 394
Sabellians 14
sacraments 1, 32, 44, 45, 50, 54, 72, 76, 77, 78, 80, 141, 164, 206, 251, 252, 253, 254, 257, 354, 355, 390, 407
sacrifice 70, 231
Safenwil 86
Salvation 43, 241, 351, 375, 378, 433
salvation history 204, 205, 206, 222, 223, 224, 304, 332
Sanctification 62, 247, 248, 426
Schleiermacher 14, 93, 94, 95, 96, 105, 234, 285, 389, 416, 424
Schlink, Edmund 282, 286, 287
Scholasticism 101, 295, 319
scientific positivism 90
Scotus, John Duns 286
Scripture 7, 11, 35, 37, 38, 41, 42, 48, 49, 54, 55, 59, 60, 61, 66, 67, 68, 69, 73, 74, 88, 98, 99, 100, 102, 103, 105, 106, 107, 110, 113, 114, 119, 120, 122, 124, 126, 143, 148, 168, 169, 170, 171, 172, 173, 176, 189, 300, 393, 407, 420, 423, 431
Second Barmen Synod 87
secular humanism 193
secular theology 192
servant 47, 106, 112, 130, 165, 195, 282
shekinah 228, 230, 263, 268, 269
sign 50, 126, 129, 130, 136, 161, 172, 253, 254, 318, 333, 347, 348, 349, 353, 356, 357, 360, 361, 380, 381, 382, 401, 402
Sign 348
Menno Simons 27, 38, 39, 59, 60, 61, 62, 63, 64, 420, 421, 422, 426, 427, 429, 430, 433, 437
sin 40, 43, 44, 47, 56, 61, 62, 63, 64, 73, 103, 104, 131, 143, 144, 158, 174, 179, 194, 210, 211, 241, 242, 324, 330, 331, 332, 336, 338, 339, 349, 352, 354, 377, 380, 382, 407
Social Democratic Party 87

Socialism 87, 196
Son 2, 3, 4, 6, 8, 10, 11, 12, 20, 35, 36, 38, 41, 46, 47, 60, 61, 62, 64, 68, 74, 85, 92, 99, 100, 101, 102, 104, 105, 109, 110, 111, 112, 113, 114, 115, 116, 117, 118, 119, 120, 121, 122, 123, 124, 129, 130, 134, 137, 140, 143, 144, 146, 147, 148, 153, 154, 159, 166, 184, 203, 204, 205, 206, 207, 208, 209, 210, 215, 216, 222, 223, 224, 225, 228, 229, 230, 231, 237, 243, 255, 257, 258, 264, 266, 268, 275, 276, 277, 293, 294, 295, 296, 297, 298, 299, 300, 301, 302, 303, 304, 305, 306, 307, 308, 309, 310, 311, 312, 313, 314, 315, 316, 317, 324, 331, 333, 334, 335, 336, 337, 338, 339, 340, 341, 342, 344, 346, 347, 348, 349, 350, 351, 352, 356, 358, 362, 363, 364, 367, 368, 370, 371, 372, 373, 375, 376, 377, 378, 379, 381, 382, 383, 389, 392, 393, 394, 395, 397, 399, 400, 401, 402, 404, 419
Son of God 64, 74, 130, 137, 144, 148, 159, 309, 310, 311, 314, 334, 348, 350
Son of man 309, 381
Sophia 411, 412
soteriology 8, 240, 253, 287, 309, 330, 403
soul 14, 32, 33, 55, 56, 62, 70, 71, 79, 118, 119, 131, 192, 195, 206, 213, 218, 235, 244, 249, 290, 319, 321, 322, 323, 325, 327, 328, 398
Space 211, 368
Spirit-history 206
Spiritual 35, 38, 39, 47, 52, 56, 68, 72, 76, 77, 192, 422, 424, 425, 426, 432, 435, 438
Spiritualists 52
spirituality 12, 15, 36, 52, 80, 260, 388, 405, 406
Spirituality 40, 405, 406, 427
spiritualization 62, 71, 72, 275
Stoicism 291
Strasbourg 66, 69, 72, 75, 76, 424, 431
subjective revelation 102, 105, 106, 107, 138, 139, 142, 162, 170
subordinationist view 111
substance 37, 41, 153, 179, 209, 226, 290, 291, 306, 319
substantialist unity 209
suffering 44, 55, 56, 57, 58, 59, 130, 166, 189, 191, 194, 203, 217, 227, 228, 229, 230, 231, 271, 272, 273, 332, 333, 399, 400, 405, 411, 413
symbolism 365

T

teacher 32, 64, 77, 84, 96, 108, 140, 170, 284
Teacher 170
tempest 199, 212, 213
Tempest 212
Temple 76, 422
Ten Commandments 151
Tertullian 11, 84, 111, 113, 208
theocentric 403
theologia crucis 229
Theology of Hope 25, 187, 189, 192, 194, 196, 197, 271, 272, 417, 418, 431
theopneustia 169
Third Reich x, 196, 283, 284
Thurneysen, Eduard 85, 86, 88, 435
Time 2, 179, 196, 368, 423, 437
Torah 351

transcendent 5, 114, 163, 183, 184,
    200, 204, 211, 215, 217, 219,
    220, 222, 230, 245, 246, 269,
    329, 330, 365, 371, 398, 399
transcendental deduction 113
Transfiguration 233, 380
Transformation 72, 435
Trinitarian 100, 184, 188, 191, 208,
    209, 215, 220, 224, 237, 264,
    265, 267, 295, 296, 341, 362,
    378, 391, 410, 417, 418, 419,
    428, 433
Trinity 1, 3, 4, 8, 10, 11, 17, 18, 19,
    25, 35, 37, 46, 71, 81, 91, 92, 99,
    100, 101, 102, 103, 105, 110,
    112, 113, 114, 118, 119, 120,
    121, 123, 146, 148, 166, 179,
    188, 204, 205, 207, 208, 209,
    210, 215, 221, 222, 223, 224,
    225, 226, 228, 229, 230, 233,
    237, 266, 267, 268, 270, 273,
    274, 276, 278, 288, 293, 294,
    295, 296, 297, 298, 299, 301,
    304, 305, 306, 307, 312, 315,
    365, 368, 378, 384, 388, 389,
    392, 393, 394, 395, 396, 398,
    406, 411, 413, 418, 420, 423,
    426, 428, 430, 432, 433, 434, 437
Triune God 25, 100, 113, 114, 183,
    184, 185, 191, 229, 247, 266,
    269, 270, 418, 426, 428

U

Ubiquitarianism 135
unique community 209
Unitarians 14
University of Basel 85
University of Berlin 93, 96, 285
University of Berne 85, 93
University of Bonn 87

V

verbum incarnandum 159
vicarious 189, 241, 333, 339

virgin birth 127, 128, 129, 130
virgin Mary 64, 126, 127, 128, 129
Visible 158

W

water 1, 55, 62, 64, 213, 214, 215,
    381, 411
Water 213
weakness 184, 230, 231, 408
Weakness 230
Weber, Otto 196, 197
Wendel, Elisabeth 197
wide space 208, 211, 218
Wilkens, Ulrich 283
wind 1, 8, 208, 218, 288, 290, 320,
    343, 366, 368, 374, 411
wine 1, 59, 69, 72, 77, 135, 358, 359,
    360, 407
wisdom xi, 56, 60, 119, 248, 266,
    296, 301, 321, 322, 412, 413
Wisdom 322, 375
Wittenberg theology 53
Wolf, Ernst 196
Word of God 7, 41, 42, 44, 46, 48,
    49, 55, 61, 63, 64, 66, 68, 76, 78,
    79, 80, 81, 84, 86, 89, 98, 99,
    102, 105, 106, 108, 110, 117,
    125, 137, 141, 142, 147, 149,
    158, 167, 168, 169, 170, 171,
    173, 174, 175, 176, 254, 255,
    256, 261, 286, 388, 432
World War II 191
written Word 98, 170
Wuppertal 190, 283

Z

Zwickau prophets 53
Zwingli, Huldrych 29

www.ingramcontent.com/pod-product-compliance
Lightning Source LLC
Chambersburg PA
CBHW050524300426
44113CB00012B/1948